Oracle PL/SQL™

INTERACTIVE WORKBOOK

Second Edition

ISBN 0-13-047320-0

9 790130 473201   93999

THE PRENTICE HALL PTR ORACLE SERIES
The Independent Voice on Oracle

Oracle
PL/SQL

INTERACTIVE WORKBOOK

Second Edition

BENJAMIN ROSENZWEIG
ELENA SILVESTROVA

PRENTICE
HALL
PTR

Upper Saddle River, New Jersey 07458
www.phptr.com

Library of Congress Cataloging-in-Publication Data

A catalog record for this book can be obtained from the Library of Congress.

Editorial/production supervision: Jessica Balch (Pine Tree Composition, Inc.)
Cover design director: Jerry Votta
Cover design: Nina Scuderi
Art director: Gail Cocker-Bogusz
Interior design: Meg Van Arsdale
Manufacturing buyer: Maura Zaldivar
Acquisitions editor: Victoria Jones
Editorial assistant: Michelle Vincenti
Marketing manager: Debby vanDijk
Full-service production coordinator: Anne R. Garcia

© 2003 Pearson Education, Inc.
Publishing as Prentice Hall PTR
Upper Saddle River, NJ 07458

Prentice Hall books are widely used by corporations and government agencies
for training, marketing, and resale.

For information regarding corporate and government bulk discounts, please contact:
Corporate and Government Sales (800)382-3419 or corpsales@pearsontechgroup.com

Other company and product names mentioned herein are the trademarks
or registered trademarks of their respective owners.

Printed in the United States of America
10 9 8 7 6 5 4 3 2 1

ISBN 0-13-047320-0

Pearson Education Ltd., *London*
Pearson Education Australia Pty, Limited, *Sydney*
Pearson Education Singapore, Pte. Ltd.
Pearson Education North Asia Ltd., *Hong Kong*
Pearson Education Canada, Ltd., *Toronto*
Pearson Educación de Mexico, S.A. de C.V.
Pearson Education-Japan, *Tokyo*
Pearson Education Malaysia, Pte. Ltd.

CONTENTS

ACKNOWLEDGMENTS

ACKNOWLEDGMENTS FROM BEN ROSENZWEIG

I would like to thank my coauthor Elena Silvestrova for being a wonderful and knowledgeable colleague to work with. I would also like to thank Douglas Scherer for giving me the opportunity to work on this book as well as for providing constant support and assistance through the entire writing process. I am indebted to Carol Brennan for her technical edits; she saved me from errors in every chapter. I would like to thank Kathryn Castelle, who did a great job reading over the manuscript and making suggestions. Finally, I would like to thank the many friends and family, especially Edward Clarin and Edward Knopping, for helping me through the long process of putting the whole book together, which included many late nights and weekends.

ACKNOWLEDGMENTS FROM ELENA SILVESTROVA

My contribution to this book reflects the help and advice of many people. I am particularly indebted to the people at Prentice Hall who diligently worked to bring this book to market. Thanks to all of my students at Columbia University, who perennially demonstrated that teaching is learning. Thanks to Carol Brennan for her valuable comments and suggestions. To Ben Rosenzweig and Douglas Scherer, thanks for making this project a rewarding and enjoyable experience. Special thanks to David Dawson, whose insightful ideas and sincere support encourage me to work hard to the very end. Most important, thanks to my mom and dad, Natalia and Victor, whose excitement, enthusiasm, inspiration, and support were exceeded only by their love.

ABOUT THE AUTHORS

Benjamin Rosenzweig is an Integration Specialist at IQ Financial Systems. He has a wide range of computer experience, including being a consultant at Oracle Corporation; creating an electronic Tibetan-English Dictionary in Katmandu, Nepal, supporting presentations centers at Goldman Sachs; and managing a trading system at TIAA-CREF. He holds a B.A. from Reed College and a certificate in database development and design from Columbia University. Benjamin has also published the *Oracle Forms Developer: The Complete Video Course* (ISBN 0-13-0321249) with Prentice Hall. His next book from Prentice Hall is *Oracle Web Application Programming for PL/SQL Developers* (ISBN: 0-13-0477311).

Elena Silvestrova, a senior software engineer for a prominent New York brokerage firm and securities dealer, has taught relational database programming in Columbia University's highly esteemed CTA program during the past four years. She was educated in database analysis and design at Columbia University and in applied mathematics at Baku State University in Azerbaijan. A U.S. citizen, Elena has lived in the United States for more than 10 years. She currently resides in New York.

INTRODUCTION

The Oracle PL/SQL Interactive Workbook, 2nd edition, presents the Oracle PL/SQL programming language in a unique and highly effective format. It challenges you to learn Oracle PL/SQL by using it rather than by simply reading about it.

Just as a grammar workbook would teach you about nouns and verbs by first showing you examples and then asking you to write sentences, the *Oracle PL/SQL Interactive Workbook* teaches you about cursors, loops, procedures, triggers, and so on by first showing you examples and then asking you to create these objects yourself.

WHO THIS BOOK IS FOR

This book is intended for anyone who needs a quick but detailed introduction to programming with Oracle's PL/SQL language. The ideal readers are those with some relational database experience, with some Oracle experience, specifically with SQL and SQL*Plus, but with little or no experience with PL/SQL or with most other programming languages.

The content of this book is based on the material that is taught in an Introduction to PL/SQL class at Columbia University's Computer Technology and Applications (CTA) program in New York City. The student body is rather diverse, in that there are some students who have years of experience with information technology (IT) and programming, but no experience with Oracle PL/SQL, and then there are those with absolutely no experience in IT or programming. The content of the book, like the class, is balanced to meet the needs of both extremes. The exercises in this book can be used as lab and homework assignments to accompany the lectures in such a PL/SQL course.

HOW THIS BOOK IS ORGANIZED

The intent of this workbook is to teach you about Oracle PL/SQL by presenting you with a series of challenges followed by detailed solutions to those challenges. The basic structure of each chapter is as follows:

Chapter

Lab

Exercises

Exercise Answers (with detailed discussion)

Self-Review Questions

Lab . . .

Test Your Thinking Questions

Each chapter contains interactive labs that introduce topics about Oracle PL/SQL. The topics are discussed briefly and then explored though exercises, which are the heart of each lab.

Each exercise consists of a series of steps that you will follow to perform a specific task, along with questions that are designed to help you discover the important things about PL/SQL programming on your own. The answers to these questions are given at the end of the Exercises, along with more in-depth discussion of the concepts explored.

The exercises are not meant to be closed-book quizzes to test your knowledge. On the contrary, they are intended to act as your guide and walk you through a task. You are encouraged to flip back and forth from the exercise question section to the exercise answer section so that, if need be, you can read the answers and discussions as you go along.

At the end of each lab is a series of multiple-choice self-review questions. These are meant to be closed-book quizzes to test how well you understood the lab material. The answers to these questions appear in Appendix A.

Finally, at the end of each chapter you will find a Test Your Thinking section, which consists of a series of projects designed to solidify all of the skills you have learned in the chapter. If you have successfully completed all of the labs in the chapter, you should be able to tackle these projects with few problems. You will find guidance and/or solutions to these in Appendix D and at the companion Web site.

ABOUT THE COMPANION WEB SITE

The companion Web site is located at

```
http://www.phptr.com/rosenzweig2e/
```

Here you will find two very important things:

- Files you will need *before* you begin reading the workbook: all of the exercises and questions are based on a sample database called STUDENT. The files required to create and install the STUDENT schema are downloadable from the Web site.
- Answers to the Test Your Thinking questions.

In addition to required files and Test Your Thinking answers, the Web site will have many other features, like message board and periodically updated information about the book. There may also be some additional PL/SQL assignments without answers that can be used for graded homework.

You should visit the companion Web site, download the student schema, and install it in your database.

WHAT YOU WILL NEED

There are software programs as well as knowledge requirements necessary to complete the exercise sections of the workbook. Note that some features covered throughout the workbook are applicable to Oracle 9i only. However, you will be able to complete a great majority of the exercise sections by using the following products:

SOFTWARE

- Oracle 7.3.4 or higher
- SQL*Plus 3.3 or higher
- Access to the Internet
- Windows 95/98/2000 or NT 4.0

ORACLE 9i

Oracle 9i is Oracle's RDBMS and its flagship product. You can use either Oracle Personal Edition or Oracle Enterprise Edition. If you use Oracle Enterprise Edition, this can be running on a remote server or locally on your own machine. Oracle 9.0.1.1.1 Enterprise Edition running locally was used to create the exercises for this book, but subsequent versions should be compatible (the Web site will also have scripts to create a database that will function for Oracle 7.3 and above, although features specified as Oracle 9i will not run in versions below Oracle 9).

Additionally, you should have access to and be familiar with SQL*Plus. This book was used running SQL*Plus version 9.0.1.0.1.

You have a number of options for how to edit and run scripts from SQL*Plus. There are also many third-party programs to edit and debug PL/SQL code. SQL*Plus is used throughout this book, since SQL*Plus comes with the Oracle Personal Edition and Enterprise Edition 9.0.1.0.1.

USING SQL*PLUS

You should be familiar with using SQL*Plus to execute SQL statements (if not, then refer to another book in the Prentice Hall Interactive Oracle Series on this topic, Morrison/Rishchert's *Oracle SQL Interactive Workbook*, 2nd ed., 2004). There are a few key differences between executing SQL statements in SQL*Plus and executing PL/SQL statements in SQL*Plus. You will be introduced to these differences so that you can work with the exercises in this book.

You can end an SQL Command in SQL*Plus in one of three ways:

- with a semicolon (;)
- with a forward slash (/) on a line by itself
- with a blank line

The semicolon (;) tells SQL*Plus that you want to run the command that you have just entered. You type the semicolon at the end of the SELECT statement and then press return. SQL*Plus will process what is in the SQL Buffer (described next).

■ FOR EXAMPLE

```
SQL> SELECT sysdate
  2 FROM dual
  3 ;

SYSDATE
---------
28-JUL-02

SQL>
```

THE SQL BUFFER

SQL*Plus will store the SQL command or PL/SQL block that you have most recently entered in an area of memory known as the SQL Buffer. The SQL Buffer will remain unchanged until you enter a new command or exit your SQL*Plus session. You can easily edit the contents of the SQL Buffer by typing the EDIT command at the SQL prompt. The default text editor will open with the contents of the SQL Buffer. You can edit and save the file and then exit the editor. This will cause the contents of the SQL Buffer to change to your last saved version.

SQL*Plus commands such as SET SERVEROUTPUT ON are not captured into the SQL Buffer, nor does SQL*Plus store the semicolon or the forward slash you type to execute a command in the SQL buffer.

When you create stored procedures, functions, or packages, you begin with the CREATE command. When you begin a PL/SQL block, you start by entering the word DECLARE or BEGIN. Typing either BEGIN, DECLARE, or CREATE will put the SQL*Plus session into PL/SQL mode.

RUNNING PL/SQL BLOCKS IN SQL*PLUS

Once you are in PL/SQL mode, you will not be able to end the block in the same manner that you ended a SQL block. The semicolon (;) can be used multiple times in a single PL/SQL block; thus when you end a line with a semicolon you will not terminate the block. You can terminate the PL/SQL block in the SQL Buffer by entering a period (.). This will end the block and leave the block in the SQL Buffer, but it will not execute it. At this point you have a choice of typing the EDIT command to edit the block or executing it with a forward slash (/) or a SQL*Plus command RUN.

■ *FOR EXAMPLE*

You may enter and execute a PL/SQL subprogram as follows:

```
SQL> BEGIN
  2 DBMS_OUTPUT.PUT_LINE ('This is a PL/SQL Block');
  3 END;
  4 .
SQL> /
This is a PL/SQL Block

PL/SQL procedure successfully completed.
```

If want to run a script file at a later date, you must remember to terminate it with a period (.) and/or forward slash (/) before saving it on your computer. If you simply want to put the code into the SQL Buffer and then execute it, you can end the script with a forward slash (/).

You should terminate PL/SQL blocks stored in the script file with the period if you want to put the code in the SQL Buffer. You should end the script with forward slash (/) if you want the PL/SQL code in the file to execute.

The failure to end your PL/SQL block with a period (.) and/or a forward slash (/) will prevent your block from executing.

ABOUT THE SAMPLE SCHEMA

The STUDENT schema contains tables and other objects meant to keep information about a registration and enrollment system for a fictitious university. There are ten tables in the system that store data about students, courses, instructors, and so on. In addition to storing contact information (addresses and telephone numbers) for students and instructors, and descriptive information about courses (costs and prerequisites), the schema also keeps track of the sections for particular courses, and the sections in which students have enrolled.

The SECTION is one of the most important tables in the schema because it stores data about the individual sections that have been created for each course. Each section record also stores information about where and when the section will meet and which instructor will teach the section. The section table is related to the COURSE and INSTRUCTOR tables.

The ENROLLMENT table is equally important because it keeps track of which students have enrolled in which sections. Each enrollment record also stores information about the student's grade and enrollment date. The enrollment table is related to the STUDENT and SECTION tables.

The schema also has a number of other tables that manage grading for each student in each section.

CONVENTIONS USED IN THIS BOOK

There are several conventions that are used in this book to try and make your learning experience easier. These are explained here.

This icon is used to flag notes or advice from the authors to you, the reader. For instance, if there is a particular topic or concept that you really need to understand for the exam, or if there's something that you need to keep in mind while working, you will find it set off from the main text like this.

This icon is used to flag tips or especially helpful tricks that will save you time or trouble. For instance, if there is a shortcut for performing a particular task or a method that the authors have found useful, you will find it set off from the main text like this.

Computers are delicate creatures and can be damaged easily. Likewise, they can be dangerous to work on if you're not careful. This icon is used to flag information and precautions that will not only save you headaches in the long run; they may even save you or your computer from harm.

This icon is used to flag passages in which there is a reference to the book's companion Web site, which is located at http://www.phptr.com/ rosenzweig2e.

About Prentice Hall Professional Technical Reference

With origins reaching back to the industry's first computer science publishing program in the 1960s, Prentice Hall Professional Technical Reference (PH PTR) has developed into the leading provider of technical books in the world today. Formally launched as its own imprint in 1986, our editors now publish over 200 books annually, authored by leaders in the fields of computing, engineering, and business.

Our roots are firmly planted in the soil that gave rise to the technological revolution. Our bookshelf contains many of the industry's computing and engineering classics: Kernighan and Ritchie's *C Programming Language,* Nemeth's *UNIX System Administration Handbook,* Horstmann's *Core Java,* and Johnson's *High-Speed Digital Design.*

PH PTR acknowledges its auspicious beginnings while it looks to the future for inspiration. We continue to evolve and break new ground in publishing by providing today's professionals with tomorrow's solutions.

CHAPTER 1

PROGRAMMING CONCEPTS

CHAPTER OBJECTIVES

In this Chapter, you will learn about:

- ✔ The Nature of a Computer Program
  and Programming Languages   Page 2
- ✔ Good Programming Practices   Page 9

Computers play a large role in the modern world. No doubt you realize how crucial they have become to running any business today; they have also become one of the sources of entertainment in our lives. You probably use computers for your everyday tasks as well, such as sending e-mail, paying bills, shopping, reading the latest news on the Internet, or even playing games.

A computer is a sophisticated device. However, it is important to remember that it is still only a device and cannot think on its own. In order to be useful, a computer needs instructions to follow. Facilities such as programming languages allow programmers to provide computers with a list of instructions called programs. These programs tell a computer what actions to perform. As a result, programming languages and computer programs play an important role in today's technology.

L A B   1 . 1

THE NATURE OF A COMPUTER PROGRAM AND PROGRAMMING LANGUAGES

LAB OBJECTIVES

After this Lab, you will be able to:

✔ Understand the Nature of Computer Programs and Programming Languages
✔ Understand the Differences between Interpreted and Compiled Languages

---

A computer needs instructions to follow because it cannot think on its own. For instance, when playing a game of solitaire you must choose which card to move. Each time a card is moved, a set of instructions has been executed to carry out the move. These instructions compose only a small part of the solitaire program. This program comprises many more instructions that allow a user to perform actions, such as beginning or ending a game, selecting a card's color, and so forth. Therefore, a computer program comprises instructions that direct the actions of the computer. In essence, a program plays the role of guide for a computer. It tells the computer what steps in what order should be taken to complete a certain task successfully.

Computer programs are created with the help of programming languages. A programming language is a set of instructions consisting of rules, syntax, numerical and logical operators, and utility functions. Programmers can use programming languages to create a computer program. There are many different programming languages available today. However, all programming languages can be divided into three major groups: machine languages, assembly languages, and high-level languages.

Words such as statement *or* command *are often used when talking about instructions issued by a program to a computer. These terms are interchangeable.*

MACHINE LANGUAGES

Machine language is the native language of a particular computer because it is defined by the hardware of the computer. Each instruction or command is a collection of zeros and ones. As a result, machine language is the hardest language for a person to understand, but it is the only language understood by the computer. All other programming languages must be translated into machine language. Consider the following example of the commands issued in the machine language.

■ FOR EXAMPLE

Consider the mathematical notation $X = X + 1$. In programming, this notation reads *the value of the variable is incremented by one*. In the following example, you are incrementing the value of the variable by 1 using machine language specific to an Intel processor.

```
1010 0001 1110 0110 0000 0001
0000 0011 0000 0110 0000 0001 0000 0000
1010 0011 1110 0110 0000 0001
```

ASSEMBLY LANGUAGES

Assembly language uses English-like abbreviations to represent operations performed on the data. A computer cannot understand assembly language directly. A program written in assembly language must be translated into machine language with the help of the special program called an *assembler*. Consider the following example of the commands issued in assembly language.

■ FOR EXAMPLE

In this example, you are increasing the value of the variable by 1 as well. This example is also specific to an Intel processor.

```
MOV AX, [01E6]
ADD AX, 0001
MOV [01E6], AX
```

HIGH-LEVEL LANGUAGES

A high-level language uses English-like instructions and common mathematical notations. High-level languages allow programmers to perform complicated calculations with a single instruction. However, it is easier to read and understand than machine and assembly languages, and it is not as time-consuming to create a program in high-level language as it is in machine or assembly language.

■ *FOR EXAMPLE*

```
variable := variable + 1;
```

This example shows the simple mathematical operation of addition. This instruction can be easily understood by anyone without programming experience and with basic mathematical knowledge.

DIFFERENCES BETWEEN INTERPRETED AND COMPILED LANGUAGES

High-level languages can be divided into two groups: interpreted and compiled. Interpreted languages are translated into machine language with the help of another program called an *interpreter*. The interpreter translates each statement in the program into machine language and executes it immediately before the next statement is examined.

A compiled language is translated into machine language with the help of the program called a *compiler*. Compilers translate English-like statements into machine language. However, all of the statements must be translated before a program can be executed. The compiled version of the program is sometimes referred to as an *executable*.

An interpreted program must be translated into machine language every time it is run. A compiled program is translated into machine language only once when it is compiled. The compiled version of the program can then be executed as many times as needed.

LAB 1.1 EXERCISES

1.1.1 UNDERSTAND THE NATURE OF COMPUTER PROGRAMS AND PROGRAMMING LANGUAGES

a) What is a program?

For the next two questions, consider this scenario: You have been hired to work for the ABC Company. One of your responsibilities is to produce a daily report that contains complicated calculations.

b) Without using a computer program to fulfill this responsibility, what potential problems do you foresee in generating this report every day?

c) Based on your observations in question b, how do you think a computer program would make that task easier?

d) What is a programming language?

For the next question, consider the following code:

```
0010 0000 1110 0110 0000 0001
0000 0011 0000 0110 1000 0000
1010 0001 1111 0110 0000 0001
```

e) What type of programming language is this code written in?

For the next question, consider the following code:

```
MOV AX, [01E9]
ADD AX, 0010
MOV [01E6], AX
```

f) What type of programming language is this code written in?

For the next question, consider the following code:

```
variable := 2 * variable - 10;
```

g) What type of programming language is this code written in?

1.1.2 UNDERSTAND THE DIFFERENCES BETWEEN INTERPRETED AND COMPILED LANGUAGES

a) What is an interpreted language?

b) What is a compiled language?

c) Which do you think will run quicker, an interpreted or a compiled program?

LAB 1.1 EXERCISE ANSWERS

This section gives you some suggested answers to the questions in Lab 1.1, with discussion related to how those answers resulted. The most important thing to realize is whether your answer works. You should figure out the implications of the answers here and what the effects are from any different answers you may come up with.

1.1.1 ANSWERS

a) What is a program?

Answer:A computer program comprises instructions that direct the actions of the computer.

b) Without using a computer program to fulfill this responsibility, what potential problems do you foresee in generating this report every day?

Answer: Programs help us with repetitive, time-consuming, and error-prone tasks. If you do not have a program that helps you create this report, it might take you a whole day to collect the needed information for the report and perform the needed calculations. As a result, you will not be able to concentrate on your other responsibilities. In addition, sooner or later you will probably make mistakes while creating the report.

c) Based on your observations in question b, how do you think a computer program would make that task easier?

Answer: Using a program guarantees fast retrieval of needed information and accurate results, assuming that the program does not contain any errors. Furthermore, once a program is created, the same set of steps is repeated on a daily basis. Consequently, a well-written program is not susceptible to human frailties such as typographical errors or the accidental exclusion of a formula.

d) What is a programming language?

Answer: A programming language is a set of instructions consisting of rules, syntax, numerical and logical operators, and utility functions.

e) What type of programming language is this code an example of?

Answer: This is an example of a machine language.

Machine language is understood directly by the computer. Each statement in machine language is represented by a string of zeros and ones.

This example illustrates the nonintuitive nature of machine language. However, a computer can read these instructions directly and execute them instantly. You can see that creating a program in a machine language can be a slow and tedious process. To facilitate program creation, programmers use higher-level languages that are closer to human language.

f) What type of programming language is this code an example of?

Answer: This is an example of an assembly language.

Assembly language uses mnemonic symbols to represent the binary code of machine language. Each assembly instruction is directly translated into a machine language instruction. You may notice that assembly language is slightly easier to understand than machine language.

g) What type of programming language is this code an example of?

Answer: This is an example of a high-level language.

Programs created in high-level languages are portable. They can be moved from one computer to another because a high-level programming language is not machine-specific. High-level languages must be translated into machine language with the help of an interpreter or a compiler.

1.1.2 ANSWERS

a) What is an interpreted language?

Answer: An interpreted language is translated into machine language with the help of another program called an interpreter. The interpreter translates statement in the program into machine language and executes it immediately before the next statement is examined.

b) What is a compiled language?

Answer: A compiled language is translated into machine language with the help of the program called a compiler. Compilers translate English-like statements into machine language.

c) Which do you think will run quicker, an interpreted or a compiled program?

Answer: Generally, interpreted programs run slower than compiled programs.

As you observed earlier, an interpreted program must be translated into machine language every time it is run. A compiled program is translated into machine language only once when it is compiled, and then it can be executed as many times as needed. As a result, an interpreted program runs slower than a compiled program.

LAB 1.1 SELF-REVIEW QUESTIONS

In order to test your progress, you should be able to answer the following questions.

1) What group of programming languages is easiest for the computer to understand?

   a) _____ The machine languages
   b) _____ The high-level languages
   c) _____ The assembly languages

2) Programs created in the machine languages are which of the following?

   a) _____ Portable
   b) _____ Machine-specific

3) Which of the following is true of interpreted programs?

   a) _____ All statements are translated and only then executed.
   b) _____ Each statement is translated and executed before the next statement.

4) Before a program written in a high-level language can be executed, which of the following must take place?

   a) _____ A program must be interpreted.
   b) _____ A program must be compiled.
   c) _____ A program can be executed immediately.

5) Which of the following is true of the interpreter?

   a) _____ It translates instructions written in assembly language into machine language.
   b) _____ It translates machine language into a high-level language.
   c) _____ It translates a high-level language into machine language.

Answers appear in Appendix A, Section 1.1.

LAB 1.2

GOOD PROGRAMMING PRACTICES

LAB OBJECTIVES

After this Lab, you will be able to:

- ✔ Understand the Nature of Good Programming Practices
- ✔ Understand Formatting Guidelines

In the previous section of this chapter you encountered the terms *computer program* and *programming language.* You will recall that a program is a set of instructions, and a programming language is a tool that allows programmers to provide computers with these instructions. However, the process of creating a computer program is not as simple as just writing down instructions. Sometimes it can become a tedious and complicated task. Before a computer can be provided with these instructions, a programmer needs to know what instructions must be specified. In essence, the process of creating a program is akin to the process of applied problem solving.

Consider this mathematical word problem:

> The 1980s speed record for human-powered vehicles was set on a measured 200-meter run by a sleek machine called Vector. Pedaling back-to-back, its two drivers averaged 69.92 miles per hour.
>
> This awkward mix of units is the way data appeared in an article reporting the event. Determine the speed of the vehicle in meters per second.[1]

This word problem involves conversion from miles per hour into meters per second. However, it contains information that has nothing to do with its solution, such as the name of the vehicle and the number of people needed to operate it. In order to achieve correct results, you must be able to filter out needed informa-

---

[1]From *Physics (with InfoTrac and Revised CD-ROM) Algebra/Trig,* 2nd edition, by E. Hecht. © 1998. Reprinted with permission of Brooks/Cole, a division of Thomson Learning. Fax 800-730-2215.

tion and discard the rest. Next, you need to know what formulas must be used for actual conversion.

This is a relatively straightforward example of a problem-solving process that can be used for academic purposes. However, in the business world, problem descriptions are often incomplete or ambiguous. They are also harder to solve. These problems require the ability to ask questions that help clarify the problem and an ability to organize the problem into logical parts. By breaking down the problem, you will be able to focus better on possible solutions and more easily manage each part. Once each part is fully understood, the solution to the overall problem will readily develop.

This technique of breaking the problem into smaller parts and solving each part is called a *top-down approach* to problem solving. When writing a program, you can also approach your task in a top-down manner. However, to solve the problem efficiently, you need to approach it in a structured manner.

STRUCTURED PROGRAMMING

Structured programming embodies a disciplined approach to writing clear code that is easy to understand, test, maintain, and modify. A program can be organized into modules called *subroutines*. These subroutines focus on a particular part of the overall problem that the program addresses. Subroutines are easier to understand and manage because they are only components of the overall program. Together, all of the subroutines compose the overall program.

Structured programming also embodies the following three attributes: sequence, selection, and iteration. These attributes, or structures, describe how statements in the program are executed. Furthermore, a program can contain any of these structures or a combination of them.

SEQUENCE

Sequence refers to the linear execution of code. In other words, control is passed from one statement to the next statement in consecutive order. Consider Figure 1.1.

Figure 1.1 contains rectangular symbols. The rectangular symbol in the diagram can represent not only a single statement, but a subroutine as well. The arrows represent the flow of control between statements. Control is passed from statement 1 to statement 2 and then to statement 3. Thus, these statements are executed in the sequential order.

SELECTION

Selection refers to the decision-making process. For example, when I am trying to choose between different activities for this weekend, I start with the knowledge

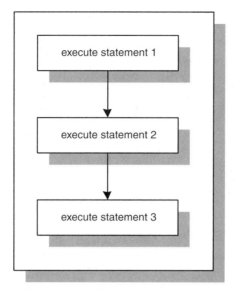

Figure 1.1 ■ Sequence Structure

that on Friday night I want to go to the movies, Saturday night I want to go dancing, and Sunday I want to spend a quiet evening at home. In order for me to choose one of the activities, I need to know what day of the week it is. The logic for my decision of the weekend activities can be illustrated as follows:

```
IF TODAY IS 'FRIDAY'
    I AM GOING TO SEE A MOVIE
IF TODAY IS 'SATURDAY'
    I AM GOING DANCING
IF TODAY IS 'SUNDAY'
    I AM SPENDING A QUIET EVENING AT HOME
```

The test conditions "TODAY IS . . ." can evaluate either to TRUE or FALSE based on the day of the week. If today happens to be Friday, the first test condition "TODAY is 'FRIDAY'" becomes TRUE, and the other test conditions become FALSE. In this case, I am going to see a movie, and the other activities can be discarded.

Figure 1.2 illustrates the general flow of control of the selection structure.

Figure 1.2 contains a diamond shape called the decision symbol. This indicates that a decision must be made or a certain test condition must be evaluated. This test condition evaluates to TRUE (Yes) or FALSE (No). If the test condition yields TRUE, statement 1 is executed. If the test condition yields FALSE, statement 2 is executed. It is important for you to remember that a rectangle can represent a set of statements or a subroutine.

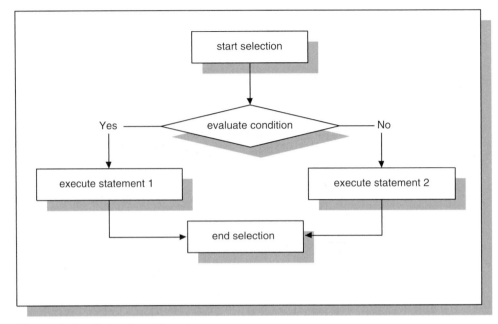

Figure 1.2 ■ **Selection Structure**

ITERATION

Iteration refers to an action that needs to be repeated a finite number of times. The number of times this action is repeated is based on some terminating factor. Consider the following example. You are reading a chapter from this book. Each chapter has a finite number of pages. In order to finish the chapter, you need to read through all of the pages. This is indicated as follows:

```
WHILE THERE ARE MORE PAGES IN THE CHAPTER TO READ
    READ THE CURRENT PAGE
    GO TO THE NEXT PAGE
```

The terminating factor in this example is the number of pages in the chapter. As soon as the last page in the chapter is read, the iteration is complete.

Figure 1.3 illustrates the general flow of control of the iteration structure.

As long as the condition evaluates to TRUE, the statements inside the iteration structure are repeated. As soon as the condition evaluates to FALSE, the flow of control is passed to the exit point of the iteration structure.

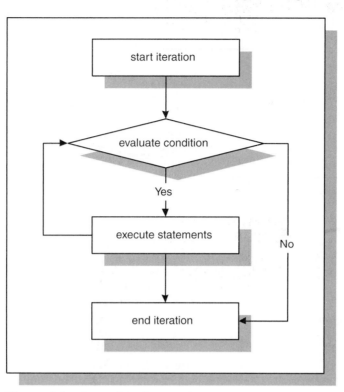

Figure 1.3 ■ Iteration Structure

DIFFERENCES BETWEEN STRUCTURED AND NONSTRUCTURED PROGRAMMING

Before structured programming became widely used, programs were simply sequential lines of code. This code was not organized into modules and did not employ many of the structures you encountered earlier in this chapter. The result was a meandering set of statements that was difficult to maintain and understand. In addition, these programs used multiple GOTO statements that allow program control to jump all over the code. Almost all programs that use GOTO statements can be rewritten using structures such as selection and iteration.

FORMATTING GUIDELINES

It was mentioned earlier that structured programming allows us to write clear code that is easy to understand, test, maintain, and modify. However, structured programming alone is not enough to create readable and manageable code. Formatting is a very important aspect of writing a program. Moreover, your formatting style should stay consistent throughout your programs.

Consider this example of a SELECT statement that has not been formatted.

■ *FOR EXAMPLE*

```
SELECT s.first_name, s.last_name, e.final_grade FROM
student s, enrollment e WHERE s.student_id = e.student_id
AND e.final_grade IS NOT NULL;
```

Even though this example contains only a very simple SELECT statement, you can see that the logic is hard to follow.

Consider the same SELECT statement with a few formatting changes.

■ *FOR EXAMPLE*

```
SELECT s.first_name, s.last_name, e.final_grade
   FROM student s, enrollment e
 WHERE s.student_id = e.student_id
   AND e.final_grade IS NOT NULL;
```

You have probably noticed that the second version of the SELECT statement is much easier to read and understand. It is important to realize that both SELECT statements are syntactically correct. They produce the same output when run.

Usually, the logic depicted in the program is more complex than that of the SELECT statement. Therefore, proper formatting of the code is extremely important for two major reasons. First, a well-formatted program will facilitate any changes made later by the program's author. In other words, even the author will understand the logic of the program more easily if he or she needs to modify the program later. Second, any person who has to maintain the program can more easily follow the logical structure of the program.

In order for the program to be readable and understandable, there are two main guidelines to follow. First, the format of the program must illustrate the logical structure of the program. You can reveal the logical structure of the program by using indentation in your code. Consider the example of the selection structure used earlier in this chapter.

■ *FOR EXAMPLE*

```
IF TODAY IS 'FRIDAY'
   I AM GOING TO SEE A MOVIE
IF TODAY IS 'SATURDAY'
   I AM GOING DANCING
IF TODAY IS 'SUNDAY'
   I AM SPENDING A QUIET EVENING AT HOME
```

You have probably noticed that each statement following the IF clause is indented. As a result, it is easier to understand what activity is taken based on the day of the week. You could take this example and format it differently.

■ *FOR EXAMPLE*

```
IF TODAY IS 'FRIDAY' I AM GOING TO SEE A MOVIE
IF TODAY IS 'SATURDAY' I AM GOING DANCING
IF TODAY IS 'SUNDAY' I AM SPENDING A QUIET EVENING AT HOME
```

This example also shows a formatted version of the selection structure. However, this formatting style does not reveal the logical structure of the selection as well as the previous example. As a matter of fact, this example looks like an extremely short story rather than a program.

Second, *your program should contain comments*. Comments will help you explain what you are trying to accomplish. However, you should be careful because too many comments can make your code confusing.

You can use the code format used in this book's examples as you write your programs. It is not the only good format available, but it will be a good example of formatting technique, which will help you to develop your own style. However, regardless of your style, you should follow these guidelines when creating a program.

LAB 1.2 EXERCISES

1.2.1 UNDERSTAND THE NATURE OF GOOD PROGRAMMING PRACTICES

a) What is a top-down approach?

b) What is structured programming?

c) Create the following selection structure: Determine which season each month of the year belongs to.

d) Create the following iteration structure: For every day of the week display its name.

e) Create the following structure: For every day that falls within the business week, display its name. For every day that falls on the weekend, display "The weekend is here, and it is here to stay!!!" *Hint:* You will need to use iteration and selection structures. The selection structure must be placed inside the iteration structure.

1.2.2 UNDERSTAND FORMATTING GUIDELINES

a) What is the reason for formatting your code?

b) What are two main guidelines of good formatting?

LAB 1.2 EXERCISE ANSWERS

This section gives you some suggested answers to the questions in Lab 1.2, with discussion related to how those answers resulted. The most important thing to realize is whether your answer works. You should figure out the implications of the answers here and what the effects are from any different answers you may come up with.

1.2.1 ANSWERS

a) What is a top-down approach?

Answer: The technique of breaking a problem into parts and solving each part is called a top-down approach to problem solving. By breaking down the problem, it is easier to focus on possible solutions and manage each part. Once each part is fully understood, the solution to the overall problem can be readily developed.

b) What is structured programming?

Answer: Structured programming embodies a disciplined approach to writing clear code that is easy to understand, test, maintain, and modify. A program can be organized into modules called subroutines. These subroutines focus on a particular part of the overall problem that the program addresses. Subroutines are easier to understand and manage because they are only components of the overall program. Together, all of the subroutines compose the overall program.

c) Create the following selection structure: Determine which season each month of the year belongs to.

Answer:Your selection structure should look similar to the following:

```
IF MONTH IN ('DECEMBER', 'JANUARY', 'FEBRUARY')
    IT IS WINTER
IF MONTH IN ('MARCH', 'APRIL', 'MAY')
    IT IS SPRING
IF MONTH IN ('JUNE', 'JULY', 'AUGUST')
    IT IS SUMMER
IF MONTH IN ('SEPTEMBER', 'OCTOBER', 'NOVEMBER')
    IT IS FALL
```

The test conditions of this selection structure use the operator IN. This operator allows you to construct the list of valid months for every season. It is important to understand the use of the parentheses. In this case, it is not done for the sake of a syntax rule. This use of parentheses allows us to define clearly the list of values for a specific month, hence helping us to outline the logic of the structure.

Now, consider the following fragment of the selection structure:

```
IF MONTH IS 'DECEMBER'
    IT IS WINTER
IF MONTH IS 'JANUARY'
    IT IS WINTER
IF MONTH IS 'FEBRUARY'
    IT IS WINTER
...
```

This selection structure results in the same outcome, yet it is much longer. As a result it does not look well structured, even though it has been formatted properly.

d) Create the following iteration structure: For every day of the week, display its name.

Answer:Your selection structure should look similar to the following:

```
WHILE THERE ARE MORE DAYS IN THE WEEK
    DISPLAY THE NAME OF THE CURRENT DAY
    GO TO THE NEXT DAY
```

Assume that you are starting your week on Monday—there are six days left. Next, you will display the name of the current day of the week, which is Monday for the first iteration. Then, you move to the next day. The next day is Tuesday, and there are five more days in the week. So, you will display the name of the current day—Tuesday—and move to the next day, and so forth. Once the name of the seventh day (Sunday) has been displayed, the iteration structure has completed.

e) Create the following structure: For every day that falls within the business week, display its name. For every day that falls on the weekend, display "The weekend is here, and it is here to stay!!!"

Answer:Your structure should look similar to the following:

```
WHILE THERE ARE MORE DAYS IN THE WEEK
    IF DAY BETWEEN 'MONDAY' AND 'FRIDAY'
        DISPLAY THE NAME OF THE CURRENT DAY
    IF DAY IN ('SATURDAY', 'SUNDAY')
        DISPLAY 'THE WEEKEND IS HERE, AND IT IS HERE TO STAY!!!'
    GO TO THE NEXT DAY
```

This structure is a combination of two structures: iteration and selection. The iteration structure will repeat its steps for each day of the week. The selection structure will display the name of the current day or the message "The weekend is. . . ."

Assume that you are starting your week on Monday again. There are six days left. Next, control of the flow is passed to the selection structure. Because the current day happens to be Monday, and it falls within the business week, its name is displayed. Then, control of the flow is passed back to the iteration structure, and you are ready to move to the next day.

The next day is Tuesday, and there are five more days in the week. So, control is passed to the iteration structure again. Tuesday also falls within the business week, so its name is displayed as well. Next, control is passed back to the iteration structure, and you go to the next day, and so forth. Once the day falls on the weekend, the message "The weekend is . . ." is displayed.

1.2.2 ANSWERS

a) What is the reason for formatting your code?

Answer:A well-formatted program is easier to understand and maintain because format can reveal the logical structure of the program.

b) What are two main guidelines of good formatting?

Answer: First, the code of the program should be indented so that the logical structure of the program is clear. Second, the program should contain comments describing what is being accomplished.

LAB 1.2 SELF-REVIEW QUESTIONS

In order to test your progress, you should be able to answer the following questions.

1) Which one is not a feature of the structured programming?

   a) _____ Iteration
   b) _____ Sequence
   c) _____ GOTO
   d) _____ Modularity

2) Structured programming allows control of the program to jump all over the code.

    a) _____ True
    b) _____ False

3) Which of the following is true about sequence structure?

    a) _____ It refers to the decision-making process.
    b) _____ It refers to the linear execution of code.
    c) _____ It refers to the repetition of code.

4) A test condition must evaluate to which of the following in order for the selection to execute?

    a) _____ TRUE
    b) _____ FALSE
    c) _____ None of the above

5) A poorly formatted SELECT statement produces output different from a well formatted SELECT statement.

    a) _____ True
    b) _____ False
    c) _____ None of the above

Answers appear in Appendix A, Section 1.2.

**LAB
1.2**

CHAPTER 1

TEST YOUR THINKING

In this chapter you learned what a program is. You also defined the concepts of the structured programming. Here are some projects that will help you test the depth of your understanding.

1) Create the following structure: Based on the value of a number, determine if it is even or odd. *Hint:* Before you decide how to define even and odd numbers, you should decide what structure must be used to achieve the desired results.

2) Create the following structure: The structure you created in the previous exercise is designed to work with a single number. Modify it so that it can work with a list of numbers.

The projects in this section are meant to have you utilize all of the skills that you have acquired throughout this chapter. The answers to these projects can be found in Appendix D and at the companion Web site to this book, located at http://www .phptr.com/rosenzweig2e. Visit the Web site periodically to share and discuss your answers.

CHAPTER 2

PL/SQL CONCEPTS

In the previous chapter, you were introduced to some elements of computer programming languages. In this chapter, you will be introduced to the elements of a specific programming language, PL/SQL, and how it fits in the client-server architecture.

PL/SQL stands for "Procedural Language Extensions to SQL." PL/SQL extends SQL by adding programming structures and subroutines available in any high-level language. In this chapter, you will see examples that will illustrate the syntax and the rules of the language.

PL/SQL is used for both server-side and client-side development. For example, database triggers (code that is attached to tables, discussed in a later chapter) on the server side and logic behind an Oracle Developer tool on the client side can be written using PL/SQL. In addition, PL/SQL can be used to develop applications for browsers such as Netscape or Internet Explorer when used in conjunction with the Oracle Application Server and the PL/SQL Web Development Toolkit.

LAB 2.1

PL/SQL IN CLIENT-SERVER ARCHITECTURE

LAB OBJECTIVES

After this Lab, you will be able to:

- ✔ Use PL/SQL Anonymous Blocks
- ✔ Understand How PL/SQL Gets Executed

Many Oracle applications are built using client-server architecture. The Oracle database resides on the server. The program that makes requests against this database resides on the client machine. This program can be written in C, Java, or PL/SQL.

Because PL/SQL is just like any other programming language, it has syntax and rules that determine how programming statements work together. It is important for you to realize that PL/SQL is not a stand-alone programming language. PL/SQL is a part of the Oracle RDBMS, and it can reside in two environments, the client and the server. As a result, it is very easy to move PL/SQL modules between server-side and client-side applications.

In both environments, any PL/SQL block or subroutine is processed by the PL/SQL engine, which is a special component of many Oracle products. Some of these products are Oracle server, Oracle Forms, and Oracle Reports. The PL/SQL engine processes and executes any PL/SQL statements and sends any SQL statements to the SQL statement processor. The SQL statement processor is always located on the Oracle server. Figure 2.1 illustrates the PL/SQL engine residing on the Oracle server.

When the PL/SQL engine is located on the server, the whole PL/SQL block is passed to the PL/SQL engine on the Oracle server. The PL/SQL engine processes the block according to Figure 2.1.

When the PL/SQL engine is located on the client, as it is in Oracle Developer Tools, the PL/SQL processing is done on the client side. All SQL statements that

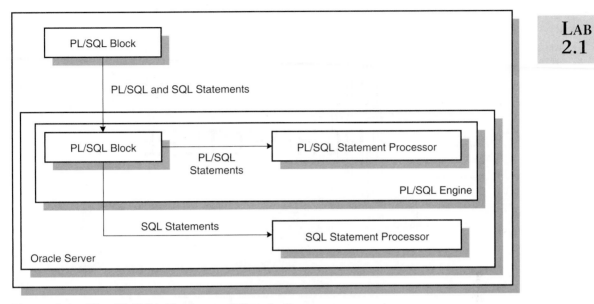

Figure 2.1 ■ The PL/SQL Engine and Oracle Server

are embedded within the PL/SQL block are sent to the Oracle server for further processing. When PL/SQL block contains no SQL statements, the entire block is executed on the client side.

Using PL/SQL has several advantages. For example, when you issue a SELECT statement in SQL*Plus against the STUDENT table, it retrieves a list of students. The SELECT statement you issued at the client computer is sent to the database server to be executed. The results of this execution are then sent back to the client. As a result, you will see rows displayed on your client machine.

Now, assume that you need to issue multiple SELECT statements. Each SELECT statement is a request against the database and is sent to the Oracle server. The results of each SELECT statement are sent back to the client. Each time a SELECT statement is executed, network traffic is generated. Hence, multiple SELECT statements will result in multiple round trip transmissions, adding significantly to the network traffic.

When these SELECT statements are combined into a PL/SQL program, they are sent to the server as a single unit. The SELECT statements in this PL/SQL program are executed at the server. The server sends the results of these SELECT statements back to the client, also as a single unit. Therefore, a PL/SQL program encompassing multiple SELECT statements can be executed at the server and have the results returned to the client in one round trip. This obviously is a more efficient process than having each SELECT statement executed independently. This model is illustrated in Figure 2.2.

Figure 2.2 compares two applications. The first application uses four independent SQL statements that generate eight trips on the network. The second application

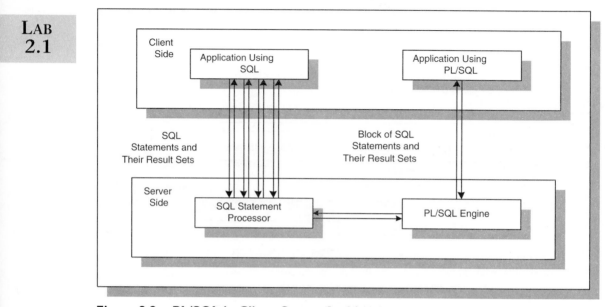

Figure 2.2 ■ PL/SQL in Client-Server Architecture

combines SQL statements into a single PL/SQL block. This PL/SQL block is then sent to the PL/SQL engine. The engine sends SQL statements to the SQL statement processor and checks the syntax of PL/SQL statements. As you can see, only two trips are generated on the network.

In addition, applications written in PL/SQL are portable. They can run in any environment that Oracle can run in. Since PL/SQL does not change from one environment to the next, different tools can use a PL/SQL script.

PL/SQL BLOCK STRUCTURE

A block is the most basic unit in PL/SQL. All PL/SQL programs are combined into blocks. These blocks can also be nested one within the other. Usually, PL/SQL blocks combine statements that represent a single logical task. Therefore, different tasks within a single program can be separated into blocks. As a result, it is easier to understand and maintain the logic of the program.

PL/SQL blocks can be divided into two groups: named and anonymous. Named PL/SQL blocks are used when creating subroutines. These subroutines are procedures, functions, and packages. The subroutines then can be stored in the database and referenced by their names later. In addition, subroutines such as procedures and functions can be defined within the anonymous PL/SQL block. These subroutines exist as long as this block is executing and cannot be referenced outside the block. In other words, subroutines defined in one PL/SQL block cannot be called by another PL/SQL block or referenced by their names later. Subroutines are discussed in Chapters 12 through 14. Anonymous PL/SQL blocks, as you have probably guessed, do not have names. As a result, they cannot be stored in the database and referenced later.

PL/SQL blocks contain three sections: declaration section, executable section, and exception-handling section. The executable section is the only mandatory section of the block. Both the declaration and exception-handling sections are optional. As a result, a PL/SQL block has the following structure:

```
DECLARE
    Declaration statements
BEGIN
    Executable statements
EXCEPTION
    Exception-handling statements
END;
```

DECLARATION SECTION

The *declaration section* is the first section of the PL/SQL block. It contains definitions of PL/SQL identifiers such as variables, constants, cursors, and so on. PL/SQL identifiers are covered in detail throughout this book.

■ FOR EXAMPLE

```
DECLARE
    v_first_name VARCHAR2(35);
    v_last_name VARCHAR2(35);
    v_counter NUMBER := 0;
```

The example given shows a declaration section of an anonymous PL/SQL block. It begins with the keyword DECLARE and contains two variable declarations and one constant declaration. The names of the variables, v_first_name and v_last_name, are followed by their datatypes and sizes. The name of the constant, v_counter, is followed by its datatype and a value assigned to it. Notice that a semicolon terminates each declaration.

EXECUTABLE SECTION

The *executable section* is the next section of the PL/SQL block. This section contains executable statements that allow you to manipulate the variables that have been declared in the declaration section.

■ FOR EXAMPLE

```
BEGIN
    SELECT first_name, last_name
      INTO v_first_name, v_last_name
```

```
         FROM student
        WHERE student_id = 123;

        DBMS_OUTPUT.PUT_LINE ('Student name: '||v_first_name||
           ' '||v_last_name);
    END;
```

The example given shows the executable section of the PL/SQL block. It begins with the keyword BEGIN and contains a SELECT INTO statement from the STUDENT table. The first and last names for student ID 123 are selected into two variables: v_first_name and v_last_name. Chapter 4 contains a detailed explanation of the SELECT INTO statement. Then the values of the variables, v_first_name and v_last_name, are displayed on the screen with the help of DBMS_OUTPUT.PUT_LINE statement. This statement will be covered later in this chapter in greater detail. The end of the executable section of this block is marked by the keyword END. The executable section of any PL/SQL block always begins with the keyword BEGIN and ends with the keyword END.

EXCEPTION-HANDLING SECTION

The *exception-handling section* is the last section of the PL/SQL block. This section contains statements that are executed when a runtime error occurs within the block. Runtime errors occur while the program is running and cannot be detected by the PL/SQL compiler. Once a runtime error occurs, control is passed to the exception-handling section of the block. The error is then evaluated, and a specific exception is raised or executed. This is best illustrated by the following example.

■ FOR EXAMPLE

```
    BEGIN
        SELECT first_name, last_name
          INTO v_first_name, v_last_name
          FROM student
         WHERE student_id = 123;

        DBMS_OUTPUT.PUT_LINE ('Student name: '||v_first_name||
           ' '||v_last_name);
    EXCEPTION
       WHEN NO_DATA_FOUND THEN
           DBMS_OUTPUT.PUT_LINE ('There is no student with '||
              'student id 123');
    END;
```

This shows the exception-handling section of the PL/SQL block. It begins with the keyword EXCEPTION. The WHEN clause evaluates which exception must be raised. In this example, there is only one exception, called NO_DATA_FOUND, and it is raised when the SELECT statement does not return any rows. If there is no record for student ID 123 in the STUDENT table, control is passed to the exception-handling section and the DBMS_OUTPUT.PUT_LINE statement is executed. Chapters 7, 10, and 11 contain more detailed explanations of the exception-handling section.

You have seen examples of the declaration section, executable section, and exception-handling section. Consider combining these examples into a single PL/SQL block.

■ FOR EXAMPLE

```
DECLARE
   v_first_name VARCHAR2(35);
   v_last_name VARCHAR2(35);
BEGIN
   SELECT first_name, last_name
     INTO v_first_name, v_last_name
     FROM student
    WHERE student_id = 123;

   DBMS_OUTPUT.PUT_LINE ('Student name: '||v_first_name||
      ' '||v_last_name);
EXCEPTION
   WHEN NO_DATA_FOUND THEN
      DBMS_OUTPUT.PUT_LINE ('There is no student with '||
         'student id 123');
END;
```

HOW PL/SQL GETS EXECUTED

Every time an anonymous PL/SQL block is executed, the code is sent to the PL/SQL engine on the server, where it is compiled. A named PL/SQL block is compiled only at the time of its creation, or if it has been changed. The compilation process includes syntax checking, binding, and p-code generation.

Syntax checking involves checking PL/SQL code for syntax or compilation errors. Syntax error occurs when a statement does not exactly correspond to the syntax of the programming language. Errors such as a misspelled keyword, a missing semicolon at the end of the statement, or an undeclared variable are examples of syntax errors.

Once the programmer corrects syntax errors, the compiler can assign a storage address to program variables that are used to hold data for Oracle. This process is called *binding*. It allows Oracle to reference storage addresses when the program is run. At the same time, the compiler checks references to the stored objects such as table names or column names in the SELECT statement, or a call to a named PL/SQL block.

Next, p-code is generated for the PL/SQL block. *P-code* is a list of instructions to the PL/SQL engine. For named blocks, p-code is stored in the database, and it is used the next time the program is executed. Once the process of compilation has completed successfully, the status of a named PL/SQL block is set to VALID, and it is also stored in the database. If the compilation process was not successful, the status of a named PL/SQL block is set to INVALID.

It is important to remember that successful compilation of the named PL/SQL block does not guarantee successful execution of this block in the future. If, at the time of execution, any one of the stored objects referenced by the block is not present in the database or not accessible to the block, execution will fail. At such time, the status of the named PL/SQL block will be changed to INVALID.

LAB 2.1 EXERCISES

2.1.1 USE PL/SQL ANONYMOUS BLOCKS

a) Why it is more efficient to combine SQL statements into PL/SQL blocks?

b) What are the differences between named and anonymous PL/SQL blocks?

For the next two questions, consider the following code:

```
DECLARE
    v_name VARCHAR2(50);
    v_total NUMBER;
BEGIN
    SELECT i.first_name||' '||i.last_name, COUNT(*)
      INTO v_name, v_total
      FROM instructor i, section s
     WHERE i.instructor_id = s.instructor_id
       AND i.instructor_id = 102
    GROUP BY i.first_name||' '||i.last_name;

    DBMS_OUTPUT.PUT_LINE
        ('Instructor '||v_name||' teaches '||v_total||
            ' courses');
```

```
EXCEPTION
   WHEN NO_DATA_FOUND THEN
      DBMS_OUTPUT.PUT_LINE ('There is no such instructor');
END;
```

The SELECT statement in the preceding example is supported by multiple versions of Oracle. However, Oracle 9i also supports the new ANSI 1999 SQL standard, and the SELECT statement can be modified as follows according to this new standard:

```
SELECT i.first_name||' '||i.last_name, COUNT(*)
  INTO v_name, v_total
  FROM instructor i
  JOIN section s
    ON (i.instructor_id = s.instructor_id)
 WHERE i.instructor_id = 102
GROUP BY i.first_name||' '||i.last_name;
```

Notice, the FROM clause contains only one table, INSTRUCTOR. Following the FROM clause is the JOIN clause that lists the second table, SECTION. Next, the ON clause lists the join condition between the two tables

```
i.instructor_id = s.instructor_id
```

which has been moved from the WHERE clause.

You will find detailed explanations and examples of the statements using new ANSI 1999 SQL standard in Appendix E and in the Oracle help. Throughout this book we will try to provide you with examples illustrating both standards; however, our main focus will remain on PL/SQL features rather than SQL.

c) Based on the example just provided, describe the structure of a PL/SQL block.

d) What happens when runtime error NO_DATA_FOUND occurs in the PL/SQL block just shown?

2.1.2 UNDERSTAND HOW PL/SQL GETS EXECUTED

a) What happens when an anonymous PL/SQL block is executed?

b) What steps are included in the compilation process of a PL/SQL block?

c) What is a syntax error?

d) How does a syntax error differ from a runtime error?

LAB 2.1 EXERCISE ANSWERS

This section gives you some suggested answers to the questions in Lab 2.1, with discussion related to how those answers resulted. The most important thing to realize is whether your answer works. You should figure out the implications of the answers here and what the effects are from any different answers you may come up with.

2.1.1 ANSWERS

a) Why it is more efficient to combine SQL statements into PL/SQL blocks?

Answer: It is more efficient to use SQL statements within PL/SQL blocks because network traffic can be decreased significantly, and an application becomes more efficient as well.

When an SQL statement is issued on the client computer, the request is made to the database on the server, and the result set is sent back to the client. As a result, a single SQL statement causes two trips on the network. If multiple SELECT statements are issued, the network traffic can increase significantly very quickly. For example, four SELECT statements cause eight network trips. If these statements are part of the PL/SQL block, there are still only two network trips made, as in the case of a single SELECT statement.

b) What are the differences between named and anonymous PL/SQL blocks?

Answer: Named PL/SQL blocks can be stored in the database and referenced later by their names. Since anonymous PL/SQL blocks do not have names, they cannot be stored in the database and referenced later.

c) Based on the example just provided, describe the structure of PL/SQL block.

Answer: PL/SQL blocks contain three sections: declaration section, executable section, and exception-handling section. The executable section is the only mandatory section of the PL/SQL block.

The declaration section holds definitions of PL/SQL identifiers such as variables, constants, and cursors. The declaration section starts with the keyword DECLARE. The declaration section

```
DECLARE
   v_name VARCHAR2(50);
   v_total NUMBER;
```

contains definitions of two variables, v_name and v_total.

The executable section holds executable statements. It starts with the keyword BEGIN and ends with the keyword END. The executable section shown in bold letters

```
BEGIN
   SELECT i.first_name||' '||i.last_name, COUNT(*)
     INTO v_name, v_total
     FROM instructor i, section s
    WHERE i.instructor_id = s.instructor_id
      AND i.instructor_id = 102
   GROUP BY i.first_name||' '||i.last_name;

   DBMS_OUTPUT.PUT_LINE
      ('Instructor '||v_name||' teaches '||v_total||
         ' courses');

EXCEPTION
   WHEN NO_DATA_FOUND THEN
      DBMS_OUTPUT.PUT_LINE ('There is no such instructor');
END;
```

contains a SELECT INTO statement that assigns values to the variables v_name and v_total, and a DBMS_OUTPUT.PUT_LINE statement that displays their values on the screen.

The exception-handling section of the PL/SQL block contains statements that are executed only if runtime errors occur in the PL/SQL block. The following exception-handling section

```
EXCEPTION
   WHEN NO_DATA_FOUND THEN
      DBMS_OUTPUT.PUT_LINE ('There is no such instructor');
```

contains the DBMS_OUTPUT.PUT_LINE statement that is executed when run-time error NO_DATA_FOUND occurs.

d) What happens when runtime error NO_DATA_FOUND occurs in the PL/SQL block just shown?

Answer: When a runtime error occurs in the PL/SQL block, control is passed to the exception-handling section of the block. The exception NO_DATA_FOUND is evaluated then with the help of the WHEN clause.

When the SELECT INTO statement

```
SELECT i.first_name||' '||i.last_name, COUNT(*)
  INTO v_name, v_total
  FROM instructor i, section s
 WHERE i.instructor_id = s.instructor_id
   AND i.instructor_id = 102
 GROUP BY i.first_name||' '||i.last_name;
```

does not return any rows, control of execution is passed to the exception-handling section of the block. Next, the DBMS_OUTPUT.PUT_LINE statement associated with the exception NO_DATA_FOUND is executed. As a result, the message "There is no such instructor" is displayed on the screen.

2.1.2 ANSWERS

a) What happens when an anonymous PL/SQL block is executed?

Answer: When an anonymous PL/SQL block is executed, the code is sent to the PL/SQL engine on the server, where it is compiled.

b) What steps are included in the compilation process of a PL/SQL block?

Answer: The compilation process includes syntax checking, binding, and p-code generation.

Syntax checking involves checking PL/SQL code for compilation errors. Once syntax errors have been corrected, a storage address is assigned to the variables that are used to hold data for Oracle. This process is called binding. Next, p-code is generated for the PL/SQL block. P-code is a list of instructions to the PL/SQL engine. For named blocks, p-code is stored in the database, and it is used the next time the program is executed.

c) What is a syntax error?

Answer: A syntax error occurs when a statement does not correspond to the syntax rules of the programming language. An undefined variable or a misplaced keyword are examples of syntax error.

d) How does a syntax error differ from a runtime error?

Answer: A syntax error can be detected by the PL/SQL compiler. A runtime error occurs while the program is running and cannot be detected by the PL/SQL compiler.

A misspelled keyword is an example of the syntax error. For example, the script

```
BEIN
   DBMS_OUTPUT.PUT_LINE ('This is a test');
END;
```

contains a syntax error. You should try to find this error.

A SELECT INTO statement returning no rows is an example of a runtime error. This error can be handled with the help of the exception-handling section of the PL/SQL block.

LAB 2.1 SELF-REVIEW QUESTIONS

In order to test your progress, you should be able to answer the following questions.

1) SQL statements combined into PL/SQL blocks cause an increase in the network traffic.

   a) _____ True
   b) _____ False

2) Which of the following sections is mandatory for a PL/SQL block?

   a) _____ Exception-handling section
   b) _____ Executable section
   c) _____ Declaration section

3) The exception-handling section in a PL/SQL block is used to

   a) _____ handle compilation errors.
   b) _____ handle runtime errors.
   c) _____ handle both compilation and runtime errors.

4) A PL/SQL compiler can detect

   a) _____ syntax errors.
   b) _____ runtime errors.
   c) _____ both compilation and runtime errors.

5) P-code is stored in the database for

   a) _____ anonymous PL/SQL blocks.
   b) _____ named PL/SQL blocks.

Answers appear in Appendix A, Section 2.1.

LAB 2.2

PL/SQL IN SQL*PLUS

LAB OBJECTIVES

After this Lab, you will be able to:

✔ Use Substitution Variables
✔ Use the DBMS_OUTPUT.PUT_LINE statement

SQL*Plus is an interactive tool that allows you to type SQL or PL/SQL statements at the command prompt. These statements are then sent to the database. Once they are processed, the results are sent back from the database and displayed on the screen. However, there are some differences between entering SQL and PL/SQL statements.

Consider the following example of a SQL statement.

■ *FOR EXAMPLE*

```
SELECT first_name, last_name
  FROM student;
```

The semicolon terminates this SELECT statement. Therefore, as soon as you type the semicolon and hit the ENTER key, the result set is displayed to you.

Now, consider the example of the PL/SQL block used in the previous Lab.

■ *FOR EXAMPLE*

```
DECLARE
   v_first_name VARCHAR2(35);
   v_last_name VARCHAR2(35);
BEGIN
   SELECT first_name, last_name
     INTO v_first_name, v_last_name
```

```
      FROM student
    WHERE student_id = 123;

    DBMS_OUTPUT.PUT_LINE ('Student name: '||v_first_name||
       ' '||v_last_name);
EXCEPTION
   WHEN NO_DATA_FOUND THEN
      DBMS_OUTPUT.PUT_LINE ('There is no student with '||
         'student id 123');
END;
.
/
```

There are two additional lines at the end of the block containing "." and "/". The "." marks the end of the PL/SQL block and is optional. The "/" executes the PL/SQL block and is required.

When SQL*Plus reads a SQL statement, it knows that the semicolon marks the end of the statement. Therefore, the statement is complete and can be sent to the database. When SQL*Plus reads a PL/SQL block, a semicolon marks the end of the individual statement within the block. In other words, it is not a block terminator. Therefore, SQL*Plus needs to know when the block has ended. As you have seen in the preceding example, it can be done with a period and a forward slash.

SUBSTITUTION VARIABLES

We noted earlier that PL/SQL is not a stand-alone programming language. It only exists as a tool within the Oracle programming environment. As a result, it does not really have capabilities to accept input from a user. However, SQL*Plus allows a PL/SQL block to receive input information with the help of substitution variables. Substitution variables cannot be used to output values, because no memory is allocated for them. SQL*Plus will substitute a variable before the PL/SQL block is sent to the database. Substitution variables are usually prefixed by the ampersand (&) character or double ampersand (&&) character. Consider the following example.

■ *FOR EXAMPLE*

```
DECLARE
   v_student_id NUMBER := &sv_student_id;
   v_first_name VARCHAR2(35);
   v_last_name VARCHAR2(35);
BEGIN
   SELECT first_name, last_name
     INTO v_first_name, v_last_name
     FROM student
    WHERE student_id = v_student_id;
```

```
        DBMS_OUTPUT.PUT_LINE ('Student name: '||v_first_name||
           ' '||v_last_name);
   EXCEPTION
      WHEN NO_DATA_FOUND THEN
          DBMS_OUTPUT.PUT_LINE ('There is no such student');
   END;
```

When this example is executed, the user is asked to provide a value for the student ID. The student's name is then retrieved from the STUDENT table if there is a record with the given student ID. If there is no record with the given student ID, the message from the exception-handling section is displayed on the screen.

The preceding example uses a single ampersand for the substitution variable. When a single ampersand is used throughout the PL/SQL block, the user is asked to provide a value for each occurrence of the substitution variable. Consider the following example.

■ FOR EXAMPLE

```
   BEGIN
      DBMS_OUTPUT.PUT_LINE ('Today is '||'&sv_day');
      DBMS_OUTPUT.PUT_LINE ('Tomorrow will be '||'&sv_day');
   END;
```

This example produces the following output:

```
   Enter value for sv_day: Monday
   old   2:    DBMS_OUTPUT.PUT_LINE ('Today is '||'&sv_day');
   new   2:    DBMS_OUTPUT.PUT_LINE ('Today is '||'Monday');
   Enter value for sv_day: Tuesday
   old   3:    DBMS_OUTPUT.PUT_LINE ('Tomorrow will be
   '||'&sv_day');
   new   3:    DBMS_OUTPUT.PUT_LINE ('Tomorrow will be
   '||'Tuesday');
   Today is Monday
   Tomorrow will be Tuesday

   PL/SQL procedure successfully completed.
```

When a substitution variable is used in the script, the output produced by the program contains the statements that show how the substitution was done. For example, consider the following lines of the output produced by the preceding example:

```
   old   2:    DBMS_OUTPUT.PUT_LINE ('Today is '||'&sv_day');
   new   2:    DBMS_OUTPUT.PUT_LINE ('Today is '||'Monday');
```

If you do not want to see these lines displayed in the output produced by the script, use the SET command option before you run the script, as shown:

```
SET VERIFY OFF;
```

Then the output appears as follows:

```
Enter value for sv_day: Monday
Enter value for sv_day: Tuesday
Today is Monday
Tomorrow will be Tuesday
```

```
PL/SQL procedure successfully completed.
```

You have probably noticed that the substitution variable sv_day appears twice in this PL/SQL block. As a result, when this example is run, the user is asked twice to provide the value for the same variable. Now, consider an altered version of the example as follows (changes are shown in bold).

■ FOR EXAMPLE

```
BEGIN
    DBMS_OUTPUT.PUT_LINE ('Today is '||'&&sv_day');
    DBMS_OUTPUT.PUT_LINE ('Tomorrow will be '||'&sv_day');
END;
```

In this example, the substitution variable sv_day is prefixed by double ampersand in the first DBMS_OUTPUT.PUT_LINE statement. As a result, this version of the example produces different output.

```
Enter value for sv_day: Monday
old   2:    DBMS_OUTPUT.PUT_LINE ('Today is '||'&&sv_day');
new   2:    DBMS_OUTPUT.PUT_LINE ('Today is '||'Monday');
old   3:    DBMS_OUTPUT.PUT_LINE ('Tomorrow will be
'||'&sv_day');
new   3:    DBMS_OUTPUT.PUT_LINE ('Tomorrow will be
'||'Monday');
Today is Monday
Tomorrow will be Monday
```

```
PL/SQL procedure successfully completed.
```

From the output shown, it is clear that the user is asked only once to provide the value for the substitution variable sv_day. As a result, both DBMS_OUTPUT.PUT_LINE statements use the value of Monday entered by the user.

When a substitution variable is assigned to the string (text) datatype, it is a good practice to enclose it with single quotes. You cannot always guarantee that a user will provide text information in single quotes. This practice will make your program less error prone. This is illustrated in the following code fragment.

■ FOR EXAMPLE

```
v_course_no VARCHAR2(5) := '&sv_course_no';
```

As mentioned earlier, substitution variables are usually prefixed by the ampersand (&) character or double ampersand (&&) characters. These are default characters that denote substitution variables. There is a special SET command option available in SQL*Plus that allows you to change the default character (&) to any other character or disable the substitution variable feature. This SET command has the following syntax:

> **SET DEFINE *character***

or

> **SET DEFINE ON**

or

> **SET DEFINE OFF**

The first set command option changes the prefix of the substitution variable from an ampersand to another character. However, it is important for you to note that this character cannot be alphanumeric or white space. The second (ON option) and third (OFF option) control whether SQL*Plus will look for substitution variables or not. In addition, the ON option changes the value of the character back to the ampersand.

DBMS_OUTPUT.PUT_LINE

You already have seen some examples of how the DBMS_OUTPUT.PUT_LINE statement can be used. This statement is used to display information on the screen. It is very helpful when you want to see how your PL/SQL block is executed. For example, you might want to see how variables change their values throughout the program, in order to debug it.

The DBMS_OUTPUT.PUT_LINE is a call to the procedure PUT_LINE. This procedure is a part of the DBMS_OUTPUT package that is owned by the Oracle user SYS.

DBMS_OUTPUT.PUT_LINE writes information to the buffer for storage. Once a program has been completed, the information from the buffer is displayed on the screen. The size of the buffer can be set between 2,000 and 1,000,000 bytes. Before you can see the output printed on the screen, one of the following statements must be entered before the PL/SQL block.

SET SERVEROUTPUT ON;

or

SET SERVEROUTPUT ON SIZE 5000;

The first SET statement enables the DBMS_OUTPUT.PUT_LINE statement, and the default value for the buffer size is used. The second SET statement not only enables the DBMS_OUTPUT.PUT_LINE statement, but also changes the buffer size from its default value to 5,000 bytes.

Similarly, if you do not want information to be displayed on the screen by the DBMS_OUTPUT.PUT_LINE statement, the following SET command can be issued prior to the PL/SQL block.

SET SERVEROUTPUT OFF;

LAB 2.2 EXERCISES

2.2.1 USE SUBSTITUTION VARIABLES

In this exercise, you will calculate the square of a number. The value of the number will be provided with the help of a substitution variable. Then the result will be displayed on the screen.

Create the following PL/SQL script:

```
-- ch02_1a.sql, version 1.0
SET SERVEROUTPUT ON
DECLARE
   v_num NUMBER := &sv_num;
   v_result NUMBER;
BEGIN
   v_result := POWER(v_num, 2);
   DBMS_OUTPUT.PUT_LINE ('The value of v_result is: '||
      v_result);
END;
```

Execute the script, and then answer the following questions:

a) If the value of v_num is equal to 10, what output is printed on the screen?

b) What is the purpose of using a substitution variable?

c) Why is it considered a good practice to enclose substitution variables with single quotes for string datatypes?

LAB
2.2

2.2.2 USE THE DBMS_OUTPUT.PUT_LINE STATEMENT

In this exercise, you will determine the day of the week based on today's date. You will then display the results on the screen.

Create the following PL/SQL script:

```
-- ch02_2a.sql, version 1.0
SET SERVEROUTPUT ON
DECLARE
    v_day VARCHAR2(20);
BEGIN
    v_day := TO_CHAR(SYSDATE, 'Day');
    DBMS_OUTPUT.PUT_LINE ('Today is '||v_day);
END;
```

Execute the script, and then answer the following questions:

a) What was printed on the screen?

b) What will be printed on the screen if the statement SET SERVEROUTPUT OFF is issued? Why?

c) How would you change the script to display the time of the day as well?

LAB 2.2 EXERCISE ANSWERS

This section gives you some suggested answers to the questions in Lab 2.2, with discussion related to how those answers resulted. The most important thing to realize is whether your answer works. You should figure out the implications of the answers here and what the effects are from any different answers you may come up with.

2.2.1 ANSWERS

a) If the value of v_num is equal to 10, what output is printed on the screen?

Answer: Your output should look like the following:

```
Enter value for v_num: 10
old    2:      v_num     NUMBER := &sv_num;
new    2:      v_num     NUMBER := 10;
The value of v_result is: 100

PL/SQL procedure successfully completed.
```

The first line of the output asks you to provide a value for the substitution variable sv_num. Then the actual substitution is shown to you in lines 2 and 3. In the second line, you can see the original statement from the PL/SQL block. In the third line, you can see the same statement with the substitution value. The next line shows the output produced by the DBMS_OUTPUT.PUT_LINE statement. Finally, the last line informs you that your PL/SQL block was executed successfully.

b) What is the purpose of using a substitution variable?

Answer: A substitution variable allows the PL/SQL block to accept information provided by the user at the time of execution. Substitution variables are used for input purposes only. They cannot be used to output values for a user.

c) Why it is considered a good practice to enclose a substitution variable with single quotes for string datatypes?

Answer: A program cannot depend wholly on a user to provide text information in single quotes. Enclosing a substitution variable with single quotes allows a program to be less error-prone.

**LAB
2.2**

a) What was printed on the screen?

Answer:Your output should look like the following:

```
Today is Friday

PL/SQL procedure successfully completed.
```

In this example, SQL*Plus does not ask you to enter the value of the v_day vari-able because no substitution variable is used. The value of v_day is computed with the help of TO_CHAR and SYSDATE functions. Then it is displayed on the screen with the help of the DBMS_OUTPUT.PUT_LINE statement.

b) What will be printed on the screen if the statement SET SERVEROUTPUT OFF is issued? Why?

Answer: If the statement SET SERVEROUTPUT OFF is issued prior to the execution of the PL/SQL block, no output will be printed on the screen. The output will look like fol-lowing:

```
PL/SQL procedure successfully completed.
```

It is important to note that when substitution variables are used, the user is prompted to enter the value for the variable regardless of the SERVEROUTPUT setting. The prompt for the user is provided by SQL*Plus and does not depend on the option chosen for the SERVEROUTPUT.

c) How would you change the script to display time of the day as well?

Answer:Your script should look similar to this script. Changes are shown in bold letters.

```
-- ch02_2b.sql, version 2.0
SET SERVEROUTPUT ON
DECLARE
   v_day VARCHAR2(20);
BEGIN
   v_day := TO_CHAR(SYSDATE, 'Day, HH24:MI');
   DBMS_OUTPUT.PUT_LINE ('Today is '|| v_day);
END;
```

The statement shown in bold has been changed in order to display time of the day as well. The output produced by this PL/SQL block is as follows:

```
Today is Friday    , 23:09

PL/SQL procedure successfully completed.
```

LAB 2.2 SELF-REVIEW QUESTIONS

In order to test your progress, you should be able to answer the following questions.

1) SQL*Plus understands a semicolon as a terminating symbol of a PL/SQL block.

a) _____ True
b) _✓_ False

2) Substitution variables are used to

a) _✓_ read input information provided by a user.
b) _____ provide a user with output information.
c) _____ both a and b.

3) PUT_LINE is one of the procedures from the DBMS_OUTPUT package.

a) _✓_ True
b) _____ False

4) DBMS_OUTPUT.PUT_LINE writes information to the buffer for storage before it is displayed on the screen.

a) _✓_ True
b) _____ False

5) The SET command SET SERVEROUTPUT ON SIZE 8000 is used to

a) _____ enable the DBMS_OUTPUT.PUT_LINE statement only.
b) _____ change the buffer size only.
c) _✓_ enable the DBMS_OUTPUT.PUT_LINE statement and change the buffer size.

Answers appear in Appendix A, Section 2.2.

CHAPTER 2

TEST YOUR THINKING

In this chapter you learned about PL/SQL concepts. You explored PL/SQL block structure, substitution variables, and the DBMS_OUTPUT.PUT_LINE statement. Here are some exercises that will help you test the depth of your understanding.

1) In order to calculate the area of a circle, the circle's radius must be squared and then multiplied by π. Write a program that calculates the area of a circle. The value for the radius should by provided with the help of a substitution variable. Use 3.14 for the value of π. Once the area of the circle is calculated, display it on the screen.

2) Rewrite the script ch02_2b.sql, version 2.0. In the output produced by the script, extra spaces appear after the day of the week. The new script must remove the extra spaces after the day of the week. The current output:

```
Today is Friday    , 23:09
```

The new output should have the format as shown:

```
Today is Friday, 23:09
```

The projects in this section are meant to have you utilize all of the skills that you have acquired throughout this chapter. The answers to these projects can be found in Appendix D and at the companion Web site to this book, located at http://www.phptr.com/rosenzweig2e. Visit the Web site periodically to share and discuss your answers.

C H A P T E R   3

GENERAL PROGRAMMING LANGUAGE FUNDAMENTALS

In the first two chapters you learned about the difference between machine language and a programming language. You have also learned how PL/SQL is different from SQL and about the PL/SQL basic block structure. This is similar to learning the history behind a foreign language and in what context it is used. In order to use the PL/SQL language, you will have to learn the key words, what they mean, and when and how to use them. First, you will encounter the different types of key words and then their full syntax. Finally, in this chapter, you will expand on simple block structure with an exploration of scope and nesting blocks.

LAB 3.1

PL/SQL PROGRAMMING FUNDAMENTALS

LAB OBJECTIVES

After this Lab, you will be able to:

✔ Make Use of PL/SQL Language Components
✔ Make Use of PL/SQL Variables
✔ Handle PL/SQL Reserved Words
✔ Make Use of Identifiers in PL/SQL
✔ Make Use of Anchored Data types
✔ Declare and Initialize Variables
✔ Understand the Scope of a Block, Nested Blocks, and Labels

In most languages, you have only two sets of characters: numbers and letters. Some languages, such as Hebrew or Tibetan, have specific characters for vowels that are not placed in line with consonants. Additionally, other languages, such as Japanese, have three character sets: one for words originally taken from the Chinese language, another set for native Japanese words, and then a third for other foreign words. In order to speak any foreign language, you have to begin by learning these character sets. Then you progress to learn how to make words from these character sets. Finally, you learn the parts of speech and you can begin talking. You can think of PL/SQL as being a more complex language because it has many character types and, additionally, many types of words or lexical units that are made from these character sets. Once you learn these, you can progress to learn the structure of the PL/SQL language.

CHARACTER TYPES

The PL/SQL engine accepts four types of characters: letters, digits, symbols (*, +, -, =, etc.), and white space. When elements from one or more of these character types are joined together, they will create a lexical unit (these lexical units can be a combination of character types). The lexical units are the words of the PL/SQL language. First you need to learn the PL/SQL vocabulary, and then you will move on to the syntax, or grammar. Soon you can start talking in PL/SQL.

Although PL/SQL can be considered a language, don't try talking to your fellow programmers in PL/SQL. For example, at a dinner table of programmers, if you say, "BEGIN, LOOP FOR PEAS IN PLATE EXECUTE EAT PEAS, END LOOP, EXCEPTION WHEN BROCCOLI FOUND EXECUTE SEND TO PRESIDENT BUSH, END EAT PEAS," you may not be considered human. This type of language is reserved for Terminators and the like.

LEXICAL UNITS

A language such as English contains different parts of speech. Each part of speech, such as a verb or noun, behaves in a different way and must be used according to specific rules. Likewise, a programming language has lexical units that are the building blocks of the language. PL/SQL lexical units fall within one of the following five groups:

1. *Identifiers.* Identifiers must begin with a letter and may be up to 30 characters long. See a PL/SQL manual for a more detailed list of restrictions; generally, if you stay with characters, numbers, and " ", and avoid reserved words, you will not run into problems.

2. *Reserved words.* Reserved words are words that PL/SQL saves for its own use (e.g., BEGIN, END, SELECT).

3. *Delimiters.* These are characters that have special meaning to PL/SQL, such as arithmetic operators and quotation marks.

4. *Literals.* A literal is any value (character, numeric, or Boolean [true/false]) that is not an identifier. 123, "Declaration of Independence," and FALSE are examples of literals.

5. *Comments.* These can be either single-line comments (i.e., --) or multiline comments (i.e., /* */).

See Appendix B, "PL/SQL Formatting Guide," for details on formatting.

In the following exercises, you will practice putting these units together.

LAB 3.1 EXERCISES

3.1.1 MAKE USE OF PL/SQL LANGUAGE COMPONENTS

Now that you have the character types and the lexical units, it is equivalent to knowing the alphabet and how to spell out words.

a) Why does PL/SQL have so many different types of characters? What are they used for?

b) What would be the equivalent of a verb and a noun in English in PL/SQL? Do you speak PL/SQL?

3.1.2 MAKE USE OF PL/SQL VARIABLES

Variables may be used to hold a temporary value.

```
Syntax : <variable-name> <data type> [optional default
assignment]
```

Variables may also be known as identifiers. There are some restrictions that you need to be familiar with: Variables must begin with a letter and may be up to 30 characters long. Consider the following example:

■ *FOR EXAMPLE*

This example contains a list of valid identifiers:

```
v_student_id
v_last_name
V_LAST_NAME
apt_#
```

It is important to note that the identifiers v_last_name and V_LAST_NAME are considered identical because PL/SQL is not case sensitive.

Next, consider an example of illegal identifiers:

■ *FOR EXAMPLE*

```
X+Y
1st_year
student ID
```

Identifier X+Y is illegal because it contains the "+" sign. This sign is reserved by PL/SQL to denote an addition operation, and it is referred to as a mathematical symbol. Identifier, `1st_year` is illegal because it starts with a number. Finally, identifier `student ID` is illegal because it contains a space.

Next, consider another example:

■ *FOR EXAMPLE*

```
SET SERVEROUTPUT ON;
DECLARE
    first&last_names VARCHAR2(30);
BEGIN
    first&last_names := 'TEST NAME';
    DBMS_OUTPUT.PUT_LINE(first&last_names);
END;
```

In this example, you declare a variable called `first&last_names`. Next, you assign a value to this variable and display this value on the screen. When run, the example produces the following output:

```
Enter value for last_names: Elena
old   2:    first&last_names VARCHAR2(30);
new   2:    firstElena VARCHAR2(30);
Enter value for last_names: Elena
old   4:    first&last_names := 'TEST NAME';
new   4:    firstElena := 'TEST NAME';
Enter value for last_names: Elena
old   5:    DBMS_OUTPUT.PUT_LINE(first&last_names);
new   5:    DBMS_OUTPUT.PUT_LINE(firstElena);
TEST NAME
PL/SQL procedure successfully completed.
```

Consider the output produced. Because there is an ampersand (&) present in the name of the variable `first&last_names`, the portion of the variable is considered to be a substitution variable (you learned about substitution variables in Chapter 2). In other words, the portion of the variable name after the ampersand (`last_names`) is treated by the PL/SQL compiler as a substitution variable. As a result, you are prompted to enter the value for the `last_names` variable every time the compiler encounters it.

It is important to realize that while this example does not produce any syntax errors, the variable `first&last_names` is still an invalid identifier because the ampersand character is reserved for substitution variables. To avoid this problem, change the name of the variable from `first&last_names` to `first_and_last_names`. Therefore, *you should use an ampersand sign in the name of a variable only when you use it as a substitution variable in your program.*

■ *FOR EXAMPLE*

```
-- ch03_1a.pls
SET SERVEROUTPUT ON
DECLARE
    v_name VARCHAR2(30);
    v_dob DATE;
    v_us_citizen BOOLEAN;
BEGIN
    DBMS_OUTPUT.PUT_LINE(v_name||'born on'||v_dob);
END;
```

a) If you ran the previous example in a SQL*Plus, what would be the result?

b) Run the example and see what happens. Explain what is happening as the focus moves from one line to the next.

3.1.3 HANDLE PL/SQL RESERVED WORDS

Reserved words are ones that PL/SQL saves for its own use (e.g., BEGIN, END, and SELECT). You cannot use reserved words for names of variables, literals, or user-defined exceptions.

■ *FOR EXAMPLE*

```
SET SERVEROUTPUT ON;
DECLARE
    exception VARCHAR2(15);
BEGIN
    exception := 'This is a test';
    DBMS_OUTPUT.PUT_LINE(exception);
END;
```

a) What would happen if you ran the preceding PL/SQL block? Would you receive an error message? If so, explain.

3.1.4 MAKE USE OF IDENTIFIERS IN PL/SQL

Take a look at the use of identifiers in the following example:

■ *FOR EXAMPLE*

```
SET SERVEROUTPUT ON;
DECLARE
    v_var1 VARCHAR2(20);
    v_var2 VARCHAR2(6);
    v_var3 NUMBER(5,3);
BEGIN
    v_var1 := 'string literal';
    v_var2 := '12.345';
    v_var3 := 12.345;
    DBMS_OUTPUT.PUT_LINE('v_var1: '||v_var1);
    DBMS_OUTPUT.PUT_LINE('v_var2: '||v_var2);
    DBMS_OUTPUT.PUT_LINE('v_var3: '||v_var3);
END;
```

In this example, you declare and initialize three variables. The values that you assign to them are literals. The first two values, 'string literal' and '12.345' are string literals because they are enclosed by single quotes. The third value, 12.345, is a numeric literal. When run, the example produces the following output:

```
v_var1: string literal
v_var2: 12.345
v_var3: 12.345
PL/SQL procedure successfully completed.
```

Consider another example that uses numeric literals:

■ *FOR EXAMPLE*

```
SET SERVEROUTPUT ON;
DECLARE
    v_var1 NUMBER(2) := 123;
    v_var2 NUMBER(3) := 123;
    v_var3 NUMBER(5,3) := 123456.123;
BEGIN
    DBMS_OUTPUT.PUT_LINE('v_var1: '||v_var1);
    DBMS_OUTPUT.PUT_LINE('v_var2: '||v_var2);
    DBMS_OUTPUT.PUT_LINE('v_var3: '||v_var3);
END;
```

a) What would happen if you ran the preceding PL/SQL block?

3.1.5 MAKE USE OF ANCHORED DATA TYPES

The data type that you assign to a variable can be based on a database object. This is called an *anchored declaration* since the variable's data type is dependent on that of the underlying object. It is wise to make use of anchored data types when possible so that you do not have to update your PL/SQL when the data types of base objects change.

```
Syntax:   <variable_name> <type attribute>%TYPE
```

The type is a direct reference to a database column.

■ *FOR EXAMPLE*

```
-- ch03_2a.pls
SET SERVEROUTPUT ON
DECLARE
    v_name student.first_name%TYPE;
    v_grade grade.numeric_grade%TYPE;
BEGIN
    DBMS_OUTPUT.PUT_LINE(NVL(v_name, 'No Name ')||
        ' has grade of '||NVL(v_grade, 0));
END;
```

a) In the previous example, what has been declared? State the data type and value.

3.1.6 DECLARE AND INITIALIZE VARIABLES

In PL/SQL, variables must be declared in order to be referenced. This is done in the initial declarative section of a PL/SQL block. Remember that each declaration must be terminated with a semicolon. Variables can be assigned using the assignment operator ":=". If you declare a variable to be a constant, it will retain the same value throughout the block; in order to do this, you must give it a value at declaration.

Type the following into a text file and run the script from a SQL*Plus session.

```
-- ch03_3a.pls
SET SERVEROUTPUT ON
DECLARE
   v_cookies_amt NUMBER := 2;
   v_calories_per_cookie CONSTANT NUMBER := 300;
BEGIN
   DBMS_OUTPUT.PUT_LINE('I ate ' || v_cookies_amt ||
      ' cookies with ' ||  v_cookies_amt *
      v_calories_per_cookie || ' calories.');
   v_cookies_amt := 3;
   DBMS_OUTPUT.PUT_LINE('I really ate ' ||
      v_cookies_amt
      || ' cookies with ' ||  v_cookies_amt *
      v_calories_per_cookie || ' calories.');
   v_cookies_amt := v_cookies_amt + 5;
   DBMS_OUTPUT.PUT_LINE('The truth is, I actually ate '
      || v_cookies_amt || ' cookies with ' ||
   v_cookies_amt * v_calories_per_cookie
      || ' calories.');
END;
```

a) What will the output be for the preceding script? Explain what is being declared and what the value of the variable is throughout the scope of the block.

■ FOR EXAMPLE

```
-- ch03_3a.pls
SET SERVEROUTPUT ON
DECLARE
   v_lname VARCHAR2(30);
   v_regdate DATE;
   v_pctincr CONSTANT NUMBER(4,2) := 1.50;
   v_counter NUMBER := 0;
   v_new_cost course.cost%TYPE;
   v_YorN BOOLEAN := TRUE;
BEGIN
      DBMS_OUTPUT.PUT.PUT_LINE(V_COUNTER);
      DBMS_OUTPUT.PUT_LINE(V_NEW_COST);
END;
```

b) In the previous example, add the following expressions to the beginning of the procedure (immediately after the BEGIN in the previous example), then explain the values of the variables at the beginning and at the end of the script.

```
v_counter := NVL(v_counter, 0) + 1;
v_new_cost := 800 * v_pctincr;
```

PL/SQL variables are held together with expressions and operators. An expression is a sequence of variables and literals, separated by operators. These expressions are then used to manipulate data, perform calculations, and compare data.

Expressions are composed of a combination of operands and operators. An *operand* is an argument to the operator; it can be a variable, a constant, a function call. An *operator* is what specifies the action (+, **, /, OR, etc.).

You can use parentheses to control the order in which Oracle evaluates an expression. Continue to add the following to your SQL script the following:

```
v_counter := ((v_counter + 5)*2) / 2;
v_new_cost := (v_new_cost * v_counter)/4;
```

c) What will the values of the variables be at the end of the script?

3.1.7 UNDERSTAND THE SCOPE OF A BLOCK, NESTED BLOCKS, AND LABELS

SCOPE OF A VARIABLE

The scope, or existence, of structures defined in the declaration section are local to that block. The block also provides the scope for exceptions that are declared and raised. Exceptions will be covered in more detail in Chapters 7, 10, and 11.

The scope of a variable is the portion of the program in which the variable can be accessed, or where the variable is visible. It usually extends from the moment of declaration until the end of the block in which the variable was declared. The visibility of a variable is the part of the program where the variable can be accessed.

```
BEGIN    -- outer block
         BEGIN -- inner block
                ...;
         END;  -- end of inner block
END;     -- end of outer block
```

LABELS AND NESTED BLOCKS

Labels can be added to a block in order to improve readability and to qualify the names of elements that exist under the same name in nested blocks. The name of the block must precede the first line of executable code (either the BEGIN or DE-CLARE) as follows:

■ FOR EXAMPLE

```
-- ch03_4a.pls
set serveroutput on
   <<find_stu_num>>
   BEGIN
       DBMS_OUTPUT.PUT_LINE('The procedure
                    find_stu_num has been executed.');
   END find_stu_num;
```

The label optionally appears after END. In SQL*Plus, the first line of a PL/SQL block cannot be a label. For commenting purposes, you may alternatively use "- -" or /*, ending with */.

Blocks can be nested in the main section or in an exception handler. A *nested block* is a block that is placed fully within another block. This has an impact on the scope and visibility of variables. The scope of a variable in a nested block is the period when memory is being allocated for the variable and extends from the moment of declaration until the END of the nested block from which it was declared. The visibility of a variable is the part of the program where the variable can be accessed.

■ FOR EXAMPLE

```
-- ch03_4b.pls
SET SERVEROUTPUT ON
<< outer_block >>
DECLARE
   v_test NUMBER := 123;
BEGIN
   DBMS_OUTPUT.PUT_LINE
       ('Outer Block, v_test: '||v_test);
   << inner_block >>
   DECLARE
      v_test NUMBER := 456;
   BEGIN
      DBMS_OUTPUT.PUT_LINE
          ('Inner Block, v_test: '||v_test);
      DBMS_OUTPUT.PUT_LINE
          ('Inner Block, outer_block.v_test: '||
            outer_block.v_test);
   END inner_block;
END outer_block;
```

This example produces the following output:

```
Outer Block, v_test: 123
Inner Block, v_test: 456
Inner Block, outer_block.v_test: 123
```

a) If the following example were run in SQL*Plus, what do you
think would be displayed?

```
-- ch03_5a.pls
SET SERVEROUTPUT ON
DECLARE
   e_show_exception_scope EXCEPTION;
   v_student_id              NUMBER := 123;
BEGIN
  DBMS_OUTPUT.PUT_LINE('outer student id is '
     ||v_student_id);
   DECLARE
     v_student_id    VARCHAR2(8) := 125;
   BEGIN
      DBMS_OUTPUT.PUT_LINE('inner student id is '
         ||v_student_id);
      RAISE e_show_exception_scope;
   END;
EXCEPTION
   WHEN e_show_exception_scope
   THEN
      DBMS_OUTPUT.PUT_LINE('When am I displayed?');
      DBMS_OUTPUT.PUT_LINE('outer student id is '
         ||v_student_id);
END;
```

b) Now run the example and see if it produces what you expected. Explain how the focus moves from one block to another in this example.

LAB 3.1 EXERCISE ANSWERS

This section gives you some suggested answers to the questions in Lab 3.1, with
discussion related to how those answers resulted. The most important thing to
realize is whether your answer works. You should figure out the implications of
the answers here and what the effects are from any different answers you may
come up with.

3.1.1 ANSWERS

a) Why does PL/SQL have so many different types of characters? What are they used for?

Answer: The PL/SQL engine recognizes different characters as having different meaning and therefore processes them differently. PL/SQL is neither a pure mathematical language nor a spoken language, yet it contains elements of both. Letters will form various lexical units such as identifiers or key words, mathematic symbols will form lexical units known as delimiters that will perform an operation, and other symbols, such as /*, indicate comments that should not be processed.

b) What would be the equivalent of a verb and a noun in English in PL/SQL? Do you speak PL/SQL?

Answer: A noun would be similar to the lexical unit known as an identifier. A verb would be similar to the lexical unit known as a delimiter. Delimiters can simply be quotation marks, but others perform a function such as to multiply "*".

3.1.2 ANSWERS

a) If you ran the previous example in a SQL*Plus, what would be the result?

Answer: Assuming `SET SERVEROUTPUT ON` *had been issued, you would get only* `born on`. *The reason is that the variables* `v_name` *and* `v_dob` *have no values.*

b) Run the example and see what happens. Explain what is happening as the focus moves from one line to the next.

Answer: Three variables are declared. When each one is declared, its initial value is null. `v_name` *is set as a varchar2VARCHAR2 with a length of 30,* `v_dob` *is set as a character type date, and* `v_us_citizen` *is set to BOOLEAN. Once the executable section begins, the variables have no value and, therefore, when the DBMS_OUTPUT is told to print their values, it prints nothing.*

This can be seen if the variables were replaced as follows: Instead of `v_name`, use `NVL(v_name, 'No Name')` and instead of `v_dob` use `NVL (v_dob, '01-Jan-1999')`. Then run the same block and you will get

```
No Name born on 01-Jan-1999
```

In order to make use of a variable, you must declare it in the declaration section of the PL/SQL block. You will have to give it a name and state its data type. You also have the option to give your variable an initial value. Note that if you do not assign a variable an initial value, it will be null. It is also possible to constrain the declaration to "not null," in which case you must assign an initial value. Variables must first be declared and then they can be referenced. PL/SQL does not allow forward references. You can set the variable to be a constant, which means it cannot change.

3.1.3 ANSWERS

a) What would happen if you ran the above PL/SQL block? Would you receive an error message? If so, explain.

Answer: In this example, you declare a variable called `exception`. *Next, you initialize this variable and display its value on the screen.*

This example illustrates an invalid use of reserved words. To the PL/SQL compiler, "exception" is a reserved word and it denotes the beginning of the exception-handling section. As a result, it cannot be used to name a variable. Consider the huge error message produced by this tiny example.

```
exception VARCHAR2(15);
      *
ERROR at line 2:
ORA-06550: line 2, column 4:
PLS-00103: Encountered the symbol "EXCEPTION" when
expecting one of the following:
begin function package pragma procedure subtype type use
<an identifier> <a double-quoted delimited-identifier>
 cursor
form current
The symbol "begin was inserted before "EXCEPTION"
to continue.
ORA-06550: line 4, column 4:
PLS-00103: Encountered the symbol "EXCEPTION" when
expecting one of the following:
begin declare exit for goto if loop mod null pragma
 raise
return select update while <an identifier>
<a double-quoted delimited-identifier> <a bin
ORA-06550: line 5, column 25:
PLS-00103: Encountered the symbol "EXCEPTION" when
expecting one of the following:
( ) - + mod not null others <an identifier>
<a double-quoted delimited-identifier> <a bind variable>
avg
count current exists max min prior sql s
ORA-06550: line 7, column 0:
PLS-00103: Encountered the symbol "end-of-file" when
expecting one of the following:
begin declare end exception exit for goto if loop
```

Here is a question you should ask yourself: If you did not know that the word "exception" is a reserved word, do you think you would attempt to debug the preceding script after looking at this error message? I know I would not.

3.1.4 ANSWERS

a) What would happen if you ran the preceding PL/SQL block?

Answer: In this example, you declare and initialize three numeric variables. The first declaration and initialization (`v_var1 NUMBER(2) := 123`*) causes an error because the value 123 exceeds the specified precision. The second variable declaration and initialization (*`v_var2 NUMBER(3) := 123`*) does not cause any errors because the value 123 corresponds to the specified precision. The last declaration and initialization (*`v_var3 NUMBER(5,3) := 123456.123`*) causes an error because the value 123456.123 exceeds the specified precision. As a result, this example produces the following output:*

```
DECLARE
*
ERROR at line 1:
ORA-06502: PL/SQL: numeric or value error
ORA-06512: at line 2
```

3.1.5 ANSWERS

a) In the previous example, what has been declared? State the data type and value.

Answer: The variable v_name was declared with the identical data type as the column first_name from the database table STUDENT - varchar2(25). Additionally, the variable v_grade was declared the identical data type as the column grade_numeric on the grade database table – number NUMBER(3). Each has a value of null.

Most Common Data Types

VARCHAR2(maximum_length)
- Stores variable-length character data.
- Takes a required parameter that specifies a maximum length up to 32,767 bytes.
- Does not use a constant or variable to specify the maximum length; an integer literal must be used.
- The maximum width of a VARCHAR2 database column is 4000 bytes.

CHAR[(maximum_length)]
- Stores fixed-length (blank-padded if necessary) character data.
- Takes an optional parameter that specifies a maximum length up to 32,767 bytes.
- Does not use a constant or variable to specify the maximum length; an integer literal must be used. If maximum length is not specified, it defaults to 1.

(cont'd.)

- The maximum width of a CHAR database column is 2000 bytes; the default is 1 byte.

NUMBER[(precision, scale)]

- Stores fixed or floating-point numbers of virtually any size.
- Precision is the total number of digits.
- Scale determines where rounding occurs.
- It is possible to specify precision and omit scale, in which case scale is 0 and only integers are allowed.
- Constants or variables cannot be used to specify precision and scale; integer literals must be used.
- Maximum precision of a NUMBER value is 38 decimal digits.
- Scale can range from –84 to 127.
- For instance, a scale of 2 rounds to the nearest hundredth (3.456 becomes 3.46).
- Scale can be negative, which causes rounding to the left of the decimal point. For example, a scale of -3 rounds to the nearest thousandth (3456 becomes 3000). A scale of zero rounds to the nearest whole number. If you do not specify the scale, it defaults to zero.

BINARY_INTEGER

- Stores signed integer variables.
- Compares to the NUMBER data type. BINARY_INTEGER variables are stored in the binary format, which takes less space.
- Calculations are faster.
- Can store any integer value in the range –2,147,483,747 through 2,147,483,747.
- This data type is primarily used for indexing a PL/SQL table. This will be explained in more depth in Chapter 16, "PL/SQL Tables." You cannot create a column in a regular table of binary_integer type.

DATE

- Stores fixed-length date values.
- Valid dates for DATE variables include January 1, 4712 B.C. to December 31, A.D. 9999.
- When stored in a database column, date values include the time of day in seconds since midnight. The date portion defaults to the first day of the current month; the time portion defaults to midnight.
- Dates are actually stored in binary format and will be displayed according to the default format.

TIMESTAMP

- This is a new data type introduced with Oracle 9i. It is an extension of the DATE data type. It stores fixed-length date values with precision down to a fraction of a second with up to 9 places after the decimal (the default is 6). Here is an example of the default this displays for this data type: '12-JAN-2002 09.51.44.000000 PM'

- The "with timezone" or "with local timezone" option allows the TIMESTAMP to be related to a particular time zone. This will then be adjusted to the time zone of the database. For example, this would allow a global database to have an entry in London and New York recorded as being the same time even though it will display as noon in New York and 5 P.M. in London.

BOOLEAN

- Stores the values TRUE and FALSE and the nonvalue NULL. Recall that NULL stands for a missing, unknown, or inapplicable value.
- Only the values TRUE and FALSE and the nonvalue NULL can be assigned to a BOOLEAN variable.
- The values TRUE and FALSE cannot be inserted into a database column.

LONG

- Stores variable-length character strings.
- The LONG data type is like the VARCHAR2 data type, except that the maximum length of a LONG value is 2 gigabytes.
- You cannot select a value longer than 4000 bytes from a LONG column into a LONG variable.
- LONG columns can store text, arrays of characters, or even short documents. You can reference LONG columns in UPDATE, INSERT, and (most) SELECT statements, but not in expressions, SQL function calls, or certain SQL clauses, such as WHERE, GROUP BY, and CONNECT BY.

LONG RAW

- Stores raw binary data of variable length up to 2 gigabytes.

LOB (Large Object)

- There are four types of LOBS: BLOB, CLOB, NCLOB, and BFILE. These can store binary objects, such as image or video files, up to 4 gigabytes in length.
- A BFILE is a large binary file stored outside the database. The maximum size is 4 gigabytes.

ROWID

- Internally, every Oracle database table has a ROWID pseudocolumn, which stores binary values called rowids.
- Rowids uniquely identify rows and provide the fastest way to access particular rows.

(cont'd.)

- Use the ROWID data type to store rowids in a readable format.
- When you select or fetch a rowid into a ROWID variable, you can use the function ROWIDTOCHAR, which converts the binary value into an 18-byte character string and returns it in that format.
- Extended rowids use a base 64 encoding of the physical address for each row. The encoding characters are A–Z, a–z, 0–9, +, and /. Row ID in Oracle 9i is as follows: OOOOOOFFFBBBBBBRRR. Each component has a meaning. The first section, OOOOOO, signifies the database segment. The next section, FFF, indicates the tablespace-relative datafile number of the datafile that contains the row. The following section, BBBBBB, is the data block that contains the row. The last section, RRR, is the row in the block (keep in mind that this may change in future versions of Oracle).

3.1.6 ANSWERS

a) What will the output be for the preceding script? Explain what is being declared and what the value of the variable is throughout the scope of the block.

Answer: The server output will be

```
I ate 2 cookies with 600 calories.
I really ate 3 cookies with 900 calories.
The truth is, I actually ate 8 cookies with
2400 calories.
PL/SQL procedure successfully completed.
```

Initially the variable v_cookies_amt *is declared to be a NUMBER with the value of 2, and the variable* v_calories_per_cookie *is declared to be a CONSTANT NUMBER with a value of 300 (since it is declared to be a tCONSTANT, it will not change its value). In the course of the procedure, the value of* v_cookies_amt *is later set to be 3, and then finally it is set to be its current value, 3 plus 5, thus becoming 8.*

b) In the previous example, add the following expressions to the beginning of the procedure, then explain the values of the variables at the beginning and at the end of the script.

Answer: Initially the variable v_lname *is declared as a data type VARCHAR2 with a length of 30 and a value of null. The variable* v_regdate *is declared as data type date with a value of null. The variable* v_pctincr *is declared as CONSTANT*

NUMBER with a length of 4 and a precision of 2 and a value of 1.15. The variable `v_counter` is declared as NUMBER with a value of 0. The variable `v_YorN` is declared as a variable of BOOLEAN data type and a value of TRUE.

The output of the procedure will be as follows (make sure you have entered SET SERVEROUTPUT ON earlier on in your SQL*Plus session):

```
1
1200
PL/SQL procedure successfully completed.
```

Once the executable section is complete, the variable `v_counter` will be changed from null to 1. The value of `v_new_cost` will change from null to 1200 (800 times 1.50).

Note that a common way to find out the value of a variable at different points in a block is to add a DBMS_OUTPUT.PUT_LINE(v_variable_name); throughout the block.

c) What will the values of the variables be at the end of the script?

Answer: The value of `v_counter` will then change from 1 to 6, which is $((1 + 5) *2))/2$, and the value of `new_cost` will go from 1200 to 1800, which is $(800 * 6)/4$. The output from running this procedure will be:

```
6
1800
PL/SQL procedure successfully completed.
```

Operators (Delimiters): the Separators in an Expression

Arithmetic (** , * , / , + , -)

Comparison(=, <> , != , < , > , <= , >= , LIKE , IN , BETWEEN , IS NULL)

Logical (AND, OR, NOT)

String (||, LIKE)

Expressions

Operator Precedence

   ** , NOT

   +, - (arithmetic identity and negation) *, / + , - , || =, <>, != , <= , >= , < , > , LIKE, BETWEEN, IN, IS NULL

  AND—logical conjunction

  OR—logical inclusion

3.1.7 ANSWERS

a) If the following example were run in SQL*Plus, what do you think would be displayed?

Answer: The following would result:

```
outer student id is 123
inner student id is 125
When am I displayed?
outer student id is 123
PL/SQL procedure successfully completed.
```

b) Now run the example and see if it produces what you expected. Explain how the focus moves from one block to another in this example.

Answer: The variable e_Show_Exception_Scope is declared as an exception type in the declaration section of the block. There is also a declaration of the variable called v_student_id of data type NUMBER that is initialized to the number 123. This variable has a scope of the entire block, but it is visible only outside of the inner block. Once the inner block begins, another variable, named v_student_id, is declared. This time it is of data type VARCHAR2(8) and is initialized to 125. This variable will have a scope and visibility only within the inner block. The use of DBMS_OUTPUT helps to show which variable is visible. The inner block raises the exception e_Show_Exception_Scope; this means that the focus will move out of the execution section and into the exception section. The focus will look for an exception named e_Show_Exception_Scope. Since the inner block has no exception with this name, the focus will move to the outer block's exception section and it will find the exception. The inner variable v_student_id is now out of scope and visibility. The outer variable v_student_id (which has always been in scope) now regains visibility. Because the exception has an IF/THEN construct, it will execute the DBMS_OUTPUT call. This is a simple use of nested blocks. Later in the book you will see more complex examples. Once you have covered exception handling in depth in Chapters 7, 10, and 11, you will see that there is greater opportunity to make use of nested blocks.

LAB 3.1 SELF-REVIEW QUESTIONS

In order to test your progress, you should be able to answer the following questions.

1) If a variable is declared as follows, what are the results?

```
v_fixed_amount CONSTANT NUMBER;
```

a) _____ A NUMBER variable called v_fixed_amount has been declared (it will remain as a constant once initialized).

b) _____ A NUMBER variable called v_fixed_amount has been declared (it will remain as null).

c) _____ An error message will result because constant initialization must be done in the executable section of the block.

d) _____ An error message will result because the declaration for the CON-STANT is missing an assignment to a NUMBER.

2) Which of the following are valid character types for PL/SQL?

a) _____ Numbers
b) _____ English letters
c) _____ Paragraph returns
d) _____ Arithmetic symbols
e) _____ Japanese Kanji

3) A variable may be used for which of the following?

a) _____ To hold a constant, such as the value of π
b) _____ To hold the value of a counter that keeps changing
c) _____ To place a value that will be inserted into the database
d) _____ To hold onto the function of an operand
e) _____ To hold any value as long as you declare it

4) Which of the following will declare a variable that is of the identical data type as the `student_id` in the database table STUDENT in the CTA database?

a) _____ v_id student_id := 123;
b) _____ v_id binary integer;
c) _____ v_id numberNUMBER := 24;
d) _____ v_id student_id%type;

5) The value of a variable is set to null after the 'end;' of the block is issued.

a) _____ True
b) _____ False

Answers appear in Appendix A, Section 3.1.

CHAPTER 3

TEST YOUR THINKING

Before starting these projects, take a look at the formatting guidelines in Appendix B. Make your variable names conform to the standard. At the top of the *declaration section,* put a comment stating which naming standard you are using.

1) Write a PL/SQL block
   a) That includes declarations for the following variables:
      A VARCHAR2 data type that can contain the string 'Introduction to Oracle PL/SQL'
      A NUMBER that can be assigned 987654.55, but not 987654.567 or 9876543.55
      A CONSTANT (you choose the correct data type) that is auto-initialized to the value '603D'
      A BOOLEAN
      A DATE data type autoinitialized to one week from today
   b) In the body of the PL/SQL block, put a DBMS_OUTPUT.PUT_LINE message for each of the variables that received an autoinitialization value.
   c) In a comment at the bottom of the PL/SQL block, state the value of your NUMBER data type.
2) Alter the PL/SQL block you created in Project 1 to conform to the following specs:
   a) Remove the DBMS_OUTPUT.PUT_LINE messages.
   b) In the body of the PL/SQL block, write a selection test (IF) that does the following (use a nested IF statement where appropriate):
      i) Check whether the VARCHAR2 you created contains the course named 'Introduction to Underwater Basketweaving'.
      ii) If it does, then put a DBMS_OUTPUT.PUT_LINE message on the screen that says so.
      iii) If it does not, then test to see if the CONSTANT you created contains the room number 603D.
      iv) If it does, then put a DBMS_OUTPUT.PUT_LINE message on the screen that states the course name and the room number that you've reached in this logic.

on the screen that states that the course and location could not be determined.

c) Add a WHEN OTHERS EXCEPTION that puts a DBMS_OUTPUT.PUT_LINE message on the screen that says that an error occurred.

The projects in this section are meant to have you utilize all of the skills that you have acquired throughout this chapter. The answers to these projects can be found in Appendix D and at the companion Web site to this book, located at http://www.phptr .com/rosenzweig2e. Visit the Web site periodically to share and discuss your answers.

C H A P T E R 4

SQL IN PL/SQL

This chapter is a collection of some fundamental elements of using SQL statements in PL/SQL blocks. In the previous chapter, you initialized variables with the ":=" syntax; in this chapter, we will introduce the method of using a SQL select statement to update the value of a variable. These variables can then be used in DML statements (INSERT, DELETE, or UPDATE). Additionally, we will demonstrate how you can use a sequence in your DML statements within a PL/SQL block much as you would in a stand-alone SQL statement.

A transaction in Oracle is a series of SQL statements that have been grouped together into a logical unit by the programmer. A programmer chooses to do this in order to maintain data integrity. Each application (SQL*Plus, Procedure Builder, and so forth) maintains a single database session for each instance of a user login. The changes to the database that have been executed by a single application session are not actually "saved" into the database until a COMMIT occurs. Work within a transaction up to and just prior to the commit can be rolled back; once a commit has been issued, work within that transaction cannot be rolled back.

In order to exert transaction control, a SAVEPOINT can be used to break down large SQL statements into individual units that are easier to manage. In this chapter, we will cover the basic elements of transaction control so you will know how to manage your PL/SQL code by use of COMMIT, ROLLBACK, and principally SAVEPOINT.

L A B   4 . 1

MAKING USE OF DML IN PL/SQL

LAB OBJECTIVES

After this Lab, you will be able to:

✔ Use the SELECT INTO Syntax for Variable Initialization
✔ Use DML in PL/SQL Block
✔ Make Use of a Sequence in a PL/SQL Block

VARIABLES INITIALIZATION WITH SELECT INTO

In PL/SQL, there are two main methods of giving value to variables in a PL/SQL block. The first one, which you learned in Chapter 2, "PL/SQL Concepts," is initialization with the ":=" syntax. In this lab we will learn how to initialize a variable with a select statement by making use of SELECT INTO syntax.

A variable that has been declared in the declaration section of the PL/SQL block can later be given a value with a SELECT statement. The correct syntax is as follows:

```
SELECT item_name
    INTO variable_name
    FROM table_name;
```

It is important to note that any single row function can be performed on the item to give the variable a calculated value.

■ FOR EXAMPLE

```
--   ch04_1a.sql
SET SERVEROUTPUT ON
DECLARE
    v_average_cost VARCHAR2(10);
```

```
BEGIN
   SELECT TO_CHAR(AVG(cost), '$9,999.99')
      INTO v_average_cost
      FROM course;
   DBMS_OUTPUT.PUT_LINE('The average cost of a '||
      'course in the CTA program is '||
      v_average_cost);
END;
```

In this example, a variable is given the value of the average cost of a course in the course table. First, the variable must be declared in the declaration section of the PL/SQL block. In this example, the variable is given the datatype of VARCHAR2(10) because of the functions used on the data. The same select statement that would produce this outcome in SQL*Plus would be

```
SELECT TO_CHAR(AVG(cost), '$9,999.99')
   FROM course;
```

The TO_CHAR function is used to format the cost; in doing this, the number datatype is converted to a character datatype. Once the variable has a value, it can be displayed to the screen in SQL*Plus using the PUT_LINE procedure of the DBMS_OUTPUT package.

LAB 4.1 EXERCISES

4.1.1 USE THE SELECT INTO SYNTAX FOR VARIABLE INITIALIZATION

Run the PL/SQL block from the pre-exercise example.

    a) What is displayed on the SQL*Plus screen? Explain the results.

    b) Take the same PL/SQL block and place the line with the DBMS_OUTPUT before the SELECT INTO statement. What is displayed on the SQL*Plus screen? Explain what the value of the variable is at each point in the PL/SQL block.

Data definition language (DDL) is not valid in a simple PL/SQL block (more advanced techniques such as procedures in the DBMS_SQL package will enable you to make use of DDL), yet data manipulation (DML) is easily achieved either by use of variables or by simply putting a DML statement into a PL/SQL block. Here is an example of a PL/SQL block that UPDATES an exiting entry in the zipcode table.

■ *FOR EXAMPLE*

```
--  ch04_2a.sql
DECLARE
   v_city zipcode.city%TYPE;
BEGIN
   SELECT 'COLUMBUS'
     INTO v_city
     FROM dual;
   UPDATE zipcode
      SET city = v_city
    WHERE ZIP = 43224;
END;
```

It is also possible to insert data into a database table in a PL/SQL block, as shown in the following example.

■ *FOR EXAMPLE*

```
--  ch04_3a.sql
DECLARE
   v_zip zipcode.zip%TYPE;
   v_user zipcode.created_by%TYPE;
   v_date zipcode.created_date%TYPE;
BEGIN
   SELECT 43438, USER, SYSDATE
     INTO v_zip, v_user, v_date
     FROM dual;
   INSERT INTO zipcode
     (ZIP, CREATED_BY ,CREATED_DATE, MODIFIED_BY,
      MODIFIED_DATE
     )
      VALUES(v_zip, v_user, v_date, v_user, v_date);
END;
```

SELECT statements that return no rows or too many rows will cause an error to occur that can be trapped by using an exception. You will learn more about handling exceptions in Chapters 7, 10, and 11.

4.1.2 USE DML IN A PL/SQL BLOCK

a) Write a PL/SQL block that will insert a new student in the student table. Use your own information for the data.

USING AN ORACLE SEQUENCE

An Oracle sequence is an Oracle database object that can be used to generate unique numbers. You can use sequences to automatically generate primary key values.

ACCESSING AND INCREMENTING SEQUENCE VALUES

Once a sequence is created, you can access its values in SQL statements with these pseudocolumns:

CURRVAL   Returns the current value of the sequence
NEXTVAL   Increments the sequence and returns the new value.

■ FOR EXAMPLE

This statement creates the sequence ESEQ:

```
CREATE SEQUENCE eseq
    INCREMENT BY 10
```

The first reference to ESEQ.NEXTVAL returns 1. The second returns 11. Each subsequent reference will return a value 10 greater than the one previous.

(Even though you will be guaranteed unique numbers, you are not guaranteed contiguous numbers. In some systems this may be a problem, for example, when generating invoice numbers.)

DRAWING NUMBERS FROM A SEQUENCE

Beginning with Oracle v7.3, a sequence value can be inserted directly into a table without first selecting it. (Previously it was necessary to use the SELECT INTO syntax and put the new sequence number into a variable and then you can insert the variable.)

■ FOR EXAMPLE

For this example, a table called test01 will be used: First the table test01 is created and then the sequence `test_seq`, then the sequence is used to populate the table.

```
--  ch04_3a.sql
CREATE TABLE test01 (col1 number);
CREATE SEQUENCE test_seq
    INCREMENT BY 5;
BEGIN
    INSERT INTO test01
```

```
          VALUES (test_seq.NEXTVAL);
END;
/
Select * FROM test01;
```

4.1.3 MAKE USE OF A SEQUENCE IN A PL/SQL BLOCK

In this last exercise for this lab, you will make use of all the material covered so far in this chapter.

   a) Write a PL/SQL block that will insert a new student in the student table. Use your own information for the data. Create two variables that are used in the select statement. Get the USER and SYSDATE for the variables. Finally, use the existing student_id_seq sequence to generate a unique id for the new student.

LAB 4.1 EXERCISE ANSWERS

This section gives you some suggested answers to the questions in Lab 4.1, with discussion related to how those answers resulted. The most important thing to realize is whether your answer works. You should figure out the implications of the answers here and what the effects are from any different answers you may come up with.

4.1.1 ANSWERS

Run the PL/SQL block from the pre-exercise example.

   a) What is displayed on the SQL*Plus screen? Explain the results.

   Answer: You will see the following result:

```
The average cost of a course in the CTA program
is $1,198.33
PL/SQL procedure successfully completed.
```

In the declaration section of the PL/SQL block, the variable v_average_cost is declared as a varchar2. In the executable section of the block, this variable is given the value of the average cost from the course table by means of the SELECT INTO syntax. The SQL function TO_CHAR is issued to format the number. The DBMS_OUTPUT is then used to show the result to the screen.

   b) Take the same PL/SQL block and place the line with the DBMS_OUTPUT before the SELECT INTO statement. What is displayed on the SQL*Plus screen? Explain what the value of the variable is at each point in the PL/SQL block.

Answer: You will see the following result:

```
The average cost of a course in the CTA program is
PL/SQL procedure successfully completed.
```

The variable v_average_cost will be set to NULL when it is first declared. Because the DBMS_OUTPUT is placed before the variable is given a value, the output for the variable will be NULL. After the SELECT INTO, the variable will be given the same value as in the original block described in question a, but it will not be displayed because there is not another DBMS_OUTPUT line in the PL/SQL block.

4.1.2 ANSWERS

a) Write a PL/SQL block that will insert a new student in the STUDENT table. Use your own information for the data.

Answer: The following is one example of how this could be handled:

```
--   ch04_4a.sql
DECLARE
   v_max_id number;
BEGIN
   SELECT MAX(student_id)
     INTO v_max_id
     FROM student;
   INSERT into student
      (student_id, last_name, zip,
       created_by, created_date,
       modified_by, modified_date,
       registration_date
      )
     VALUES (v_max_id + 1, 'Rosenzweig',
             11238, 'BROSENZ ', '01-JAN-99',
             'BROSENZ', '01-JAN-99', '01-JAN-99'
            );
END;
```

In order to generate a unique ID, the maximum student_id is selected into a variable and then it is incremented by one. It is important to remember in this example that there is foreign key on the zip item in the student table, which means that the zipcode you choose to enter must be in the ZIPCODE table.

4.1.3 ANSWERS

a) Write a PL/SQL block that will insert a new student in the STUDENT table. Use your own information for the data. Create two variables that are used in the select statement. Get the USER and SYSDATE for the variables. Finally, use the existing `student_id_seq` sequence to generate a unique id for the new student.

Answer: The following is one example of how this could be handled:

```
--   ch04_5a.sql
DECLARE
    v_user student.created_by%TYPE;
    v_date student.created_date%TYPE;
BEGIN
    SELECT USER, sysdate
      INTO  v_user, v_date
      FROM dual;
    INSERT INTO student
       (student_id, last_name, zip,
        created_by, created_date, modified_by,
        modified_date, registration_date
       )
       VALUES (student_id_seq.nextval, 'Smith',
               11238, v_user, v_date, v_user, v_date,
               v_date
               );
END;
```

In the declaration section of the PL/SQL block, two variables are declared. They are both set to be datatypes within the student table using the %TYPE method of declaration. This ensures the datatypes match the columns of the tables into which they will be inserted. The two variables `v_user` and `v_date` are given values from the system by means of SELECT INTO. The value of the `student_id` is generated by using the next value of the `student_id_seq` sequence.

LAB 4.1 SELF-REVIEW QUESTIONS

In order to test your progress, you should be able to answer the following questions.

1) Which of the following are valid methods to initialize value for a variable?

    a) _____ Declare a sequence
    b) _____ The ":=" syntax
    c) _____ SET SERVEROUTPUT ON
    d) _____ SELECT INTO statement

2) Which of the following are valid DML or DDL statements in a PL/SQL Block?

    a) _____ INSERT
    b) _____ CREATE TABLE
    c) _____ CREATE SEQUENCE
    d) _____ UPDATE

3) Complete the following statement with the correct syntax for inserting a sequence in a PL/SQL BLOCK.

```
INSERT INTO STUDENT (student_id, last_name)
```

a) _____ VALUES (student_id_seq.currval, 'Smith');
b) _____ VALUES ('Smith', student_id_seq.currval);
c) _____ VALUES (student_id_seq.nextval, 'Smith');
d) _____ VALUES (nextval, 'Smith');

4) Which of the following are true statements about an Oracle sequence?

a) _____ It can use a DML statement only in stand-alone SQL, not in a PL/SQL block.
b) _____ It is a database object.
c) _____ It is useful for generating contiguous numbers for invoicing.
d) _____ It can be used to generate unique primary keys.

Answers appear in Appendix A, Section 4.1.

LAB 4.2

MAKING USE OF SAVEPOINT

LAB OBJECTIVES

After this Lab, you will be able to:

✔ Make Use of COMMIT, ROLLBACK and SAVEPOINT in a PL/SQL Block

---

Transactions are a means to break programming code into manageable units. Grouping transactions into smaller elements is a standard practice that ensures an application will save only correct data. Initially, any application will have to connect to the database in order to access the data. It is important to point out that when a user is issuing DML statements in an application, the changes are not visible to other users until a COMMIT or ROLLBACK has been issued. Oracle guarantees a read-consistent view of the data. Until that point, all data that have been inserted or updated will be held in memory and only available to the current user. The rows that have been changed will be locked by the current user and will not be available for updating to other users until the locks have been released. A COMMIT or a ROLLBACK statement will release these locks. Transactions can be controlled more readily by marking points of the transaction with the SAVEPOINT command.

For more details on transaction control (such as row locking issues), see the companion volume, Oracle DBA Interactive Workbook, *by Douglas Scherer and Melanie Caffrey (Prentice Hall, 2000).*

- **COMMIT**—Makes events within a transaction permanent
- **ROLLBACK**—Erases events within a transaction

Additionally, you can use a SAVEPOINT to control transactions. Transactions are defined in the PL/SQL block from one SAVEPOINT to another. The use of the SAVEPOINT command allows you to break your SQL statements into units so that in a given PL/SQL block, some units can be *committed* (saved to the database) and some can be *rolled back* (undone) and so forth.

Note that there is a distinction between transaction and a PL/SQL block. The start and end of a PL/SQL block do not necessarily mean the start and end of a transaction.

In order to demonstrate the need for transaction control, we will examine a two-step data-manipulation process. For example, suppose that the fees for all courses in the CTA database that had a prerequisite course needed to be increased by 10 percent and at the same time all courses that did not have a prerequisite needed to be decreased by 10 percent. This is a two-step process. If one step had been successful but the second step was not, then the data concerning course cost would be inconsistent in the database. Because this adjustment is based on a change in percentage, there would be no way to track what part of this course adjustment had been successful and what had not been.

■ FOR EXAMPLE

In this example, you see one PL/SQL block that performs two updates on the cost item in the course table. In the first step (this code is commented for the purpose of emphasizing each update), the cost is updated with a cost that is 10 percent less whenever the course does not have a prerequisite. In the second step, the cost is increased by 10 percent when the course has a prerequisite.

```
--   ch04_6a.sql
BEGIN
-- STEP 1
   UPDATE course
      SET cost = cost  - (cost * 0.10)
    WHERE prerequisite IS NULL;
-- STEP 2
   UPDATE course
      SET cost = cost  + (cost * 0.10)
    WHERE prerequisite IS NOT NULL;
END;
```

Let's assume that the first update statement succeeds, but the second update statement fails because the network went down. The data in the course table is now inconsistent because courses with no prerequisite have had their cost reduced but courses with prerequisites have not been adjusted. To prevent this sort of situation, statements must be combined into a transaction. So, either both statements will succeed, or both statements will fail.

A transaction usually combines SQL statements that represent a logical unit of work. The transaction begins with the first SQL statement issued after the previous transaction, or the first SQL statement issued after connecting to the database. The transaction ends with the COMMIT or ROLLBACK statement.

COMMIT

When a COMMIT statement is issued to the database, the transaction has ended, and the following statements are true:

- All work done by the transaction becomes permanent.
- Other users can see changes in data made by the transaction.
- Any locks acquired by the transaction are released.

A COMMIT statement has the following syntax:

```
COMMIT [WORK];
```

The word WORK is optional and is used to improve readability. Until a transaction is committed, only the user executing that transaction can see changes in the data made by his session.

■ FOR EXAMPLE

Suppose User A issues the following command on a student table that exists in another schema but has a public synonym of student:

```
--  ch04_6a.sql
INSERT INTO student
    (student_id, last_name, zip, registration_date,
     created_by, created_date, modified_by,
     modified_date
    )
    VALUES (student_id_seq.nextval, 'Tashi', 10015,
            '01-JAN-99', 'STUDENTA', '01-JAN-99',
            'STUDENTA', '01-JAN-99'
           );
```

Then User B enters the following command to query table known by its public synonym student, while logged on to his session.

```
SELECT *
    FROM student
    WHERE last_name = 'Tashi';
```

Then User A issues the following command:

```
COMMIT;
```

Now if User B enters the same query again, he will not see the same results.

In this next example, there are two sessions: User A and User B. User A inserts a record into the student table. User B queries the student table, but does not get the record that was inserted by User A. User B cannot see the information because User A has not committed the work. When User A commits the transaction, User B, upon resubmitting the query, sees the records inserted by User A.

 Note that this is covered in more depth in the companion volume, Oracle DBA Interactive Workbook, *by Douglas Scherer and Melanie Caffrey (Prentice Hall, 2000).*

ROLLBACK

When a ROLLBACK statement is issued to the database, the transaction has ended, and the following statements are true:

- All work done by the user is undone, as if it hadn't been issued.
- Any locks acquired by the transaction are released.

A ROLLBACK statement has the following syntax:

```
ROLLBACK [WORK];
```

The *WORK* keyword is optional and is available for increased readability.

SAVEPOINT

The ROLLBACK statement undoes all work done by the user in a specific transaction. With the SAVEPOINT command, however, only part of the transaction can be undone. A SAVEPOINT command has the following syntax:

```
SAVEPOINT name;
```

The word name is the SAVEPOINT's name. Once a SAVEPOINT is defined, the program can roll back to the SAVEPOINT. A ROLLBACK statement, then, has the following syntax:

```
ROLLBACK [WORK] to SAVEPOINT name;
```

When a ROLLBACK to SAVEPOINT statement is issued to the database, the following statements are true:

- Any work done since the SAVEPOINT is undone. The SAVEPOINT remains active, however, until a full COMMIT or ROLLBACK is issued. It can be rolled back to again, if desired.
- Any locks and resources acquired by the SQL statements since the SAVEPOINT will be released.
- The transaction is not finished, because SQL statements are still pending.

LAB 4.2 EXERCISES

4.2.1 MAKE USE OF COMMIT, ROLLBACK, AND SAVEPOINT IN A PL/SQL BLOCK

Log into the CTA schema and enter the following series of commands. (Optionally, you can write the PL/SQL block in a text file and then run the script from the SQL*Plus prompt.)

```
--  ch04_7a.sql
BEGIN
   INSERT INTO student
      ( student_id, Last_name, zip, registration_date,
        created_by, created_date, modified_by,
        modified_date
      )
      VALUES ( student_id_seq.nextval, 'Tashi', 10015,
               '01-JAN-99', 'STUDENTA', '01-JAN-99',
               'STUDENTA','01-JAN-99'
             );
   SAVEPOINT A;
   INSERT INTO student
      ( student_id, Last_name, zip, registration_date,
        created_by, created_date, modified_by,
        modified_date
      )
      VALUES (student_id_seq.nextval, 'Sonam', 10015,
               '01-JAN-99', 'STUDENTB','01-JAN-99',
               'STUDENTB', '01-JAN-99'
             );
   SAVEPOINT B;
   INSERT INTO student
      ( student_id, Last_name, zip, registration_date,
        created_by, created_date, modified_by,
        modified_date
      )
```

```
      VALUES (student_id_seq.nextval, 'Norbu', 10015,
              '01-JAN-99', 'STUDENTB', '01-JAN-99',
              'STUDENTB', '01-JAN-99'
           );
   SAVEPOINT C;
   ROLLBACK TO B;
END;
```

a) If you issue the following command, what would you expect to
see? Why?

```
SELECT *
  FROM student
 WHERE last_name = 'Norbu';
```

b) Try it. What happened? Why?

Now issue

```
ROLLBACK to SAVEPOINT A;
```

c) What happened?

d) If you issue the following, what do you expect to see?

```
SELECT last_name
  FROM student
 WHERE last_name = 'Tashi';
```

e) Issue the command and explain your findings.

*SAVEPOINT is often used before a complicated section of the transac-
tion. If this part of the transaction fails, it can be rolled back, allowing
the earlier part to continue.*

*It is important to note the distinction between transactions and PL/SQL
blocks. When a block starts, it does not mean that the transaction
starts. Likewise, the start of the transaction need not coincide with the
start of a block.*

LAB 4.2 EXERCISE ANSWERS

This section gives you some suggested answers to the questions in Lab 4.2, with discussion related to how those answers resulted. The most important thing to realize is whether your answer works. You should figure out the implications of the answers here and what the effects are from any different answers you may come up with.

4.2.1 ANSWERS

a) If you issue the following command, what would you expect to see? Why?

```
SELECT *
  FROM student
 WHERE last_name = 'Norbu';
```

Answer: You will not be able to see any data because the ROLLBACK to (SAVEPOINT) B has undone the last insert statement where the student 'Norbu' was inserted.

b) Try it. What happened? Why?

Answer: When you issue this command, you will get the message "no rows se-lected."

Three students were inserted in this PL/SQL block. First, Sonam in SAVEPOINT A, then Tashi in SAVEPOINT B, and finally Norbu was inserted in SAVEPOINT C. Then when the command ROLLBACK to B was issued, the insert of Norbu was undone.

Now issue

```
ROLLBACK to SAVEPOINT A;
```

c) What happened?

Answer: The insert in SAVEPOINT B was just undone. This deleted the insert of Tashi who was inserted in SAVEPOINT B.

d) If you issue the following, what do you expect to see?

```
SELECT last_name
FROM student
WHERE last_name = 'Tashi';
```

Answer: You will see the data for Tashi.

e) Issue the command and explain your findings.

Answer: You will see one entry for Tashi, as follows:

```
LAST_NAME
-------------------------
Tashi
```

Tashi was the only student that was successfully entered into the database. The ROLL-BACK to SAVEPOINT A undid the insert statement for Norbu and Sonam.

A Single PL/SQL Block Can Contain Multiple Transactions

For Example:

```
Declare
    v_Counter NUMBER;
BEGIN
    v_counter := 0;
    FOR i IN 1..100
    LOOP
        v_counter := v_counter + 1;
        IF v_counter = 10
        THEN
            COMMIT;
            v_counter := 0;
        END IF;
    END LOOP;
END;
```

In this example, as soon as the value of v_counter becomes equal to 10, the work is committed. So, there will be a total of 10 transactions contained in this one PL/SQL block.

LAB 4.2 SELF-REVIEW QUESTIONS

In order to test your progress, you should be able to answer the following questions.

1) User A can ROLLBACK User B's insert statement.

    a) _____ True
    b) _____ False

2) When a COMMIT has been issued, which of the following are true? (Choose all that apply.)

a) _____ All memory holds on the data have been released.
b) _____ All data inserts are available to other users.
c) _____ You have to get married.
d) _____ The transaction is not finished because SQL statements are still pending.

3) What defines a logical unit of work?

a) _____ From one SAVEPOINT to the next.
b) _____ From one ROLLBACK to the next.
c) _____ From one COMMIT to the next.
d) _____ All of the above.

4) Which of the following is an advantage of using SAVEPOINTS in a PL/SQL block?

a) _____ It prevents inconsistent data.
b) _____ It allows one to group code into manageable units.
c) _____ It prevents one from duplicating a primary key.
d) _____ It locks rows and prevents other users from updating the same row.

Answers appear in Appendix A, Section 4.2.

CHAPTER 4

TEST YOUR THINKING

In the chapter discussion, you learned how to use numerous SQL techniques in a PL/SQL block. First, you learned how to use SELECT INTO to generate values for a variable. Then you learned the various DML methods, including the use of a sequence. Finally, you learned how to manage transactions by using savepoints. Complete the following projects by writing the code for each step and running it and then going on to the next step.

1) Create a table called CHAP4 with two columns; one is ID (a number) and the second is NAME, which is a varchar2(20).
2) Create a sequence called CHAP4_SEQ that increments by units of 5.
3) Write a PL/SQL block that performs the following in this order:
   a) Declares 2 variables, one for the v_name and one for v_id. The v_name variable can be used throughout the block for holding the name that will be inserted; realize that the value will change in the course of the block.
   b) The block then inserts into the table the name of the student that is enrolled in the most classes and uses a sequence for the ID; afterward there is SAVEPOINT A.
   c) Then the student with the least enrollments is inserted; afterward there is SAVEPOINT B.
   d) Then the instructor who is teaching the maximum number of courses is inserted in the same way. Afterward there is SAVE-POINT C.
   e) Using a SELECT INTO statement, hold the value of the instructor in the variable v_id.
   f) Undo the instructor insert by use of rollback.
   g) Insert the instructor teaching the least amount of courses but do not use the sequence to generate the ID; instead use the value from the first instructor whom you have since undone.
   h) Now insert the instructor teaching the most number of courses and use the sequence to populate his ID.

Add DBMS_OUTPUT throughout the block to display the values of the variables as they change. (This is good practice for debugging.)

The answers to Test Your Thinking can be found in Appendix D and on the web site.

CHAPTER 5

CONDITIONAL CONTROL: IF STATEMENTS

In almost every program that you write, you need to make decisions. For example, if it is the end of the fiscal year, bonuses must be distributed to the employees based on their salaries. In order to compute employee bonuses, a program needs to have a conditional control. In other words, it needs to employ a selection structure (you learned about selection structure in Chapter 1).

Conditional control allows you to control the flow of the execution of the program based on a condition. In programming terms, it means that the statements in the program are not executed sequentially. Rather, one group of statements or another will be executed depending on how the condition is evaluated.

In PL/SQL, there are three types of conditional control: IF, ELSIF, and CASE statements. In this chapter, you will explore two types of conditional control—IF and ELSIF—and how these types can be nested one inside of another. CASE statements are discussed in the next chapter.

LAB 5.1

IF STATEMENTS

LAB OBJECTIVES

After this Lab, you will be able to:

✔ Use IF-THEN Statements
✔ Use IF-THEN-ELSE Statements

An IF statement has two forms: IF-THEN and IF-THEN-ELSE. An IF-THEN state-ment allows you to specify only one group of actions to take. In other words, this group of actions is taken only when a condition evaluates to TRUE. An IF-THEN-ELSE statement allows you to specify two groups of actions, and the second group of actions is taken when a condition evaluates to FALSE or NULL.

IF-THEN STATEMENTS

An IF-THEN statement is the most basic kind of a conditional control and has the following structure:

```
IF CONDITION THEN
    STATEMENT 1;
    ...
    STATEMENT N;
END IF;
```

The reserved word IF marks the beginning of the IF statement. Statements 1 through *N* are a sequence of executable statements that consist of one or more of the standard programming structures. The word CONDITION between keywords IF and THEN determines whether these statements are executed. END IF is a re-served phrase that indicates the end of the IF-THEN construct.

This flow of the logic from the preceding structure of the IF-THEN statement is il-lustrated in the Figure 5.1.

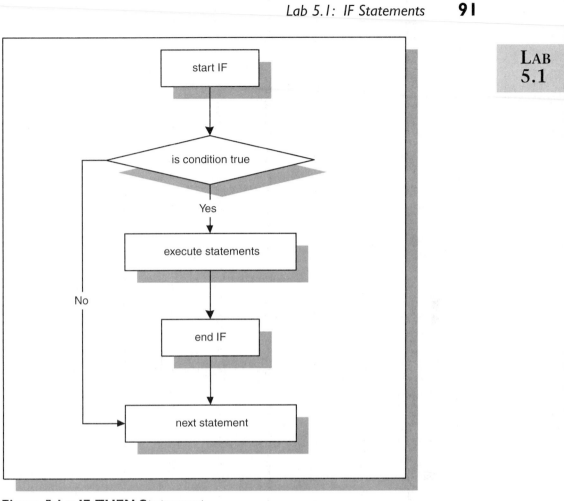

Figure 5.1 ■ IF-THEN Statement

When an IF-THEN statement is executed, a condition is evaluated to either TRUE or FALSE. If the condition evaluates to TRUE, control is passed to the first executable statement of the IF-THEN construct. If the condition evaluates to FALSE, control is passed to the first executable statement after the END IF statement.

Consider the following example. You have two numeric values stored in the variables, v_num1 and v_num2. You need to arrange your values so that the smaller value is always stored in v_num1, and the larger value is always stored in the v_num2.

■ FOR EXAMPLE

```
DECLARE
    v_num1 NUMBER := 5;
    v_num2 NUMBER := 3;
    v_temp NUMBER;
```

```
BEGIN
    -- if v_num1 is greater than v_num2 rearrange their values
    IF v_num1 > v_num2 THEN
        v_temp := v_num1;
        v_num1 := v_num2;
        v_num2 := v_temp;
    END IF;

    -- display the values of v_num1 and v_num2
    DBMS_OUTPUT.PUT_LINE ('v_num1 = '||v_num1);
    DBMS_OUTPUT.PUT_LINE ('v_num2 = '||v_num2);
END;
```

In this example, condition v_num1 > v_num2 evaluates to TRUE because 5 is greater that 3. Next, the values are rearranged so that 3 is assigned to v_num1, and 5 is assigned to v_num2. It is done with the help of the third variable, v_temp, which is used for temporary storage.

This example produces the following output:

```
v_num1 = 3
v_num2 = 5

PL/SQL procedure successfully completed.
```

IF-THEN-ELSE STATEMENT

An IF-THEN statement specifies the sequence of statements to execute only if the condition evaluates to TRUE. When this condition evaluates to FALSE, there is no special action to take except to proceed with execution of the program.

An IF-THEN-ELSE statement enables you to specify two groups of statements. One group of statements is executed when the condition evaluates to TRUE. Another group of statements is executed when the condition evaluates to FALSE. This is indicated as follows:

```
IF CONDITION THEN
    STATEMENT 1;
ELSE
    STATEMENT 2;
END IF;
STATEMENT 3;
```

When CONDITION evaluates to TRUE, control is passed to STATEMENT 1; when CONDITION evaluates to FALSE, control is passed to STATEMENT 2. After the IF-THEN-ELSE construct has completed, STATEMENT 3 is executed. This flow of the logic is illustrated in the Figure 5.2.

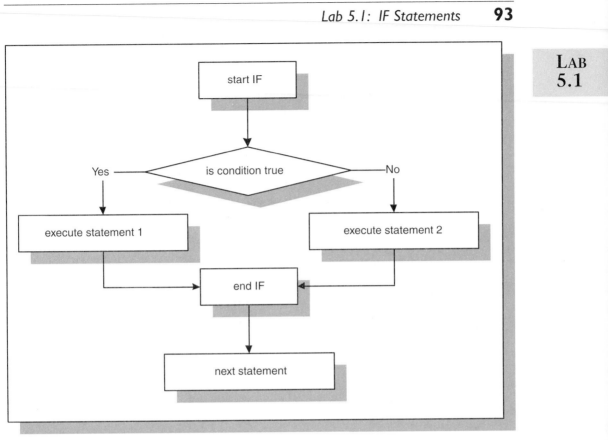

Figure 5.2 ■ IF-THEN-ELSE Statement

The IF-THEN-ELSE construct should be used when trying to choose be-tween two mutually exclusive actions. Consider the following example:

```
DECLARE
   v_num NUMBER := &sv_user_num;
BEGIN
   -- test if the number provided by the user is even
   IF MOD(v_num,2) = 0  THEN
      DBMS_OUTPUT.PUT_LINE (v_num||' is even number');
   ELSE
      DBMS_OUTPUT.PUT_LINE (v_num||' is odd number');
   END IF;
   DBMS_OUTPUT.PUT_LINE ('Done');
END;
```

It is important to realize that for any given number only one of the DBMS_OUTPUT.PUT_LINE statements is executed. Hence, the IF-THEN-ELSE con-struct enables you to specify two and only two mutually exclusive actions.

When run, this example produces the following output:

```
Enter value for v_user_num: 24
old    2:     v_num   NUMBER := &v_user_num;
new    2:     v_num   NUMBER := 24;
24 is even number
Done

PL/SQL procedure successfully completed.
```

NULL CONDITION

In some cases, a condition used in an IF statement can be evaluated to NULL instead of TRUE or FALSE. For the IF-THEN construct, the statements will not be executed if an associated condition evaluates to NULL. Next, control will be passed to the first executable statement after END IF. For the IF-THEN-ELSE construct, the statements specified after the keyword ELSE will be executed if an associated condition evaluates to NULL.

■ FOR EXAMPLE

```
DECLARE
   v_num1 NUMBER := 0;
   v_num2 NUMBER;
BEGIN
   IF v_num1 = v_num2 THEN
       DBMS_OUTPUT.PUT_LINE ('v_num1 = v_num2');
   ELSE
       DBMS_OUTPUT.PUT_LINE ('v_num1 != v_num2');
   END IF;
END;
```

This example produces the following output:

```
v_num1 != v_num2

PL/SQL procedure successfully completed.
```

The condition

```
v_num1 = v_num2
```

is evaluated to NULL because a value is not assigned to the variable v_num2. Therefore, variable v_num2 is NULL. Notice that the IF-THEN-ELSE construct is behaving as if the condition evaluated to FALSE, and the second DBMS_OUTPUT.PUT_LINE statement is executed.

LAB 5.1 EXERCISES

5.1.1 USE THE **IF-THEN** STATEMENT

In this exercise, you will use the IF-THEN statement to test whether the date provided by the user falls on the weekend. In other words, if the day happens to be Saturday or Sunday.

Create the following PL/SQL script:

```
-- ch05_1a.sql, version 1.0
SET SERVEROUTPUT ON
DECLARE
    v_date DATE := TO_DATE('&sv_user_date', 'DD-MON-YYYY');
    v_day VARCHAR2(15);
BEGIN
    v_day := RTRIM(TO_CHAR(v_date, 'DAY'));

    IF v_day IN ('SATURDAY', 'SUNDAY') THEN
        DBMS_OUTPUT.PUT_LINE (v_date||' falls on weekend');
    END IF;

    --- control resumes here
    DBMS_OUTPUT.PUT_LINE ('Done...');
END;
```

In order to test this script fully, execute it twice. For the first run, enter '09-JAN-2002', and for the second run, enter '13-JAN-2002'. Execute the script, and then answer the following questions:

a) What output was printed on the screen (for both dates)?

b) Explain why the output produced for the two dates is different.

Remove the RTRIM function from the assignment statement for v_day as follows:

```
v_day := TO_CHAR(v_date, 'DAY');
```

Run the script again, entering '13-JAN-2002' for v_date.

c) What output was printed on the screen? Why?

d) Rewrite this script using the LIKE operator instead of the IN operator, so that it produces the same results for the dates specified earlier.

e) Rewrite this script using the IF-THEN-ELSE construct. If the date specified does not fall on the weekend, display a message to the user saying so.

5.1.2 USE THE IF-THEN-ELSE STATEMENT

In this exercise, you will use the IF-THEN-ELSE statement to check how many students are enrolled in course number 25, section 1. If there are 15 or more students enrolled, section 1 of course number 25 is full. Otherwise, section 1 of course number 25 is not full and more students can register for it. In both cases, a message should be displayed to the user indicating whether section 1 is full. Try to answer the questions before you run the script. Once you have answered the questions, run the script and check your answers. *Note that the SELECT INTO statement uses ANSI 1999 SQL standard.*

Create the following PL/SQL script:

```
-- ch05_2a.sql, version 1.0
SET SERVEROUTPUT ON
DECLARE
   v_total NUMBER;
BEGIN
   SELECT COUNT(*)
     INTO v_total
     FROM enrollment e
     JOIN section s USING (section_id)
    WHERE s.course_no = 25
      AND s.section_no = 1;

   -- check if section 1 of course 25 is full
   IF v_total >= 15 THEN
      DBMS_OUTPUT.PUT_LINE
         ('Section 1 of course 25 is full');
```

```
         ELSE
             DBMS_OUTPUT.PUT_LINE
                 ('Section 1 of course 25 is not full');
         END IF;
         -- control resumes here
     END;
```

Notice that the SELECT INTO statement uses an equijoin. The join condition is listed in the JOIN clause, indicating columns that are part of the primary key and foreign key constraints. In this example, column SECTION_ID of the ENROLLMENT table has a foreign key constraint defined on it. This constraint references column SECTION_ID of the SECTION table, which, in turn, has a primary key constraint defined on it.

You will find detailed explanations and examples of the statements using new ANSI 1999 SQL standard in Appendix E and in the Oracle help. Throughout this book we try to provide you with examples illustrating both standards; however, our main focus is on PL/SQL features rather than SQL.

In the previous versions of Oracle, this statement would look as follows:

```
     SELECT COUNT(*)
       INTO v_total
       FROM enrollment e, section s
      WHERE e.section_id = s.section_id
        AND s.course_no = 25
        AND s.section_no = 1;
```

Try to answer the following questions first and then execute the script:

   a) What DBMS_OUTPUT.PUT_LINE statement will be displayed if there are 15 students enrolled in section 1 of course number 25?

   b) What DBMS_OUTPUT.PUT_LINE statement will be displayed if there are 3 students enrolled in section 1 of course number 25?

c) What DBMS_OUTPUT.PUT_LINE statement will be displayed if there is no section 1 for course number 25?

d) How would you change this script so that both course and section numbers are provided by a user?

e) How would you change this script so that if there are less than 15 students enrolled in section 1 of course number 25, a message indicating how many students can still be enrolled is displayed?

LAB 5.1 EXERCISE ANSWERS

This section gives you some suggested answers to the questions in Lab 5.1, with discussion related to how those answers resulted. The most important thing to realize is whether your answer works. You should figure out the implications of the answers here and what the effects are from any different answers you may come up with.

5.1.1 ANSWERS

a) What output was printed on the screen (for both dates)?

Answer: The first output produced for the date is 09-JAN-2002. The second output produced for the date is 13-JAN-2002.

```
Enter value for sv_user_date: 09-JAN-2002
old    2:    v_date DATE := TO_DATE('&sv_user_date', 'DD-MON-
YYYY');
new    2:    v_date DATE := TO_DATE('09-JAN-2002', 'DD-MON-
YYYY');
Done...

PL/SQL procedure successfully completed.
```

When the value of 09-JAN-2002 is entered for v_date, the day of the week is determined for the variable v_day with the help of the functions TO_CHAR and RTRIM. Next, the following condition is evaluated:

```
v_day IN ('SATURDAY', 'SUNDAY')
```

Because the value of v_day is 'WEDNESDAY,' the condition evaluates to FALSE. Then, control is passed to the first executable statement after END IF. As a result, 'Done...' is displayed on the screen.

```
Enter value for sv_user_date: 13-JAN-2002
old   2:    v_date DATE := TO_DATE('&sv_user_date', 'DD-MON-
YYYY');
new   2:    v_date DATE := TO_DATE('13-JAN-2002', 'DD-MON-
YYYY');
13-JAN-02 falls on weekend
Done...

PL/SQL procedure successfully completed.
```

The value of v_day is derived from the value of v_date. Next, the condition of the IF-THEN statement is evaluated. Because it evaluates to TRUE, the statement after the keyword THEN is executed. So, '13-JAN-2002 falls on weekend' is displayed on the screen. Next, control is passed to the last DBMS_OUTPUT.PUT_LINE statement, and 'Done . . .' is displayed on the screen.

b) Explain why the output produced for the two dates is different.

Answer: The first date, 09-JAN-2002, is a Wednesday. As a result, the condition, v_day IN ('SATURDAY,' 'SUNDAY'), does not evaluate to TRUE. So, control is transferred to the statement after END IF, and 'Done...' is displayed on the screen.

The second date, 13-JAN-2002, is a Sunday. Because Sunday falls on a weekend, the condition evaluates to TRUE, and the message '13-JAN-2002 falls on weekend' is displayed on the screen. Next, the last DBMS_OUTPUT.PUT_LINE statement is executed, and 'Done . . .' is displayed on the screen.

Remove the RTRIM function from the assignment statement for v_day as follows:

```
v_day := TO_CHAR(v_date, 'DAY');
```

Run the script again, entering '13-JAN-2002' for v_date.

c) What output was printed on the screen? Why?

Answer: Your script should look similar to the following. Changes are shown in bold letters.

```
-- ch05_1b.sql, version 2.0
SET SERVEROUTPUT ON
DECLARE
   v_date DATE := TO_DATE('&sv_user_date', 'DD-MON-YYYY');
   v_day VARCHAR2(15);
BEGIN
   v_day := TO_CHAR(v_date, 'DAY');
```

```
      IF v_day IN ('SATURDAY', 'SUNDAY') THEN
          DBMS_OUTPUT.PUT_LINE (v_date||' falls on weekend');
      END IF;

      --- control resumes here
      DBMS_OUTPUT.PUT_LINE ('Done...');
   END;
```

This script produces the following output:

```
Enter value for sv_user_date: 13-JAN-2002
old    2:     v_date DATE := TO_DATE('&sv_user_date', 'DD-MON-
YYYY');
new    2:     v_date DATE := TO_DATE('13-JAN-2002', 'DD-MON-
YYYY');
Done...

PL/SQL procedure successfully completed.
```

In the original example, the variable v_day is calculated with the help of the statement, RTRIM(TO_CHAR(v_date, 'DAY')). First, the function TO_CHAR returns the day of the week padded with blanks. The size of the value retrieved by the function TO_CHAR is always 9 bytes. Next, the RTRIM function removes trailing spaces.

In the statement

```
v_day := TO_CHAR(v_date, 'DAY')
```

the TO_CHAR function is used without the RTRIM function. Therefore, trailing blanks are not removed after the day of the week has been derived. As a result, the condition of the IF-THEN statement evaluates to FALSE even though given date falls on the weekend, and control is passed to the last DBMS_OUTPUT.PUT_LINE statement.

d) Rewrite this script using the LIKE operator instead of the IN operator, so that it produces the same results for the dates specified earlier.

Answer: Your script should look similar to the following. Changes are shown in bold letters.

```
-- ch05_1c.sql, version 3.0
SET SERVEROUTPUT ON
DECLARE
   v_date DATE := TO_DATE('&sv_user_date', 'DD-MON-YYYY');
   v_day VARCHAR2(15);
BEGIN
   v_day := RTRIM(TO_CHAR(v_date, 'DAY'));

   IF v_day LIKE 'S%' THEN
       DBMS_OUTPUT.PUT_LINE (v_date||' falls on weekend');
   END IF;
```

```
--- control resumes here
   DBMS_OUTPUT.PUT_LINE ('Done...');
END;
```

Both days, Saturday and Sunday, are the only days of the week that start with the letter 'S'. As a result, there is no need to spell out the names of the days or specify any additional letters for the LIKE operator.

e) Rewrite this script using the IF-THEN-ELSE construct. If the date specified does not fall on the weekend, display a message to the user saying so.

Answer: Your script should look similar to the following. Changes are shown in bold letters.

```
-- ch05_1d.sql, version 4.0
SET SERVEROUTPUT ON
DECLARE
   v_date DATE := TO_DATE('&sv_user_date', 'DD-MON-YYYY');
   v_day VARCHAR2(15);
BEGIN
   v_day := RTRIM(TO_CHAR(v_date, 'DAY'));

   IF v_day IN ('SATURDAY', 'SUNDAY') THEN
      DBMS_OUTPUT.PUT_LINE (v_date||' falls on weekend');
   ELSE
      DBMS_OUTPUT.PUT_LINE (v_date||
         ' does not fall on the weekend');
   END IF;

   -- control resumes here
   DBMS_OUTPUT.PUT_LINE('Done...');
END;
```

In order to modify the script, the ELSE part was added to the IF statement. The rest of the script has not been changed.

5.1.2 ANSWERS

a) What DBMS_OUTPUT.PUT_LINE statement will be displayed if there are 15 students enrolled in section 1 of course number 25?

Answer: If there are 15 or more students enrolled in section 1 of course number 25, the first DBMS_OUTPUT.PUT_LINE statement is displayed on the screen.

The condition

```
v_total >= 15
```

evaluates to TRUE, and as a result, the statement

```
DBMS_OUTPUT.PUT_LINE ('Section 1 of course 25 is full');
```

is executed.

b) What DBMS_OUTPUT.PUT_LINE statement will be displayed if there are 3 students enrolled in section 1 of course number 25?

Answer: If there are 3 students enrolled in section 1 of course number 25, the second DBMS_OUTPUT.PUT_LINE statement is displayed on the screen.

The condition

```
v_total >= 15
```

evaluates to FALSE, and the ELSE part on the IF-THEN-ELSE statement is executed. As a result, the statement

```
DBMS_OUTPUT.PUT_LINE ('Section 1 of course 25 is not full');
```

is executed.

c) What DBMS_OUTPUT.PUT_LINE statement will be displayed if there is no section 1 for course number 25?

Answer: If there is no section 1 for course number 25, the ELSE part of the IF-THEN-ELSE statement will be executed. So the second DBMS_OUTPUT.PUT_LINE statement will be displayed on the screen.

The COUNT function used in the SELECT statement

```
SELECT COUNT(*)
  INTO v_total
  FROM enrollment e
  JOIN section s USING (section_id)
 WHERE s.course_no = 25
   AND s.section_no = 1;
```

returns 0. The condition of the IF-THEN-ELSE statement evaluates to FALSE. Therefore, the ELSE part of the IF-THEN-ELSE statement is executed, and the second DBMS_OUTPUT.PUT_LINE statement is displayed on the screen.

d) How would you change this script so that both the course and section numbers are provided by a user?

Answer: Two additional variables must be declared and initialized with the help of the substitution variables as follows. Your script should look similar to this script. Changes are shown in bold letters.

```
-- ch05_2b.sql, version 2.0
SET SERVEROUTPUT ON
```

```
DECLARE
   v_total NUMBER;
   v_course_no CHAR(6) := '&sv_course_no';
   v_section_no NUMBER := &sv_section_no;
BEGIN
   SELECT COUNT(*)
     INTO v_total
     FROM enrollment e
     JOIN section s USING (section_id)
   WHERE s.course_no = v_course_no
     AND s.section_no = v_section_no;

   -- check if a specific section of a course is full
   IF v_total >= 15 THEN
      DBMS_OUTPUT.PUT_LINE
         ('Section 1 of course 25 is full');
   ELSE
      DBMS_OUTPUT.PUT_LINE
         ('Section 1 of course 25 is not full');
   END IF;
   -- control resumes here
END;
```

e) How would you change this script so that if there were less than 15 students enrolled in section 1 of course number 25, a message indicating how many students could still be enrolled would be displayed?

Answer: Your script should look similar to this script. Changes are shown in bold letters.

```
-- ch05_2c.sql, version 3.0
SET SERVEROUTPUT ON
DECLARE
   v_total NUMBER;
   v_students NUMBER;
BEGIN
   SELECT COUNT(*)
     INTO v_total
     FROM enrollment e
     JOIN section s USING (section_id)
    WHERE s.course_no = 25
      AND s.section_no = 1;

   -- check if section 1 of course 25 is full
   IF v_total >= 15 THEN
      DBMS_OUTPUT.PUT_LINE
         ('Section 1 of course 25 is full');
   ELSE
      v_students := 15 - v_total;
      DBMS_OUTPUT.PUT_LINE (v_students||
```

```
                        ' students can still enroll into section 1 '||
                        'of course 25');
              END IF;
              -- control resumes here
         END;
```

Notice that if the IF-THEN-ELSE statement evaluates to FALSE, the statements associated with the ELSE part are executed. In this case, the value of the variable `v_total` is subtracted from 15. The result of this operation indicates how many more students can enroll in section 1 of course number 25.

LAB 5.1 SELF-REVIEW QUESTIONS

In order to test your progress, you should be able to answer the following questions.

1) An IF construct is a control statement for which of the following?

    a) _____ Sequence structure
    b) _____ Iteration structure
    c) _____ Selection structure

2) In order for the statements of an IF-THEN construct to be executed, the condition must evaluate to which of the following?

    a) _____ TRUE
    b) _____ FALSE
    c) _____ NULL

3) When a condition of the IF-THEN-ELSE construct is evaluated to NULL, control is passed to the first executable statement after END IF.

    a) _____ True
    b) _____ False

4) How many actions can you specify in an IF-THEN-ELSE statement?

    a) _____ One
    b) _____ Two
    c) _____ Four
    d) _____ As many as you require

5) The IF-THEN-ELSE construct should be used to achieve which of the following?

    a) _____ Three mutually exclusive actions
    b) _____ Two mutually exclusive actions
    c) _____ Two actions that are not mutually exclusive

Answers appear in Appendix A, Section 5.1.

L A B 5 . 2

ELSIF STATEMENTS

LAB OBJECTIVES

After this Lab, you will be able to:

✔ Use the ELSIF Statement

An ELSIF statement has the following structure:

```
IF CONDITION 1 THEN
    STATEMENT 1;
ELSIF CONDITION 2 THEN
    STATEMENT 2;
ELSIF CONDITION 3 THEN
    STATEMENT 3;
...
ELSE
    STATEMENT N;
END IF;
```

The reserved word IF marks the beginning of an ELSIF construct. The words CONDITION 1 through CONDITION N are a sequence of the conditions that evaluate to TRUE or FALSE. These conditions are mutually exclusive. In other words, if CONDITION 1 evaluates to TRUE, STATEMENT 1 is executed, and control is passed to the first executable statement after the reserved phrase END IF. The rest of the ELSIF construct is ignored. When CONDITION 1 evaluates to FALSE, control is passed to the ELSIF part and CONDITION 2 is evaluated, and so forth. If none of the specified conditions yield TRUE, control is passed to the ELSE part of the ELSIF construct. An ELSIF statement can contain any number of ELSIF clauses. This flow of the logic is illustrated in Figure 5.3.

Figure 5.3 shows that if condition 1 evaluates to TRUE, statement 1 is executed, and control is passed to the first statement after END IF. If condition 1 evaluates to FALSE, control is passed to condition 2. If condition 2 yields TRUE, statement

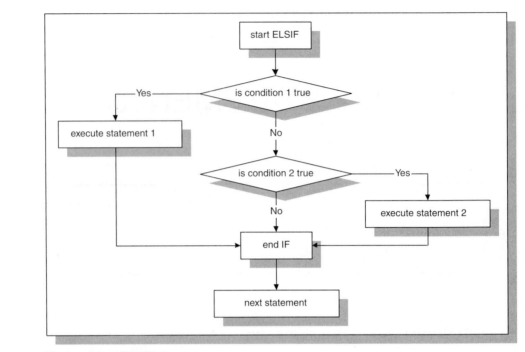

Figure 5.3 ■ ESLIF Statement

2 is executed. Otherwise, control is passed to the statement following END IF, and so forth. Consider the following example.

■ *FOR EXAMPLE*

```
DECLARE
   v_num NUMBER := &sv_num;
BEGIN
   IF v_num < 0 THEN
      DBMS_OUTPUT.PUT_LINE (v_num||' is a negative number');
   ELSIF v_num = 0 THEN
      DBMS_OUTPUT.PUT_LINE (v_num||' is equal to zero');
   ELSE
      DBMS_OUTPUT.PUT_LINE (v_num||' is a positive number');
   END IF;
END;
```

The value of v_num is provided at runtime and evaluated with the help of the ELSIF statement. If the value of v_num is less that zero, the first DBMS_OUTPUT.PUT_LINE statement executes, and the ELSIF construct terminates. If the value of v_num is greater than zero, both conditions

v_num < 0 and **v_num = 0**

evaluate to FALSE, and the ELSE part of the ELSIF construct executes.

Assume that the value of v_num equals 5 at runtime. This example produces the following output:

```
Enter value for sv_num: 5
old    2:    v_num   NUMBER := &sv_num;
new    2:    v_num   NUMBER := 5;
5 is a positive number

PL/SQL procedure successfully completed.
```

Remember the following information about an ELSIF statement:

- *Always match IF with an END IF.*
- *There must be a space between END and IF. When the space is omitted, the compiler produces the following error:*

```
ERROR at line 22:
ORA-06550: line 22, column 4:
PLS-00103: Encountered the symbol ";" when expecting one
of the following: if
```

> *As you can see, this error message is not very clear, and it can take you some time to correct it, especially if you have not encountered it before.*

- *There is no second "E" in "ELSIF".*
- *Conditions of an ELSIF statement must be mutually exclusive. These conditions are evaluated in sequential order, from the first to the last. Once a condition evaluates to TRUE, the remaining conditions of the ELSIF statement are not evaluated at all. Consider this example of an ELSIF construct:*

```
IF v_num >= 0 THEN
   DBMS_OUTPUT.PUT_LINE ('v_num is greater than 0');
ELSIF v_num =< 10 THEN
   DBMS_OUTPUT.PUT_LINE ('v_num is less than 10');
ELSE
   DBMS_OUTPUT.PUT_LINE
      ('v_num is less than ? or greater than ?');
END IF;
```

> *Assume that the value of v_num is equal to 5. Both conditions of the ELSIF statement can evaluate to TRUE because 5 is greater than 0, and 5 is less than 10. However, once the first condition, v_num >= 0, evaluates to TRUE, the rest of the ELSIF construct is ignored.*

For any value of v_num *that is greater than or equal to 0 and less than or equal to 10, these conditions are not mutually exclusive. Therefore, the DBMS_OUTPUT.PUT_LINE statement associated with the ELSIF clause will not execute for any such value of* v_num. *In order for the second condition, v_num <= 10, to yield TRUE, the value of* v_num *must be less than 0.*

How would you rewrite this ELSIF construct to capture any value of v_num *between 0 and 10 and display it on the screen with a single condition?*

When using an ELSIF construct, it is not necessary to specify what action should be taken if none of the conditions evaluate to TRUE. In other words, an ELSE clause is not required in the ELSIF construct. Consider the following example:

■ FOR EXAMPLE

```
DECLARE
    v_num NUMBER := &sv_num;
BEGIN
    IF v_num < 0 THEN
        DBMS_OUTPUT.PUT_LINE (v_num||' is a negative number');
    ELSIF v_num > 0 THEN
        DBMS_OUTPUT.PUT_LINE (v_num||' is a positive number');
    END IF;
    DBMS_OUTPUT.PUT_LINE ('Done...');
END;
```

As you can see, there is no action specified when v_num is equal to zero. If the value of v_num is equal to zero, both conditions will evaluate to FALSE, and the ELSIF statement will not execute at all. When a value of zero is specified for v_num, this example produces the following output.

```
Enter value for sv_num: 0
old    2:    v_num  NUMBER := &sv_num;
new    2:    v_num  NUMBER := 0;
Done...

PL/SQL procedure successfully completed.
```

You probably noticed that for all IF statement examples, the reserved words IF, ELSIF, ELSE, and END IF are entered on a separate line and aligned with the word IF. In addition, all executable statements in the IF construct are indented. The format of the IF construct makes no difference to the compiler. However, the meaning of the formatted IF construct becomes obvious to us.

The IF-THEN-ELSE statement

```
IF x = y THEN v_text := 'YES'; ELSE v_text := 'NO';   END
IF;
```

is equivalent to

```
IF x = y THEN
    v_text := 'YES';
ELSE
    v_text := 'NO';
END IF;
```

The formatted version of the IF construct is easier to read and understand.

LAB 5.2 EXERCISES

5.2.1 USE THE ELSIF STATEMENT

In this exercise, you will use an ELSIF statement to display a letter grade for a student registered for a specific section of course number 25.

Create the following PL/SQL script:

```
-- ch05_3a.sql, version 1.0
SET SERVEROUTPUT ON
DECLARE
   v_student_id NUMBER := 102;
   v_section_id NUMBER := 89;
   v_final_grade NUMBER;
   v_letter_grade CHAR(1);
BEGIN
   SELECT final_grade
     INTO v_final_grade
     FROM enrollment
    WHERE student_id = v_student_id
      AND section_id = v_section_id;

   IF v_final_grade BETWEEN 90 AND 100 THEN
      v_letter_grade := 'A';
   ELSIF v_final_grade BETWEEN 80 AND 89 THEN
      v_letter_grade := 'B';
   ELSIF v_final_grade BETWEEN 70 AND 79 THEN
      v_letter_grade := 'C';
   ELSIF v_final_grade BETWEEN 60 AND 69 THEN
      v_letter_grade := 'D';
```

```
      ELSE
         v_letter_grade := 'F';
      END IF;

      -- control resumes here
      DBMS_OUTPUT.PUT_LINE ('Letter grade is: '||
         v_letter_grade);
   END;
```

Note, that you may need to change the values for the variables v_stu-dent_id and v_section_id as you see fit in order to test some of your answers.

Try to answer the following questions first, and then execute the script:

a) What letter grade will be displayed on the screen:

   i) if the value of v_final_grade is equal to 85?

   ii) if the value of v_final_grade is NULL?

   iii) if the value of v_final_grade is greater than 100?

b) How would you change this script so that a message 'v_final_grade is null' is displayed if v_final_grade is NULL?

c) How would you change this script so that student ID and sec-tion ID are provided by a user?

d) How would you change the script to define a letter grade with-out specifying the upper limit of the final grade? In the state-ment, v_final_grade BETWEEN 90 and 100, number 100 is the upper limit.

LAB 5.2 EXERCISE ANSWERS

This section gives you some suggested answers to the questions in Lab 5.2, with discussion related to how those answers resulted. The most important thing to realize is whether your answer works. You should figure out the implications of the answers here and what the effects are from any different answers you may come up with.

5.2.1 ANSWERS

a) What letter grade will displayed on the screen
   i) if the value of v_final_grade is equal to 85?
   ii) if the value of v_final_grade is NULL?
   iii) if the value of v_final_grade is greater than 100?

   Answer: If the value of v_final_grade *is equal to 85, the value "B" of the letter grade will be displayed on the screen.*

The conditions of the ELSIF statement are evaluated in sequential order. The first condition

   v_final_grade BETWEEN 90 AND 100

evaluates to FALSE, and control is passed to the first ELSIF part of the ELSIF statement. Then, the second condition

   v_final_grade BETWEEN 80 AND 89

evaluates to TRUE, and the letter "B" is assigned to the variable v_letter_grade. Control is then passed to first executable statement after END IF, and message

   Letter grade is: B

is displayed on the screen.

   If the value of v_final_grade *is NULL, value "F" of the letter grade will be displayed of the screen.*

If the value of the v_final_grade is undefined or NULL, then all conditions of the ESLIF statement evaluate to NULL (notice, they do not evaluate to FALSE). As a result, the ELSE part of the ELSIF statement is executed, and letter "F" is assigned to the v_letter_grade.

   If the value of v_final_grade *is greater than 100, value "F" of the letter grade will be displayed of the screen.*

The conditions specified for the ELSIF statement cannot handle a value of v_final_grade greater than 100. So, for any student whose letter grade should be A+, will result in a letter grade of "F." After the ELSIF statement has terminated, "The letter grade is: F" is displayed on the screen.

**LAB
5.2**

b) How would you change this script so that a message "v_final_grade is null" is displayed if v_final_grade is NULL?

Answer: Your script should look similar to this script. Changes are shown in bold letters.

```
-- ch05_3b.sql, version 2.0
SET SERVEROUTPUT ON
DECLARE
   v_student_id NUMBER := 102;
   v_section_id NUMBER := 89;
   v_final_grade NUMBER;
   v_letter_grade CHAR(1);
BEGIN
   SELECT final_grade
     INTO v_final_grade
     FROM enrollment
    WHERE student_id = v_student_id
      AND section_id = v_section_id;

   IF v_final_grade IS NULL THEN
      DBMS_OUTPUT.PUT_LINE('v_final_grade is null');
   ELSIF v_final_grade BETWEEN 90 AND 100 THEN
      v_letter_grade := 'A';
   ELSIF v_final_grade BETWEEN 80 AND 89 THEN
      v_letter_grade := 'B';
   ELSIF v_final_grade BETWEEN 70 AND 79 THEN
      v_letter_grade := 'C';
   ELSIF v_final_grade BETWEEN 60 AND 69 THEN
      v_letter_grade := 'D';
   ELSE
      v_letter_grade := 'F';
   END IF;

   -- control resumes here
   DBMS_OUTPUT.PUT_LINE ('Letter grade is: '||
      v_letter_grade);
END;
```

One more condition has been added to the ELSIF statement. The condition

   v_final_grade BETWEEN 90 AND 100

becomes the first ELSIF condition. Now, if the value of v_final_grade is NULL, the message "v_final_grade is null" is displayed on the screen. However, there is no value assigned to the variable v_letter_grade. The message "Letter grade is:" is displayed on the screen as well.

c) How would you change this script so that both the student ID and the section ID are provided by a user?

Answer:Your script should look similar to this script. Changes are shown in bold letters.

```
-- ch05_3c.sql, version 3.0
SET SERVEROUTPUT ON
DECLARE
   v_student_id NUMBER := &sv_student_id;
   v_section_id NUMBER := &sv_section_id;
   v_final_grade NUMBER;
   v_letter_grade CHAR(1);
BEGIN
   SELECT final_grade
     INTO v_final_grade
     FROM enrollment
    WHERE student_id = v_student_id
      AND section_id = v_section_id;

   IF v_final_grade BETWEEN 90 AND 100 THEN
      v_letter_grade := 'A';
   ELSIF v_final_grade BETWEEN 80 AND 89 THEN
      v_letter_grade := 'B';
   ELSIF v_final_grade BETWEEN 70 AND 79 THEN
      v_letter_grade := 'C';
   ELSIF v_final_grade BETWEEN 60 AND 69 THEN
      v_letter_grade := 'D';
   ELSE
      v_letter_grade := 'F';
   END IF;

   -- control resumes here
   DBMS_OUTPUT.PUT_LINE ('Letter grade is: '||
      v_letter_grade);
END;
```

d) How would you change the script to define a letter grade without specifying the upper limit of the final grade? In the statement, v_final_grade BETWEEN 90 and 100, number 100 is the upper limit.

Answer:Your script should look similar to following. Changes are shown in bold letters.

```
-- ch05_3d.sql, version 4.0
SET SERVEROUTPUT ON
DECLARE
   v_student_id NUMBER := 102;
```

```
    v_section_id NUMBER := 89;
    v_final_grade NUMBER;
    v_letter_grade CHAR(1);
BEGIN
    SELECT final_grade
      INTO v_final_grade
      FROM enrollment
     WHERE student_id = v_student_id
       AND section_id = v_section_id;

    IF v_final_grade >= 90 THEN
        v_letter_grade := 'A';
    ELSIF v_final_grade >= 80 THEN
        v_letter_grade := 'B';
    ELSIF v_final_grade >= 70 THEN
        v_letter_grade := 'C';
    ELSIF v_final_grade >= 60 THEN
        v_letter_grade := 'D';
    ELSE
        v_letter_grade := 'F';
    END IF;

    --- control resumes here
    DBMS_OUTPUT.PUT_LINE ('Letter grade is: '||
        v_letter_grade);
END;
```

In this example, there is no upper limit specified for the variable v_final_grade because the BETWEEN operator has been replaced with ">=" operator. Thus, this script is able to handle a value of v_final_grade that is greater than 100. Instead of assigning letter "F" to v_letter_grade (in version 1.0 of the script), the letter "A" is assigned to the variable v_letter_grade. As a result, this script produces more accurate results.

LAB 5.2 SELF-REVIEW QUESTIONS

In order to test your progress, you should be able to answer the following questions.

1) An ELSIF construct can have only one ELSIF clause present.

a) _____ True
b) _____ False

2) There are multiple ELSE clauses present in an ELSIF construct.

a) _____ True
b) _____ False

3) What part of the ELSIF statement is executed when all of the conditions speci-fied evaluate to NULL?

    a) _____ IF part
    b) _____ One of the ELSIF parts
    c) _____ ELSE part
    d) _____ ELSIF statement is not executed at all

4) When the conditions of the ELSIF statement are not mutually exclusive, which of the following occur?

    a) _____ ELSIF statement causes an error.
    b) _____ ELSIF statement is not executed at all.
    c) _____ Statements associated with the first condition that evaluates to TRUE are executed.
    d) _____ Statements associated with the last condition that evaluates to TRUE are executed.

5) An ELSIF statement without the ELSE part causes a syntax error.

    a) _____ True
    b) _____ False

Answers appear in Appendix A, Section 5.2.

L A B 5 . 3

NESTED IF STATEMENTS

LAB OBJECTIVES

After this Lab, you will be able to:

✔ Use Nested IF Statements

You have encountered different types of conditional controls: IF-THEN statement, IF-THEN-ELSE statement, and ELSIF statement. These types of conditional controls can be nested inside of another—for example, an IF statement can be nested inside an ELSIF and vice versa. Consider the following:

■ *FOR EXAMPLE*

```
DECLARE
    v_num1 NUMBER := &sv_num1;
    v_num2 NUMBER := &sv_num2;
    v_total NUMBER;
BEGIN
    IF v_num1 > v_num2 THEN
        DBMS_OUTPUT.PUT_LINE ('IF part of the outer IF');
        v_total := v_num1 - v_num2;
    ELSE
        DBMS_OUTPUT.PUT_LINE ('ELSE part of the outer IF');
        v_total := v_num1 + v_num2;

        IF v_total < 0 THEN
            DBMS_OUTPUT.PUT_LINE ('Inner IF');
            v_total := v_total * (-1);
        END IF;

    END IF;
    DBMS_OUTPUT.PUT_LINE ('v_total = '||v_total);
END;
```

The IF-THEN-ELSE statement is called an outer IF statement because it encompasses the IF-THEN statement (shown in bold letters). The IF-THEN statement is called an inner IF statement because it is enclosed by the body of the IF-THEN-ELSE statement.

Assume that the value for v_num1 and v_num2 are –4 and 3 respectively. First, the condition

```
v_num1 > v_num2
```

of the outer IF statement is evaluated. Since –4 is not greater than 3, the ELSE part of the outer IF statement is executed. As a result, the message

```
ELSE part of the outer IF
```

is displayed, and the value of v_total is calculated. Next, the condition

```
v_total < 0
```

of the inner IF statement is evaluated. Since that value of v_total is equal –1, the condition yields TRUE, and message

```
Inner IF
```

is displayed. Next, the value of v_total is calculated again. This logic is demonstrated by the output produced by the example:

```
Enter value for sv_num1: -4
old    2:    v_num1   NUMBER := &sv_num1;
new    2:    v_num1   NUMBER := -4;
Enter value for sv_num2: 3
old    3:    v_num2   NUMBER := &sv_num2;
new    3:    v_num2   NUMBER := 3;
ELSE part of the outer IF
Inner IF
v_total = 1

PL/SQL procedure successfully completed.
```

LOGICAL OPERATORS

So far in this chapter, you have seen examples of different IF statements. All of these examples used test operators, such as >, <, and =, to test a condition. Logical operators can be used to evaluate a condition, as well. In addition, they allow a programmer to combine multiple conditions into a single condition if there is such a need.

■ *FOR EXAMPLE*

```
DECLARE
    v_letter CHAR(1) := '&sv_letter';
```

```
BEGIN
   IF (v_letter >= 'A' AND v_letter <= 'Z') OR
      (v_letter >= 'a' AND v_letter <= 'z')
   THEN
      DBMS_OUTPUT.PUT_LINE ('This is a letter');
   ELSE
      DBMS_OUTPUT.PUT_LINE ('This is not a letter');

      IF v_letter BETWEEN '0' and '9' THEN
         DBMS_OUTPUT.PUT_LINE ('This is a number');
      ELSE
         DBMS_OUTPUT.PUT_LINE ('This is not a number');
      END IF;

   END IF;
END;
```

**LAB
5.3**

In this example, the condition

```
(v_letter >= 'A' AND v_letter <= 'Z') OR
(v_letter >= 'a' AND v_letter <= 'z')
```

uses logical operators AND and OR. There are two conditions

```
(v_letter >= 'A' AND v_letter <= 'Z')
```

and

```
(v_letter >= 'a' AND v_letter <= 'z')
```

combined into one with the help of the OR operator. It is also important for you to realize the purpose of the parentheses. In this example, they are used to improve readability only, because the operator AND takes precedence over the operator OR.

When the symbol "?" is entered at runtime, this example produces the following output:

```
Enter value for sv_letter: ?
old   2:    v_letter CHAR(1) := '&sv_letter';
new   2:    v_letter CHAR(1) := '?';
This is not a letter
This is not a number

PL/SQL procedure successfully completed.
```

LAB 5.3 EXERCISES

5.3.1 USE NESTED IF STATEMENTS

In this exercise, you will use nested IF statements. This script will convert the value of a temperature from one system to another. If the temperature is supplied in Fahrenheit, it will be converted to Celsius, and vice versa.

Create the following PL/SQL script:

```
-- ch05_4a.sql, version 1.0
SET SERVEROUTPUT ON
DECLARE
    v_temp_in NUMBER := &sv_temp_in;
    v_scale_in CHAR := '&sv_scale_in';
    v_temp_out NUMBER;
    v_scale_out CHAR;
BEGIN
    IF v_scale_in != 'C' AND v_scale_in != 'F' THEN
        DBMS_OUTPUT.PUT_LINE ('This is not a valid scale');
    ELSE
        IF v_scale_in = 'C' THEN
            v_temp_out := ( (9 * v_temp_in) / 5 ) + 32;
            v_scale_out := 'F';
        ELSE
            v_temp_out := ( (v_temp_in - 32) * 5 ) / 9;
            v_scale_out := 'C';
        END IF;
        DBMS_OUTPUT.PUT_LINE ('New scale is: '||
            v_scale_out);
        DBMS_OUTPUT.PUT_LINE ('New temperature is: '||
            v_temp_out);
    END IF;
END;
```

Execute the script, and then answer the following questions:

a) What output is printed on the screen if the value of 100 is entered for the temperature, and the letter "C" is entered for the scale?

b) Try to run this script without providing a value for the temperature. What message will be displayed on the screen? Why?

c) Try to run this script providing an invalid letter for the temperature scale, for example, letter "V." What message will be displayed on the screen? Why?

d) Rewrite this script so that if an invalid letter is entered for the scale, `v_temp_out` is initialized to zero and `v_scale_out` is initialized to C.

LAB 5.3 EXERCISE ANSWERS

This section gives you some suggested answers to the questions in Lab 5.3, with discussion related to how those answers resulted. The most important thing to realize is whether your answer works. You should figure out the implications of the answers here and what the effects are from any different answers you may come up with.

5.3.1 ANSWERS

a) What output is printed on the screen if the value of 100 is entered for the temperature, and the letter "C" is entered for the scale?

Answer: Your output should look like the following:

```
Enter value for sv_temp_in: 100
old    2:      v_temp_in     NUMBER := &sv_temp_in;
new    2:      v_temp_in     NUMBER := 100;
Enter value for sv_scale_in: C
old    3:      v_scale_in    CHAR := '&sv_scale_in';
new    3:      v_scale_in    CHAR := 'C';
New scale is: F
New temperature is: 212

PL/SQL procedure successfully completed.
```

Once the values for `v_temp_in` and `v_scale_in` have been entered, the condition

```
v_scale_in != 'C' AND v_scale_in != 'F'
```

of the outer IF statement evaluates to FALSE, and control is passed to the ELSE part of the outer IF statement. Next, the condition

```
v_scale_in = 'C'
```

of the inner IF statement evaluates to TRUE, and the values of the variables `v_temp_out` and `v_scale_out` are calculated. Control is then passed back to the outer IF statement, and the new value for the temperature and the scale are displayed on the screen.

b) Try to run this script without providing a value for the temperature. What message will be displayed on the screen? Why?

Answer: If the value for the temperature is not entered, the script will not compile at all.

The compiler will try to assign a value to `v_temp_in` with the help of the substitution variable. Because the value for `v_temp_in` has not been entered, the assignment statement will fail, and the following error message will be displayed.

```
Enter value for sv_temp_in:
old   2:     v_temp_in    NUMBER := &sv_temp_in;
new   2:     v_temp_in    NUMBER := ;
Enter value for sv_scale_in: C
old   3:     v_scale_in   CHAR := '&sv_scale_in';
new   3:     v_scale_in   CHAR := 'C';
    v_temp_in      NUMBER := ;
                              *
ERROR at line 2:
ORA-06550: line 2, column 27:
PLS-00103: Encountered the symbol ";" when expecting one of
the following:
( - + mod not null <an identifier>
<a double-quoted delimited-identifier> <a bind variable> avg
count current exists max min prior sql stddev sum variance
cast <a string literal with character set specification>
<a number> <a single-quoted SQL string>
The symbol "null" was substituted for ";" to continue.
```

You have probably noticed that even though the mistake seems small and insignificant, the error message is fairly long and confusing.

c) Try to run this script providing an invalid letter for the temperature scale, for example, letter "V." What message will be displayed on the screen? Why?

Answer: If an invalid letter is entered for the scale, the message "This is not a valid scale" will be displayed on the screen.

The condition of the outer IF statement will evaluate to TRUE. As a result, the inner IF statement will not be executed at all, and the message "This is not a valid scale" will be displayed on the screen.

Assume that letter "V" was typed by mistake. This example will produce the following output:

```
Enter value for sv_temp_in: 45
old    2:     v_temp_in     NUMBER := &sv_temp_in;
new    2:     v_temp_in     NUMBER := 45;
Enter value for sv_scale_in: V
old    3:     v_scale_in    CHAR := '&sv_scale_in';
new    3:     v_scale_in    CHAR := 'V';
This is not a valid scale

PL/SQL procedure successfully completed.
```

d) Rewrite this script so that if an invalid letter is entered for the scale, `v_temp_out` is initialized to zero and `v_scale_out` is initialized to C.

Answer: Your script should look similar to the following script. Changes are shown in bold letters. Notice that the two last DBMS_OUTPUT.PUT_LINE statements have been moved from the body of the outer IF statement.

```
-- ch05_4b.sql, version 2.0
DECLARE
    v_temp_in NUMBER := &sv_temp_in;
    v_scale_in CHAR := '&sv_scale_in';
    v_temp_out NUMBER;
    v_scale_out CHAR;
BEGIN
    IF v_scale_in != 'C' AND v_scale_in != 'F' THEN
        DBMS_OUTPUT.PUT_LINE ('This is not a valid scale');
        v_temp_out := 0;
        v_scale_out := 'C';
    ELSE
        IF v_scale_in = 'C' THEN
            v_temp_out := ( (9 * v_temp_in) / 5 ) + 32;
            v_scale_out := 'F';
        ELSE
            v_temp_out := ( (v_temp_in - 32) * 5 ) / 9;
            v_scale_out := 'C';
        END IF;
    END IF;
    DBMS_OUTPUT.PUT_LINE ('New scale is: '||v_scale_out);
    DBMS_OUTPUT.PUT_LINE ('New temperature is: '||
        v_temp_out);
END;
```

The preceding script produces the following output:

```
Enter value for sv_temp_in: 100
old    2:     v_temp_in     NUMBER := &sv_temp_in;
```

```
new    2:    v_temp_in    NUMBER := 100;
Enter value for sv_scale_in: V
old    3:    v_scale_in    CHAR := '&sv_scale_in';
new    3:    v_scale_in    CHAR := 'V';
This is not a valid scale.
New scale is: C
New temperature is: 0

PL/SQL procedure successfully completed.
```

LAB 5.3 SELF-REVIEW QUESTIONS

In order to test your progress, you should be able to answer the following questions.

1) What types of IF statements can be nested one inside another?

a) _____ IF-THEN statement can only be nested inside ELSIF statement.
b) _____ IF-THEN-ELSE statement cannot be nested at all.
c) _____ Any IF statement can be nested inside another IF statement.

2) How many IF statements can be nested one inside another?

a) _____ One
b) _____ Two
c) _____ Any number

3) Only a single logical operator can be used with a condition of an IF statement.

a) _____ True
b) _____ False

4) When using nested IF statements, their conditions do not need to be mutually exclusive.

a) _____ True
b) _____ False

5) When the condition of the outer IF statement evaluates to FALSE, which of the following happens?

a) _____ Control is transferred to the inner IF statement.
b) _____ The error message is generated.
c) _____ Control is transferred to the first executable statement after the outer END IF statement.

Answers appear in Appendix A, Section 5.3.

C H A P T E R 5

TEST YOUR THINKING

In this chapter you learned about different types of IF statements. You also learned that all of these different IF statements can be nested one inside another. Here are some exercises that will help you test the depth of your understanding.

1) Rewrite ch05_1a.sql. Instead of getting information from the user for the variable `v_date`, define its value with the help of the function SYS-DATE. After it has been determined that a certain day falls on the weekend, check to see if the time is before or after noon. Display the time of the day together with the day.

2) Create a new script. For a given instructor, determine how many sections he or she is teaching. If the number is greater than or equal to 3, display a message saying that the instructor needs a vacation. Otherwise, display a message saying how many sections this instructor is teaching.

3) Execute the two PL/SQL blocks below and explain why they produce different output for the same value of the variable v_num. Remember to issue the SET SERVEROUTPUT ON command before running this script.

```
-- Block 1
DECLARE
    v_num NUMBER := NULL;
BEGIN
    IF v_num > 0 THEN
        DBMS_OUTPUT.PUT_LINE ('v_num is greater than 0');
    ELSE
        DBMS_OUTPUT.PUT_LINE
            ('v_num is not greater than 0');
    END IF;
END;

-- Block 2
DECLARE
    v_num NUMBER := NULL;
BEGIN
    IF v_num > 0 THEN
```

```
            DBMS_OUTPUT.PUT_LINE ('v_num is greater than 0');
        END IF;
        IF NOT (v_num > 0) THEN
            DBMS_OUTPUT.PUT_LINE
                ('v_num is not greater than 0');
        END IF;
    END;
```

The projects in this section are meant to have you utilize all of the skills that you have acquired throughout this chapter. The answers to these projects can be found in Appendix D and at the companion Web site to this book, located at http://www .phptr.com/rosenzweig2e. Visit the Web site periodically to share and discuss your answers.

C H A P T E R   6

CONDITIONAL CONTROL: CASE STATEMENTS

In the previous chapter, you explored the concept of conditional control via IF and ELSIF statements. In this chapter, you will continue by examining different types of CASE statements and expressions. They are new PL/SQL features and are not supported by PL/SQL in versions prior to Oracle 9i. You will also learn how to use NULLIF and COALESCE functions that are considered an extension of CASE.

LAB 6.1

CASE STATEMENTS

LAB OBJECTIVES

After this Lab, you will be able to:

✔ Use CASE Statements
✔ Use Searched CASE Statements

A CASE statement has two forms: CASE and searched CASE. A CASE statement allows you to specify a *selector* that determines which group of actions to take. A searched CASE statement does not have a selector; it has search conditions that are evaluated in order to determine which group of actions to take.

CASE STATEMENTS

A CASE statement has the following structure:

```
CASE SELECTOR
    WHEN EXPRESSION 1 THEN STATEMENT 1;
    WHEN EXPRESSION 2 THEN STATEMENT 2;
    ...
    WHEN EXPRESSION N THEN STATEMENT N;
    ELSE STATEMENT N+1;
END CASE;
```

The reserved word CASE marks the beginning of the CASE statement. A *selector* is a value that determines which WHEN clause should be executed. Each WHEN clause contains an EXPRESSION and one or more executable statements associated with it. The ELSE clause is optional and works similar to the ELSE clause used in that IF-THEN-ELSE statement. END CASE is a reserved phrase that indicates the end of the CASE statement. This flow of the logic from the preceding structure of the CASE statement is illustrated in Figure 6.1.

Note that the selector is evaluated only once. The WHEN clauses are evaluated sequentially. The value of an expression is compared to the value of the selector. If

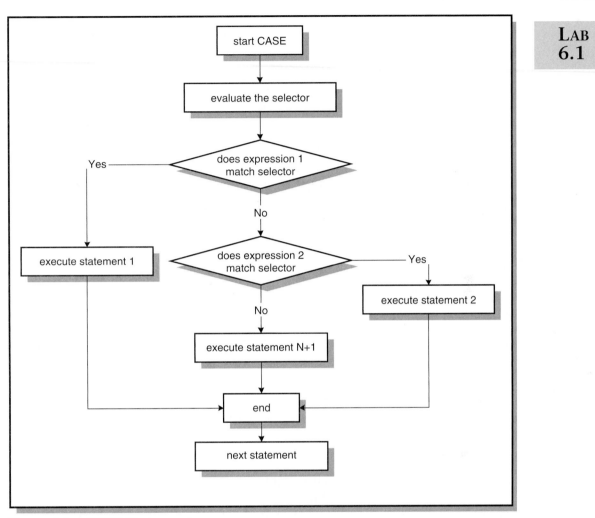

Figure 6.1 ■ CASE Statement

they are equal, the statement associated with a particular WHEN clause is executed, and subsequent WHEN clauses are not evaluated. If no expression matches the value of the selector, the ELSE clause is executed.

Recall the example of the IF-THEN-ELSE statement used in the previous chapter.

■ *FOR EXAMPLE*

```
DECLARE
    v_num NUMBER := &sv_user_num;
BEGIN
    -- test if the number provided by the user is even
```

```
        IF MOD(v_num,2) = 0   THEN
            DBMS_OUTPUT.PUT_LINE (v_num||' is even number');
        ELSE
            DBMS_OUTPUT.PUT_LINE (v_num||' is odd number');
        END IF;
        DBMS_OUTPUT.PUT_LINE ('Done');
    END;
```

Consider the new version of the same example with the CASE statement instead of the IF-THEN-ELSE statement.

■ FOR EXAMPLE

```
DECLARE
    v_num NUMBER := &sv_user_num;
    v_num_flag NUMBER;
BEGIN
    v_num_flag := MOD(v_num,2);

    -- test if the number provided by the user is even
    CASE v_num_flag
        WHEN 0 THEN
            DBMS_OUTPUT.PUT_LINE (v_num||' is even number');
        ELSE
            DBMS_OUTPUT.PUT_LINE (v_num||' is odd number');
    END CASE;
    DBMS_OUTPUT.PUT_LINE ('Done');
END;
```

In this example, a new variable, v_num_flag, is used as a selector for the CASE statement. If the MOD function returns 0, then the number is even; otherwise it is odd. If v_num is assigned the value of 7, this example produces the following output:

```
Enter value for sv_user_num: 7
old   2:    v_num NUMBER := &sv_user_num;
new   2:    v_num NUMBER := 7;
7 is odd number
Done

PL/SQL procedure successfully completed.
```

SEARCHED CASE STATEMENTS

A searched CASE statement has search conditions that yield Boolean values: TRUE, FALSE, or NULL. When a particular search condition evaluates to TRUE, the group of statements associated with this condition is executed. This is indicated as follows:

```
CASE
   WHEN SEARCH CONDITION 1 THEN STATEMENT 1;
   WHEN SEARCH CONDITION 2 THEN STATEMENT 2;
   ...
   WHEN SEARCH CONDITION N THEN STATEMENT N;
   ELSE STATEMENT N+1;
END CASE;
```

When a search condition evaluates to TRUE, control is passed to the statement associated with it. If no search condition yields TRUE, then statements associated with the ELSE clause are executed. This flow of logic from the preceding structure of the searched CASE statement is illustrated in Figure 6.2.

Consider the modified version of the example that you have seen previously in this lab.

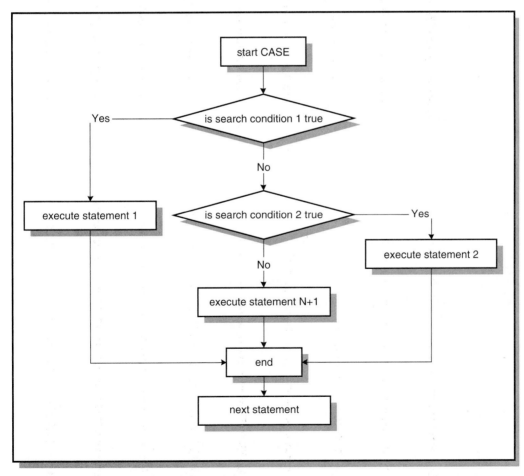

Figure 6.2 ■ Searched CASE Statement

■ *FOR EXAMPLE*

```
DECLARE
    v_num NUMBER := &sv_user_num;
BEGIN
    -- test if the number provided by the user is even
    CASE
        WHEN MOD(v_num,2) = 0 THEN
            DBMS_OUTPUT.PUT_LINE (v_num||' is even number');
        ELSE
            DBMS_OUTPUT.PUT_LINE (v_num||' is odd number');
    END CASE;
    DBMS_OUTPUT.PUT_LINE ('Done');
END;
```

Notice that this example is almost identical to the previous example.

In the previous example, the variable v_num_flag was used as a selector, and the result of the MOD function was assigned to it. The value of the selector was then compared to the value of the expression. In this example, you are using a searched CASE statement, so there is no selector present. The variable v_num is used as part of the search conditions, so there is no need to declare variable v_num_flag. This example produces the same output when the same value is provided for the v_num:

```
Enter value for sv_user_num: 7
old    2:    v_num NUMBER := &sv_user_num;
new    2:    v_num NUMBER := 7;
7 is odd number
Done

PL/SQL procedure successfully completed.
```

DIFFERENCES BETWEEN CASE AND SEARCHED CASE STATEMENTS

It is important to note the differences between the CASE and searched CASE statements. You have seen that the searched CASE statement does not have a selector. In addition, its WHEN clauses contain search conditions that yield a Boolean value similar to the IF statement, not expressions that can yield a value of any type except a PL/SQL record, an index-by-table, a nested table, a vararray, BLOB, BFILE, or an object type. You will encounter some of these types in the future chapters. Consider the following two code fragments based on the examples you have seen earlier in this chapter.

■ *FOR EXAMPLE*

```
DECLARE
   v_num NUMBER := &sv_user_num;
   v_num_flag NUMBER;
BEGIN
   v_num_flag := MOD(v_num,2);

   -- test if the number provided by the user is even
   CASE v_num_flag
      WHEN 0 THEN
         DBMS_OUTPUT.PUT_LINE (v_num||' is even number');
...
```

■ *FOR EXAMPLE*

```
DECLARE
   v_num NUMBER := &sv_user_num;
BEGIN
   -- test if the number provided by the user is even
   CASE
      WHEN MOD(v_num,2) = 0 THEN
...
```

In the first code fragment, `v_num_flag` is the selector. It is a PL/SQL variable that has been defined as NUMBER. Because the value of the expression is compared to the value of the selector, the expression must return a similar datatype. The expression '0' contains a number, so its datatype is also numeric. In the second code fragment, each searched expression evaluates to TRUE or FALSE just like conditions of an IF statement.

Next, consider an example of the CASE statement that generates a syntax error because the datatype returned by the expressions does not match the datatype assigned to the selector.

■ *FOR EXAMPLE*

```
DECLARE
   v_num NUMBER := &sv_num;
   v_num_flag NUMBER;
BEGIN
   CASE v_num_flag
      WHEN MOD(v_num,2) = 0 THEN
         DBMS_OUTPUT.PUT_LINE (v_num||' is even number');
      ELSE
         DBMS_OUTPUT.PUT_LINE (v_num||' is odd number');
   END CASE;
   DBMS_OUTPUT.PUT_LINE ('Done');
END;
```

In this example, the variable v_num_flag has been defined as a NUMBER. However, the result of each expression yields Boolean datatype. As a result, this example produces the following syntax error:

```
Enter value for sv_num: 7
old    2:     v_num NUMBER := &sv_num;
new    2:     v_num NUMBER := 7;
   CASE v_num_flag
           *
ERROR at line 5:
ORA-06550: line 5, column 9:
PLS-00615: type mismatch found at 'V_NUM_FLAG' between
CASE operand and WHEN operands
ORA-06550: line 5, column 4:
PL/SQL: Statement ignored
```

Consider a modified version of this example where v_num_flag has been defined as a Boolean variable.

■ FOR EXAMPLE

```
DECLARE
    v_num NUMBER := &sv_num;
    v_num_flag Boolean;
BEGIN
    CASE v_num_flag
        WHEN MOD(v_num,2) = 0 THEN
            DBMS_OUTPUT.PUT_LINE (v_num||' is even number');
        ELSE
            DBMS_OUTPUT.PUT_LINE (v_num||' is odd number');
    END CASE;
    DBMS_OUTPUT.PUT_LINE ('Done');
END;
```

If v_num is assigned the value of 7 again, this example produces the following output:

```
Enter value for sv_num: 7
old    2:     v_num NUMBER := &sv_num;
new    2:     v_num NUMBER := 7;
7 is odd number
Done

PL/SQL procedure successfully completed.
```

At first glance this seems to be the output that you would expect. However, consider the output produced by this example when the value of 4 is assigned to the variable v_num:

```
Enter value for sv_num: 4
old    2:    v_num NUMBER := &sv_num;
new    2:    v_num NUMBER := 4;
4 is odd number
Done

PL/SQL procedure successfully completed.
```

Notice that the second run of the example produced an incorrect output even though it did not generate any syntax errors. When the value 4 is assigned to the variable v_num, the expression

```
MOD(v_num,2) = 0
```

yields TRUE, and it is compared to the selector v_num_flag. However, the v_num_flag has not been initialized to any value, so it is NULL. Because NULL does not equal to TRUE, the statement associated with the ELSE clause is executed.

LAB 6.1 EXERCISES

6.1.1 USE THE CASE STATEMENT

In this exercise, you will use the CASE statement to display the name of a day on the screen based on the number of the day in a week. In other words, if the number of a day of the week is 3, then it is Tuesday.

Create the following PL/SQL script:

```
-- ch06_1a.sql, version 1.0
SET SERVEROUTPUT ON
DECLARE
   v_date DATE := TO_DATE('&sv_user_date', 'DD-MON-YYYY');
   v_day VARCHAR2(1);
BEGIN
   v_day := TO_CHAR(v_date, 'D');
   CASE v_day
      WHEN '1' THEN
         DBMS_OUTPUT.PUT_LINE ('Today is Sunday');
      WHEN '2' THEN
         DBMS_OUTPUT.PUT_LINE ('Today is Monday');
      WHEN '3' THEN
         DBMS_OUTPUT.PUT_LINE ('Today is Tuesday');
      WHEN '4' THEN
         DBMS_OUTPUT.PUT_LINE ('Today is Wednesday');
      WHEN '5' THEN
         DBMS_OUTPUT.PUT_LINE ('Today is Thursday');
```

```
            WHEN '6' THEN
                DBMS_OUTPUT.PUT_LINE ('Today is Friday');
            WHEN '7' THEN
                DBMS_OUTPUT.PUT_LINE ('Today is Saturday');
        END CASE;
    END;
```

Execute the script, and then answer the following questions:

a) If the value of v_date equals '15-JAN-2002', what output is printed on the screen?

b) How many times is the CASE selector v_day evaluated?

c) Rewrite this script using the ELSE clause in the CASE statement.

d) Rewrite this script using the searched CASE statement.

6.1.2 USE THE SEARCHED CASE STATEMENT

In this exercise, you will modify the script ch05_3d.sql used in the previous chapter. The original script uses the ELSIF statement to display a letter grade for a student registered for a specific section of course number 25. The new version will use a searched CASE statement to achieve the same result. Try to answer the questions before you run the script. Once you have answered the questions, run the script and check your answers. *Note that you may need to change the values for the variables* v_student_id *and* v_section_id *as you see fit in order to test some of your answers.*

Create the following PL/SQL script:

```
-- ch06_2a.sql, version 1.0
SET SERVEROUTPUT ON
DECLARE
    v_student_id NUMBER := 102;
    v_section_id NUMBER := 89;
    v_final_grade NUMBER;
    v_letter_grade CHAR(1);
```

```
BEGIN
    SELECT final_grade
      INTO v_final_grade
      FROM enrollment
     WHERE student_id = v_student_id
       AND section_id = v_section_id;

    CASE
        WHEN v_final_grade >= 90 THEN v_letter_grade := 'A';
        WHEN v_final_grade >= 80 THEN v_letter_grade := 'B';
        WHEN v_final_grade >= 70 THEN v_letter_grade := 'C';
        WHEN v_final_grade >= 60 THEN v_letter_grade := 'D';
        ELSE v_letter_grade := 'F';
    END CASE;
    -- control resumes here
    DBMS_OUTPUT.PUT_LINE ('Letter grade is: '||
        v_letter_grade);
END;
```

Try to answer the following questions first, and then execute the script:

a) What letter grade will be displayed on the screen:

  i) if the value of `v_final_grade` is equal to 60?

  ii) if the value of `v_final_grade` is greater than 60 and less than 70?

  iii) if the value of `v_final_grade` is NULL?

b) How would you change this script so that a message "There is no final grade" is displayed if `v_final_grade` is null? In addition, make sure that the message "Letter grade is: " is not displayed on the screen.

c) Rewrite this script, changing the order of the searched conditions as follows:

```
CASE
    WHEN v_final_grade >= 60 THEN v_letter_grade := 'D';
    WHEN v_final_grade >= 70 THEN v_letter_grade := 'C';
    WHEN v_final_grade >= 80 THEN ...
    WHEN v_final_grade >= 90 THEN ...
    ELSE ...
```

Execute the script and explain the output produced.

**LAB
6.1**

LAB 6.1 EXERCISE ANSWERS

This section gives you some suggested answers to the questions in Lab 6.1, with discussion related to how those answers resulted. The most important thing to realize is whether your answer works. You should figure out the implications of the answers here and what the effects are from any different answers you may come up with.

6.1.1 ANSWERS

a) If the value of v_date equals '15-JAN-2002', what output is printed on the screen?

Answer: Your output should look like the following:

```
Enter value for sv_user_date: 15-JAN-2002
old    2:    v_date DATE := TO_DATE('&sv_user_date', 'DD-
MON-YYYY');
new    2:    v_date DATE := TO_DATE('15-JAN-2002', 'DD-MON-
YYYY');
Today is Tuesday

PL/SQL procedure successfully completed.
```

When the value of 15-JAN-2002 is entered for v_date, the number of the day of the week is determined for the variable v_day with the help of the TO_CHAR function. Next, each expression of the CASE statement is compared sequentially to the value of the selector. Because the value of the selector equals 3, the DBMS_OUTPUT.PUT_LINE statement associated with the third WHEN clause is executed. As a result, the message 'Today is Tuesday' is displayed on the screen. The rest of the expressions are not evaluated, and control is passed to the first executable statement after END CASE.

b) How many times is the CASE selector v_day evaluated?

Answer: The CASE selector v_day is evaluated only once. However, the WHEN clauses are checked sequentially. When the value of the expression in the WHEN clause equals the value of the selector, the statements associated with the WHEN clause are executed.

c) Rewrite this script using the ELSE clause in the CASE statement.

Answer: Your script should look similar to the following. Changes are shown in bold letters.

```
-- ch06_1b.sql, version 2.0
SET SERVEROUTPUT ON
DECLARE
   v_date DATE := TO_DATE('&sv_user_date', 'DD-MON-YYYY');
   v_day VARCHAR2(1);
BEGIN
   v_day := TO_CHAR(v_date, 'D');
   CASE v_day
      WHEN '1' THEN
         DBMS_OUTPUT.PUT_LINE ('Today is Sunday');
      WHEN '2' THEN
         DBMS_OUTPUT.PUT_LINE ('Today is Monday');
      WHEN '3' THEN
         DBMS_OUTPUT.PUT_LINE ('Today is Tuesday');
      WHEN '4' THEN
         DBMS_OUTPUT.PUT_LINE ('Today is Wednesday');
      WHEN '5' THEN
         DBMS_OUTPUT.PUT_LINE ('Today is Thursday');
      WHEN '6' THEN
         DBMS_OUTPUT.PUT_LINE ('Today is Friday');
      ELSE DBMS_OUTPUT.PUT_LINE ('Today is Saturday');
   END CASE;
END;
```

Notice that the last WHEN clause has been replaced by the ELSE clause. If '19-JAN-2002' is provided at runtime, the example produces the following output:

```
Enter value for sv_user_date: 19-JAN-2002
old    2:    v_date DATE := TO_DATE('&sv_user_date', 'DD-
MON-YYYY');
new    2:    v_date DATE := TO_DATE('19-JAN-2002', 'DD-MON-
YYYY');
Today is Saturday

PL/SQL procedure successfully completed.
```

None of the expressions listed in the WHEN clauses are equal to the value of the selector because the date '19-JAN-2002' falls on Saturday, which is the seventh day of the week. As a result, the ELSE clause is executed, and the message 'Today is Saturday' is displayed on the screen.

d) Rewrite this script using the searched CASE statement.

Answer: Your script should look similar to the following. Changes are shown in bold letters.

```
-- ch06_1c.sql, version 1.0
SET SERVEROUTPUT ON
DECLARE
   v_date DATE := TO_DATE('&sv_user_date', 'DD-MON-YYYY');
```

**LAB
6.1**

```
BEGIN
   CASE
      WHEN TO_CHAR(v_date, 'D') = '1' THEN
         DBMS_OUTPUT.PUT_LINE ('Today is Sunday');
      WHEN TO_CHAR(v_date, 'D') = '2' THEN
         DBMS_OUTPUT.PUT_LINE ('Today is Monday');
      WHEN TO_CHAR(v_date, 'D') = '3' THEN
         DBMS_OUTPUT.PUT_LINE ('Today is Tuesday');
      WHEN TO_CHAR(v_date, 'D') = '4' THEN
         DBMS_OUTPUT.PUT_LINE ('Today is Wednesday');
      WHEN TO_CHAR(v_date, 'D') = '5' THEN
         DBMS_OUTPUT.PUT_LINE ('Today is Thursday');
      WHEN TO_CHAR(v_date, 'D') = '6' THEN
         DBMS_OUTPUT.PUT_LINE ('Today is Friday');
      WHEN TO_CHAR(v_date, 'D') = '7' THEN
         DBMS_OUTPUT.PUT_LINE ('Today is Saturday');
   END CASE;
END;
```

Notice that in the new version of the example there is no need to declare variable v_day because the searched CASE statement does not need a selector. The expression that you used to assign a value to the variable v_day is now used as part of the searched conditions. When run, this example produces output identical to the output produced by the original version:

```
Enter value for sv_user_date: 15-JAN-2002
old   2:    v_date DATE := TO_DATE('&sv_user_date', 'DD-
MON-YYYY');
new   2:    v_date DATE := TO_DATE('15-JAN-2002', 'DD-MON-
YYYY');
Today is Tuesday

PL/SQL procedure successfully completed.
```

6.1.2 ANSWERS

a) What letter grade will be displayed on the screen:
   i) if the value of v_final_grade is equal to 60?
   ii) if the value of v_final_grade is greater than 60 and less than 70?
   iii) if the value of v_final_grade is NULL?

Answer: If the value of v_final_grade is equal to 60, value "D" of the letter grade will be displayed on the screen.

The searched conditions of the CASE statement are evaluated in sequential order. The searched condition

```
WHEN v_final_grade >= 60 THEN
```

yields TRUE, and as a result, letter "D" is assigned to the variable
`v_letter_grade`. Control is then passed to the first executable statement after
END IF, and the message "Letter grade is: D" is displayed on the screen.

> *If the value of* `v_final_grade` *is greater than 60 and less than 70, value "D" of
> the letter grade will be displayed on the screen.*

If the value of the `v_final_grade` falls between 60 and 70, then the searched
condition

> **WHEN v_final_grade >= 70 THEN**

yields FALSE because the value of the variable `v_final_grade` is less that 70.
However, the next searched condition

> **WHEN v_final_grade >= 60 THEN**

of the CASE statement evaluates to TRUE, and letter "D" is assigned to the variable `v_letter_grade`.

> *If the value of* `v_final_grade` *is NULL, value "F" of the letter grade will be dis-
> played on the screen.*

All searched conditions of the CASE statement evaluate to FALSE because NULL
cannot be compared to a value. Such a comparison will always yield FALSE, and
as a result, the ELSE clause is executed.

b) How would you change this script so that a message "There is no final grade" is
displayed if `v_final_grade` is NULL? In addition, make sure that the message
"Letter grade is:" is not displayed on the screen.

> *Answer: Your script should look similar to this script. Changes are shown in bold letters.*

```
-- ch06_2b.sql, version 2.0
SET SERVEROUTPUT ON
DECLARE
   v_student_id NUMBER := &sv_student_id;
   v_section_id NUMBER := 89;
   v_final_grade NUMBER;
   v_letter_grade CHAR(1);
BEGIN
   SELECT final_grade
     INTO v_final_grade
     FROM enrollment
    WHERE student_id = v_student_id
      AND section_id = v_section_id;

   CASE -- outer CASE
     WHEN v_final_grade IS NULL THEN
```

```
                    DBMS_OUTPUT.PUT_LINE ('There is no final grade.');
                ELSE
                    CASE -- inner CASE
                        WHEN v_final_grade >= 90
                            THEN v_letter_grade := 'A';
                        WHEN v_final_grade >= 80
                            THEN v_letter_grade := 'B';
                        WHEN v_final_grade >= 70
                            THEN v_letter_grade := 'C';
                        WHEN v_final_grade >= 60
                            THEN v_letter_grade := 'D';
                        ELSE v_letter_grade := 'F';
                    END CASE;
                    -- control resumes here after inner CASE terminates
                    DBMS_OUTPUT.PUT_LINE ('Letter grade is: '||
                        v_letter_grade);
            END CASE;
            -- control resumes here after outer CASE terminates
        END;
```

In order to achieve the desired results, you are nesting CASE statements one inside the other just like IF statements in the previous chapter. The outer CASE statement evaluates the value of the variable v_final_grade. If the value of v_final_grade is NULL, then the message "There is no final grade." is displayed on the screen. If the value of v_final_grade is not NULL, then the ELSE part of the outer CASE statement is executed.

Notice that in order to display the letter grade only when there is a final grade, you have associated the statement

```
    DBMS_OUTPUT.PUT_LINE ('Letter grade is: '||v_letter_grade);
```

with the ELSE clause of the outer CASE statement. This guarantees that the message "Letter grade…" will be displayed on the screen only when the variable v_final_grade is not NULL.

In order to test this script fully, you have also introduced a substitution variable. This enables you to run the script for the different values of v_student_id. For the first run, enter value of 136, and for the second run enter the value of 102.

The first output displays the message "There is no final grade." and does not display the message "Letter grade…":

```
    Enter value for sv_student_id: 136
    old    2:    v_student_id NUMBER := &sv_student_id;
    new    2:    v_student_id NUMBER := 136;
    There is no final grade.

    PL/SQL procedure successfully completed.
```

The second run produced output similar to the output produced by the original version:

```
Enter value for sv_student_id: 102
old    2:    v_student_id NUMBER := &sv_student_id;
new    2:    v_student_id NUMBER := 102;
Letter grade is: A

PL/SQL procedure successfully completed.
```

c) Rewrite this script changing the order of the searched conditions as follows:

```
CASE
    WHEN v_final_grade >= 60 THEN v_letter_grade := 'D';
    WHEN v_final_grade >= 70 THEN v_letter_grade := 'C';
    WHEN v_final_grade >= 80 THEN ...
    WHEN v_final_grade >= 90 THEN ...
    ELSE ...
```

Execute the script and explain the output produced.

Answer: Your script should look similar to the following script. Changes are shown in bold letters.

```
-- ch06_2c.sql, version 3.0
SET SERVEROUTPUT ON
DECLARE
    v_student_id NUMBER := 102;
    v_section_id NUMBER := 89;
    v_final_grade NUMBER;
    v_letter_grade CHAR(1);
BEGIN
    SELECT final_grade
      INTO v_final_grade
      FROM enrollment
     WHERE student_id = v_student_id
       AND section_id = v_section_id;

    CASE
        WHEN v_final_grade >= 60 THEN v_letter_grade := 'D';
        WHEN v_final_grade >= 70 THEN v_letter_grade := 'C';
        WHEN v_final_grade >= 80 THEN v_letter_grade := 'B';
        WHEN v_final_grade >= 90 THEN v_letter_grade := 'A';
        ELSE v_letter_grade := 'F';
    END CASE;
    -- control resumes here
    DBMS_OUTPUT.PUT_LINE ('Letter grade is: '||
        v_letter_grade);
END;
```

This script produces the following output:

```
Letter grade is: D

PL/SQL procedure successfully completed.
```

The first searched condition of the CASE statement evaluates to TRUE, because the value of `v_final_grade` *equals 92, and it is greater than 60.*

You learned earlier that the searched conditions are evaluated sequentially. Therefore, the statements associated with the first condition that yields TRUE are executed, and the rest of the searched conditions are discarded. In this example, the searched condition

```
WHEN v_final_grade >= 60 THEN
```

evaluates to TRUE, and the value of "D" is assigned to the variable `v_letter_grade`. Then control is passed to the first executable statement after END CASE, and the message "Letter grade is: D" is displayed on the screen. In order for this script to assign the letter grade correctly, the CASE statement may be modified as follows:

```
CASE
    WHEN v_final_grade < 60 THEN v_letter_grade := 'F';
    WHEN v_final_grade < 70 THEN v_letter_grade := 'D';
    WHEN v_final_grade < 80 THEN v_letter_grade := 'C';
    WHEN v_final_grade < 90 THEN v_letter_grade := 'B';
    WHEN v_final_grade < 100 THEN v_letter_grade := 'A';
END CASE;
```

However, there is a small problem with this CASE statement also. What do you think will happen when `v_final_grade` is greater than 100?

 With the CASE constructs, as with the IF constructs, a group of statements that is executed will generally depend on the order in which its condition is listed.

LAB 6.1 SELF-REVIEW QUESTIONS

In order to test your progress, you should be able to answer the following questions.

1) A CASE construct is a control statement for which of the following?

a) _____ Sequence structure
b) _____ Iteration structure
c) _____ Selection structure

2) The ELSE clause is required part of a CASE construct.

    a) _____ True
    b) _____ False

3) A selector in a CASE statement

    a) _____ is evaluated as many times as there are WHEN clauses.
    b) _____ is evaluated once per CASE statement.
    c) _____ is not evaluated at all.

4) When all conditions of the searched CASE construct evaluate to NULL

    a) _____ Control is passed to the first executable statement after END CASE if there is no ELSE clause present.
    b) _____ Control is passed to the first executable statement after END CASE if there is an ELSE clause present.
    c) _____ CASE statement causes a syntax error if there is no ELSE clause present.

5) CASE statements cannot be nested one inside the other

    a) _____ False
    b) _____ True

Answers appear in Appendix A, Section 6.1.

L A B   6 . 2

CASE EXPRESSIONS

LAB OBJECTIVES

After this Lab, you will be able to:

✔ Use CASE Expressions

In Chapter 3, you encountered various PL/SQL expressions. You will recall that the result of an expression yields a single value that is assigned to a variable. In a similar manner, a CASE expression evaluates to a single value that is then assigned to a variable.

A CASE expression has a structure almost identical to a CASE statement. Thus, it also has two forms: CASE and searched CASE. Consider an example of a CASE statement used in the previous lab of this chapter:

■ *FOR EXAMPLE*

```
DECLARE
    v_num NUMBER := &sv_user_num;
    v_num_flag NUMBER;
BEGIN
    v_num_flag := MOD(v_num,2);

    -- test if the number provided by the user is even
    CASE v_num_flag
        WHEN 0 THEN
            DBMS_OUTPUT.PUT_LINE (v_num||' is even number');
        ELSE
            DBMS_OUTPUT.PUT_LINE (v_num||' is odd number');
    END CASE;
    DBMS_OUTPUT.PUT_LINE ('Done');
END;
```

Consider the new version of the same example, with the CASE expression instead of the CASE statement:

■ *FOR EXAMPLE*

```
DECLARE
    v_num NUMBER := &sv_user_num;
    v_num_flag NUMBER;
    v_result VARCHAR2(30);
BEGIN
    v_num_flag := MOD(v_num,2);

    v_result :=
        CASE v_num_flag
            WHEN 0 THEN v_num||' is even number'
            ELSE v_num||' is odd number'
        END;
    DBMS_OUTPUT.PUT_LINE (v_result);
    DBMS_OUTPUT.PUT_LINE ('Done');
END;
```

In this example, a new variable, v_result, is used to hold the value returned by the CASE expression. If v_num is assigned the value of 8, this example produces the following output:

```
Enter value for sv_user_num: 8
old    2:    v_num NUMBER := &sv_user_num;
new    2:    v_num NUMBER := 8;
8 is even number
Done

PL/SQL procedure successfully completed.
```

It is important to note some syntax differences between a CASE statement and a CASE expression. Consider the following code fragments:

Case Statement	Case Expression
```CASE v_num_flag WHEN 0 THEN DBMS_OUTPUT.PUT_LINE (v_num||' is even number'); ELSE DBMS_OUTPUT.PUT_LINE (v_num||' is odd number');END CASE;```	```CASE v_num_flag WHEN 0 THEN v_num|| ' is even number' ELSE v_num|| ' is odd number'END;```

In the CASE statement, the WHEN and ELSE clauses each contain a single executable statement. Each executable statement is terminated by a semicolon. In the CASE expression, the WHEN and ELSE clauses each contain an expression that is not terminated by a semicolon. There is one semicolon present after the reserved word END, which terminates the CASE expression. Finally, the CASE statement is terminated by the reserved phrase END CASE.

Next, consider another version of the previous example, with the searched CASE expression:

■ *FOR EXAMPLE*

```
DECLARE
   v_num NUMBER := &sv_user_num;
   v_result VARCHAR2(30);
BEGIN
   v_result :=
      CASE
         WHEN MOD(v_num,2) = 0 THEN v_num||' is even number'
         ELSE v_num||' is odd number'
      END;
   DBMS_OUTPUT.PUT_LINE (v_result);
   DBMS_OUTPUT.PUT_LINE ('Done');
END;
```

In this example, there is no need to declare variable v_num_flag because the searched CASE expression does not need a selector value, and the result of the MOD function is incorporated into the search condition. When run, this example produces output identical to the previous version:

```
Enter value for sv_user_num: 8
old    2:     v_num NUMBER := &sv_user_num;
new    2:     v_num NUMBER := 8;
8 is even number
Done

PL/SQL procedure successfully completed.
```

You learned earlier that a CASE expression returns a single value that is then assigned to a variable. In the examples that you saw earlier, this assignment operation was accomplished via the assignment operator, :=. You may recall that there is another way to assign a value to a PL/SQL variable, via a SELECT INTO statement. Consider an example of the CASE expression used in a SELECT INTO statement:

■ *FOR EXAMPLE*

```
DECLARE
   v_course_no NUMBER;
   v_description VARCHAR2(50);
   v_prereq VARCHAR2(35);
BEGIN
   SELECT course_no, description,
          CASE
```

```
        WHEN prerequisite IS NULL THEN
             'No prerequisite course required'
        ELSE TO_CHAR(prerequisite)
     END prerequisite
  INTO v_course_no, v_description, v_prereq
  FROM course
 WHERE course_no = 20;

   DBMS_OUTPUT.PUT_LINE ('Course: '||v_course_no);
   DBMS_OUTPUT.PUT_LINE ('Description: '||v_description);
   DBMS_OUTPUT.PUT_LINE ('Prerequisite: '||v_prereq);
END;
```

In this example, you are displaying course number, description, and the number of a prerequisite course on the screen. Furthermore, if a given course does not have a prerequisite course, a message stating so is displayed on the screen. In order to achieve the desired results, a CASE expression is used as one of the columns in the SELECT INTO statement. Its value is assigned to the variable v_prereq. *Notice that there is no semicolon after the reserved word END of the CASE expression.*

This example produces the following output:

```
Course: 20
Description: Intro to Computers
Prerequisite: No prerequisite course required

PL/SQL procedure successfully completed.
```

Course 20 does not have a prerequisite course. As a result, the searched condition

```
WHEN prerequisite IS NULL THEN
```

evaluates to TRUE, and the value "No prerequisite course required" is assigned to the variable v_prereq.

It is important to note why function TO_CHAR is used in the ELSE clause of the CASE expression:

```
CASE
    WHEN prerequisite IS NULL THEN 'No prerequisite course
    required'
    ELSE TO_CHAR(prerequisite)
END
```

A CASE expression returns a single value, thus, a single datatype. Therefore, it is important to ensure that regardless of what part of a CASE expression is executed, it always returns the same datatype. In the preceding CASE expression, the WHEN clause returns the VARCHAR2 datatype. The ELSE clause returns the value of the PREREQUISITE column of the COURSE table. This column has been defined as NUMBER, so it is necessary to convert it to the string datatype.

When the TO_CHAR function is not used, the CASE expression causes the following syntax error:

```
                    ELSE prerequisite
                         *
    ERROR at line 9:
    ORA-06550: line 9, column 19:
    PL/SQL: ORA-00932: inconsistent datatypes
    ORA-06550: line 6, column 4:
    PL/SQL: SQL Statement ignored
```

LAB 6.2 EXERCISES

6.2.1 USE THE CASE EXPRESSION

In this exercise, you will modify the script ch06_2a.sql. Instead of using a searched CASE statement, you will use a searched CASE expression to display a letter grade for a student registered for a specific section of course number 25.

Answer the following questions:

a) Modify the script ch06_2a.sql. Substitute the CASE statement with the searched CASE expression, and assign the value returned by the expression to the variable v_letter_grade.

b) Run the script created in part a and explain the output produced.

c) Rewrite the script created in part a so that the result of the CASE expression is assigned to the v_letter_grade variable via a SELECT INTO statement.

LAB 6.2 EXERCISE ANSWERS

This section gives you some suggested answers to the questions in Lab 6.2, with discussion related to how those answers resulted. The most important thing to realize is whether your answer works. You should figure out the implications of the answers here and what the effects are from any different answers you may come up with.

6.2.1 ANSWERS

a) Modify the script ch06_2a.sql. Substitute the CASE statement with the searched CASE expression, and assign the value returned by the expression to the variable `v_letter_grade`.

Answer: Your script should look similar to the script below. Changes are shown in bold letters.

```
-- ch06_3a.sql, version 1.0
SET SERVEROUTPUT ON
DECLARE
    v_student_id NUMBER := 102;
    v_section_id NUMBER := 89;
    v_final_grade NUMBER;
    v_letter_grade CHAR(1);
BEGIN
    SELECT final_grade
      INTO v_final_grade
      FROM enrollment
     WHERE student_id = v_student_id
       AND section_id = v_section_id;

    v_letter_grade :=
       CASE
          WHEN v_final_grade >= 90 THEN 'A'
          WHEN v_final_grade >= 80 THEN 'B'
          WHEN v_final_grade >= 70 THEN 'C'
          WHEN v_final_grade >= 60 THEN 'D'
          ELSE 'F'
       END;
    -- control resumes here
    DBMS_OUTPUT.PUT_LINE ('Letter grade is: '||
       v_letter_grade);
END;
```

In the original version of the script (ch06_2a.sql), you used a searched CASE statement in order to assign a value to the variable `v_letter_grade` as follows:

```
CASE
    WHEN v_final_grade >= 90 THEN v_letter_grade := 'A';
    WHEN v_final_grade >= 80 THEN v_letter_grade := 'B';
    WHEN v_final_grade >= 70 THEN v_letter_grade := 'C';
    WHEN v_final_grade >= 60 THEN v_letter_grade := 'D';
    ELSE v_letter_grade := 'F';
END CASE;
```

**LAB
6.2**

Notice that the variable v_letter_grade was used as part of the CASE statement. In the new version of the script, the CASE expression

```
CASE
   WHEN v_final_grade >= 90 THEN 'A'
   WHEN v_final_grade >= 80 THEN 'B'
   WHEN v_final_grade >= 70 THEN 'C'
   WHEN v_final_grade >= 60 THEN 'D'
   ELSE 'F'
END;
```

does not contain any references to the variable v_letter_grade. Each search condition is evaluated. As soon as a particular condition evaluates to TRUE, its corresponding value is returned and then assigned to the variable v_letter_grade.

b) Run the script created in part a and explain the output produced.

Answer:Your output should look similar to the following:

```
Letter grade is: A

PL/SQL procedure successfully completed.
```

The SELECT INTO statement returns a value of 92 that is assigned to the variable v_final_grade. *As a result, the first searched condition of the CASE expression evaluates to TRUE and returns a value of 'A'. This value is then assigned to the variable* v_letter_grade *and displayed on the screen via the DBMS_OUTPUT.PUT_LINE statement.*

c) Rewrite the script created in part a so that the result of the CASE expression is assigned to the v_letter_grade variable via a SELECT INTO statement.

Answer:Your script should look similar to the following. Changes are shown in bold letters.

```
-- ch06_3b.sql, version 2.0
SET SERVEROUTPUT ON
DECLARE
   v_student_id NUMBER := 102;
   v_section_id NUMBER := 89;
   v_letter_grade CHAR(1);
BEGIN
   SELECT CASE
              WHEN final_grade >= 90 THEN 'A'
              WHEN final_grade >= 80 THEN 'B'
              WHEN final_grade >= 70 THEN 'C'
              WHEN final_grade >= 60 THEN 'D'
              ELSE 'F'
          END
```

```
      INTO v_letter_grade
      FROM enrollment
    WHERE student_id = v_student_id
      AND section_id = v_section_id;

    -- control resumes here
    DBMS_OUTPUT.PUT_LINE ('Letter grade is: '||
        v_letter_grade);
END;
```

In the previous version of the script, the variable `v_final_grade` was used to hold the value of the numeric grade.

```
SELECT final_grade
  INTO v_final_grade
  FROM enrollment
 WHERE student_id = v_student_id
   AND section_id = v_section_id;
```

This value was used by the CASE expression to assign proper letter grade to the variable `v_letter_grade`.

```
CASE
    WHEN v_final_grade >= 90 THEN 'A'
    WHEN v_final_grade >= 80 THEN 'B'
    WHEN v_final_grade >= 70 THEN 'C'
    WHEN v_final_grade >= 60 THEN 'D'
    ELSE 'F'
END;
```

In the current version of the script, the CASE expression is used as part of the SELECT INTO statement. As a result, the column FINAL_GRADE can be used by the CASE expression

```
CASE
    WHEN final_grade >= 90 THEN 'A'
    WHEN final_grade >= 80 THEN 'B'
    WHEN final_grade >= 70 THEN 'C'
    WHEN final_grade >= 60 THEN 'D'
    ELSE 'F'
END
```

as part of the searched conditions in order to assign a value to the variable `v_letter_grade`.

LAB 6.2 SELF-REVIEW QUESTIONS

In order to test your progress, you should be able to answer the following questions.

1) A CASE expression

    a) _____ returns a single value.
    b) _____ returns multiple values.
    c) _____ does not return values at all

2) A CASE expression is terminated by

    a) _____ END CASE.
    b) _____ CASE.
    c) _____ END.

3) A CASE expression never has a selector.

    a) _____ True
    b) _____ False

4) When all conditions of a CASE expression evaluate to NULL, the expression

    a) _____ returns NULL if there is no ELSE clause present.
    b) _____ causes a syntax error if there is no ELSE clause present.

5) A CASE expression may return a single datatype only.

    a) _____ True
    b) _____ False

Answers appear in Appendix A, Section 6.2.

L A B   6 . 3

NULLIF AND COALESCE FUNCTIONS

LAB OBJECTIVES

After this Lab, you will be able to:

✔ Use the NULLIF Function
✔ Use the COALESCE Function

The NULLIF and COALESCE functions are defined by the ANSI 1999 standard to be "CASE abbreviations." Both functions can be used as a variety of the CASE expression.

NULLIF FUNCTION

The NULLIF function compares two expressions. If they are equal, then the function returns NULL; otherwise, it returns the value of the first expression. The NULLIF has the following structure:

```
NULLIF (expression1, expression2)
```

If expression1 is equal to expression2, then NULLIF returns NULL. If expression1 does not equal expression2, NULLIF returns expression1. Note that the NULLIF function does the opposite of the NVL function. If the first expression is NULL, then NVL returns the second expression. If the first expression is not NULL, then NVL returns the first expression.

The NULLIF function is equivalent to the following CASE expression:

```
CASE
    WHEN expression1 = expression2 THEN NULL
    ELSE expression1
END
```

Consider the following example of NULLIF:

■ *FOR EXAMPLE*

```
DECLARE
    v_num NUMBER := &sv_user_num;
    v_remainder NUMBER;
BEGIN
    -- calculate the remainder and if it is zero return a NULL
    v_remainder := NULLIF(MOD(v_num,2),0);
    DBMS_OUTPUT.PUT_LINE ('v_remainder: '||v_remainder);
END;
```

This is example is somewhat similar to an example that you have seen earlier in this chapter. A value is assigned to the variable v_num at run-time. Next, this value is divided by 2, and its remainder is compared to 0 via the NULLIF function. If the remainder equals 0, the NULLIF function returns NULL; otherwise it returns the remainder. The value returned by the NULLIF function is stored in the variable v_remainder and displayed on the screen via the DBMS_OUTPUT.PUT_LINE statement. When run, the example produces the output shown below. For the first run, 5 is assigned to the variable v_num:

```
Enter value for sv_user_num: 5
old    2:    v_num NUMBER := &sv_user_num;
new    2:    v_num NUMBER := 5;
v_remainder: 1

PL/SQL procedure successfully completed.
```

For the second run, 4 is assigned to the variable v_num:

```
Enter value for sv_user_num: 4
old    2:    v_num NUMBER := &sv_user_num;
new    2:    v_num NUMBER := 4;
v_remainder:

PL/SQL procedure successfully completed.
```

In the first run, 5 is not divisible by 2, and the NULLIF function returns the value of the remainder. In the second run, 4 is divisible by 2, and the NULLIF function returns NULL as the value of the remainder.

The NULLIF function has a restriction: *You cannot assign a **literal** NULL to expression1.* You learned about literals in Chapter 3. Consider another output produced by the preceding example. For this run, the variable v_num is assigned NULL:

```
Enter value for sv_user_num: NULL
old    2:    v_num NUMBER := &sv_user_num;
new    2:    v_num NUMBER := NULL;
```

```
v_remainder:

PL/SQL procedure successfully completed.
```

When NULL is assigned to the variable v_num, both the MOD and NULLIF functions return NULL. This example does not produce any errors because the literal NULL is assigned to the variable v_num, and it is not used as the first expression of the NULLIF function. Next, consider this modified version of the preceding example:

■ FOR EXAMPLE

```
DECLARE
   v_remainder NUMBER;
BEGIN
   -- calculate the remainder and if it is zero return a
   NULL
   v_remainder := NULLIF(NULL,0);
   DBMS_OUTPUT.PUT_LINE ('v_remainder: '||v_remainder);
END;
```

In the previous version of this example, the MOD function is used as expression1. In this version, the literal NULL is used in place of the MOD function, and as a result, this example produces the following syntax error:

```
   v_remainder := NULLIF(NULL,0);
                        *
ERROR at line 5:
ORA-06550: line 5, column 26:
PLS-00619: the first operand in the NULLIF expression must
not be NULL
ORA-06550: line 5, column 4:
PL/SQL: Statement ignored
```

COALESCE FUNCTION

The COALESCE function compares each expression to NULL from the list of expressions and returns the value of the first non-null expression. The COALESCE function has the following structure:

```
COALESCE (expression1, expression2, …, expressionN)
```

If expression1 evaluates to NULL, then expression2 is evaluated. If expression2 does not evaluate to NULL, then the function returns expression2. If expression2 also evaluates to NULL, then the next expression is evaluated. If all expressions evaluate to NULL, the function returns NULL.

Note that the COALESCE function is like a nested NVL function:

```
NVL(expression1, NVL(expression2, NVL(expression3,…)))
```

The COALESCE function can also be used as an alternative to a CASE expression. For example,

```
COALESCE (expression1, expression2)
```

is equivalent to

```
CASE
    WHEN expression1 IS NOT NULL THEN expression1
    ELSE expression2
END
```

If there are more than two expressions to evaluate, then

```
COALESCE (expression1, expression2, …, expressionN)
```

is equivalent to

```
CASE
    WHEN expression1 IS NOT NULL THEN expression1
    ELSE COALESCE (expression2, …, expressionN)
END
```

Consider the following example of the COALESCE function:

■ FOR EXAMPLE

```
SELECT e.student_id, e.section_id, e.final_grade,
       g.numeric_grade,
       COALESCE(e.final_grade, g.numeric_grade, 0) grade
  FROM enrollment e, grade g
 WHERE e.student_id = g.student_id
   AND e.section_id = g.section_id
   AND e.student_id = 102
   AND g.grade_type_code = 'FI';
```

This SELECT statement returns the following output:

STUDENT_ID	SECTION_ID	FINAL_GRADE	NUMERIC_GRADE	GRADE
102	86		85	85
102	89	92	92	92

The value of GRADE equals the value of the NUMERIC_GRADE in the first row. The COALESCE function compares the value of the FINAL_GRADE to NULL. If it is NULL, then the value of the NUMERIC_GRADE is compared to NULL. Because the value of the NUMERIC_GRADE is not NULL, the COALESCE function returns the value of the NUMERIC_GRADE. The value of GRADE equals the value of FINAL_GRADE in the second row. The COALESCE function returns the value of FINAL_GRADE because it is not NULL.

The COALESCE function shown in the previous example is equivalent to the following NVL statement and CASE expression:

```
NVL(e.final_grade, NVL(g.numeric_grade, 0))

CASE
   WHEN e.final_grade IS NOT NULL THEN e.final_grade
   ELSE COALESCE(g.numeric_grade, 0)
END
```

The COALESCE function has the following restriction: *At least one of its expressions must not contain a literal NULL.* Consider the following example and its output:

**LAB
6.3**

■ *FOR EXAMPLE*

```
SELECT COALESCE(NULL, 3, 8)
   FROM DUAL;


COALESCE(NULL,3,8)
------------------
                 3
```

Next, consider this modified version of the same SELECT statement and the syntax error it generates

■ *FOR EXAMPLE*

```
SELECT COALESCE(NULL, NULL, NULL)
   FROM DUAL;


SELECT COALESCE(NULL, NULL, NULL)
       *
ERROR at line 1:
ORA-00938: not enough arguments for function
```

The SELECT statement causes a syntax error because all of the expressions in the COALESCE function contain the literal NULL.

LAB 6.3 EXERCISES

6.3.1 USE THE NULLIF FUNCTION

In this exercise, you will modify the following script. Instead of using the searched CASE expression, you will use the NULLIF function. *Note that the SELECT INTO statement uses ANSI 1999 SQL standard.*

You will find detailed explanations and examples of the statements using new ANSI 1999 SQL standard in Appendix E and in Oracle help. Throughout this book we try to provide you with examples illustrating both standards; however our main focus is on PL/SQL features rather than SQL.

**LAB
6.3**

```
-- ch06_4a.sql, version 1.0
SET SERVEROUTPUT ON
DECLARE
   v_final_grade NUMBER;
BEGIN
   SELECT CASE
                WHEN e.final_grade = g.numeric_grade THEN NULL
                ELSE g.numeric_grade
             END
        INTO v_final_grade
        FROM enrollment e
        JOIN grade g
          ON (e.student_id = g.student_id
         AND e.section_id = g.section_id)
       WHERE e.student_id = 102
         AND e.section_id = 86
         AND g.grade_type_code = 'FI';

       DBMS_OUTPUT.PUT_LINE ('Final grade: '||v_final_grade);
   END;
```

In the preceding script, the value of the final grade is compared to the value of the numeric grade. If these values are equal, the CASE expression returns NULL. In the opposite case, the CASE expression returns the numeric grade. The result of the CASE expression is then displayed on the screen via the DBMS_OUTPUT.PUT_LINE statement.

Answer the following questions:

a) Modify script ch06_4a.sql. Substitute the CASE expression with the NULLIF function.

b) Run the modified version of the script and explain the output produced.

c) Change the order of columns in the NULLIF function. Run the modified version of the script and explain the output produced.

6.3.2 USE THE COALESCE FUNCTION

In this exercise, you will modify the following script. Instead of using the searched CASE expression, you will use the COALESCE function.

**LAB
6.3**

```
-- ch06_5a.sql, version 1.0
SET SERVEROUTPUT ON
DECLARE
    v_num1 NUMBER := &sv_num1;
    v_num2 NUMBER := &sv_num2;
    v_num3 NUMBER := &sv_num3;
    v_result NUMBER;
BEGIN
    v_result := CASE
                    WHEN v_num1 IS NOT NULL THEN v_num1
                    ELSE
                        CASE
                            WHEN v_num2 IS NOT NULL THEN v_num2
                            ELSE v_num3
                        END
                END;
    DBMS_OUTPUT.PUT_LINE ('Result: '||v_result);
END;
```

In the preceding script, the list consisting of three numbers is evaluated as follows: If the value of the first number is not NULL, then the outer CASE expression returns the value of the first number. Otherwise, control is passed to the inner CASE expression, which evaluates the second number. If the value of the second number is not NULL, then the inner CASE expression returns the value of the second number; in the opposite case, it returns the value of the third number.

The preceding CASE expression is equivalent to the following two CASE expressions:

```
CASE
    WHEN v_num1 IS NOT NULL THEN v_num1
    WHEN v_num2 IS NOT NULL THEN v_num2
    ELSE v_num3
END
```

```
CASE
   WHEN v_num1 IS NOT NULL THEN v_num1
   ELSE COALESCE(v_num2, v_num3)
END
```

Answer the following questions:

a) Modify script ch06_5a.sql. Substitute the CASE expression with the COALESCE function.

b) Run the modified version of the script and explain the output produced. Use the following values for the list of numbers: NULL, 1, 2.

c) What output will be produced by the modified version of the script if NULL is provided for all three numbers? Try to explain your answer before you run the script.

LAB 6.3 EXERCISE ANSWERS

This section gives you some suggested answers to the questions in Lab 6.3, with discussion related to how those answers resulted. The most important thing to realize is whether your answer works. You should figure out the implications of the answers here and what the effects are from any different answers you may come up with.

6.3.1 ANSWERS

a) Modify the script ch06_4a.sql. Substitute the CASE expression with the NULLIF function.

Answer:Your script should look similar to the following script. Changes are shown in bold letters.

```
-- ch06_4b.sql, version 2.0
SET SERVEROUTPUT ON
DECLARE
   v_final_grade NUMBER;
```

```
BEGIN
   SELECT NULLIF(g.numeric_grade, e.final_grade)
     INTO v_final_grade
     FROM enrollment e
     JOIN grade g
       ON (e.student_id = g.student_id
      AND e.section_id = g.section_id)
    WHERE e.student_id = 102
      AND e.section_id = 86
      AND g.grade_type_code = 'FI';

   DBMS_OUTPUT.PUT_LINE ('Final grade: '||v_final_grade);
END;
```

In the original version of the script, you used CASE expression in order to assign a value to the variable v_final_grade as follows:

```
CASE
   WHEN e.final_grade = g.numeric_grade THEN NULL
   ELSE g.numeric_grade
END
```

The value stored in the column FINAL_GRADE is compared to the value stored in the column NUMERIC_GRADE. If these values are equal, then NULL is assigned to the variable v_final_grade; otherwise, the value stored in the column NUMERIC_GRADE is assigned to the variable v_letter_grade.

In the new version of the script you substitute the CASE expression with the NULLIF function as follows:

```
NULLIF(g.numeric_grade, e.final_grade)
```

It is important to note that the NUMERIC_GRADE column is referenced first in the NULLIF function. You will recall that the NULLIF function compares expression1 to expression2. If expression1 equals expression2, the NULLIF functions returns NULL. If expression1 does not equal expression2, the NULLIF function returns expression1. In order to return the value stored in the column NUMERIC_GRADE, you must reference it first in the NULLIF function.

b) Run the modified version of the script and explain the output produced.

Answer: Your output should look similar to the following:

```
Final grade: 85
```

```
PL/SQL procedure successfully completed.
```

The NULLIF function compares values stored in the columns NUMERIC_GRADE and FINAL_GRADE. Because the column FINAL_GRADE is not populated, the NULLIF function returns the value stored in the column NUMERIC_GRADE. This value is assigned to the variable `v_final_grade` *and displayed on the screen with the help of the* *DBMS_OUTPUT.PUT_LINE statement.*

c) Change the order of columns in the NULLIF function. Run the modified version of the script and explain the output produced.

Answer: Your script should look similar to the following. Changes are shown in bold letters.

```
-- ch06_4c.sql, version 3.0
SET SERVEROUTPUT ON
DECLARE
   v_final_grade NUMBER;
BEGIN
   SELECT NULLIF(e.final_grade, g.numeric_grade)
     INTO v_final_grade
     FROM enrollment e
     JOIN grade g
       ON (e.student_id = g.student_id
       AND e.section_id = g.section_id)
    WHERE e.student_id = 102
      AND e.section_id = 86
      AND g.grade_type_code = 'FI';

   DBMS_OUTPUT.PUT_LINE ('Final grade: '||v_final_grade);
END;
```

The example produces the following output:

Final grade:

PL/SQL procedure successfully completed.

In this version of the script, the columns NUMERIC_GRADE and FINAL_GRADE are listed in the opposite order as follows:

NULLIF(e.final_grade, g.numeric_grade)

The value stored in the column FINAL_GRADE is compared to the value stored in the column NUMERIC_GRADE. Because these values are not equal, the NULLIF function returns the value of the column FINAL_GRADE. This column is not populated, so NULL is assigned to the variable `v_final_grade`.

6.3.2 ANSWERS

a) Modify the script ch06_5a.sql. Substitute the CASE expression with the COALESCE function.

Answer: Your script should look similar to the following script. Changes are shown in bold letters.

```
-- ch06_5b.sql, version 2.0
SET SERVEROUTPUT ON
DECLARE
    v_num1 NUMBER := &sv_num1;
    v_num2 NUMBER := &sv_num2;
    v_num3 NUMBER := &sv_num3;
    v_result NUMBER;
BEGIN
    v_result := COALESCE(v_num1, v_num2, v_num3);
    DBMS_OUTPUT.PUT_LINE ('Result: '||v_result);
END;
```

In the original version of the script you used nested CASE expression in order to assign a value to the variable v_result as follows:

```
CASE
    WHEN v_num1 IS NOT NULL THEN v_num1
    ELSE
        CASE
            WHEN v_num2 IS NOT NULL THEN v_num2
            ELSE v_num3
        END
END;
```

In the new version of the script you substitute the CASE expression with the COALESCE function as follows:

```
COALESCE(v_num1, v_num2, v_num3)
```

Based on the values stored in the variables v_num1, v_num2, and v_num3, the COALESCE function returns the first non-null variable.

b) Run the modified version of the script and explain the output produced. Use the following values for the list of numbers: NULL, 1, 2.

Answer: Your output should look similar to the following:

```
Enter value for sv_num1: null
old    2:    v_num1 NUMBER := &sv_num1;
new    2:    v_num1 NUMBER := null;
Enter value for sv_num2: 1
old    3:    v_num2 NUMBER := &sv_num2;
new    3:    v_num2 NUMBER := 1;
Enter value for sv_num3: 2
old    4:    v_num3 NUMBER := &sv_num3;
new    4:    v_num3 NUMBER := 2;
Result: 1

PL/SQL procedure successfully completed.
```

The COALESCE function evaluates its expressions in the sequential order. The variable v_num1 is evaluated first. Because the variable v_num1 is NULL, the COALESCE function evaluates the variable v_num2 next. Because the variable v_num2 is not NULL, the COALSECE function returns the value of the variable v_num2. This value is assigned to the variable v_result and is displayed on the screen via DBMS_OUTPUT.PUT_LINE statement.

c) What output will be produced by the modified version of the script if NULL is provided for all three numbers? Try to explain your answer before you run the script.

LAB 6.3

Answer: The variables v_num1, v_num2, and v_num3 are evaluated in the sequential order by the COALESCE function. When NULL is assigned to these variables, none of the evaluations produce a non-null result. So the COALESCE function returns NULL when all expressions evaluate to NULL.

Your output should look similar to the following:

```
Enter value for sv_num1: null
old    2:    v_num1 NUMBER := &sv_num1;
new    2:    v_num1 NUMBER := null;
Enter value for sv_num2: null
old    3:    v_num2 NUMBER := &sv_num2;
new    3:    v_num2 NUMBER := null;
Enter value for sv_num3: null
old    4:    v_num3 NUMBER := &sv_num3;
new    4:    v_num3 NUMBER := null;
Result:

PL/SQL procedure successfully completed.
```

LAB 6.3 SELF-REVIEW QUESTIONS

In order to test your progress, you should be able to answer the following questions.

1) A NULLIF function returns NULL if
    a) _____ expression1 equals expression2.
    b) _____ expression1 does not equal expression2.

2) A NULLIF function is just like NVL function.
    a) _____ True
    b) _____ False

3) You can specify literal NULL in the first expression of the NULLIF function.
    a) _____ True
    b) _____ False

4) A COALESCE function returns
    a) _____ first null expression.
    b) _____ first non-null expression.
    c) _____ first expression only.

5) You can never specify literal NULL as one of the expressions in the COALESCE function.
    a) _____ True
    b) _____ False

Answers appear in Appendix A, Section 6.3.

**LAB
6.3**

CHAPTER 6

TEST YOUR THINKING

In this chapter you learned about different types of CASE statements and expressions. You also learned about NULLIF and COALESCE functions. Here are some exercises based on the scripts created in this section in Chapter 5 that will help you test the depth of your understanding.

1) Create the following script. Modify the script created in this section in Chapter 5 (Question 1 of the Test Your Thinking section). You can use either the CASE statement or the searched CASE statement. Your output should look similar to the output produced by the example created in Chapter 5.

2) Create the following script. Modify the script created in this section in Chapter 5 (Question 2 of the Test Your Thinking section). You can use either the CASE statement or the searched CASE statement. Your output should look similar to the output produced by the example created in Chapter 5.

3) Execute the following two SELECT statements and explain why they produce different output:

```
SELECT e.student_id, e.section_id, e.final_grade,
       g.numeric_grade,
       COALESCE(g.numeric_grade, e.final_grade) grade
  FROM enrollment e, grade g
 WHERE e.student_id = g.student_id
   AND e.section_id = g.section_id
   AND e.student_id = 102
   AND g.grade_type_code = 'FI';

SELECT e.student_id, e.section_id, e.final_grade,
       g.numeric_grade,
       NULLIF(g.numeric_grade, e.final_grade) grade
  FROM enrollment e, grade g
 WHERE e.student_id = g.student_id
   AND e.section_id = g.section_id
   AND e.student_id = 102
   AND g.grade_type_code = 'FI';
```

The projects in this section are meant to have you utilize all of the skills that you have acquired throughout this chapter. The answers to these projects can be found in Appendix D and at the companion Web site to this book, located at http://www .phptr.com/rosenzweig2e. Visit the Web site periodically to share and discuss your answers.

CHAPTER 7

ERROR HANDLING AND BUILT-IN EXCEPTIONS

In Chapter 2, you encountered two types of errors that can be found in a program: compilation errors and runtime errors. You will recall that there is a special section in a PL/SQL block that handles runtime errors. This section is called the exception-handling section, and in it, runtime errors are referred to as exceptions. The exception-handling section allows programmers to specify what actions should be taken when a specific exception occurs.

In PL/SQL, there are two types of exceptions: built-in exceptions and user-defined exceptions. In this chapter, you will learn how you can handle certain kinds of runtime errors with the help of built-in exceptions. User-defined exceptions are discussed in Chapters 10 and 11.

LAB 7.1

HANDLING ERRORS

LAB OBJECTIVES

After this Lab, you will be able to:

✔ Understand the Importance of Error Handling

The following example will help to illustrate some of the differences between compilation and runtime errors.

■ *FOR EXAMPLE*

```
DECLARE
    v_num1 INTEGER := &sv_num1;
    v_num2 INTEGER := &sv_num2;
    v_result NUMBER;
BEGIN
    v_result = v_num1 / v_num2;
    DBMS_OUTPUT.PUT_LINE ('v_result: '||v_result);
END;
```

This example is a very simple program. There are two variables, v_num1 and v_num2. A user supplies values for these variables. Next, v_num1 is divided by v_num2, and the result of this division is stored in the third variable, v_result. Finally, the value of v_result is displayed on the screen.

Now, assume that a user supplies values of 3 and 5 for the variables, v_num1 and v_num2, respectively. As a result, the example produces the following output:

```
Enter value for sv_num1: 3
old   2:    v_num1 integer := &sv_num1;
new   2:    v_num1 integer := 3;
Enter value for sv_num2: 5
old   3:    v_num2 integer := &sv_num2;
new   3:    v_num2 integer := 5;
   v_result = v_num1 / v_num2;
```

```
                   *
ERROR at line 6:
ORA-06550: line 6, column 13:
PLS-00103: Encountered the symbol "=" when expecting one
of the following:
:= . ( @ % ;
ORA-06550: line 7, column 4:
PLS-00103: Encountered the symbol "DBMS_OUTPUT"
ORA-06550: line 7, column 49:
PLS-00103: Encountered the symbol ";" when expecting one
of the following:
. ( * % & - + / mod rem return RETURNING_ an exponent (**)
and or ||
```

You have probably noticed that the example did not execute successfully. A syntax error has been encountered at line 6. Close inspection of the example shows that the statement

```
v_result = v_num1 / v_num2;
```

contains an equal sign operator where an assignment operator should be used. The statement should be rewritten as follows:

```
v_result := v_num1 / v_num2;
```

Once the corrected example is run again, the following output is produced:

```
Enter value for sv_num1: 3
old   2:     v_num1 integer := &sv_num1;
new   2:     v_num1 integer := 3;
Enter value for sv_num2: 5
old   3:     v_num2 integer := &sv_num2;
new   3:     v_num2 integer := 5;
v_result: .6

PL/SQL procedure successfully completed.
```

As you can see, the example now executes successfully because the syntax error has been corrected.

Next, if you change the values of variables v_num1 and v_num2 to 4 and 0, respectively, the following output is produced:

```
Enter value for sv_num1: 4
old   2:     v_num1 integer := &sv_num1;
new   2:     v_num1 integer := 4;
Enter value for sv_num2: 0
```

```
old    3:     v_num2 integer := &sv_num2;
new    3:     v_num2 integer := 0;
DECLARE
*
ERROR at line 1:
ORA-01476: divisor is equal to zero
ORA-06512: at line 6
```

Even though this example does not contain syntax errors, it was terminated prematurely because the value entered for v_num2, the divisor, was 0. As you may recall, division by 0 is undefined, and thus leads to an error.

This example illustrates a runtime error that cannot be detected by the compiler. In other words, for some of the values entered for the variables v_num1 and v_num2, this example executes successfully. For other values entered for the variables v_num1 and v_num2, this example cannot execute. As a result, the runtime error occurs. You will recall that the compiler cannot detect runtime errors. In this case, a runtime error occurs because the compiler does not know the result of the division of v_num1 by v_num2. This result can be determined only at runtime. Hence, this error is referred to as a runtime error.

In order to handle this type of error in the program, an exception handler must be added. The exception-handling section has the following structure:

```
EXCEPTION
    WHEN EXCEPTION_NAME THEN
        ERROR-PROCESSING STATEMENTS;
```

The exception-handling section is placed after the executable section of the block. The preceeding example can be rewritten in the following manner.

■ FOR EXAMPLE

```
DECLARE
    v_num1 integer := &sv_num1;
    v_num2 integer := &sv_num2;
    v_result number;
BEGIN
    v_result := v_num1 / v_num2;
    DBMS_OUTPUT.PUT_LINE ('v_result: '||v_result);
EXCEPTION
    WHEN ZERO_DIVIDE THEN
        DBMS_OUTPUT.PUT_LINE
            ('A number cannot be divided by zero.');
END;
```

The section of the example in bold letters shows the exception-handling section of the block. When this version of the example is executed with the values of 4 and 0 for variables v_num1 and v_num2, respectively, the following output is produced:

```
Enter value for sv_num1: 4
old    2:    v_num1 integer := &sv_num1;
new    2:    v_num1 integer := 4;
Enter value for sv_num2: 0
old    3:    v_num2 integer := &sv_num2;
new    3:    v_num2 integer := 0;
A number cannot be divided by zero.

PL/SQL procedure successfully completed.
```

This output shows that once an attempt to divide v_num1 by v_num2 was made, the exception-handling section of the block was executed. Therefore, the error message specified by the exception-handling section was displayed on the screen.

This version of the output illustrates several advantages of using an exception-handling section. You have probably noticed that the output looks cleaner compared to the previous version. Even though the error message is still displayed on the screen, the output is more informative. In short, it is oriented more toward a user than a programmer.

It is important for you to realize that on many occasions, a user does not have access to the code. Therefore, references to line numbers and keywords in a program are not significant to most users.

An exception-handling section allows a program to execute to completion, instead of terminating prematurely. Another advantage offered by the exception-handling section is isolation of error-handling routines. In other words, all error-processing code for a specific block is located in a single section. As a result, the logic of the program becomes easier to follow and understand. Finally, adding an exception-handling section enables event-driven processing of errors. As in the example shown earlier, in the case of a specific exception event, such as division by 0, the exception-handling section was executed, and the error message specified by the DBMS_OUTPUT.PUT_LINE statement was displayed on the screen.

LAB 7.1 EXERCISES

7.1.1 UNDERSTANDING THE IMPORTANCE OF ERROR HANDLING

In this exercise, you will calculate the value of the square root of a number and display it on the screen.

Create the following PL/SQL script:

```
-- ch07_1a.sql, version 1.0
SET SERVEROUTPUT ON;
DECLARE
    v_num NUMBER := &sv_num;
BEGIN
    DBMS_OUTPUT.PUT_LINE ('Square root of '||v_num||
        ' is '||SQRT(v_num));
EXCEPTION
    WHEN VALUE_ERROR THEN
        DBMS_OUTPUT.PUT_LINE ('An error has occurred');
END;
```

In the preceding script, the exception VALUE_ERROR, is raised when conversion or type mismatch errors occur. This exception is covered in greater detail in Lab 7.2 of this chapter. In order to test this script fully, execute it two times. For the first run, enter a value of 4 for the variable v_num. For the second run, enter the value of –4 for the variable v_num. Execute the script, and then answer the following questions:

a) What output was printed on the screen (for both runs)?

b) Why do you think an error message was generated when the script was run a second time?

c) Assume that you are not familiar with the exception VALUE_ERROR. How would you change this script to avoid this runtime error?

LAB 7.1 EXERCISE ANSWERS

This section gives you some suggested answers to the questions in Lab 7.1, with discussion related to how those answers resulted. The most important thing to realize is whether your answer works. You should figure out the implications of the answers here and what the effects are from any different answers you may come up with.

7.1.1 ANSWERS

a) What output was printed on the screen (for both runs)?

Answer: The first version of the output is produced when the value of v_num *is equal to 4. Your output should look like the following:*

```
Enter value for sv_num: 4
old     2:     v_num NUMBER := &sv_num;
new     2:     v_num NUMBER := 4;
Square root of 4 is 2

PL/SQL procedure successfully completed.
```

The second version of the output is produced when v_num *is equal to −4. Your output should look like the following:*

```
Enter value for sv_num: -4
old     2:     v_num NUMBER := &sv_num;
new     2:     v_num NUMBER := -4;
An error has occurred

PL/SQL procedure successfully completed.
```

b) Why do you think an error message was generated when the script was run a second time?

Answer: Error message "An error has occurred" was generated for the second run of example because a runtime error has occurred. The built-in function SQRT is unable to accept a negative number as its argument. Therefore, the exception VALUE_ERROR was raised, and the error message was displayed on the screen.

c) Assume that you are not familiar with the exception VALUE_ERROR. How would you change this script to avoid this runtime error?

Answer: The new version of the program should look similar to the program below. All changes are shown in bold letters.

```
-- ch07_1b.sql, version 2.0
SET SERVEROUTPUT ON;
DECLARE
   v_num NUMBER := &sv_num;
BEGIN
   IF v_num >= 0 THEN
      DBMS_OUTPUT.PUT_LINE ('Square root of '||v_num||
         ' is '||SQRT(v_num));
   ELSE
      DBMS_OUTPUT.PUT_LINE ('A number cannot be negative');
   END IF;
END;
```

Notice that before you calculate the square root of a number, you can check to see if the number is greater than or equal to 0 with the help of the IF-THEN-ELSE statement. If the number is negative, the message "A number cannot be negative" is displayed on the screen. When the value of –4 is entered for the variable v_num, this script produces the following output:

```
Enter value for sv_num: -4
old    2:    v_num NUMBER := &sv_num;
new    2:    v_num NUMBER := -4;
A number cannot be negative

PL/SQL procedure successfully completed.
```

LAB 7.1 SELF-REVIEW QUESTIONS

In order to test your progress, you should be able to answer the following questions.

1) A compiler can detect a runtime error.

a) _____ True
b) _____ False

2) Without an exception-handling section, a PL/SQL block cannot be compiled.

a) _____ True
b) _____ False

3) An exception is raised when which of the following occurs?

a) _____ A compilation error is encountered.
b) _____ A runtime error is encountered.

4) An exception-handling section of a PL/SQL block is placed

a) _____ after the reserved word END.
b) _____ before the reserved word END.
c) _____ before the reserved word BEGIN.

5) The exception ZERO_DIVIDE is raised when number 1 is divided by number 2 and

a) _____ number 1 is equal to 0.
b) _____ number 2 is equal to 0.
c) _____ both numbers are equal to 0.

Answers appear in Appendix A, Section 7.1.

LAB 7.2

BUILT-IN EXCEPTIONS

LAB OBJECTIVES

After this Lab, you will be able to:

✔ Use Built-In Exceptions

As mentioned earlier, a PL/SQL block has the following structure:

```
DECLARE
   ...
BEGIN
   EXECUTABLE STATEMENTS;
EXCEPTION
   WHEN EXCEPTION_NAME THEN
      ERROR-PROCESSING STATEMENTS;
END;
```

When an error occurs that raises a built-in exception, the exception is said to be raised implicitly. In other words, if a program breaks an Oracle rule, control is passed to the exception-handling section of the block. At this point, the error-processing statements are executed. It is important for you to realize that after the exception-handling section of the block has executed, the block terminates. Control will not return to the executable section of the block. The following example illustrates this point.

■ FOR EXAMPLE

```
DECLARE
   v_student_name VARCHAR2(50);
BEGIN
   SELECT first_name||' '||last_name
     INTO v_student_name
     FROM student
    WHERE student_id = 101;
```

```
        DBMS_OUTPUT.PUT_LINE ('Student name is '||
            v_student_name);
    EXCEPTION
        WHEN NO_DATA_FOUND THEN
            DBMS_OUTPUT.PUT_LINE ('There is no such student');
    END;
```

**LAB
7.2**

This example produces the following output:

There is no such student

PL/SQL procedure successfully completed.

Because there is no record in the STUDENT table with student ID 101, the SELECT INTO statement does not return any rows. As a result, control passes to the exception-handling section of the block, and the error message "There is no such student" is displayed on the screen. Even though there is a DBMS_OUTPUT.PUT_LINE statement right after the SELECT statement, it will not be executed because control has been transferred to the exception-handling section. Control will never return to the executable section of this block, which contains the first DBMS_OUTPUT.PUT_LINE statement.

You have probably noticed that, while every Oracle runtime error has a number associated with it, it must be handled by its name in the exception-handling section. One of the outputs from the example used in the previous lab of this chapter has the following error message:

ORA-01476: divisor is equal to zero

where ORA-01476 stands for the error number. This error number refers to the error named ZERO_DIVIDE. Some common Oracle runtime errors are predefined in PL/SQL as exceptions.

The following list explains some commonly used predefined exceptions and how they are raised:

- NO_DATA_FOUND—This exception is raised when a SELECT INTO statement that makes no calls to group functions, such as SUM or COUNT, does not return any rows. For example, you issue a SELECT INTO statement against the STUDENT table where student ID equals 101. If there is no record in the STUDENT table passing this criteria (student ID equals 101), the NO_DATA_FOUND exception is raised.

    When a SELECT INTO statement calls a group function, such as COUNT, the result set is never empty. When used in a SELECT INTO statement against the STUDENT table, function COUNT will return 0 for the value of student ID 123. Hence, a SELECT statement that calls a group function will never raise the NO_DATA_FOUND exception.

- TOO_MANY_ROWS—This exception is raised when a SELECT INTO statement returns more than one row. By definition, a SELECT INTO can return only a single row. If a SELECT INTO statement returns more than one row, the definition of the SELECT INTO statement is violated. This causes the TOO_MANY_ROWS exception to be raised.

  For example, you issue a SELECT INTO statement against the STUDENT table for a specific zipcode. There is a big chance that this SELECT statement will return more than one row because many students can live in the same zipcode area.

- ZERO_DIVIDE—This exception is raised when a division operation is performed in the program and a divisor is equal to zero. An example in the previous lab of this chapter illustrates how this exception is raised.

- LOGIN_DENIED—This exception is raised when a user is trying to login to Oracle with an invalid username or password.

- PROGRAM_ERROR—This exception is raised when a PL/SQL program has an internal problem.

- VALUE_ERROR—This exception is raised when a conversion or size mismatch error occurs. For example, you select a student's last name into a variable that has been defined as VARCHAR2(5). If the student's last name contains more than five characters, the VALUE_ERROR exception is raised.

- DUP_VALUE_ON_INDEX—This exception is raised when a program tries to store a duplicate value in the column or columns that have a unique index defined on them. For example, you are trying to insert a record into the SECTION table for the course number "25," section 1. If a record for the given course and section number already exists in the SECTION table, the DUP_VAL_ON_INDEX exception is raised because these columns have a unique index defined on them.

So far, you have seen examples of programs able to handle a single exception only. For example, a PL/SQL block contains an exception handler with a single exception ZERO_DIVIDE. However, many times you need to handle different exceptions in the PL/SQL block. Moreover, often you need to specify different actions that must be taken when a particular exception is raised, as the following illustrates.

■ *FOR EXAMPLE*

```
DECLARE
    v_student_id NUMBER := &sv_student_id;
    v_enrolled VARCHAR2(3) := 'NO';
BEGIN
    DBMS_OUTPUT.PUT_LINE
        ('Check if the student is enrolled');
    SELECT 'YES'
      INTO v_enrolled
      FROM enrollment
     WHERE student_id = v_student_id;
```

```
      DBMS_OUTPUT.PUT_LINE
          ('The student is enrolled into one course');
   EXCEPTION
      WHEN NO_DATA_FOUND THEN
          DBMS_OUTPUT.PUT_LINE ('The student is not enrolled');

      WHEN TOO_MANY_ROWS THEN
          DBMS_OUTPUT.PUT_LINE
               ('The student is enrolled in too many courses');
   END;
```

Notice that this example contains two exceptions in a single exception-handling section. The first exception, NO_DATA_FOUND, will be raised if there are no records in the ENROLLMENT table for a particular student. The second exception, TOO_MANY_ROWS, will be raised if a particular student is enrolled in more than one course.

Consider what happens if you run this example for three different values of student ID: 102, 103, and 319.

The first run of the example (student ID is 102) produces the following output:

```
Enter value for sv_student_id: 102
old    2:    v_student_id NUMBER := &sv_student_id;
new    2:    v_student_id NUMBER := 102;
Check if the student is enrolled
Student is enrolled in too many courses

PL/SQL procedure successfully completed.
```

The first time, a user entered 102 for the value of student ID. Next, the first DBMS_ OUTPUT.PUT_LINE statement is executed, and the message "Check if the . . ." is displayed on the screen. Then the SELECT INTO statement is executed. You have probably noticed that the DBMS_OUTPUT.PUT_LINE statement following the SELECT INTO statement was not executed. When the SELECT INTO statement is executed for student ID 102, multiple rows are returned. Because the SELECT INTO statement can return only a single row, control is passed to the exception-handling section of the block. Next, the PL/SQL block raises the proper exception. As a result, the message "The student is enrolled into many courses" is displayed on the screen, and this message is specified by the exception TOO_MANY_ROWS.

It is important for you to note that built-in exceptions are raised implicitly. Therefore, you only need to specify what action must be taken in the case of a particular exception.

A second run of the example (student ID is 103) produces the following output:

```
Enter value for sv_student_id: 103
old   2:    v_student_id NUMBER := &sv_student_id;
new   2:    v_student_id NUMBER := 103;
Check if the student is enrolled
The student is enrolled into one course

PL/SQL procedure successfully completed.
```

In this second run, a user entered 103 for the value of student ID. As a result, the first DBMS_OUTPUT.PUT_LINE statement is executed, and the message "Check if the . . ." is displayed on the screen. Then the SELECT INTO statement is executed. When the SELECT INTO statement is executed for student ID 103, a single row is returned. Next, the DBMS_OUTPUT.PUT_LINE statement following the SELECT INTO statement is executed. As a result, the message "The student is enrolled into one course" is displayed on the screen. Notice that for this value of the variable v_student_id, no exception has been raised.

A third run of the example (student ID is 319) produces the following output:

```
Enter value for sv_student_id: 319
old   2:    v_student_id NUMBER := &sv_student_id;
new   2:    v_student_id NUMBER := 319;
Check if the student is enrolled
The student is not enrolled

PL/SQL procedure successfully completed.
```

This time, a user entered 319 for the value of student ID. The first DBMS_OUTPUT.PUT_LINE statement is executed, and the message "Check if the . . ." is displayed on the screen. Then the SELECT INTO statement is executed. When the SELECT INTO statement is executed for student ID 319, no rows are returned. As a result, control is passed to the exception-handling section of the PL/SQL block, and the proper exception is raised. In this case, the NO_DATA_FOUND exception is raised because the SELECT INTO statement failed to return a single row. Thus, the message "The student is not enrolled" is displayed on the screen.

So far, you have seen examples of exception-handling sections that have particular exceptions, such as NO_DATA_FOUND or ZERO_DIVIDE. However, you cannot always predict beforehand what exception might be raised by your PL/SQL block. In cases like this, there is a special exception handler called OTHERS. All predefined Oracle errors (exceptions) can be handled with the use of the OTHERS handler.

Consider the following:

■ FOR EXAMPLE

```
DECLARE
   v_instructor_id NUMBER := &sv_instructor_id;
   v_instructor_name VARCHAR2(50);
BEGIN
   SELECT first_name||' '||last_name
     INTO v_instructor_name
     FROM instructor
    WHERE instructor_id = v_instructor_id;

   DBMS_OUTPUT.PUT_LINE ('Instructor name is '||
      v_instructor_name);
EXCEPTION
   WHEN OTHERS THEN
      DBMS_OUTPUT.PUT_LINE ('An error has occurred');
END;
```

When run, this example produces the following output:

```
Enter value for sv_instructor_id: 100
old   2:    v_instructor_id NUMBER := &sv_instructor_id;
new   2:    v_instructor_id NUMBER := 100;
An error has occurred

PL/SQL procedure successfully completed.
```

This demonstrates not only the use of the OTHERS exception handler, but also a bad programming practice. The exception OTHERS has been raised because there is no record in the INSTRUCTOR table for instructor ID 100.

This is a simple example, where it is possible to guess what exception handlers should be used. However, in many instances you may find a number of programs that have been written with a single exception handler, OTHERS. This is a bad programming practice, because such use of this exception handler does not give you or your user good feedback. You do not really know what error has occurred. Your user does not know whether he or she entered some information incorrectly. There are special error-reporting functions, SQLCODE and SQLERRM, that are very useful when used with the OTHERS handler. You will learn about them in Chapter 11.

LAB 7.2 EXERCISES

7.2.1 USE BUILT-IN EXCEPTIONS

In this exercise, you will learn more about some built-in exceptions discussed earlier in the chapter.

Create the following PL/SQL script:

```
-- ch07_2a.sql, version 1.0
SET SERVEROUTPUT ON
DECLARE
   v_exists NUMBER(1);
   v_total_students NUMBER(1);
   v_zip CHAR(5):= '&sv_zip';
BEGIN
   SELECT count(*)
     INTO v_exists
     FROM zipcode
    WHERE zip = v_zip;

   IF v_exists != 0 THEN
      SELECT COUNT(*)
        INTO v_total_students
        FROM student
       WHERE zip = v_zip;
      DBMS_OUTPUT.PUT_LINE
          ('There are '||v_total_students||' students');
   ELSE
      DBMS_OUTPUT.PUT_LINE (v_zip||' is not a valid zip');
   END IF;

EXCEPTION
   WHEN VALUE_ERROR OR INVALID_NUMBER THEN
      DBMS_OUTPUT.PUT_LINE ('An error has occurred');
END;
```

This script contains two exceptions, VALUE_ERROR and INVALID_NUMBER. However, only one exception handler is written for both exceptions. You can combine different exceptions in a single exception handler when you want to handle both exceptions in a similar way. Often the exceptions VALUE_ERROR and INVALID_NUMBER are used in a single exception handler because these Oracle errors refer to the conversion problems that may occur at runtime.

In order to test this script fully, execute it three times. For the first run, enter "07024," for the second run, enter "00914," and for the third run, enter "12345" for the variable `v_zip`. Execute the script, and then answer the following questions:

a) What output was printed on the screen (for all values of zip)?

b) Explain why no exception has been raised for these values of the variable `v_zip`.

c) Insert a record into the STUDENT table with a zip having the value of "07024."

```
INSERT INTO student (student_id, salutation, first_name,
    last_name, zip, registration_date, created_by,
    created_date, modified_by, modified_date)
VALUES (STUDENT_ID_SEQ.NEXTVAL, 'Mr.', 'John', 'Smith',
    '07024', SYSDATE, 'STUDENT', SYSDATE, 'STUDENT',
    SYSDATE);
```

Run the script again for the same value of zip ("07024"). What output was printed on the screen? Why?

d) How would you change the script to display a student's first name and last name instead of displaying the total number of students for any given value of a zip? Remember, only one record can be returned by a SELECT INTO statement.

LAB 7.2 EXERCISE ANSWERS

This section gives you some suggested answers to the questions in Lab 7.2, with discussion related to how those answers resulted. The most important thing to realize is whether your answer works. You should figure out the implications of the answers here and what the effects are from any different answers you may come up with.

7.2.1 ANSWERS

a) What output was printed on the screen (for all values of zip)?

Answer: The first version of the output is produced when the value of zip is 07024. The second version of the output is produced when the value of zip is 00914. The third version of the output is produced when the value of zip is 12345.

Your output should look like the following:

```
Enter value for sv_zip: 07024
old    4:    v_zip CHAR(5):= '&sv_zip';
new    4:    v_zip CHAR(5):= '07024';
There are 9 students

PL/SQL procedure successfully completed.
```

When "07024" is entered for the variable `v_zip`, the first SELECT INTO statement is executed. This SELECT INTO statement checks whether the value of zip is valid, or, in other words, if a record exists in the ZIPCODE table for a given value of zip. Next, the value of the variable `v_exists` is evaluated with the help of the IF statement. For this run of the example, the IF statement evaluates to TRUE, and, as a result, the SELECT INTO statement against the STUDENT table is evaluated. Next, the DBMS_OUTPUT.PUT_LINE following the SELECT INTO statement is executed, and the message "There are 9 students" is displayed on the screen.

Your output should look like the following:

```
Enter value for sv_zip: 00914
old    4:    v_zip CHAR(5):= '&sv_zip';
new    4:    v_zip CHAR(5):= '00914';
There are 0 students

PL/SQL procedure successfully completed.
```

For the second run, the value 00914 is entered for the variable `v_zip`. The SELECT INTO statement against the STUDENT table returns one record, and the message "There are 0 students" is displayed on the screen.

Because the SELECT INTO statement against the STUDENT table uses a group function, COUNT, there is no reason to use the exception NO_DATA_FOUND, because the COUNT function will always return data.

Your output should look like the following:

```
Enter value for sv_zip: 12345
old    4:    v_zip CHAR(5):= '&sv_zip';
new    4:    v_zip CHAR(5):= '12345';
12345 is not a valid zip

PL/SQL procedure successfully completed.
```

For the third run, the value 12345 is entered for the variable `v_zip`. The SELECT INTO statement against the ZIPCODE table is executed. Next, the variable `v_exists` is evaluated with the help of the IF statement. Because the value of `v_exists` equals 0, the IF statement evaluates to FALSE. As a result, the ELSE part of the IF statement is executed. The message "12345 is not a valid zip" is displayed on the screen.

b) Explain why no exception has been raised for these values of the variable `v_zip`.

Answer:The exceptions VALUE_ERROR or INVALID_NUMBER have not been raised because there was no conversion or type mismatch error. Both variables, `v_exists` and `v_total_students`, have been defined as NUMBER(1).

The group function COUNT used in the SELECT INTO statement returns a NUMBER datatype. Moreover, on both occasions, a single digit number is returned by the COUNT function. As a result, neither exception has been raised.

c) Insert a record into the STUDENT table with a zip having the value of "07024." Run the script again for the same value of zip ("07024"). What output was printed on the screen? Why?

Answer: After a student has been added, your output should look like the following:

```
Enter value for sv_zip: 07024
old    4:    v_zip CHAR(5):= '&sv_zip';
new    4:    v_zip CHAR(5):= '07024';
An error has occurred

PL/SQL procedure successfully completed.
```

Once the student has been inserted into the STUDENT table with a zip having a value of "07024," the total number of students changes to 10 (remember, previously this number was 9). As a result, the SELECT INTO statement against the STUDENT table causes an error, because the variable `v_total_students` has been defined as NUMBER(1). This means that only a single-digit number can be stored in this variable. The number 10 is a two-digit number, so the exception INVALID_NUMBER is raised. As a result, the message "An error has occurred" is displayed on the screen.

d) How would you change the script to display a student's first name and last name instead of displaying the total number of students for any given value of zip? Remember, only one record can be returned by a SELECT INTO statement.

Answer: The new version of your program should look similar to this program. All changes are shown in bold letters.

```
-- ch07_2b.sql, version 2.0
SET SERVEROUTPUT ON
DECLARE
    v_exists NUMBER(1);
    v_student_name VARCHAR2(30);
    v_zip CHAR(5):= '&sv_zip';
BEGIN
```

```
    SELECT count(*)
      INTO v_exists
      FROM zipcode
     WHERE zip = v_zip;

    IF v_exists != 0 THEN
        SELECT first_name||' '||last_name
          INTO v_student_name
          FROM student
         WHERE zip = v_zip
           AND rownum = 1;
        DBMS_OUTPUT.PUT_LINE ('Student name is '||
           v_student_name);
    ELSE
        DBMS_OUTPUT.PUT_LINE (v_zip||' is not a valid zip');
    END IF;

EXCEPTION
    WHEN VALUE_ERROR OR INVALID_NUMBER THEN
        DBMS_OUTPUT.PUT_LINE ('An error has occurred');

    WHEN NO_DATA_FOUND THEN
        DBMS_OUTPUT.PUT_LINE
           ('There are no students for this value of '||
              'zip code');
END;
```

This version of the program contains several changes. The variable v_total_students has been replaced by the variable v_student_name. The SELECT INTO statement against the STUDENT table has been changed as well. Another condition has been added to the WHERE clause:

rownum = 1

You have seen from the previous runs of this program that for any given value of zip there could be multiple records in the STUDENT table. Because a SELECT INTO statement returns only a single row, the condition rownum = 1 has been added to it. Another way to deal with multiple rows returned by the SELECT INTO statement is to add the exception TOO_MANY_ROWS.

Finally, another exception has been added to the program. The SELECT INTO statement against the STUDENT table does not contain any group functions. Therefore, for any given value of zip, the SELECT INTO statement may not return any data, and it causes an error. As a result, the exception NO_DATA_FOUND will be raised.

LAB 7.2 SELF-REVIEW QUESTIONS

In order to test your progress, you should be able to answer the following questions.

1) How does a built-in exception get raised?

   a) _____ Implicitly

   b) _____ Explicitly

2) An Oracle error, or exception, is referred to by its

   a) _____ Number.

   b) _____ Name.

   c) _____ Both.

3) When a group function is used in the SELECT INTO statement, exception NO_DATA_FOUND is raised if there are no rows returned.

   a) _____ True

   b) _____ False

4) When an exception is raised and executed, control is passed back to the PL/SQL block.

   a) _____ True

   b) _____ False

5) An exception-handling section of a PL/SQL block may contain a single exception handler only.

   a) _____ True

   b) _____ False

Answers appear in Appendix A, Section 7.2.

CHAPTER 7

TEST YOUR THINKING

In this chapter you learned about built-in exceptions. Here are some projects that will help you test the depth of your understanding.

1) Create the following script: Check to see whether there is a record in the STUDENT table for a given student ID. If there is no record for the given student ID, insert a record into the STUDENT table for the given student ID.

2) Create the following script: For a given instructor ID, check to see whether it is assigned to a valid instructor. Then check the number of sections that are taught by this instructor and display this information on the screen.

The projects in this section are meant to have you utilize all of the skills that you have acquired throughout this chapter. The answers to these projects can be found in Appendix D and at the companion Web site to this book, located at: http://www .phptr.com/rosenzweig2e. Visit the Web site periodically to share and discuss your answers.

C H A P T E R   8

ITERATIVE CONTROL

<table>
<tr><td colspan="2">CHAPTER OBJECTIVES</td></tr>
<tr><td colspan="2">In this Chapter, you will learn about:</td></tr>
<tr><td>✔ Simple Loops</td><td>Page 194</td></tr>
<tr><td>✔ WHILE Loops</td><td>Page 208</td></tr>
<tr><td>✔ Numeric FOR Loops</td><td>Page 219</td></tr>
<tr><td>✔ Nested Loops</td><td>Page 232</td></tr>
</table>

Generally, computer programs are written because certain tasks must be executed a number of times. For example, many companies need to process transactions on a monthly basis. A program allows the completion of this task by being executed at the end of each month.

Similarly, programs incorporate instructions that need to be executed repeatedly. For example, a program may need to write a number of records to a table. By using a loop, the program is able to write the desired number of records to a table. In other words, loops are programming facilities that allow a set of instructions to be executed repeatedly.

In PL/SQL, there are four types of loops: simple loops, WHILE loops, numeric FOR loops, and cursor FOR loops. In this chapter, you will explore simple loops, WHILE loops, numeric FOR loops, and nested loops. Cursor FOR loops are discussed later in the book.

L A B 8 . 1

SIMPLE LOOPS

LAB OBJECTIVES

After this Lab, you will be able to:

✔ Use Simple Loops with EXIT Conditions
✔ Use Simple Loops with EXIT WHEN Conditions

A simple loop, as you can see from its name, is the most basic kind of loop and has the following structure:

```
LOOP
    STATEMENT 1;
    STATEMENT 2;
    ...
    STATEMENT N;
END LOOP;
```

The reserved word LOOP marks the beginning of the simple loop. Statements 1 through N are a sequence of statements that is executed repeatedly. These statements consist of one or more of the standard programming structures. END LOOP is a reserved phrase that indicates the end of the loop construct.

The flow of logic from this structure is illustrated in Figure 8.1.

Every time the loop is iterated, a sequence of statements is executed, and then control is passed back to the top of the loop. The sequence of statements will be executed an infinite number of times, because there is no statement specifying when the loop must terminate. Hence, a simple loop is called an infinite loop because there is no means to exit the loop. A properly constructed loop needs to have an exit condition that determines when the loop is complete. This exit condition has two forms: EXIT and EXIT WHEN.

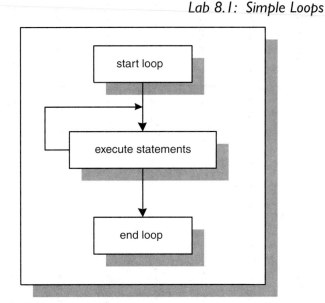

Figure 8.1 ■ Simple Loop

EXIT

The EXIT statement causes a loop to terminate when the EXIT condition evaluates to TRUE. The EXIT condition is evaluated with the help of an IF statement. When the EXIT condition is evaluated to TRUE, control is passed to the first executable statement after the END LOOP statement. This is indicated by the following:

```
LOOP
    STATEMENT 1;
    STATEMENT 2;
    IF CONDITION THEN
        EXIT;
    END IF;
END LOOP;
STATEMENT 3;
```

In this example, you can see that after the EXIT condition evaluates to TRUE, control is passed to STATEMENT 3, which is the first executable statement after the END LOOP statement.

 The EXIT statement is valid only when placed inside of a loop. When placed outside of a loop, it will cause a syntax error. To avoid this error, use the RETURN statement to terminate a PL/SQL block before its normal end is reached as follows:

```
BEGIN
    DBMS_OUTPUT.PUT_LINE ('Line 1');
    RETURN;
```

```
      DBMS_OUTPUT.PUT_LINE ('Line 2');
END;
```

This example produces the output:

Line 1

PL/SQL procedure successfully completed.

Because the RETURN statement terminates the PL/SQL block, the second DBMS_OUTPUT.PUT_LINE statement is never executed.

EXIT WHEN

The EXIT WHEN statement causes a loop to terminate only if the EXIT WHEN condition evaluates to TRUE. Control is then passed to the first executable statement after the END LOOP statement. The structure of a loop using an EXIT WHEN clause is as follows:

```
LOOP
    STATEMENT 1;
    STATEMENT 2;
    EXIT WHEN CONDITION;
END LOOP;
STATEMENT 3;
```

This flow of logic from the EXIT and EXIT WHEN statements is illustrated in Figure 8.2.

Figure 8.2 shows that during each iteration, the loop executes a sequence of statements. Control is then passed to the EXIT condition of the loop. If the EXIT condition evaluates to FALSE, control is passed to the top of the loop. The sequence of statements will be executed repeatedly until the EXIT condition evaluates to TRUE. When the EXIT condition evaluates to TRUE, the loop is terminated, and control is passed to the next executable statement following the loop.

Figure 8.2 also shows that the EXIT condition is included in the body of the loop. Therefore, the decision about loop termination is made inside the body of the loop, and the body of the loop, or a part of it, will always be executed at least once. However, the number of iterations of the loop depends on the evaluation of the EXIT condition and is not known until the loop completes.

As mentioned earlier, Figure 8.2 illustrates that the flow of logic for the structure of EXIT and EXIT WHEN statements is the same even though two different forms of EXIT condition are used. In other words,

```
IF CONDITION THEN
    EXIT;
END IF;
```

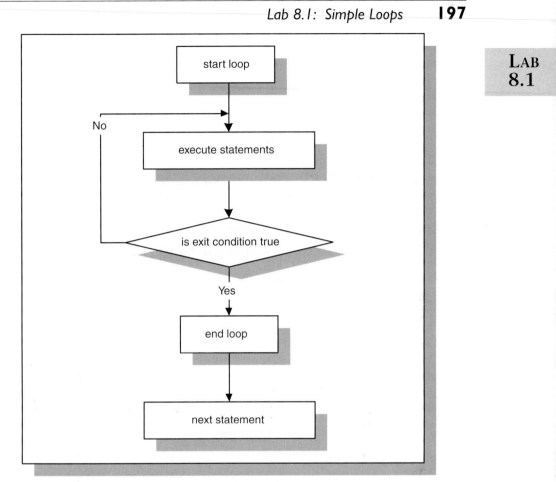

Figure 8.2 ■ Simple Loop with the EXIT Condition

is equivalent to

```
EXIT WHEN CONDITION;
```

*It is important to note that when the EXIT statement is used without
an EXIT condition, the simple loop will execute only once. Consider the
following example.*

```
DECLARE
    v_counter NUMBER := 0;
BEGIN
    LOOP
        DBMS_OUTPUT.PUT_LINE ('v_counter = '||v_counter);
        EXIT;
    END LOOP;
END;
```

**LAB
8.1**

This example produces the following output:

```
v_counter = 0
```

```
PL/SQL procedure successfully completed.
```

Because the EXIT statement is used without an EXIT condition, the loop is terminated as soon as the EXIT statement is executed.

LAB 8.1 EXERCISES

8.1.1 USE SIMPLE LOOPS WITH EXIT CONDITIONS

In this exercise, you will use the EXIT condition to terminate a simple loop, and a special variable, v_counter, which keeps count of the loop iterations. With each iteration of the loop, the value of v_counter will be incremented and displayed on the screen.

Create the following PL/SQL script:

```
-- ch08_1a.sql, version 1.0
SET SERVEROUTPUT ON
DECLARE
   v_counter BINARY_INTEGER := 0;
BEGIN
   LOOP
      -- increment loop counter by one
      v_counter := v_counter + 1;
      DBMS_OUTPUT.PUT_LINE ('v_counter = '||v_counter);

      -- if EXIT condition yields TRUE exit the loop
      IF v_counter = 5 THEN
         EXIT;
      END IF;

   END LOOP;
   -- control resumes here
   DBMS_OUTPUT.PUT_LINE ('Done…');
END;
```

The statement

```
v_counter := v_counter + 1
```

is used often when working with a loop. Variable `v_counter` *is a loop counter that tracks the number of times the statements in the body of the loop are executed. You will notice that for each iteration of the loop, its value is incremented by 1. However, it is very important to initialize the variable* `v_counter` *for successful termination of the loop. If* `v_counter` *is not initialized, its value is NULL. Then, the statement*

```
v_counter := v_counter + 1
```

will never increment the value of `v_counter` *by one, because NULL + 1 evaluates to NULL. As result, the EXIT condition will never yield TRUE, and the loop will become infinite.*

Execute the script, and then answer the following questions.

a) What output was printed on the screen?

b) How many times was the loop executed?

c) What is the EXIT condition for this loop?

d) How many times will the value of the variable `v_counter` be displayed if the DBMS_OUTPUT.PUT_LINE statement is used after the END IF statement?

e) Why does the number of times the loop counter value is displayed on the screen differ when the DBMS_OUTPUT.PUT_LINE statement is placed after the END IF statement?

f) Rewrite this script using the EXIT WHEN condition instead of the EXIT condition, so that it produces the same result.

8.1.2 USE SIMPLE LOOPS WITH *EXIT WHEN* CONDITIONS

In this exercise, you will use the EXIT WHEN condition to terminate the loop. You will add a number of sections for a given course number. Try to answer the questions before you run the script. Once you have answered the questions, run the script and check your answers.

Create the following PL/SQL script:

```
-- ch08_2a.sql, version 1.0
SET SERVEROUTPUT ON
DECLARE
   v_course course.course_no%type := 430;
   v_instructor_id instructor.instructor_id%type := 102;
   v_sec_num section.section_no%type := 0;
BEGIN
   LOOP
      -- increment section number by one
      v_sec_num := v_sec_num + 1;
      INSERT INTO section
         (section_id, course_no, section_no,
         instructor_id, created_date, created_by,
         modified_date, modified_by)
      VALUES
         (section_id_seq.nextval, v_course, v_sec_num,
         v_instructor_id, SYSDATE, USER, SYSDATE,
         USER);

      -- if number of sections added is four exit the loop
      EXIT WHEN v_sec_num = 4;
   END LOOP;

   -- control resumes here
   COMMIT;
EXCEPTION
   WHEN OTHERS THEN
      DBMS_OUTPUT.PUT_LINE ('An error has occurred');
END;
```

Notice that the INSERT statement contains an Oracle built-in function called USER. At first glance, this function looks like a variable that has not been declared. This function returns the name of the current user. In other words, it will return the login name that you use when connecting to Oracle.

Try to answer the following questions first, and then execute the script:

a) How many sections will be added for the specified course number?

b) How many times will the loop be executed if the course number is not valid?

c) How would you change this script to add 10 sections for the specified course number?

d) How would you change the script to add only even-numbered sections (maximum section number is 10) for the specified course number?

e) How many times will the loop be executed in this case?

LAB 8.1 EXERCISE ANSWERS

This section gives you some suggested answers to the questions in Lab 8.1, with discussion related to how those answers resulted. The most important thing to realize is whether your answer works. You should figure out the implications of the answers here and what the effects are from any different answers you may come up with.

8.1.1 ANSWERS

a) What output was printed on the screen?

Answer: Your output should look like the following:

```
v_counter = 1
v_counter = 2
v_counter = 3
v_counter = 4
v_counter = 5
Done...

PL/SQL procedure successfully completed.
```

Every time the loop is run, the statements in the body of the loop are executed. In this script, the value of v_counter is incremented by 1 and displayed on the screen. The EXIT condition is evaluated for each value of v_counter. Once the value of v_counter increases to 5, the loop is terminated. For the first iteration of the loop, the value of v_counter is equal to 1, and it is displayed on the screen, and so forth. After the loop has terminated, "Done..." is displayed on the screen.

b) How many times was the loop executed?

Answer: The loop was executed five times.

Once the value of v_counter increases to 5, the IF statement

```
IF v_counter = 5 THEN
    EXIT;
END IF;
```

evaluates to TRUE, and the loop is terminated.

The loop counter tracks the number of times the loop is executed. You will notice that in this exercise, the maximum value of v_counter is equal to the number of times the loop is iterated.

c) What is the EXIT condition for this loop?

Answer: The EXIT condition for this loop is v_counter = 5.

The EXIT condition is used as a part of an IF statement. The IF statement evaluates the EXIT condition to TRUE or FALSE, based on the current value of v_counter.

d) How many times will the value of the variable v_counter be displayed if the DBMS_OUTPUT.PUT_LINE statement is used after the END IF statement?

Answer: The value of v_counter *will be displayed four times.*

```
LOOP
    v_counter := v_counter + 1;
    IF v_counter = 5 THEN
        EXIT;
    END IF;
    DBMS_OUTPUT.PUT_LINE ('v_counter = '||v_counter);
END LOOP;
```

Assume that the loop has iterated four times already. Then the value of v_counter is incremented by 1, so v_counter is equal to 5. Next, the IF statement evaluates the EXIT condition. The EXIT condition yields TRUE, and the loop is terminated. The DBMS_OUTPUT.PUT_LINE statement is not executed for the fifth iteration of the loop because control is passed to the next executable statement after the END LOOP statement. Thus, only four values of v_counter are displayed on the screen.

e) Why does the number of times the loop counter value is displayed on the screen differ when the DBMS_OUTPUT.PUT_LINE statement is placed after the END IF statement?

Answer:When the DBMS_OUTPUT.PUT_LINE statement is placed before the IF statement, the value of v_counter *is displayed on the screen first.Then it is evaluated by the IF statement.The fifth iteration of the loop "v_counter = 5" is displayed first, then the EXIT condition yields TRUE and the loop is terminated.*

When the DBMS_OUTPUT.PUT_LINE statement is placed after the END IF statement, the EXIT condition is evaluated prior to the execution of the DBMS_OUTPUT.PUT_ LINE statement.Thus, for the fifth iteration of the loop, the EXIT condition evaluates to TRUE before the value of v_counter *is displayed on the screen by the DBMS_OUTPUT.PUT_LINE statement.*

f) Rewrite this script using the EXIT WHEN condition instead of the EXIT condition, so that it produces the same result.

Answer:Your script should look similar to the following script. Changes are shown in bold letters.

```
-- ch08_1b.sql, version 2.0
SET SERVEROUTPUT ON
DECLARE
   v_counter BINARY_INTEGER := 0;
BEGIN
   LOOP
      -- increment loop counter by one
      v_counter := v_counter + 1;
      DBMS_OUTPUT.PUT_LINE ('v_counter = '||v_counter);

      -- if EXIT WHEN condition yields TRUE exit the loop
      EXIT WHEN v_counter = 5;
   END LOOP;

   -- control resumes here
   DBMS_OUTPUT.PUT_LINE ('Done...');
END;
```

Notice that the IF statement has been replaced by the EXIT WHEN statement. The rest of the statements in the body of the loop do not need to be changed.

**LAB
8.1**

a) How many sections will be added for the specified course number?

Answer: Four sections were added for the given course number.

b) How many times will the loop be executed if the course number is not valid?

Answer: The loop will be executed one time.

If the course number is not valid, the INSERT statement

```
INSERT INTO section
    (section_id, course_no, section_no, instructor_id,
     created_date, created_by, modified_date, modified_by)
VALUES
    (section_id_seq.nextval, v_course, v_sec_num,
     v_instructor_id, SYSDATE, USER, SYSDATE, USER);
```

will cause an exception to be raised. As soon as an exception is raised, control is passed out of the loop to the exception handler. Therefore, if the course number is not valid, the loop will be executed only once.

c) How would you change this script to add 10 sections for the specified course number?

Answer: Your script should look similar to the following script. Changes are shown in bold letters.

```
-- ch08_2b.sql, version 2.0
DECLARE
    v_course course.course_no%type := 430;
    v_instructor_id instructor.instructor_id%type := 102;
    v_sec_num section.section_no%type := 0;
BEGIN
    LOOP
        -- increment section number by one
        v_sec_num := v_sec_num + 1;
        INSERT INTO section
            (section_id, course_no, section_no,
             instructor_id, created_date, created_by,
             modified_date, modified_by)
        VALUES
            (section_id_seq.nextval, v_course, v_sec_num,
             v_instructor_id, SYSDATE, USER, SYSDATE,
             USER);
```

```
           -- if number of sections added is ten exit the loop
           EXIT WHEN v_sec_num = 10;
      END LOOP;

      -- control resumes here
      COMMIT;
   EXCEPTION
      WHEN OTHERS THEN
           DBMS_OUTPUT.PUT_LINE ('An error has occurred');
   END;
```

In order to add 10 sections for the given course number, the test value of v_sec_num in the EXIT condition is changed to 10.

Note that before you execute this version of the script you need to delete records from the SECTION table that were added when you executed the original example. If you did not run the original script, you do not need to delete records from the SECTION table.

The SECTION table has a unique constraint defined on the COURSE_NO and SECTION_NO columns. In other words, the combination of course and section numbers allows you to uniquely identify each row of the table. When the original script is executed, it creates four records in the SECTION table for course number 430, section numbers 1, 2, 3, and 4. When the new version of this script is executed, the unique constraint defined on the SECTION table is violated because there already are records corresponding to course number 430 and section numbers 1, 2, 3, and 4. Therefore, these rows must be deleted from the SECTION table as follows:

```
DELETE FROM section
 WHERE course_no = 430
   AND section_no <= 4;
```

Once these records are deleted from the SECTION table, you can execute the new version of the script.

d) How would you change the script to add only even-numbered sections (maximum section number is 10) for the specified course number?

Answer: Your script should look similar to the following script. Changes are shown in bold letters. In order to run this script, you will need to delete records from the SECTION table that were added by the previous version. With each iteration of the loop, the value of v_sec_num *should be incremented by two, as shown:*

```
-- ch08_2c.sql, version 3.0
SET SERVEROUTPUT ON
DECLARE
   v_course course.course_no%type := 430;
   v_instructor_id instructor.instructor_id%type := 102;
```

```
      v_sec_num section.section_no%type := 0;
BEGIN
   LOOP
      -- increment section number by two
      v_sec_num := v_sec_num + 2;
      INSERT INTO section
         (section_id, course_no, section_no,
         instructor_id, created_date, created_by,
         modified_date, modified_by)
      VALUES
         (section_id_seq.nextval, v_course, v_sec_num,
         v_instructor_id, SYSDATE, USER, SYSDATE,
         USER);

      -- if number of sections added is ten exit the loop
      EXIT WHEN v_sec_num = 10;
   END LOOP;

   -- control resumes here
   COMMIT;
EXCEPTION
   WHEN OTHERS THEN
      DBMS_OUTPUT.PUT_LINE ('An error has occurred');
END;
```

e) How many times will the loop be executed in this case?

Answer: The loop is executed five times when even-numbered sections are added for the given course number.

LAB 8.1 SELF-REVIEW QUESTIONS

In order to test your progress, you should be able to answer the following questions.

1) How many times is a simple loop executed if there is no EXIT condition specified?

a) _____ The loop does not execute at all.
b) _____ The loop executes once.
c) _____ The loop executes an infinite number of times.

2) How many times is a simple loop executed if the EXIT statement is used without an EXIT condition?

a) _____ The loop does not execute at all.
b) _____ The loop executes once.
c) _____ The loop executes an infinite number of times.

3) What value must the EXIT condition evaluate to in order for the loop to terminate?

a) _____ TRUE
b) _____ FALSE
c) _____ NULL

4) What statement must be executed before control can be passed from the body of the loop to the first executable statement outside of the loop?

a) _____ LOOP statement
b) _____ END LOOP statement
c) _____ EXIT statement
d) _____ RETURN statement

5) A simple loop will execute a minimum of which of the following?

a) _____ Zero times
b) _____ One time
c) _____ Infinite number of times

Answers appear in Appendix A, Section 8.1.

L A B   8 . 2

WHILE LOOPS

LAB OBJECTIVES

After this Lab, you will be able to:

✔ Use WHILE Loops

A WHILE loop has the following structure:

```
WHILE CONDITION LOOP
    STATEMENT 1;
    STATEMENT 2;
    ...
    STATEMENT N;
END LOOP;
```

The reserved word WHILE marks the beginning of a loop construct. The word CONDITION is the test condition of the loop that evaluates to TRUE or FALSE. The result of this evaluation determines whether the loop is executed. Statements 1 through N are a sequence of statements that is executed repeatedly. The END LOOP is a reserved phrase that indicates the end of the loop construct.

This flow of the logic is illustrated in Figure 8.3.

Figure 8.3 shows that the test condition is evaluated prior to each iteration of the loop. If the test condition evaluates to TRUE, the sequence of statements is executed, and control is passed to the top of the loop for the next evaluation of the test condition. If the test condition evaluates to FALSE, the loop is terminated, and control is passed to the next executable statement following the loop.

As mentioned earlier, before the body of the loop can be executed, the test condition must be evaluated. The decision as to whether to execute the statements in the body of the loop is made prior to entering the loop. As a result, the loop will not be executed at all if the test condition yields FALSE.

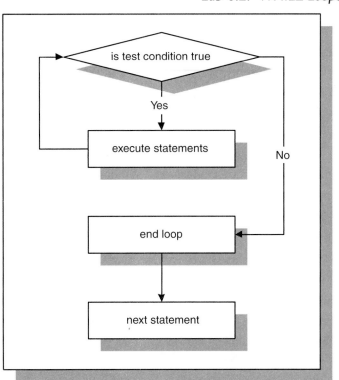

Figure 8.3 ■ WHILE Loop

■ FOR EXAMPLE

```
DECLARE
    v_counter NUMBER := 5;
BEGIN
    WHILE v_counter < 5 LOOP
        DBMS_OUTPUT.PUT_LINE ('v_counter = '||v_counter);

        -- decrement the value of v_counter by one
        v_counter := v_counter - 1;
    END LOOP;
END;
```

In this example, the body of the loop is not executed at all because the test condition of the loop evaluates to FALSE.

While the test condition of the loop must evaluate to TRUE at least once for the statements in the loop to execute, it is important to insure that the test condition will eventually evaluate to FALSE, as well. Otherwise, the WHILE loop will execute continually.

**LAB
8.2**

■ *FOR EXAMPLE*

```
DECLARE
   v_counter NUMBER := 1;
BEGIN
   WHILE v_counter < 5 LOOP
      DBMS_OUTPUT.PUT_LINE('v_counter = '||v_counter);

      -- decrement the value of v_counter by one
      v_counter := v_counter - 1;
   END LOOP;
END;
```

This is an example of an infinite WHILE loop. The test condition always evaluates to TRUE, because the value of v_counter is decremented by 1 and is always less than 5.

It is important to note that Boolean expressions can also be used to determine when the loop should terminate.

```
DECLARE
   v_test BOOLEAN := TRUE;
BEGIN
   WHILE v_test LOOP
      STATEMENTS;

      IF TEST_CONDITION THEN
         v_test := FALSE;
      END IF;

   END LOOP;
END;
```

When using a Boolean expression as a test condition of a loop, you must make sure that a different value is eventually assigned to the Boolean variable in order to exit the loop. Otherwise, the loop will become infinite.

PREMATURE TERMINATION OF THE LOOP

The EXIT and EXIT WHEN statements can be used inside the body of a WHILE loop. If the EXIT condition evaluates to TRUE before the test condition evaluates to FALSE, the loop is terminated prematurely. If the test condition yields FALSE before the EXIT condition yields TRUE, there is no premature termination of the loop. This is indicated as follows:

```
WHILE TEST_CONDITION LOOP
    STATEMENT 1;
    STATEMENT 2;

    IF EXIT_CONDITION THEN
        EXIT;
    END IF;
END LOOP;
STATEMENT 3;
```

or

```
WHILE TEST_CONDITION LOOP
    STATEMENT 1;
    STATEMENT 2;
    EXIT WHEN EXIT_CONDITION;
END LOOP;
STATEMENT 3;
```

Consider the following example.

■ FOR EXAMPLE

```
DECLARE
    v_counter NUMBER := 1;
BEGIN
    WHILE v_counter <= 5 LOOP
        DBMS_OUTPUT.PUT_LINE ('v_counter = '||v_counter);

        IF v_counter = 2 THEN
            EXIT;
        END IF;

        v_counter := v_counter + 1;
    END LOOP;
END;
```

Before the statements in the body of the WHILE loop are executed, the test condition

v_counter <= 5

must evaluate to TRUE. Then, the value of v_counter is displayed on the screen and incremented by one. Next, the EXIT condition

v_counter = 2

is evaluated, and as soon as the value of v_counter reaches 2, the loop is terminated.

Notice that according to the test condition, the loop should execute five times. However, the loop is executed only twice, because the EXIT condition is present inside the body of the loop. Therefore, the loop terminates prematurely.

Now you will try to reverse the test condition and EXIT condition.

■ FOR EXAMPLE

```
DECLARE
    v_counter NUMBER := 1;
BEGIN
    WHILE v_counter <= 2 LOOP
        DBMS_OUTPUT.PUT_LINE ('v_counter = '||v_counter);
        v_counter := v_counter + 1;

        IF v_counter = 5 THEN
            EXIT;
        END IF;
    END LOOP;
END;
```

In this example, the test condition is

v_counter <= 2

and the EXIT condition is

v_counter = 5

In this case, the loop is executed twice as well. However, it does not terminate prematurely, because the EXIT condition never evaluates to TRUE. As soon as the value of v_counter reaches 3, the test condition evaluates to FALSE, and the loop is terminated.

Both examples, when run, produce the following output:

v_counter = 1
v_counter = 2

PL/SQL procedure successfully completed.

These examples demonstrate not only the use of the EXIT statement inside the body of the WHILE loop, but also a bad programming practice. In the first example, the test condition can be changed so that there is no need to use an EXIT condition, because essentially they both are used to terminate the loop. In the second example, the EXIT condition is useless, because its terminal value is never reached. *You should never use unnecessary code in your program.*

LAB 8.2 EXERCISES

8.2.1 USE WHILE LOOPS

In this exercise, you will use a WHILE loop to calculate the sum of the integers between 1 and 10.

Create the following PL/SQL script:

```
-- ch08_3a.sql, version 1.0
SET SERVEROUTPUT ON
DECLARE
   v_counter BINARY_INTEGER := 1;
   v_sum NUMBER := 0;
BEGIN
   WHILE v_counter <= 10 LOOP
      v_sum := v_sum + v_counter;
      DBMS_OUTPUT.PUT_LINE ('Current sum is: '||v_sum);

      -- increment loop counter by one
      v_counter := v_counter + 1;
   END LOOP;

   -- control resumes here
   DBMS_OUTPUT.PUT_LINE ('The sum of integers between 1 '||
      'and 10 is: '||v_sum);
END;
```

Execute the script, and then answer the following questions:

a) What output was printed on the screen?

b) What is the test condition for this loop?

c) How many times was the loop executed?

d) How many times will the loop be executed
  i) if v_counter is not initialized?
  ii) if v_counter is initialized to 0?
  iii) if v_counter is initialized to 10?

e) How will the value of v_sum change based on the initial value of v_counter from the previous question?

f) What will be the value of v_sum if it is not initialized?

g) How would you change the script to calculate the sum of the even integers between 1 and 100?

LAB 8.2 EXERCISE ANSWERS

This section gives you some suggested answers to the questions in Lab 8.2, with discussion related to how those answers resulted. The most important thing to realize is whether your answer works. You should figure out the implications of the answers here and what the effects are from any different answers you may come up with.

8.2.1 ANSWERS

a) What output was printed on the screen?

Answer: Your output should look like the following:

```
Current sum is: 1
Current sum is: 3
Current sum is: 6
Current sum is: 10
Current sum is: 15
Current sum is: 21
Current sum is: 28
Current sum is: 36
Current sum is: 45
Current sum is: 55
The sum of integers between 1 and 10 is: 55

PL/SQL procedure successfully completed.
```

Every time the loop is run, the value of v_counter is checked in the test condition. While the value of v_counter is less than or equal to 10, the statements inside the body of the loop are executed. In this script, the value of v_sum is calculated and displayed on the screen. Next, the value of v_counter is incremented, and control is passed to the top of the loop. Once the value of v_counter increases to 11, the loop is terminated.

For the first iteration of the loop, the value of v_sum is equal to 1, according to the statement

```
v_sum := v_sum + v_counter
```

After the value of v_sum is calculated, the value of v_counter is incremented by 1. Then, for the second iteration of the loop, the value of v_sum is equal to 3, because 2 is added to the old value of v_sum.

After the loop has terminated, "The sum of integers..." and "Done ..." are displayed on the screen.

b) What is the test condition for this loop?

Answer:The test condition for this loop is v_counter <= 10 *.*

c) How many times was the loop executed?

Answer:The loop was executed 10 times.

Once the value of v_counter reaches 11, the test condition

```
v_counter <= 10
```

evaluates to FALSE, and the loop is terminated.

As mentioned earlier, the loop counter tracks the number of times the loop is executed. You will notice that in this exercise, the maximum value of v_counter is equal to the number of times the loop is iterated.

d) How many times will the loop be executed:
i) if v_counter is not initialized?
ii) if v_counter is initialized to 0?
iii) if v_counter is initialized to 10?

Answer: If the value of v_counter *is not initialized to some value, the loop will not execute at all.*

In order for the loop to execute at least once, the test condition must evaluate to TRUE at least once. If the value of v_counter is only declared and not initialized, it is NULL. *It is important to remember that null variables cannot be compared to other variables or values.* Therefore, the test condition

```
v_counter <= 10
```

never evaluates to TRUE, and the loop is not executed at all.

If v_counter *is initialized to 0, the loop will execute 11 times instead of 10, since the minimum value of* v_counter *has decreased by 1.*

When v_counter is initialized to 0, the range of integers for which the test condition of the loop evaluates to TRUE becomes 0 to 10. The given range of the integers has eleven numbers in it. As a result, the loop will iterate eleven times.

If v_counter *is initialized to 10, the loop will execute once.*

When the initial value of v_counter is equal to 10, the test condition evaluates to TRUE for the first iteration of the loop. Inside the body of the loop, the value of v_counter is incremented by one. As a result, for the second iteration of the loop, the test condition evaluates to FALSE, since 11 is not less than or equal to 10, and control is passed to the next executable statement after the loop.

e) How will the value of v_sum change based on the initial value of v_counter from the previous question?

Answer:When v_counter *is not initialized, the loop is not executed at all. Therefore, the value of* v_sum *does not change from its initial value; it stays 0.*

When v_counter *is initialized to 0, the loop is executed 11 times. The value of* v_sum *is calculated 11 times, as well. However, after the loop completes, the value of v_sum is 55, because 0 is added to* v_sum *during first iteration of the loop.*

When v_counter *is initialized to 10, the loop is executed once. As a result, the value of* v_sum *is incremented only once by 10. After the loop is complete, the value of* v_sum *is equal to 10.*

f) What will be the value of v_sum if it is not initialized?

Answer:The value of v_sum will be NULL if is not initialized to some value.

The value of v_sum in the statement

```
v_sum := v_sum + 1
```

will always be equal to NULL, because NULL + 1 is NULL. It was mentioned earlier that NULL variables cannot be compared to other variable or values. *Similarly, calculations cannot be performed on null variables.*

g) How would you change the script to calculate the sum of even integers between 1 and 100?

Answer:Your answer should be similar to the following. Changes are shown in bold letters.

Notice that the value of v_counter *is initialized to 2, and with each iteration of the loop, the value of* v_counter *is incremented by 2, as well.*

```
-- ch08_3b.sql, version 2.0
SET SERVEROUTPUT ON
DECLARE
   v_counter BINARY_INTEGER := 2;
   v_sum NUMBER := 0;
BEGIN
   WHILE v_counter <= 100 LOOP
      v_sum := v_sum + v_counter;
      DBMS_OUTPUT.PUT_LINE ('Current sum is: '||v_sum);

      -- increment loop counter by two
      v_counter := v_counter + 2;
   END LOOP;

   -- control resumes here
   DBMS_OUTPUT.PUT_LINE ('The sum of even integers between
      '||'1 and 100 is: '||v_sum);
END;
```

LAB 8.2 SELF-REVIEW QUESTIONS

In order to test your progress, you should be able to answer the following questions.

1) How many times is a WHILE loop executed if the test condition always evaluates to FALSE?

   a) _____ The loop does not execute at all.
   b) _____ The loop executes once.
   c) _____ The loop executes an infinite number of times.

2) How many times is a WHILE loop executed if the test condition always evaluates to TRUE?

   a) _____ The loop does not execute at all.
   b) _____ The loop executes once.
   c) _____ The loop executes an infinite number of times.

3) What value must the test condition evaluate to in order for the loop to terminate?

   a) _____ TRUE
   b) _____ FALSE
   c) _____ NULL

**LAB
8.2**

4) What causes a WHILE loop to terminate prematurely?

   a) _____ The EXIT condition evaluates to TRUE before the test condition evaluates to FALSE.

   b) _____ The test condition evaluates to FALSE before the EXIT condition evaluates to TRUE.

   c) _____ Both test and EXIT conditions evaluate to FALSE.

5) A WHILE loop will execute a minimum of

   a) _____ zero times.

   b) _____ one time.

   c) _____ infinite number of times.

Answers appear in Appendix A, Section 8.2.

LAB 8.3

NUMERIC FOR LOOPS

LAB OBJECTIVES

After this Lab, you will be able to:

✔ Use Numeric FOR Loops with the IN Option
✔ Use Numeric FOR Loops with the REVERSE Option

A numeric FOR loop is called numeric because it requires an integer as its terminating value. Its structure is as follows:

```
FOR loop_counter IN[REVERSE] lower_limit..upper_limit LOOP
    STATEMENT 1;
    STATEMENT 2;
    ...
    STATEMENT N;
END LOOP;
```

The reserved word FOR marks the beginning of a FOR loop construct. The variable, `loop_counter`, is an implicitly defined index variable. There is no need to define the loop counter in the declaration section of the PL/SQL block. This variable is defined by the loop construct. Lower_limit and upper_limit are two integer numbers that define the number of iterations for the loop. The values of the lower_limit and upper_limit are evaluated once, for the first iteration of the loop. At this point, it is determined how many times the loop will iterate. Statements 1 through *N* are a sequence of statements that is executed repeatedly. END LOOP is a reserved phrase that marks the end of the loop construct.

The reserved word IN or IN REVERSE must be present when defining the loop. If the REVERSE keyword is used, the loop counter will iterate from the upper limit to the lower limit. However, the syntax for the limit specification does not change. The lower limit is always referenced first. The flow of this logic is illustrated in Figure 8.4.

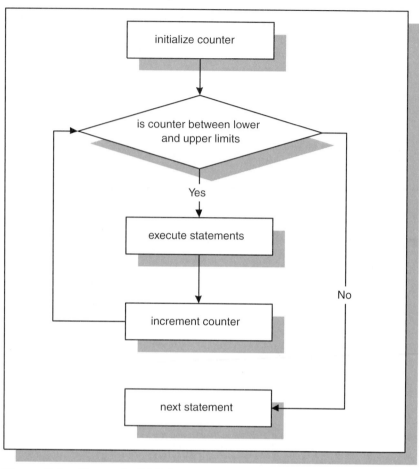

Figure 8.4 ■ Numeric FOR Loop

Figure 8.4 shows that the loop counter is initialized to the lower limit for the first iteration of the loop only. However, the value of the loop counter is tested for each iteration of the loop. As long as the value of v_counter ranges from the lower limit to the upper limit, the statements inside the body of the loop are executed. When the value of the loop counter does not satisfy the range specified by the lower limit and the upper limit, control is passed to the first executable statement outside the loop.

■ *FOR EXAMPLE*

```
BEGIN
    FOR v_counter IN 1..5 LOOP
        DBMS_OUTPUT.PUT_LINE ('v_counter = '||v_counter);
    END LOOP;
END;
```

**LAB
8.3**

In this example, there is no declaration section for the PL/SQL block because the only variable used, v_counter, is the loop counter. Numbers 1..5 specify the range of the integer numbers for which this loop is executed.

Notice that there is no statement

```
v_counter := v_counter + 1
```

anywhere, inside or outside the body of the loop. The value of v_counter is incremented implicitly by the FOR loop itself.

This example produces the following output when run:

**LAB
8.3**

```
v_counter = 1
v_counter = 2
v_counter = 3
v_counter = 4
v_counter = 5

PL/SQL procedure successfully completed.
```

As a matter of fact, if you include the statement

```
v_counter := v_counter + 1
```

in the body of the loop, the PL/SQL script will compile with errors. Consider the following example.

■ FOR EXAMPLE

```
BEGIN
    FOR v_counter IN 1..5 LOOP
        v_counter := v_counter + 1;
        DBMS_OUTPUT.PUT_LINE ('v_counter = '|| v_counter);
    END LOOP;
END;
```

When this example is run, the following error message is produced:

```
BEGIN
*
ERROR at line 1:
ORA-06550: line 3, column 7:
PLS-00363: expression 'V_COUNTER' cannot be used as an
assignment target
ORA-06550: line 3, column 7:
PL/SQL: Statement ignored
```

It is important to remember that the loop counter is implicitly defined and incremented when a numeric FOR loop is used. As a result, it cannot be referenced outside the body of the FOR loop. Consider the following example:

```
BEGIN
    FOR v_counter IN 1..5 LOOP
        DBMS_OUTPUT.PUT_LINE ('v_counter = '||v_counter);
    END LOOP;
    DBMS_OUTPUT.PUT_LINE ('Counter outside the loop is '||
        v_counter);
END;
```

When this example is run, the following error message is produced:

```
DBMS_OUTPUT.PUT_LINE ('Counter outside the loop is '||
v_counter);
                   *
ERROR at line 5:
ORA-06550: line 5, column 53:
PLS-00201: identifier 'V_COUNTER' must be declared
ORA-06550: line 5, column 4:
PL/SQL: Statement ignored
```

Because the loop counter is declared implicitly by the loop, the variable v_counter *cannot be referenced outside the loop. As soon as the loop completes, the loop counter ceases to exist.*

USING THE REVERSE OPTION IN THE LOOP

Earlier in this section, you encountered two options that are available when the value of the loop counter is evaluated, IN and IN REVERSE. You have seen examples already that demonstrate the usage of the IN option for the loop. The next example demonstrates the usage of the IN REVERSE option for the loop.

■ FOR EXAMPLE

```
BEGIN
    FOR v_counter IN REVERSE 1..5 LOOP
        DBMS_OUTPUT.PUT_LINE ('v_counter = '||v_counter);
    END LOOP;
END;
```

When this example is run, the following output is produced:

```
v_counter = 5
v_counter = 4
```

```
v_counter = 3
v_counter = 2
v_counter = 1
```

PL/SQL procedure successfully completed.

As mentioned before, even though the REVERSE keyword is present, the lower limit of the loop is referenced first. However, it is important to note that the loop counter is evaluated from the upper limit to the lower limit. For the first iteration of the loop, `v_counter` (in our case it is a loop counter) is initialized to 5 (upper limit). Then its value is displayed on the screen. For the second iteration of the loop, the value of `v_counter` is decreased by 1, and displayed on the screen.

**LAB
8.3**

Notice that the number of times the body of the loop is executed is not affected by the option used, IN or IN REVERSE. Only the values assigned to the lower limit and the upper limit determine how many times the body of the loop is executed.

PREMATURE TERMINATION OF THE LOOP

The EXIT and EXIT WHEN statements can be used inside the body of a numeric FOR loop. If the EXIT condition evaluates to TRUE before the loop counter reaches its terminal value, the FOR loop is terminated prematurely. If the loop counter reaches its terminal value before the EXIT condition yields TRUE, there is no premature termination of the FOR loop. Consider the following:

```
FOR LOOP_COUNTER IN LOWER_LIMIT..UPPER_LIMIT LOOP
    STATEMENT 1;
    STATEMENT 2;
    IF EXIT_CONDITION THEN
        EXIT;
    END IF;
END LOOP;
STATEMENT 3;
```

or

```
FOR LOOP_COUNTER IN LOWER_LIMIT..UPPER_LIMIT LOOP
    STATEMENT 1;
    STATEMENT 2;
    EXIT WHEN EXIT_CONDITION;
END LOOP;
STATEMENT 3;
```

Consider the following example of a FOR loop that uses the EXIT WHEN condition. This condition is causing the loop to terminate prematurely.

■ *FOR EXAMPLE*

```
BEGIN
   FOR v_counter IN 1..5 LOOP
      DBMS_OUTPUT.PUT_LINE ('v_counter = '||v_counter);
      EXIT WHEN v_counter = 3;
   END LOOP;
END;
```

Notice that according to the range specified, the loop should execute five times. However, the loop is executed only three times because the EXIT condition is present inside the body of the loop. Thus, the loop terminates prematurely.

LAB 8.3 EXERCISES

8.3.1 USE NUMERIC *FOR* LOOPS WITH THE *IN* OPTION

In this exercise, you will use a numeric FOR loop to calculate a factorial of 10 (10! = 1*2*3...*10).

Create the following PL/SQL script:

```
-- ch08_4a.sql, version 1.0
SET SERVEROUTPUT ON
DECLARE
   v_factorial NUMBER := 1;
BEGIN
   FOR v_counter IN 1..10 LOOP
      v_factorial := v_factorial * v_counter;
   END LOOP;
   -- control resumes here
   DBMS_OUTPUT.PUT_LINE ('Factorial of ten is: '||
      v_factorial);
END;
```

Execute the script, and then answer the following questions:

a) What output was printed on the screen?

b) How many times was the loop executed?

c) What is the value of the loop counter before the loop?

d) What is the value of the loop counter after the loop?

e) How many times will the loop be executed if the value of `v_counter` is incremented by 5 inside the body of the loop?

f) Rewrite this script using the REVERSE option. What will the value of `v_factorial` be after the loop is completed?

8.3.2 USE NUMERIC FOR LOOPS WITH THE REVERSE OPTION

In this exercise, you will use the REVERSE option to specify the range of numbers used by the loop to iterate. You will display a list of even numbers starting from 10 going down to 0. Try to answer the questions before you run the script. Once you have answered the questions, run the script and check your results.

Create the following PL/SQL script:

```
-- ch08_5a.sql, version 1.0
SET SERVEROUTPUT ON
BEGIN
    FOR v_counter IN REVERSE 0..10 LOOP
        -- if v_counter is even, display its value on the
        -- screen
        IF MOD(v_counter, 2) = 0 THEN
            DBMS_OUTPUT.PUT_LINE ('v_counter = '||v_counter);
        END IF;
    END LOOP;
    -- control resumes here
    DBMS_OUTPUT.PUT_LINE ('Done...');
END;
```

As in the previous exercises, answer the following questions first, and then execute the script:

a) What output will be printed on the screen?

b) How many times will the body of the loop be executed?

c) How many times will the value of `v_counter` be displayed on the screen?

d) How would you change this script to start the list from 0 and go up to 10?

e) How would you change the script to display only odd numbers on the screen?

f) How many times will the loop be executed in this case?

LAB 8.3 EXERCISE ANSWERS

This section gives you some suggested answers to the questions in Lab 8.3, with discussion related to how those answers resulted. The most important thing to realize is whether your answer works. You should figure out the implications of the answers here and what the effects are from any different answers you may come up with.

8.3.1 ANSWERS

a) What output was printed on the screen?

Answer: Your output should look like the following:

```
Factorial of ten is: 3628800
Done...

PL/SQL procedure successfully completed.
```

Every time the loop is run, the value of `v_counter` is incremented by 1 implicitly, and the current value of the factorial is calculated. Once the value of `v_counter` increases to 10, the loop is run for the last time. At this point, the final value of the factorial is calculated, and the loop is terminated. After the loop has terminated, control is passed to the first statement outside of the loop—in this case, DBMS_OUTPUT.PUT_LINE.

b) How many times was the loop executed?

Answer:The loop was executed ten times according to the range specified by the lower limit and the upper limit of the loop. In this example, the lower limit is equal to 1, and upper limit is equal to 10.

c) What is the value of the loop counter before the loop?

Answer:The loop counter is defined implicitly by the loop.Therefore, before the loop, the loop counter is undefined and has no value.

d) What is the value of the loop counter after the loop?

Answer: Similarly, after the loop has completed, the loop counter is undefined again and can hold no value.

e) How many times will the loop be executed if the value of v_counter is incremented by 5 inside the body of the loop?

Answer: If the value of v_counter *is incremented by 5 inside the body of the loop, the PL/SQL block will not compile successfully. As a result, it will not execute at all.*

In this example, variable v_counter is a loop counter. Therefore, its value can be incremented only implicitly by the loop. Any executable statement that causes v_counter to change its current value leads to compilation errors.

f) Rewrite this script using the REVERSE option.What will the value of v_factorial be after the loop is completed?

Answer:Your script should look similar to the following script. Changes are shown in bold letters.

The value of v_factorial *will be equal to 3628800 after the loop is completed.*

```
-- ch08_4b.sql, version 2.0
SET SERVEROUTPUT ON
DECLARE
   v_factorial NUMBER := 1;
BEGIN
   FOR v_counter IN REVERSE 1..10 LOOP
      v_factorial := v_factorial * v_counter;
   END LOOP;
   -- control resumes here
   DBMS_OUTPUT.PUT_LINE ('Factorial of ten is: '||
      v_factorial);
END;
```

The preceding script produces the following output:

```
Factorial of ten is: 3628800
Done...

PL/SQL procedure successfully completed.
```

The value of `v_factorial` computed by this loop is equal to the value of `v_factorial` computed by the original loop. You will notice that in some cases it does not matter which option, IN or REVERSE, you are using to obtain the final result. You will also notice that in other cases, the result produced by the loop can differ significantly.

8.3.2 ANSWERS

a) What output will be printed on the screen?

Answer: Your output should look like the following:

```
v_counter = 10
v_counter = 8
v_counter = 6
v_counter = 4
v_counter = 2
v_counter = 0
Done...

PL/SQL procedure successfully completed.
```

Notice that the values of `v_counter` are displayed in decreasing order from 10 to 0 because the REVERSE option is used. Remember that regardless of the option used, the lower limit is referenced first.

b) How many times will the body of the loop be executed?

Answer: The body of the loop will be executed eleven times, since the range of the integer numbers specified varies from 0 to 10.

c) How many times will the value of `v_counter` be displayed on the screen?

Answer: The value of `v_counter` will be displayed on the screen six times, since the IF statement will evaluate to TRUE only for even integers.

d) How would you change this script to start the list from 0 and go up to 10?

Answer: Your script should look similar to the script shown below. Changes are shown in bold letters.

To start the list of integers from 0 and go up to 10, the IN option needs to be used in the loop.

```
-- ch08_5b.sql, version 1.0
SET SERVEROUTPUT ON
BEGIN
    FOR v_counter IN 0..10 LOOP
        -- if v_counter is even, display its value on the
        -- screen
        IF MOD(v_counter, 2) = 0 THEN
            DBMS_OUTPUT.PUT_LINE ('v_counter = '||v_counter);
        END IF;
    END LOOP;
    -- control resumes here
    DBMS_OUTPUT.PUT_LINE ('Done...');
END;
```

This example produces the following output:

```
v_counter = 0
v_counter = 2
v_counter = 4
v_counter = 6
v_counter = 8
v_counter = 10
Done...

PL/SQL procedure successfully completed.
```

Notice that when the IN option is used, the value of v_counter is initialized to 0, and, with each iteration of the loop, it is incremented by 1. When the RE-VERSE option is used, v_counter is initialized to 10, and its value is decremented by 1 with each iteration of the loop.

e) How would you change the script to display only odd numbers on the screen?

Answer: Your script should look similar to the following script. Changes are shown in bold letters.

```
-- ch08_5c.sql, version 3.0
SET SERVEROUTPUT ON
BEGIN
    FOR v_counter IN REVERSE 0..10 LOOP
        -- if v_counter is even, display its value on the
        -- screen
        IF MOD(v_counter, 2) != 0 THEN
            DBMS_OUTPUT.PUT_LINE ('v_counter = '||v_counter);
        END IF;
    END LOOP;
    -- control resumes here
    DBMS_OUTPUT.PUT_LINE ('Done...');
END;
```

Notice that only the test condition of the IF statement is changed in order to display the list of odd integers, and the following output is produced:

```
v_counter = 9
v_counter = 7
v_counter = 5
v_counter = 3
v_counter = 1
Done...
```

```
PL/SQL procedure successfully completed.
```

f) How many times will the loop be executed in this case?

Answer: In this case the loop will be executed eleven times.

Based on the test condition used in the IF statement, even or odd integers are displayed on the screen. Depending on the test condition, the number of times v_counter is displayed on the screen varies. However, the loop is executed eleven times as long as the number range specified is 0 to 10.

LAB 8.3 SELF-REVIEW QUESTIONS

In order to test your progress, you should be able to answer the following questions.

1) How many times is a numeric FOR loop executed if the value of the lower limit is equal to the value of the upper limit?

    a) _____ The loop does not execute at all.
    b) _____ The loop executes once.
    c) _____ The loop executes an infinite number of times.

2) How many times is the numeric FOR loop executed if the value of the lower limit is greater than the value of the upper limit?

    a) _____ The loop does not execute at all.
    b) _____ The loop executes once.
    c) _____ The loop executes an infinite number of times.

3) What is the value of the loop counter prior to entering the loop?

    a) _____ 0
    b) _____ I
    c) _____ Undefined

4) What is the value of the loop counter after termination of the loop?

    a) _____ Same as upper limit
    b) _____ Same as lower limit
    c) _____ Undefined

5) When the REVERSE option is used, the value of the loop counter is initialized to which of the following?

    a) _____ Lower limit
    b) _____ Upper limit
    c) _____ NULL

Answers appear in Appendix A, Section 8.3.

LAB
8.3

L A B   8 . 4

NESTED LOOPS

LAB OBJECTIVES

After this Lab, you will be able to:

✔ Use Nested Loops

You have explored three types of loops: simple loops, WHILE loops, and numeric FOR loops. Any of these three types of loops can be nested inside one another. For example, a simple loop can be nested inside a WHILE loop and vice versa. Consider the following example:

■ *FOR EXAMPLE*

```
DECLARE
   v_counter1 INTEGER := 0;
   v_counter2 INTEGER;
BEGIN
   WHILE v_counter1 < 3 LOOP
      DBMS_OUTPUT.PUT_LINE ('v_counter1: '||v_counter1);
      v_counter2 := 0;
      LOOP
         DBMS_OUTPUT.PUT_LINE ('v_counter2: '||v_counter2);
         v_counter2 := v_counter2 + 1;
         EXIT WHEN v_counter2 >= 2;
      END LOOP;
      v_counter1 := v_counter1 + 1;
   END LOOP;
END;
```

In this example, the WHILE loop is called an outer loop because it encompasses the simple loop. The simple loop is called an inner loop because it is enclosed by the body of the WHILE loop.

The outer loop is controlled by the loop counter, v_counter1, and it will execute providing the value of v_counter1 is less than 3. With each iteration of the loop, the value of v_counter1 is displayed on the screen. Next, the value of v_counter2 is initialized to 0. It is important to note that v_counter2 is not initialized at the time of the declaration. The simple loop is placed inside the body of the WHILE loop, and the value of v_counter2 must be initialized every time before control is passed to the simple loop.

Once control is passed to the inner loop, the value of v_counter2 is displayed on the screen and incremented by 1. Next, the EXIT WHEN condition is evaluated. If the EXIT WHEN condition evaluates to FALSE, control is passed back to the top of the simple loop. If the EXIT WHEN condition evaluates to TRUE, control is passed to the first executable statement outside of the loop. In our case, control is passed back to the outer loop, and the value of v_counter1 is incremented by 1, and the test condition of the WHILE loop is evaluated again.

This logic is demonstrated by the output produced by the example:

```
v_counter1: 0
v_counter2: 0
v_counter2: 1
v_counter1: 1
v_counter2: 0
v_counter2: 1
v_counter1: 2
v_counter2: 0
v_counter2: 1

PL/SQL procedure successfully completed.
```

Notice that for each value of v_counter1, there are two values of v_counter2 displayed. For the first iteration of the outer loop, the value of v_counter1 is equal to 0. Once control is passed to the inner loop, the value of v_counter2 is displayed on the screen twice, and so forth.

LOOP LABELS

Earlier in the book, you read about labeling of PL/SQL blocks. Loops can be labeled in a similar manner, as follows:

```
<<label_name>>
FOR LOOP_COUNTER IN LOWER_LIMIT..UPPER_LIMIT LOOP
    STATEMENT 1;
    ...
    STATEMENT N;
END LOOP label_name;
```

The label must appear right before the beginning of the loop. This syntax example shows that the label can be optionally used at the end of the loop statement. It is very helpful to label nested loops because labels improve readability. Consider the following example.

■ *FOR EXAMPLE*

```
BEGIN
    <<outer_loop>>
    FOR i IN 1..3 LOOP
        DBMS_OUTPUT.PUT_LINE ('i = '||i);
        <<inner_loop>>
        FOR j IN 1..2 LOOP
            DBMS_OUTPUT.PUT_LINE ('j = '||j);
        END LOOP inner_loop;
    END LOOP outer_loop;
END;
```

**LAB
8.4**

For both outer and inner loops, the statement END LOOP must be used. If the loop label is added to each END LOOP statement, it becomes easier to understand which loop is being terminated.

Loop labels can also be used when referencing loop counters.

■ *FOR EXAMPLE*

```
BEGIN
    <<outer>>
    FOR v_counter IN 1..3 LOOP
        <<inner>>
        FOR v_counter IN 1..2 LOOP
            DBMS_OUTPUT.PUT_LINE ('outer.v_counter '||
                outer.v_counter);
            DBMS_OUTPUT.PUT_LINE ('inner.v_counter '||
                inner.v_counter);
        END LOOP inner;
    END LOOP outer;
END;
```

In this example, both the inner and outer loops use the same loop counter, v_counter. In order to reference both the outer and inner values of v_counter, loop labels are used. This example produces the following output:

```
outer.v_counter 1
inner.v_counter 1
outer.v_counter 1
inner.v_counter 2
outer.v_counter 2
```

```
inner.v_counter 1
outer.v_counter 2
inner.v_counter 2
outer.v_counter 3
inner.v_counter 1
outer.v_counter 3
inner.v_counter 2
```

PL/SQL procedure successfully completed.

Your program is able to differentiate between two variables having the same name because loop labels are used when the variables are referenced. If no loop labels are used when v_counter is referenced, the output produced by this script will change significantly. Basically, once control is passed to the inner loop, the value of v_counter from the outer loop is unavailable. When control is passed back to the outer loop, the value of v_counter becomes available again.

In this example, the same name for two different loop counters is used to demonstrate another use of loop labels. However, it is not considered a good programming practice to use the same name for different variables.

LAB 8.4 EXERCISES

8.4.1 USE NESTED LOOPS

In this exercise, you will use nested numeric FOR loops.

Create the following PL/SQL script:

```
-- ch08_6a.sql, version 1.0
SET SERVEROUTPUT ON
DECLARE
   v_test NUMBER := 0;
BEGIN
   <<outer_loop>>
   FOR i IN 1..3 LOOP
      DBMS_OUTPUT.PUT_LINE('Outer Loop');
      DBMS_OUTPUT.PUT_LINE('i = '||i);
      DBMS_OUTPUT.PUT_LINE('v_test = '||v_test);
      v_test := v_test + 1;

      <<inner_loop>>
      FOR j IN 1..2 LOOP
         DBMS_OUTPUT.PUT_LINE('Inner Loop');
         DBMS_OUTPUT.PUT_LINE('j = '||j);
         DBMS_OUTPUT.PUT_LINE('i = '||i);
         DBMS_OUTPUT.PUT_LINE('v_test = '||v_test);
```

```
        END LOOP inner_loop;
    END LOOP outer_loop;
END;
```

Execute the script, and then answer the following questions:

a) What output was printed on the screen?

b) How many times was the outer loop executed?

c) How many times was the inner loop executed?

d) What are the values of the loop counters, i and j, after both loops terminate?

e) Rewrite this script using the REVERSE option for both loops. How many times will each loop be executed in this case?

LAB 8.4 EXERCISE ANSWERS

This section gives you some suggested answers to the questions in Lab 8.4, with discussion related to how those answers resulted. The most important thing to realize is whether your answer works. You should figure out the implications of the answers here and what the effects are from any different answers you may come up with.

8.4.1 ANSWERS

a) What output was printed on the screen?

Answer: Your output should look like the following:

```
Outer Loop
i = 1
v_test = 0
Inner Loop
j = 1
```

```
i = 1
v_test = 1
Inner Loop
j = 2
i = 1
v_test = 1
Outer Loop
i = 2
v_test = 1
Inner Loop
j = 1
i = 2
v_test = 2
Inner Loop
j = 2
i = 2
v_test = 2
Outer Loop
i = 3
v_test = 2
Inner Loop
j = 1
i = 3
v_test = 3
Inner Loop
j = 2
i = 3
v_test = 3
```

PL/SQL procedure successfully completed.

Every time the outer loop is run, the value of the loop counter is incremented by 1 implicitly and displayed on the screen. In addition, the value of v_test is displayed on the screen and is incremented by 1, as well. Next, control is passed to the inner loop.

Every time the inner loop is run, the value of the inner loop counter is incremented by 1 and displayed on the screen, along with the value of the outer loop counter and the variable v_test.

b) How many times was the outer loop executed?

Answer:The outer loop was executed three times, according to the range specified by the lower limit and the upper limit of the loop. In this example, the lower limit is equal to 1, and the upper limit is equal to 3.

c) How many times was the inner loop executed?

Answer:The inner loop was executed six times.

For each iteration of the outer loop, the inner loop was executed twice. However, the outer loop was executed three times. Overall, the inner loop was executed six times.

d) What are the values of the loop counters, i and j, after both loops terminate?

Answer: After both loops terminate, both loop counters are undefined again and can hold no values. As mentioned earlier, the loop counter ceases to exist once the numeric FOR loop is terminated.

e) Rewrite this script using the REVERSE option for both loops. How many times will each loop be executed in this case?

Answer: Your script should be similar to the script below. Changes are shown in bold letters.

The outer loop will execute three times, and the inner loop will execute six times.

```
-- ch08_6b.sql, version 2.0
SET SERVEROUTPUT ON
DECLARE
   v_test NUMBER := 0;
BEGIN
   <<outer_loop>>
   FOR i IN REVERSE 1..3 LOOP
      DBMS_OUTPUT.PUT_LINE('Outer Loop');
      DBMS_OUTPUT.PUT_LINE('i = '||i);
      DBMS_OUTPUT.PUT_LINE('v_test = '||v_test);
      v_test := v_test + 1;

      <<inner_loop>>
      FOR j IN REVERSE 1..2 LOOP
         DBMS_OUTPUT.PUT_LINE('Inner Loop');
         DBMS_OUTPUT.PUT_LINE('j = '||j);
         DBMS_OUTPUT.PUT_LINE('i = '||i);
         DBMS_OUTPUT.PUT_LINE('v_test = '||v_test);
      END LOOP inner_loop;
   END LOOP outer_loop;
END;
```

This script produces the following output:

```
Outer Loop
i = 3
v_test = 0
Inner Loop
j = 2
i = 3
v_test = 1
```

```
Inner Loop
j = 1
i = 3
v_test = 1
Outer Loop
i = 2
v_test = 1
Inner Loop
j = 2
i = 2
v_test = 2
Inner Loop
j = 1
i = 2
v_test = 2
Outer Loop
i = 1
v_test = 2
Inner Loop
j = 2
i = 1
v_test = 3
Inner Loop
j = 1
i = 1
v_test = 3
```

```
PL/SQL procedure successfully completed.
```

Notice that the output produced by this example has changed significantly from the output in the previous example. The values of the loop counters are decremented because the REVERSE option is used. However, the value of the variable v_test was not affected by using the REVERSE option.

LAB 8.4 SELF-REVIEW QUESTIONS

In order to test your progress, you should be able to answer the following questions.

1) What types of PL/SQL loop can be nested one inside another?

a) _____ A simple loop can only be nested inside WHILE loop.
b) _____ A WHILE loop can only be nested inside simple loop.
c) _____ Any loop can be nested inside another loop.

2) When nested loops are used, you must use loop labels.

a) _____ True
b) _____ False

3) When a loop label is defined, you must use it with an END LOOP statement.

a) _____ True
b) _____ False

4) When nested loops are used, it is recommended that you use the same name for the loop counters.

a) _____ True
b) _____ False

5) If the loop label is defined, you must use it when the loop counter is referenced.

a) _____ True
b) _____ False

Answers appear in Appendix A, Section 8.4.

CHAPTER 8

TEST YOUR THINKING

In this chapter you learned about simple loops, WHILE loops, and numeric FOR loops. You also learned that all these loops can be nested one inside another. Here are some projects that will help you test the depth of your understanding:

1) Rewrite script ch08_1a.sql using a WHILE loop instead of a simple loop. Make sure that the output produced by this script does not differ from the output produced by the script ch08_1a.sql.
2) Rewrite script ch08_4a.sql using a simple loop instead of a numeric FOR loop. Make sure that the output produced by this script does not differ from the output produced by the script ch08_4a.sql.
3) Rewrite script ch08_6a.sql. A simple loop should be used as the outer loop, and a WHILE loop should be used as the inner loop.

The projects in this section are meant to have you utilize all of the skills that you have acquired throughout this chapter. The answers to these projects can be found in Appendix D and at the companion Web site to this book, located at http://www .phptr.com/rosenzweig2e. Visit the Web site periodically to share and discuss your answers.

C H A P T E R 9

INTRODUCTION TO CURSORS

C ursors are memory areas that allow you to allocate an area of memory and access the information retrieved from a SQL statement. For example, you use a cursor to operate on all the rows of the STUDENT table for those students taking a particular course (having associated entries in the ENROLLMENT table). In this chapter, you will learn to declare an explicit cursor that enables a user to process many rows returned by a query and allows the user to write code that will process each row one at a time.

L A B   9 . 1

CURSOR MANIPULATION

LAB OBJECTIVES

After this Lab, you will be able to:

✔ Make Use of Record Types
✔ Process an Explicit Cursor
✔ Make Use of Cursor Attributes
✔ Put It All Together

In order for Oracle to process an SQL statement, it needs to create an area of memory known as the context area; this will have the information needed to process the statement. This information includes the number of rows processed by the statement, a pointer to the parsed representation of the statement (parsing an SQL statement is the process whereby information is transferred to the server, at which point the SQL statement is evaluated as being valid). In a query, the active set refers to the rows that will be returned.

A cursor is a handle, or pointer, to the context area. Through the cursor, a PL/SQL program can control the context area and what happens to it as the statement is processed. Two important features about the cursor are as follows:

1. Cursors allow you to fetch and process rows returned by a SELECT statement, one row at a time.
2. A cursor is named so that it can be referenced.

TYPES OF CURSORS

There are two types of cursors:

1. An *implicit* cursor is automatically declared by Oracle every time an SQL statement is executed. The user will not be aware of this happening and will not be able to control or process the information in an implicit cursor.

2. An *explicit* cursor is defined by the program for any query that returns more than one row of data. That means the programmer has declared the cursor within the PL/SQL code block. This declaration allows for the application to sequentially process each row of data as it is returned by the cursor.

IMPLICIT CURSOR

In order to better understand the capabilities of an explicit cursor, you first need to run through the process of an implicit cursor. The process is as follows:

- Any given PL/SQL block issues an implicit cursor whenever an SQL statement is executed, as long as an explicit cursors does not exist for that SQL statement.
- A cursor is automatically associated with every DML (Data Manipulation) statement (UPDATE, DELETE, INSERT).
- All UPDATE and DELETE statements have cursors that identify the set of rows that will be affected by the operation.
- An INSERT statement needs a place to receive the data that is to be inserted in the database; the implicit cursor fulfills this need.
- The most recently opened cursor is called the 'SQL%' cursor.

THE PROCESSING OF AN IMPLICIT CURSOR.   The implicit cursor is used to process INSERT, UPDATE, DELETE, and SELECT INTO statements. During the processing of an implicit cursor, Oracle automatically performs the OPEN, FETCH, and CLOSE operations.

 An implicit cursor cannot tell you how many rows were affected by an update. SQL%ROWCOUNT returns numbers of rows updated. It can be used as follows:

```
SET SERVEROUTPUT ON
BEGIN
   UPDATE student
      SET first_name = 'B'
    WHERE first_name LIKE 'B%';
   DBMS_OUTPUT.PUT_LINE(SQL%ROWCOUNT);
END;
```

Consider the following example of an implicit cursor.

■ FOR EXAMPLE

```
SET SERVEROUTPUT ON;
DECLARE
   v_first_name VARCHAR2(35);
```

```
        v_last_name VARCHAR2(35);
BEGIN
    SELECT first_name, last_name
      INTO v_first_name, v_last_name
      FROM student
     WHERE student_id = 123;
    DBMS_OUTPUT.PUT_LINE ('Student name: '||
        v_first_name||' '||v_last_name);
EXCEPTION
    WHEN NO_DATA_FOUND THEN
        DBMS_OUTPUT.PUT_LINE
        ('There is no student with student ID 123');
END;
```

It is important to note that Oracle automatically associates an implicit cursor with the SELECT INTO statement and fetches the values for the variables, v_first_name and v_last_name. Once the SELECT INTO statement completes, Oracle closes the implicit cursor.

Unlike implicit cursor, explicit cursor is defined by the program for any query that returns more than one row of data. So you need to process an explicit cursor as follows. First you declare a cursor. Next, you open earlier declared cursor. Next, you fetch earlier declared and opened cursor. Finally, you close the cursor.

EXPLICIT CURSOR

The only means of generating an explicit cursor is for the cursor to be named in the DECLARE section of the PL/SQL block.

The advantages of declaring an explicit cursor over the indirect implicit cursor are that the explicit cursor gives more programmatic control to the programmer. Implicit cursors are less efficient than explicit cursors, and thus it is harder to trap data errors.

The process of working with an explicit cursor consists of the following steps:

1. *Declaring* the cursor. This initializes the cursor into memory.
2. *Opening* the cursor. The previously declared cursor can now be opened; memory is allotted.
3. *Fetching* the cursor. Previously declared and opened cursor can now retrieve data; this is the process of fetching the cursor.
4. *Closing* the cursor. Previously declared, opened, and fetched cursor must now be closed to release memory allocation.

DECLARING A CURSOR

Declaring a cursor defines the name of the cursor and associates it with a SELECT statement. The first step is to Declare the Cursor with the following syntax:

```
CURSOR c_cursor_name IS select statement
```

The naming conventions that are used in the Oracle Interactive Series advise you always to name a cursor as c_cursorname. By using a c_ in the beginning of the name, it will always be clear to you that the name is referencing a cursor.

It is not possible to make use of a cursor unless the complete cycle of (1) declaring, (2) opening, (3) fetching, and finally (4) closing has been performed. In order to explain these four steps, the following examples will have code fragments for each step and finally will show you the complete process.

■ FOR EXAMPLE

This is a PL/SQL fragment that demonstrates the first step of declaring a cursor. A cursor named C_MyCursor is declared as a select statement of all the rows in the zipcode table that have the item state equal to 'NY'.

```
DECLARE
    CURSOR C_MyCursor IS
        SELECT *
          FROM zipcode
         WHERE state = 'NY';
    . . .
        <code would continue here with Opening, Fetching
        and closing of the cursor>
```

Cursor names follow the same rules of scope and visibility that apply to the PL/SQL identifiers. Because the name of the cursor is a PL/SQL identifier, it must be declared before it is referenced. Any valid select statement can be used to define a cursor, including joins and statements with the UNION or MINUS clause.

RECORD TYPES

A record is a composite data structure, which means that it is composed of more than one element. Records are very much like a row of a database table, but each element of the record does not stand on its own. PL/SQL supports three kinds of records: (1) table-based, (2) cursor-based, (3) programmer-defined.

A table-based record is one whose structure is drawn from the list of columns in the table. A cursor-based record is one whose structure matches the elements of a predefined cursor. To create a table-based or cursor-based record, use the %ROWTYPE attribute.

```
<record_name>    <table_name or cursor_name>%ROWTYPE
```

■ FOR EXAMPLE

```
-- ch09_1a.sql
SET SERVEROUTPUT ON
DECLARE
   vr_student student%ROWTYPE;
BEGIN
   SELECT *
     INTO vr_student
     FROM student
    WHERE student_id = 156;
   DBMS_OUTPUT.PUT_LINE (vr_student.first_name||' '
      ||vr_student.last_name||' has an ID of 156');
EXCEPTION
   WHEN no_data_found
      THEN
            RAISE_APPLICATION_ERROR(-2001,'The Student '||
               'is not in the database');
END;
```

The variable `vr_student` is a record type of the existing database table student. That is, it has the same components as a row in the student table. A cursor-based record is much the same, except that it is drawn from the select list of an explicitly declared cursors. When referencing elements of the record, you use the same syntax that you use with tables.

```
record_name.item_name
```

In order to define a variable that is based on a cursor record, the cursor must first be declared. In the following lab, you will start by declaring a cursor and then proceed with the process of opening the cursor, fetching from the cursor, and finally closing the cursor.

A table-based record is drawn from a particular table structure. Consider the following code fragment.

■ FOR EXAMPLE

```
DECLARE
   vr_zip ZIPCODE%ROWTYPE;
   vr_instructor INSTRUCTOR%ROWTYPE;
```

Record vr_zip has structure similar to a row of the ZIPCODE table. Its elements are CITY, STATE, and ZIP. It is important to note that if CITY column of the ZIPCODE table has been defined as VARCHAR2(15), the attribute CITY of the vr_zip record will have the same datatype structure. Similarly, record vr_instructor is based on the row of the INSTRUCTOR table.

LAB 9.1 EXERCISES

9.1.1 MAKE USE OF RECORD TYPES

Here is an example of a record type in an anonymous PL/SQL block.

■ *FOR EXAMPLE*

```
SET SERVEROUTPUT ON;
DECLARE
 vr_zip ZIPCODE%ROWTYPE;
BEGIN
    SELECT *
      INTO vr_zip
      FROM zipcode
     WHERE rownum < 2;
    DBMS_OUTPUT.PUT_LINE('City: '||vr_zip.city);
    DBMS_OUTPUT.PUT_LINE('State: '||vr_zip.state);
    DBMS_OUTPUT.PUT_LINE('Zip: '||vr_zip.zip);
END;
```

a) What will happen when the preceding example is run in a SQL*Plus session?

A cursor-based record is based on the list of elements of a predefined cursor.

b) Explain how the record type vr_student_name is being used in the following example.

■ *FOR EXAMPLE*

```
DECLARE
    CURSOR c_student_name IS
        SELECT first_name, last_name
          FROM student;
    vr_student_name c_student_name%ROWTYPE;
```

In the next Lab you will learn how to process an explicit cursor. Afterward you will address record types within that process.

9.1.2 PROCESS AN EXPLICIT CURSOR

a) Write the declarative section of a PL/SQL block that defines a cursor named c_student, based on the student table with the last_name and the first_name concatenated into one item called name and leaving out the created_by and modified_by columns. Then declare a record based on this cursor.

OPENING A CURSOR

The next step in controlling an explicit cursor is to open it. When the Open cursor statement is processed, the following four actions will take place automatically:

1. The variables (including bind variables) in the WHERE clause are examined.
2. Based on the values of the variables, the active set is determined and the PL/SQL engine executes the query for that cursor. Variables are examined at cursor open time only.
3. The PL/SQL engine identifies the active set of data—the rows from all involved tables that meet the WHERE clause criteria.
4. The active set pointer is set to the first row.

The syntax for opening a cursor is

```
OPEN cursor_name;
```

A pointer into the active set is also established at the cursor open time. The pointer determines which row is the next to be fetched by the cursor. More than one cursor can be open at a time.

b) Add the necessary lines to the PL/SQL block that you just wrote to open the cursor.

FETCHING ROWS IN A CURSOR

After the cursor has been declared and opened, you can then retrieve data from the cursor. The process of getting the data from the cursor is referred to as fetching the cursor. There are two methods of fetching a cursor, done with the following command:

```
FETCH cursor_name INTO PL/SQL variables;
```

or

```
FETCH cursor_name INTO PL/SQL record;
```

When the cursor is fetched, the following occurs:

1. The fetch command is used to retrieve one row at a time from the active set. This is generally done inside a loop. The values of each row in the active set can then be stored into the corresponding variables or PL/SQL record one at a time, performing operations on each one successively.

2. After each FETCH, the active set pointer is moved forward to the next row. Thus, each fetch will return successive rows of the active set, until the entire set is returned. The last FETCH will not assign values to the output variables; they will still contain their prior values.

■ FOR EXAMPLE

```
-- ch09_2a.sql
SET SERVEROUTPUT ON
DECLARE
    CURSOR c_zip IS
        SELECT *
          FROM zipcode;
    vr_zip c_zip%ROWTYPE;
BEGIN
    OPEN c_zip;
    LOOP
        FETCH c_zip INTO vr_zip;
        EXIT WHEN c_zip%NOTFOUND;
        DBMS_OUTPUT.PUT_LINE(vr_zip.zip||
            ' '||vr_zip.city||' '||vr_zip.state);
    END LOOP;
END;
```

The lines in italics have not yet been covered but are essential for the code to run correctly. They will be explained later in this chapter.

c) In Chapter 3 you learned how to construct a loop. For the PL/SQL block that you have been writing, add a loop. Inside the loop

FETCH the cursor into the record. Include a DBMS_OUTPUT line inside the loop so that each time the loop iterates, all the information in the record is displayed in a SQL*Plus session.

CLOSING A CURSOR

Once all of the rows in the cursor have been processed (retrieved), the cursor should be closed. This tells the PL/SQL engine that the program is finished with the cursor, and the resources associated with it can be freed. The syntax for closing the cursor is

```
CLOSE cursor_name;
```

Once a cursor is closed, it is no longer valid to fetch from it. Likewise, it is not possible to close an already closed cursor (either one will result in an Oracle error).

d) Continue with the code you have developed by adding a close statement to the cursor. Is your code complete now?

Next, consider another example.

■ FOR EXAMPLE

```
SET SERVEROUTPUT ON;
DECLARE
    CURSOR c_student_name IS
        SELECT first_name, last_name
          FROM student
         WHERE rownum <= 5;
    vr_student_name c_student_name%ROWTYPE;
BEGIN
    OPEN c_student_name;
    LOOP
        FETCH c_student_name INTO vr_student_name;
        EXIT WHEN c_student_name%NOTFOUND;
        DBMS_OUTPUT.PUT_LINE('Student name: '||
            vr_student_name.first_name||'
            '||vr_student_name.last_name);
    END LOOP;
    CLOSE c_student_name;
END;
```

e) Explain what is occurring in this PL/SQL block. What will be the output from the preceding example?

f) Next, consider the same example with single modification. Notice that the DBMS_OUTPUT.PUT_LINE statement has been moved outside the loop (shown in bold letters). Execute this example, and try to explain why this version of the script produces different output.

■ FOR EXAMPLE

```
SET SERVEROUTPUT ON;
DECLARE
    CURSOR c_student_name IS
        SELECT first_name, last_name
            FROM student
            WHERE rownum <= 5;
    vr_student_name c_student_name%ROWTYPE;
BEGIN
    OPEN c_student_name;
    LOOP
        FETCH c_student_name INTO vr_student_name;
        EXIT WHEN c_student_name%NOTFOUND;
    END LOOP;
    CLOSE c_student_name;
    DBMS_OUTPUT.PUT_LINE('Student name: '||
        vr_student_name.first_name||'
        '||vr_student_name.last_name);
END;
```

A programmer-defined record is based on the record type defined by a programmer. First you declare a record type, and next, you declare a record based on the record type defined in the previous step as follows:

```
type type_name IS RECORD
    (field_name 1 DATATYPE 1,
     field_name 2 DATATYPE 2,
     ...
     field_name N DATATYPE N);

  record_name TYPE_NAME%ROWTYPE;
```

Consider the following code fragment.

**LAB
9.1**

■ *FOR EXAMPLE*

```
SET SERVEROUTPUT ON;
DECLARE
    -- declare user-defined type
    TYPE instructor_info IS RECORD
        (instructor_id instructor.instructor_id%TYPE,
         first_name instructor.first_name%TYPE,
         last_name instructor.last_name%TYPE,
         sections NUMBER(1));
    -- declare a record based on the type defined above
    rv_instructor instructor_info;
```

In this code fragment, you define your own type, instructor_info. This type contains four attributes: instructor's ID, first and last names, and number of sections taught by this instructor. Next, you declare a record based on the type just described. As a result, this record has structure similar to the type, instructor_info. Consider the following example.

■ *FOR EXAMPLE*

```
SET SERVEROUTPUT ON;
DECLARE
    TYPE instructor_info IS RECORD
        (first_name instructor.first_name%TYPE,
         last_name instructor.last_name%TYPE,
         sections NUMBER);
    rv_instructor instructor_info;
BEGIN
    SELECT RTRIM(i.first_name),
           RTRIM(i.last_name), COUNT(*)
      INTO rv_instructor
      FROM instructor i, section s
     WHERE i.instructor_id = s.instructor_id
       AND i.instructor_id = 102
    GROUP BY i.first_name, i.last_name;
    DBMS_OUTPUT.PUT_LINE('Instructor, '||
       rv_instructor.first_name||'
       '||rv_instructor.last_name||
         ', teaches '||rv_instructor.sections||'
           section(s)');
EXCEPTION
    WHEN NO_DATA_FOUND THEN
        DBMS_OUTPUT.PUT_LINE
            ('There is no such instructor');
END;
```

g) Explain what is declared in the previous example. Describe what is happening to the record and explain how this results in the output.

9.1.3 MAKE USE OF CURSOR ATTRIBUTES

Table 9.1 lists the attributes of a cursor, which are used to determine the result of a cursor operation when *fetched* or *opened*.

a) Now that you know cursor attributes, you can use one of these to exit the loop within the code you developed in the previous example. Are you able to make a fully executable block now? If not, explain why.

Cursor attributes can be used with implicit cursors by using the prefix SQL, for example, SQL%ROWCOUNT.

If you use a SELECT INTO syntax in your PL/SQL block, you will be creating an implicit cursor. You can then use these attributes on the implicit cursor.

■ *FOR EXAMPLE*

```
-- ch09_3a.sql
SET SERVEROUTPUT ON
DECLARE
    v_city zipcode.city%type;
BEGIN
    SELECT city
```

Table 9.1 ■ Explicit Cursor Attributes

Cursor Attribute	Syntax	Explanation
%NOTFOUND	cursor_name%NOTFOUND	A Boolean attribute that returns TRUE if the previous FETCH did not return a row, and FALSE if it did.
%FOUND	cursor_name%FOUND	A Boolean attribute that returns TRUE if the previous FETCH returned a row, and FALSE if it did not.
%ROWCOUNT	cursor_name%ROWCOUNT	# of records fetched from a cursor at that point in time.
%ISOPEN	Cursor_name%ISOPEN	A Boolean attribute that returns TRUE if cursor is open, FALSE if it is not.

```
        INTO v_city
        FROM zipcode
       WHERE zip = 07002;
    IF SQL%ROWCOUNT = 1
    THEN
       DBMS_OUTPUT.PUT_LINE(v_city ||' has a '||
          'zipcode of 07002');
    ELSIF SQL%ROWCOUNT = 0
    THEN
       DBMS_OUTPUT.PUT_LINE('The zipcode 07002 is '||
          ' not in the database');
    ELSE
       DBMS_OUTPUT.PUT_LINE('Stop harassing me');
    END IF;
END;
```

b) What will happen if this code is run? Describe what is happening in each phase of the example.

c) Rerun this block, changing 07002 to 99999. What do you think will happen? Explain.

d) Now, try running this file. Did it run as you expected? Why or why not? What could be done to improve the way it handles a possible error condition?

9.1.4 PUT IT ALL TOGETHER

Here is an example of the complete cycle of declaring, opening, fetching, and closing a cursor, including use of cursor attributes.

```
-- ch09_4a.sql
1> DECLARE
2>    v_sid        student.student_id%TYPE;
3>    CURSOR c_student IS
4>       SELECT student_id
5>          FROM student
6>          WHERE student_id < 110;
7> BEGIN
8>    OPEN c_student;
9>    LOOP
10>       FETCH c_student INTO v_sid;
```

```
11>        EXIT WHEN c_student%NOTFOUND;
12>            DBMS_OUTPUT.PUT_LINE('STUDENT ID : '||v_sid);
13>     END LOOP;
14>     CLOSE c_student;
15> EXCEPTION
16>    WHEN OTHERS
17>    THEN
18>        IF c_student%ISOPEN
19>        THEN
20>            CLOSE c_student;
21>        END IF;
22> END;
```

a) Describe what is happening in each phase of example
ch09_4a.sql. Use the line numbers to reference the example.

b) Modify the example to make use of the cursor attributes
%FOUND and %ROWCOUNT.

c) Fetch a cursor that has a data from the student table into a
%ROWTYPE. Only select students with a student_id under
110. The columns are the STUDENT_ID, LAST_NAME,
FIRST_NAME, and a count of the number of classes they are
enrolled in (using the enrollment table). Fetch the cursor with a
loop and then output all the columns. You will have to use an
alias for the enrollment count.

LAB 9.1 EXERCISE ANSWERS

a) What will happen when the preceding example is run in a SQL*Plus session?

*Answer: In this example, you select a single row for the ZIPCODE table into vr_zip
record. Next, you display each element of the record on the screen. Notice that in order
to reference each attribute of the record, dot notation is used. When run, the example
produces the following output:*

```
City: Santurce
State: PR
```

```
Zip: 00914
PL/SQL procedure successfully completed.
```

b) Explain how the record type vr_student_name is being used in the following example.

Answer: Record `vr_student_name` *has structure similar to a row returned by the SELECT statement defined in the cursor. It contains two attributes, student's first and last names.*

It is important to note that a cursor-based record can be declared only after its corresponding cursor has been declared; otherwise, a compilation error will occur.

9.1.2 ANSWERS

a) Write the declarative section of a PL/SQL block that defines a cursor named c_student based on the student table with the last_name and the first_name concatenated into one item called name and leaving out the created_by and modified_by columns. Then declare a record based on this cursor.

Answer:

```
DECLARE
    CURSOR c_student is
        SELECT first_name||'   '||Last_name name
            FROM student;
    vr_student c_student%ROWTYPE;
```

b) Add the necessary lines to the PL/SQL block that you just wrote to open the cursor.

Answer: The following lines should be added to the lines in a).

```
BEGIN
    OPEN c_student;
```

c) In Chapter 3 you learned how to construct a loop. For the PL/SQL block that you have been writing, add a loop. Inside the loop FETCH the cursor into the record. Include a DBMS_OUTPUT line inside the loop so that each time the loop iterates, all the information in the record is displayed in a SQL*Plus session.

Answer: The following lines should be added:

```
LOOP
    FETCH c_student INTO vr_student;
    DBMS_OUTPUT.PUT_LINE(vr_student.name);
```

d) Continue with the code you have developed by adding a close statement to the cursor. Is your code complete now?

Answer:The following lines should be added:

```
CLOSE c_student;
```

The code is not complete since there is not a proper way to exit the loop.

e) Explain what is occurring in this PL/SQL block. What will be the output from the preceding example?

Answer: In this example, you declare a cursor that returns five student names. Next, you declare a cursor-based record. In the body of the program you process explicit cursors via the cursor loop. In the body of the loop, you assign each record returned by the cursor to the cursor-based record, `vr_student_name`. *Next, you display its contents on the screen. When run, the example produces the following output:*

```
Student name: George Eakheit
Student name: Leonard Millstein
Student name: Austin V. Cadet
Student name: Tamara Zapulla
Student name: Jenny Goldsmith
PL/SQL procedure successfully completed.
```

f) Next, consider the same example with single modification. Notice that the DBMS_OUTPUT.PUT_LINE statement has been moved outside the loop (shown in bold letters). Execute this example, and try to explain why this version of the script produces different output.

Answer:The DBMS_OUTPUT.PUT_LINE has been moved outside the loop. First the loop will process the five student records. The values for each record will be placed in the record vr_student_name, but each time the loop iterates it will replace the value in the record with a new value. When the five iterations of the loop are finished, it will exit because of the EXIT WHEN condition, leaving the vr_student_name record with the last value that was in the cursor. This is the only value that will be displayed via the DBMS_OUTPUT.PUT_LINE, which comes after the loop is closed.

g) Explain what is declared in the previous example. Describe what is happening to the record and explain how this results in the output.

Answer: In this example, you declare a record called `vr_instructor`. *This record is based on the type you defined previously. In the body of the PL/SQL block, you initialize this record with the help of the SELECT INTO statement, and display its value on the screen. It is important to note that the columns of the SELECT INTO statement are listed in the same order the attributes are defined in* `instructor_info` *type. So there is no need to use dot notation for this record initialization. When run, this example produces the following output:*

```
Instructor, Tom Wojick, teaches 9 section(s)
PL/SQL procedure successfully completed.
```

9.1.3 ANSWERS

a) Now that you know cursor attributes, you can use one of these to exit the loop within the code you developed in the previous example. Are you able to make a fully executable block now? If not, explain why.

Answer: You can make use of attribute %NOTFOUND to close the loop. It would also be a wise idea to add an exception clause to the end of the block to close the cursor if it is still open. If you add the following statements to the end of your block, it will be complete.

```
      EXIT WHEN c_student%NOTFOUND;
   END LOOP;
   CLOSE c_student;
EXCEPTION
   WHEN OTHERS
   THEN
      IF c_student%ISOPEN
      THEN
         CLOSE c_student;
      END IF;
END;
```

b) What will happen if this code is run? Describe what is happening in each phase of the example.

Answer: The PL/SQL block ch09_3a would display the following output:

```
Bayonne has a zipcode of 07002
PL/SQL procedure successfully completed.
```

The declaration section declares a variable, v_city, anchored to the datatype of the city item in the zipcode table. The SELECT statement causes an implicit cursor to be opened, fetched, and then closed. The IF clause makes use of the attribute %ROWCOUNT to determine if the implicit cursor has a rowcount of 1 or not. If it does have a row count of 1, then the first DBMS_OUTPUT line will be displayed. You should notice that this example does not handle a situation where the rowcount is greater than 1. Since the zipcode table's primary key is the zipcode, this could happen.

c) Rerun this block changing 07002 to 99999. What do you think will happen? Explain.

Answer:The PL/SQL block would display the following:

```
DECLARE
ERROR at line 1:
ORA-01403: no data found
ORA-06512: at line 4
```

A select statement in a PL/SQL block that does not return any rows will raise a no data found exception. Since there was no exception handler, the preceding error would be displayed.

d) Now, try running this file. Did it run as you expected? Why or why not? What could be done to improve the way it handles a possible error condition?

Answer:You may have expected the second and third condition of the IF statement to capture the instance of a %ROWCOUNT equal to 0. Now that you understand that a SELECT statement that returns no rows will raise a NO_DATA_FOUND exception, it would be a good idea to handle this by adding a <%WHEN NO_DATA_FOUND> exception to the existing block.You can add a %ROWCOUNT in the exception, either to display the rowcount in a DBMS_OUTPUT or to put an IF statement to display various possibilities.

9.1.4 ANSWERS

a) Describe what is happening in each phase of example `ch09_4a.sql`. Use the line numbers to reference the example.

Answer:The example illustrates a cursor fetch loop, in which multiple rows of data are returned from the query.The cursor is declared in the declaration section of the block (1–6) just like other identifiers. In the executable section of the block (7–15), a cursor is opened using the OPEN (8) statement. Because the cursor returns multiple rows, a loop is used to assign returned data to the variables with a FETCH statement (10). Because the loop statement has no other means of termination, there must be an exit condition specified. In this case, one of the attributes for the cursor is %NOTFOUND (12).The cursor is then closed to free the memory allocation (14).Additionally, if the exception handler is called, there is a check to see if the cursor is open (18) and if it is closed (20).

b) Modify the example to make use of the cursor attributes %FOUND and %ROWCOUNT.

Answer:Your modification should look like this:

```
-- ch09_5a.sql
SET SERVEROUTPUT ON
DECLARE
    v_sid        student.student_id%TYPE;
    CURSOR c_student IS
```

```
               SELECT student_id
                 FROM student
                WHERE student_id < 110;
       BEGIN
          OPEN c_student;
          LOOP
            FETCH c_student INTO v_sid;
            IF c_student%FOUND THEN
            DBMS_OUTPUT.PUT_LINE
              ('Just FETCHED row '
                 ||TO_CHAR(c_student%ROWCOUNT)||
                 ' Student ID: '||v_sid);
            ELSE
               EXIT;
            END IF;
          END LOOP;
          CLOSE c_student;
       EXCEPTION
          WHEN OTHERS
          THEN
             IF c_student%ISOPEN
             THEN
                CLOSE c_student;
             END IF;
       END;
```

There has been a modification to the loop structure. Instead of having an exit condition, an IF statement is being used. The IF statement is making use of the cursor attribute %FOUND. This attribute returns true when a row has been "found" in the cursor and false when it has not. The next attribute %ROWCOUNT returns a number, which is the current row number of the cursor.

c) Fetch a cursor that has a data from the Student table into a %ROWTYPE. Only select students with a STUDENT_ID under 110. The columns are the STUDENT_ID, LAST_NAME, FIRST_NAME, and a count of the number of classes each student is enrolled in (using the ENROLLMENT table). Fetch the cursor with a loop and then output all the columns. You will have to use an alias for the enrollment count.

Answer: One method of doing this would be as follows:

```
-- ch09_6a.sql
SET SERVEROUTPUT ON
DECLARE
   CURSOR c_student_enroll IS
      SELECT s.student_id, first_name, last_name,
             COUNT(*) enroll,
             (CASE
```

```
                WHEN count(*) = 1 Then ' class.'
                WHEN count(*) is null then
                            ' no classes.'
            ELSE ' classes.'
        END) class
    FROM student s, enrollment e
   WHERE s.student_id = e.student_id
     AND s.student_id <110
   GROUP BY s.student_id, first_name, last_name;
  r_student_enroll     c_student_enroll%ROWTYPE;
BEGIN
   OPEN c_student_enroll;
   LOOP
      FETCH c_student_enroll INTO r_student_enroll;
      EXIT WHEN c_student_enroll%NOTFOUND;
      DBMS_OUTPUT.PUT_LINE('Student INFO: ID '||
         r_student_enroll.student_id||' is '||
         r_student_enroll.first_name|| ' ' ||
         r_student_enroll.last_name||
         ' is enrolled in '||r_student_enroll.enroll||
         r_student_enroll.class);
   END LOOP;
   CLOSE c_student_enroll;
EXCEPTION
   WHEN OTHERS
   THEN
    IF c_student_enroll %ISOPEN
      THEN
    CLOSE c_student_enroll;
    END IF;
END;
```

Remember that the CASE syntax was introduced in Oracle 9i. This means that the previous statement will not run in Oracle 8 or 8i. You can change the CASE statement to a DECODE statement as follows:
```
DECODE( count(*), 1, ' class. ', null, ' no
classes.', 'classes') class
```

In the declarative section, a cursor c_student_enroll *is defined as well as a record, which is the type of a row of the cursor. The cursor loop structure makes use of an exit condition with the %NOTFOUND cursor attribute. When there are no more rows, the %NOTFOUND will be false and will cause the loop to exit. While the cursor is open and loop is processing, it will fetch a row of the cursor in a record one at a time. The DBMS output will cause each row to be displayed to the screen. Finally, the cursor is closed, and an exception clause will also close the cursor if any error is raised.*

Assorted Tips on Cursors

Cursor SELECT LIST

Match the Select list with PL/SQL variables or PL/SQL record components.

The number of variables must be equal to the number of columns or expressions in the Select list. The number of the components of a record must match the columns or expressions in the Select list.

Cursor Scope

The scope of a cursor declared in the main block (or an enclosing block) extends to the sub-blocks.

Expressions in a Cursor SELECT List

PL/SQL variables, expressions, and even functions can be included in the Cursor Select list.

Column Aliases in Cursors

An alternative name you provide to a column or expression in the Select list.

In an Explicit cursor column, aliases are required for calculated columns when

- You FETCH into a record declared with %ROWTYPE declaration against that cursor
- You want to reference the calculated column in the program

LAB 9.1 SELF-REVIEW QUESTIONS

In order to test your progress, you should be able to answer the following questions.

1) Implicit cursors are the only way to fetch and manage data from the database.

   a) _____ True
   b) _____ False

2) What are cursor attributes used for?

   a) _____ Controlling cursors
   b) _____ Populating cursors
   c) _____ Ordering pizza
   d) _____ Closing cursors

3) Number the following steps in processing a cursor.

  a) _____ Fetch
  b) _____ Declare
  c) _____ Close
  d) _____ Open
  e) _____ Dance

4) What is the difference between an implicit and an explicit cursor?

  a) _____ An implicit cursor is easier to manage.
  b) _____ Cursor attributes can only be used on explicit cursors.
  c) _____ It is easier to trap errors with implicit cursors.
  d) _____ Explicit cursors give the programmer greater control.

5) What must be done to place a cursor in memory?

  a) _____ It must be fetched.
  b) _____ It must be pinned.
  c) _____ It must be memorized verbatim.
  d) _____ It must be declared.

Answers appear in Appendix A, Section 9.1.

LAB 9.2

USING CURSOR FOR LOOPS AND NESTING CURSORS

LAB OBJECTIVES

After this Lab, you will be able to:

✔ Use a Cursor FOR Loop
✔ Process Nested Cursors

There is an alternative method of handling cursors. It is called the cursor FOR loop because of the simplified syntax that is used. When using the cursor FOR loop, the process of opening, fetching, and closing is handled implicitly. This makes the blocks much simpler to code and easier to maintain.

The cursor FOR loop specifies a sequence of statements to be repeated once for each row returned by the cursor. Use the cursor FOR loop if you need to FETCH and PROCESS each and every record from a cursor.

■ FOR EXAMPLE

Assume the existence of a table called log with one column.

```
create table table_log
       (description VARCHAR2(250));
-- ch09_7a.sql
DECLARE
   CURSOR c_student IS
       SELECT student_id, last_name, first_name
         FROM student
        WHERE student_id < 110;
BEGIN
   FOR r_student IN c_student
```

```
        LOOP
            INSERT INTO table_log
                VALUES(r_student.last_name);
        END LOOP;
    END;
```

LAB 9.2 EXERCISES

9.2.1 USE A CURSOR FOR LOOP

a) Write a PL/SQL block that will reduce the cost of all courses by 5% for courses having an enrollment of eight students or more. Use a cursor FOR loop that will update the course table.

9.2.2 PROCESS NESTED CURSORS

Cursors can be nested inside each other. Although this may sound complex, it is really just a loop inside a loop, much like nested loops, which were covered in the previous chapter. If you had one parent cursor and two child cursors, then each time the parent cursor makes a single loop, it will loop through each child cursor once and then begin a second round. In the following two examples, you will encounter a nested cursor with a single child cursor.

■ FOR EXAMPLE

```
SET SERVEROUTPUT ON
-- ch09_8a.sql
 1    DECLARE
 2        v_zip zipcode.zip%TYPE;
 3        v_student_flag CHAR;
 4        CURSOR c_zip IS
 5            SELECT zip, city, state
 6              FROM zipcode
 7             WHERE state = 'CT';
 8        CURSOR c_student IS
 9            SELECT first_name, last_name
10              FROM student
11             WHERE zip = v_zip;
12    BEGIN
13        FOR r_zip IN c_zip
14        LOOP
15            v_student_flag := 'N';
```

```
16              v_zip := r_zip.zip;
17              DBMS_OUTPUT.PUT_LINE(CHR(10));
18              DBMS_OUTPUT.PUT_LINE('Students living in '||
19                  r_zip.city);
20              FOR r_student in c_student
21              LOOP
22                 DBMS_OUTPUT.PUT_LINE(
23                     r_student.first_name||
24                     ' '||r_student.last_name);
25                 v_student_flag := 'Y';
26              END LOOP;
27              IF v_student_flag = 'N'
28                 THEN
29                 DBMS_OUTPUT.PUT_LINE
                        ('No Students for this zipcode');
30              END IF;
31          END LOOP;
32   END;
```

There are two cursors in this example. The first is a cursor of the zipcodes, and the second cursor is a list of students. The variable `v_zip` is initialized in line 16 to be the zipcode of the current record of the `c_zip` cursor. The `c_student` cursor ties in the `c_zip` cursor by means of this variable. Thus, when the cursor is processed in lines 20–26, it is retrieving students who have the zipcode of the current record for the parent cursor. The parent cursor is processed from lines 13–31. Each iteration of the parent cursor will only execute the DBMS_OUTPUT in lines 16 and 17 once. The DBMS_OUTPUT in line 22 will be executed once for each iteration of the child loop, producing a line of output for each student. The DBMS statement in line 29 will only execute if the inner loop did not execute. This was accomplished by setting a variable `v_student_flag`. The variable is set to N in the beginning of the parent loop. If the child loop executes at least once, the variable will be set to Y. After the child loop has closed, a check is made with an IF statement to determine the value of the variable. If it is still N, then it can be safely concluded that the inner loop did not process. This will then allow the last DBMS statement to execute. Nested cursors are more often parameterized. You will see parameters in cursors explained in depth in Lab 8.3, "Using Parameters in Cursors."

a) Write a PL/SQL block with two cursor FOR loops. The parent cursor will call the `student_id`, `first_name`, and `last_name` from the student table for students with a `student_id` less than 110 and output one line with this information. For each student, the child cursor will loop through

all the courses that the student is enrolled in, outputting the
`course_no` and the description.

The following is an example of a nested cursor. Review the code.

■ *FOR EXAMPLE*

```
SET SERVEROUTPUT ON
-- ch09_9a.sql
DECLARE
    v_amount course.cost%TYPE;
    v_instructor_id  instructor.instructor_id%TYPE;
    CURSOR c_inst IS
        SELECT first_name, last_name, instructor_id
          FROM instructor;
    CURSOR c_cost IS
        SELECT c.cost
          FROM course c, section s, enrollment e
         WHERE s.instructor_id = v_instructor_id
           AND c.course_no = s.course_no
           AND s.section_id = e.section_id;
BEGIN
    FOR r_inst IN c_inst
    LOOP
        v_instructor_id := r_inst.instructor_id;
        v_amount := 0;
        DBMS_OUTPUT.PUT_LINE(
            'Amount generated by instructor '||
            r_inst.first_name||' '||r_inst.last_name
            ||' is');
        FOR r_cost IN c_cost
        LOOP
            v_amount := v_amount + NVL(r_cost.cost, 0);
        END LOOP;
        DBMS_OUTPUT.PUT_LINE
        ('       '||TO_CHAR(v_amount,'$999,999'));
    END LOOP;
END;
```

b) Before you run the preceding code, analyze what it is doing and
determine what you think the result would be. Explain what is
happening in each phase of the PL/SQL block and what is happening to the variables as control is passing through parent and
child cursor.

c) Run the code and see what the result is. Is it what you expected? Explain the difference.

LAB 9.2 EXERCISE ANSWERS

9.2.1 ANSWERS

a) Write a PL/SQL block that will reduce the cost of all courses by 5% for courses having an enrollment of eight students or more. Use a cursor FOR loop that will update the course table.

Answer: Your block should look like this:

```
-- ch09_10a.sql
DECLARE
    CURSOR c_group_discount IS
        SELECT DISTINCT s.course_no
          FROM section s, enrollment e
         WHERE s.section_id = e.section_id
           GROUP BY s.course_no, e.section_id, s.section_id
           HAVING COUNT(*)>=8;
BEGIN
    FOR r_group_discount IN c_group_discount    LOOP
        UPDATE course
           SET cost = cost * .95
           WHERE course_no = r_group_discount.course_no;
    END LOOP;
    COMMIT;
END;
```

The cursor c_group_discount *is declared in the declarative section. The proper SQL is used to generate the select statement to answer the question given. The cursor is processed in a FOR loop—in each iteration of the loop the SQL update statement will be executed. This means it does not have to be opened, fetched, and closed. Also, it means that a cursor attribute does not have to be used to create an exit condition for the loop that is processing the cursor.*

9.2.2 ANSWERS

a) Write a PL/SQL block with two cursors FOR loops. The parent cursor will call the student_id, first_name, and last_name from the student table for students with a student_id less than 110 and output one line with this information. For each student, the child cursor will loop through all the courses that the student is enrolled in, outputting the `course_no` and the description.

Answer:Your block should look be similar to this:

```
-- ch09_11a.sql
DECLARE
   v_sid student.student_id%TYPE;
   CURSOR c_student IS
      SELECT student_id, first_name, last_name
        FROM student
       WHERE student_id < 110;
   CURSOR c_course IS
      SELECT c.course_no, c.description
        FROM course c, section s, enrollment e
       WHERE c.course_no = s.course_no
         AND s.section_id = e.section_id
         AND e.student_id = v_sid;
BEGIN
   FOR r_student IN c_student
   LOOP
      v_sid := r_student.student_id;
      DBMS_OUTPUT.PUT_LINE(chr(10));
      DBMS_OUTPUT.PUT_LINE(' The Student '||
         r_student.student_id||' '||
         r_student.first_name||' '||
         r_student.last_name);
      DBMS_OUTPUT.PUT_LINE(' is enrolled in the '||
         'following courses: ');
      FOR r_course IN c_course
      LOOP
         DBMS_OUTPUT.PUT_LINE(r_course.course_no||
            '    '||r_course.description);
      END LOOP;
   END LOOP;
END;
```

The select statements for the two cursors are defined in the declarative section of the PL/SQL block. A variable to store the `student_id` *from the parent cursor is also declared. The course cursor is the child cursor, and, since it makes use of the variable* `v_sid`, *the variable must be declared first. Both cursors are processed with a FOR loop, which eliminates the need for OPEN, FETCH, and CLOSE. When the parent student loop is processed, the first step is to initialize the variable* `v_sid`, *and the value is then used when the child loop is processed. DBMS_OUTPUT is used so that display is generated for each cursor loop. The parent cursor will display the student name once, and the child cursor will display the name of each course in which the student is enrolled.*

b) Before you run the preceding code, analyze what it is doing and determine what you think the result would be. Explain what is happening in each phase of the PL/SQL block and what is happening to the variables as control is passing through parent and child cursor.

Answer: The declaration section contains a declaration for two variables. The first is v_amount *of the datatype matching that of the cost in the course table; the second is the* v_instructor_id *of the datatype matching the* instructor_id *in the instructor table. There are also two declarations for two cursors. The first is for* c_inst, *which is comprised of the* first_name, last_name, *and* instructor_id *for an instructor from the instructor table. The second cursor,* c_cost, *will produce a result set of the cost of the course taken for each student enrolled in a course by the instructor that matches the variable* v_instructor_id. *These two cursors will be run in nested fashion. First, the cursor* c_inst *is opened in a FOR loop. The value of the variable* v_instructor_id *is initialized to match the* instructor_id *of the current row of the* c_inst *cursor. The variable* v_amount *is initialized to 0. The second cursor is open within the loop for the first cursor. This means that for each iteration of the cursor* c_inst, *the second cursor will be opened, fetched, and closed. The second cursor will loop through all the cost generated by each student enrolled in a course for the instructor, which is current of the* c_inst *cursor. Each time the nest loop iterates, it will increase the variable* v_amount *by adding the current cost in the* c_cost *loop. Prior to opening the* c_cost *loop, there is a DBMS_OUTPUT to display the instructor name. After the* c_cost *cursor loop is closed, it will display the total amount generated by all the enrollments of the current instructor.*

c) Run the code and see what the result is. Is it what you expected? Explain the difference.

Answer: The result set would be as follows:

```
Generated by instructor Fernand   Hanks
$16,915
Generated by instructor Tom    Wojick
$18,504
Generated by instructor Nina    Schorin
$30,137
Generated by instructor Gary    Pertez
$24,044
Generated by instructor Anita   Morris
$13,389
Generated by instructor Todd    Smythe
$14,940
Generated by instructor Rick    Chow
$0
Generated by instructor Charles   Lowry
$12,175
```

```
Generated by instructor Marilyn   Frantzen
$13,224
PL/SQL procedure successfully completed.
```

In this example, the nested cursor is tied to the current row of the outer cursor by means of the variable `v_instructor_id.` *A more common way of doing this is to pass a parameter to a cursor. You will learn more about how to achieve this in Chapter 15, "Advanced Cursors."*

LAB 9.2 SELF-REVIEW QUESTIONS

In order to test your progress, you should be able to answer the following questions.

1) In a cursor FOR loop, cursor and loop handling is carried out implicitly.

    a) _____ True
    b) _____ False

2) In a cursor FOR loop, it is necessary to declare the rowtype for the cursor.

    a) _____ True
    b) _____ False

3) Is it necessary to open, fetch, and close a cursor in a cursor FOR loop?

    a) _____ Yes
    b) _____ No

4) The child loop in a nested cursor is passed through how many times for each cycle of the parent?

    a) _____ Three
    b) _____ One or more
    c) _____ Two
    d) _____ It depends on the individual code.

5) If the SELECT statement of the cursor makes use of a variable, when should the variable be declared?

    a) _____ It is a bind variable and therefore does not need to be declared.
    b) _____ In the declarative section.
    c) _____ Before the cursor that is using it.
    d) _____ It will be self-declared upon initialization.

Answers appear in Appendix A, Section 9.2.

CHAPTER 9

TEST YOUR THINKING

In this chapter, you learned how to process data with a cursor. Additionally, you learned how to simplify the code by using a cursor FOR loop. You also encountered the more complex example of nesting cursors within cursors.

1) Write a nested cursor where the parent cursor calls information about each section of a course. The child cursor counts the enrollment. The only output is one line for each course with the Course Name and Section Number and the total enrollment.

2) Write an anonymous PL/SQL block that finds all the courses that have at least one section that is at its maximum enrollment. If there are no courses that meet that criterion, then pick two courses and create that situation for each.

  a) For each of those courses, add another section. The instructor for the new section should be taken from the existing records in the instruct table. Use the instructor who is signed up to teach the least number of courses. Handle the fact that, during the execution of your program, the instructor teaching the most courses may change.

  b) Use any exception-handling techniques you think are useful to capture error conditions.

The projects in this section are meant to have you utilize all of the skills that you have acquired throughout this chapter. The answers to these projects can be found in Appendix D and at the companion Web site to this book, located at http://www.phptr .com/rosenzweig2e. Visit the Web site periodically to share and discuss your answers.

CHAPTER 10

EXCEPTIONS

In Chapter 7, you explored the concept of error handling and built-in exceptions. In this chapter you will continue by examining whether an exception can catch a runtime error occurring in the declaration, executable, or exception-handling section of a PL/SQL block. You will also learn how to define your own exceptions and how to re-raise an exception.

LAB 10.1

EXCEPTION SCOPE

> ## LAB OBJECTIVE
>
> After this Lab, you will be able to:
>
> ✔ Understand the Scope of an Exception

You are already familiar with the term *scope*—for example, the scope of a variable. Even though variables and exceptions serve different purposes, the same scope rules apply to them. Now examine the scope of an exception by means of an example.

■ FOR EXAMPLE

```
DECLARE
    v_student_id NUMBER := &sv_student_id;
    v_name VARCHAR2(30);
BEGIN
    SELECT RTRIM(first_name)||' '||RTRIM(last_name)
      INTO v_name
      FROM student
     WHERE student_id = v_student_id;

    DBMS_OUTPUT.PUT_LINE ('Student name is '||v_name);
EXCEPTION
    WHEN NO_DATA_FOUND THEN
        DBMS_OUTPUT.PUT_LINE ('There is no such student');
END;
```

In this example, you display the student's name on the screen. If there is no record in the STUDENT table corresponding to the value of v_student_id provided by the user, the exception NO_DATA_FOUND is raised. Therefore, you can say that the exception NO_DATA_FOUND covers this block, or this block is the scope of this exception. In other words, *the scope of an exception is the portion of the block that is covered by this exception.*

Now, you can expand on that:

■ FOR EXAMPLE

```
DECLARE
    v_student_id NUMBER := &sv_student_id;
    v_name VARCHAR2(30);
    v_total NUMBER(1);

-- outer block
BEGIN
    SELECT RTRIM(first_name)||' '||RTRIM(last_name)
      INTO v_name
      FROM student
     WHERE student_id = v_student_id;
    DBMS_OUTPUT.PUT_LINE ('Student name is '||v_name);

    -- inner block
    BEGIN
       SELECT COUNT(*)
         INTO v_total
         FROM enrollment
        WHERE student_id = v_student_id;
       DBMS_OUTPUT.PUT_LINE ('Student is registered for '||
           v_total||' course(s)');
    EXCEPTION
       WHEN VALUE_ERROR OR INVALID_NUMBER THEN
           DBMS_OUTPUT.PUT_LINE ('An error has occurred');
    END;

EXCEPTION
    WHEN NO_DATA_FOUND THEN
        DBMS_OUTPUT.PUT_LINE ('There is no such student');
END;
```

The part of the example shown in bold letters has been added to the original version of the example. The new version of the example has an inner block added to it. This block has a structure similar to the outer block. It has a SELECT INTO statement and an exception section to handle errors. When a VALUE_ERROR or an INVALID_NUMBER error occurs in the inner block, the exception is raised.

It is important that you realize that the exceptions VALUE_ERROR and INVALID_NUMBER have been defined for the inner block only. Therefore, they can be raised in the inner block only. If one of these errors occurs in the outer block, this program will be unable to terminate successfully.

On the other hand, the exception NO_DATA_FOUND has been defined in the outer block; therefore, it is global to the inner block. This version of the example will never raise the exception NO_DATA_FOUND in the inner block. Why do you think this is the case?

It is important to note that if you define an exception in a block, it is local to that block. However, it is global to any blocks enclosed by that block. In other words, in the case of nested blocks, any exception defined in the outer block becomes global to its inner blocks.

Note what happens when the example is changed so that the exception NO_DATA_FOUND can be raised by the inner block.

■ FOR EXAMPLE

```
DECLARE
    v_student_id NUMBER := &sv_student_id;
    v_name VARCHAR2(30);
    v_registered CHAR;

-- outer block
BEGIN
    SELECT RTRIM(first_name)||' '||RTRIM(last_name)
      INTO v_name
      FROM student
     WHERE student_id = v_student_id;
    DBMS_OUTPUT.PUT_LINE ('Student name is '||v_name);

    -- inner block
    BEGIN
        SELECT 'Y'
          INTO v_registered
          FROM enrollment
         WHERE student_id = v_student_id;
        DBMS_OUTPUT.PUT_LINE ('Student is registered');
    EXCEPTION
        WHEN VALUE_ERROR OR INVALID_NUMBER THEN
            DBMS_OUTPUT.PUT_LINE ('An error has occurred');
    END;

EXCEPTION
    WHEN NO_DATA_FOUND THEN
        DBMS_OUTPUT.PUT_LINE ('There is no such student');
END;
```

The part of the example shown in bold letters has been added to the original version of the example. The new version of the example has a different SELECT INTO statement. To answer the question posed earlier, the exception NO_DATA_FOUND can be raised by the inner block because the SELECT INTO statement does not contain a group function, COUNT(). This function always returns a result, so when no rows are returned by the SELECT INTO statement, the value returned by the COUNT(*) equals zero.

Now, run this example with the value of 284 for student ID. As a result, the following output is produced:

```
Enter value for sv_student_id: 284
old   2:    v_student_id NUMBER := &sv_student_id;
new   2:    v_student_id NUMBER := 284;
Student name is Salewa Lindeman
There is no such student

PL/SQL procedure successfully completed.
```

You have probably noticed that this example produces only a partial output. Even though you are able to see the student's name, the error message is displayed saying that this student does not exist. This error message is displayed because the exception NO_DATA_FOUND is raised in the inner block.

The SELECT INTO statement of the outer block returns the student's name, and it is displayed on the screen by the DBMS_OUTPUT.PUT_LINE statement. Next, control is passed to the inner block. The SELECT INTO statement of the inner block does not return any rows. As a result, the error occurs.

Next, PL/SQL tries to find a handler for the exception NO_DATA_FOUND in the inner block. Because there is no such handler in the inner block, control is transferred to the exception section of the outer block. The exception section of the outer block contains the handler for the exception NO_DATA_FOUND. So this handler executes, and the message "There is no such student" is displayed on the screen. The process is called exception propagation, and it will be discussed in detail in Lab 10.3.

It is important to realize that this example has been shown for illustrative purposes only. In its current version, it is not very useful. The SELECT INTO statement of the inner block is prone to another exception, TOO_MANY_ROWS, that is not handled by this example. In addition, the error message "There is no such student" is not very descriptive when the exception NO_DATA_FOUND is raised by the inner block.

LAB 10.1 EXERCISES

10.1.1 UNDERSTAND THE SCOPE OF AN EXCEPTION

In this exercise, you will display the number of students in each zipcode (you still use the first 50 zipcodes only). You will use nested PL/SQL blocks to achieve the desired results. The original PL/SQL script will not contain any exception handlers. Therefore, you will be asked to identify possible errors that may occur and define exception handlers for them.

Create the following PL/SQL script:

```
-- ch10_1a.sql, version 1.0
SET SERVEROUTPUT ON
DECLARE
   CURSOR zip_cur IS
      SELECT zip
        FROM zipcode
       WHERE rownum <= 50
     ORDER BY zip;
   v_total NUMBER(1);

-- outer block
BEGIN
   FOR zip_rec IN zip_cur LOOP

      -- inner block
      BEGIN
         SELECT count(*)
           INTO v_total
           FROM student
          WHERE zip = zip_rec.zip;

         IF v_total != 0 THEN
            DBMS_OUTPUT.PUT_LINE ('There is(are) '||
               v_total||' student(s) for zipcode '||
               zip_rec.zip);
         END IF;
      END;
   END LOOP;
   DBMS_OUTPUT.PUT_LINE ('Done...');
END;
```

Execute the script, and then answer the following questions:

a) What output was printed on the screen?

b) The first run of this example was successful. The output produced by the example shows that there are 9 students for zip-code 07024. What will happen if there are 10 students with a zip code 07024? What output will be produced? Note that in order to answer this question you will need to add a record to the STUDENT table as follows:

```
INSERT INTO student
    (student_id, salutation, first_name, last_name,
     street_address, zip, phone, employer, registration_date,
     created_by, created_date, modified_by, modified_date)
VALUES
    (STUDENT_ID_SEQ.NEXTVAL, 'Mr.', 'John', 'Smith', '100
     Main St.', '07024', '718-555-5555', 'ABC Co.',
     SYSDATE, USER, SYSDATE, USER, SYSDATE);
```

c) Based on the error message produced by the example in the previous question, what exception handler must be added to the script?

d) How would you change this script so that when an error occurs, the cursor loop does not terminate prematurely?

LAB 10.1 EXERCISE ANSWERS

This section gives you some suggested answers to the questions in Lab 10.1, with discussion related to how those answers resulted. The most important thing to realize is whether your answer works. You should figure out the implications of the answers here and what the effects are from any different answers you may come up with.

10.1.1 ANSWERS

a) What output was printed on the screen?

Answer:Your output should look like the following:

```
There is(are) 1 student(s) for zipcode 01247
There is(are) 1 student(s) for zipcode 02124
There is(are) 1 student(s) for zipcode 02155
There is(are) 1 student(s) for zipcode 02189
There is(are) 1 student(s) for zipcode 02563
There is(are) 1 student(s) for zipcode 06483
There is(are) 1 student(s) for zipcode 06605
There is(are) 1 student(s) for zipcode 06798
There is(are) 3 student(s) for zipcode 06820
There is(are) 3 student(s) for zipcode 06830
There is(are) 1 student(s) for zipcode 06850
```

```
There is(are) 1 student(s) for zipcode 06851
There is(are) 1 student(s) for zipcode 06853
There is(are) 1 student(s) for zipcode 06870
There is(are) 1 student(s) for zipcode 06877
There is(are) 2 student(s) for zipcode 06880
There is(are) 1 student(s) for zipcode 06902
There is(are) 2 student(s) for zipcode 06903
There is(are) 1 student(s) for zipcode 06905
There is(are) 1 student(s) for zipcode 06907
There is(are) 2 student(s) for zipcode 07003
There is(are) 1 student(s) for zipcode 07008
There is(are) 6 student(s) for zipcode 07010
There is(are) 2 student(s) for zipcode 07011
There is(are) 2 student(s) for zipcode 07012
There is(are) 2 student(s) for zipcode 07016
There is(are) 1 student(s) for zipcode 07023
There is(are) 9 student(s) for zipcode 07024
There is(are) 1 student(s) for zipcode 07029
There is(are) 2 student(s) for zipcode 07036
There is(are) 1 student(s) for zipcode 07040
There is(are) 5 student(s) for zipcode 07042
There is(are) 1 student(s) for zipcode 07044
There is(are) 5 student(s) for zipcode 07047
Done...

PL/SQL procedure successfully completed.
```

b) The first run of this example was successful. The output produced by the example shows that there are 9 students for zipcode 07024. What will happen if there are 10 students with a zipcode 07024? What output will be produced? Note that in order to answer this question you will need to add a record to the STUDENT table as follows:

```
INSERT INTO student
    (student_id, salutation, first_name, last_name,
    street_address, zip, phone, employer, registration_date,
    created_by, created_date, modified_by, modified_date)
VALUES
    (STUDENT_ID_SEQ.NEXTVAL, 'Mr.', 'John', 'Smith', '100
    Main St.', '07024', '718-555-5555', 'ABC Co.',
    SYSDATE, USER, SYSDATE, USER, SYSDATE);
```

Answer: The example will produce a partial output only. When the total number of students is calculated for zipcode 07024, the error occurs.

The SELECT INTO statement returns a value of 10. However, the variable v_total has been defined so that it is able to hold only single digit numbers. Be-

cause 10 is a two-digit number, the error occurs during the execution of the SE-
LECT INTO statement. As a result, an error message is displayed on the screen.

The following output contains only a portion of the output produced by the example:

```
There is(are) 1 student(s) for zipcode 01247
...
There is(are) 1 student(s) for zipcode 07023
DECLARE
*
ERROR at line 1:
ORA-06502: PL/SQL: numeric or value error: number
precision too large
ORA-06512: at line 13
```

Notice that as soon as the error occurs, the example terminates because there is
no exception handler for this error.

c) Based on the error message produced by the example in the previous question,
what exception handler must be added to the script?

*Answer: The error message produced by the example in the previous question referred
to a numeric or value error. Therefore, an exception VALUE_ERROR or INVALID_NUM-
BER must be added to the script.*

Your script should look similar to the following script. Changes are shown in bold letters.

```
-- ch10_1b.sql, version 2.0
DECLARE
   CURSOR zip_cur IS
      SELECT zip
        FROM zipcode
       WHERE rownum <= 50
    ORDER BY zip;
   v_total NUMBER(1);

-- outer block
BEGIN
   FOR zip_rec IN zip_cur LOOP

      -- inner block
      BEGIN
         SELECT count(*)
           INTO v_total
           FROM student
          WHERE zip = zip_rec.zip;
```

```
                IF v_total != 0 THEN
                   DBMS_OUTPUT.PUT_LINE ('There is(are) '||
                      v_total||' student(s) for zipcode '||
                      zip_rec.zip);
                END IF;
           END;
        END LOOP;
        DBMS_OUTPUT.PUT_LINE ('Done...');
   EXCEPTION
      WHEN VALUE_ERROR OR INVALID_NUMBER THEN
         DBMS_OUTPUT.PUT_LINE ('An error has occurred');
   END;
```

When run, this version of the example produces the following output (only a portion of the output is shown):

```
There is(are) 1 student(s) for zipcode 01247
...
There is(are) 1 student(s) for zipcode 07023
An error has occurred

PL/SQL procedure successfully completed.
```

Notice that because an exception handler has been added to the script, it was able to terminate successfully.

d) How would you change this script so that when an error occurs, the cursor loop does not terminate prematurely?

Answer: Your script should look similar to the script shown. All changes are shown in bold letters.

```
-- ch10_1c.sql, version 3.0
DECLARE
   CURSOR zip_cur IS
      SELECT zip
        FROM zipcode
       WHERE rownum <= 50
    ORDER BY zip;
   v_total NUMBER(1);

-- outer block
BEGIN
   FOR zip_rec IN zip_cur LOOP
```

```
    -- inner block
    BEGIN
       SELECT count(*)
         INTO v_total
         FROM student
        WHERE zip = zip_rec.zip;

       IF v_total != 0 THEN
          DBMS_OUTPUT.PUT_LINE ('There is(are) '||
             v_total||' student(s) for zipcode '||
             zip_rec.zip);
       END IF;
    EXCEPTION
       WHEN VALUE_ERROR OR INVALID_NUMBER THEN
          DBMS_OUTPUT.PUT_LINE
          ('An error has occurred');
    END;
  END LOOP;
  DBMS_OUTPUT.PUT_LINE ('Done...');
END;
```

In order for the cursor loop to be able to execute after an exception has occurred, the exception handler must be moved inside the loop in the inner block. In this case, once an exception has occurred, control is transferred to the exception handler of the block. Once the exception is raised, control is passed to the next executable statement of the outer block. That statement is END LOOP. If the end of the loop has not been reached and there are more records to process, control is passed to the top of the loop, and the inner block is executed again. As a result, this version of the script produces the following output (again, only a portion of the output is shown):

```
There is(are) 1 student(s) for zipcode 01247
...
There is(are) 1 student(s) for zipcode 07023
An error has occurred
There is(are) 1 student(s) for zipcode 07029
There is(are) 2 student(s) for zipcode 07036
There is(are) 1 student(s) for zipcode 07040
There is(are) 5 student(s) for zipcode 07042
There is(are) 1 student(s) for zipcode 07044
There is(are) 5 student(s) for zipcode 07047
Done...

PL/SQL procedure successfully completed.
```

LAB 10.1 SELF-REVIEW QUESTIONS

In order to test your progress, you should be able to answer the following questions.

1) An exception defined in the inner block can be raised in

   a) _____ both inner and outer blocks.
   b) _____ the outer block only.
   c) _____ the inner block only.

2) If an exception has been raised in the inner block and has been handled in the outer block, control is transferred back to inner block for further execution of the script.

   a) _____ True
   b) _____ False

3) If an exception has been raised in the outer block, and its handler is defined in the inner block, which of the following will occur?

   a) _____ Control will be passed to the inner block to handle the raised exception.
   b) _____ The script will terminate due to an exception that is not handled.

4) An exception defined inside the body of the loop

   a) _____ terminates this loop after it has been raised.
   b) _____ allows the loop to proceed with next iteration.
   c) _____ causes an error.

5) A WHEN clause of the exception-handling section of a PL/SQL block can reference a single exception only.

   a) _____ True
   b) _____ False

Answers appear in Appendix A, Section 10.1.

LAB 10.2

USER-DEFINED EXCEPTIONS

LAB OBJECTIVE

After this Lab, you will be able to:

✔ Use User-Defined Exceptions

Often in your programs you may need to handle problems that are specific to the program you write. For example, your program asks a user to enter a value for student_id. This value is then assigned to the variable v_student_id that is used later in the program. Generally, you want a positive number for an id. By mistake, the user enters a negative number. However, no error has occurred because student_id has been defined as a number, and the user has supplied a legitimate numeric value. Therefore, you may want to implement your own exception to handle this situation.

This type of an exception is called a user-defined exception because it is defined by the programmer. As a result, before the exception can be used, it must be declared. A user-defined exception is declared in the declarative part of a PL/SQL block as shown:

```
DECLARE
    exception_name EXCEPTION;
```

Notice that this declaration looks similar to a variable declaration. You specify an exception name followed by the keyword EXCEPTION. Consider the following code fragment.

■ FOR EXAMPLE

```
DECLARE
    e_invalid_id EXCEPTION;
```

In the example, the name of the exception is prefixed by the letter "e." This is not a required syntax; rather, it allows you to differentiate between variable names and exception names.

Once an exception has been declared, the executable statements associated with this exception are specified in the exception-handling section of the block. The format of the exception-handling section is the same as for built-in exceptions. Consider the following code fragment.

■ *FOR EXAMPLE*

```
DECLARE
    e_invalid_id EXCEPTION;
BEGIN
    ...
EXCEPTION
    WHEN e_invalid_id THEN
        DBMS_OUTPUT.PUT_LINE ('An id cannot be negative');
END;
```

You already know that built-in exceptions are raised implicitly. In other words, when a certain error occurs, a built-in exception associated with this error is raised. Of course, you are assuming that you have included this exception in the exception-handling section of your program. For example, a TOO_MANY_ROWS exception is raised when a SELECT INTO statement returns multiple rows. Next, you will explore how a user-defined exception is raised.

A user-defined exception must be raised explicitly. In other words, you need to specify in your program under which circumstances an exception must be raised, as shown:

```
DECLARE
    exception_name EXCEPTION;
BEGIN
    ...
    IF CONDITION THEN
        RAISE exception_name;
    ELSE
        ...
    END IF;
EXCEPTION
    WHEN exception_name THEN
        ERROR-PROCESSING STATEMENTS;
END;
```

In the structure just shown, the circumstances under which a user-defined exception must be raised are determined with the help of the IF-THEN-ELSE statement. If CONDITION evaluates to TRUE, a user-defined exception is raised. If CONDITION evaluates to FALSE, the program proceeds with its normal execution. In other words, the statements associated with the ELSE part of the IF-THEN-ELSE statement are executed. Any form of the IF statement can be used to check when a user-defined exception must be raised.

In the next modified version of the earlier example used in this lab, you will see that the exception e_invalid_id is raised when a negative number is entered for the variable v_student_id.

■ FOR EXAMPLE

```
DECLARE
    v_student_id STUDENT.STUDENT_ID%TYPE := &sv_student_id;
    v_total_courses NUMBER;
    e_invalid_id EXCEPTION;
BEGIN
    IF v_student_id < 0 THEN
        RAISE e_invalid_id;
    ELSE
        SELECT COUNT(*)
          INTO v_total_courses
          FROM enrollment
         WHERE student_id = v_student_id;
        DBMS_OUTPUT.PUT_LINE ('The student is registered for
            '||v_total_courses||' courses');
    END IF;
    DBMS_OUTPUT.PUT_LINE ('No exception has been raised');
EXCEPTION
    WHEN e_invalid_id THEN
        DBMS_OUTPUT.PUT_LINE ('An id cannot be negative');
END;
```

In this example, the exception e_invalid_id is raised with the help of IF-THEN-ELSE statement. Once a user supplies a value for the v_student_id, the sign of this numeric value is checked. If the value is less than zero, the IF-THEN-ELSE statement evaluates to TRUE, and the exception e_invalid_id is raised. Therefore, the control transfers to the exception-handling section of the block. Next, statements associated with this exception are executed. In this case, the message "An id cannot be negative" is displayed on the screen. If the value entered for the v_student_id is positive, the IF-THEN-ELSE statement yields FALSE, and the ELSE part of the IF-THEN-ELSE statement is executed.

Run this example for two values of v_student_id: 102 and –102.

A first run of the example (student ID is 102) produces the output shown:

```
Enter value for sv_student_id: 102
old   2:    v_student_id STUDENT.STUDENT_ID%TYPE :=
&sv_student_id;
```

```
new    2:    v_student_id STUDENT.STUDENT_ID%TYPE := 102;
The student is registered for 2 courses
No exception has been raised

PL/SQL procedure successfully completed.
```

For this run, you entered a positive value for the variable v_student_id. As a result, the IF-THEN-ELSE statement evaluates to FALSE, and the ELSE part of the statement executes. The SELECT INTO statement determines how many records are in the ENROLLMENT table for a given student_id. Next, the message "The student is registered for 2 courses" statement is displayed on the screen. At this point, the IF-THEN-ELSE statement is complete. So the control is transferred to the DBMS_OUTPUT.PUT_LINE statement that follows END IF. As a result, another message is displayed on the screen.

A second run of the example (student ID is –102) produces the following output:

```
Enter value for sv_student_id: -102
old    2:    v_student_id STUDENT.STUDENT_ID%TYPE :=
&sv_student_id;
new    2:    v_student_id STUDENT.STUDENT_ID%TYPE := -102;
An id cannot be negative

PL/SQL procedure successfully completed.
```

For the second run, a negative value was entered for the variable v_student_id. The IF-THEN-ELSE statement evaluates to TRUE, and the exception e_invalid_id is raised. As a result, control is transferred to the exception-handling section of the block, and the error message "An id cannot be negative" is displayed on the screen.

It is important for you to note that the RAISE statement must be used in conjunction with an IF statement. Otherwise, control of the execution will be transferred to the exception-handling section of the block for every single execution. Consider the following example:

```
DECLARE
   e_test_exception EXCEPTION;
BEGIN
   DBMS_OUTPUT.PUT_LINE ('Exception has not been raised');
   RAISE e_test_exception;
   DBMS_OUTPUT.PUT_LINE ('Exception has been raised');
EXCEPTION
   WHEN e_test_exception THEN
      DBMS_OUTPUT.PUT_LINE ('An error has occurred');
END;
```

Every time this example is run, the following output is produced:

```
Exception has not been raised
An error has occurred

PL/SQL procedure successfully completed.
```

Even though no error has occurred, control is transferred to the exception-handling section. It is important for you to check to see if the error has occurred before raising the exception associated with that error.

Just like for built-in exceptions, the same scope rules apply to user-defined exceptions. An exception declared in the inner block must be raised in the inner block and defined in the exception-handling section of the inner block. Consider the following example.

■ FOR EXAMPLE

```
-- outer block
BEGIN
   DBMS_OUTPUT.PUT_LINE ('Outer block');

   -- inner block
   DECLARE
      e_my_exception EXCEPTION;
   BEGIN
      DBMS_OUTPUT.PUT_LINE ('Inner block');
   EXCEPTION
      WHEN e_my_exception THEN
         DBMS_OUTPUT.PUT_LINE ('An error has occurred');
   END;

   IF 10 > &sv_number THEN
      RAISE e_my_exception;
   END IF;
END;
```

In this example, the exception, e_my_exception, has been declared in the inner block. However, you are trying to raise this exception in the outer block. This example causes a syntax error because the exception declared in the inner block ceases to exists once the inner block terminates. As a result, this example produces the following output:

```
Enter value for sv_number: 11
old   12:    IF 10 > &sv_number THEN
new   12:    IF 10 > 11 THEN
       RAISE e_my_exception;
                   *
ERROR at line 13:
```

```
ORA-06550: line 13, column 13:
PLS-00201: identifier 'E_MY_EXCEPTION' must be declared
ORA-06550: line 13, column 7:
PL/SQL: Statement ignored
```

Notice that the error message

```
PLS-00201: identifier 'E_MY_EXCEPTION' must be declared
```

is the same error message you get when trying to use a variable that has not been declared.

LAB 10.2 EXERCISES

10.2.1 USE USER-DEFINED EXCEPTIONS

In this exercise, you will define an exception that will allow you to raise an error if an instructor teaches ten or more sections.

Create the following PL/SQL script:

```
-- ch10_2a.sql, version 1.0
SET SERVEROUTPUT ON
DECLARE
   CURSOR instruct_cur IS
      SELECT instructor_id, COUNT(*) tot_sec
        FROM section
      GROUP BY instructor_id;

   v_name VARCHAR2(30);
   e_too_many_sections EXCEPTION;
BEGIN
   FOR instruct_rec IN instruct_cur LOOP
      IF instruct_rec.tot_sec >= 10 THEN
         RAISE e_too_many_sections;
      ELSE
         SELECT RTRIM(first_name)||' '||RTRIM(last_name)
           INTO v_name
           FROM instructor
          WHERE instructor_id = instruct_rec.instructor_id;

         DBMS_OUTPUT.PUT_LINE ('Instructor, '||v_name||
            ', teaches '|| instruct_rec.tot_sec||
            ' sections');
      END IF;
   END LOOP;
EXCEPTION
```

```
      WHEN e_too_many_sections THEN
          DBMS_OUTPUT.PUT_LINE
              ('This instructor teaches too much');
   END;
```

Execute the script, and then answer the following questions:

a) What output was printed on the screen?

b) What is the condition that causes the user-defined exception to be raised?

c) How would you change the script so that the cursor FOR loop processes all records returned by the cursor? In other words, once an exception is raised, the cursor FOR loop should not terminate.

d) How would you change the script to display an instructor's name in the error message as well?

LAB 10.2 EXERCISE ANSWERS

This section gives you some suggested answers to the questions in Lab 10.2, with discussion related to how those answers resulted. The most important thing to realize is whether your answer works. You should figure out the implications of the answers here and what the effects are from any different answers you may come up with.

10.2.1 ANSWERS

a) What output was printed on the screen?

Answer: Your output should look like the following:

```
Instructor, Fernand Hanks, teaches 9 sections
This instructor teaches too much

PL/SQL procedure successfully completed.
```

b) What is the condition that causes the user-defined exception to be raised?

Answer:The user-defined exception is raised if the condition

```
instruct_rec.tot_sec >= 10
```

evaluates to TRUE. In other words, if an instructor teaches ten or more sections, the exception e_too_many_sections *is raised.*

c) How would you change the script so that the cursor FOR loop processes all records returned by the cursor? In other words, once an exception is raised, the cursor FOR loop should not terminate.

Answer:Your script should look similar to the script shown. All changes are shown in bold letters.

```
-- ch10_2b.sql, version 2.0
SET SERVEROUTPUT ON
DECLARE
   CURSOR instruct_cur IS
      SELECT instructor_id, COUNT(*) tot_sec
        FROM section
        GROUP BY instructor_id;

   v_name VARCHAR2(30);
   e_too_many_sections EXCEPTION;
BEGIN
   FOR instruct_rec IN instruct_cur LOOP
      -- inner block
      BEGIN
         IF instruct_rec.tot_sec >= 10 THEN
            RAISE e_too_many_sections;
         ELSE
            SELECT RTRIM(first_name)||' '||RTRIM(last_name)
              INTO v_name
              FROM instructor
             WHERE instructor_id = instruct_rec.
              instructor_id;

            DBMS_OUTPUT.PUT_LINE ('Instructor, '||v_name||
               ', teaches '||instruct_rec.tot_sec||
               ' sections');
         END IF;
      EXCEPTION
         WHEN e_too_many_sections THEN
            DBMS_OUTPUT.PUT_LINE
               ('This instructor teaches too much');
      END; -- end inner block
   END LOOP;
END;
```

There are several changes in the new version of this script. First, the inner block has been created inside the body of the cursor FOR loop. Next, the exception-handling section has been moved from the outer block to the inner block.

In this script, the exception has been declared in the outer block, but it is raised in the inner block. This does not cause any errors because the exception, e_too_many_sections, is global to the inner block. Hence, it can be raised anywhere in the inner block.

The new version of this script produces the output shown:

```
Instructor, Fernand Hanks, teaches 9 sections
This instructor teaches too much
This instructor teaches too much
This instructor teaches too much
This instructor teaches too much
This instructor teaches too much
This instructor teaches too much
Instructor, Charles Lowry, teaches 9 sections

PL/SQL procedure successfully completed.
```

d) How would you change the script to display an instructor's name in the error message as well?

Answer:Your script should look similar to the script shown.All changes are shown in bold letters.

```
-- ch10_2c.sql, version 3.0
SET SERVEROUTPUT ON
DECLARE
    CURSOR instruct_cur IS
        SELECT instructor_id, COUNT(*) tot_sec
          FROM section
      GROUP BY instructor_id;

    v_name VARCHAR2(30);
    e_too_many_sections EXCEPTION;
BEGIN
    FOR instruct_rec IN instruct_cur LOOP
        BEGIN
            SELECT RTRIM(first_name)||' '||RTRIM(last_name)
              INTO v_name
              FROM instructor
             WHERE instructor_id = instruct_rec.instructor_id;

            IF instruct_rec.tot_sec >= 10 THEN
                RAISE e_too_many_sections;
            ELSE
```

```
                    DBMS_OUTPUT.PUT_LINE ('Instructor, '||v_name||
                         ', teaches '||instruct_rec.tot_sec||
                         ' sections');
              END IF;
           EXCEPTION
           WHEN e_too_many_sections THEN
              DBMS_OUTPUT.PUT_LINE ('Instructor, '||v_name||
                   ', teaches too much');
           END;
        END LOOP;
     END;
```

In order to achieve the desired result, the SELECT INTO statement has been moved outside the IF-THEN-ELSE statement. This change allows you to get an instructor's name regardless of the number of sections he or she teaches. As a result, you are able to include an instructor's name in the error message, thus improving the error message itself.

The new version of the output is shown:

```
Instructor, Fernand Hanks, teaches 9 sections
Instructor, Tom Wojick, teaches too much
Instructor, Nina Schorin, teaches too much
Instructor, Gary Pertez, teaches too much
Instructor, Anita Morris, teaches too much
Instructor, Todd Smythe, teaches too much
Instructor, Marilyn Frantzen, teaches too much
Instructor, Charles Lowry, teaches 9 sections

PL/SQL procedure successfully completed.
```

This version of the output is oriented more toward a user than the previous versions because it displays the name of the instructor in every message. The previous versions of the output were confusing because it was not clear which instructor caused this error. For example, consider the output produced by the first version of this script:

```
Instructor, Fernand Hanks, teaches 9 sections
This instructor teaches too much
```

It is not clear to a user whether the message "This instructor teaches too much" is caused by the fact that Fernand Hanks teaches nine sections, or whether another instructor teaches more than nine sections.

Remember, you have created this script, and you know the exception that you have defined. However, as mentioned earlier, most of the time, a user does not have access to your program. Therefore, it is important for you to provide clear error messages in your programs.

LAB 10.2 SELF-REVIEW QUESTIONS

In order to test your progress, you should be able to answer the following questions.

1) In order to use a user-defined exception, it must be

a) _____ declared.
b) _____ declared and raised.

2) How does any user-defined exception get raised?

a) _____ Implicitly
b) _____ Explicitly

3) If a user-defined exception has been declared in the inner block, it can be raised in the outer block.

a) _____ True
b) _____ False

4) When a user-defined exception is raised and executed, control is passed back to the PL/SQL block.

a) _____ True
b) _____ False

5) A user-defined exception is raised with the help of which of the following?

a) _____ IF-THEN and RAISE statements
b) _____ IF-THEN statement only
c) _____ RAISE statement only

Answers appear in Appendix A, Section 10.2.

LAB 10.3

EXCEPTION PROPAGATION

LAB OBJECTIVES

After this Lab, you will be able to:

✔ Understand How Exceptions Propagate
✔ Re-raise Exceptions

You already have seen how different types of exceptions are raised when a runtime error occurs in the executable portion of the PL/SQL block. However, a runtime error may occur in the declaration section of the block or in the exception-handling section of the block. The rules that govern how exceptions are raised in these situations are referred to as exception propagation.

Consider the first case: A runtime error occurred in the executable section of the PL/SQL block. This case should be treated as a review because the examples that you have seen earlier in this chapter show how an exception is raised when an error occurs in the executable section of the block.

If there is an exception specified associated with a particular error, control is passed to the exception-handling section of the block. Once the statements associated with the exception are executed, control is passed to the host environment or to the enclosing block. If there is no exception handler for this error, the exception is propagated to the enclosing block (outer block). Then the steps just described are repeated again. If no exception handler is found, the execution of the program halts, and control is transferred to the host environment.

Next, take a look at a second case: A runtime error occurred in the declaration section of the block. If there is no outer block, the execution of the program halts, and control is passed to the host environment. Consider the following script.

■ *FOR EXAMPLE*

```
DECLARE
    v_test_var CHAR(3):= 'ABCDE';
```

```
BEGIN
   DBMS_OUTPUT.PUT_LINE ('This is a test');
EXCEPTION
   WHEN INVALID_NUMBER OR VALUE_ERROR THEN
      DBMS_OUTPUT.PUT_LINE ('An error has occurred');
END;
```

When executed, this example produces the output shown:

```
DECLARE
*
ERROR at line 1:
ORA-06502: PL/SQL: numeric or value error: character
string buffer too small
ORA-06512: at line 2
```

As you can see, the assignment statement in the declaration section of the block causes an error. Even though there is an exception handler for this error, the block is not able to execute successfully. Based on this example you may conclude that when a runtime error occurs in the declaration section of the PL/SQL block, the exception-handling section of this block is not able to catch the error.

Next, consider an example with nested PL/SQL blocks.

■ FOR EXAMPLE

```
--outer block
BEGIN
   -- inner block
   DECLARE
      v_test_var CHAR(3):= 'ABCDE';
   BEGIN
      DBMS_OUTPUT.PUT_LINE ('This is a test');
   EXCEPTION
      WHEN INVALID_NUMBER OR VALUE_ERROR THEN
         DBMS_OUTPUT.PUT_LINE ('An error has occurred in '||
            'the inner block');
   END;
EXCEPTION
   WHEN INVALID_NUMBER OR VALUE_ERROR THEN
      DBMS_OUTPUT.PUT_LINE ('An error has occurred in the '||
         'program');
END;
```

When executed, this example produces the output shown:

```
An error has occurred in the program

PL/SQL procedure successfully completed.
```

In this example, the PL/SQL block is enclosed by another block, and the program is able to complete. This is possible because the exception defined in the outer block is raised when the error occurs in the declaration section of the inner block. Therefore, you can conclude that *when a runtime error occurs in the declaration section of the inner block, the exception immediately propagates to the enclosing (outer) block.*

Finally, consider a third case: A runtime error occurred in the exception-handling section of the block. Just like in the previous case, if there is no outer block, the execution of the program halts, and control is passed to the host environment. Consider the following script.

■ FOR EXAMPLE

```
DECLARE
    v_test_var CHAR(3) := 'ABC';
BEGIN
    v_test_var := '1234';
    DBMS_OUTPUT.PUT_LINE ('v_test_var: '||v_test_var);
EXCEPTION
    WHEN INVALID_NUMBER OR VALUE_ERROR THEN
        v_test_var := 'ABCD';
        DBMS_OUTPUT.PUT_LINE ('An error has occurred');
END;
```

When executed, this example produces the output shown:

```
DECLARE
*
ERROR at line 1:
ORA-06502: PL/SQL: numeric or value error: character
string buffer too small
ORA-06512: at line 8
ORA-06502: PL/SQL: numeric or value error: character
string buffer too small
```

As you can see, the assignment statement in the executable section of the block causes an error. Therefore, control is transferred to the exception-handling section of the block. However, the assignment statement in the exception-handling section of the block raises the same error. As a result, the output of this example contains the same error message twice. The first message is generated by the assignment statement in the executable section of the block, and the second message is generated by the assignment statement of the exception-handling section of this block. Based on this example, you may conclude that *when a runtime error occurs in the exception-handling section of the PL/SQL block, the exception-handling section of this block is not able to prevent the error.*

Next, consider an example with nested PL/SQL blocks.

■ *FOR EXAMPLE*

```
--outer block
BEGIN
   -- inner block
   DECLARE
      v_test_var CHAR(3) := 'ABC';
   BEGIN
      v_test_var := '1234';
      DBMS_OUTPUT.PUT_LINE ('v_test_var: '||v_test_var);
   EXCEPTION
      WHEN INVALID_NUMBER OR VALUE_ERROR THEN
         v_test_var := 'ABCD';
         DBMS_OUTPUT.PUT_LINE ('An error has occurred in '||
            'the inner block');
   END;
EXCEPTION
   WHEN INVALID_NUMBER OR VALUE_ERROR THEN
      DBMS_OUTPUT.PUT_LINE ('An error has occurred in the '||
         'program');
END;
```

When executed, this example produces the output shown:

```
An error has occurred in the program

PL/SQL procedure successfully completed.
```

In this example, the PL/SQL block is enclosed by another block, and the program is able to complete. This is possible because the exception defined in the outer block is raised when the error occurs in the exception-handling section of the inner block. Therefore, you can conclude that *when a runtime error occurs in the exception-handling section of the inner block, the exception immediately propagates to the enclosing block.*

In the previous two examples, an exception is raised implicitly by a runtime error in the exception-handling section of the block. However, an exception can be raised in the exception-handling section of the block explicitly by the RAISE statement. Consider the following example.

■ *FOR EXAMPLE*

```
--outer block
DECLARE
   e_exception1 EXCEPTION;
   e_exception2 EXCEPTION;
BEGIN
   -- inner block
```

```
BEGIN
   RAISE e_exception1;
EXCEPTION
   WHEN e_exception1 THEN
       RAISE e_exception2;
   WHEN e_exception2 THEN
       DBMS_OUTPUT.PUT_LINE ('An error has occurred in '||
           'the inner block');
   END;
EXCEPTION
   WHEN e_exception2 THEN
       DBMS_OUTPUT.PUT_LINE ('An error has occurred in '||
           'the program');
END;
```

This example produces the output shown:

An error has occurred in the program

PL/SQL procedure successfully completed.

Here two exceptions are declared: e_exception1 and e_exception2. Exception e_exception1 is raised in the inner block via the statement RAISE. In the exception-handling section of the block, exception e_exception1 tries to raise e_exception2. Even though there is an exception handler for the exception e_exception2 in the inner block, control is transferred to the outer block. This happens because only one exception can be raised in the exception-handling section of the block. Only after one exception has been handled can another be raised, but two or more exceptions cannot be raised simultaneously.

When a PL/SQL block is not enclosed by another block, control is transferred to the host environment, and the program is not able to complete successfully. Then the following error message is displayed.

```
DECLARE
*
ERROR at line 1:
ORA-06510: PL/SQL: unhandled user-defined exception
ORA-06512: at line 10
ORA-06510: PL/SQL: unhandled user-defined exception
```

RE-RAISING AN EXCEPTION

On some occasions you may want to be able to stop your program if a certain type of error occurs. In other words, you may want to handle an exception in the inner block and then pass it to the outer block. This process is called re-raising an exception. The following example helps to illustrate this point.

■ FOR EXAMPLE

```
-- outer block
DECLARE
    e_exception EXCEPTION;
BEGIN
    -- inner block
    BEGIN
        RAISE e_exception;
    EXCEPTION
        WHEN e_exception THEN
            RAISE;
    END;
EXCEPTION
    WHEN e_exception THEN
        DBMS_OUTPUT.PUT_LINE ('An error has occurred');
END;
```

In this example, the exception e_exception is declared in the outer block. Then it is raised in the inner block. As a result, control is transferred to the exception-handling section of the inner block. The statement RAISE in the exception-handling section of the block causes the exception to propagate to the exception-handling section of the outer block. Notice that when the RAISE statement is used in the exception-handling section of the inner block, it is not followed by the exception name.

When run, this example produces the output shown:

The error has occurred

PL/SQL procedure successfully completed.

It is important to note that when an exception is re-raised in the block that is not enclosed by any other block, the program is unable to complete successfully. Consider the following example:

```
DECLARE
    e_exception EXCEPTION;
BEGIN
    RAISE e_exception;
EXCEPTION
    WHEN e_exception THEN
        RAISE;
END;
```

When run, this example produces the following output:

```
DECLARE
*
ERROR at line 1:
ORA-06510: PL/SQL: unhandled user-defined exception
ORA-06512: at line 7
```

LAB 10.3 EXERCISES

10.3.1 UNDERSTAND HOW EXCEPTIONS PROPAGATE

In this exercise, you will use nested PL/SQL blocks to practice exception propagation. You will be asked to experiment with the script via exceptions. Try to answer the questions before you run the script. Once you have answered the questions, run the script and check your answers.

Create the following PL/SQL script:

```
-- ch10_3a.sql, version 1.0
SET SERVEROUTPUT ON
DECLARE
   v_my_name VARCHAR2(15) := 'ELENA SILVESTROVA';
BEGIN
   DBMS_OUTPUT.PUT_LINE ('My name is '||v_my_name);

   DECLARE
      v_your_name VARCHAR2(15);
   BEGIN
      v_your_name := '&sv_your_name';
      DBMS_OUTPUT.PUT_LINE ('Your name is '||v_your_name);
   EXCEPTION
      WHEN VALUE_ERROR THEN
         DBMS_OUTPUT.PUT_LINE ('Error in the inner block');
         DBMS_OUTPUT.PUT_LINE ('This name is too long');
   END;

EXCEPTION
   WHEN VALUE_ERROR THEN
      DBMS_OUTPUT.PUT_LINE ('Error in the outer block');
      DBMS_OUTPUT.PUT_LINE ('This name is too long');
END;
```

Answer the following questions first, and then execute the script:

a) What exception is raised by the assignment statement in the declaration section of the outer block?

b) Once this exception (based on the previous question) is raised, will the program terminate successfully? You should explain your answer.

c) How would you change this script so that the exception is able to handle an error caused by the assignment statement in the declaration section of the outer block?

d) Change the value of the variable from "Elena Silvestrova" to "Elena." Then change the script so that if there is an error caused by the assignment statement of the inner block, it is handled by the exception-handling section of the outer block.

10.3.2 RE-RAISE EXCEPTIONS

In this exercise, you will check the number of sections for each course. If a course does not have a section associated with it, you will raise an exception, e_no_sections. Again, try to answer the questions before you run the script. Once you have answered the questions, run the script and check your answers.

Create the following PL/SQL script:

```
-- ch10_4a.sql, version 1.0
SET SERVEROUTPUT ON
DECLARE
   CURSOR course_cur IS
      SELECT course_no
         FROM course;

   v_total NUMBER;
   e_no_sections EXCEPTION;
BEGIN
   FOR course_rec in course_cur LOOP
      BEGIN
         SELECT COUNT(*)
```

```
            INTO v_total
            FROM section
           WHERE course_no = course_rec.course_no;

        IF v_total = 0 THEN
           RAISE e_no_sections;
        ELSE
           DBMS_OUTPUT.PUT_LINE ('Course, '||
              course_rec.course_no||' has '||
              v_total||' sections');
        END IF;
     EXCEPTION
        WHEN e_no_sections THEN
           DBMS_OUTPUT.PUT_LINE ('There are no sections '||
              'for course '||course_rec.course_no);
     END;
   END LOOP;
 END;
```

Answer the following questions first, and then execute the script:

a) What exception will be raised if there are no sections for a given course number?

b) If the exception e_no_sections is raised, will the cursor FOR loop terminate? Explain your answer.

c) Change this script so that the exception e_no_sections is re-raised in the outer block.

LAB 10.3 EXERCISE ANSWERS

This section gives you some suggested answers to the questions in Lab 10.3, with discussion related to how those answers resulted. The most important thing to realize is whether your answer works. You should figure out the implications of the answers here and what the effects are from any different answers you may come up with.

10.3.1 ANSWERS

a) What exception is raised by the assignment statement in the declaration section of the outer block?

Answer: The exception VALUE_ERROR is raised by the assignment statement of the outer block.

The variable v_my_name is declared as VARCHAR2(15). However, the value that is assigned to this variable contains seventeen letters. As a result, the assignment statement causes a runtime error.

b) Once this exception (based on the previous question) is raised, will the program terminate successfully? You should explain your answer.

Answer: When that exception VALUE_ERROR is raised, the script is not able to complete successfully because the error occurred in the declaration section of the outer block. Since the outer block is not enclosed by any other block, control is transferred to the host environment. As a result, an error message will be generated when this example is run.

c) How would you change this script so that the exception is able to handle an error caused by the assignment statement in the declaration section of the outer block?

Answer: In order for the exception to handle the error generated by the assignment statement in the declaration section of the outer block, the assignment statement must be moved to the executable section of this block. All changes are shown in bold letters.

```
-- ch10_3b.sql, version 2.0
SET SERVEROUTPUT ON
DECLARE
   v_my_name VARCHAR2(15);
BEGIN
   v_my_name := 'ELENA SILVESTROVA';
   DBMS_OUTPUT.PUT_LINE ('My name is '||v_my_name);

   DECLARE
      v_your_name VARCHAR2(15);
   BEGIN
      v_your_name := '&sv_your_name';
      DBMS_OUTPUT.PUT_LINE ('Your name is '||v_your_name);
   EXCEPTION
      WHEN VALUE_ERROR THEN
         DBMS_OUTPUT.PUT_LINE ('Error in the inner block');
         DBMS_OUTPUT.PUT_LINE ('This name is too long');
   END;
```

```
EXCEPTION
   WHEN VALUE_ERROR THEN
      DBMS_OUTPUT.PUT_LINE ('Error in the outer block');
      DBMS_OUTPUT.PUT_LINE ('This name is too long');
END;
```

The new version of this script produces the following output:

```
Enter value for sv_your_name: TEST A NAME
old    9:          v_your_name := '&sv_your_name';
new    9:          v_your_name := 'TEST A NAME';
Error in the outer block
This name is too long

PL/SQL procedure successfully completed.
```

**LAB
10.3**

d) Change the value of the variable from "Elena Silvestrova" to "Elena". Then change the script so that if there is an error caused by the assignment statement of the inner block, it is handled by the exception-handling section of the outer block.

Answer: Note that when the value of the variable used in the outer block is changed from "Elena Silvestrova" to "Elena", it allows the script to pass control of the execution to the inner block. In the previous versions of this example, the inner block was never executed because the VALUE_ERROR exception was always encountered in the outer block.

Your script should look similar to the script below. All changes are shown in bold letters.

```
-- ch10_3c.sql, version 3.0
SET SERVEROUTPUT ON
DECLARE
   v_my_name VARCHAR2(15) := 'ELENA';
BEGIN
   DBMS_OUTPUT.PUT_LINE ('My name is '||v_my_name);

   DECLARE
      v_your_name VARCHAR2(15) := '&sv_your_name';
   BEGIN
      DBMS_OUTPUT.PUT_LINE ('Your name is '||v_your_name);
   EXCEPTION
      WHEN VALUE_ERROR THEN
         DBMS_OUTPUT.PUT_LINE ('Error in the inner block');
         DBMS_OUTPUT.PUT_LINE ('This name is too long');
   END;

EXCEPTION
   WHEN VALUE_ERROR THEN
      DBMS_OUTPUT.PUT_LINE ('Error in the outer block');
      DBMS_OUTPUT.PUT_LINE ('This name is too long');
END;
```

In this version of the example, the assignment statement was moved from the executable section of the inner block to the declaration section of this block. As a result, if an exception is raised by the assignment statement of the inner block, control is transferred to the exception section of the outer block.

You can modify this example in a different manner that allows you to achieve the same result.

**LAB
10.3**

```
-- ch10_3d.sql, version 4.0
SET SERVEROUTPUT ON
DECLARE
   v_my_name VARCHAR2(15) := 'ELENA';
BEGIN
   DBMS_OUTPUT.PUT_LINE ('My name is '||v_my_name);

   DECLARE
      v_your_name VARCHAR2(15);
   BEGIN
      v_your_name := '&sv_your_name';
      DBMS_OUTPUT.PUT_LINE ('Your name is '||v_your_name);
   EXCEPTION
      WHEN VALUE_ERROR THEN
          RAISE;
   END;

EXCEPTION
   WHEN VALUE_ERROR THEN
       DBMS_OUTPUT.PUT_LINE ('Error in the outer block');
       DBMS_OUTPUT.PUT_LINE ('This name is too long');
END;
```

In this version of the example, the RAISE statement was used in the exception-handling section of the inner block. As a result, the exception is re-raised in the outer block.

Both versions of this example produce very similar output. The first output is generated by the third version of the example, and the second output is generated by the fourth version of the example.

```
Enter value for sv_your_name: THIS NAME MUST BE REALLY
LONG
old    6:          v_your_name VARCHAR2(15) := '&sv_your_name';
new    6:          v_your_name VARCHAR2(15) := 'THIS NAME MUST
BE REALLY LONG';
My name is ELENA
Error in the outer block
This name is too long

PL/SQL procedure successfully completed.
```

```
Enter value for sv_your_name: THIS NAME MUST BE REALLY
LONG
old    8:        v_your_name := '&sv_your_name';
new    8:        v_your_name := 'THIS NAME MUST BE REALLY
LONG';
My name is ELENA
Error in the outer block
This name is too long

PL/SQL procedure successfully completed.
```

Notice that the only difference between the two versions of the output is the line number of the bind variable. In the first version of the output, the assignment statement takes place in the declaration section of the inner block. In the second version of the output, the assignment statement occurs in the executable section of the inner block. However, all messages displayed on the screen are identical in both versions of the output.

10.3.2 ANSWERS

a) What exception will be raised if there are no sections for a given course number?

Answer: If there are no sections for a given course number, the exception e_no_sec-
tions *is raised.*

b) If the exception e_no_sections is raised, will the cursor FOR loop terminate? Explain your answer.

Answer: If the exception e_no_sections *is raised, the cursor FOR loop will continue its normal execution. This is possible because the inner block, in which this exception is raised and handled, is located inside the body of the loop. As a result, the example produces the following output:*

```
Course, 10 has 1 sections
Course, 20 has 4 sections
Course, 25 has 9 sections
There are no sections for course 80
Course, 100 has 5 sections
Course, 120 has 6 sections
Course, 122 has 5 sections
Course, 124 has 4 sections
Course, 125 has 5 sections
Course, 130 has 4 sections
Course, 132 has 2 sections
Course, 134 has 3 sections
Course, 135 has 4 sections
Course, 140 has 3 sections
Course, 142 has 3 sections
```

```
Course, 144 has 1 sections
Course, 145 has 2 sections
Course, 146 has 2 sections
Course, 147 has 1 sections
Course, 204 has 1 sections
Course, 210 has 1 sections
Course, 220 has 1 sections
Course, 230 has 2 sections
Course, 240 has 2 sections
Course, 310 has 1 sections
Course, 330 has 1 sections
Course, 350 has 3 sections
Course, 420 has 1 sections
Course, 430 has 2 sections
Course, 450 has 1 sections

PL/SQL procedure successfully completed.
```

**LAB
10.3**

c) Change this script so that the exception e_no_sections is re-raised in the outer block.

Answer: Your script should look similar to the script shown. All changes are shown in bold letters.

```
-- ch10_4b.sql, version 2.0
SET SERVEROUTPUT ON
DECLARE
   CURSOR course_cur IS
      SELECT course_no
        FROM course;

   v_total NUMBER;
   e_no_sections EXCEPTION;
BEGIN
   FOR course_rec in course_cur LOOP
      BEGIN
         SELECT COUNT(*)
           INTO v_total
           FROM section
          WHERE course_no = course_rec.course_no;

         IF v_total = 0 THEN
            RAISE e_no_sections;
         ELSE
            DBMS_OUTPUT.PUT_LINE ('Course, '||
               course_rec.course_no||' has '||
               v_total||' sections');
         END IF;
      EXCEPTION
```

```
            WHEN e_no_sections THEN
                RAISE;
        END;
    END LOOP;
EXCEPTION
    WHEN e_no_sections THEN
        DBMS_OUTPUT.PUT_LINE ('There are no sections for '||
            'the course');
END;
```

In this version of the example, the exception-handling section of the inner block was modified. The DBMS_OUTPUT.PUT_LINE statement has been replaced by the RAISE statement. In addition, the exception-handling section was included in the outer block.

Notice that the error message has been modified as well. There is no course number displayed by the error message. This change is necessary because the exception-handling section of the outer block is located outside of the cursor FOR loop. Therefore, the course number is not visible by the exception. When run, this version produces the following output:

```
Course, 10 has 1 sections
Course, 20 has 4 sections
Course, 25 has 9 sections
There are no sections for the course

PL/SQL procedure successfully completed.
```

In order to produce the error message that contains the course number, the script should be modified as follows:

```
-- ch10_4c.sql, version 3.0
SET SERVEROUTPUT ON
DECLARE
    CURSOR course_cur IS
        SELECT course_no
          FROM course;

    v_total NUMBER;
    v_course_no NUMBER;
    e_no_sections EXCEPTION;
BEGIN
    FOR course_rec in course_cur LOOP
        v_course_no := course_rec.course_no;
        BEGIN
            SELECT COUNT(*)
              INTO v_total
              FROM section
             WHERE course_no = course_rec.course_no;
```

```
            IF v_total = 0 THEN
                RAISE e_no_sections;
            ELSE
                DBMS_OUTPUT.PUT_LINE ('Course, '||
                    course_rec.course_no||' has '||v_total||
                    ' sections');
            END IF;
        EXCEPTION
            WHEN e_no_sections THEN
                RAISE;
        END;
    END LOOP;
EXCEPTION
    WHEN e_no_sections THEN
        DBMS_OUTPUT.PUT_LINE ('There are no sections for '||
            'the course '||v_course_no);
END;
```

In this version of the example, there is a new variable, v_course_no, that holds
the current course number. Notice that the assignment statement for this variable is the first executable statement of the cursor FOR loop. This arrangement
guarantees that the variable will have a value assigned to it before the
e_no_sections exception is raised. When run, the example produces the following output:

```
Course, 10 has 1 sections
Course, 20 has 4 sections
Course, 25 has 9 sections
There are no sections for the course 80

PL/SQL procedure successfully completed.
```

LAB 10.3 SELF-REVIEW QUESTIONS

In order to test your progress, you should be able to answer the following questions.

1) When an exception is raised in the declaration section of the inner block, it
   propagates to the

   a) _____ exception-handling section of this block.
   b) _____ exception-handling section of the enclosing (outer) block.
   c) _____ host environment and causes a syntax error.

2) When an exception is raised in the declaration section of the outer block, it
   propagates to the

   a) _____ exception-handling section of this block.
   b) _____ host environment and causes a syntax error.

3) When an exception is raised in the executable section of the inner block, it propagates to the

a) _____ exception-handling section of this block.
b) _____ exception-handling section of the enclosing block.
c) _____ host environment and causes a syntax error.

4) When an exception is re-raised in the inner block, control is transferred to the

a) _____ exception-handling section of this block.
b) _____ exception-handling section of the enclosing block.

**LAB
10.3**

5) To re-raise an exception, one must issue which of the following statements?

a) _____ RAISE exception_name
b) _____ RAISE
c) _____ There is no need to issue any statements.

Answers appear in Appendix A, Section 10.3.

CHAPTER 10

TEST YOUR THINKING

In this chapter you learned about built-in exceptions. Here are some projects that will help you test the depth of your understanding.

1) Create the following script. For each section determine the number of students registered. If this number is equal to or greater than 15, raise the user-defined exception `e_too_many_students` and display the error message. Otherwise, display how many students are in a section. Make sure that your program is able to process all sections.

2) Modify the script you created in the previous exercise. Once the exception `e_too_many_students` has been raised in the inner block, re-raise it in the outer block.

The projects in this section are meant to have you utilize all of the skills that you have acquired throughout this chapter. The answers to these projects can be found in Appendix D and at the companion Web site to this book, located at http://www.phptr .com/rosenzweig2e. Visit the Web site periodically to share and discuss your answers.

C H A P T E R   1 1

EXCEPTIONS: ADVANCED CONCEPTS

In Chapters 7 and 10, you encountered the concept of error handling, built-in exceptions, and user-defined exceptions. You also learned about the scope of an exception, and how to re-raise an exception.

In this chapter you will conclude your exploration of error handling and exceptions with a study of advanced topics. After working through this chapter, you will be able to associate an error number with an error message. You also will be able to trap a runtime error having an Oracle error number but no name by which it can be referenced.

L A B   1 1 . 1

RAISE_APPLICATION_ERROR

LAB OBJECTIVE

After this Lab, you will be able to:

✔ Use RAISE_APPLICATION_ERROR

RAISE_APPLICATION_ERROR is a special built-in procedure provided by Oracle. This procedure allows programmers to create meaningful error messages for a specific application. The RAISE_APLICATION_ERROR procedure works with user-defined exceptions. The syntax of the RAISE_APPLICATION_ERROR is

```
RAISE_APPLICATION_ERROR(error_number, error_message);
```

or

```
RAISE_APPLICATION_ERROR(error_number, error_message,
    keep_errors);
```

As you can see, there are two forms of the RAISE_APPLICATION_ERROR procedure. The first form contains only two parameters: error_number and error_message. The error_number is a number of the error that a programmer associates with a specific error message, and can be any number between −20,999 and −20,000. The error_message is the text of the error, and it can contain up to 512 characters.

The second form of RAISE_APPLICATION_ERROR contains one additional parameter: keep_errors. Keep_errors is an optional Boolean parameter. If keep_errors is set to TRUE, the new error will be added to the list of errors that has been raised already. If keep_errors is set to FALSE, the new error replaces the list of errors that has been raised already. The default value for the parameter keep_errors is FALSE.

It is important for you to note that the RAISE_APPLICATION_ERROR procedure works with unnamed user-defined exceptions. It associates the number of the error with the text of the error. Therefore, the user-defined exception does not have a name associated with it.

Consider the following example used in Chapter 10. This example illustrates the use of the named user-defined exception and the RAISE statement. Within the example you will be able to compare a modified version using the unnamed user-defined exception and the RAISE_APPLICATION_ERROR procedure.

■ FOR EXAMPLE

First, view the original example from Chapter 10. Notice that the named user-defined exception and the RAISE statement are shown in bold letters.

```
DECLARE
    v_student_id STUDENT.STUDENT_ID%TYPE := &sv_student_id;
    v_total_courses NUMBER;
    e_invalid_id EXCEPTION;
BEGIN
    IF v_student_id < 0 THEN
        RAISE e_invalid_id;
    ELSE
        SELECT COUNT(*)
          INTO v_total_courses
          FROM enrollment
         WHERE student_id = v_student_id;
        DBMS_OUTPUT.PUT_LINE ('The student is registered for
            '||v_total_courses||' courses');
    END IF;
    DBMS_OUTPUT.PUT_LINE ('No exception has been raised');
EXCEPTION
    WHEN e_invalid_id THEN
        DBMS_OUTPUT.PUT_LINE ('An id cannot be negative');
END;
```

Now, compare the modified example as follows (changes are shown in bold letters):

```
DECLARE
    v_student_id STUDENT.STUDENT_ID%TYPE := &sv_student_id;
    v_total_courses NUMBER;
BEGIN
    IF v_student_id < 0 THEN
        RAISE_APPLICATION_ERROR
            (-20000, 'An id cannot be negative');
    ELSE
        SELECT COUNT(*)
          INTO v_total_courses
          FROM enrollment
         WHERE student_id = v_student_id;
```

```
      DBMS_OUTPUT.PUT_LINE ('The student is registered for
          '||v_total_courses||' courses');
   END IF;
END;
```

The second version of the example does not contain the name of the exception, the RAISE statement, nor the error-handling section of the PL/SQL block. Instead, it has a single RAISE_APPLICATION_ERROR statement.

Even though the RAISE_APPLICATION_ERROR is a built-in procedure, it can be referred to as a statement when used in the PL/SQL block.

Both versions of the example achieve the same result: The processing stops if a negative number is provided for v_student_id. However, the second version of this example produces the output that has the look and feel of an error message. Now, run both versions of the example with the value of –4 for the variable v_student_id.

The first version of the example produces the following output:

```
Enter value for sv_student_id: -4
old    2: v_student_id STUDENT.STUDENT_ID%TYPE := &sv_
student_id;
new    2: v_student_id STUDENT.STUDENT_ID%TYPE := -4;
An id cannot be negative

PL/SQL procedure successfully completed.
```

The second version of the example produces the following output:

```
Enter value for sv_student_id: -4
old    2:     v_student_id STUDENT.STUDENT_ID%TYPE :=
&sv_student_id;
new    2:     v_student_id STUDENT.STUDENT_ID%TYPE := -4;
DECLARE
*
ERROR at line 1:
ORA-20000: An id cannot be negative
ORA-06512: at line 6
```

The output produced by the first version of the example contains the error message "An id cannot be negative" and the message "PL/SQL completed . . .". The error message "An id cannot . . ." in the output generated by the second version of the example looks like the error message generated by the system, because the error number ORA-20000 precedes the error message.

The RAISE_APPLICATION_ERROR procedure can work with built-in exceptions as well. Consider the following example:

■ *FOR EXAMPLE*

```
DECLARE
    v_student_id STUDENT.STUDENT_ID%TYPE := &sv_student_id;
    v_name VARCHAR2(50);
BEGIN
    SELECT first_name||' '||last_name
      INTO v_name
      FROM student
     WHERE student_id = v_student_id;
    DBMS_OUTPUT.PUT_LINE (v_name);
EXCEPTION
    WHEN NO_DATA_FOUND THEN
        RAISE_APPLICATION_ERROR (-20001, 'This ID is invalid');
END;
```

When the value of 100 is entered for the student ID, the example produces the output shown:

```
Enter value for sv_student_id: 100
old    2:    v_student_id STUDENT.STUDENT_ID%TYPE :=
&sv_student_id;
new    2:    v_student_id STUDENT.STUDENT_ID%TYPE := 100;
DECLARE
*
ERROR at line 1:
ORA-20001: This ID is invalid
ORA-06512: at line 12
```

The built-in exception NO_DATA_FOUND is raised because there is no record in the STUDENT table corresponding to this value of the student ID. However, the number of the error message does not refer to the exception NO_DATA_FOUND. It refers to the error message "This ID is invalid."

The RAISE_APPLICATION_ERROR procedure allows programmers to return error messages in a manner that is consistent with Oracle errors. However, it is important for you to note that it is up to a programmer to maintain the relationship between the error numbers and the error messages. For example, you have designed an application to maintain the enrollment information on students. In this application you have associated the error text "This ID is invalid" with the error number ORA-20001. This error message can be used by your application for any invalid ID. Once you have associated the error number (ORA-20001) with a specific error message (This ID is invalid), you should not assign this error number to another error message. If you do not maintain the relationship between error numbers and error messages, the error-handling interface of your application might become very confusing to the users and to yourself.

LAB 11.1 EXERCISES

11.1.1 USE RAISE_APPLICATION_ERROR

In this exercise, you calculate how many students are registered for each course. You then display a message on the screen that contains the course number and the number of students registered for it. The original PL/SQL script will not contain any exception handlers, so you will be asked to add the RAISE_APPLICATION_ERROR statement.

Create the following PL/SQL script:

```
-- ch11_1a.sql, version 1.0
SET SERVEROUTPUT ON
DECLARE
   CURSOR course_cur IS
      SELECT course_no, section_id
        FROM section
      ORDER BY course_no, section_id;
   v_cur_course SECTION.COURSE_NO%TYPE := 0;
   v_students NUMBER(3) := 0;
   v_total NUMBER(3) := 0;
BEGIN
   FOR course_rec IN course_cur LOOP
      IF v_cur_course = 0 THEN
         v_cur_course := course_rec.course_no;
      END IF;

      SELECT COUNT(*)
        INTO v_students
        FROM enrollment
       WHERE section_id = course_rec.section_id;

      IF v_cur_course = course_rec.course_no THEN
         v_total := v_total + v_students;
      ELSE
         DBMS_OUTPUT.PUT_LINE ('Course '||v_cur_course||
            ' has '||v_total||' student(s)');
         v_cur_course := course_rec.course_no;
         v_total := 0;
      END IF;
   END LOOP;
   DBMS_OUTPUT.PUT_LINE ('Done...');
END;
```

Take a closer look this script. As you learned earlier, this script determines the number of students registered for each course. It then displays the course number and the number of students on the screen. In order to achieve these results, the cursor needs to be defined on the SECTION table. This cursor retrieves the course numbers and section IDs. It also now defines three variables: v_cur_course, v_students, and v_total.

The variable v_cur_course holds the number of the current course. There are duplicate course numbers in the SECTION table, because a course can have multiple sections. In order to display the number of students for each course rather than each section, you need to store the number of the current course. For example, course 10 has three sections: 1, 2, and 3. Section 1 has 3 students, section 2 has 5 students, and section 3 has 10 students. Therefore, course 10 has 18 students. Once this number is calculated, the message "10 has 18 student(s)" can be displayed on the screen. As a result, you need to compare the variable v_cur_course to the course number returned by the cursor.

The variable v_students holds the number of students registered for a specific section of a course. As long as the value of the variable v_cur_course equals the value of the course_rec.course_no, the variable v_students is added to the current value of the variable v_total, which holds the total number of students registered for a given course.

Notice that in the body of the cursor FOR loop, there are two IF statements. The first IF statement

```
IF v_cur_course = 0 THEN
   v_cur_course := course_rec.course_no;
END IF;
```

is executed only once, for the first iteration of the cursor FOR loop. This IF statement guarantees that the value of course_rec.course_no is assigned to the variable v_cur_course before any further processing.

The second IF statement

```
IF v_cur_course = course_rec.course_no THEN
   v_total := v_total + v_students;
ELSE
   DBMS_OUTPUT.PUT_LINE ('Course '||v_cur_course||' has '||
      v_total||' student(s)');
   v_cur_course := course_rec.course_no;
   v_total := 0;
END IF;
```

compares the value of v_cur_course to the value of the course_rec.course_no. For the first iteration of the cursor FOR loop, this condition of the IF statement evaluates to TRUE, and the value of v_students is added to the current value of `v_total`. For the next iteration of the cursor FOR loop, the IF statement evaluates to TRUE if the course number has not changed. However, if the course number has changed, this IF statement evaluates to FALSE, and the ELSE part of the IF statement is executed. Therefore, the DBMS_OUTPUT.PUT_LINE statement displays the course information on the screen, the value of the `course_rec.course_no` is assigned to the variable `v_cur_course`, and the value of the variable `v_total` is set to 0 again. Why do you think the variable `v_total` must be set to 0?

Execute the script, and then answer the following questions:

a) What output was printed on the screen?

b) Modify this script so that if a course has more than 20 students enrolled in it, an error message is displayed indicating that this course has too many students enrolled.

c) Execute the new version of the script. What output was printed on the screen?

d) Generally, when an exception is raised and handled inside a loop, the loop does not terminate prematurely. Why do you think the cursor FOR loop terminates as soon as RAISE_APPLICATION_ERROR executes?

LAB 11.1 EXERCISE ANSWERS

This section gives you some suggested answers to the questions in Lab 11.1, with discussion related to how those answers resulted. The most important thing to realize is whether your answer works. You should figure out the implications of the answers here and what the effects are from any different answers you may come up with.

11.1.1 ANSWERS

a) What output was printed on the screen?

Answer:

```
Course 10 has 1 student(s)
Course 20 has 6 student(s)
```

```
Course 25 has 40 student(s)
Course 100 has 7 student(s)
Course 120 has 19 student(s)
Course 122 has 20 student(s)
Course 124 has 3 student(s)
Course 125 has 6 student(s)
Course 130 has 6 student(s)
Course 132 has 0 student(s)
Course 134 has 2 student(s)
Course 135 has 2 student(s)
Course 140 has 7 student(s)
Course 142 has 3 student(s)
Course 144 has 0 student(s)
Course 145 has 0 student(s)
Course 146 has 1 student(s)
Course 147 has 0 student(s)
Course 204 has 0 student(s)
Course 210 has 0 student(s)
Course 220 has 0 student(s)
Course 230 has 2 student(s)
Course 240 has 1 student(s)
Course 310 has 0 student(s)
Course 330 has 0 student(s)
Course 350 has 9 student(s)
Course 420 has 0 student(s)
Course 430 has 0 student(s)
Done...
```

PL/SQL procedure successfully completed.

Notice that each course number is displayed a single time only.

b) Modify this script so that if a course has more than 20 students enrolled in it, an error message is displayed indicating that this course has too many students enrolled.

Answer: Your script should look similar to the script shown. All changes are shown in bold letters.

```
-- ch11_1b.sql, version 2.0
SET SERVEROUTPUT ON
DECLARE
   CURSOR course_cur IS
      SELECT course_no, section_id
        FROM section
       ORDER BY course_no, section_id;
   v_cur_course SECTION.COURSE_NO%TYPE := 0;
   v_students NUMBER(3) := 0;
   v_total NUMBER(3) := 0;
```

```
BEGIN
   FOR course_rec IN course_cur LOOP
      IF v_cur_course = 0 THEN
         v_cur_course := course_rec.course_no;
      END IF;

      SELECT COUNT(*)
        INTO v_students
        FROM enrollment
       WHERE section_id = course_rec.section_id;

      IF v_cur_course = course_rec.course_no THEN
         v_total := v_total + v_students;
         IF v_total > 20 THEN
            RAISE_APPLICATION_ERROR (-20002, 'Course '||
               v_cur_course||' has too many students');
         END IF;
      ELSE
         DBMS_OUTPUT.PUT_LINE ('Course '||v_cur_course||
            'has '||v_total||' student(s)');
         v_cur_course := course_rec.course_no;
         v_total := 0;
      END IF;
   END LOOP;
   DBMS_OUTPUT.PUT_LINE ('Done...');
END;
```

Consider the result if you were to add another IF statement to this script, one in which the IF statement checks whether the value of the variable exceeds 20. If the value of the variable does exceed 20, the RAISE_APPLICATION_ERROR statement executes, and the error message is displayed on the screen.

c) Execute the new version of the script. What output was printed on the screen?

Answer: Your output should look similar to the following:

```
Course 10 has 1 student(s)
Course 20 has 6 student(s)
DECLARE
*
ERROR at line 1:
ORA-20002: Course 25 has too many students
ORA-06512: at line 21
```

Course 25 has 40 students enrolled. As a result, the IF statement

```
IF v_total > 20 THEN
    RAISE_APPLICATION_ERROR (-20002, 'Course '||
        v_cur_course||' has too many students');
END IF;
```

evaluates to TRUE, and the unnamed user-defined error is displayed on the screen.

d) Generally, when an exception is raised and handled inside a loop, the loop does not terminate prematurely. Why do you think the cursor FOR loop terminates as soon as RAISE_APPLICATION_ERROR executes?

Answer: When the RAISE_APPLICATION_ERROR procedure is used to handle a user-defined exception, control is passed to the host environment as soon as the error is handled. Therefore, the cursor FOR loop terminates prematurely. In this case, it terminates as soon as the course that has more than 20 students registered for it is encountered.

When a user-defined exception is used with the RAISE statement, the exception propagates from the inner block to the outer block. For example:

```
-- outer block
BEGIN
    FOR record IN cursor LOOP
        -- inner block
        BEGIN
            RAISE my_exception;
        EXCEPTION
            WHEN my_exception THEN
                DBMS_OUTPUT.PUT_LINE ('An error has occurred');
        END;
    END LOOP;
END;
```

In this example, the exception `my_exception` is raised and handled in the inner block. Control of the execution is passed to the outer block once the exception `my_exception` is raised. As a result, the cursor FOR loop will not terminate prematurely.

When the RAISE_APPLICATION_ERROR procedure is used, control is always passed to the host environment. The exception does not propagate from the inner block to the outer block. Therefore, any loop defined in the outer block will terminate prematurely if an error has been raised in the inner block, with the help of the RAISE_APPLICATION_ERROR procedure.

LAB 11.1 SELF-REVIEW QUESTIONS

In order to test your progress, you should be able to answer the following questions.

1) The RAISE_APPLICATION_ERROR works with which of the following?

    a) _____ Named user-defined exceptions only
    b) _____ Unnamed user-defined exceptions only
    c) _____ Built-in and unnamed user-defined exceptions

2) The RAISE_APPLICATION_ERROR procedure requires which of the following parameters?

    a) _____ error_number, error_text, keep_error
    b) _____ error_text, keep_error
    c) _____ error_number, error_text

3) The error number used in the RAISE_APPLICATION_ERROR must be which of the following?

    a) _____ A number between −20,000 and −20,999
    b) _____ A number between 20,000 and 20,999

4) The RAISE_APLICATION_ERROR halts the execution of the program.

    a) _____ True
    b) _____ False

5) When the parameter keep_error is set to TRUE, which of the following occurs?

    a) _____ An error message is displayed on the screen.
    b) _____ An error number is displayed on the screen.
    c) _____ A new error message is added to the list of raised error messages.

Answers appear in Appendix A, Section 11.1.

L A B   1 1 . 2

EXCEPTION_INIT PRAGMA

LAB OBJECTIVE

After this Lab, you will be able to:

✔ Use EXCEPTION_INIT Pragma

Often your programs need to handle an Oracle error having a particular number associated with it, but no name by which it can be referenced. As a result, you are unable to write a handler to trap this error. In a case like this, you can use a construct called *pragma*. A pragma is a special instruction to the PL/SQL compiler. It is important to note that pragmas are processed at the time of the compilation. The *EXCEPTION_INIT pragma* allows you to associate an Oracle error number with a name of a user-defined error. Once you associate an error name with an Oracle error number, you can reference the error and write a handler for it.

The EXCEPTION_INIT pragma appears in the declaration section of a block as shown:

```
DECLARE
   exception_name EXCEPTION;
   PRAGMA EXCEPTION_INIT(exception_name, error_code);
```

Notice that the declaration of the user-defined exception appears before the EXCEPTION_INIT pragma where it is used. The EXCEPTION_INIT pragma has two parameters: exception_name and error_code. The exception_name is the name of your exception, and the error_code is the number of the Oracle error you want to associate with your exception. Consider the following:

■ FOR EXAMPLE

```
DECLARE
   v_zip ZIPCODE.ZIP%TYPE := '&sv_zip';
BEGIN
   DELETE FROM zipcode
```

```
        WHERE zip = v_zip;
        DBMS_OUTPUT.PUT_LINE ('Zip '||v_zip||
           ' has been deleted');
        COMMIT;
    END;
```

In this example, the record corresponding to the value of zipcode provided by a user is deleted from the ZIPCODE table. Next, the message that a specific zipcode has been deleted is displayed on the screen.

Compare the results running this example entering 06870 for the value of v_zip. The example produces the following output:

```
Enter value for sv_zip: 06870
old   2:    v_zip ZIPCODE.ZIP%TYPE := '&sv_zip';
new   2:    v_zip ZIPCODE.ZIP%TYPE := '06870';
DECLARE
*
ERROR at line 1:
ORA-02292: integrity constraint (STUDENT.STU_ZIP_FK)
violated - child record found
ORA-06512: at line 4
```

The error message generated by this example occurs because you are trying to delete a record from the ZIPCODE table while its child records exist in the STU-DENT table, thus violating the referential integrity constraint STU_ZIP_FK. In other words, there is a record with a foreign key (STU_ZIP_FK) in the STUDENT table (child table) that references a record in the ZIPCODE table (parent table).

Notice that this error has Oracle error number ORA-02292 assigned to it, but it does not have a name. As a result, you need to associate this error number with a user-defined exception, so you can handle this error in the script.

Contrast the example if you modify it as follows (all changes are shown in bold letters):

■ FOR EXAMPLE

```
DECLARE
    v_zip ZIPCODE.ZIP%TYPE := '&sv_zip';
    e_child_exists EXCEPTION;
    PRAGMA EXCEPTION_INIT(e_child_exists, -2292);
BEGIN
    DELETE FROM zipcode
     WHERE zip = v_zip;
    DBMS_OUTPUT.PUT_LINE ('Zip '||v_zip||
       ' has been deleted');
    COMMIT;
```

```
EXCEPTION
   WHEN e_child_exists THEN
      DBMS_OUTPUT.PUT_LINE ('Delete students for this '||
         'zipcode first');
END;
```

In this example, you declare the exception `e_child_exists`. Then you associate the exception with the error number –2292. It is important to note you do not use ORA-02292 in the EXCEPTION_INIT pragma. Next, you add the exception-handling section to the PL/SQL block, so you trap this error. Notice that even though the exception `e_child_exists` is user-defined, you do not use the RAISE statement, as you saw in Chapter 10. Why do you think you don't use the RAISE statement?

When you run this example using the same value of zipcode, the following output is produced:

```
Enter value for sv_zip: 06870
old    2:    v_zip ZIPCODE.ZIP%TYPE := '&sv_zip';
new    2:    v_zip ZIPCODE.ZIP%TYPE := '06870';
Delete students for this zipcode first

PL/SQL procedure successfully completed.
```

Notice that this output contains a new error message displayed by the DBMS_OUTPUT.PUT_LINE statement. This version of the output is more descriptive than the previous version. Remember that the user of the program probably does not know about the referential integrity constraints existing in the database. Therefore, the EXCEPTION_INIT pragma improves the readability of your error-handling interface. If the need arises, you can use multiple EXCEPTION_INIT pragmas in your program.

LAB 11.2 EXERCISES

11.2.1 USE EXCEPTION_INIT PRAGMA

In this exercise, you insert a record in the COURSE table. The original PL/SQL script does not contain any exception handlers, so you are asked to define an exception and add the EXCEPTION_INIT pragma.

Create the following PL/SQL script:

```
-- ch11_2a.sql, version 1.0
SET SERVEROUTPUT ON
BEGIN
   INSERT INTO course
      (course_no, description, created_by, created_date)
```

```
VALUES
    (COURSE_NO_SEQ.NEXTVAL, 'TEST COURSE', USER, SYSDATE);
COMMIT;
DBMS_OUTPUT.PUT_LINE ('One course has been added');
END;
```

Execute the script, and then answer the following questions:

a) What output is printed on the screen?

b) Explain why the script does not execute successfully.

c) Add a user-defined exception to the script, so that the error generated by the INSERT statement is handled.

d) Run the new version of the script. Explain the output produced by the new version of the script.

LAB 11.2 EXERCISE ANSWERS

This section gives you some suggested answers to the questions in Lab 11.2, with discussion related to how those answers resulted. The most important thing to realize is whether your answer works. You should figure out the implications of the answers here and what the effects are from any different answers you may come up with.

11.2.1 ANSWERS

a) What output is printed on the screen?

Answer: Your output should look like the following:

```
BEGIN
*
ERROR at line 1:
ORA-02290: check constraint
(STUDENT.CRSE_MODIFIED_DATE_NNULL) violated
ORA-06512: at line 2
```

b) Explain why the script does not execute successfully.

Answer: The script does not execute successfully because a NULL is inserted for the MODIFIED_BY and MODIFIED_DATE columns.

The MODIFED_BY and MODIFIED_DATE columns have check constraints defined on them. These constraints can be viewed by querying one of the data dictionary tables. The data dictionary comprises tables owned by the user SYS. These tables provide the database with information that it uses to manage itself.

Consider the following SELECT statement against one of Oracle's data dictionary tables, USER_CONSTRAINTS. This table contains information on various constraints defined on each table of the STUDENT schema.

```
SELECT constraint_name, search_condition
FROM user_constraints
WHERE table_name = 'COURSE';
```

```
CONSTRAINT_NAME                 SEARCH_CONDITION
-----------------------------   --------------------------
CRSE_CREATED_DATE_NNULL         "CREATED_DATE" IS NOT NULL
CRSE_MODIFIED_BY_NNULL          "MODIFIED_BY" IS NOT NULL
CRSE_MODIFIED_DATE_NNULL        "MODIFIED_DATE" IS NOT NULL
CRSE_DESCRIPTION_NNULL          "DESCRIPTION" IS NOT NULL
CRSE_COURSE_NO_NNULL            "COURSE_NO" IS NOT NULL
CRSE_CREATED_BY_NNULL           "CREATED_BY" IS NOT NULL
CRSE_PK
CRSE_CRSE_FK

8 rows selected.
```

Notice that the last two rows refer to the primary and foreign key constraints, so there are no search conditions specified.

Based on the results produced by the preceding SELECT statement, there are six columns having a NOT NULL constraint. However, the INSERT statement

```
INSERT INTO course
    (course_no, description, created_by, created_date)
VALUES
    (COURSE_NO_SEQ.NEXTVAL, 'TEST COURSE',USER, SYSDATE);
```

has only four columns having NOT NULL constraints. The columns MODIFIED_BY and MODIFIED_DATE are not included in the INSERT statement. Any column of a table not listed in the INSERT statement has NULL assigned to it when a new record is added to the table. If a column has a NOT NULL constraint and is not listed in the INSERT statement, the INSERT statement fails and causes an error.

c) Add a user-defined exception to the script, so that the error generated by the INSERT statement is handled.

Answer: Your script should look similar to the script shown. All changes are shown in bold letters.

```
-- ch11_2b.sql, version 2.0
SET SERVEROUTPUT ON
DECLARE
   e_constraint_violation EXCEPTION;
   PRAGMA EXCEPTION_INIT(e_constraint_violation, -2290);
BEGIN
   INSERT INTO course
      (course_no, description, created_by, created_date)
   VALUES
      (COURSE_NO_SEQ.NEXTVAL, 'TEST COURSE', USER, SYSDATE);
   COMMIT;
   DBMS_OUTPUT.PUT_LINE ('One course has been added');
EXCEPTION
   WHEN e_constraint_violation THEN
      DBMS_OUTPUT.PUT_LINE ('INSERT statement is '||
         'violating a constraint');
END;
```

In this script, you declared the e_constraint_violation exception. Then, using the EXCEPTION_INIT pragma to associate the exception with the Oracle error number ORA-02290, the handler is written for the new exception e_constraint_violation.

d) Run the new version of the script. Explain the output produced by the new version of the script.

Answer: Your output should look similar to the following:

```
INSERT statement is violating a constraint

PL/SQL procedure successfully completed.
```

Once you define an exception and associate an Oracle error number with it, you can write an exception handler for it. As a result, as soon as the INSERT statement causes an error, control of the execution is transferred to the exception-handling section of the block. Then, the message "INSERT statement . . ." is displayed on the screen. Notice that once an exception is raised, the execution of the program does not halt. The script completes successfully.

LAB 11.2 SELF-REVIEW QUESTIONS

In order to test your progress, you should be able to answer the following questions.

1) A pragma is

    a) _____ a special procedure provided by Oracle.
    b) _____ a special instruction to the compiler.

2) A pragma is processed during

    a) _____ runtime.
    b) _____ compile time.

3) The EXCEPTION_INIT pragma associates a

    a) _____ built-in exception with a user-defined error number.
    b) _____ user-defined exception with a user-defined error number.
    c) _____ user-defined exception with an Oracle error number.

4) The EXCEPTION_INIT pragma needs which of the following parameters?

    a) _____ error_number only
    b) _____ error_name only
    c) _____ error_name and error_number

5) Which of the following is a valid error_number parameter?

    a) _____ ORA-02292
    b) _____ 2292
    c) _____ −2292

Answers appear in Appendix A, Section 11.2.

L A B   1 1 . 3

SQLCODE AND SQLERRM

LAB OBJECTIVE

After this Lab, you will be able to:

✔ Use SQLCODE and SQLERRM

In Chapter 7, you learned about the Oracle exception OTHERS. You will recall that all Oracle errors can be trapped with the help of the OTHERS exception handler. Consider the following example.

■ *FOR EXAMPLE*

```
DECLARE
    v_zip VARCHAR2(5) := '&sv_zip';
    v_city VARCHAR2(15);
    v_state CHAR(2);
BEGIN
    SELECT city, state
      INTO v_city, v_state
      FROM zipcode
     WHERE zip = v_zip;
    DBMS_OUTPUT.PUT_LINE (v_city||', '||v_state);
EXCEPTION
    WHEN OTHERS THEN
        DBMS_OUTPUT.PUT_LINE ('An error has occurred');
END;
```

When "07458" is entered for the value of zipcode, this example produces the following output:

```
Enter value for sv_zip: 07458
old   2:    v_zip VARCHAR2(5) := '&sv_zip';
```

```
new    2:    v_zip VARCHAR2(5) := '07458';
An error has occurred

PL/SQL procedure successfully completed.
```

This output informs you that an error has occurred at runtime. However, you do not know what the error is and what caused it. Maybe there is no record in the ZIPCODE table corresponding to the value provided at runtime, or maybe there is a datatype mismatch caused by the SELECT INTO statement. As you can see, even though this is a simple example, there are a number of possible runtime errors that can occur.

Of course, you cannot always know all of the possible runtime errors that may occur when a program is running. Therefore, it is a good practice to have the OTHERS exception handler in your script. To improve the error-handling interface of your program, Oracle provides you with two built-in functions, SQLCODE and SQLERRM, used with the OTHERS exception handler. The SQLCODE function returns the Oracle error number, and the SQLERRM function returns the error message. The maximum length of a message returned by the SQLERRM function is 512 bytes.

Consider what happens if you modify the preceding by adding the SQLCODE and SQLERRM functions as follows (all changes are shown in bold letters):

■ FOR EXAMPLE

```
DECLARE
   v_zip VARCHAR2(5) := '&sv_zip';
   v_city VARCHAR2(15);
   v_state CHAR(2);
   v_err_code NUMBER;
   v_err_msg VARCHAR2(200);
BEGIN
   SELECT city, state
     INTO v_city, v_state
     FROM zipcode
    WHERE zip = v_zip;
   DBMS_OUTPUT.PUT_LINE (v_city||', '||v_state);
EXCEPTION
   WHEN OTHERS THEN
      v_err_code := SQLCODE;
      v_err_msg := SUBSTR(SQLERRM, 1, 200);
      DBMS_OUTPUT.PUT_LINE ('Error code: '||v_err_code);
      DBMS_OUTPUT.PUT_LINE ('Error message: '||v_err_msg);
END;
```

When executed, this example produces the output shown:

```
Enter value for sv_zip: 07458
old    2:     v_zip VARCHAR2(5) := '&sv_zip';
new    2:     v_zip VARCHAR2(5) := '07458';
Error code: -6502
Error message: ORA-06502: PL/SQL: numeric or value error

PL/SQL procedure successfully completed.
```

In this example, you declare two variables: `v_err_code` and `v_err_msg`. Then, in the exception-handling section of the block, you assign SQLCODE to the variable `v_err_code`, and SQLERRM to the variable `v_err_msg`. Next, you use the DBMS_OUTPUT.PUT_LINE statements to display the error number and the error message on the screen.

Notice that this output is more informative than the output produced by the previous version of the example because it displays the error message. Once you know which runtime error has occurred in your program, you can take steps to prevent this error's recurrence.

Generally, the SQLCODE function returns a negative number for an error number. However, there are a few exceptions:

- When SQLCODE is referenced outside the exception section, it returns 0 for the error code. The value of 0 means successful completion.

- When SQLCODE is used with the user-defined exception, it returns +1 for the error code.

- SQLCODE returns a value of 100 when the NO_DATA_FOUND exception is raised.

The SQLERRM function accepts an error number as a parameter, and it returns an error message corresponding to the error number. Usually, it works with the value returned by SQLCODE. However, you can provide the error number yourself if such a need arises. Consider the following example:

■ FOR EXAMPLE

```
BEGIN
   DBMS_OUTPUT.PUT_LINE ('Error code: '||SQLCODE);
   DBMS_OUTPUT.PUT_LINE ('Error message1: '||
      SQLERRM(SQLCODE));
   DBMS_OUTPUT.PUT_LINE ('Error message2: '||SQLERRM(100));
   DBMS_OUTPUT.PUT_LINE ('Error message3: '||SQLERRM(200));
   DBMS_OUTPUT.PUT_LINE ('Error message4: '||
      SQLERRM(-20000));
END;
```

In this example, SQLCODE and SQLERRM are used in the executable section of the PL/SQL block. The SQLERRM function accepts the value of the SQLCODE in the second DBMS_OUTPUT.PUT_LINE statement. In the following DBMS_OUPUT.PUT_LINE statements, the SQLERRM accepts the values of 100, 200, and –20,000 respectively. When executed, this example produces the output shown:

```
Error code: 0
Error message1: ORA-0000: normal, successful completion
Error message2: ORA-01403: no data found
Error message3:  -200: non-ORACLE exception
Error message4: ORA-20000:

PL/SQL procedure successfully completed.
```

The first DBMS_OUTPUT.PUT_LINE statement displays the value of the SQLCODE function. Since there is no exception raised, it returns 0. Next, the value returned by the SQLCODE function is accepted as a parameter by SQLERRM. This function returns the message "ORA-0000: normal, ..." Next, SQLERRM accepts 100 as its parameter and returns "ORA-01402: no data . . . ." Notice that when the SQLERRM accepts 200 as its parameter, it is not able to find an Oracle exception that corresponds to the error number 200. Finally, when the SQLERRM accepts –20,000 as its parameter, no error message is returned. Remember that –20,000 is an error number that can be associated with a named user-defined exception.

LAB 11.3 EXERCISES

11.3.1 USE SQLCODE AND SQLERRM

In this exercise, you add a new record to the ZIPCODE table. The original PL/SQL script does not contain any exception handlers. You are asked to add an exception-handling section to this script.

Create the following PL/SQL script:

```
-- ch11_3a.sql, version 1.0
SET SERVEROUTPUT ON
BEGIN
   INSERT INTO ZIPCODE
      (zip, city, state, created_by, created_date,
       modified_by, modified_date)
   VALUES (
      '10027', 'NEW YORK', 'NY', USER, SYSDATE, USER,
      SYSDATE);
   COMMIT;
END;
```

Execute the script and answer the following questions:

a) What output is printed on the screen?

b) Modify the script so that the script completes successfully, and the error number and message are displayed on the screen.

c) Run the new version of the script. Explain the output produced by the new version of the script.

LAB 11.3 EXERCISE ANSWERS

This section gives you some suggested answers to the questions in Lab 11.3, with discussion related to how those answers resulted. The most important thing to realize is whether your answer works. You should figure out the implications of the answers here and what the effects are from any different answers you may come up with.

11.3.1 ANSWERS

a) What output is printed on the screen?

Answer: Your output should look like the following:

```
BEGIN
*
ERROR at line 1:
ORA-00001: unique constraint (STUDENT.ZIP_PK) violated
ORA-06512: at line 2
```

The INSERT statement

```
INSERT INTO ZIPCODE (zip, city, state, created_by,
   created_date, modified_by, modified_date)
VALUES ('10027', 'NEW YORK', 'NY', USER, SYSDATE, USER,
   SYSDATE);
```

causes an error because a record with zipcode 10027 already exists in the ZIP-CODE table. Column ZIP of the ZIPCODE table has a primary key constraint defined on it. Therefore, when you try to insert another record with the value of

ZIP already existing in the ZIPCODE table, the error message "ORA-00001: unique constraint . . ." is generated.

b) Modify the script so that the script completes successfully, and the error number and message are displayed on the screen.

Answer: Your script should resemble the script shown. All changes are shown in bold letters.

**LAB
11.3**

```
-- ch11_3b.sql, version 2.0
SET SERVEROUTPUT ON
BEGIN
    INSERT INTO ZIPCODE (zip, city, state, created_by,
        created_date, modified_by, modified_date)
    VALUES ('10027', 'NEW YORK', 'NY', USER, SYSDATE, USER,
        SYSDATE);
    COMMIT;
EXCEPTION
    WHEN OTHERS THEN
        DECLARE
            v_err_code NUMBER := SQLCODE;
            v_err_msg VARCHAR2(100) := SUBSTR(SQLERRM, 1, 100);
        BEGIN
            DBMS_OUTPUT.PUT_LINE ('Error code: '||v_err_code);
            DBMS_OUTPUT.PUT_LINE ('Error message: '||
                v_err_msg);
        END;
END;
```

In this script, you add an exception-handling section with the OTHERS exception handler. Notice that two variables v_err_code and v_err_msg, are declared, in the exception-handling section of the block, adding an inner PL/SQL block.

c) Run the new version of the script. Explain the output produced by the new version of the script.

Answer: Your output should look similar to the following:

```
Error code: -1
Error message: ORA-00001: unique constraint
(STUDENT.ZIP_PK) violated

PL/SQL procedure successfully completed.
```

Because the INSERT statement causes an error, control is transferred to the OTHERS exception handler. The SQLCODE function returns –1, and the SQLERRM function returns the text of the error corresponding to the error code –1. Once the exception-handling section completes its execution, control is passed to the host environment.

LAB 11.3 SELF-REVIEW QUESTIONS

In order to test your progress, you should be able to answer the following questions.

1) The SQLCODE function returns an Oracle error number.

    a) _____ True
    b) _____ False

2) The SQLERRM function returns the error text corresponding to a specific error number.

    a) _____ True
    b) _____ False

3) When the SQLERRM function cannot return an error message corresponding to a particular error number, which of the following occurs?

    a) _____ SQLERRM causes an error.
    b) _____ SQLERRM does not return anything.
    c) _____ SQLERRM returns "non-ORACLE exception" message.

4) What is the maximum length of the error text returned by the SQLERRM function?

    a) _____ 450 bytes
    b) _____ 550 bytes
    c) _____ 512 bytes

5) The SQLCODE function always returns a negative number.

    a) _____ True
    b) _____ False

Answers appear in Appendix A, Section 11.3.

LAB 11.3

CHAPTER 11

TEST YOUR THINKING

In this chapter you learned about advanced concepts of exception-handling techniques. Here are some projects that will help you test the depth of your understanding.

1) Create the following script. Modify the script created in this section in Chapter 10 (Question 1 of the Test Your Thinking section). Raise a user-defined exception with the RAISE_APPLICATION_ERROR statement. Otherwise, display how many students there are in a section. Make sure your program is able to process all sections.

2) Create the following script. Try to add a record to the INSTRUCTOR table without providing values for the columns MODIFIED_BY and MODIFIED_DATE. Define an exception and associate it with the Oracle error number, so that the error generated by the INSERT statement is handled.

3) Modify the script created in the previous exercise. Instead of declaring a user-defined exception, add the OTHERS exception handler to the exception-handling section of the block. Then display the error number and the error message on the screen.

The projects in this section are meant to have you utilize all of the skills that you have acquired throughout this chapter. The answers to these projects can be found in Appendix D and at the companion Web site to this book, located at http://www.phptr .com/rosenzweig2e. Visit the Web site periodically to share and discuss your answers.

C H A P T E R   1 2

PROCEDURES

PL/SQL STORED CODE

All the PL/SQL that you have written up to this point has been anonymous blocks that were run as scripts and compiled by the database server at runtime. Now you will begin to use modular code. Modular code is a methodology to build a program from distinct parts (modules), each of which performs a specific function or task toward the final objective of the program. Once modular code is stored on the database server, it becomes a database object, or subprogram, that is available to other program units for repeated execution. In order to save code into the database, the source code needs to be sent to the server so that it can be compiled into p-code and stored in the database. In the first lab, you will learn more about stored code and how to write one type of stored code known as procedures. In the second lab, you will learn about passing parameters into and out of procedures.

LAB 12.1

CREATING PROCEDURES

> ### LAB OBJECTIVES
>
> After this Lab, you will be able to:
>
> ✔ Create Procedures
> ✔ Query the Data Dictionary for Information on Procedures

BENEFITS OF MODULAR CODE

A PL/SQL module is any complete logical unit of work. There are four types of PL/SQL modules: (1) anonymous blocks that are run with a text script (this is the type you have used until now), (2) procedures, (3) functions, and (4) packages.

There are two main benefits to using modular code: (1) It is more reusable and (2) it is more manageable.

You create a procedure either in SQL*Plus or in one of the many tools for creating and debugging stored PL/SQL code. If you are using SQL*Plus, you will need to write your code in a text editor and then run it at the SQL*Plus prompt.

BLOCK STRUCTURE

The block structure is common for all the module types. The block begins with a header (for named blocks only), which consists of (1) the name of the module, and (2) a parameter list (if used).

The Declaration section consists of variable, cursors, and subblocks that will be needed in the next section.

The main part of the module is the Execution section, where all the calculations and processing is performed. This will contain executable code such as IF-THEN-ELSE, LOOPS, calls to other PL/SQL modules, and so on.

The last section of the module is an optional exception handler, which is where the code to handle exceptions is placed.

ANONYMOUS BLOCK

Until this chapter, you have only been writing anonymous blocks. Anonymous blocks are very much the same as modules, which were just introduced (except anonymous blocks do not have headers). There are important distinctions, though. As the name implies, anonymous blocks have no name and thus cannot be called by another block. They are not stored in the database and must be compiled and then run each time the script is loaded.

The PL/SQL block in a subprogram is a named block that can accept parameters and can be invoked from an application that can communicate with the Oracle database server. A subprogram can be compiled and stored in the database. This allows the programmer to reuse the program. It also provides for easier maintenance of code. Subprograms are either procedures or functions.

PROCEDURES

A procedure is a module performing one or more actions; it does not need to return any values. The syntax for creating a procedure is as follows:

```
CREATE OR REPLACE PROCEDURE name
    [(parameter[, parameter, ...])]
AS
    [local declarations]
BEGIN
    executable statements
[EXCEPTION
    exception handlers]
END [name];
```

A procedure may have 0 to many parameters. This will be covered in the next lab. Every procedure has two parts: (1) the header portion, which comes before AS (sometimes you will see IS—they are interchangeable), keyword (this contains the procedure name and the parameter list), and (2) the body, which is everything after the IS keyword. The word REPLACE is optional. When the word RE-PLACE is not used in the header of the procedure, in order to change the code in the procedure, the procedure must be dropped first and then re-created. Since it is very common to change the code of the procedure, especially when it is under development, it is strongly recommended to use the OR REPLACE option.

LAB 12.1 EXERCISES

12.1.1 CREATE PROCEDURES

In this exercise, you will run a script that creates a procedure. Using a text editor such as Notepad, create a file with the following script.

```
-- ch12_01a.sql
CREATE OR REPLACE PROCEDURE Discount
AS
  CURSOR c_group_discount
  IS
    SELECT distinct s.course_no, c.description
      FROM section s, enrollment e, course c
     WHERE s.section_id = e.section_id
       AND c.course_no = s.course_no
     GROUP BY s.course_no, c.description,
              e.section_id, s.section_id
     HAVING COUNT(*) >=8;
BEGIN
   FOR r_group_discount IN c_group_discount
   LOOP
      UPDATE course
         SET cost = cost * .95
       WHERE course_no = r_group_discount.course_no;
      DBMS_OUTPUT.PUT_LINE
        ('A 5% discount has been given to'||
         r_group_discount.course_no||' '||
         r_group_discount.description
        );
   END LOOP;
END;
```

At the SQL*Plus session, run the script.

a) What did you see on your screen? Explain what happened.

In order to execute in SQL*Plus use the following syntax:

```
EXECUTE Procedure_name
```

b) Execute the Discount procedure. How did you accomplish this? What are the results that you see in your SQL*Plus screen?

c) The script did not contain a COMMIT. Discuss the issues involved with placing a COMMIT in the procedure and indicate where the COMMIT could be placed.

12.1.2 QUERY THE DATA DICTIONARY FOR INFORMATION ON PROCEDURES

There are two main views in the data dictionary that provide information on stored code. They are the USER_OBJECTS view, to give information about the objects, and the USER_SOURCE, to give the text of the source code. Remember, the data dictionary also has an ALL_ and DBA_ version of these views.

a) Write the select statement to get pertinent information from the USER_OBJECTS view about the Discount procedure you just wrote. Run the query and describe the results.

b) Write the SELECT statement to display the source code from the USER_SOURCE view for the Discount procedure.

LAB 12.1 EXERCISE ANSWERS

12.1.1 ANSWERS

a) What did you see on your screen? Explain what happened.

Answer: `Procedure created.` *The procedure named Discount was compiled into p-code and stored in the database for later execution. Note if you saw an error—this is due to a typing mistake. Recheck the code against the example in the book and recompile.*

b) Execute the Discount procedure. How did you accomplish this? What are the results that you see in your SQL*Plus screen?

Answer:

```
SQL> EXECUTE Discount

5% discount has been given to 25  Adv. Word Perfect
.... (through each course with an enrollment over 8)
PL/SQL procedure successfully completed.
```

c) The script did not contain a COMMIT. Discuss the issues involved with placing a COMMIT in the procedure and indicate where the COMMIT could be placed.

Answer: There is no COMMIT in this procedure, which means the procedure will not up-date the database. A COMMIT needs to be issued after the procedure is run, if you want the changes to be made. Alternatively, you can enter a COMMIT either before or after the END LOOP. If you put the COMMIT before the END LOOP, then you are committing changes after every loop. If you put the COMMIT after the END LOOP, then the changes will not be committed until after the procedure is near completion. It is wiser to take the second option. This way you are better prepared for handling errors.

If you receive an error, then type the command:

```
Show error
```

You can also add to the command:

```
L start_line_number end_line_number
```

to see a portion of the code in order to isolate errors.

12.1.2 ANSWERS

a) Write the SELECT statement to get pertinent information from the USER_OBJECTS view about the Discount procedure you just wrote. Run the query and describe the results.

Answer:

```
SELECT object_name, object_type, status
  FROM user_objects
 WHERE object_name = 'DISCOUNT';
```

The result is:

```
OBJECT_NAME            OBJECT_TYPE        STATUS
--------------------   ----------------   ------
DISCOUNT               PROCEDURE          VALID
```

The status indicates where the procedure was complied successfully. An invalid proce-dure cannot be executed.

b) Write the select statement to display the source code from the USER_SOURCE view for the Discount procedure.

Answer:

```
SQL> column text format a70
     SELECT TO_CHAR(line, 99)||'>', text
```

```
      FROM user_source
    WHERE name = 'DISCOUNT'
```

 A procedure can become invalid if the table it is based on is deleted or changed. You can recompile an invalid procedure with the command

```
alter procedure procedure_name compile
```

L A B   1 2 . 2

PASSING PARAMETERS IN AND OUT OF PROCEDURES

> ## LAB OBJECTIVE
>
> After this Lab, you will be able to:
>
> ✔ Use IN and OUT Parameters with Procedures

PARAMETERS

Parameters are the means to pass values to and from the calling environment to the server. These are the values that will be processed or returned via the execution of the procedure. There are three types of parameters: IN, OUT, and IN OUT.

MODES

Modes specify whether the parameter passed is read in or a receptacle for what comes out.

Figure 12.1 illustrates the relationship between the parameters when they are in the procedure header versus when the procedure is executed.

FORMAL AND ACTUAL PARAMETERS

Formal parameters are the names specified within parentheses as part of the header of a module. Actual parameters are the values—expressions specified within parentheses as a parameter list—when a call is made to the module. The formal parameter and the related actual parameter must be of the same or compatible datatypes. Table 12.1 explains the three types of parameters.

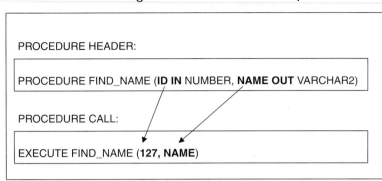

Figure 12.1 ■ Matching Procedure Call to Procedure Header

PASSING OF CONSTRAINTS (DATATYPE) WITH PARAMETER VALUES

Formal parameters do not require constraints in datatype—for example, instead of specifying a constraint such as VARCHAR2(60), you just say VARCHAR2 against the parameter name in the formal parameter list. The constraint is passed with the value when a call is made.

MATCHING ACTUAL AND FORMAL PARAMETERS

Two methods can be used to match actual and formal parameters: positional notation and named notation. Positional notation is simply association by position: The order of the parameters used when executing the procedure matches the

Table 12.1 ■ Three Types of Parameters

Mode	Description	Usage
IN	Passes a value into the program	• Read only value
		• Constants, literals, expressions
		• Cannot be changed within program Default Mode
OUT	Passes a value back from the program	• Write only value
		• Cannot assign default values
		• Has to be a variable
		• Value assigned only if the program is successful
IN OUT	Passes values in and also sends values back	• Has to be a variable
		• Values will be read and then written

order in the procedure's header exactly. Named notation is explicit association using the symbol =>.

> Syntax: formal_parameter_name => argument_value

In named notation, the order does not matter. If you mix notation, list positional notation before named notation.

Default values can be used if a call to the program does not include a value in the parameter list. Note that it makes no difference which style is used; they will both function similarly.

LAB 12.2 EXERCISES

12.2.1 USE IN AND OUT PARAMETERS WITH PROCEDURES

Create the following text file in a text editor. Run the script at a SQL*Plus session.

```
-- ch12_02a.sql
CREATE OR REPLACE PROCEDURE find_sname
  (i_student_id IN NUMBER,
   o_first_name OUT VARCHAR2,
   o_last_name OUT VARCHAR2
   )
AS
BEGIN
   SELECT first_name, last_name
     INTO o_first_name, o_last_name
     FROM student
    WHERE student_id = i_student_id;
EXCEPTION
   WHEN OTHERS
   THEN
      DBMS_OUTPUT.PUT_LINE('Error in finding student_id:
         '||i_student_id);
END find_sname;
```

a) Explain what is happening in the find_sname procedure. What parameters are being passed into and out of the procedure? How would you call the procedure?

Call the find_sname script with the following anonymous block:

```
-- ch12_03a.sql
DECLARE
   v_local_first_name student.first_name%TYPE;
   v_local_last_name student.last_name%TYPE;
BEGIN
   find_sname
      (145, v_local_first_name, v_local_last_name);
   DBMS_OUTPUT.PUT_LINE
      ('Student 145 is: '||v_local_first_name||
      ' '|| v_local_last_name||'.'
      );
END;
```

b) Explain the relationship between the parameters that are in the procedures header definition versus the parameters that are passed IN and OUT of the procedure.

LAB 12.2 EXERCISE ANSWERS

12.2.1 ANSWERS

a) Explain what is happening in the find_sname procedure. What parameters are being passed into and out of the procedure? How would you call the procedure?

Answer: The procedure takes in a `student_id` *via the parameter named* `i_student_id`. *It passes out the parameters* `o_first_name` *and* `o_last_name`. *The procedure is a simple SELECT statement retrieving the* `first_name` *and* `last_name` *from the Student table where the* `student_id` *matches the value of the* `i_student_id`, *which is the only in parameter that exists in the procedure. To call the procedure, a value must be passed in for the* `i_student_id` *parameter.*

b) Explain the relationship between the parameters that are in the procedures header definition versus the parameters that are passed out and in of the procedure.

Answer:When calling the procedure find_sname, a valid student_id *should be passed in for the* i_student_id. *If it is not a valid* student_id, *the exception will be raised. Two variables must also be listed when calling the procedure. These variables,* v_local_first_name *and* v_local_last_name, *are used to hold the values of the parameters that are being passed out. After the procedure has been executed, the local variables will have value and can then be displayed with a DBMS_OUTPUT.PUT _LINE.*

LAB 12.2 SELF-REVIEW QUESTIONS

In order to test your progress, you should be able to answer the following questions.

1) The benefits of module code are that it (check all that apply)

    a) _____ takes IN and OUT parameters.
    b) _____ can be called by many types of calling environments.
    c) _____ is stored in the database.
    d) _____ is always valid.

2) All module code contains the following components (check all that apply):

    a) _____ Header
    b) _____ Footer
    c) _____ Declaration
    d) _____ Exception
    e) _____ Execution

3) If a procedure has an IN parameter, then it must have an OUT parameter.

    a) _____ True
    b) _____ False

4) Which are valid parameter definitions in the header of a parameter? (check all that apply)

    a) _____ P_LAST_NAME IN OUT VARCHAR2(20)
    b) _____ P_STUDID OUT IN NUMBER
    c) _____ P_ZIPCODE NUMBER
    d) _____ P_COURSE_COST IN NUMBER := 1095

5) The view USER_SOURCE only contains the code of valid procedures.

    a) _____ True
    b) _____ False

Answers appear in Appendix A, Section 12.2.

CHAPTER 12

TEST YOUR THINKING

In this chapter, we have learned about creating procedures, with and without the use of parameters. Additionally, you learned about where information and source code for these procedures can be found.

1) Write a procedure with no parameters. The procedure will let you know if the current day is a weekend or a weekday. Additionally, it will let you know the user name and current time. It will also let you know how many valid and invalid procedures are in the database.

2) Write a procedure that takes in a zipcode, city, and state and inserts the values into the zipcode table. There should be a check to see if the zipcode is already in the database. If it is, an exception will be raised and an error message will be displayed. Write an anonymous block that uses the procedure and inserts your zipcode.

The projects in this section are meant to have you utilize all of the skills that you have acquired throughout this chapter. The answers to these projects can be found in Appendix D and at the companion Web site to this book, located at http://www.phptr .com/rosenzweig2e. Visit the Web site periodically to share and discuss your answers.

C H A P T E R   1 3

FUNCTIONS

A function that is stored in the database is much like a procedure in that it is a named PL/SQL block that can take parameters and be invoked. There are key differences both in the way it is created and how it is used. In this chapter, you will cover the basics of how to create, make use of, and drop a function.

L A B   1 3 . 1

CREATING AND USING FUNCTIONS

LAB OBJECTIVES

After this Lab, you will be able to:

✔ Create Stored Functions
✔ Make Use of Functions
✔ Invoke Functions in SQL Statements
✔ Write Complex Functions

FUNCTION BASICS

Functions are another type of stored code and are very similar to procedures. The significant difference is that a function is a PL/SQL block that returns a single value. Functions can accept one, many, or no parameters, but a function must have a return clause in the executable section of the function. The datatype of the return value must be declared in the header of the function. A function is not a stand-alone executable in the way that a procedure is: It must be used in some context. You can think of it as a sentence fragment. A function has output that needs to be assigned to a variable, or it can be used in a SELECT statement.

FUNCTION SYNTAX

The syntax for creating a function is as follows:

```
CREATE [OR REPLACE] FUNCTION function_name
   (parameter list)
    RETURN datatype
IS
BEGIN
```

```
      <body>
      RETURN (return_value);
END;
```

The function does not necessarily have any parameters, but it must have a RE-TURN value declared in the header, and it must return values for all the varying possible execution streams. The RETURN statement does not have to appear as the last line of the main execution section, and there may be more than one RE-TURN statement (there should be a RETURN statement for each exception). A function may have IN, OUT, or IN OUT parameters, but you rarely see anything except IN parameters since it is bad programming practice to do otherwise.

■ FOR EXAMPLE

```
-- ch13_01a.sql ver 1.0
CREATE OR REPLACE FUNCTION show_description
   (i_course_no course.course_no%TYPE)
RETURN varchar2
AS
   v_description varchar2(50);
BEGIN
   SELECT description
     INTO v_description
     FROM course
    WHERE course_no = i_course_no;
   RETURN v_description;
EXCEPTION
   WHEN NO_DATA_FOUND
   THEN
     RETURN('The Course is not in the database');
   WHEN OTHERS
   THEN
     RETURN('Error in running show_description');
END;
```

LAB 13.1 EXERCISES

13.1.1 CREATE STORED FUNCTIONS

a) Put the create script for the function in the preceding example into a text file. Open SQL*Plus, log into the student schema, and run the script from the preceding example. What do you expect to see? Explain the function line by line.

b) Create another function using the following script. Explain what is happening in this function. Pay close attention to the method of creating the Boolean return.

```
-- ch13_01b.sql, version 1.0
CREATE OR REPLACE FUNCTION id_is_good
  (i_student_id IN NUMBER)
  RETURN BOOLEAN
AS
  v_id_cnt NUMBER;
BEGIN
  SELECT COUNT(*)
    INTO v_id_cnt
    FROM student
   WHERE student_id = i_student_id;
   RETURN 1 = v_id_cnt;
EXCEPTION
  WHEN OTHERS
  THEN
    RETURN FALSE;
END id_is_good;
```

13.1.2 MAKE USE OF FUNCTIONS

In this exercise, you will learn how to make use of the stored functions that you created in Exercise 13.1.1.

a) Use the following anonymous block to run the function. When prompted, enter 350. Then try other numbers. What is produced?

```
SET SERVEROUTPUT ON
DECLARE
  v_description VARCHAR2(50);
BEGIN
  v_description := show_description(&sv_cnumber);
  DBMS_OUTPUT.PUT_LINE(v_description);
END;
```

b) Now create a similar anonymous block to make use of the function id_is_good. Try running it for a number of different IDs.

13.1.3 INVOKE FUNCTIONS IN SQL STATEMENTS

a) Now you will try another method of using a stored function. Before you type the following SELECT statement, think about what the function show_description is doing. Will this statement produce an error? If not, then what will be displayed?

```
SELECT course_no, show_description(course_no)
  FROM course;
```

13.1.4 WRITE COMPLEX FUNCTIONS

a) Create the function with the following script. Before you execute the function, analyze this script and explain line by line what the function will perform. When could you use this function?

```
-- ch13_01c.sql, version 1.0
CREATE OR REPLACE FUNCTION new_instructor_id
    RETURN instructor.instructor_id%TYPE
AS
    v_new_instid instructor.instructor_id%TYPE;
BEGIN
    SELECT INSTRUCTOR_ID_SEQ.NEXTVAL
      INTO v_new_instid
      FROM dual;
    RETURN v_new_instid;
EXCEPTION
    WHEN OTHERS
    THEN
      DECLARE
        v_sqlerrm VARCHAR2(250)
            := SUBSTR(SQLERRM,1,250);
      BEGIN
        RAISE_APPLICATION_ERROR(-20003,
            'Error in     instructor_id: '||v_sqlerrm);
    END;
END new_instructor_id;
```

LAB 13.1 EXERCISE ANSWERS

13.1.1 ANSWERS

a) Put the create script for the function in the preceding example into a text file. Open SQL*Plus, log into the student schema, and run the script from the preceding example. What do you expect to see? Explain the function line by line.

*Answer: When a function has been compiled without errors, the SQL*Plus session will return*

```
Function created.
```

which indicates that the function was successfully compiled. The script is for the function show_description. *The function heading indicates that the function takes in a parameter of the number datatype and returns a VARCHAR2. The function makes use of a VARCHAR2(5) variable called* v_description. *The function gives the variable the value of the description of the course, whose number is passed into the function. The return value is then the variable. There are two exceptions. The first is the WHEN NO_DATA_FOUND exception, the one most likely to occur. The second exception is the WHEN OTHERS exception, which is being used as a catchall for any other error that may occur. It is important for you to note that the RETURN clause is one of the last statements in the function. The reason is that the program focus will return to the calling environment once the RETURN clause is issued.*

b) Create another function using the following script. Explain what is happening in this function. Pay close attention to the method of creating the Boolean return.

Answer: The function id_is_good *is a check to see if the ID passed in exists in the database. The function takes in a number (which is assumed to be a student ID) and returns a BOOLEAN value. The function uses the variable* v_id_cnt *as a means to process the data. The SELECT statement determines a count of the number of students with the numeric value that was passed in. If the student is in the database, because the* student_id *is the primary key, the value of* v_id_cnt *will be 1. If the student is not in the database, the SELECT statement will throw the focus down to the exception section, where the function returns a value of FALSE. The function makes use of a very interesting method to return TRUE. If the student is in the database, then* v_id_cnt *will equal 1, thus the code* RETURN 1 = v_id_cnt *will actually return a value of TRUE when* v_id_cnt *equals 1.*

13.1.2 ANSWERS

a) Use the following anonymous block to run the function. When prompted, enter 350. Then try other numbers. What is produced?

Answer: Since there is a lexical parameter of &cnumber in the PL/SQL block, the user will be prompted as follows:

```
Enter value for cnumber:
```

If you enter "350," you will see the following:

```
old   4:   v_descript := show_description(&sv_cnumber);
new   4:   v_descript := show_description(350);
Intro to SQL
PL/SQL procedure successfully completed.
```

This means that the value for `&sv_cnumber` *has been replaced with 350. The function* `show_description` *returns a VARCHAR2 value, which is the course description for the course number that is passed in. The PL/SQL block initializes the* `v_description` *value with the return from the* `show_description` *function. This value is then displayed with the* `DBMS_OUTPUT` *package.*

b) Now create a similar anonymous block to make use of the function `id_is_good`. Try running it for a number of different IDs.

Answer: The following is one method of testing the `id_is_good` *function:*

```
DECLARE
   V_id number;
BEGIN
   V_id := &id;
   IF id_is_good(v_id)
   THEN
      DBMS_OUTPUT.PUT_LINE
         ('Student ID: '||v_id||' is a valid.');
   ELSE
      DBMS_OUTPUT.PUT_LINE
         ('Student ID: '||v_id||' is not valid.');
   END IF;
END;
```

This PL/SQL block evaluates the return from the function and then determines which output to project. Since the function id_is_good returns a Boolean, the easiest way to make use of this function is to run it and use the result (which will be either true or false) in an IF statement. Remember that when testing a Boolean function id_is_good the line 'IF id_is_good(v_id)' means if the function id_is_good for the variable will result in a return of 'true' then do the following. The ELSE will then cover if the function returns 'false'.

13.1.3 ANSWERS

a) Now try another method of using a stored function. Before you type the following SELECT statement, think about what the function show_description is doing. Will this statement produce an error? If not, then what will be displayed?

```
SELECT course_no, show_description(course_no)
    FROM course;
```

Answer: This SELECT statement will be identical to the SELECT statement that follows:

```
SELECT course_no, description
    FROM course.
```

Functions can be used in a SQL statement. In fact, you have been using them all along and may not have realized it. As a simple example, imagine using the function UPPER in a select statement.

```
SELECT UPPER('bill') FROM DUAL;
```

The Oracle-supplied function UPPER is a function that returns the upper case value of the parameter that was passed in.

Note that for a user-defined function to be called in a SQL expression it must be a ROW function, not a GROUP function, and the datatypes must be SQL datatypes. The datatypes cannot be PL/SQL datatypes like Boolean, table, or record. Additionally, the function is not allowed to have any DML (insert, update, delete).

 Note that in order to use a function in a SQL select statement, the function must have a certain level of purity. This is accomplished with the PRAGMA RESTRICT_REFERENCES clause. This will be discussed in detail in the next chapter in the context of functions within packages.

LAB 13.1 SELF-REVIEW QUESTIONS

In order to test your progress, you should be able to answer the following questions.

1) What are the distinguishing characteristics that make functions different from procedures? (check all that apply)

a) _____ Functions require a PRAGMA RESTRICT clause.
b) _____ Functions only take IN parameters.
c) _____ Functions are stored in the database.
d) _____ Functions require a return value.

2) The parameters of a function must be labeled IN or the function will not compile successfully.

a) _____ True
b) _____ False

3) Which statement(s) will cause control to return to the calling environment in a function? (check all that apply)

a) _____ The raising of an exception
b) _____ The initialization of an OUT parameter
c) _____ Writing to a database table
d) _____ The RETURN statement

4) IN OUT parameters are permissible in functions.

a) _____ True
b) _____ False
c) _____ The function will compile with an IN OUT parameter, but it is not advisable to use them.

5) If a function declares a user-defined exception but never explicitly raises the exception, which of the following will be true?

a) _____ The function will not be able to compile.
b) _____ The function will fail a purity level check.
c) _____ The exception will never be raised.
d) _____ As long as the exception has a RETURN clause, there is no error in having a user-defined exception and not calling it.

Answers appear in Appendix A, Section 13.1.

CHAPTER 13

TEST YOUR THINKING

In this chapter, you have learned about functions. Here are some projects that will help you test the depth of your understanding.

1) Write a stored function called `new_student_id` that takes in no parameters and returns a `student.student_id%TYPE`. The value returned will be used when inserting a new student into the CTA application. It will be derived by using the formula: `student_id_seq.NEXTVAL`.

2) Write a stored function called `zip_does_not_exist` that takes in a `zipcode.zip%TYPE` and returns a Boolean. The function will return TRUE if the zipcode passed into it does not exist. It will return a FALSE if the zipcode exists. *Hint:* An example of how it might be used is as follows:

```
DECLARE
    cons_zip CONSTANT zipcode.zip%TYPE := '&sv_zipcode';
    e_zipcode_is_not_valid EXCEPTION;
BEGIN
    IF zipcode_does_not_exist(cons_zip);
    THEN
        RAISE e_zipcode_is_not_valid;
    ELSE
      -- An insert of an instructor's record which
      -- makes use of the checked zipcode might go here.
        NULL;
    END IF;
EXCEPTION
    WHEN e_zipcode_is_not_valid
    THEN
        RAISE_APPLICATION_ERROR
            (-20003, 'Could not find zipcode '||
            cons_zip||'.'
            );
END;
```

3) Create a new function. For a given instructor, determine how many sections he or she is teaching. If the number is greater or equal to 3, return a message saying the instructor needs a vacation. Otherwise, return a message saying how many sections this instructor is teaching.

The answers to Test Your Thinking can be found in Appendix D and on the Web site.

C H A P T E R   1 4

PACKAGES

A package is a collection of PL/SQL objects grouped together under one package name. Packages include procedures, functions, cursors, declarations, types, and variables. There are numerous benefits in collecting objects into a package. In this chapter, you learn what these benefits are and how to use them.

LAB 14.1

THE BENEFITS
OF UTILIZING PACKAGES

LAB OBJECTIVES

After this Lab, you will be able to:

- ✔ Create Package Specifications
- ✔ Create Package Bodies
- ✔ Call Stored Packages
- ✔ Create Private Objects
- ✔ Create Package Variables and Cursors

There are numerous benefits of using packages as a method to bundle your functions and procedures, the first being that a well-designed package is a logical grouping of objects—such as functions, procedures, global variables, and cursors. All of the code (parse tree and pseudocode [p-code]) is loaded on the first call of the package. This means that the first call to the package is very expensive (involves a lot of processing on the server), but all subsequent calls will result in an improved performance. Packages are therefore often used in applications where procedures and functions are used repeatedly.

There is also an additional level of security using packages. When a user executes a procedure in a package (or stored procedures and functions), the procedure operates with the same permissions as its owner. Packages also allow the creation of private functions and procedures, which can only be called from other functions and procedures in the package. This enforces information hiding. The structure of the package also encourages top-down design.

THE PACKAGE SPECIFICATION

The package specification contains information about the contents of the package, but not the code for the procedures and functions. It also contains declarations of global/public variables. Anything placed in the declarative section of a PL/SQL block may be coded in a package specification. All objects placed in the package specification are called public objects. Any function or procedure not in the package specification but coded in a package body is called a private function or procedure.

THE PACKAGE BODY

The package body contains the actual executable code for the objects described in the package specification. The package body contains code for all procedures and functions described in the specification and may additionally contain code for objects not declared in the specification; the latter type of packaged object is invisible outside the package and is referred to as hidden. When creating stored packages, the package specification and body can be compiled separately.

RULES FOR THE PACKAGE BODY

There are a number of rules that must be followed in package body code: (1) There must be an exact match between the cursor and module headers and their definitions in package specification; (2) do not repeat declaration of variables, exceptions, type, or constants in the specification again in the body; and (3) any element declared in the specification can be referenced in the body.

REFERENCING PACKAGE ELEMENTS

Use the following notation when calling packaged elements from outside of the package: `package_name.element`.

You do not need to qualify elements when declared and referenced inside the body of the package or when declared in a specification and referenced inside the body of the same package.

LAB 14.1 EXERCISES

14.1.1 CREATE PACKAGE SPECIFICATIONS

In this exercise, you will learn more about table-based and cursor-based records discussed earlier in the chapter.

Create the following PL/SQL script:

■ *FOR EXAMPLE*

```
-- ch14_1a.sql
 1   CREATE OR REPLACE PACKAGE manage_students
 2   AS
 3     PROCEDURE find_sname
 4        (i_student_id IN student.student_id%TYPE,
 5          o_first_name OUT student.first_name%TYPE,
 6          o_last_name OUT student.last_name%TYPE
 7        );
 8     FUNCTION id_is_good
 9        (i_student_id IN student.student_id%TYPE)
10        RETURN BOOLEAN;
11   END manage_students;
```

Answer the following questions:

a) Type the preceding code into a text file. Then run the script in a SQL*Plus session. Explain what happened.

b) If the following script was run from a SQL*PLUS session, what would the result be and why?

```
-- ch14_2a.sql
SET SERVEROUTPUT ON
DECLARE
    v_first_name student.first_name%TYPE;
    v_last_name student.last_name%TYPE;
BEGIN
    manage_students.find_sname
        (125, v_first_name, v_last_name);
    DBMS_OUTPUT.PUT_LINE(v_first_name||' '||v_last_name);
END;
```

c) Create a package specification for a package named student_ta_api. The package contains the procedure discount from Chapter 12 and the function new_instructor_id from Chapter 13.

14.1.2 CREATE PACKAGE BODIES

Now we will create the body of the manage_students package, which was specified in the previous section.

■ *FOR EXAMPLE*

```
-- ch14_3a.sql
1    CREATE OR REPLACE PACKAGE BODY manage_students
2    AS
3      PROCEDURE find_sname
4        (i_student_id IN student.student_id%TYPE,
5         o_first_name OUT student.first_name%TYPE,
6         o_last_name OUT student.last_name%TYPE
7         )
8      IS
9       v_student_id  student.student_id%TYPE;
10     BEGIN
11        SELECT first_name, last_name
12          INTO o_first_name, o_last_name
13          FROM student
14         WHERE student_id = i_student_id;
15      EXCEPTION
16        WHEN OTHERS
17        THEN
18          DBMS_OUTPUT.PUT_LINE
19      ('Error in finding student_id: '||v_student_id);
20      END find_sname;
21      FUNCTION id_is_good
22        (i_student_id IN student.student_id%TYPE)
23        RETURN BOOLEAN
24      IS
25        v_id_cnt number;
26      BEGIN
27        SELECT COUNT(*)
28          INTO v_id_cnt
29          FROM student
30         WHERE student_id = i_student_id;
31        RETURN 1 = v_id_cnt;
32      EXCEPTION
33      WHEN OTHERS
34      THEN
35        RETURN FALSE;
36      END id_is_good;
37    END manage_students;
```

a) Type the preceding code into a text file. Then run the script in a SQL*Plus session. Explain what happens.

b) Create a package body for the package named cta_api that you just created.

14.1.3 CALL STORED PACKAGES

Now we will use elements of the manage_student package in another code block.

■ *FOR EXAMPLE*

```
-- ch14_4a.sql
DECLARE
  v_first_name student.first_name%TYPE;
  v_last_name student.last_name%TYPE;
BEGIN
  IF manage_students.id_is_good(&v_id)
  THEN
     manage_students.find_sname(&&v_id, v_first_name,
        v_last_name);
     DBMS_OUTPUT.PUT_LINE('Student No. '||&&v_id||' is '
        ||v_last_name||', '||v_first_name);
  ELSE
     DBMS_OUTPUT.PUT_LINE
     ('Student ID: '||&&v_id||' is not in the database.');
  END IF;
END;
```

a) The previous example displays how a procedure within a package is executed. What results do you expect if you run this PL/SQL block?

b) Run the script and see the results. How does this compare with what you expected? Explain what the script is accomplishing line by line.

c) Create a script testing the cta_api package.

14.1.4 CREATE PRIVATE OBJECTS

PUBLIC AND PRIVATE PACKAGE ELEMENTS

Public elements are elements defined in the package specification. If an object is defined only in the package body, then it is private.

Private elements cannot be accessed directly by any programs outside of the package.

You can think of the package specification as being a "menu" of packaged items that are available to users; there may be other objects working behind the scenes, but they aren't accessible. They cannot be called or utilized in any way; they are available as part of the internal "menu" of the package and can only be called by other elements of the package.

a) Replace the last lines of the manage_students package specification with the following and recompile the package specification:

```
11      PROCEDURE display_student_count;
12   END manage_students;
```

Replace the end of the body with the following and recompile the package body:

```
37   FUNCTION student_count_priv
38     RETURN NUMBER
39     IS
40     v_count NUMBER;
41     BEGIN
42     select count(*)
43     into v_count
44     from student;
45     return v_count;
46     EXCEPTION
47     WHEN OTHERS
48       THEN
49       return(0);
50     END student_count_priv;
51     PROCEDURE display_student_count
52     is
53     v_count NUMBER;
54     BEGIN
55     v_count := student_count_priv;
```

```
56      DBMS_OUTPUT.PUT_LINE
57          ('There are '||v_count||' students.');
58      END display_student_count;
59   END manage_students;
```

What have you added to the manage_student package?

b) If you run the following from your SQL*PLUS session, what are the results?

```
DECLARE
    V_count NUMBER;
BEGIN
    V_count := Manage_students.student_count_priv;
    DBMS_OUTPUT.PUT_LINE(v_count);
END;
```

c) If you were to run the following, what do you expect to see?

```
SET SERVEROUTPUT ON
Execute manage_students.display_student_count;
```

d) Add a private function to the school_api called get_course_descript_private. It accepts a course.course_no%TYPE and returns a course.description%TYPE. It searches for and returns the course description for the course number passed to it. If the course does not exist or if an error occurs, it returns a NULL.

14.1.5 CREATE PACKAGE VARIABLES AND CURSORS

The first time a package is called within a user session, the code in the initialization section of the package will be executed if it exists. This is only done once and is not repeated if other procedures or functions for that package are called by the user.

Variables, cursors, and user-defined datatypes used by numerous procedures and functions can be declared once at the beginning of the package and can then be used by the functions and procedures within the package without having to declare them again.

a) Add a package wide variable called v_current_date to cta_api; additionally, add an initialization section that assigns the current sysdate to the variable v_current_date.

LAB 14.1 EXERCISE ANSWERS

14.1.1 ANSWERS

a) Type the preceding code into a text file. Then run the script in a SQL*Plus session. Explain what happens.

Answer: The specification for the package manage_students has been compiled into the database. The specification for the package now indicates that there is one procedure and one function. The procedure find_sname requires one IN parameter, which is the student ID, and it returns two OUT parameters, one being the student's first name and the other being the student's last name. The function id_is_good takes in a single parameter of a student ID and returns a Boolean (true or false). Although the body has not yet been entered into the database, the package is still available for other applications. For example, if you included a call to one of these procedures in another stored procedure, that procedure would compile (but would not execute).

b) If the following script is run from a SQL*PLUS session, what are the results and why?

*Answer: The procedure cannot run because only the specification for the procedure exists in the database, not the body. The SQL*Plus session returns the following:*

```
ERROR at line 1:
ORA-04068: existing state of packages has been discarded
ORA-04067: not executed, package body
           "STUDENT.MANAGE_STUDENTS" does not exist
ORA-06508: PL/SQL: could not find program
           unit being called
ORA-06512: at line 5
```

c) Create a package specification named school_api. The package contains the procedure named discount from Chapter 12, and the function named new_instructor_id from Chapter 13.

Answer:

```
1    CREATE OR REPLACE PACKAGE  school_api as
2         PROCEDURE discount_cost;
3         FUNCTION new_instructor_id
4            RETURN instructor.instructor_id%TYPE;
5      END school_api;
```

14.1.2 Answers

a) Type the preceding code into a text file. Then run the script in a SQL*Plus session. Explain what happens.

Answer: The package body manage_students is compiled into the database. The package contains the procedure manage_students.find_sname, which accepts the parameter student_id and returns the student's last_name and first_name from the Student table.

b) Create a package body for the package named cta_api that you just created.

Answer:

```
-- ch14_5a.sql
1 CREATE OR REPLACE PACKAGE BODY school_api AS
2    PROCEDURE discount_cost
3    IS
4       CURSOR c_group_discount
5       IS
6       SELECT distinct s.course_no, c.description
7         FROM section s, enrollment e, course c
8        WHERE s.section_id = e.section_id
9       GROUP BY s.course_no, c.description,
10               e.section_id, s.section_id
11      HAVING COUNT(*) >=8;
12    BEGIN
14       FOR r_group_discount IN c_group_discount
14       LOOP
15       UPDATE course
16          SET cost = cost * .95
17        WHERE course_no = r_group_discount.course_no;
18        DBMS_OUTPUT.PUT_LINE
19          ('A 5% discount has been given to'
20          ||r_group_discount.course_no||'
21        '||r_group_discount.description);
22      END LOOP;
23     END discount_cost;
24    FUNCTION new_instructor_id
25       RETURN instructor.instructor_id%TYPE
26    IS
27       v_new_instid instructor.instructor_id%TYPE;
28    BEGIN
29       SELECT INSTRUCTOR_ID_SEQ.NEXTVAL
30         INTO v_new_instid
31         FROM dual;
32       RETURN v_new_instid;
33    EXCEPTION
34       WHEN OTHERS
```

```
35              THEN
36                 DECLARE
37                    v_sqlerrm VARCHAR2(250) :=
                          SUBSTR(SQLERRM,1,250);
38                 BEGIN
39                    RAISE_APPLICATION_ERROR(-20003,
40                       'Error in    instructor_id: '||v_sqlerrm);
41                 END;
42           END new_instructor_id;
43      END school_api;
```

14.1.3 ANSWERS

a) The previous example displays how a procedure within a package is executed. What results do you expect to see when you run this PL/SQL block?

Answer:This is a correct PL/SQL block for running the function and the procedure in the package manage_students. *If an existing* student_id *is entered, then the name of the student is displayed. If the id is not valid, then the error message is displayed.*

b) Run the script and observe the results. How does this compare with what you expected? Explain what the script is accomplishing line by line.

Answer: Initially the following appears:

```
Enter value for v_id:
If you enter "145," then you see:
old 5: IF manage_students.id_is_good(&v_id)
new 5: IF manage_students.id_is_good(145)
old  7: manage_students.find_sname(&&v_id, v_first_name,
new  7: manage_students.find_sname(145, v_first_name,
old  9: DBMS_OUTPUT.PUT_LINE('Student No. '||&&v_id||
        ' is '
new 9: DBMS_OUTPUT.PUT_LINE('Student No. '||145||' is '
old 14: ('Student ID: '||&&v_id||' is not in the
        database.');
new 14: ('Student ID: '||145||' is not in the
        database.');
Student No. 145 is Lefkowitz, Paul
PL/SQL procedure successfully completed.
```

The function id_is_good returns TRUE for an existing student_id such as 145. The control then flows to the first part of the IF statement and the procedure manage_students.find_sname finds the first and last name for student_id 145, which happens to be Lefkowitz, Paul.

c) Create a script that tests the cta_api package.

Answer:
```
SET SERVEROUTPUT ON
DECLARE
    V_instructor_id instructor.instructor_id%TYPE;
BEGIN
    cta_api.Discount;
    v_instructor_id := cta_api.new_instructor_id;
    DBMS_OUTPUT.PUT_LINE
        ('The new id is: '||v_instructor_id);
END;
```

14.1.4 ANSWERS

a) What have you added to the manage_student package?

Answer: A private function, student_count_privs, and a public procedure, display_student_count, calling the private function.

b) If you run the following from your SQL*PLUS session, what are the results?

Answer: Since the private function, student_count_privs, cannot be called from outside the package, you receive an error message as follows:

```
ERROR at line 1:
ORA-06550: line 4, column 31:
PLS-00302: component 'STUDENT_COUNT_PRIV'
           must be  declared
ORA-06550: line 4, column 3:
PL/SQL: Statement ignored
```

It appears as if the private function does not exist. This is important to keep in mind. You can see this can be useful when you are writing PL/SQL packages used by other developers. In order to simplify the package for them, they only need to see the package specification. This way they know what is being passed into the procedures and functions and what is being returned. They do not need to see the inner workings. If a number of procedures make use of the same logic, it may make more sense to put them into a private function called by the procedures.

c) If you run the following, what do you expect to see?

Answer: This is a valid method of running a procedure. A line is displayed indicating the number of students in the database. Note that the procedure in the package manage_students is using the private function student_count_priv to retrieve the student count.

Note that if you forget to include a procedure or function in a package specification, it becomes private. On the other hand, if you declare a procedure or function in the package specification, and then you do not define it when you create the body, you receive the following error message:

```
PLS-00323: subprogram or cursor 'procedure_name' is
declared in a package specification and must be
defined in the package body
```

d) Add a private function to the school_api called get_course_descript_private. It accepts a course.course_no%TYPE and returns a course.description%TYPE. It searches for and returns the course description for the course number passed to it. If the course does not exist, or if an error occurs, it returns a NULL.

Answer: Add the following lines to the package body: There is nothing that needs to be added to the package specification, since you are only adding a private object.

```
43     FUNCTION get_course_descript_private
44       (i_course_no   course.course_no%TYPE)
45       RETURN course.description%TYPE
46     IS
47        v_course_descript course.description%TYPE;
48     BEGIN
49        SELECT description
50          INTO v_course_descript
51          FROM course
52         WHERE course_no = i_course_no;
53        RETURN v_course_descript;
54     EXCEPTION
55       WHEN OTHERS
56       THEN
57          RETURN NULL;
58     END get_course_descript_private;
59  END school_api;
```

14.1.5 ANSWERS

a) Add a package-wide variable called v_current_date to school_api. Additionally, add an initialization section that assigns the current sysdate to the variable v_current_date.

Answer: Add the following line to the beginning of the package specification:

```
1   CREATE OR REPLACE PACKAGE  school_api as
2      v_current_date DATE;
3      PROCEDURE Discount;
4      FUNCTION new_instructor_id
5          RETURN instructor.instructor_id%TYPE;
6   END school_api;
```

Add the following to the end of the package body:

```
59   BEGIN
60     SELECT trunc(sysdate, 'DD')
```

```
61         INTO v_current_date
62         FROM dual;
63    END school_api;
```

LAB 14.1 SELF-REVIEW QUESTIONS

In order to test your progress, you should be able to answer the following questions.

1) The main advantages to grouping procedures and functions into packages are (check all that apply):

   a) _____ It follows the trendy object method of programming.
   b) _____ It is a more efficient way of utilizing the processor memory.
   c) _____ It makes greater use of the security privileges of various users.
   d) _____ It is a more efficient method to maximize tablespace storage.
   e) _____ It keeps you on good terms with the DBA.

2) If user Tashi has SELECT privilege on the student table and user Sonam does not, then Sonam can make use of a procedure created by Tashi to get access to the student table if he has execute privileges on Tashi's procedure.

   a) _____ True
   b) _____ False

3) All procedures and functions in a package body must be declared in the package specification.

   a) _____ True
   b) _____ False

4) The initialization section of a package refers to

   a) _____ another term for the package header.
   b) _____ the first part of the package.
   c) _____ the executable code at the end of the package.
   d) _____ the evolutionary rudiments in code that are left over from program-ming methods of cavemen.

5) The package specification is merely a formality for other programmers to let them know what parameters are being passed in and out of the procedures and functions. It hides the program logic but in actuality it is not necessary and is in-corporated into the package body.

   a) _____ True
   b) _____ False

Answers appear in Appendix A, Section 14.1.

CHAPTER 14

TEST YOUR THINKING

In this chapter, you have learned about packages. Here are some projects that will help you test the depth of your understanding.

1) Add a procedure to the student_api package called remove_student. This procedure accepts a student_id and returns nothing. Based on the student id passed in, it removes the student from the database. If the student does not exist or there is a problem removing the student (such as a foreign key constraint violation), then let the calling program handle it.

2) Alter remove_student in the student_api package body to accept an additional parameter. This new parameter is a VARCHAR2 and is called p_ri. Make p_ri default to "R." The new parameter may contain a value of "R" or "C." If "R" is received, it represents DELETE RESTRICT and the procedure acts as it does now. If there are enrollments for the student, the delete is disallowed. If a "C" is received, it represents DELETE CASCADE. This functionally means that the remove_student procedure locates all records for the student in all of the CTA tables and removes them from the database before attempting to remove the student from the student table. Decide how to handle the situation where the user passes in a code other than "C" or "R."

The projects in this section are meant to have you utilize all of the skills that you have acquired throughout this chapter. The answers to these projects can be found in Appendix D and at the companion Web site to this book, located at http://www.phptr.com/rosenzweig2e. Visit the Web site periodically to share and discuss your answers.

C H A P T E R   1 5

ADVANCED CURSORS

In the previous chapter you mastered the basic concepts of cursors. In this chapter you will learn how to dynamically alter the WHERE clause of a cursor by passing parameters to when you call the cursor. You will also learn about cursor variables. Cursor variables are like C pointers; they hold the address or memory location of an object of some type. Cursor variables are very useful for passing query result sets between PL/SQL stored subprograms and various clients. Neither PL/SQL nor any of its clients owns a result set. They simply share a pointer to the query work area that identifies the result set.

L A B   1 5 . 1

USING PARAMETERS
WITH CURSORS
AND FOR UPDATE CURSORS

LAB OBJECTIVES

After this Lab, you will be able to:

✔ Use Parameters in a Cursor
✔ Use a FOR UPDATE Cursor
✔ Use the WHERE CURRENT OF Clause

CURSORS WITH PARAMETERS

A cursor can be declared with parameters. This enables a cursor to generate a specific result set, which is, on the one hand, narrow, but, on the other hand, reusable. A cursor of all the data from the ZIPCODE table may be very useful, but it would be more useful for certain data processing if it held information for only one state. At this point, you know how to create such a cursor. But wouldn't it be more useful if you could create a cursor that could accept a parameter of a state and then run through only the city and zip for that state?

■ *FOR EXAMPLE*

```
CURSOR c_zip (p_state IN zipcode.state%TYPE) IS
    SELECT zip, city, state
      FROM zipcode
     WHERE state = p_state;
```

The main points to keep in mind for parameters in cursors are as follows:

- Cursor parameters make the cursor more reusable.
- Cursor parameters can be assigned default values.
- The scope of the cursor parameters is local to the cursor.
- The mode of the parameters can only be IN.

When a cursor has been declared as taking a parameter, it must be called with a value for that parameter. The c_zip cursor that was just declared is called as follows:

```
OPEN c_zip (parameter_value)
```

The same cursor could be opened with a FOR CURSOR loop as follows:

```
FOR r_zip IN c_zip('NY')
LOOP  ...
```

LAB 15.1 EXERCISES

15.1.1 USE PARAMETERS IN A CURSOR

a) Complete the code for the parameter cursor that was begun in the preceding example. Include a DBMS_OUTPUT line that displays the zipcode, city, and state. This is identical to the process you have already used in a FOR CURSOR loop, only now, when you open the cursor, you pass a parameter.

b) The following PL/SQL code is complex. It involves all of the topics covered so far in this chapter. There is a nested cursor with three levels, meaning a grandparent cursor, a parent cursor, and a child cursor. Before running this script, review the code and identify the levels of nesting in the code. When you describe each level of the code, explain what parameters are being passed into the cursor and why. What do you think the result will be from running this statement?

```
-- ch15_1a.sql
SET SERVEROUTPUT ON
1     DECLARE
2        CURSOR c_student IS
3           SELECT first_name, last_name, student_id
4             FROM student
5            WHERE last_name LIKE 'J%';
6        CURSOR c_course
7             (i_student_id IN
```

```
                                          student.student_id%TYPE)
 8        IS
 9            SELECT c.description, s.section_id sec_id
10              FROM course c, section s, enrollment e
11            WHERE e.student_id = i_student_id
12              AND c.course_no = s.course_no
13              AND s.section_id = e.section_id;
14        CURSOR c_grade(i_section_id IN
                              section.section_id%TYPE,
15                      i_student_id IN
                              student.student_id%TYPE)
16            IS
17            SELECT gt.description grd_desc,
18                TO_CHAR
19                    (AVG(g.numeric_grade), '999.99')
                                        num_grd
20                FROM enrollment e,
21                    grade g, grade_type gt
22              WHERE e.section_id = i_section_id
23                AND e.student_id = g.student_id
24                AND e.student_id = i_student_id
25                AND e.section_id = g.section_id
26                AND g.grade_type_code =
                              gt.grade_type_code
27            GROUP BY gt.description ;
28      BEGIN
29        FOR r_student IN c_student
30        LOOP
31          DBMS_OUTPUT.PUT_LINE(CHR(10));
32          DBMS_OUTPUT.PUT_LINE(r_student.first_name||
33              ' '||r_student.last_name);
34          FOR r_course IN
                    c_course(r_student.student_id)
35          LOOP
36            DBMS_OUTPUT.PUT_LINE
                  ('Grades for course :'||
37              r_course.description);
38            FOR r_grade IN c_grade(r_course.sec_id,
39                              r_student.student_id)
40            LOOP
41                DBMS_OUTPUT.PUT_LINE(r_grade.num_grd||
42                  ' '||r_grade.grd_desc);
43            END LOOP;
44          END LOOP;
45        END LOOP;
46      END;
```

c) Now run the code and see if you were correct. Analyze the code line by line and explain what is being processed and then displayed for each line.

15.1.2 USE A FOR UPDATE CURSOR

The cursor FOR UPDATE clause is only used with a cursor when you want to update tables in the database. Generally, when you execute a SELECT statement, you are not locking any rows. The purpose of using the FOR UPDATE clause is to lock the rows of the tables that you want to update, so that another user cannot perform an update until you perform your update and release the lock. The next COMMIT or ROLLBACK statement releases the lock. The FOR UPDATE clause will change the manner in which the cursor operates in only a few respects. When you open a cursor, all rows that meet the restriction criteria are identified as part of the active set. Using the FOR UPDATE clause will lock these rows that have been identified in the active set. If the FOR UPDATE clause is used, then rows may not be fetched from the cursor until a COMMIT has been issued. It is important for you to consider where to place the COMMIT. Be careful to consider issues covered in the transaction management topic in Chapter 4.

The syntax is simply to add FOR UPDATE to the end of the cursor definition. If there are multiple items being selected, but you only want to lock one of them, then end the cursor definition with the following syntax:

```
FOR UPDATE OF <item_name>
```

■ FOR EXAMPLE

```
-- ch15_2a.sql
DECLARE
  CURSOR c_course IS
    SELECT course_no, cost
      FROM course FOR UPDATE;
BEGIN
  FOR r_course IN c_course
  LOOP
     IF r_course.cost < 2500
     THEN
        UPDATE course
           SET cost = r_course.cost + 10
         WHERE course_no = r_course.course_no;
     END IF;
  END LOOP;
END;
```

This example shows how to update the cost of all courses with a cost under $2500. It will increment them by 10.

a) In the example just given, where should the COMMIT be placed? What are the issues involved in deciding where to place a COMMIT in this example?

■ *FOR EXAMPLE*

```
-- ch15_3a.sql
DECLARE
    CURSOR c_grade(
        i_student_id IN enrollment.student_id%TYPE,
        i_section_id IN enrollment.section_id%TYPE)
    IS
        SELECT final_grade
          FROM enrollment
         WHERE student_id = i_student_id
           AND section_id = i_section_id
          FOR UPDATE;
    CURSOR c_enrollment IS
        SELECT e.student_id, e.section_id
          FROM enrollment e, section s
         WHERE s.course_no = 135
           AND e.section_id = s.section_id;
BEGIN
    FOR r_enroll IN c_enrollment
    LOOP
        FOR r_grade IN c_grade(r_enroll.student_id,
                               r_enroll.section_id)
        LOOP
            UPDATE enrollment
               SET final_grade  = 90
             WHERE student_id = r_enroll.student_id
               AND section_id = r_enroll.section_id;
        END LOOP;
    END LOOP;
END;
```

b) What do you think will happen if you run the code in this example? After making your analysis, run the code, and then perform a SELECT statement to determine if your guess is correct.

c) Where should the COMMIT go in the preceding example? Explain the considerations.

FOR UPDATE OF can be used when creating a cursor for update that is based on multiple tables. FOR UPDATE OF locks the rows of a stable that both contain one of the specified columns and are members of the active set. In other words, it is the means of specifying which table you want to lock. If the FOR UPDATE OF clause is used, then rows may not be fetched from the cursor until a COMMIT has been issued.

■ FOR EXAMPLE

```
-- ch15_4a.sql
DECLARE
    CURSOR c_stud_zip IS
        SELECT s.student_id, z.city
          FROM student s, zipcode z
         WHERE z.city = 'Brooklyn'
           AND s.zip = z.zip
          FOR UPDATE OF phone;
BEGIN
  FOR r_stud_zip IN c_stud_zip
  LOOP
     UPDATE student
        SET phone = '718'||SUBSTR(phone,4)
       WHERE student_id = r_stud_zip.student_id;
  END LOOP;
END;
```

d) What changes to the database will take place if the preceding example is run? Explain specifically what is being locked as well as when it is locked and when it is released.

15.1.3 USE THE *WHERE CURRENT OF* CLAUSE

Use WHERE CURRENT OF when you want to update the most recently fetched row. WHERE CURRENT OF can only be used with a FOR UPDATE OF cursor. The advantage of the WHERE CURRENT OF clause is that it enables you to eliminate the WHERE clause in the UPDATE statement.

■ FOR EXAMPLE

```
-- ch15_5a.sql
DECLARE
```

```
        CURSOR c_stud_zip IS
           SELECT s.student_id, z.city
             FROM student s, zipcode z
            WHERE z.city = 'Brooklyn'
              AND s.zip = z.zip
              FOR UPDATE OF phone;
BEGIN
   FOR r_stud_zip IN c_stud_zip
   LOOP
      DBMS_OUTPUT.PUT_LINE(r_stud_zip.student_id);
      UPDATE student
         SET phone = '718'||SUBSTR(phone,4)
       WHERE CURRENT OF c_stud_zip;
   END LOOP;
END;
```

a) Compare the last two examples. Explain their similarities and differences. What has been altered by using the WHERE CURRENT OF clause? What is the advantage of doing this?

The FOR UPDATE and WHERE CURRENT OF syntax can be used with cursors that are performing a delete as well as an update.

LAB 15.1 EXERCISE ANSWERS

15.1.1 ANSWERS

a) Complete the code for the parameter cursor that was begun in the preceding example. Include a DBMS_OUTPUT line that displays the zipcode, city, and state. This is identical to the process you have already used in a FOR CURSOR loop, only now, when you open the cursor, you pass a parameter.

Answer: Your block should look like this:

```
-- ch15_17a.sql
DECLARE
   CURSOR c_zip (p_state IN zipcode.state%TYPE) IS
      SELECT zip, city, state
        FROM zipcode
       WHERE state = p_state
BEGIN
   FOR r_zip IN c_zip('NJ')
```

```
        LOOP   ...
           DBMS_OUTPUT.PUT_LINE(r_zip.city||
               ' '||r_zip.zip');
        END LOOP;
    END;
```

To complete the block, the cursor declaration must be surrounded by DECLARE and BEGIN. The cursor is opened by passing the parameter "NJ," and then, for each iteration of the cursor loop, the zipcode and the city are displayed by using the built-in package DBMS_OUTPUT.

b) The following PL/SQL code is complex. It involves all the topics covered in this chapter. There is a nested cursor with three levels, meaning a grandparent cursor, a parent cursor, and a child cursor. Before running this script, review the code and identify the levels of nesting in the code. When you describe each level of the code, explain what parameters are being passed into the cursor and why. What do you think the result will be from running this statement?

Answer: The grandparent cursor, c_student, *is declared in lines 2–5. It takes no parameters and is a collection of students with a last name beginning with J. The parent cursor is declared in lines 6–13. The parent cursor,* c_course, *takes in the parameter of the* student_ID *to generate a list of courses taken by that student. The child cursor,* c_grade, *is declared in lines 14–27. It takes in two parameters, both the* section_id *and the* student_id. *In this way it can generate an average of the different grade types for that student for that course. The grandparent cursor loop begins on line 29, and only the student name is displayed with DBMS_OUTPUT. The parent cursor loop begins on line 35. It takes the parameter of the* student_id *from the grandparent cursor. Only the description of the course is displayed. The child cursor loop begins on line 40. It takes in the parameter of the* section_id *from the parent cursor and the* student_id *from the grandparent cursor. The grades are then displayed. The grandparent cursor loop ends on line 45, the parent cursor on line 44, and, finally, the child on line 43.*

c) Now run the code and see if you are correct. Analyze the code line by line and explain what is being processed and displayed for each line.

Answer: The output will be a student name, followed by the courses he or she is taking and the average grade he or she has earned for each grade type. If you did not get the correct answer, try commenting out different sections of the block and see what happens. This will help you to understand what is happening in each step.

15.1.2 ANSWERS

a) In the example just given, where should the COMMIT be placed? What are the issues involved in deciding where to place a COMMIT in this example?

Answer: Placing a COMMIT after each update can be costly. But if there are a lot of updates and the COMMIT comes after the block loop, then there is a risk of a rollback segment not being large enough. Normally, the COMMIT would go after the loop, except when the transaction count is high, and then you might want to code something that does a COMMIT for each 10,000 records. If this were part of a large procedure, you may want to put a SAVEPOINT after the loop. Then, if you need to rollback this update at a later point, it would be an easy task.

b) What do you think will happen if you run the code in this example? After making your analysis, run the code and then perform a SELECT statement to determine if your guess is correct.

Answer: The `final_grade` *for all students enrolled in course 135 will be updated to 90. There are two cursors here. One cursor captures the students who are enrolled in course 135 into the active set. The other cursor takes the* `student_id` *and the* `section_id` *from this active set and selects the corresponding* `final_grade` *from the enrollment table and locks the entire enrollment table. The enrollment cursor loop is begun first, and then it passes the* `student_id` *and the* `section_id` *as an IN parameters for the second cursor loop of the* `c_grade` *cursor, which performs the update.*

c) Where should the COMMIT go in the preceding example? Explain the considerations.

Answer: The COMMIT should go immediately after the update to ensure that each update is committed into the database.

d) What changes to the database will take place if the preceding example is run? Explain specifically what is being locked as well as when it is locked and when it is released.

Answer: The phone numbers of students living in Brooklyn are being updated to change the area code to 718. The cursor declaration is only locking the phone column of the student table. The lock is never released because there is no COMMIT or ROLLBACK statement.

15.1.3 ANSWERS

a) Compare the last two examples. Explain their similarities and differences. What has been altered by using the WHERE CURRENT OF clause? What is the advantage of doing this?

Answer: These two statements perform the same update. The WHERE CURRENT OF clause allows you to eliminate a match in the UPDATE statement, because the update is being performed for the current record of the cursor only.

L A B   1 5 . 2

CURSOR VARIABLES

LAB OBJECTIVE

After this Lab, you will be able to:

✔ Make Use of Cursor Variables

Up to this point in this book you have seen cursors used to gather specific data from a single SELECT statement. In Chapter 14, "Packages," you learned how to bring a number of procedures into a large program called a package. A package may have one cursor that is used by a few procedures. In this case, each of the procedures that use the same cursor would have to declare, open, fetch, and close the cursor. In the current version of PL/SQL, cursors can be declared and manipulated like any other PL/SQL variable. This type of variable is called a cursor variable or a REF CURSOR. A cursor variable is just a reference or a handle to a static cursor. It permits a programmer to pass this reference to the same cursor among all the program's units that need access to the cursor. A cursor variable binds the cursor's SELECT statement dynamically at runtime.

Explicit cursors are used to name a work area that holds the information of a multirow query. A cursor variable may be used to point to the area in memory where the result of a multirow query is stored. The cursor always refers to the same information in a work area, while a cursor variable can point to different work areas. Cursors are static, and cursor variables can be seen as dynamic because they are not tied to any one specific query. Cursor variables give you easy access to centralized data retrieval.

You can use a cursor variable to pass the result set of a query between stored procedures and various clients. A query work area remains accessible as long as a cursor variable points to it. So you can freely pass a cursor variable from one scope to another. There are two types of cursor variables; one is called strong and the other is called weak.

To execute a multirow query, the Oracle server opens a work area called a cursor to store processing information. To access the information, you either name the work area, or you use a cursor variable that points to the work area. A cursor always refers to the same work area, and a cursor variable can refer to different work areas. Hence, cursors and cursor variables are not interoperable. An explicit cursor is static and is associated with one SQL statement. A cursor variable can be associated with different statements at runtime. Primarily you use a cursor variable to pass a pointer to query results sets between PL/SQL stored subprograms and various clients, such as a client Oracle Developer Forms application. None of them owns the result set; they simply share a pointer to the query work area that stores the result set. You can declare a cursor variable on the client side, open and fetch from it on the server side, and then continue to fetch from it on the client side.

Cursor variables differ from cursors the way constants differ from variables. A cursor is static; a cursor variable is dynamic. In PL/SQL a cursor variable has a REF CURSOR data type, where REF stands for reference and CURSOR stands for the class of the object. You will now learn the syntax for declaring and using a cursor variable.

To create a cursor variable, you first need to define a REF CURSOR type and then declare a variable of that type.

Before you declare the REF CURSOR of a strong type, you must first declare a record that has the data types of the result set of the SELECT statement that you plan to use (note that this is not necessary for a weak REF CURSOR).

■ FOR EXAMPLE

```
TYPE inst_city_type IS RECORD
(first_name instructor.first_name%TYPE;
 last_name  instructor.last_name%TYPE;
 city       zipcode.city%TYPE;
 state      zipcode.state%TYPE)
```

Second, you must declare a composite data type for the cursor variable that is of the type REF CURSOR. The syntax is as follows:

```
TYPE ref_type_name is REF CURSOR [RETURN return_type];
```

The ref_type_name is a type specified in subsequent declarations. The return type represents a record type for a strong cursor; a weak cursor does not have a specific return type but can handle any combination of data items in a SELECT statement. The REF CURSOR keyword indicates that the new type will be a pointer to the defined type. The return_type indicates the types of SELECT list that are eventually returned by the cursor variable. The return type must be a record type.

■ FOR EXAMPLE

```
TYPE inst_city_cur IS REF CURSOR RETURN inst_city_type;
```

A cursor variable can be strong (restrictive) or weak (nonrestrictive). A strong cursor variable is a REF CURSOR type definition that specifies a return_type; a weak definition does not. PL/SQL enables you to associate a strong type with type-comparable queries only, while a weak type can be associated with any query. This makes a strong cursor variable less error prone but weak REF CURSORS types more flexible.

These are the key steps for handling a cursor variable:

1. Define and declare the cursor variable.

   Open the cursor variable. Associate a cursor variable with a multirow SELECT statement, execute the query, and identify the result set. An OPEN FOR statement can open the same cursor variable for different queries. You do not need to close a cursor variable before reopening it. Keep in mind that when you reopen a cursor variable for a different query, the previous query is lost.

2. Fetch rows from the result set.

   Retrieve rows from the result set one at a time. Note that the return type of the cursor variable must be compatible with the variable named in the INTO clause of the FETCH statement.

   The FETCH statement retrieves rows from the result set one at a time. PL/SQL verifies that the return type of the cursor variable is compatible with the INTO clause of the FETCH statement. For each query column value returned, there must be a type type-comparable variable in the INTO clause. Also, the number of query column values must equal the number of variables. In case of a mismatch in number or type, the error occurs at compiletime for strongly typed cursor variables and at runtime for weakly typed cursor variables.

3. Close the cursor variable.

The next example is a complete example showing the use of a cursor variable in a package.

■ FOR EXAMPLE

```
-- csh15_18a.sql
CREATE OR REPLACE PACKAGE course_pkg AS
  TYPE course_rec_typ IS RECORD
     (first_name     student.first_name%TYPE,
      last_name      student.last_name%TYPE,
      course_no      course.course_no%TYPE,
      description    course.description%TYPE,
      section_no     section.section_no%TYPE
      );
  TYPE course_cur IS REF CURSOR RETURN course_rec_typ;
  PROCEDURE get_course_list
     (p_student_id    NUMBER ,
```

```
                    p_instructor_id NUMBER ,
                    course_list_cv IN OUT course_cur);
          END course_pkg;

          CREATE OR REPLACE PACKAGE BODY course_pkg AS
             PROCEDURE get_course_list
               (p_student_id    NUMBER ,
                p_instructor_id NUMBER ,
                course_list_cv IN OUT course_cur)
             IS
             BEGIN
               IF p_student_id IS NULL AND p_instructor_id
                 IS NULL THEN
                 OPEN course_list_cv FOR
                   SELECT 'Please choose a student-' First_name,
                          'instructor combination'    Last_name,
                      NULL        course_no,
                      NULL        description,
                      NULL        section_no
                      FROM dual;
                ELSIF p_student_id IS NULL  THEN
                  OPEN course_list_cv FOR
                    SELECT s.first_name    first_name,
                        s.last_name      last_name,
                        c.course_no      course_no,
                        c.description    description,
                        se.section_no    section_no
                 FROM    instructor i, student s,
                         section se, course c, enrollment e
                 WHERE   i.instructor_id = p_instructor_id
                    AND  i.instructor_id = se.instructor_id
                    AND  se.course_no     = c.course_no
                    AND  e.student_id     = s.student_id
                    AND  e.section_id     = se.section_id
                    ORDER BY  c.course_no, se.section_no;
                 ELSIF p_instructor_id IS NULL   THEN
                   OPEN course_list_cv FOR
                        SELECT i.first_name    first_name,
                        i.last_name      last_name,
                        c.course_no      course_no,
                        c.description    description,
                        se.section_no    section_no
                 FROM    instructor i, student s,
                         section se, course c, enrollment e
                 WHERE   s.student_id = p_student_id
                    AND  i.instructor_id = se.instructor_id
                    AND  se.course_no     = c.course_no
                    AND  e.student_id     = s.student_id
                    AND  e.section_id     = se.section_id
```

```
      ORDER BY  c.course_no, se.section_no;
      END IF;
  END get_course_list;

END course_pkg;
```

You can pass query results sets between PL/SQL stored subprograms and various clients. This works because PL/SQL and its clients share a pointer to the query work area identifying the result set. This can be done in a client program like SQL*Plus by defining a host variable with a data type of REFCURSOR to hold the query result generated from a REF CURSOR in a stored program. In order to see what is being stored in the SQL*Plus variable, use the SQL*Plus PRINT command. Optionally you can have the SQL*Plus command SET AUTOPRINT ON to display the query results automatically.

LAB 15.2 EXERCISES

15.2.1 MAKE USE OF CURSOR VARIABLES

a) Take a look at the previous example and explain why the package has two different TYPE declarations. Also explain how the procedure get_course_list is making use of the cursor variable.

b) Create a SQL*Plus variable that is a cursor variable type.

c) Execute the procedure course_pkg.get_course_list, with three different types of variable combinations to show the three possible results sets. After you execute the procedure, display the values of the SQL*Plus variable you declared in question (a).

d) Create another package called student_info_pkg that has a single procedure called get_student_info. The get_student_info package will have three parameters. The first one is the student_id and the second is a number called p_choice; the last is a weak cursor variable. The p_choice indicates what information will be delivered about the student. The p_choice indicates what information will deliver about the student. If it is 1, then return the information about the student from the STUDENT table. If it is 2, then list all the courses the student is enrolled in with the student names of the fellow students enrolled in the same section as the student with the student_id that was passed in. If it is 3, then return the instructor name for that student, with the information about the courses that the student is enrolled in.

e) Run the get_student_info procedure in SQL*Plus and display the results.

LAB 15.2 EXERCISE ANSWERS

15.2.1 ANSWERS

a) Take a look at the previous example and explain why the package has two different TYPE declarations. Also explain how the procedure get_course_list is making use of the cursor variable.

Answer: In script ch15_18a there are two declarations of a TYPE in the package header. The first is for the record type course_rec_type. This record type is declared to define the result set of the SELECT statements that will be used for the cursor variable. When data items in a record do not match a single table, it is necessary to create a record type. The second TYPE declaration is for the cursor variable also known as REF CURSOR. The variable has the name, course_cur, and it is declared as a strong cursor, meaning that it can only be used for a single record type. The record type is, course_rec_type. The procedure get_course_list in the course_pkg is made so that it can return a cursor variable that holds three different result sets. Each of the result sets is of the same record type. The first type is for when both IN parameters of student ID and instructor ID are null. This will produce a result set that is a message, 'Please choose a student-instructor combination.' The next way the procedure runs is if the instructor_id is passed in but the student_id is null (note that the logic of the procedure is a reverse negative; saying in the second clause of the IF statement p_student_id IS NULL, means when the instructor_id is passed in). This will run a SELECT statement to populate the cursor variable that holds a list of all the courses this instructor teaches and the students enrolled in these classes. The last way this can run is for a student_id and no instructor_id. This will produce a result set of all the courses the student is enrolled in and the instructors for each section. Also note that while the cursor variable is opened it is never closed.

b) Create a SQL*Plus variable that is a cursor variable type.

Answer:

```
SQL> VARIABLE course_cv REFCURSOR
```

c) Execute the procedure course_pkg.get_course_list, with three different types of variable combinations to show the three possible results sets. After you execute the procedure, display the values of the SQL*Plus variable you declared in question (a).

Answer: There are three ways to execute this procedure. The first way would be to pass a student ID and not an instructor ID.

```
SQL> exec course_pkg.get_course_list(102,
     NULL, :course_cv);

PL/SQL procedure successfully completed.

SQL> print course_cv
```

FIRST_NAME	LAST_NAME	COURSE_NO	DESCRIPTION	SECTION_NO
Charles	Lowry	25	Intro to Programming	2
Nina	Schorin	25	Intro to Programming	5

The next method would be to pass an instructor ID and not a student ID.

```
SQL> exec course_pkg.get_course_list(NULL, 102,
     :course_cv);

PL/SQL procedure successfully completed.

SQL> print course_cv
```

FIRST_NAME	LAST_NAME	COURSE_NO	DESCRIPTION	SECTION_NO
Jeff	Runyan	10	DP Overview	2
Dawn	Dennis	25	Intro to Programming	4
May	Jodoin	25	Intro to Programming	4
Jim	Joas	25	Intro to Programming	4
Arun	Griffen	25	Intro to Programming	4
Alfred	Hutheesing	25	Intro to Programming	4
Lula	Oates	100	Hands-On Windows	1
Regina	Bose	100	Hands-On Windows	1
Jenny	Goldsmith	100	Hands-On Windows	1
Roger	Snow	100	Hands-On Windows	1
Rommel	Frost	100	Hands-On Windows	1
Debra	Boyce	100	Hands-On Windows	1
Janet	Jung	120	Intro to Java Programming	4
John	Smith	124	Advanced Java Programming	1

Charles	Caro	124 Advanced Java Programming	1
Sharon	Thompson	124 Advanced Java Programming	1
Evan	Fielding	124 Advanced Java Programming	1
Ronald	Tangaribuan	124 Advanced Java Programming	1
N	Kuehn	146 Java for C/C++ Programmers	2
Derrick	Baltazar	146 Java for C/C++ Programmers	2
Angela	Torres	240 Intro to the Basic Language	2

**LAB
15.2**

The last method would be not to pass either the student ID or the instructor ID.

```
SQL> exec course_pkg.get_course_list(NULL, NULL,
     :course_cv);

PL/SQL procedure successfully completed.

SQL>  print course_cv

FIRST_NAME             LAST_NAME               C DESCRIPTION      S
---------------------- ----------------------- - ----------------
Please choose a student-  instructor combination
```

d) Create another package called student_info_pkg that has a single procedure called get_student_info. The get_student_info package will have three parameters. The first one is the student_id and the second is also a number called p_choice; the last is a weak cursor variable. The p_choice indicates what information will be delivered about the student. If it is 1, then return the information about the student from the STUDENT table. If it is 2, then list all the courses the student is enrolled in, with the student names of the fellow students enrolled in the same section as the student with the student_id that was passed in. If it is 3, then return the instructor name for that student, with the information about the courses that the student is enrolled in.

Answer:

```
CREATE OR REPLACE PACKAGE student_info_pkg AS

  TYPE student_details IS REF CURSOR;

  PROCEDURE get_student_info
    (p_student_id    NUMBER ,
     p_choice        NUMBER ,
     details_cv IN OUT student_details);
END student_info_pkg;

CREATE OR REPLACE PACKAGE BODY student_info_pkg AS
  PROCEDURE get_student_info
    (p_student_id    NUMBER ,
     p_choice        NUMBER ,
     details_cv IN OUT student_details)
```

```
IS
BEGIN
  IF p_choice = 1  THEN
    OPEN details_cv FOR
      SELECT s.first_name      first_name,
             s.last_name       last_name,
             s.street_address  address,
             z.city            city,
             z.state           state,
             z.zip             zip
      FROM   student s, zipcode z
      WHERE  s.student_id = p_student_id
        AND  z.zip = s.zip;
  ELSIF p_choice = 2 THEN
    OPEN details_cv  FOR
      SELECT c.course_no      course_no,
             c.description    description,
             se.section_no    section_no,
             s.first_name     first_name,
             s.last_name      last_name
      FROM   student s,  section se,
             course c, enrollment e
      WHERE  se.course_no    = c.course_no
        AND  e.student_id    = s.student_id
        AND  e.section_id    = se.section_id
        AND  se.section_id in (SELECT e.section_id
                                 FROM student s,
                                      enrollment e
                                WHERE s.student_id =
                                      p_student_id
                                  AND s.student_id =
                                      e.student_id)
      ORDER BY  c.course_no;
  ELSIF p_choice = 3 THEN
    OPEN details_cv FOR
      SELECT i.first_name     first_name,
             i.last_name      last_name,
             c.course_no      course_no,
             c.description    description,
             se.section_no    section_no
      FROM   instructor i, student s,
             section se, course c, enrollment e
      WHERE  s.student_id = p_student_id
        AND  i.instructor_id = se.instructor_id
        AND  se.course_no    = c.course_no
        AND  e.student_id    = s.student_id
        AND  e.section_id    = se.section_id
      ORDER BY  c.course_no, se.section_no;
  END IF;
```

```
   END get_student_info;

END student_info_pkg;
```

e) Run the get_student_info procedure in SQL*Plus and display the results.

Answer:

```
SQL> VARIABLE student_cv REFCURSOR
SQL> execute student_info_pkg.GET_STUDENT_INFO
     (102, 1, :student_cv);
PL/SQL procedure successfully completed.

SQL>  print student_cv
FIRST_ LAST_NAM ADDRESS            CITY            ST ZIP
------ -------- ------------------ --------------- -- -----
Fred   Crocitto 101-09 120th St.   Richmond Hill   NY 11419

SQL> execute student_info_pkg.GET_STUDENT_INFO
                       (102, 2,  :student_cv);
PL/SQL procedure successfully completed.

SQL> print student_cv
COURSE_NO DESCRIPTION            SECTION_NO FIRST_NAME LAST_NAME
--------- ------------------     ---------- ---------- ----------
       25 Intro to Programming            2 Fred       Crocitto
       25 Intro to Programming            2 Judy       Sethi
       25 Intro to Programming            2 Jenny      Goldsmith
       25 Intro to Programming            2 Barbara    Robichaud
       25 Intro to Programming            2 Jeffrey    Citron
       25 Intro to Programming            2 George     Kocka
       25 Intro to Programming            5 Fred       Crocitto
       25 Intro to Programming            5 Hazel      Lasseter
       25 Intro to Programming            5 James      Miller
       25 Intro to Programming            5 Regina     Gates
       25 Intro to Programming            5 Arlyne     Sheppard
       25 Intro to Programming            5 Thomas     Edwards
       25 Intro to Programming            5 Sylvia     Perrin
       25 Intro to Programming            5 M.         Diokno
       25 Intro to Programming            5 Edgar      Moffat
       25 Intro to Programming            5 Bessie     Heedles
       25 Intro to Programming            5 Walter     Boremmann
       25 Intro to Programming            5 Lorrane    Velasco

SQL> execute student_info_pkg.GET_STUDENT_INFO
                          (214, 3,   :student_cv);
PL/SQL procedure successfully completed.
```

```
SQL> print student_cv
FIRST_NAME  LAST_NAME    COURSE_NO   DESCRIPTION               SECTION_NO
----------  -----------  ----------  ------------------------  ----------
Marilyn     Frantzen     120 Intro to Java Programming              1
Fernand     Hanks        122 Intermediate Java Programming          5
Gary        Pertez       130 Intro to Unix                          2
Marilyn     Frantzen     145 Internet Protocols                     1
```

Rules for Using Cursor Variables

- You cannot use cursor variables with remote subprograms on another server.
- Do not use FOR UPDATE with OPEN FOR in processing a cursor variable.
- You cannot use comparison operators to test cursor variables.
- A cursor variable cannot be assigned a null value.
- A REF CURSOR types cannot be used in a CREATE TABLE or VIEW statements.
- A stored procedure that uses a cursor variable can only be used as a query block data source; it cannot be used for a DML block data source. Using a ref cursor is ideal for queries that are dependent only on variations in SQL statements and not PL/SQL.

LAB 15.2 SELF-REVIEW QUESTIONS

In order to test your progress, you should be able to answer the following questions.

1) The main benefit of using parameters with cursors is that it makes the cursor reusable.

a) _____ True
b) _____ False

2) Which of the following are acceptable types of parameters to be used with cursors?

a) _____ IN
b) _____ OUT
c) _____ %ROWTYPE
d) _____ IN OUT

3) By adding the keywords FOR UPDATE at the end of a cursor, you are

a) _____ simply alerting the DBA that you are updating a table.
b) _____ freeing up rollback segments for the update.
c) _____ locking the indicated rows for an update.
d) _____ creating a bind variable.

4) Adding the keywords WHERE CURRENT OF to a FOR UPDATE cursor causes which of the following to take place?

a) _____ The DBA gets annoyed.
b) _____ Rows are locked and unlocked one at a time.
c) _____ The update occurs for the current record in the cursor.
d) _____ The scope of the cursor is increased.

5) The principal difference between a FOR UPDATE cursor without a WHERE CURRENT OF clause and one with a WHERE CURRENT OF clause is that

a) _____ without the clause the update needs to have a WHERE clause.
b) _____ rows are only locked with the extra clause present.
c) _____ only the items specified in the WHERE CURRENT OF clause are locked.
d) _____ processing will only occur for the current row of the cursor.

Answers appear in Appendix A, Section 15.2.

C H A P T E R   1 6

STORED CODE

In Chapter 11 you learned about procedures, in Chapter 12 you learned about functions, and in Chapter 13 you learned about the process of grouping functions and procedures into a package. Now you will learn more about what it means to have code bundled into a package. There are numerous data dictionary views that can be accessed to gather information about the objects in a package.

Functions in packages are also required to meet additional restrictions in order to be used in a SELECT statement. In this chapter, you learn what they are and how to enforce them. You will also learn an advanced technique to overload a function or procedure so that it executes different code, depending on the type of the parameter passed in.

**LAB
16.1**

LAB 16.1

GATHERING STORED CODE INFORMATION

LAB OBJECTIVES

After this Lab, you will be able to:

✔ Get Stored Code Information from the Data Dictionary
✔ Enforce Purity Level with RESTRICT_REFERENCES Pragma
✔ Overload Modules

Stored programs are stored in compiled form in the database. Information about the stored programs is accessible through various data dictionary views. In Chapter 11 you learned about the two data dictionary views USER_OBJECTS and USER_SOURCE. Additionally, you learned about the USER_TRIGGERS view in Chapter 8. There are a few more data dictionary views that are useful for obtaining information about stored code. In this lab, you will learn how to take advantage of these.

LAB 16.1 EXERCISES

16.1.1 GET STORED CODE INFORMATION FROM THE DATA DICTIONARY

Answer the following questions:

a) Query the data dictionary to determine all the stored procedures, functions, and packages in the current schema of the database. Also include the current status of the stored code. Write the SELECT statement.

b) Type the following script into a text file and run the script in SQL*Plus. It creates the function `scode_at_line`. Explain what the purpose of this function is. What is accomplished by running it? When does a developer find it useful?

■ FOR EXAMPLE

```
-- ch16_1a.sql
CREATE OR REPLACE FUNCTION scode_at_line
    (i_name_in IN VARCHAR2,
     i_line_in IN INTEGER := 1,
     i_type_in IN VARCHAR2 := NULL)
RETURN VARCHAR2
IS
    CURSOR scode_cur IS
        SELECT text
          FROM user_source
         WHERE name = UPPER (i_name_in)
           AND (type = UPPER (i_type_in)
            OR i_type_in IS NULL)
           AND line = i_line_in;
    scode_rec scode_cur%ROWTYPE;
BEGIN
    OPEN scode_cur;
    FETCH scode_cur INTO scode_rec;
    IF scode_cur%NOTFOUND
        THEN
            CLOSE scode_cur;
            RETURN NULL;
    ELSE
        CLOSE scode_cur;
        RETURN scode_rec.text;
    END IF;
END;
```

c) Type DESC USER_ERRORS. What do you see? In what way do you think this view is useful for you?

d) Type the following script to force an error.

```
CREATE OR REPLACE PROCEDURE FORCE_ERROR
as
BEGIN
    SELECT course_no
```

```
        INTO v_temp
        FROM course;
END;
```

Now type:

```
SHO ERR
```

What do you see?

e) How can you retrieve information from the USER_ERRORS view?

f) Type DESC USER_DEPENDENCIES. What do you see? How can you make use of this view?

g) Type the following:

```
SELECT referenced_name
FROM user_dependencies
WHERE name = 'SCHOOL_API';
```

Analyze what you see and explain how it is useful.

h) Type DESC `school_api`. What do you see?

i) Explain what you are seeing. How is this different from the USER_DEPENDENCIES view?

16.1.2 ENFORCE PURITY LEVEL WITH RESTRICT_REFERENCES PRAGMA

Answer the following questions:

a) Add the following function to the `school_api` package specification that you created in Chapter 13:

```
6       FUNCTION total_cost_for_student
7          (i_student_id IN student.student_id%TYPE)
8       RETURN course.cost%TYPE;
9    END school_api;
```

Append to the body:

```
60   FUNCTION total_cost_for_student
61      (i_student_id IN student.student_id%TYPE)
62       RETURN course.cost%TYPE
63   IS
64      v_cost course.cost%TYPE;
65   BEGIN
66      SELECT sum(cost)
67        INTO v_cost
68        FROM course c, section s, enrollment e
69       WHERE c.course_no = s.course_no
70         AND e.section_id = s.section_id
71         AND e.student_id = i_student_id;
72      RETURN v_cost;
73   EXCEPTION
74      WHEN OTHERS THEN
75         RETURN NULL;
76   END total_cost_for_student;
77   BEGIN
78     SELECT trunc(sysdate, 'DD')
79       INTO v_current_date
80       FROM dual;
81   END school_api;
```

If you performed the following SELECT statement, what would you expect to see?

```
SELECT school_api.total_cost_for_student(student_id),
       student_id
FROM student;
```

A pragma is a special directive to the PL/SQL compiler. You use the RESTRICT_REFERENCES pragma to tell the compiler about the purity level of a packaged function.

To assert the purity level, use the syntax:

```
PRAGMA RESTRICT_REFERENCES
     (function_name, WNDS [,WNPS], [,RNDS] [,RNPS])
```

b) Alter the package specification for school_api as follows:

```
6       FUNCTION total_cost_for_student
7          (i_student_id IN student.student_id%TYPE)
8          RETURN course.cost%TYPE;
9          PRAGMA RESTRICT_REFERENCES
10             (total_cost_for_student, WNDS, WNPS, RNPS);
11   END school_api;
```

Now run the SELECT statement from question (a). What do you expect to see?

c) What is the "purity level" of the function school_api. total_cost_for_student?

d) If you add the following three lines, will the package compile without error?

```
81      UPDATE STUDENT
82         SET employer = 'Prenctice Hall'
83        WHERE employer is null;
84   END school_api;
```

16.1.3 OVERLOAD MODULES

When you overload modules, you give two or more modules the same name. The parameter lists of the modules must differ in a manner significant enough for the compiler (and runtime engine) to distinguish between the different versions.

You can overload modules in three contexts:

1. In a local module in the same PL/SQL block
2. In a package specification
3. In a package body

a) Add the following lines to the package specification of school_api. Then recompile the package specification. Explain what you have created.

```
11      PROCEDURE get_student_info
12          (i_student_id   IN   student.student_id%TYPE,
13           o_last_name    OUT  student.last_name%TYPE,
```

```
14        o_first_name    OUT student.first_name%TYPE,
15        o_zip           OUT student.zip%TYPE,
16        o_return_code OUT NUMBER);
17    PROCEDURE get_student_info
18        (i_last_name    IN student.last_name%TYPE,
19         i_first_name   IN student.first_name%TYPE,
20         o_student_id   OUT student.student_id%TYPE,
21         o_zip          OUT student.zip%TYPE,
22         o_return_code OUT NUMBER);
23  END school_api;
```

b) Add the following code to the body of the package
   `school_api`. Explain what has been accomplished.

```
77    PROCEDURE get_student_info
78     (i_student_id   IN   student.student_id%TYPE,
79      o_last_name    OUT  student.last_name%TYPE,
80      o_first_name   OUT  student.first_name%TYPE,
81      o_zip          OUT  student.zip%TYPE,
82      o_return_code  OUT NUMBER)
83    IS
84    BEGIN
85      SELECT last_name, first_name, zip
86        INTO o_last_name, o_first_name, o_zip
87        FROM student
88       WHERE student.student_id = i_student_id;
89      o_return_code := 0;
90    EXCEPTION
91      WHEN NO_DATA_FOUND
92      THEN
93         DBMS_OUTPUT.PUT_LINE
               ('Student ID is not valid.');
94         o_return_code := -100;
95         o_last_name := NULL;
96         o_first_name := NULL;
97         o_zip    := NULL;
98      WHEN OTHERS
99        THEN
100        DBMS_OUTPUT.PUT_LINE
               ('Error in procedure get_student_info');
101   END get_student_info;
102   PROCEDURE get_student_info
103    (i_last_name    IN student.last_name%TYPE,
104     i_first_name   IN student.first_name%TYPE,
105     o_student_id   OUT student.student_id%TYPE,
106     o_zip          OUT student.zip%TYPE,
107     o_return_code OUT NUMBER)
```

```
108  IS
109  BEGIN
110    SELECT student_id, zip
111      INTO o_student_id, o_zip
112      FROM student
113      WHERE UPPER(last_name)  = UPPER(i_last_name)
114      AND UPPER(first_name) = UPPER(i_first_name);
115    o_return_code := 0;
116  EXCEPTION
117    WHEN NO_DATA_FOUND
118      THEN
119        DBMS_OUTPUT.PUT_LINE
                ('Student name is not valid.');
120        o_return_code := -100;
121        o_student_id := NULL;
122        o_zip    := NULL;
123    WHEN OTHERS
124      THEN
125        DBMS_OUTPUT.PUT_LINE
                ('Error in procedure get_student_info');
126  END get_student_info;
127    BEGIN
128      SELECT TRUNC(sysdate, 'DD')
129        INTO v_current_date
130        FROM dual;
131  END school_api;
```

c) Write a PL/SQL block using the overloaded function you just created.

LAB 16.1 EXERCISE ANSWERS

16.1.1 ANSWERS

a) Query the data dictionary to determine all the stored procedures, functions, and packages in the current schema of the database. Also include the current status of the stored code.

Answer: You can use the USER_OBJECTS view you learned about in Chapter 11. This view has information about all database objects in the schema of the current user. Re-

member, if you want to see all the objects in other schemas that the current user has access to, then use the ALL_OBJECTS view. There is also a DBA_OBJECTS view for a list of all objects in the database regardless of privilege. The STATUS will either be VALID or INVALID. An object can change status from VALID to INVALID if an underlying table is altered or privileges on a referenced object have been revoked from the creator of the function, procedure, or package. The following SELECT statement produces the answer you are looking for.

```
SELECT OBJECT_TYPE, OBJECT_NAME, STATUS
FROM   USER_OBJECTS
WHERE  OBJECT_TYPE IN
       ('FUNCTION', 'PROCEDURE', 'PACKAGE',
        'PACKAGE_BODY')
ORDER BY OBJECT_TYPE;
```

b) Type the following script into a text file and run the script in SQL*Plus. It creates the function `scode_at_line`. Explain the purpose of this function. What is accomplished by running it? When does a developer find it useful?

Answer: The `scode_at_line` *function provides an easy mechanism for retrieving the text from a stored program for a specified line number. This is useful if a developer receives a compilation error message referring to a particular line number in an object. The developer can then make use of this function to find out the text that is in error.*

The procedure uses three parameters:

```
name_in The name of the stored object.
line_in The line number of the line you wish to retrieve.
The default value is 1.
type_in The type of object you want to view. The default
for type_in is NULL.
```

The default values are designed to make this function as easy as possible to use.

*The output from a call to SHOW ERRORS in SQL*Plus displays the line number in which an error occurred, but the line number doesn't correspond to the line in your text file. Instead, it relates directly to the line number stored with the source code in the USER_SOURCE view.*

c) Type DESC USER_ERRORS. What do you see? In what way do you think this view is useful for you?

Answer: The view stores current errors on the user's stored objects. The text file contains the text of the error. This is useful in determining the details of a compilation error. The next exercise walks you through using this view.

Name	Null?	Type
NAME	NOT NULL	VARCHAR2(30)
TYPE		VARCHAR2(12)
SEQUENCE	NOT NULL	NUMBER
LINE	NOT NULL	NUMBER
POSITION	NOT NULL	NUMBER
TEXT	NOT NULL	VARCHAR2(2000) ---

d) Type the following script to force an error. Now type SHO ERR. What do you see?

Answer:

```
Errors for PROCEDURE FORCE_ERROR:
LINE/COL ERROR
-------- ---------------------------------------------
4/4      PL/SQL: SQL Statement ignored
5/9       PLS-00201: identifier 'V_TEMP' must be declared
```

e) How can you retrieve information from the USER_ERRORS view?

Answer:

```
SELECT line||'/'||position "LINE/COL", TEXT "ERROR"
FROM user_errors
WHERE name = 'FORCE_ERROR'
```

It is important for you to know how to retrieve this information from the USER_ ERRORS view since the SHO ERR command only shows you the most recent errors. If you run a script creating a number of objects, then you have to rely on the USER_ ERRORS view.

f) Type DESC USER_DEPENDENCIES. What do you see?

Answer: The DEPENDENCIES view is useful for analyzing the impact that may occur from table changes or changes to other stored procedures. If tables are about to be redesigned, an impact assessment can be made from the information in USER_ DEPENDENCIES. ALL_DEPENDENCIES and DBA_DEPENDENCIES show all dependencies for procedures, functions, package specifications, and package bodies.

Name	Null?	Type
NAME	NOT NULL	VARCHAR2(30)
TYPE		VARCHAR2(12)
REFERENCED_OWNER		VARCHAR2(30)
REFERENCED_NAME	NOT NULL	VARCHAR2(30)
REFERENCED_TYPE		VARCHAR2(12)
REFERENCED_LINK_NAME		VARCHAR2(30)

g) Type the following:

```
SELECT referenced_name
FROM user_dependencies
WHERE name = 'SCHOOL_API';
```

Analyze what you see and explain how it is useful.

Answer:

```
REFERENCED_NAME
------------------------------
DUAL
DUAL
STANDARD
STANDARD
DBMS_STANDARD
DBMS_OUTPUT
DBMS_OUTPUT
INSTRUCTOR_ID_SEQ
COURSE
COURSE
ENROLLMENT
INSTRUCTOR
INSTRUCTOR
SECTION
STUDENT
STUDENT
DBMS_OUTPUT
DUAL
SCHOOL_API
```

This list of dependencies for the school_api package lists all objects referenced in the package. This includes tables, sequences, and procedures (even Oracle-supplied packages). This information is very useful when you are planning a change to the database structure. You can easily pinpoint what the ramifications are for any database changes.

h) Type DESC school_api. What do you see?

Answer:

```
PROCEDURE DISCOUNT
FUNCTION NEW_INSTRUCTOR_ID RETURNS NUMBER(8)
FUNCTION TOTAL_COST_FOR_STUDENT RETURNS NUMBER(9,2)
Argument Name     Type                 In/Out Default?
------------------------------- ---------------------
I_STUDENT_ID      NUMBER(8)                 IN
```

DEPTREE

There is also an Oracle-supplied utility called DEPTREE that shows you, for a given object, which other objects are dependent upon it. There are three pieces to this utility. You need to have DBA access to the database in order to use this utility.

```
utldtree.sql script
DEPTREE_FILL(type, schema, object_name) procedure
ideptree view
```

First, run utldtree.sql in your schema. This creates the necessary objects to map the dependencies. The location of utldtree.sql is dependent on your particular installation, so ask your DBA. (c:\orant\rdbms80\admin\utldtree.sql)

($ORACLE_HOME/rdbms/admin/utldtree.sql)

Second, fill the deptree e_temptab table by running DEPTREE_FILL.

Example: SQL> exec DEPTREE_FILL('TABLE', USER, 'MESSAGE_LOG')

Third, look at the deptree information in the ideptree view.

Example: SQL> SELECT * FROM ideptree;

The result contains the following kind of information:

```
DEPENDENCIES
------------------------------------------
TABLE CTA.MESSAGE_LOG
PACKAGE BODY CTA.API
TRIGGER CTA.COURSE_AFTER_I
PACKAGE CTA.API
PACKAGE BODY CTA.API
```

---

i) Explain what you are seeing. How is this different from the USER_
DEPENDENCIES view?

Answer: The DESC command you have been using to describe the columns in a table is also used for procedures, packages, and functions. The DESC command shows all the parameters with their default values and an indication of whether they are IN or OUT. If the object is a function, then the return datatype is displayed. This is very different from the USER_DEPENDENCIES view, which has information on all the objects that are referenced in a package, function, or procedure.

16.1.2 ANSWERS

a) If you perform the following SELECT statement, what do you expect to see?

Answer: At first glance you may have thought you would see a list of student_ids *with the total cost for the courses they took. But instead you see the following error:*

```
ERROR at line 1:
ORA-06571: Function TOTAL_COST_FOR_STUDENT
does not guarantee not to update database
```

Although functions can be used in a SELECT statement, if a function is in a package, it requires some additional definitions to enforce its purity.

Requirements for Stored Functions in SQL

Need a hand with this? I used this command from my shell prompt:

1. The function must be stored in the database (not in the library of an Oracle tool).

2. The function must be a row-specific function and not a column or group function.

3. As for all functions (whether to be used in SQL statements or not), parameters must be the IN mode.

4. Datatypes of the function parameters and the function RETURN clause must be recognized within the Oracle server. (Not, as of yet, BOOLEAN, BINARY_ INTEGER, PL/SQL tables, PL/SQL records, and programmer-defined subtypes. Maybe in the future—keep your fingers crossed).

There are numerous function side effects that must be considered. Modification of database tables in stored functions may have ripple effects on queries using the function. Modification of package variables can have an impact on other stored functions or procedures, or in turn the SQL statement using the stored function. Stored functions in the WHERE clause may subvert the query optimization process. A SQL statement may use a stand-alone function or package function as an operator on one or more columns, provided the function returns a valid Oracle database type.

A user-defined function may select from database tables or call other procedures or functions, whether stand-alone or packaged. When a function is used in a SELECT statement, it may not modify data in any database table with an INSERT, UPDATE, or DELETE statement, or read or write package variables across user sessions.

The Oracle server automatically enforces the rules for stand-alone functions, but not with a stored function in a package. The purity level (the extent to which the function is free of side effects) of a function in a package must be stated explicitly. This is done via a pragma.

The reason the error message was received is because the pragma was not used. You will now learn how to make use of a pragma.

b) Alter the package specification for `school_api` as follows. Run the SELECT statement from question (a). What do you expect to see?

Answer: The pragma restriction is added to the package specification and ensures that the function `total_cost_for_student` *has met the required purity restriction for a function to be in a SELECT statement. The SELECT statement now functions properly and projects a list of the total cost for each student and the student's ID.*

Rules for Using Pragma Restrictions

Only the WNDS level is mandatory.

You need a separate pragma statement for each packaged function used in an SQL statement.

The pragma must come after the function declaration in the package specification.

---

c) What is the "purity level" of the function `school_api. total_cost_for_student`?

Answer: The extent to which a function is free of side effects is called the purity level of the function. The function is now very pure. It has the following levels of purity: (1) WNDS means write no database state; that is, it does not make any changes to database tables. (2) WNPS means the function writes no package state; that is, the function does not alter the values of any package variables. (3) RNPS means it reads no package state; that is, no package variables are read in order to calculate the return for the function. There is also a RNDS pragma, which means no database tables are read. If this is added, the function is too pure for the needs here and cannot be used in a SELECT statement.

Table 16.1 shows a summary of the codes and their meanings.

Table 16.1 ■ Pragma Restricitons

Purity Level	Code Description	Assertion
WNDS	Writes No Database State	No modification of any database table.
WNPS	Writes No Package State	No modification of any packaged variable.
RNDS	Reads No Database State	No reading of any database table.
RNPS	Reads No Package State	No reading of any package variables.

d) If you add the following three lines, does the package compile without any errors?

Answer: No. You added an update statement and violated the purity level of the pragma restriction WNDS—writes no database state. You receive the following error message when you try to compile the new package:

```
Errors for PACKAGE BODY SCHOOL_API:
LINE/COL ERROR
-------- ----------------------------------------------
0/0       PL/SQL: Compilation unit analysis terminated
60/2      PLS-00452: Subprogram 'TOTAL_COST_FOR_STUDENT'
                     violates its  associated pragma
```

16.1.3 ANSWERS

a) Add the following lines to the package specification `school_api`. Then compile the package specification. Explain what you created.

Answer: No, you have not created Frankenstein, it's just an overloaded procedure. The specification has two procedures with the same name and different IN parameters both in number and in datatype. The OUT parameters are also different in number and datatype. This overloaded function accepts either of the two sets of IN parameters and performs the version of the function corresponding to the datatype passed in.

b) Add the following code to the package body `school_api`. Explain what you accomplished.

Answer: A single function name, `get_student_info`, *accepts either a single IN parameter of* `student_id` *or two parameters consisting of a student's* `last_name` *and* `first_name`. *If a number is passed in, then the procedure looks for the name and zipcode of the student. If it finds them, they are returned as well as a return code of 0. If they cannot be found, then null values are returned and a return code of −100. If two VARCHAR2 parameters are passed in, then the procedure searches for the* `student_id` *corresponding to the names passed in. As with the other version of this procedure, if a match is found the procedure returns a* `student_id`, *the student's zipcode, and a return code of 0. If a match is not found, then the values returned are null as well as an exit code of −100.*

PL/SQL uses overloading in many common functions and built-in packages. For example, TO_CHAR converts both numbers and dates to strings. Overloading makes it easy for other programmers to use your code in an API.

The main benefits of overloading are as follows: (1) Overloading simplifies the call interface of packages and reduces many program names to one. (2) Modules are easier to use and hence more likely to be used. The software determines the context. (3) The volume of code is reduced because code required for different datatypes is often the same.

The rules for overloading are as follows: (1) The compiler must be able to distinguish between the two calls at runtime. Distinguishing between the uses of the overloaded module is what is important and not solely the spec or header. (2) The formal parameters must differ in number, order, or datatype family. (3) You cannot overload the names of stand-alone modules. (4) Functions differing only in RETURN datatypes cannot be overloaded.

c) Write a PL/SQL block using the overloaded function you just created.

Answer: A suitable bride for Frankenstein is as follows:

```
SET SERVEROUTPUT ON
PROMPT ENTER A student_id
ACCEPT p_id
PROMPT ENTER a differnt student's first name surrounded
PROMPT by quotes
ACCEPT p_first_name
PROMPT Now enter the last name surrounded by quotes
ACCEPT p_last_name
DECLARE
    v_student_ID   student.student_id%TYPE;
    v_last_name    student.last_name%TYPE;
    v_first_name   student.first_name%TYPE;
    v_zip          student.zip%TYPE;
    v_return_code NUMBER;
BEGIN
    school_api.get_student_info
        (&&p_id, v_last_name, v_first_name,
         v_zip,v_return_code);
    IF v_return_code = 0
    THEN
      DBMS_OUTPUT.PUT_LINE
          ('Student with ID '||&&p_id||' is '||v_first_name
          ||' '||v_last_name
          );
    ELSE
    DBMS_OUTPUT.PUT_LINE
        ('The ID '||&&p_id||'is not in the database'
         );
    END IF;
    school_api.get_student_info
        (&&p_last_name , &&p_first_name, v_student_id,
         v_zip , v_return_code);
    IF v_return_code = 0
    THEN
```

```
        DBMS_OUTPUT.PUT_LINE
          (&&p_first_name||' '|| &&p_last_name||
           ' has an ID of '||v_student_id
          );
    ELSE
    DBMS_OUTPUT.PUT_LINE
      (&&p_first_name||' '|| &&p_last_name||
       'is not in the database'
       );
    END IF;
  END;
```

It is important for you to realize the benefits of using a && variable. The value for the variable need only be entered once, but if you run the code a second time, you will not be prompted to enter the value again since it is now in memory.

Here are a few things to keep in mind when you overload functions or procedures. These two procedures cannot be overloaded:

```
    PROCEDURE calc_total (reg_in IN CHAR);
    PROCEDURE calc_total (reg_in IN VARCHAR2).
```

In these two versions of `calc_total` *the two different IN variables cannot be distinguished from each other. In the following example, an anchored type (%TYPE) is relied on to establish the datatype of the second calc's parameter.*

```
    DECLARE
    PROCEDURE calc (comp_id_IN IN NUMBER)
        IS
    BEGIN ... END;
    PROCEDURE calc
    (comp_id_IN IN company.comp_id%TYPE)
        IS
    BEGIN ... END;
```

PL/SQL does not find a conflict at compile time with overloading even though `comp_id` *is a numeric column. Instead, you get the following message at runtime:*

```
PLS-00307: too many declarations of '<program>' match this
call
```

LAB 16.1 SELF-REVIEW QUESTIONS

In order to test your progress, you should be able to answer the following questions.

1) What is the purpose of the USER_ERRORS view?
   a) _____ It prevents you from having to make use of the SHO ERR command.
   b) _____ It has the details on database objects in an invalid state.
   c) _____ It is a record of all compilation errors you have ever made.
   d) _____ It has no purpose but to take up database space.

2) The DESC command behaves like an overloaded procedure.
   a) _____ True
   b) _____ False

3) All functions require a pragma restriction to be used in an SQL statement.
   a) _____ True
   b) _____ False

4) What does the purity level of a pragma restriction mean?

   a) _____ It refers to whether it is kosher or not.
   b) _____ It tells you if the function can be used in a SELECT statement.
   c) _____ It shows the effect executing the function will have on other objects in the database or the package.
   d) _____ It tells you if the function is overloaded.

5) What is the principal benefit of an overloaded function?

   a) _____ An overloaded function is able to bypass any pragma restriction.
   b) _____ An overloaded function behaves differently depending on the type of data passed in when it is called.
   c) _____ It is just a lot of hype—overloaded functions have no benefit.
   d) _____ An overloaded function is like a ghost function.

Answers appear in Appendix A, Section 16.1.

CHAPTER 16

TEST YOUR THINKING

In this chapter you learned about stored code. Here are some projects to help you test the depth of your understanding. Add the following to the `school_api`.

1) Add a function in school_api package specification called get_course_descript. The caller takes a course.cnumber%TYPE parameter and it returns a course.description%TYPE.

2) Create a function in the school_api package body called get_course_description. A caller passes in a course number and it returns the course description. Instead of searching for the description itself, it makes a call to get_course_descript_private. It passes its course number to get_course_descript_private. It passes back to the caller the description it gets back from get_course_descript_private.

Add a PRAGMA RESTRICT_REFERENCES for get_course_description specifying the following: writes no database state, writes no package state, and reads no package state.

The projects in this section are meant to have you utilize all of the skills that you have acquired throughout this chapter. The answers to these projects can be found in Appendix D and at the companion Web site to this book, located at http://www.phptr .com/rosenzweig2e. Visit the Web site periodically to share and discuss your answers.

C H A P T E R   1 7

TRIGGERS

In Chapters 12 through 16, you explored the concepts of stored code and different types of named PL/SQL blocks, such as procedures, functions, and packages. In this chapter, you will learn about another type of named PL/SQL block called a database trigger. You will also learn about different characteristics of triggers and their usage in the database.

L A B   1 7 . 1

WHAT TRIGGERS ARE

> ## LAB OBJECTIVES
>
> After this Lab, you will be able to:
>
> ✔ Understand What a Trigger Is
> ✔ Use BEFORE and AFTER Triggers

A database trigger is a named PL/SQL block stored in a database and executed implicitly when a *triggering event* occurs. An act of executing a trigger is referred to as *firing a trigger*. A triggering event is a DML (INSERT, UPDATE, or DELETE) statement executed against a database table. A trigger can fire before or after a triggering event. For example, if you have defined a trigger to fire before an INSERT statement on the STUDENT table, this trigger fires each time before you insert a row in the STUDENT table.

The general syntax for creating a trigger is as follows (the reserved words and phrases surrounded by brackets are optional):

```
CREATE [OR REPLACE] TRIGGER trigger_name
{BEFORE|AFTER} triggering_event ON table_name
[FOR EACH ROW]
[WHEN condition]
DECLARE
    Declaration statements
BEGIN
    Executable statements
EXCEPTION
    Exception-handling statements
END;
```

The reserved word CREATE specifies that you are creating a new trigger. The reserved word REPLACE specifies that you are modifying an existing trigger. REPLACE is optional. However, note that both CREATE and REPLACE are present most of the time. Consider the following situation. You create a trigger as follows:

```
CREATE TRIGGER trigger_name
   ...
```

In a few days you decide to modify this trigger. If you do not include the reserved word REPLACE in the CREATE clause of the trigger, an error message will be generated when you compile the trigger. The error message states that the name of your trigger is already used by another object. Once REPLACE is included in the CREATE clause of the trigger, there is less of a chance for an error because, if it is a new trigger, it is created, and if it is an old trigger, it is replaced.

The trigger_name references the name of the trigger. BEFORE or AFTER specifies when the trigger fires (before or after the triggering event). The triggering_event references a DML statement issued against the table. The table_name is the name of the table associated with the trigger. The clause FOR EACH ROW specifies that a trigger is a row trigger and fires once for each row either inserted, updated, or deleted. You will encounter row and statement triggers in the next lab of this chapter. A WHEN clause specifies a condition that must evaluate to TRUE for the trigger to fire. For example, this condition may specify a certain restriction on the column of a table. Next, the trigger body is defined. *It is important for you to realize that if you drop a table, the table's database triggers are dropped as well.*

You should be careful when using the reserved word REPLACE for a number of reasons. First, if you happen to use REPLACE and the name of an existing stored function, procedure, or package, it will be replaced by the trigger. Second, when you use the reserved word REPLACE and decide to associate a different table with your trigger, an error message is generated. For example, assume you created a trigger STUDENT_BI on the STUDENT table. Next, you decide to modify this trigger and associate it with the ENROLLMENT table. As a result, the following error message is generated:

```
ERROR at line 1:
ORA-04095: trigger 'STUDENT_BI' already exists on another
table, cannot replace it
```

Triggers are used for different purposes. Some uses for triggers are as follows:

- Enforcing complex business rules that cannot be defined by using integrity constraints
- Maintaining complex security rules
- Automatically generating values for derived columns
- Collecting statistical information on table accesses
- Preventing invalid transactions
- Providing value auditing

The body of a trigger is a PL/SQL block. However, there are several restrictions that you need to know to create a trigger:

- A trigger may not issue a transactional control statement such as COMMIT, SAVEPOINT, or ROLLBACK. When the trigger fires, all operations performed become part of a transaction. When this transaction is committed or rolled back, the operations performed by the trigger are committed or rolled back as well.

- Any function or procedure called by a trigger may not issue a transactional control statement.

- It is not permissible to declare LONG or LONG RAW variables in the body of a trigger.

BEFORE TRIGGERS

Consider the following example of a trigger on the STUDENT table mentioned earlier in this chapter. This trigger fires before the INSERT statement on the STUDENT table and populates STUDENT_ID, CREATED_DATE, MODIFIED_DATE, CREATED_BY, and MODIFIED_BY columns. Column STUDENT_ID is populated with the number generated by the STUDENT_ID_SEQ sequence, and columns CREATED_DATE, MODIFIED_DATE, CREATED_USER, and MODIFIED_USER are populated with the current date and the current user name information, respectively.

■ FOR EXAMPLE

```
CREATE OR REPLACE TRIGGER student_bi
BEFORE INSERT ON student
FOR EACH ROW
DECLARE
   v_student_id STUDENT.STUDENT_ID%TYPE;
BEGIN
   SELECT STUDENT_ID_SEQ.NEXTVAL
     INTO v_student_id
     FROM dual;
   :NEW.student_id := v_student_id;
   :NEW.created_by := USER;
   :NEW.created_date := SYSDATE;
   :NEW.modified_by := USER;
   :NEW.modified_date := SYSDATE;
END;
```

This trigger fires before each INSERT statement on the STUDENT table. Notice that the name of the trigger is STUDENT_BI, where STUDENT references the name of the table on which the trigger is defined, and the letters BI mean BEFORE INSERT. There is no specific requirement for naming triggers; however, this approach to naming a trigger is descriptive because the name of the trigger contains the name of the table affected by the triggering event, the time of the triggering event (before or after), and the triggering event itself.

In the body of the trigger, there is a pseudorecord, :NEW, allowing you to access a row currently being processed. In other words, a row is being inserted into the STUDENT table. The :NEW pseudorecord is of a type TRIGGERING_ TABLE%TYPE, so, in this case, it is of the STUDENT%TYPE type. In order to access individual members of the pseudorecord :NEW, dot notation is used. In other words, :NEW.CREATED_BY refers to the member, CREATED_BY, of the :NEW pseudorecord, and the name of the record is separated by the dot from the name of its member.

Before you create this trigger, consider the following INSERT statement on the STUDENT table:

```
INSERT INTO student (student_id, first_name, last_name,
   zip, registration_date, created_by, created_date,
   modified_by, modified_date)
VALUES (STUDENT_ID_SEQ.NEXTVAL, 'John', 'Smith', '00914',
   SYSDATE, USER, SYSDATE, USER, SYSDATE);
```

This INSERT statement contains values for the columns STUDENT_ID, CREATED_BY, CREATED_DATE, MODIFIED_BY, and MODIFIED_DATE. It is important to note that for every row you insert into the STUDENT table, the values for these columns must be provided, and they are always derived in the same fashion. Why do you think the values for these columns must be provided when inserting a record into the STUDENT table?

Once the trigger shown earlier is created, there is no need to include these columns in the INSERT statement, because the trigger will populate them with the required information. Therefore, the INSERT statement can be modified as follows:

```
INSERT INTO student (first_name, last_name, zip,
   registration_date)
VALUES ('John', 'Smith', '00914', SYSDATE);
```

Notice that this version of the INSERT statement looks significantly shorter than the previous version. The columns STUDENT_ID, CREATED_BY, CREATED_DATE, MODIFIED_BY, and MODIFIED_DATE are not present. However, their values are provided by the trigger. As a result, there is no need to include them in the INSERT statement, and there is less of a chance for a transaction error.

You should use BEFORE triggers in the following situations:

- When a trigger provides values for derived columns before an INSERT or UPDATE statement is completed. For example, the column FINAL_GRADE in the ENROLLMENT table holds the value of the student's final grade for a specific course. This value is calculated based on the student performance for the duration of the course.

- When a trigger determines whether an INSERT, UPDATE, or DELETE statement should be allowed to complete. For example, when you insert a record into the INSTRUCTOR table, a trigger can verify whether the value provided for the column ZIP is valid, or, in other words, if there is a record in the ZIPCODE table corresponding to the value of zip that you provided.

AFTER TRIGGERS

Assume there is a table called STATISTICS having the following structure:

```
Name                             Null?     Type
------------------------------   --------  ----
TABLE_NAME                                 VARCHAR2(30)
TRANSACTION_NAME                           VARCHAR2(10)
TRANSACTION_USER                           VARCHAR2(30)
TRANSACTION_DATE                           DATE
```

This table is used to collect statistical information on different tables of the database. For example, you can record who deleted records from the INSTRUCTOR table and when they were deleted.

Consider the following example of a trigger on the INSTRUCTOR table. This trigger fires after an UPDATE or DELETE statement is issued on the INSTRUCTOR table.

■ FOR EXAMPLE

```
CREATE OR REPLACE TRIGGER instructor_aud
AFTER UPDATE OR DELETE ON INSTRUCTOR
DECLARE
    v_type VARCHAR2(10);
BEGIN
    IF UPDATING THEN
        v_type := 'UPDATE';
    ELSIF DELETING THEN
        v_type := 'DELETE';
    END IF;
    UPDATE statistics
        SET transaction_user = USER,
            transaction_date = SYSDATE
      WHERE table_name = 'INSTRUCTOR'
        AND transaction_name = v_type;

    IF SQL%NOTFOUND THEN
        INSERT INTO statistics
        VALUES ('INSTRUCTOR', v_type, USER, SYSDATE);
    END IF;
END;
```

This trigger fires after an UPDATE or DELETE statement on the INSTRUCTOR table. In the body of the trigger, there are two Boolean functions, UPDATING and DELETING. The function UPDATING evaluates to TRUE if an UPDATE statement is issued on the table, and the function DELETING evaluates to TRUE if a DELETE statement is issued on the table. There is another Boolean function called INSERTING. As you have probably guessed, this function evaluates to TRUE when an INSERT statement is issued against the table.

This trigger updates a record or inserts a new record into the STATISTICS table when an UPDATE or DELETE operation is issued against the INSTRUCTOR table. First, the trigger determines the type of the DML statement issued against the IN-STRUCTOR table. The type of the DML statement is determined with the help of the UPDATING and DELETING functions.

Next, the trigger tries to update a record in the STATISTICS table where TABLE_NAME is equal to INSTRUCTOR and TRANSACTION_NAME is equal to the current transaction (UPDATE or DELETE). Then the status of the UPDATE statement is checked with the help of SQL%NOTFOUND constructor. The SQL%NOTFOUND constructor evaluates to TRUE if the update statement does not update any rows and FALSE otherwise. So if SQL%NOTFOUND evaluates to TRUE, a new record is added to the STATISTICS table.

Once this trigger is created on the INSTRUCTOR table, any UPDATE or DELETE operation causes modification of old records or creation of new records in the STATISTICS table. Furthermore, you can enhance this trigger by calculating how many rows are updated or deleted from the INSTRUCTOR table.

You should use AFTER triggers in the following situations:

- When a trigger should fire after a DML statement is executed.
- When a trigger performs actions not specified in a BEFORE trigger.

LAB 17.1 EXERCISES

17.1.1 UNDERSTAND WHAT A TRIGGER IS

In this exercise, you need to determine the trigger firing event, its type, and so on, based on the CREATE clause of the trigger.

Consider the following CREATE clause:

```
CREATE TRIGGER student_au
AFTER UPDATE ON STUDENT
FOR EACH ROW
WHEN (NVL(NEW.ZIP, ' ') <> OLD.ZIP)
    Trigger Body...
```

In the WHEN statement of the CREATE clause, there is a pseudorecord, :OLD, allowing you to access a row currently being processed. It is important for you to note that neither :NEW nor :OLD are prefixed by the colon (:) when they are used in the condition of the WHEN statement.

You are already familiar with the pseudorecord :NEW. The :OLD pseudorecord allows you to access the current information of the record being updated. In other words, it is information currently present in the STUDENT table for a specified record. The :NEW pseudorecord allows you to access the new information for the current record. In other words, :NEW indicates the updated values. For example, consider the following UPDATE statement:

```
UPDATE student
   SET zip = '01247'
 WHERE zip = '02189';
```

The value "01247" of the ZIP column is a new value, and the trigger references it as :NEW.ZIP. The value "02189" in the ZIP column is the previous value and is referenced as :OLD.ZIP.

It is important for you to note that :OLD is undefined for INSERT statements and :NEW is undefined for DELETE statements. However, the PL/SQL compiler does not generate syntax errors when :OLD or :NEW is used in triggers where the triggering event is an INSERT or DELETE operation. In this case, the field values are set to NULL for :OLD and :NEW pseudorecords.

Answer the following questions:

a) Assume a trigger named STUDENT_AU already exists in the database. If you use the CREATE clause to modify the existing trigger, what error message is generated? Explain your answer.

b) If an update statement is issued on the STUDENT table, how many times does this trigger fire?

c) How many times does this trigger fire if an update statement is issued against the STUDENT table, but the ZIP column is not changed?

d) Why do you think there is a NVL function present in the WHEN statement of the CREATE clause?

17.1.2 USE *BEFORE* AND *AFTER* TRIGGERS

In this exercise, you create a trigger on the INSTRUCTOR table firing before an INSERT statement is issued against the table. The trigger determines the values for the columns CREATED_BY, MODIFIED_BY, CREATED_DATE, and MODIFIED_DATE. In addition, it determines if the value of zip provided by an INSERT statement is valid.

Create the following trigger:

```
-- ch17_1a.sql, version 1.0
CREATE OR REPLACE TRIGGER instructor_bi
BEFORE INSERT ON INSTRUCTOR
FOR EACH ROW
DECLARE
   v_work_zip CHAR(1);
BEGIN
   :NEW.CREATED_BY := USER;
   :NEW.CREATED_DATE := SYSDATE;
   :NEW.MODIFIED_BY := USER;
   :NEW.MODIFIED_DATE := SYSDATE;

   SELECT 'Y'
     INTO v_work_zip
     FROM zipcode
    WHERE zip = :NEW.ZIP;
EXCEPTION
   WHEN NO_DATA_FOUND THEN
      RAISE_APPLICATION_ERROR
         (-20001, 'Zip code is not valid!');
END;
```

Answer the following questions:

a) If an INSERT statement issued against the INSTRUCTOR table is missing a value for the column ZIP, does the trigger raise an exception? Explain your answer.

b) Modify this trigger so that another error message is displayed when an INSERT statement is missing a value for the column ZIP.

c) Modify this trigger so there is no need to supply the value for the instructor's ID at the time of the INSERT statement.

LAB 17.1 EXERCISE ANSWERS

This section gives you some suggested answers to the questions in Lab 17.1, with discussion related to how those answers resulted. The most important thing to realize is whether your answer works. You should figure out the implications of the answers here and what the effects are from any different answers you may come up with.

17.1.1 ANSWERS

a) Assume a trigger named STUDENT_AU already exists in the database. If you use this CREATE clause to modify the existing trigger, what error message is generated? Explain your answer.

Answer: An error message stating STUDENT_AU name is already used by another object is displayed on the screen. The CREATE clause has the ability to create new objects in the database, but it is unable to handle modifications. In order to modify the existing trigger, the REPLACE statement must be added to the CREATE clause. In this case, the old version of the trigger is dropped without warning, and the new version of the trigger is created.

b) If an update statement is issued on the STUDENT table, how many times does this trigger fire?

Answer: The trigger fires as many times as there are rows affected by the triggering event, because the FOR EACH ROW statement is present in the CREATE trigger clause.

When the FOR EACH ROW statement is not present in the CREATE trigger clause, the trigger fires once for the triggering event. In this case, if the following UPDATE statement

```
UPDATE student
   SET zip = '01247'
 WHERE zip = '02189';
```

is issued against the STUDENT table, it updates 10 records and the trigger fires only once instead of 10 times.

c) How many times does this trigger fire if an update statement is issued against the STUDENT table, but the ZIP column is not changed?

Answer: The trigger does not fire, because the condition of the WHEN statement evaluates to FALSE.

The condition

```
(NVL(NEW.ZIP, ' ') <> OLD.ZIP)
```

of the WHEN statement compares the new value of zipcode to the old value of zipcode. If the value of the zipcode is not changed, this condition evaluates to FALSE. As a result, this trigger does not fire if an UPDATE statement does not modify the value of zipcode for a specified record.

d) Why do you think there is a NVL function present in the WHEN statement of the CREATE clause?

Answer: If an UPDATE statement does not modify the column ZIP, the value of the field NEW.ZIP is undefined. In other words, it is NULL. A NULL value of ZIP cannot be compared with a non-NULL value of ZIP. Therefore, the NVL function is present in the WHEN condition.

Because the column ZIP has a NOT NULL constraint defined, there is no need to use the NVL function for the OLD.ZIP field. For an UPDATE statement issued against the STUDENT table, there is always a value of ZIP currently present in the table.

17.1.2 ANSWERS

a) If an INSERT statement issued against the INSTRUCTOR table is missing the value for the column ZIP, does the trigger raise an exception? Explain your answer.

Answer: Yes, the trigger raises an exception. When an INSERT statement does not provide a value for the column ZIP, the value of the :NEW.ZIP is NULL. This value is used in the WHERE clause of the SELECT INTO statement. As a result, the SELECT INTO statement is unable to return data. Therefore, the exception NO_DATA_FOUND is raised by the trigger.

b) Modify this trigger so that another error message is displayed when an INSERT statement is missing a value for the column ZIP.

Answer: Your script should look similar to the following script. All changes are shown in bold letters.

```
-- ch17_1b.sql, version 2.0
CREATE OR REPLACE TRIGGER instructor_bi
BEFORE INSERT ON INSTRUCTOR
FOR EACH ROW
DECLARE
   v_work_zip CHAR(1);
BEGIN
   :NEW.CREATED_BY := USER;
   :NEW.CREATED_DATE := SYSDATE;
   :NEW.MODIFIED_BY := USER;
   :NEW.MODIFIED_DATE := SYSDATE;

   IF :NEW.ZIP IS NULL THEN
      RAISE_APPLICATION_ERROR
         (-20002, 'Zip code is missing!');
   ELSE
      SELECT 'Y'
        INTO v_work_zip
        FROM zipcode
       WHERE zip = :NEW.ZIP;
   END IF;
EXCEPTION
   WHEN NO_DATA_FOUND THEN
      RAISE_APPLICATION_ERROR
         (-20001, 'Zip code is not valid!');
END;
```

Notice that an IF-ELSE statement is added to the body of the trigger. This IF-ELSE statement evaluates the value of :NEW.ZIP. If the value of :NEW.ZIP is NULL, the IF-ELSE statement evaluates to TRUE, and another error message is displayed stating that the value of ZIP is missing. If the IF-ELSE statement evaluates to FALSE, the control is passed to the ELSE part of the statement, and the SELECT INTO statement is executed.

c) Modify this trigger so there is no need to supply the value for the instructor's ID at the time of the INSERT statement.

Answer: Your version of the trigger should look similar to the one shown. All changes are shown in bold letters.

```
-- ch17_1c.sql, version 3.0
CREATE OR REPLACE TRIGGER instructor_bi
BEFORE INSERT ON INSTRUCTOR
FOR EACH ROW
DECLARE
   v_work_zip CHAR(1);
   v_instructor_id INSTRUCTOR.INSTRUCTOR_ID%TYPE;
BEGIN
   :NEW.CREATED_BY := USER;
```

```
        :NEW.CREATED_DATE := SYSDATE;
        :NEW.MODIFIED_BY := USER;
        :NEW.MODIFIED_DATE := SYSDATE;

        SELECT 'Y'
          INTO v_work_zip
          FROM zipcode
         WHERE zip = :NEW.ZIP;

        SELECT INSTRUCTOR_ID_SEQ.NEXTVAL
          INTO v_instructor_id
          FROM dual;

        :NEW.INSTRUCTOR_ID := v_instructor_id;
    EXCEPTION
        WHEN NO_DATA_FOUND THEN
            RAISE_APPLICATION_ERROR
                (-20001, 'Zip code is not valid!');
    END;
```

The original version of this trigger does not derive a value for the instructor's ID. Therefore, an INSERT statement issued against the INSTRUCTOR table has to populate the INSTRUCTOR_ID column as well. The new version of the trigger populates the value of the INSTRUCTOR_ID column, so that the INSERT statement does not have to do it.

Generally, it is a good idea to populate columns holding IDs in the trigger because when a user issues an INSERT statement, he or she might not know that an ID must be populated at the time of the insert. Furthermore, a user may not know—and more than likely does not know—how to operate sequences to populate the ID.

LAB 17.1 SELF-REVIEW QUESTIONS

In order to test your progress, you should be able to answer the following questions.

1) A trigger can fire for which of the following?

    a) _____ Before a triggering event
    b) _____ After a triggering event
    c) _____ Before or after a triggering event

2) How is a trigger executed?

    a) _____ Explicitly when a triggering event occurs
    b) _____ Implicitly when a triggering event occurs

3) In order for a trigger to fire, the WHEN condition must evaluate to which of the
following?

    a) _____ True
    b) _____ False

4) A BEFORE INSERT trigger fires for which of the following?

    a) _____ Before an UPDATE is issued against the triggering table
    b) _____ After an INSERT is issued against the triggering table
    c) _____ Before an INSERT is issued against the triggering table

5) When a SELECT statement is issued against the triggering table, which of the following triggers fire?

    a) _____ BEFORE trigger
    b) _____ AFTER trigger
    c) _____ BEFORE trigger and AFTER trigger
    d) _____ Triggers are not fired at all.

Answers appear in Appendix A, Section 17.1.

L A B   1 7 . 2

TYPES OF TRIGGERS

LAB OBJECTIVES

After this Lab, you will be able to:

✔ Use Row and Statement Triggers
✔ Use INSTEAD OF Triggers

In the previous lab of this chapter, you encountered the term *row trigger*. A row trigger is fired as many times as there are rows affected by the triggering statement. When the statement FOR EACH ROW is present in the CREATE TRIGGER clause, the trigger is a row trigger. Consider the following code:

■ *FOR EXAMPLE*

```
CREATE OR REPLACE TRIGGER course_au
AFTER UPDATE ON COURSE
FOR EACH ROW
...
```

In this code fragment, the statement FOR EACH ROW is present in the CREATE TRIGGER clause. Therefore, this trigger is a row trigger. If an UPDATE statement causes 20 records in the COURSE table to be modified, this trigger fires 20 times.

A statement trigger is fired once for the triggering statement. In other words, a statement trigger fires once, regardless of the number of rows affected by the triggering statement. To create a statement trigger, you omit the FOR EACH ROW in the CREATE TRIGGER clause. Consider the following code fragment:

■ *FOR EXAMPLE*

```
CREATE OR REPLACE TRIGGER enrollment_ad
AFTER DELETE ON ENROLLMENT
...
```

This trigger fires once after a DELETE statement is issued against the ENROLL-MENT table. Whether the DELETE statement removes one row or five rows from the ENROLLMENT table, this trigger fires only once.

Statement triggers should be used when the operations performed by the trigger do not depend on the data in the individual records. For example, if you want to limit access to a table to business hours only, a statement trigger is used. Consider the following example.

■ FOR EXAMPLE

```
CREATE OR REPLACE TRIGGER instructor_biud
BEFORE INSERT OR UPDATE OR DELETE ON INSTRUCTOR
DECLARE
    v_day VARCHAR2(10);
BEGIN
    v_day := RTRIM(TO_CHAR(SYSDATE, 'DAY'));
    IF v_day LIKE ('S%') THEN
        RAISE_APPLICATION_ERROR (-20000, 'A table cannot be '||
            'modified during off hours');
    END IF;
END;
```

This is a statement trigger on the INSTRUCTOR table, and it fires before an INSERT, UPDATE, or DELETE statement is issued. First, the trigger determines the day of the week. If the day happens to be Saturday or Sunday, an error message is generated. When the following UPDATE statement on the INSTRUCTOR table is issued on Saturday or Sunday

```
UPDATE instructor
   SET zip = 10025
 WHERE zip = 10015;
```

the trigger generates the error message shown below:

```
update INSTRUCTOR
       *
ERROR at line 1:
ORA-20000: A table cannot be modified during off hours
ORA-06512: at "STUDENT.INSTRUCTOR_BIUD", line 6
ORA-04088: error during execution of trigger
'STUDENT.INSTRUCTOR_BIUD'
```

Notice that this trigger checks for a specific day of the week. However, it does not check the time of day. You can create a more sophisticated trigger that checks what day of the week it is and if the current time is between 9:00 A.M. and 5:00 P.M. If the day falls on the business week and the time of the day is not between 9:00 A.M. and 5:00 P.M., the error is generated.

INSTEAD OF TRIGGERS

So far you have seen triggers that are defined on the database tables. PL/SQL provides another kind of trigger that is defined on database views. A view is a custom representation of data and can be referred to as a "stored query." Consider the following example of the view created against the COURSE table.

■ FOR EXAMPLE

```
CREATE VIEW course_cost AS
    SELECT course_no, description, cost
      FROM course;
```

It is important to note that once a view is created, it does not contain or store any data. The data is derived from the SELECT statement associated with the view. Based on the preceding example, the COURSE_COST view contains three columns that are selected from the COURSE table.

Similar to tables, views can be manipulated via INSERT, UPDATE, or DELETE statements, with some restrictions. However, it is important to note that when any of these statements are issued against a view, the corresponding data are modified in the underlying tables. For example, consider an UPDATE statement against the COURSE_COST view.

■ FOR EXAMPLE

```
UPDATE course_cost
   SET cost = 2000
 WHERE course_no = 450;
```

Once the UPDATE statement is executed, both SELECT statements against the COURSE_COST view and the COURSE table return the same value of the cost for course number 450.

```
SELECT *
  FROM course_cost
 WHERE course_no = 450;
```

COURSE_NO	DESCRIPTION	COST
450	DB Programming in Java	2000

```
SELECT course_no, cost
  FROM course
 WHERE course_no = 450;
```

COURSE_NO	COST
450	2000

As mentioned earlier, there are restrictions placed on some views as to whether they can be modified by INSERT, UPDATE, or DELETE statements. Specifically, these restrictions apply to the underlying SELECT statement that is also referred to as a "view query." Thus, if a view query performs any of the operations or contains any of the following constructs, a view cannot be modified by an UPDATE, INSERT, or DELETE statement:

- Set operations such as UNION, UNION ALL, INTERSECT, MINUS
- Group functions such as AVG, COUNT, MAX, MIN, SUM
- GROUP BY or HAVING clauses
- CONNECT BY or START WITH clauses
- The DISTINCT operator
- ROWNUM pseudocolumn

■ FOR EXAMPLE

Consider the following view created on the INSTRUCTOR and SECTION tables:

```
CREATE VIEW instructor_summary AS
    SELECT i.instructor_id, COUNT(s.section_id) total_courses
      FROM instructor i
      LEFT OUTER JOIN section s
        ON (i.instructor_id = s.instructor_id)
    GROUP BY i.instructor_id;
```

Note that the SELECT statement is written in the ANSI 1999 SQL standard. It uses the outer join between the INSTRUCTOR and SECTION tables. The LEFT OUTER JOIN indicates that an instructor record in the INSTRUCTOR table that does not have a corresponding record in the SECTION table is included in the result set with TOTAL_COURSES equal to zero.

You will find detailed explanations and examples of the statements using the new ANSI 1999 SQL standard in Appendix E and in the Oracle help. Throughout this book we try to provide you with examples illustrating both standards; however, our main focus is on PL/SQL features rather than SQL.

In the previous versions of Oracle, this statement would look as follows:

```
SELECT i.instructor_id, COUNT(s.section_id) total_courses
  FROM instructor i, section s
 WHERE i.instructor_id = s.instructor_id (+)
GROUP BY i.instructor_id;
```

This view is not updatable because it contains the group function, COUNT(). As a result, the following DELETE statement

```
DELETE FROM instructor_summary
 WHERE instructor_id = 109;
```

causes the error shown:

```
DELETE FROM instructor_summary
           *
ERROR at line 1:
ORA-01732: data manipulation operation not legal on this view
```

You will recall that PL/SQL provides a special kind of trigger that can be defined on database views. This trigger is called an *INSTEAD OF trigger and is created as a row trigger.* An INSTEAD OF trigger fires instead of the triggering statement (INSERT, UPDATE, DELETE) that has been issued against a view and directly modifies the underlying tables.

Consider an INSTEAD OF trigger defined on the INSTRUCTOR_SUMMARY view created earlier. This trigger deletes a record from the INSTRUCTOR table for the corresponding value of the instructor's ID.

■ FOR EXAMPLE

```
CREATE OR REPLACE TRIGGER instructor_summary_del
INSTEAD OF DELETE ON instructor_summary
FOR EACH ROW
BEGIN
    DELETE FROM instructor
      WHERE instructor_id = :OLD.INSTRUCTOR_ID;
END;
```

Once the trigger is created, the DELETE statement against the INSTRUCTOR_ SUMMARY view does not generate any errors.

```
DELETE FROM instructor_summary
 WHERE instructor_id = 109;


1 row deleted.
```

When the DELETE statement is issued, the trigger deletes a record from the INSTRUCTOR table corresponding to the specified value of INSTRUCTOR_ID. Consider the same DELETE statement with a different instructor ID:

```
DELETE FROM instructor_summary
  WHERE instructor_id = 101;
```

When this DELETE statement is issued, it causes the error shown:

```
DELETE FROM instructor_summary
*
ERROR at line 1:
ORA-02292: integrity constraint (STUDENT.SECT_INST_FK)
violated - child record found
ORA-06512: at "STUDENT.INSTRUCTOR_SUMMARY_DEL", line 2
```

```
ORA-04088: error during execution of trigger
'STUDENT.INSTRUCTOR_SUMMARY_DEL'
```

The INSTRUCTOR_SUMMARY view joins the INSTRUCTOR and SECTION tables based on the INSTRUCTOR_ID column that is present in both tables. The INSTRUCTOR_ID column in the INSTRUCTOR table has is a primary key constraint defined on it. The INSTRUCTOR_ID column in the SECTION table has a foreign key constraint that references the INSTRUCTOR_ID column of the INSTRUCTOR table. Thus, the SECTION table is considered a child table of the INSTRUCTOR table.

The original DELETE statement does not cause any errors because there is no record in the SECTION table corresponding to the instructor ID of 109. In other words, the instructor with the ID of 109 does not teach any courses.

The second DELETE statement causes an error because the INSTEAD OF trigger tries to delete a record from the INSTRUCTOR table, the parent table. However, there is a corresponding record in the SECTION table, the child table, with the instructor ID of 101. This causes an integrity constraint violation error. It may seem that one more DELETE statement should be added to the INSTEAD OF trigger, as shown below.

```
CREATE OR REPLACE TRIGGER instructor_summary_del
INSTEAD OF DELETE ON instructor_summary
FOR EACH ROW
BEGIN
   DELETE FROM section
    WHERE instructor_id = :OLD.INSTRUCTOR_ID;
   DELETE FROM instructor
    WHERE instructor_id = :OLD.INSTRUCTOR_ID;
END;
```

Notice that the new DELETE statement removes records from the SECTION table before the INSTRUCTOR table because the SECTION table contains child records of the INSTRUCTOR table. However, the DELETE statement against the INSTRUCTOR_SUMMARY view causes another error:

```
DELETE FROM instructor_summary
 WHERE instructor_id = 101;

DELETE FROM instructor_summary
            *
ERROR at line 1:
ORA-02292: integrity constraint (STUDENT.GRTW_SECT_FK)
violated - child record found
ORA-06512: at "STUDENT.INSTRUCTOR_SUMMARY_DEL", line 2
ORA-04088: error during execution of trigger
'STUDENT.INSTRUCTOR_SUMMARY_DEL'
```

This time, the error refers to a different foreign key constraint that specifies the relationship between the SECTION and the GRADE_TYPE_WEIGHT tables. In this case, the child records are found in the GRADE_TYPE_WEIGHT table. This means that before deleting records from the SECTION table, the trigger must delete all corresponding records from the GRADE_TYPE_WEIGHT table. However, the GRADE_TYPE_WEIGHT table has child records in the GRADE table, so the trigger must delete records from the GRADE table first.

This example illustrates the complexity of designing an INSTEAD OF trigger. To design such a trigger, you must be aware of two important factors: the relationship among tables in the database, and the ripple effect that a particular design may introduce. This example suggests deleting records from four underlying tables. However, it is important to realize that those tables contain information that relates not only to the instructors and the sections they teach, but also to the students and the sections they are enrolled in.

LAB
17.2

LAB 17.2 EXERCISES

17.2.1 USE ROW AND STATEMENT TRIGGERS

In this exercise, you create a trigger that fires before an INSERT statement is issued against the COURSE table.

Create the following trigger:

```
-- ch17_2a.sql, version 1.0
CREATE OR REPLACE TRIGGER course_bi
BEFORE INSERT ON COURSE
FOR EACH ROW
DECLARE
   v_course_no COURSE.COURSE_NO%TYPE;
BEGIN
   SELECT COURSE_NO_SEQ.NEXTVAL
     INTO v_course_no
     FROM DUAL;
   :NEW.COURSE_NO := v_course_no;
   :NEW.CREATED_BY := USER;
   :NEW.CREATED_DATE := SYSDATE;
   :NEW.MODIFIED_BY := USER;
   :NEW.MODIFIED_DATE := SYSDATE;
END;
```

Answer the following questions:

a) What type of trigger is created on the COURSE table (row or statement)? Explain your answer.

b) Based on the answer you provided for question (a), explain why this particular type is chosen for the trigger.

c) When an INSERT statement is issued against the COURSE table, which actions are performed by the trigger?

d) Modify this trigger so that if there is a prerequisite course supplied at the time of the insert, its value is checked against the existing courses in the COURSE table.

17.2.2 USE INSTEAD OF TRIGGERS

In this exercise, you create a view STUDENT_ADDRESS and an INSTEAD OF trigger that fires instead of an INSERT statement issued against the view.

Create the following view:

```
CREATE VIEW student_address AS
    SELECT s.student_id, s.first_name, s.last_name,
           s.street_address, z.city, z.state, z.zip
      FROM student s
      JOIN zipcode z
        ON (s.zip = z.zip);
```

Note that the SELECT statement is written in the ANSI 1999 SQL standard.

 You will find detailed explanations and examples of the statements using new ANSI 1999 SQL standard in Appendix E and in the Oracle help. Throughout this book we try to provide you with examples illustrating both standards; however, our main focus is on PL/SQL features rather than SQL.

Create the following INSTEAD OF trigger:

```
-- ch17_3a.sql, version 1.0
CREATE OR REPLACE TRIGGER student_address_ins
INSTEAD OF INSERT ON student_address
FOR EACH ROW
```

```
BEGIN
    INSERT INTO STUDENT
        (student_id, first_name, last_name, street_address,
        zip, registration_date, created_by, created_date,
        modified_by, modified_date)
    VALUES
        (:NEW.STUDENT_ID, :NEW.FIRST_NAME, :NEW.LAST_NAME,
        :NEW.STREET_ADDRESS, :NEW.ZIP, SYSDATE, USER,
        SYSDATE, USER, SYSDATE);
END;
```

Issue the following INSERT statements:

```
INSERT INTO student_address
VALUES (STUDENT_ID_SEQ.NEXTVAL, 'John', 'Smith',
        '123 Main Street', 'New York', 'NY', '10019');

INSERT INTO student_address
VALUES (STUDENT_ID_SEQ.NEXTVAL, 'John', 'Smith',
        '123 Main Street', 'New York', 'NY', '12345');
```

Answer the following questions:

a) What output is produced after each INSERT statement is issued?

b) Explain why the second INSERT statement causes an error.

c) Modify the trigger so that it checks the value of the zipcode provided by the INSERT statement against the ZIPCODE table and raises an error if there is no such value.

d) Modify the trigger so that it checks the value of the zipcode provided by the INSERT statement against the ZIPCODE table. If there is no corresponding record in the ZIPCODE table, the trigger should create a new record for the given value of zip before adding a new record to the STUDENT table.

LAB 17.2

LAB 17.2 EXERCISE ANSWERS

This section gives you some suggested answers to the questions in Lab 17.2, with discussion related to how those answers resulted. The most important thing to realize is whether your answer works. You should figure out the implications of the answers here and what the effects are from any different answers you may come up with.

17.2.1 ANSWERS

a) What type of trigger is created on the COURSE table (row or statement)? Explain your answer.

Answer: The trigger created on the COURSE table is a row trigger because the CREATE TRIGGER clause contains the statement FOR EACH ROW. It means this trigger fires every time a record is added to the COURSE table.

b) Based on the answer you provided for question (a), explain why this particular type is chosen for the trigger.

Answer: This trigger is a row trigger because its operations depend on the data in the individual records. For example, for every record inserted into the COURSE table, the trigger calculates the value for the column COURSE_NO. All values in this column must be unique, because it is defined as a primary key. A row trigger guarantees every record added to the COURSE table has a unique number assigned to the COURSE_NO column.

c) When an INSERT statement is issued against the COURSE table, which actions are performed by the trigger?

Answer: First, the trigger assigns a number derived from the sequence COURSE_NO_SEQ to the variable v_course_no *via the SELECT INTO statement. Second, the variable* v_course_no *is assigned to the field COURSE_NO of the :NEW pseudorecord. Finally, the values containing the current user's name and date are assigned to the fields CREATED_BY, MODIFIED_BY, CREATED_DATE, and MODIFIED_DATE of the :NEW pseudorecord.*

d) Modify this trigger so that if there is a prerequisite course supplied at the time of the insert, its value is checked against the existing courses in the COURSE table.

Answer: The trigger you created should look similar to the following trigger. All changes are shown in bold letters.

```
-- ch17_2b.sql, version 2.0
CREATE OR REPLACE TRIGGER course_bi
BEFORE INSERT ON COURSE
FOR EACH ROW
```

```
DECLARE
    v_course_no COURSE.COURSE_NO%TYPE;
    v_prerequisite COURSE.COURSE_NO%TYPE;
BEGIN
    IF :NEW.PREREQUISITE IS NOT NULL THEN
        SELECT course_no
          INTO v_prerequisite
          FROM course
         WHERE course_no = :NEW.PREREQUISITE;
    END IF;
    SELECT COURSE_NO_SEQ.NEXTVAL
      INTO v_course_no
      FROM DUAL;
    :NEW.COURSE_NO := v_course_no;
    :NEW.CREATED_BY := USER;
    :NEW.CREATED_DATE := SYSDATE;
    :NEW.MODIFIED_BY := USER;
    :NEW.MODIFIED_DATE := SYSDATE;
EXCEPTION
    WHEN NO_DATA_FOUND THEN
        RAISE_APPLICATION_ERROR
            (-20002, 'Prerequisite is not valid!');
END;
```

Notice that because the PREREQUISITE is not a required column, or, in other words, there is no NOT NULL constraint defined against it, the IF statement validates the existence of the incoming value. Next, the SELECT INTO statement validates that the prerequisite already exists in the COURSE table. If there is no record corresponding to the prerequisite course, the NO_DATA_FOUND exception is raised and the error message "Prerequisite is not valid!" is displayed on the screen.

Once this version of the trigger is created, the INSERT statement

```
INSERT INTO COURSE (description, cost, prerequisite)
VALUES ('Test Course', 0, 999);
```

causes the following error:

```
INSERT INTO COURSE (description, cost, prerequisite)
*
ERROR at line 1:
ORA-20002: Prerequisite is not valid!
ORA-06512: at "STUDENT.COURSE_BI", line 21
ORA-04088: error during execution of trigger
'STUDENT.COURSE_BI'
```

17.2.2 ANSWERS

a) What output is produced after each INSERT statement is issued?

Answer: Your output should look similar to the following:

```
INSERT INTO student_address
VALUES (STUDENT_ID_SEQ.NEXTVAL, 'John', 'Smith',
       '123 Main Street', 'New York', 'NY', '10019');

1 row created.

INSERT INTO student_address
VALUES (STUDENT_ID_SEQ.NEXTVAL, 'John', 'Smith',
       '123 Main Street', 'New York', 'NY', '12345');
VALUES (STUDENT_ID_SEQ.NEXTVAL, 'John', 'Smith',
       '123 Main Street', 'New York',
       *
ERROR at line 2:
ORA-02291: integrity constraint (STUDENT.STU_ZIP_FK)
violated - parent key not found
ORA-06512: at "STUDENT.STUDENT_ADDRESS_INS", line 2
ORA-04088: error during execution of trigger 'STUDENT.
STUDENT_ADDRESS_INS'
```

b) Explain why the second INSERT statement causes an error.

Answer: The second INSERT statement causes an error because it violates the foreign key constraint on the STUDENT table. The value of the zipcode provided at the time of an insert does not have a corresponding record in the ZIPCODE table.

The ZIP column of the STUDENT table has a foreign key constraint STU_ZIP_FK defined on it. It means that each time a record is inserted into the STUDENT table, the incoming value of zipcode is checked by the system in the ZIPCODE table. If there is a corresponding record, the INSERT statement against the STUDENT table does not cause errors. For example, the first INSERT statement is successful because the ZIPCODE table contains a record corresponding to the value of zip '10019'. The second insert statement causes an error because there is no record in the ZIPCODE table corresponding to the value of zip '12345'.

c) Modify the trigger so that it checks the value of the zipcode provided by the INSERT statement against the ZIPCODE table and raises an error if there is no such value.

Answer: Your trigger should look similar to the following trigger. All changes are shown in bold letters.

```
-- ch17_3b.sql, version 2.0
CREATE OR REPLACE TRIGGER student_address_ins
INSTEAD OF INSERT ON student_address
```

```
FOR EACH ROW
DECLARE
    v_zip VARCHAR2(5);
BEGIN
    SELECT zip
      INTO v_zip
      FROM zipcode
     WHERE zip = :NEW.ZIP;

    INSERT INTO STUDENT
        (student_id, first_name, last_name, street_address,
         zip, registration_date, created_by, created_date,
         modified_by, modified_date)
    VALUES
        (:NEW.STUDENT_ID, :NEW.FIRST_NAME, :NEW.LAST_NAME,
         :NEW.STREET_ADDRESS, :NEW.ZIP, SYSDATE, USER,
         SYSDATE, USER, SYSDATE);

EXCEPTION
    WHEN NO_DATA_FOUND THEN
        RAISE_APPLICATION_ERROR
            (-20002, 'Zip code is not valid!');
END;
```

In this version of the trigger, the incoming value of zipcode is checked against the ZIPCODE table via the SELECT INTO statement. If the SELECT INTO statement does not return any rows, the NO_DATA_FOUND exception is raised and the error message stating 'Zip code is not valid!' is displayed on the screen.

Once this trigger is created, the second INSERT statement produces the following output:

```
INSERT INTO student_address
VALUES (STUDENT_ID_SEQ.NEXTVAL, 'John', 'Smith',
        '123 Main Street', 'New York', 'NY', '12345');
VALUES (STUDENT_ID_SEQ.NEXTVAL, 'John', 'Smith',
        '123 Main Street', 'New York',
        *
ERROR at line 2:
ORA-20002: Zip code is not valid!
ORA-06512: at "STUDENT.STUDENT_ADDRESS_INS", line 18
ORA-04088: error during execution of trigger
'STUDENT.STUDENT_ADDRESS_INS'
```

d) Modify the trigger so that it checks the value of the zipcode provided by the INSERT statement against the ZIPCODE table. If there is no corresponding record in the ZIPCODE table, the trigger should create a new record for the given value of zip before adding a new record to the STUDENT table.

Answer: Your trigger should look similar to the following trigger. All changes are shown in bold letters.

```
-- ch17_3c.sql, version 3.0
CREATE OR REPLACE TRIGGER student_address_ins
INSTEAD OF INSERT ON student_address
FOR EACH ROW
DECLARE
   v_zip VARCHAR2(5);
BEGIN
   BEGIN
      SELECT zip
        INTO v_zip
        FROM zipcode
       WHERE zip = :NEW.ZIP;
   EXCEPTION
      WHEN NO_DATA_FOUND THEN
         INSERT INTO ZIPCODE
            (zip, city, state, created_by, created_date,
             modified_by, modified_date)
         VALUES
            (:NEW.ZIP, :NEW.CITY, :NEW.STATE, USER,
             SYSDATE, USER, SYSDATE);
   END;
   INSERT INTO STUDENT
      (student_id, first_name, last_name, street_address,
       zip, registration_date, created_by, created_date,
       modified_by, modified_date)
   VALUES
      (:NEW.STUDENT_ID, :NEW.FIRST_NAME, :NEW.LAST_NAME,
       :NEW.STREET_ADDRESS, :NEW.ZIP, SYSDATE, USER,
       SYSDATE, USER, SYSDATE);
END;
```

Just like in the previous version, the existence of the incoming value of zipcode is checked against the ZIPCODE table via the SELECT INTO statement. When a new value of zipcode is provided by the INSERT statement, the SELECT INTO statement does not return any rows. As a result, the NO_DATA_FOUND exception is raised and the INSERT statement against the ZIPCODE table is executed. Next, control is passed to the INSERT statement against the STUDENT table.

It is important to realize that the SELECT INTO statement and the exception-handling section have been placed in the inner block. This placement ensures that once the exception NO_DATA_FOUND is raised the trigger does not terminate but proceeds with its normal execution.

Once this trigger is created, the second INSERT statement completes successfully:

```
INSERT INTO student_address
VALUES (STUDENT_ID_SEQ.NEXTVAL, 'John', 'Smith',
        '123 Main Street', 'New York', 'NY', '12345');
```

```
1 row created.
```

LAB 17.2 SELF-REVIEW QUESTIONS

In order to test your progress, you should be able to answer the following questions.

1) How many times does a row trigger fire if a DML (INSERT, UPDATE, or DELETE) operation is issued against a table?

a) _____ As many times as there are rows affected by the DML operation
b) _____ Once per DML operation

2) How many times does a statement trigger fire if a DML (INSERT, UPDATE, or DELETE) operation is issued against a table?

a) _____ As many times as there are rows affected by the DML operation
b) _____ Once per DML operation

3) What does the statement FOR EACH ROW mean?

a) _____ A trigger is a statement trigger.
b) _____ A trigger is a row trigger.

4) INSTEAD OF triggers are defined on which of the following?

a) _____ Table
b) _____ View
c) _____ None of the above

5) INSTEAD OF triggers must always be which of the following?

a) _____ Statement trigger
b) _____ Row trigger

Answers appear in Appendix A, Section 17.2.

LAB 17.3

MUTATING TABLE ISSUES

LAB OBJECTIVE

After this Lab, you will be able to:

✔ Understand Mutating Tables

A table having a DML statement issued against it is called *mutating table*. For a trigger, it is the table on which this trigger is defined. If a trigger tries to read or modify such a table, it causes a mutating table error. As a result, a SQL statement issued in the body of the trigger may not read or modify a mutating table.

Note that prior to Oracle 8i, there was another restriction on the SQL statement issued in the body of a trigger that caused a different type of error called a constraining table error. A table read from for a referential integrity constraint is called a *constraining table*. So an SQL statement issued in the body of a trigger could not modify the columns of a constraining table having primary, foreign, or unique constraints defined of them. However, staring with Oracle 8i, there is no such restriction.

Consider the following example of a trigger causing a mutating table error. It is important for you to note that a mutating table error is a runtime error.

■ *FOR EXAMPLE*

```
CREATE OR REPLACE TRIGGER section_biu
BEFORE INSERT OR UPDATE ON section
FOR EACH ROW
DECLARE
   v_total NUMBER;
   v_name VARCHAR2(30);
BEGIN
   SELECT COUNT(*)
     INTO v_total
     FROM section   -- SECTION is MUTATING
    WHERE instructor_id = :NEW.INSTRUCTOR_ID;
```

```
   -- check if the current instructor is overbooked
   IF v_total >= 10 THEN
      SELECT first_name||' '||last_name
        INTO v_name
        FROM instructor
       WHERE instructor_id = :NEW.instructor_id;

         RAISE_APPLICATION_ERROR (-20000, 'Instructor, '||
            v_name||', is overbooked');
      END IF;
   EXCEPTION
      WHEN NO_DATA_FOUND THEN
         RAISE_APPLICATION_ERROR (-20001,
            'This is not a valid instructor');
   END;
```

This trigger fires before an INSERT or UPDATE statement is issued on the SECTION table. The trigger checks whether the specified instructor is teaching too many sections. If the number of sections taught by an instructor is equal to or greater than 10, the trigger issues an error message stating that this instructor teaches too much.

Now, consider the following UPDATE statement issued against the SECTION table:

```
UPDATE section
   SET instructor_id = 101
 WHERE section_id = 80;
```

When this UPDATE statement is issued against the SECTION table, the following error message is displayed:

```
UPDATE section
*
ERROR at line 1:
ORA-04091: table STUDENT.SECTION is mutating,
trigger/function may not see it
ORA-06512: at "STUDENT.SECTION_BIU", line 5
ORA-04088: error during execution of trigger
'STUDENT.SECTION_BIU'
```

Notice that the error message is stating that the SECTION table is mutating and the trigger may not see it. This error message is generated because there is a SELECT INTO statement,

```
SELECT COUNT(*)
  INTO v_total
  FROM section
 WHERE instructor_id = :NEW.INSTRUCTOR_ID;
```

issued against the SECTION table that is being modified and is therefore mutating.

In order to correct this problem, the following steps must be accomplished:

1. An existing trigger must be modified so that it records the instructor's ID, queries the INSTRUCTOR table, and records the instructor's name.
2. In order to record the instructor's ID and name as described in the preceding step, two global variables must be declared with the help of a package.
3. A new trigger must be created on the SECTION table. This trigger should be a statement-level trigger that fires after the INSERT or UPDATE statement has been issued. It will check the number of courses that are taught by a particular instructor and will raise an error if the number is equal to or greater than 10.

Consider the following package:

```
CREATE OR REPLACE PACKAGE instructor_adm AS
    v_instructor_id   instructor.instructor_id%TYPE;
    v_instructor_name varchar2(50);
END;
```

Notice that this package does not have a package body and is used to declare two global variables only, v_instructor_id and v_instructor_name.

Next, the existing trigger SECTION_BIU is modified as follows:

```
CREATE OR REPLACE TRIGGER section_biu
BEFORE INSERT OR UPDATE ON section
FOR EACH ROW
BEGIN
   IF :NEW.INSTRUCTOR_ID IS NOT NULL THEN
      BEGIN
         instructor_adm.v_instructor_id :=
            :NEW.INSTRUCTOR_ID;
         SELECT first_name||' '||last_name
           INTO instructor_adm.v_instructor_name
           FROM instructor
          WHERE instructor_id =
                instructor_adm.v_instructor_id;
      EXCEPTION
         WHEN NO_DATA_FOUND THEN
            RAISE_APPLICATION_ERROR
               (-20001, 'This is not a valid instructor');
      END;
   END IF;
END;
```

In this version of the trigger, the global variables `v_instructor_id` and `v_instructor_name` are initialized if the incoming value of the instructor's ID is not null. Notice that the variable names are prefixed by the package name. This type of notation is called *dot notation*.

Finally, a new trigger is created on the SECTION table as follows:

```
CREATE OR REPLACE TRIGGER section_aiu
AFTER INSERT OR UPDATE ON section
DECLARE
   v_total INTEGER;
BEGIN
   SELECT COUNT(*)
     INTO v_total
     FROM section
    WHERE instructor_id = instructor_adm.v_instructor_id;

   -- check if the current instructor is overbooked
   IF v_total >= 10 THEN
      RAISE_APPLICATION_ERROR (-20000, 'Instructor, '||
         instructor_adm.v_instructor_name||
         ', is overbooked');
   END IF;
END;
```

This trigger checks the number of courses that are taught by a particular instructor and raises an error if the number is equal to or greater than 10. This is accomplished with the help of two global variables, `v_instructor_id` and `v_instructor_name`. As mentioned earlier, these variables are populated by the SECTION_BIU trigger that fires before the UPDATE statement is issued against the SECTION table.

As a result, the UPDATE statement used earlier

```
UPDATE section
   SET instructor_id = 101
 WHERE section_id = 80;
```

causes a different error

```
UPDATE section
      *
ERROR at line 1:
ORA-20000: Instructor, Fernand Hanks, is overbooked
ORA-06512: at "STUDENT.SECTION_AIU", line 11
ORA-04088: error during execution of trigger
'STUDENT.SECTION_AIU'
```

Notice that this error has been generated by the trigger SECTION_AIU and does not contain any message about a mutating table. Next, consider a similar UPDATE statement for a different instructor ID that does not cause any errors:

```
UPDATE section
   SET instructor_id = 109
 WHERE section_id = 80;
```

1 row updated.

LAB 17.3 EXERCISES

17.3.1 UNDERSTAND MUTATING TABLES

In this exercise, you modify a trigger that causes a mutating table error when an INSERT statement is issued against the ENROLLMENT table.

Create the following trigger:

```
-- ch17_4a.sql, version 1.0
CREATE OR REPLACE TRIGGER enrollment_biu
BEFORE INSERT OR UPDATE ON enrollment
FOR EACH ROW
DECLARE
   v_total NUMBER;
   v_name VARCHAR2(30);
BEGIN
   SELECT COUNT(*)
     INTO v_total
     FROM enrollment
    WHERE student_id = :NEW.STUDENT_ID;

   -- check if the current student is enrolled into too
   -- many courses
   IF v_total >= 3 THEN
      SELECT first_name||' '||last_name
        INTO v_name
        FROM student
       WHERE student_id = :NEW.STUDENT_ID;

      RAISE_APPLICATION_ERROR (-20000, 'Student, '||v_name||
         ', is registered for 3 courses already');
   END IF;
EXCEPTION
   WHEN NO_DATA_FOUND THEN
      RAISE_APPLICATION_ERROR
         (-20001, 'This is not a valid student');
END;
```

Issue the following INSERT and UPDATE statements:

```
INSERT INTO ENROLLMENT
    (student_id, section_id, enroll_date, created_by,
    created_date, modified_by, modified_date)
VALUES
    (184, 98, SYSDATE, USER, SYSDATE, USER, SYSDATE);

INSERT INTO ENROLLMENT
    (student_id, section_id, enroll_date, created_by,
    created_date, modified_by, modified_date)
VALUES
    (407, 98, SYSDATE, USER, SYSDATE, USER, SYSDATE);

UPDATE ENROLLMENT
    SET student_id = 404
 WHERE student_id = 407;
```

**LAB
17.3**

Answer the following questions:

a) What output is produced after the INSERT and UPDATE statements are issued?

b) Explain why two of the statements did not succeed.

c) Modify the trigger so that it does not cause a mutating table error when an UPDATE statement is issued against the ENROLLMENT table.

LAB 17.3 EXERCISE ANSWERS

This section gives you some suggested answers to the questions in Lab 17.3, with discussion related to how those answers resulted. The most important thing to realize is whether your answer works. You should figure out the implications of the answers here and what the effects are from any different answers you may come up with.

a) What output is produced after the INSERT and UPDATE statements are issued?

Answer: Your output should look as follows:

```
INSERT INTO ENROLLMENT
    (student_id, section_id, enroll_date, created_by,
    created_date, modified_by, modified_date)
VALUES
    (184, 98, SYSDATE, USER, SYSDATE, USER, SYSDATE);
INSERT INTO ENROLLMENT
              *
ERROR at line 1:
ORA-20000: Student, Salewa Zuckerberg, is registered for 3
courses already
ORA-06512: at "STUDENT.ENROLLMENT_BIU", line 17
ORA-04088: error during execution of trigger
'STUDENT.ENROLLMENT_BIU'
INSERT INTO ENROLLMENT
    (student_id, section_id, enroll_date, created_by,
    created_date, modified_by, modified_date)
VALUES
    (407, 98, SYSDATE, USER, SYSDATE, USER, SYSDATE);

1 row created.

UPDATE enrollment
SET student_id = 404
WHERE student_id = 407;

UPDATE enrollment
*
ERROR at line 1:
ORA-04091: table STUDENT.ENROLLMENT is mutating,
trigger/function may not see it
ORA-06512: at "STUDENT.ENROLLMENT_BIU", line 5
ORA-04088: error during execution of trigger 'STUDENT.
ENROLLMENT_BIU'
```

b) Explain why neither of the statements succeed.

Answer: The INSERT statement does not succeed because it tries to create a record in the ENROLLMENT table for a student that is already registered for three courses.

The IF statement

```
-- check if the current student is enrolled into too many
-- courses
```

```
    IF v_total >= 3 THEN
       SELECT first_name||' '||last_name
         INTO v_name
         FROM student
        WHERE student_id = :NEW.STUDENT_ID;

       RAISE_APPLICATION_ERROR (-20000, 'Student, '||v_name||
            ', is registered for 3 courses already');
    END IF;
```

in the body of the trigger evaluates to TRUE, and as a result the RAISE_
APPLICATION_ERROR statement raises a user-defined exception.

*The UPDATE statement does not succeed, because a trigger tries to read data from the
mutating table.*

The SELECT INTO

```
    SELECT COUNT(*)
      INTO v_total
      FROM enrollment
     WHERE student_id = :NEW.STUDENT_ID;
```

statement is issued against the ENROLLMENT table that is being modified and
therefore is mutating.

c) Modify the trigger so that it does not cause a mutating table error when an UP-
DATE statement is issued against the ENROLLMENT table.

Answer: First, create a package to hold the student's ID and name as follows:

```
    CREATE OR REPLACE PACKAGE student_adm AS
       v_student_id   student.student_id%TYPE;
       v_student_name varchar2(50);
    END;
```

Next, the existing trigger, SECTION_BIU, is modified as follows:

```
    CREATE OR REPLACE TRIGGER enrollment_biu
    BEFORE INSERT OR UPDATE ON enrollment
    FOR EACH ROW
    BEGIN
       IF :NEW.STUDENT_ID IS NOT NULL THEN
          BEGIN
             student_adm.v_student_id := :NEW.STUDENT_ID;

             SELECT first_name||' '||last_name
               INTO student_adm.v_student_name
               FROM student
              WHERE student_id = student_adm.v_student_id;
```

```
        EXCEPTION
            WHEN NO_DATA_FOUND THEN
                RAISE_APPLICATION_ERROR
                    (-20001, 'This is not a valid student');
        END;
    END IF;
END;
```

Finally, create a new statement-level trigger on the ENROLLMENT table as follows:

```
CREATE OR REPLACE TRIGGER enrollment_aiu
AFTER INSERT OR UPDATE ON enrollment
DECLARE
    v_total INTEGER;
BEGIN
    SELECT COUNT(*)
      INTO v_total
      FROM enrollment
     WHERE student_id = student_adm.v_student_id;
    -- check if the current student is enrolled into too
    -- many courses
    IF v_total >= 3 THEN
        RAISE_APPLICATION_ERROR (-20000, 'Student, '||
            student_adm.v_student_name||
            ', is registered for 3 courses already ');
    END IF;
END;
```

Once the package and two triggers are created, the UPDATE statement does not cause a mutating table error.

LAB 17.3 SELF-REVIEW QUESTIONS

In order to test your progress, you should be able to answer the following questions.

1) You are allowed to issue any SQL statement in the body of a trigger.

   a) _____ True
   b) _____ False

2) It is always permissible to issue a SELECT statement in the body of a trigger. However, it is not always permissible to issue an INSERT, UPDATE, or DELETE statement.

   a) _____ True
   b) _____ False

3) Which of the following is an SQL statement restriction?

a) _____ No SQL statement may be issued against any table in the body of a trigger.

b) _____ No SQL statement may be issued against the mutating table in the body of a trigger.

c) _____ A SQL statement can be issued only against the mutating table in the body of a trigger.

4) Which of the following is a mutating table?

a) _____ A table having a SELECT statement issued against it
b) _____ A table having a trigger defined on it
c) _____ A table being modified by a DML statement

5) Which of the following is a constraining table?

a) _____ A table having a SELECT statement issued against it
b) _____ A table having a trigger defined on it
c) _____ A table needing to be read from for a referential integrity constraint

Answers appear in Appendix A, Section 17.3.

LAB
17.3

C H A P T E R   1 7

TEST YOUR THINKING

In this chapter you learned about triggers. Here are some projects that will help you test the depth of your understanding:

1) Create the following trigger: Create or modify a trigger on the ENROLLMENT table that fires before an INSERT statement. Make sure all columns that have NOT NULL and foreign key constraints defined on them are populated with their proper values.

2) Create the following trigger: Create or modify a trigger on the SECTION table that fires before an UPDATE statement. Make sure that the trigger validates incoming values so that there are no constraint violation errors.

The projects in this section are meant to have you utilize all of the skills that you have acquired throughout this chapter. The answers to these projects can be found in Appendix D and at the companion Web site to this book, located at http://www.phptr .com/rosenzweig2e. Visit the Web site periodically to share and discuss your answers.

C H A P T E R 1 8

COLLECTIONS

Throughout this book you have explored different types of PL/SQL identifiers or variables that represent individual elements (for example, a variable that represents a grade of a particular student). However, often in your programs you want to have the ability to represent a group of elements (for example, the grades for a class of students). In order to support this technique, PL/SQL provides collection datatypes that work just like arrays available in other third-generation programming languages.

A *collection* is a group of elements of the same datatype. Each element is identified by a unique subscript that represents its position in the collection. In this chapter you will learn about two collection datatypes: *table* and *varray*. In addition, you will learn about multilevel collections that have been introduced in Oracle 9i and are not supported by the previous releases.

L A B   1 8 . 1

PL/SQL TABLES

LAB OBJECTIVES

After this Lab, you will be able to:

✔ Use Index-By Tables
✔ Use Nested Tables

A PL/SQL table is similar to one-column database table. The rows of a PL/SQL table are not stored in any predefined order, yet when they are retrieved in a variable each row is assigned a consecutive subscript starting at 1, as shown in the in Figure 18.1.

10	number (1)
1	number (2)
39	number (3)
57	number (4)
3	number (5)

Figure 18.1 ■ PL/SQL Table

Figure 18.1 shows a PL/SQL table consisting of integer numbers. Each number is assigned a unique subscript that corresponds to its position in the table. For example, number 3 has subscript 5 assigned to it because it is stored in the fifth row of the PL/SQL table.

There are two types of PL/SQL tables: *index-by tables* and *nested tables*. They have the same structure, and their rows are accessed in the same way via subscript notation as shown in Figure 18.1. The main difference between these two types is that nested tables can be stored in a database column, and the index-by tables cannot.

INDEX-BY TABLES

The general syntax for creating an index-by table is as follows (the reserved words and phrases surrounded by brackets are optional):

```
TYPE type_name IS TABLE OF element_type [NOT NULL]
    INDEX BY BINARY_INTEGER;
table_name TYPE_NAME;
```

Notice that there are two steps in the declaration of an index-by table. First, a table structure is defined using the TYPE statement, where TYPE_NAME is the name of the type that is used in the second step to declare an actual table. An ELEMENT_TYPE is any PL/SQL datatype, such as NUMBER, VARCHAR2, or DATE, with some restrictions. The majority of restricted datatypes are beyond the scope of this book and are not mentioned in this chapter. However, you can find the complete list in Oracle help available online. Second, the actual table is declared based on the type specified in the previous step. Consider the following code fragment.

■ FOR EXAMPLE

```
DECLARE
    TYPE last_name_type IS TABLE OF student.last_name%TYPE
        INDEX BY BINARY_INTEGER;
    last_name_tab last_name_type;
```

In this example, type `last_name_type` is declared based on the column LAST_NAME of the STUDENT table. Next, the actual index-by table `last_name_tab` is declared as LAST_NAME_TYPE.

As mentioned earlier, the individual elements of a PL/SQL table are referenced via subscript notation as follows:

```
table_name(subscript)
```

This technique is demonstrated in the following example.

**LAB
18.1**

■ FOR EXAMPLE

```
DECLARE
    CURSOR name_cur IS
        SELECT last_name
          FROM student
         WHERE rownum <= 10;

    TYPE last_name_type IS TABLE OF student.last_name%TYPE
        INDEX BY BINARY_INTEGER;
    last_name_tab last_name_type;

    v_counter INTEGER := 0;
BEGIN
    FOR name_rec IN name_cur LOOP
        v_counter := v_counter + 1;
        last_name_tab(v_counter) := name_rec.last_name;
        DBMS_OUTPUT.PUT_LINE ('last_name('||v_counter||'): '||
            last_name_tab(v_counter));
    END LOOP;
END;
```

In this example, the index-by table `last_name_tab` is populated with last names from the STUDENT table. Notice that the variable `v_counter` is used as a subscript to reference individual table elements. This example produces the following output:

```
last_name(1): Crocitto
last_name(2): Landry
last_name(3): Enison
last_name(4): Moskowitz
last_name(5): Olvsade
last_name(6): Mierzwa
last_name(7): Sethi
last_name(8): Walter
last_name(9): Martin
last_name(10): Noviello
```

PL/SQL procedure successfully completed.

It is important to note that referencing a nonexistent row raises the NO_DATA_FOUND exception as follows:

```
DECLARE
    CURSOR name_cur IS
        SELECT last_name
          FROM student
         WHERE rownum <= 10;
```

```
    TYPE last_name_type IS TABLE OF student.last_name%TYPE
        INDEX BY BINARY_INTEGER;
    last_name_tab last_name_type;

    v_counter INTEGER := 0;
BEGIN
    FOR name_rec IN name_cur LOOP
        v_counter := v_counter + 1;
        last_name_tab(v_counter) := name_rec.last_name;
        DBMS_OUTPUT.PUT_LINE ('last_name('||v_counter||
            '): '||last_name_tab(v_counter));
    END LOOP;
    DBMS_OUTPUT.PUT_LINE ('last_name(11): '||
        last_name_tab(11));
END;
```

This example produces the output shown below:

```
last_name(1): Crocitto
last_name(2): Landry
last_name(3): Enison
last_name(4): Moskowitz
last_name(5): Olvsade
last_name(6): Mierzwa
last_name(7): Sethi
last_name(8): Walter
last_name(9): Martin
last_name(10): Noviello
DECLARE
*
ERROR at line 1:
ORA-01403: no data found
ORA-06512: at line 19
```

Notice that the DBMS_OUTPUT.PUT_LINE statement shown in bold letters raises the NO_DATA_FOUND exception because it references the eleventh row of the table, even though the table contains only ten rows.

NESTED TABLES

The general syntax for creating a nested table is as follows (the reserved words and phrases surrounded by brackets are optional):

```
TYPE type_name IS TABLE OF element_type [NOT NULL];
table_name TYPE_NAME;
```

Notice that this declaration is very similar to the declaration of an index-by table except that there is no

```
INDEX BY BINARY_INTEGER
```

clause. Just like in the case of an index-by table, there are restrictions that apply to an ELEMENT_TYPE of a nested table. These restrictions are listed in Oracle help available online.

It is important to note that a nested table must be initialized before its individual elements can be referenced. Consider the modified version of the example used earlier in this lab. Notice that the last_name_type is defined as a nested table (there is no INDEX BY clause).

■ FOR EXAMPLE

```
DECLARE
   CURSOR name_cur IS
      SELECT last_name
        FROM student
       WHERE rownum <= 10;

   TYPE last_name_type IS TABLE OF student.last_name%TYPE;
   last_name_tab last_name_type;

   v_counter INTEGER := 0;
BEGIN
   FOR name_rec IN name_cur LOOP
      v_counter := v_counter + 1;
      last_name_tab(v_counter) := name_rec.last_name;
      DBMS_OUTPUT.PUT_LINE ('last_name('||v_counter||'): '||
         last_name_tab(v_counter));
   END LOOP;
END;
```

This example causes the following error:

```
DECLARE
*
ERROR at line 1:
ORA-06531: Reference to uninitialized collection
ORA-06512: at line 14
```

The example causes an error because *a nested table is automatically NULL when it is declared.* In other words, there are no individual elements yet because the nested table itself is NULL. In order to reference the individual elements of the nested table, it must be initialized with the help of a system-defined function called *constructor.* The constructor has the same name as the nested table type. For example,

```
last_name_tab := last_name_type('Rosenzweig',
    'Silvestrova');
```

This statement initializes the `last_name_tab` table to two elements. Note that most of the time, it is not known in advance what values should constitute a particular nested table. So, the following statement produces an empty but non-null nested table.

```
last_name_tab := last_name_type();
```

Notice that there are no arguments passed to a constructor.

Consider a modified version of the example shown previously.

■ FOR EXAMPLE

```
DECLARE
    CURSOR name_cur IS
        SELECT last_name
         FROM student
         WHERE rownum <= 10;

    TYPE last_name_type IS TABLE OF student.last_name%TYPE;
    last_name_tab last_name_type := last_name_type();

    v_counter INTEGER := 0;
BEGIN
    FOR name_rec IN name_cur LOOP
        v_counter := v_counter + 1;
        last_name_tab.EXTEND;
        last_name_tab(v_counter) := name_rec.last_name;

        DBMS_OUTPUT.PUT_LINE ('last_name('||v_counter||'): '||
            last_name_tab(v_counter));
    END LOOP;
END;
```

In this version, the nested table is initialized at the time of the declaration. This means that it is empty, but non-null. In the cursor loop, there is a statement with one of the collection methods, EXTEND. This method allows you to increase the size of the collection. Note that *the EXTEND method cannot be used with index-by tables.* You will see detailed explanation of various collection methods later in this chapter.

Next, the nested table is assigned values just like the index-by table in the original version of the example. When run, the script produces the following output:

```
last_name(1): Crocitto
last_name(2): Landry
last_name(3): Enison
last_name(4): Moskowitz
last_name(5): Olvsade
last_name(6): Mierzwa
last_name(7): Sethi
last_name(8): Walter
last_name(9): Martin
last_name(10): Noviello

PL/SQL procedure successfully completed.
```

It is important to note the difference between NULL collection and empty collection. If a collection has not been initialized, referencing its individual elements causes the following error:

```
DECLARE
    TYPE integer_type IS TABLE OF INTEGER;
    integer_tab integer_type;

    v_counter integer := 1;
BEGIN
    DBMS_OUTPUT.PUT_LINE (integer_tab(v_counter));
END;

DECLARE
*
ERROR at line 1:
ORA-06531: Reference to uninitialized collection
ORA-06512: at line 7
```

If a collection has been initialized so that it is empty, referencing its individual elements causes a different error:

```
DECLARE
    TYPE integer_type IS TABLE OF INTEGER;
    integer_tab integer_type := integer_type();

    v_counter integer := 1;
BEGIN
    DBMS_OUTPUT.PUT_LINE (integer_tab(v_counter));
END;
```

```
DECLARE
*
ERROR at line 1:
ORA-06533: Subscript beyond count
ORA-06512: at line 7
```

COLLECTION METHODS

In the previous examples, you have seen one of the collection methods, EXTEND. A *collection method* is a built-in function that is called using a dot notation as follows:

```
collection_name.method_date
```

The following list explains collection methods that allow you to manipulate or gain information about a particular collection:

- EXISTS—Returns TRUE if a specified element exists in a collection. This method can be used to avoid raising SUBSCRIPT_OUTSIDE_LIMIT exceptions.
- COUNT—Returns the total number of elements in a collection.
- EXTEND—Increases the size of a collection.
- DELETE—Deletes either all elements, elements in the specified range, or a particular element from a collection. Note that PL/SQL keeps placeholders of the deleted elements.
- FIRST and LAST—Return subscripts of the first and last elements of a collection. Note that if first elements of a nested table are deleted, the FIRST method returns a value greater than one. If elements have been deleted from the middle of a nested table, the LAST method returns a value greater than the COUNT method.
- PRIOR and NEXT—Return subscripts that precede and succeed a specified collection subscript.
- TRIM—Removes either one or a specified number of elements from the end of a collection. Note that PL/SQL does not keep placeholders for the trimmed elements.

 Note that DELETE and TRIM methods cannot be used with index-by tables.

Consider the following example, which illustrates the use of various collection methods.

■ *FOR EXAMPLE*

```
DECLARE
   TYPE index_by_type IS TABLE OF NUMBER
      INDEX BY BINARY_INTEGER;
   index_by_table index_by_type;

   TYPE nested_type IS TABLE OF NUMBER;
   nested_table nested_type := nested_type(1, 2, 3, 4, 5,
      6, 7, 8, 9, 10);

BEGIN
   -- Populate index by table
   FOR i IN 1..10 LOOP
      index_by_table(i) := i;
   END LOOP;

   IF index_by_table.EXISTS(3) THEN
      DBMS_OUTPUT.PUT_LINE ('index_by_table(3) = '||
         index_by_table(3));
   END IF;

   -- delete 10th element from a collection
   nested_table.DELETE(10);
   -- delete elements 1 through 3 from a collection
   nested_table.DELETE(1,3);
   index_by_table.DELETE(10);

   DBMS_OUTPUT.PUT_LINE ('nested_table.COUNT = '||
      nested_table.COUNT);
   DBMS_OUTPUT.PUT_LINE ('index_by_table.COUNT = '||
      index_by_table.COUNT);

   DBMS_OUTPUT.PUT_LINE ('nested_table.FIRST = '||
      nested_table.FIRST);
   DBMS_OUTPUT.PUT_LINE ('nested_table.LAST = '||
      nested_table.LAST);
   DBMS_OUTPUT.PUT_LINE ('index_by_table.FIRST = '||
      index_by_table.FIRST);
   DBMS_OUTPUT.PUT_LINE ('index_by_table.LAST = '||
      index_by_table.LAST);

   DBMS_OUTPUT.PUT_LINE ('nested_table.PRIOR(2) = '||
      nested_table. PRIOR(2));
   DBMS_OUTPUT.PUT_LINE ('nested_table.NEXT(2) = '||
      nested_table.NEXT(2));
   DBMS_OUTPUT.PUT_LINE ('index_by_table.PRIOR(2) = '||
      index_by_table.PRIOR(2));
```

```
    DBMS_OUTPUT.PUT_LINE ('index_by_table.NEXT(2) = '||
        index_by_table.NEXT(2));

    -- Trim last two elements
    nested_table.TRIM(2);
    -- Trim last element
    nested_table.TRIM;

    DBMS_OUTPUT.PUT_LINE('nested_table.LAST = '||
        nested_table.LAST);
END;
```

Consider the output returned by the example:

```
index_by_table(3) = 3
nested_table.COUNT = 6
index_by_table.COUNT = 9
nested_table.FIRST = 4
nested_table.LAST = 9
index_by_table.FIRST = 1
index_by_table.LAST = 9
nested_table.PRIOR(2) =
nested_table.NEXT(2) = 4
index_by_table.PRIOR(2) = 1
index_by_table.NEXT(2) = 3
nested_table.LAST = 7

PL/SQL procedure successfully completed.
```

The first line of the output

```
index_by_table(3) = 3
```

is produced because the EXISTS method returns TRUE, and as a result, the IF statement

```
IF index_by_table.EXISTS(3) THEN
    DBMS_OUTPUT.PUT_LINE ('index_by_table(3) = '||
        index_by_table(3));
END IF;
```

evaluates to TRUE as well.

The second and third lines of the output

```
nested_table.COUNT = 6
index_by_table.COUNT = 9
```

show the results of method COUNT after some elements were deleted from the index-by and nested tables.

Next, lines four through seven of the output

```
nested_table.FIRST = 4
nested_table.LAST = 9
index_by_table.FIRST = 1
index_by_table.LAST = 9
```

show the results of FIRST and LAST methods. Notice that the FIRST method applied to the nested table returns 4 because the first three elements were deleted earlier.

Next, lines eight through eleven of the output

```
nested_table.PRIOR(2) =
nested_table.NEXT(2) = 4
index_by_table.PRIOR(2) = 1
index_by_table.NEXT(2) = 3
```

show the results of PRIOR and NEXT methods. Notice that the PRIOR method applied to the nested table returns NULL because the first element was deleted earlier.

Finally, the last line of the output

```
nested_table.LAST = 7
```

shows the value of the last subscript after the last three elements were removed. As mentioned earlier, once the DELETE method is issued, the PL/SQL keeps placeholders of the deleted elements. Therefore, the first call of the TRIM method removed ninth and tenth elements from the nested table, and the second call of the TRIM method removed eighth element of the nested table. As a result, the LAST method returned value 7 as the last subscript of the nested table.

LAB 18.1 EXERCISES

18.1.1 USE INDEX-BY TABLES

In this exercise, you will learn more about index-by tables discussed earlier in the chapter.

Create the following PL/SQL script:

```
-- ch18_1a.sql, version 1.0
SET SERVEROUTPUT ON
```

```
DECLARE
    CURSOR course_cur IS
        SELECT description
            FROM course;

    TYPE course_type IS TABLE OF course.description%TYPE
        INDEX BY BINARY_INTEGER;
    course_tab course_type;

    v_counter INTEGER := 0;
BEGIN
    FOR course_rec IN course_cur LOOP
        v_counter := v_counter + 1;
        course_tab(v_counter) := course_rec.description;
    END LOOP;
END;
```

Answer the following questions:

a) Explain the script ch18_1a.sql.

b) Modify the script so that rows of the index-by table are displayed on the screen.

c) Modify the script so that only first and last rows of the index-by table are displayed on the screen.

d) Modify the script by adding the following statements and explain the output produced:

   i) Display the total number of elements in the index-by table after it has been populated on the screen.

   ii) Delete the last element, and display the total number of elements of the index-by table again.

   iii) Delete the fifth element, and display the total number of elements and the subscript of the last element of the index-by table again.

**LAB
18.1**

In this exercise, you will learn more about nested tables discussed earlier in this chapter.

Answer the following questions:

a) Modify the script 18_1a.sql used in Exercise 18.1.1. Instead of using an index-by table, use a nested table.

b) Modify the script by adding the following statements and explain the output produced:

i) Delete the last element of the nested table, and then reassign a new value to it. Execute the script.

ii) Trim the last element of the nested table, and then reassign a new value to it. Execute the script.

c) How would you modify the script created, so that there is no error generated when a new value is assigned to the trimmed element?

LAB 18.1 EXERCISE ANSWERS

This section gives you some suggested answers to the questions in Lab 18.1, with discussion related to how those answers resulted. The most important thing to realize is whether your answer works. You should figure out the implications of the answers here and what the effects are from any different answers you may come up with.

a) Explain the script ch18_1a.sql.

Answer: The declaration section of the script contains definition of the index-by table type, `course_type`. *This type is based on the column DESCRIPTION of the table COURSE. Next, the actual index-by table is declared as* `course_tab`.

The executable section of the script populates the `course_tab` table in the cursor FOR loop. Each element of the index-by table is referenced by its subscript, `v_counter`. For each iteration of the loop, the value of `v_counter` is incremented by 1 so that each new description value is stored in the new row of the index-by table.

b) Modify the script so that rows of the index-by table are displayed on the screen.

Answer: Your script should look similar to the following script. Changes are shown in bold letters.

```
-- ch18_1b.sql, version 2.0
SET SERVEROUTPUT ON
DECLARE
   CURSOR course_cur IS
      SELECT description
        FROM course;

   TYPE course_type IS TABLE OF course.description%TYPE
      INDEX BY BINARY_INTEGER;
   course_tab course_type;

   v_counter INTEGER := 0;
BEGIN
   FOR course_rec IN course_cur LOOP
      v_counter := v_counter + 1;
      course_tab(v_counter):= course_rec.description;
      DBMS_OUTPUT.PUT_LINE('course('||v_counter||'): '||
         course_tab(v_counter));
   END LOOP;
END;
```

Consider another version of the same script.

```
-- ch18_1c.sql, version 3.0
SET SERVEROUTPUT ON
DECLARE
   CURSOR course_cur IS
      SELECT description
        FROM course;

   TYPE course_type IS TABLE OF course.description%TYPE
      INDEX BY BINARY_INTEGER;
   course_tab course_type;

   v_counter INTEGER := 0;
BEGIN
   FOR course_rec IN course_cur LOOP
      v_counter := v_counter + 1;
```

```
            course_tab(v_counter) := course_rec.description;
      END LOOP;

      FOR i IN 1..v_counter LOOP
         DBMS_OUTPUT.PUT_LINE('course('||i||'): '||
            course_tab(i));
      END LOOP;
   END;
```

When run, both versions produce the same output:

```
course(1): DP Overview
course(2): Intro to Computers
course(3): Intro to Programming
course(4): Structured Programming Techniques
course(5): Hands-On Windows
course(6): Intro to Java Programming
course(7): Intermediate Java Programming
course(8): Advanced Java Programming
course(9): JDeveloper
course(10): Intro to Unix
course(11): Basics of Unix Admin
course(12): Advanced Unix Admin
course(13): Unix Tips and Techniques
course(14): Structured Analysis
course(15): Project Management
course(16): Database Design
course(17): Internet Protocols
course(18): Java for C/C++ Programmers
course(19): GUI Programming
course(20): Intro to SQL
course(21): Oracle Tools
course(22): PL/SQL Programming
course(23): Intro to Internet
course(24): Intro to the Basic Language
course(25): Operating Systems
course(26): Network Administration
course(27): JDeveloper Lab
course(28): Database System Principles
course(29): JDeveloper Techniques
course(30): DB Programming in Java

PL/SQL procedure successfully completed.
```

c) Modify the script so that only first and last rows of the index-by table are displayed on the screen.

Answer: Your script should look similar to the following script. Changes are shown in bold letters.

```
-- ch18_1d.sql, version 4.0
SET SERVEROUTPUT ON
DECLARE
    CURSOR course_cur IS
        SELECT description
          FROM course;

    TYPE course_type IS TABLE OF course.description%TYPE
        INDEX BY BINARY_INTEGER;
    course_tab course_type;

    v_counter INTEGER := 0;
BEGIN
    FOR course_rec IN course_cur LOOP
        v_counter := v_counter + 1;
        course_tab(v_counter) := course_rec.description;
    END LOOP;
    DBMS_OUTPUT.PUT_LINE('course('||course_tab.FIRST||'): '||
        course_tab(course_tab.FIRST));
    DBMS_OUTPUT.PUT_LINE('course('||course_tab.LAST||'): '||
        course_tab(course_tab.LAST));
END;
```

Consider the statements

course_tab(course_tab.FIRST) and **course_tab(course_tab.LAST)**

used in this example. While these statements look somewhat different from the statements that you have seen so far, they produce the same effect as

course_tab(1) and **course_tab(30)**

statements because, as mentioned earlier, the FIRST and LAST methods return *the subscripts* of the first and last elements of a collection, respectively. In this example, the index-by table contains 30 elements, where the first element has subscript of 1, and the last element has subscript of 30.

This version of the script produces the following output:

```
course(1): DP Overview
course(30): DB Programming in Java

PL/SQL procedure successfully completed.
```

d) Modify the script by adding the following statements and explain the output produced:

i) Display the total number of elements in the index-by table after it has been populated on the screen.

ii) Delete the last element, and display the total number of elements of the index-by table again.

iii) Delete the fifth element, and display the total number of elements and the subscript of the last element of the index-by table again.

Answer: Your script should look similar to the following script. All changes are shown in bold letters.

```
-- ch18_1e.sql, version 5.0
SET SERVEROUTPUT ON
DECLARE
   CURSOR course_cur IS
      SELECT description
      FROM course;

   TYPE course_type IS TABLE OF course.description%TYPE
      INDEX BY BINARY_INTEGER;
   course_tab course_type;

   v_counter INTEGER := 0;
BEGIN
   FOR course_rec IN course_cur LOOP
      v_counter := v_counter + 1;
      course_tab(v_counter) := course_rec.description;
   END LOOP;

   -- Display the total number of elements in the index-by
   -- table
   DBMS_OUTPUT.PUT_LINE ('1. Total number of elements: '||
      course_tab.COUNT);

   -- Delete the last element of the index-by table
   -- Display the total number of elements in the index-by
   -- table
   course_tab.DELETE(course_tab.LAST);
   DBMS_OUTPUT.PUT_LINE ('2. Total number of elements: '||
      course_tab.COUNT);

   -- Delete the fifth element of the index-by table
   -- Display the total number of elements in the index-by
   -- table
   -- Display the subscript of the last element of the
   -- index-by table
   course_tab.DELETE(5);
   DBMS_OUTPUT.PUT_LINE ('3. Total number of elements: '||
      course_tab.COUNT);
   DBMS_OUTPUT.PUT_LINE ('3. The subscript of the last '||
      'element: '||course_tab.LAST);
END;
```

When run, this example produces the following output:

```
1. Total number of elements: 30
2. Total number of elements: 29
3. Total number of elements: 28
3. The subscript of the last element: 29

PL/SQL procedure successfully completed.
```

First, the total number of the elements in the index-by table is calculated via the COUNT method and displayed on the screen. Second, the last element is deleted via DELETE and LAST methods, and the total number of the elements in the index-by table is displayed on the screen again. Third, the fifth element is deleted, and the total number of the elements in the index-by table and the subscript of the last element are displayed on the screen.

Consider the last two lines on the output. After the fifth element of the index-by table is deleted, the COUNT method returns value 28, and the LAST method returns the value 29. Usually, the values returned by the COUNT and LAST methods are equal. However, when an element is deleted from the middle of the index-by table, the value returned by the LAST method is greater than the value returned by the COUNT method because *the COUNT method ignores deleted elements*.

18.1.2 ANSWERS

a) Modify the script 18_1a.sql used in Exercise 18.1.1. Instead of using an index-by table, use a nested table.

Answer: Your script should look similar to the following script. Changes are shown in bold letters.

```
-- ch18_2a.sql, version 1.0
SET SERVEROUTPUT ON
DECLARE
   CURSOR course_cur IS
      SELECT description
        FROM course;

   TYPE course_type IS TABLE OF course.description%TYPE;
   course_tab course_type := course_type();

   v_counter INTEGER := 0;
BEGIN
   FOR course_rec IN course_cur LOOP
      v_counter := v_counter + 1;
      course_tab.EXTEND;
      course_tab(v_counter) := course_rec.description;
   END LOOP;
END;
```

b) Modify the script by adding the following statements and explain the output produced:

i) Delete the last element of the nested table, and then reassign a new value to it. Execute the script.

Answer: Your script should look similar to the following script. Changes are shown in bold letters.

```
-- ch18_2b.sql, version 2.0
SET SERVEROUTPUT ON
DECLARE
    CURSOR course_cur IS
        SELECT description
          FROM course;

    TYPE course_type IS TABLE OF course.description%TYPE;
    course_tab course_type := course_type();

    v_counter INTEGER := 0;
BEGIN
    FOR course_rec IN course_cur LOOP
        v_counter := v_counter + 1;
        course_tab.EXTEND;
        course_tab(v_counter) := course_rec.description;
    END LOOP;

    course_tab.DELETE(30);
    course_tab(30) := 'New Course';
END;
```

ii) Trim the last element of the nested table, and then reassign a new value to it. Execute the script.

Answer: Your script should look similar to the following script. Changes are shown in bold letters.

```
-- ch18_2c.sql, version 3.0
SET SERVEROUTPUT ON
DECLARE
    CURSOR course_cur IS
        SELECT description
          FROM course;

    TYPE course_type IS TABLE OF course.description%TYPE;
    course_tab course_type := course_type();

    v_counter INTEGER := 0;
BEGIN
```

```
   FOR course_rec IN course_cur LOOP
      v_counter := v_counter + 1;
      course_tab.EXTEND;
      course_tab(v_counter) := course_rec.description;
   END LOOP;

   course_tab.TRIM;
   course_tab(30) := 'New Course';
END;
```

When run, this version of the script produces the following error:

```
DECLARE
*
ERROR at line 1:
ORA-06533: Subscript beyond count
ORA-06512: at line 18
```

In the previous version of the script, the last element of the nested table is re-moved via the DELETE method. As mentioned earlier, when the DELETE method is used, the PL/SQL keeps a placeholder of the deleted element. Therefore, the statement

```
course_tab(30) := 'New Course';
```

does not cause any errors.

In the current version of the script, the last element of the nested table is re-moved via the TRIM method. In this case, the PL/SQL does not keep placeholder of the trimmed element because the TRIM method manipulates the internal size of a collection. As a result, the reference to the trimmed elements causes 'Sub-script beyond count' error.

c) How would you modify the script created above, so that there is no error gener-ated when a new value is assigned to the trimmed element?

Answer: Your script should look similar to the following script. Changes are shown in bold letters.

```
-- ch18_2d.sql, version 4.0
SET SERVEROUTPUT ON
DECLARE
   CURSOR course_cur IS
      SELECT description
        FROM course;

   TYPE course_type IS TABLE OF course.description%TYPE;
   course_tab course_type := course_type();
```

```
      v_counter INTEGER := 0;
BEGIN
   FOR course_rec IN course_cur LOOP
      v_counter := v_counter + 1;
      course_tab.EXTEND;
      course_tab(v_counter) := course_rec.description;
   END LOOP;

   course_tab.TRIM;
   course_tab.EXTEND;
   course_tab(30) := 'New Course';
END;
```

In order to reference the trimmed element, the EXTEND method is use to increase the size on the collection. As a result, the assignment statement

```
course_tab(30) := 'New Course';
```

does not cause any errors.

LAB 18.1 SELF-REVIEW QUESTIONS

In order to test your progress, you should be able to answer the following questions.

1) The main difference between the index-by and nested tables is that

a) _____ nested tables can be stored in a database column, and index-by tables cannot.

b) _____ index-by tables can be stored in a database column, and nested tables cannot.

2) An index-by table is indexed by what datatype?

a) _____ NUMBER
b) _____ INTEGER
c) _____ BINARY_INTEGER
d) _____ PLS_INTEGER

3) A nested table must be initialized prior to its use.

a) _____ True
b) _____ False

4) If a PL/SQL table contains one element

   a) _____ the FIRST method returns value of one, and the LAST method returns NULL.

   b) _____ the FIRST method returns NULL, and the LAST method returns value of one.

   c) _____ the FIRST and LAST methods return a value of one.

   d) _____ referring to these methods causes an error.

5) If a PL/SQL table has eight elements, the DELETE (3, 7) method deletes

   a) _____ the third and seventh elements of the collection.

   b) _____ the third element and ignores the seventh element of the collection.

   c) _____ elements three to seven.

Answers appear in Appendix A, Section 18.1.

LAB 18.2

VARRAYS

> ## LAB OBJECTIVE
>
> After this Lab, you will be able to:
>
> ✔ Use Varrays

As mentioned earlier, a varray is another collection type, and it stands for variable-size arrays. Similar to PL/SQL tables, each element of a varray is assigned a consecutive subscript starting at 1, as shown in Figure 18.2.

Figure 18.2 shows a varray consisting of five integer numbers. Each number is assigned a unique subscript that corresponds to its position in the varray.

It is important to note that a varray has a maximum size. In other words, a subscript of a varray has a fixed lower bound equal to 1, and an upper bound that is extensible if such a need arises. In Figure 18.2, the upper bound of a varray is 5, but it can be extended to 6, 7, 8, and so on up to 10. Therefore, a varray can contain a number of elements, varying from zero (empty array) to its maximum size. You will recall that PL/SQL tables do not have a maximum size that must be specified explicitly.

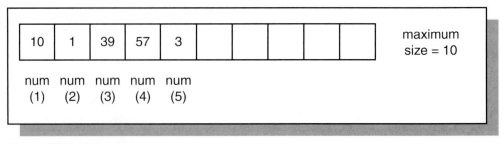

Figure 18.2 ■ Varray

The general syntax for creating a varray is as follows (the reserved words and phrases surrounded by brackets are optional):

```
TYPE type_name IS {VARRAY | VARYING ARRAY} (size_limit) OF
element_type [NOT NULL];
varray_name TYPE_NAME;
```

First, a varray structure is defined using the TYPE statement, where TYPE_NAME is the name of the type that is used in the second step to declare an actual varray. Notice that there are two variations of the type, VARRAY and VARYING ARRAY. A SIZE_LIMIT is a positive integer literal that specifies the upper bound of a varray. Just like in the case of PL/SQL tables, there are restrictions that apply to an ELEMENT_TYPE of a varray. These restrictions are listed in Oracle help available online. Second, the actual varray is declared based on the type specified in the first step.

LAB 18.2

Consider the following code fragment:

■ FOR EXAMPLE

```
DECLARE
    TYPE last_name_type IS VARRAY(10) OF student.
    last_name%TYPE;
    last_name_varray last_name_type;
```

In this example, type `last_name_type` is declared as a varray of ten elements based on the column LAST_NAME of the STUDENT table. Next, the actual varray `last_name_varray` is declared based on the LAST_NAME_TYPE.

Similar to nested tables, a varray is automatically NULL when it is declared and must be initialized before its individual elements can be referenced. So consider a modified version of the example used in the previous lab. Instead of using nested table, this version uses varray (changes are highlighted in bold).

■ FOR EXAMPLE

```
DECLARE
    CURSOR name_cur IS
        SELECT last_name
          FROM student
         WHERE rownum <= 10;

    TYPE last_name_type IS VARRAY(10) OF student.
    last_name%TYPE;
    last_name_varray last_name_type := last_name_type();

    v_counter INTEGER := 0;
BEGIN
```

```
    FOR name_rec IN name_cur LOOP
        v_counter := v_counter + 1;
        last_name_varray.EXTEND;
        last_name_varray(v_counter) := name_rec.last_name;
        DBMS_OUTPUT.PUT_LINE ('last_name('||v_counter||'): '||
            last_name_varray(v_counter));
    END LOOP;
END;
```

This example produces the following output:

```
last_name(1): Crocitto
last_name(2): Landry
last_name(3): Enison
last_name(4): Moskowitz
last_name(5): Olvsade
last_name(6): Mierzwa
last_name(7): Sethi
last_name(8): Walter
last_name(9): Martin
last_name(10): Noviello

PL/SQL procedure successfully completed.
```

Based on the preceding example, you may realize that collection methods seen in the previous lab can be used with varrays as well. Consider the following example, which illustrates the use of various collection methods when applied to a varray.

■ FOR EXAMPLE

```
DECLARE
    TYPE varray_type IS VARRAY(10) OF NUMBER;
    varray varray_type := varray_type(1, 2, 3, 4, 5, 6);

BEGIN
    DBMS_OUTPUT.PUT_LINE ('varray.COUNT = '||varray.COUNT);
    DBMS_OUTPUT.PUT_LINE ('varray.LIMIT = '||varray.LIMIT);

    DBMS_OUTPUT.PUT_LINE ('varray.FIRST = '||varray.FIRST);
    DBMS_OUTPUT.PUT_LINE ('varray.LAST = '||varray.LAST);

    varray.EXTEND(2, 4);
    DBMS_OUTPUT.PUT_LINE ('varray.LAST = '||varray.LAST);
    DBMS_OUTPUT.PUT_LINE ('varray('||varray.LAST||') = '||
        varray(varray.LAST));
```

```
    -- Trim last two elements
    varray.TRIM(2);
    DBMS_OUTPUT.PUT_LINE('varray.LAST = '||varray.LAST);
END;
```

Consider the output returned by the example:

```
varray.COUNT = 6
varray.LIMIT = 10
varray.FIRST = 1
varray.LAST = 6
varray.LAST = 8
varray(8) = 4
varray.LAST = 6

PL/SQL procedure successfully completed.
```

The first two lines of output

```
varray.COUNT = 6
varray.LIMIT = 10
```

show the results of the COUNT and LIMIT methods, respectively. You will recall that the COUNT method returns the number of elements that a collection contains. The collection has been initialized to six elements, so the COUNT method returns a value of 6.

The next line of output corresponds to another collection method, LIMIT. This method returns the maximum number of elements that a collection can contain and is usually used with varrays only because varrays have an upper bound specified at the time of declaration. The collection VARRAY has an upper bound of ten, so the LIMIT method returns a value of 10. When used with nested tables, the LIMIT method returns NULL because nested tables do not have a maximum size.

The third and fourth lines of the output

```
varray.FIRST = 1
varray.LAST = 6
```

show the results of the FIRST and LAST methods.

The fifth and six lines of the output

```
varray.LAST = 8
varray(8) = 4
```

show the results of LAST method and the value of the eighth element of the collection after the EXTEND method increased the size of the collection. Notice that the EXTEND method

```
varray.EXTEND(2, 4);
```

appends two copies on the fourth element to the collection. As a result, the seventh and eighth elements both contain a value of 4.

Next, the last line of output

```
varray.LAST = 6
```

shows the value of the last subscript after the last two elements were removed via the TRIM method.

It is important to note that you cannot use the DELETE method with a varray to remove its elements. Unlike PL/SQL tables, varrays are dense, and using the DELETE method causes an error, as illustrated in the following example:

```
DECLARE
    TYPE varray_type IS VARRAY(3) OF CHAR(1);
    varray varray_type := varray_type('A', 'B', 'C');

BEGIN
    varray.DELETE(3);
END;

    varray.DELETE(3);
    *
ERROR at line 6:
ORA-06550: line 6, column 4:
PLS-00306: wrong number or types of arguments in call to
'DELETE'
ORA-06550: line 6, column 4:
PL/SQL: Statement ignored
```

LAB 18.2 EXERCISES

18.2.1 USE VARRAYS

In this exercise, you will learn more about varrays. You will need to debug the following script, which populates `city_varray` with 10 cities selected from the ZIPCODE table and displays its individual elements on the screen.

Create the following PL/SQL script:

```
-- ch18_3a.sql, version 1.0
SET SERVEROUTPUT ON
DECLARE
    CURSOR city_cur IS
        SELECT city
          FROM zipcode
         WHERE rownum <= 10;

    TYPE city_type IS VARRAY(10) OF zipcode.city%TYPE;
    city_varray city_type;

    v_counter INTEGER := 0;
BEGIN
    FOR city_rec IN city_cur LOOP
        v_counter := v_counter + 1;
        city_varray(v_counter) := city_rec.city;
        DBMS_OUTPUT.PUT_LINE('city_varray('||v_counter||
            '): '||city_varray(v_counter));
    END LOOP;
END;
```

Execute the script, and then answer the following questions:

a) What output was printed on the screen? Explain it.

b) Modify the script so that no errors are returned at runtime.

c) Modify the script as follows: Double the size of the varray and populate the last ten elements with the first ten elements. In other words, the value of the eleventh element should be equal to the value of the first element; the value of the twelfth element should be equal to the value of the second element; and so forth.

LAB 18.2 EXERCISE ANSWERS

This section gives you some suggested answers to the questions in Lab 18.2, with discussion related to how those answers resulted. The most important thing to realize is whether your answer works. You should figure out the implications of the answers here and what the effects are from any different answers you may come up with.

18.2.1 ANSWERS

a) What output was printed on the screen? Explain it.

Answer: Your output should look similar to the following:

```
DECLARE
*
ERROR at line 1:
ORA-06531: Reference to uninitialized collection
ORA-06512: at line 14
```

You will recall that when a varray is declared, it is automatically NULL. In other words, the collection itself is NULL, not its individual elements. Therefore, before it can be used, it must be initialized via the constructor function with the same name as the varray type. Furthermore, once the collection is initialized, the EXTEND method must be used before its individual elements can be referenced in the script.

b) Modify the script so that no errors are returned at runtime.

Answer: Your script should look similar to the following script. Changes are shown in bold letters.

```
-- ch18_3b.sql, version 2.0
SET SERVEROUTPUT ON
DECLARE
    CURSOR city_cur IS
        SELECT city
          FROM zipcode
         WHERE rownum <= 10;

    TYPE city_type IS VARRAY(10) OF zipcode.city%TYPE;
    city_varray city_type := city_type();

    v_counter INTEGER := 0;
BEGIN
    FOR city_rec IN city_cur LOOP
        v_counter := v_counter + 1;
        city_varray.EXTEND;
        city_varray(v_counter) := city_rec.city;
```

```
      DBMS_OUTPUT.PUT_LINE('city_varray('||v_counter||
          '): '||city_varray(v_counter));
    END LOOP;
  END;
```

When run, this script produces the following output:

```
city_varray(1):  Santurce
city_varray(2):  North Adams
city_varray(3):  Dorchester
city_varray(4):  Tufts Univ. Bedford
city_varray(5):  Weymouth
city_varray(6):  Sandwich
city_varray(7):  Ansonia
city_varray(8):  Middlefield
city_varray(9):  Oxford
city_varray(10): New Haven

PL/SQL procedure successfully completed.
```

c) Modify the script as follows: Double the size of the varray and populate the last ten elements with the first ten elements. In other words, the value of the eleventh element should be equal to the value of the first element; the value of the twelfth element should be equal to the value of the second element; and so forth.

Answer: Your script should look similar to the following script. Changes are shown in bold letters.

```
-- ch18_3c.sql, version 3.0
SET SERVEROUTPUT ON
DECLARE
   CURSOR city_cur IS
      SELECT city
        FROM zipcode
       WHERE rownum <= 10;

   TYPE city_type IS VARRAY(20) OF zipcode.city%TYPE;
   city_varray city_type := city_type();

   v_counter INTEGER := 0;
BEGIN
   FOR city_rec IN city_cur LOOP
      v_counter := v_counter + 1;
      city_varray.EXTEND;
      city_varray(v_counter) := city_rec.city;
   END LOOP;
```

```
        FOR i IN 1..v_counter LOOP
           -- extend the size of varray by 1 and copy the
           -- current element to the last element
           city_varray.EXTEND(1, i);
        END LOOP;

        FOR i IN 1..20 LOOP
           DBMS_OUTPUT.PUT_LINE('city_varray('||i||
              '): '||city_varray(i));
        END LOOP;
     END;
```

In the preceding script, you increase the maximum size of the varray to 20 at the time of `city_type` declaration. After the first 10 elements of the varray are populated, the last ten elements are populated via numeric FOR loop and the EXTEND method as follows:

```
     FOR i IN 1..v_counter LOOP
        -- extend the size of varray by 1 and copy the current
        -- element to the last element
        city_varray.EXTEND(1, i);
     END LOOP;
```

In this loop, the loop counter is implicitly incremented by one. So for the first iteration of the loop, the size of the varray is increased by one and the first element of the varray is copied to the eleventh element. In the same manner, the second element of the varray is copied to the twelfth element, and so forth.

In order to display all elements of the varray, the DBMS_OUTPUT.PUT_LINE statement has been moved to its own numeric FOR loop that iterates 20 times.

When run, this script produces the following output:

```
     city_varray(1): Santurce
     city_varray(2): North Adams
     city_varray(3): Dorchester
     city_varray(4): Tufts Univ. Bedford
     city_varray(5): Weymouth
     city_varray(6): Sandwich
     city_varray(7): Ansonia
     city_varray(8): Middlefield
     city_varray(9): Oxford
     city_varray(10): New Haven
     city_varray(11): Santurce
     city_varray(12): North Adams
     city_varray(13): Dorchester
     city_varray(14): Tufts Univ. Bedford
```

```
city_varray(15): Weymouth
city_varray(16): Sandwich
city_varray(17): Ansonia
city_varray(18): Middlefield
city_varray(19): Oxford
city_varray(20): New Haven

PL/SQL procedure successfully completed.
```

LAB 18.2 SELF-REVIEW QUESTIONS

In order to test your progress, you should be able to answer the following questions.

1) One of the differences between the nested tables and varrays is that

    a) _____ nested tables can be sparse, and varrays cannot.
    b) _____ varrays can be sparse, and nested tables cannot.

2) A varray has an upper bound that

    a) _____ can be extended without any limits.
    b) _____ can be extended to its maximum size.
    c) _____ is fixed and cannot be extended to all.

3) A varray must be initialized prior to its use.

    a) _____ True
    b) _____ False

4) If a varray has maximum size of 5 and contains 2 elements

    a) _____ the LIMIT and COUNT methods return the same value of 5.
    b) _____ the LIMIT and COUNT methods return the same value of 2.
    c) _____ the LIMIT method returns the value of 5, and the COUNT method returns the value of 2.

5) If a varray has eight elements, the DELETE (3, 7) method

    a) _____ deletes the third and seventh elements of the collection.
    b) _____ deletes the third element and ignores the seventh element of the collection.
    c) _____ deletes the elements three to seven.
    d) _____ causes an error.

Answers appear in Appendix A, Section 18.2.

LAB 18.3

MULTILEVEL COLLECTIONS

LAB OBJECTIVE

After this Lab, you will be able to:

✔ Use Multilevel Collections

So far you have seen various examples of collections with the element type based on a scalar type, such as NUMBER and VARCHAR2. In Oracle 9i, PL/SQL provides you with the ability to create collections whose element type is based on a collection type. Such collections are called *multilevel collections*. You will recall that multilevel collections is a new feature and is not supported by Oracle versions prior to 9i.

Consider a varrray of varrays shown in Figure 18.3.

Figure 18.3 shows a varray of varrays or nested varray. A varray of varrays consists of three elements, where each individual element is a varray consisting of four integer numbers. As a result, in order to reference an individual element of a varray of varrays, you use the following notation:

```
varray_name(subscript of the outer varray)(subscript of
the inner varray)
```

For example, the varray(1)(3) in Figure 18.3 equals 6; similarly, varray(2)(1) equals 1.

Consider an example based on Figure 18.3.

■ *FOR EXAMPLE*

```
DECLARE
   TYPE varray_type1 IS VARRAY(4) OF INTEGER;
   TYPE varray_type2 IS VARRAY(3) OF varray_type1;
```

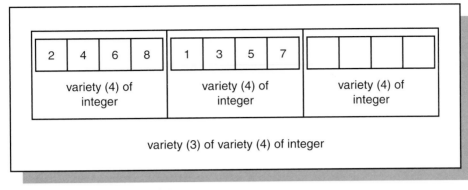

Figure 18.3 ▪ A Varray of Varrays

```
   varray1 varray_type1 := varray_type1(2, 4, 6, 8);
   varray2 varray_type2 := varray_type2(varray1);
BEGIN
   DBMS_OUTPUT.PUT_LINE ('Varray of integers');
   FOR i IN 1..4 LOOP
      DBMS_OUTPUT.PUT_LINE ('varray1('||i||'): ' ||
         varray1(i));
   END LOOP;

   varray2.EXTEND;
   varray2(2) := varray_type1(1, 3, 5, 7);

   DBMS_OUTPUT.PUT_LINE (chr(10)||
      'Varray of varrays of integers');
   FOR i IN 1..2 LOOP
      FOR j IN 1..4 LOOP
         DBMS_OUTPUT.PUT_LINE
            ('varray2('||i||')('||j||'): '||varray2(i)(j));
      END LOOP;
   END LOOP;
END;
```

In this declaration portion of the example, you define two varray types. The first type, `varray_type1`, is based on the INTEGER datatype and can contain up to four elements. The second type, `varray_type2`, is based on the `varray_type1` and can contain up to six elements. Next, you declare two varrays based on the types just described. The first varray, `varray1`, is declared as `varray_type1` and initialized so that its four elements are populated with the first four even numbers. The second varray, `varray2`, is declared as `varray_type2`, so that each individual element is a varray consisting of four integer numbers, and initialized so that it first varray element is populated.

In the executable portion of the example, you display the values of the `varray1` on the screen. Next, you extend the upper bound of the `varray2` by one, and populate its second element as follows:

```
varray2(2) := varray_type1(1, 3, 5, 7);
```

Notice that you are using a constructor corresponding to the `varray_type1` because each element of the `varray2` is based on the `varray1` collection. In other words, the same result could be achieved via the following two statements:

```
varray1 := varray_type1(1, 3, 5, 7);
varray2 := varray_type2(varray1);
```

**LAB
18.3**

Once the second element of the `varray2` is populated, you display results on the screen via nested numeric FOR loops.

This example produces the following output:

```
Varray of integers
varray1(1): 2
varray1(2): 4
varray1(3): 6
varray1(4): 8

Varray of varrays of integers
varray2(1)(1): 2
varray2(1)(2): 4
varray2(1)(3): 6
varray2(1)(4): 8
varray2(2)(1): 1
varray2(2)(2): 3
varray2(2)(3): 5
varray2(2)(4): 7

PL/SQL procedure successfully completed.
```

LAB 18.3 EXERCISES

18.3.1 USE MULTILEVEL COLLECTIONS

In this exercise, you will learn more about multilevel collections.

Create the following PL/SQL script:

```
-- ch18_4a.sql, version 1.0
SET SERVEROUTPUT ON
DECLARE
```

```
      TYPE table_type1 IS TABLE OF integer INDEX BY
      BINARY_INTEGER;
      TYPE table_type2 IS TABLE OF table_type1 INDEX BY
      BINARY_INTEGER;

      table_tab1 table_type1;
      table_tab2 table_type2;

   BEGIN
      FOR i IN 1..2 LOOP
         FOR j IN 1..3 LOOP
            IF i = 1 THEN
               table_tab1(j) := j;
            ELSE
               table_tab1(j) := 4 - j;
            END IF;
            table_tab2(i)(j) := table_tab1(j);
            DBMS_OUTPUT.PUT_LINE ('table_tab2('||
               i||')('||j||'): '||table_tab2(i)(j));
         END LOOP;
      END LOOP;
   END;
```

LAB
18.3

Execute the script, and then answer the following questions:

a) Execute the script ch18_4a.sql and explain the output produced.

b) Modify the script so that instead of using multilevel index-by tables it uses a nested table of index-by tables.

c) Modify the script so that instead of using multilevel index-by tables it uses a nested table of varrays.

LAB 18.3 EXERCISE ANSWERS

This section gives you some suggested answers to the questions in Lab 18.3, with discussion related to how those answers resulted. The most important thing to realize is whether your answer works. You should figure out the implications of the answers here and what the effects are from any different answers you may come up with.

a) Execute the script ch18_4a.sql and explain the output produced.

Answer: Your output should look similar to the following:

```
table_tab2(1)(1): 1
table_tab2(1)(2): 2
table_tab2(1)(3): 3
table_tab2(2)(1): 3
table_tab2(2)(2): 2
table_tab2(2)(3): 1

PL/SQL procedure successfully completed.
```

The script ch18_4a.sql uses multilevel index-by tables or an index-by table of index-by tables. The declaration portion of the script defines a multilevel index-by table `table_tab2`. *Each row of this table is an index-by table consisting of three rows. The executable portion of the script populates the multilevel table via nested numeric FOR loops. In the first iteration of the outer loop, the inner loop populates the index-by table* `table_tab1` *with values 1, 2, 3, and the first row of the multilevel table* `table_tab2`. *In the second iteration of the outer loop, the inner loop populates the index-by table* `table_tab1` *with values 3, 2, 1, and the second row of the multilevel table* `table_tab2`.

b) Modify the script so that instead of using multilevel index-by tables it uses a nested table of index-by tables.

Answer: Your script should look similar to the following script. Changes are shown in bold letters.

```
-- ch18_4b.sql, version 2.0
SET SERVEROUTPUT ON
DECLARE
   TYPE table_type1 IS TABLE OF integer INDEX BY
BINARY_INTEGER;
   TYPE table_type2 IS TABLE OF table_type1;

   table_tab1 table_type1;
   table_tab2 table_type2 := table_type2();

BEGIN
   FOR i IN 1..2 LOOP
      table_tab2.EXTEND;
      FOR j IN 1..3 LOOP
         IF i = 1 THEN
            table_tab1(j) := j;
         ELSE
```

```
            table_tab1(j) := 4 - j;
         END IF;
         table_tab2(i)(j) := table_tab1(j);
         DBMS_OUTPUT.PUT_LINE ('table_tab2('||
            i||')('||j||'): '||table_tab2(i)(j));
      END LOOP;
   END LOOP;
END;
```

In this version of the script, the `table_type2` is declared as a nested table of index-by tables. Next, `table_tab2` is initialized prior to its use, and its size is extended before a new element is assigned a value.

c) Modify the script so that instead of using multilevel index-by tables it uses a nested table of varrays.

Answer: Your script should look similar to the following script. Changes are shown in bold letters.

```
-- ch18_4c.sql, version 3.0
SET SERVEROUTPUT ON
DECLARE
   TYPE table_type1 IS VARRAY(3) OF integer;
   TYPE table_type2 IS TABLE OF table_type1;

   table_tab1 table_type1 := table_type1();
   table_tab2 table_type2 := table_type2(table_tab1);

BEGIN
   FOR i IN 1..2 LOOP
      table_tab2.EXTEND;
      table_tab2(i) := table_type1();
      FOR j IN 1..3 LOOP
         IF i = 1 THEN
            table_tab1.EXTEND;
            table_tab1(j) := j;
         ELSE
            table_tab1(j) := 4 - j;
         END IF;
         table_tab2(i).EXTEND;
         table_tab2(i)(j):= table_tab1(j);
         DBMS_OUTPUT.PUT_LINE ('table_tab2('||
            i||')('||j||'): '||table_tab2(i)(j));
      END LOOP;
   END LOOP;
END;
```

In this declaration section of the script, the `table_type1` is defined as a varray with three integer elements, and the `table_type2` is declared as a nested table of varrays. Next, `table_tab1` and `table_tab2` are initialized prior to their uses.

In the executable portion of the script, the size of the `table_tab2` is incremented via the EXTEND method and its individual elements are initialized as follows:

```
table_tab2(i) := table_type1();
```

Notice that that each element is initialized via the constructor associated with the varray type `table_type1`. Furthermore, in order to populate a nested table, a new varray element must be added to the each nested table element as shown:

```
table_tab2(i).EXTEND;
```

In other words, for the first iteration of the outer loop, there are three varray elements added to the first element of the nested table. Without this statement, the script causes the following error:

```
DECLARE
*
ERROR at line 1:
ORA-06533: Subscript beyond count
ORA-06512: at line 20
```

When run, this script produces output identical to the original example:

```
table_tab2(1)(1): 1
table_tab2(1)(2): 2
table_tab2(1)(3): 3
table_tab2(2)(1): 3
table_tab2(2)(2): 2
table_tab2(2)(3): 1

PL/SQL procedure successfully completed.
```

LAB 18.3 SELF-REVIEW QUESTIONS

In order to test your progress, you should be able to answer the following questions.

1) Multilevel collections are not supported by Oracle 8i.

   a) _____ True
   b) _____ False

2) A varray of varrays has an upper bound

a) _____ that is fixed and cannot be extended to all.
b) _____ that can be extended to its maximum size.
c) _____ that can be extended without any limits.

3) There is no need to initialize a nested table of index-by tables prior to its use.

a) _____ True
b) _____ False

Consider the following script for the next two questions:

**LAB
18.3**

```
DECLARE
    TYPE varray_type1 IS VARRAY(3) OF INTEGER;
    TYPE varray_type2 IS VARRAY(10) OF varray_type1;

    varray1 varray_type1 := varray_type1(1, 2, 3);
    varray2 varray_type2 := varray_type2(varray1,
    varray_type1(4, 5, 6));

    var1 INTEGER;
BEGIN
    var1 := varray2(2)(3);
    varray2.EXTEND;
    varray2(3) := varray_type1(0);
    varray2(3).EXTEND;
END;
```

4) Based on the preceding script, what is the value of the variable VAR1?

a) _____ There is no value because the script generates an error.
b) _____ 2
c) _____ 6

5) The statement varray2(3).EXTEND

a) _____ adds a third element to the third element of VARRAY2.
b) _____ adds a second element to the third element of VARRAY2.
c) _____ causes a 'Subscript beyond count' error.

Answers appear in Appendix A, Section 18.3.

CHAPTER 18

TEST YOUR THINKING

In this chapter, you learned about collections and multilevel collections. Here are some projects that will help you test the depth of your understanding.

1) Create the following script. Create an index-by table and populate it with the instructor's full name. In other words, each row of the index-by table should contain first name, middle initial, and last name. Display this information on the screen.

2) Modify the script created in 1). Instead of using an index-by table, use a varray.

3) Modify the script created in 2). Create an additional varray and populate it with unique course numbers that each instructor teaches. Display instructor's name and the list of courses he or she teaches.

4) Find and explain errors in the following script:

```
DECLARE
    TYPE varray_type1 IS VARRAY(7) OF INTEGER;
    TYPE table_type2 IS TABLE OF varray_type1 INDEX BY
    BINARY_INTEGER;

    varray1 varray_type1 := varray_type1(1, 2, 3);
    table2 table_type2 := table_type2(varray1,
    varray_type1(8, 9, 0));

BEGIN
    DBMS_OUTPUT.PUT_LINE ('table2(1)(2): '||table2(1)(2));

FOR i IN 1..10 LOOP
    varray1.EXTEND;
    varray1(i) := i;
    DBMS_OUTPUT.PUT_LINE ('varray1('||i||'): '||
        varray1(i));
    END LOOP;
END;
```

The projects in this section are meant to have you utilize all of the skills that you have acquired throughout this chapter. The answers to these projects can be found in Appendix D and at the companion Web site to this book, located at http://www.phptr.com/rosenzweig2e. Visit the Web site periodically to share and discuss your answers.

CHAPTER 19

RECORDS

In Chapter 9, you were briefly introduced to the concept of a record type. You have learned that a record is a composite data structure that allows you to combine various yet related data into a logical unit. You have also learned that PL/SQL supports three kinds of record types: table based, cursor based, and user defined. In this chapter, you will revisit table-based and cursor-based record types and learn about user-defined record type. In addition, you will learn about records that contain collections and other records (called nested records) and collections of records.

L A B   1 9 . 1

RECORDS

LAB OBJECTIVES

After this Lab, you will be able to:

✔ Use Table-Based and Cursor-Based Records
✔ Use User-Defined Records

A record structure is somewhat similar to a row of a database table. Each data item is stored in a field with its own name and datatype. For example, suppose you have various data about a company, such as name, address, and number of employees. A record containing a field for each of these items allows you to treat a company as a logical unit, thus making it easier to organize and represent company's information.

TABLE-BASED AND CURSOR-BASED RECORDS

The %ROWTYPE attribute enables you to create table-based and cursor-based records. It is similar to the %TYPE attribute that is used to define scalar variables. Consider the following example of a table-based record.

■ *FOR EXAMPLE*

```
DECLARE
   course_rec course%ROWTYPE;
BEGIN
   SELECT *
     INTO course_rec
     FROM course
    WHERE course_no = 25;

   DBMS_OUTPUT.PUT_LINE ('Course No: '||
      course_rec.course_no);
```

```
            DBMS_OUTPUT.PUT_LINE ('Course Description: '||
               course_rec.description);
            DBMS_OUTPUT.PUT_LINE ('Prerequisite: '||
               course_rec.prerequisite);
      END;
```

The `course_rec` record has the same structure as a row from the COURSE table. As a result, there is no need to reference individual record fields when the SELECT INTO statement populates the `course_rec` record. However, *note that a record does not have a value of its own; rather, each individual field holds a value.* Therefore, to display record information on the screen, individual fields are referenced using the dot notation, as shown in the DBMS_OUTPUT.PUT_LINE statements.

When run, this example produces the following output:

```
Course No: 25
Course Description: Intro to Programming
Prerequisite: 140

PL/SQL procedure successfully completed.
```

As mentioned previously, a record does not have a value of its own. For this reason, you cannot test records for nullity, equality, or inequality. In other words, the statements

```
IF course_rec IS NULL THEN …
IF course_rec1 = course_rec2 THEN …
```

are illegal and will cause syntax errors.

Next, consider an example of a cursor-based record.

■ FOR EXAMPLE

```
DECLARE
   CURSOR student_cur IS
      SELECT first_name, last_name, registration_date
        FROM student
       WHERE rownum <= 4;

   student_rec student_cur%ROWTYPE;
BEGIN
   OPEN student_cur;
   LOOP
      FETCH student_cur INTO student_rec;
      EXIT WHEN student_cur%NOTFOUND;
```

```
        DBMS_OUTPUT.PUT_LINE ('Name: '||
            student_rec.first_name||' '||
            student_rec.last_name);
        DBMS_OUTPUT.PUT_LINE ('Registration Date: '||
            student_rec.registration_date);
    END LOOP;
END;
```

The `student_rec` record has the same structure as the rows returned by the STUDENT_CUR cursor. As a result, similar to the previous example, there is no need to reference individual fields when data is fetched from the cursor to the record.

When run, this example produces the following output:

```
Name: Fred Crocitto
Registration Date: 22-JAN-99
Name: J. Landry
Registration Date: 22-JAN-99
Name: Laetia Enison
Registration Date: 22-JAN-99
Name: Angel Moskowitz
Registration Date: 22-JAN-99

PL/SQL procedure successfully completed.
```

Note that because a cursor-based record is defined based on the rows returned by a select statement of a cursor, its declaration must be proceeded by a cursor declaration. In other words, *a cursor-based record is dependent on a particular cursor and cannot be declared prior to its cursor.* Consider a modified version of the previous example. The cursor-based record variable is declared before the cursor, and as a result, when run, this example causes a syntax error.

■ *FOR EXAMPLE*

```
DECLARE
    student_rec student_cur%ROWTYPE;

    CURSOR student_cur IS
        SELECT first_name, last_name, registration_date
        FROM student
        WHERE rownum <= 4;

BEGIN
    OPEN student_cur;
    LOOP
        FETCH student_cur INTO student_rec;
        EXIT WHEN student_cur%NOTFOUND;
```

```
        DBMS_OUTPUT.PUT_LINE ('Name: '||
            student_rec.first_name||' '||
            student_rec.last_name);
        DBMS_OUTPUT.PUT_LINE ('Registration Date: '||
            student_rec.registration_date);
    END LOOP;
END;


student_rec student_cur%ROWTYPE;
                    *
ERROR at line 2:
ORA-06550: line 2, column 16:
PLS-00320: the declaration of the type of this expression
is incomplete or malformed
ORA-06550: line 2, column 16:
PL/SQL: Item ignored
ORA-06550: line 12, column 30:
PLS-00320: the declaration of the type of this expression
is incomplete or malformed
ORA-06550: line 12, column 7:
PL/SQL: SQL Statement ignored
ORA-06550: line 16, column 10:
PLS-00320: the declaration of the type of this expression
is incomplete or malformed
ORA-06550: line 15, column 7:
PL/SQL: Statement ignored
ORA-06550: line 17, column 52:
PLS-00320: the declaration of the type of this expression
is incomplete or malformed
ORA-06550: line 17, column 7:
PL/SQL: Statement ignored
```

USER-DEFINED RECORDS

So far, you have seen how to create records based on a table or a cursor. However, you may need to create a record that is not based on any table or any one cursor. For such situations, PL/SQL provides a user-defined record type that allows you to have complete control over the record structure.

The general syntax for creating a user-defined record is as follows (the reserved words and phrases surrounded by brackets are optional):

```
TYPE type_name IS RECORD
    (field_name1 datatype1 [NOT NULL] [ := DEFAULT
      EXPRESSION],
     field_name2 datatype2 [NOT NULL] [ := DEFAULT
      EXPRESSION],
```

```
    ...
    field_nameN datatypeN [NOT NULL] [ := DEFAULT
    EXPRESSION]);

record_name TYPE_NAME;
```

First, a record structure is defined using the TYPE statement, where TYPE_NAME is the name of the record type that is used in the second step to declare the actual record. Enclosed in the parentheses are declarations of each record field with its name and datatype. You may also specify a NOT NULL constraint and/or assign a default value. Second, the actual record is declared based on the type specified in the previous step. Consider the following example.

■ FOR EXAMPLE

```
DECLARE
    TYPE time_rec_type IS RECORD
        (curr_date DATE,
         curr_day  VARCHAR2(12),
         curr_time VARCHAR2(8) := '00:00:00');

        time_rec TIME_REC_TYPE;
BEGIN
    SELECT sysdate
      INTO time_rec.curr_date
      FROM dual;

    time_rec.curr_day := TO_CHAR(time_rec.curr_date, 'DAY');
    time_rec.curr_time :=
        TO_CHAR(time_rec.curr_date, 'HH24:MI:SS');

    DBMS_OUTPUT.PUT_LINE ('Date: '||time_rec.curr_date);
    DBMS_OUTPUT.PUT_LINE ('Day: '||time_rec.curr_day);
    DBMS_OUTPUT.PUT_LINE ('Time: '||time_rec.curr_time);
END;
```

In this example, the `time_rec_type` is a user-defined record type that contains three fields. Notice that the last field, `curr_time`, has been initialized to a particular value. The `time_rec` is a user-defined record based on the `time_rec_type`. Notice that, different from the previous examples, each record field is assigned a value individually. When run, the script produces the following output:

```
Date: 30-MAR-02
Day: SATURDAY
Time: 18:12:59


PL/SQL procedure successfully completed.
```

As mentioned earlier, when declaring a record type you may specify a NOT NULL constraint for individual fields. It is important to note that such fields must be initialized. Consider an example that causes a syntax error because a record field has not been initialized after a NOT NULL constraint has been defined on it.

■ *FOR EXAMPLE*

```
DECLARE
   TYPE sample_type IS RECORD
      (field1 NUMBER(3),
       field2 VARCHAR2(3) NOT NULL);

   sample_rec sample_type;

BEGIN
   sample_rec.field1 := 10;
   sample_rec.field2 := 'ABC';

   DBMS_OUTPUT.PUT_LINE ('sample_rec.field1 = '||
      sample_rec.field1);
   DBMS_OUTPUT.PUT_LINE ('sample_rec.field2 = '||
      sample_rec.field2);
END;
```

```
       field2 VARCHAR2(3) NOT NULL);
       *
ERROR at line 4:
ORA-06550: line 4, column 8:
PLS-00218: a variable declared NOT NULL must have an
initialization assignment
```

Next, consider the correct version of the preceding example and its output.

■ *FOR EXAMPLE*

```
DECLARE
   TYPE sample_type IS RECORD
      (field1 NUMBER(3),
       field2 VARCHAR2(3) NOT NULL := 'ABC');
       -- initialize a NOT NULL field

   sample_rec sample_type;

BEGIN
   sample_rec.field1 := 10;

   DBMS_OUTPUT.PUT_LINE ('sample_rec.field1 = '||
      sample_rec.field1);
```

```
        DBMS_OUTPUT.PUT_LINE ('sample_rec.field2 = '||
            sample_rec.field2);
END;
```

sample_rec.field1 = 10
sample_rec.field2 = ABC

PL/SQL procedure successfully completed.

RECORD COMPATIBILITY

You have seen that a record is defined by its name, structure, and type. However, it is important to realize that two records may have the same structure yet be of a different type. As a result, there are certain restrictions that apply to the operations between different record types. Consider the following example.

▇ *FOR EXAMPLE*

```
DECLARE
    TYPE name_type1 IS RECORD
        (first_name VARCHAR2(15),
         last_name VARCHAR2(30));

    TYPE name_type2 IS RECORD
        (first_name VARCHAR2(15),
         last_name VARCHAR2(30));

    name_rec1 name_type1;
    name_rec2 name_type2;
BEGIN
    name_rec1.first_name := 'John';
    name_rec1.last_name  := 'Smith';
    name_rec2 := name_rec1; -- illegal assignment
END;
```

In this example, both records have the same structure; however, each record is of a different type. As a result, these records are not compatible with each other on the record level. In other words, an aggregate assignment statement will cause an error as follows:

```
    name_rec2 := name_rec1; -- illegal assignment
                *
ERROR at line 15:
ORA-06550: line 15, column 17:
PLS-00382: expression is of wrong type
ORA-06550: line 15, column 4:
PL/SQL: Statement ignored
```

In order to assign name_rec1 to name_rec2, you can assign each field of name_rec1 to the corresponding field of name_rec2, or you can declare name_rec2 so that it has the same datatype as name_rec1, as follows:

■ FOR EXAMPLE

```
DECLARE
    TYPE name_type1 IS RECORD
        (first_name VARCHAR2(15),
         last_name VARCHAR2(30));

    name_rec1 name_type1;
    name_rec2 name_type1;
BEGIN
    name_rec1.first_name := 'John';
    name_rec1.last_name  := 'Smith';
    name_rec2 := name_rec1; -- no longer illegal assignment
END;
```

It is important to note that the assignment restriction just mentioned applies to the user-defined records. In other words, *you can assign a table-based or a cursor-based record to a user-defined record as long as they have the same structure.* Consider the following example.

■ FOR EXAMPLE

```
DECLARE
    CURSOR course_cur IS
        SELECT *
          FROM course
         WHERE rownum <= 4;

    TYPE course_type IS RECORD
        (course_no NUMBER(38),
         description VARCHAR2(50),
         cost NUMBER(9,2),
         prerequisite NUMBER(8),
         created_by VARCHAR2(30),
         created_date DATE,
         modified_by VARCHAR2(30),
         modified_date DATE);

    course_rec1 course%ROWTYPE;        -- table-based record
    course_rec2 course_cur%ROWTYPE;    -- cursor-based record
    course_rec3 course_type;           -- user-defined record
BEGIN
    -- Populate table-based record
    SELECT *
```

```
        INTO course_rec1
       FROM course
      WHERE course_no = 10;

   -- Populate cursor-based record
   OPEN course_cur;
   LOOP
      FETCH course_cur INTO course_rec2;
      EXIT WHEN course_cur%NOTFOUND;
   END LOOP;

   course_rec1 := course_rec2;
   course_rec3 := course_rec2;
END;
```

In this example, each record is a different type; however, they are compatible with each other because all records have the same structure. As a result, this example does not cause any syntax errors.

LAB 19.1 EXERCISES

19.1.1 USE TABLE-BASED AND CURSOR-BASED RECORDS

In this exercise, you will learn more about table-based and cursor-based records.

Create the following PL/SQL script:

```
-- ch19_1a.sql, version 1.0
SET SERVEROUTPUT ON
DECLARE
   zip_rec zipcode%ROWTYPE;

BEGIN
   SELECT *
     INTO zip_rec
     FROM zipcode
    WHERE rownum < 2;
END;
```

Answer the following questions:

a) Explain the script ch19_1a.sql.

b) Modify the script so that `zip_rec` data is displayed on the screen.

c) Modify the script created in the previous exercise (ch19_1b.sql) so that `zip_rec` is defined as a cursor-based record.

d) Modify the script created in the previous exercise (ch19_1c.sql). Change the structure of the `zip_rec` record so that it contains total number of students in a given city, state, and zipcode. Do not include audit columns such as CREATED_BY and CREATED_DATE in the record structure.

19.1.2 USE USER-DEFINED RECORDS

In this exercise, you will learn more about user-defined records.

Create the following PL/SQL script:

```
-- ch19_2a.sql, version 1.0
SET SERVEROUTPUT ON
DECLARE
   CURSOR zip_cur IS
      SELECT zip, COUNT(*) students
        FROM student
       GROUP BY zip;

   TYPE zip_info_type IS RECORD
      (zip_code VARCHAR2(5),
       students INTEGER);

   zip_info_rec zip_info_type;
BEGIN
   FOR zip_rec IN zip_cur LOOP
      zip_info_rec.zip_code := zip_rec.zip;
      zip_info_rec.students := zip_rec.students;
   END LOOP;
END;
```

Answer the following questions:

a) Explain the script ch19_2a.sql.

b) Modify the script so that `zip_info_rec` data is displayed on the screen only for the first five records returned by the ZIP_CUR cursor.

c) Modify the script created in the previous exercise (ch19_2b.sql). Change the structure of the `zip_info_rec` record so that it also contains total number of instructors for a given zipcode. Populate this new record and display its data on the screen for the first five records returned by the ZIP_CUR cursor.

LAB 19.1 EXERCISE ANSWERS

This section gives you some suggested answers to the questions in Lab 19.1, with discussion related to how those answers resulted. The most important thing to realize is whether your answer works. You should figure out the implications of the answers here and what the effects are from any different answers you may come up with.

19.1.1 ANSWERS

a) Explain the script ch19_1a.sql.

Answer:The declaration portion of the script contains a declaration of the table-based record, `zip_rec`, that has the same structure as a row from the ZIPCODE table.The executable portion of the script populates the `zip_rec` record via the SELECT INTO statement with a row from the ZIPCODE table. Notice that a restriction applied to the ROWNUM enforces the SELECT INTO statement always returns a random single row. As mentioned earlier, there is no need to reference individual record fields when the SELECT INTO statement populates the `zip_rec` record because `zip_rec` has a structure identical to a row of the ZIPCODE table.

b) Modify the script so that `zip_rec` data is displayed on the screen.

Answer:Your script should look similar to the following script. Changes are shown in bold letters.

```
-- ch19_1b.sql, version 2.0
SET SERVEROUTPUT ON
DECLARE
    zip_rec zipcode%ROWTYPE;

BEGIN
    SELECT *
      INTO zip_rec
      FROM zipcode
     WHERE rownum < 2;

    DBMS_OUTPUT.PUT_LINE ('Zip:            '||
       zip_rec.zip);
    DBMS_OUTPUT.PUT_LINE ('City:           '||
       zip_rec.city);
    DBMS_OUTPUT.PUT_LINE ('State:          '||
       zip_rec.state);
    DBMS_OUTPUT.PUT_LINE ('Created By:     '||
       zip_rec.created_by);
    DBMS_OUTPUT.PUT_LINE ('Created Date:   '||
       zip_rec.created_date);
    DBMS_OUTPUT.PUT_LINE ('Modified By:    '||
       zip_rec.modified_by);
    DBMS_OUTPUT.PUT_LINE ('Modified Date:  '||
       zip_rec.modified_date);
END;
```

When run, both versions produce the same output:

```
Zip:            00914
City:           Santurce
State:          PR
Created By:     AMORRISO
Created Date:   03-AUG-99
Modified By:    ARISCHER
Modified Date: 24-NOV-99

PL/SQL procedure successfully completed.
```

c) Modify the script created in the previous exercise (ch19_1b.sql) so that
zip_rec is defined as a cursor-based record.

*Answer: Your script should look similar to the following script. Changes are shown in bold
letters.*

```
-- ch19_1c.sql, version 3.0
SET SERVEROUTPUT ON
DECLARE
    CURSOR zip_cur IS
```

```
      SELECT *
        FROM zipcode
        WHERE rownum < 4;

   zip_rec zip_cur%ROWTYPE;
BEGIN
   OPEN zip_cur;
   LOOP
      FETCH zip_cur INTO zip_rec;
      EXIT WHEN zip_cur%NOTFOUND;

      DBMS_OUTPUT.PUT_LINE ('Zip:           '||
         zip_rec.zip);
      DBMS_OUTPUT.PUT_LINE ('City:          '||
         zip_rec.city);
      DBMS_OUTPUT.PUT_LINE ('State:         '||
         zip_rec.state);
      DBMS_OUTPUT.PUT_LINE ('Created By:    '||
         zip_rec.created_by);
      DBMS_OUTPUT.PUT_LINE ('Created Date:  '||
         zip_rec.created_date);
      DBMS_OUTPUT.PUT_LINE ('Modified By:   '||
         zip_rec.modified_by);
      DBMS_OUTPUT.PUT_LINE ('Modified Date: '||
         zip_rec.modified_date);
   END LOOP;
END;
```

The declaration portion of the script contains a definition of the ZIP_CUR cursor that returns four records from the ZIPCODE table. In this case, the number of records returned by the cursor has been chosen for one reason only, so that the cursor loop iterates more than once. Next, it contains the definition of the cursor-based record, `zip_rec`.

The executable portion of the script populates the `zip_rec` record and displays its data on the screen via the simple cursor loop.

This version of the script produces the following output:

```
Zip:           00914
City:          Santurce
State:         PR
Created By:    AMORRISO
Created Date:  03-AUG-99
Modified By:   ARISCHER
Modified Date: 24-NOV-99
Zip:           01247
City:          North Adams
State:         MA
```

```
Created By:     AMORRISO
Created Date:   03-AUG-99
Modified By:    ARISCHER
Modified Date:  24-NOV-99
Zip:            02124
City:           Dorchester
State:          MA
Created By:     AMORRISO
Created Date:   03-AUG-99
Modified By:    ARISCHER
Modified Date:  24-NOV-99

PL/SQL procedure successfully completed.
```

d) Modify the script created in the previous exercise (ch19_1c.sql). Change the structure of the `zip_rec` record so that it contains total number of students in a given city, state, and zipcode. Do not include audit columns such as CREATED_BY, CREATED_DATE, MODIFIED_BY, and MODIFIED_DATE in the record structure.

Answer: Your script should look similar to the following script. All changes are shown in bold letters.

```
-- ch19_1d.sql, version 4.0
SET SERVEROUTPUT ON SIZE 40000
DECLARE
   CURSOR zip_cur IS
      SELECT city, state, z.zip, COUNT(*) students
        FROM zipcode z, student s
       WHERE z.zip = s.zip
       GROUP BY city, state, z.zip;

   zip_rec zip_cur%ROWTYPE;
BEGIN
   OPEN zip_cur;
   LOOP
      FETCH zip_cur INTO zip_rec;
      EXIT WHEN zip_cur%NOTFOUND;

      DBMS_OUTPUT.PUT_LINE ('Zip:       '||zip_rec.zip);
      DBMS_OUTPUT.PUT_LINE ('City:      '||zip_rec.city);
      DBMS_OUTPUT.PUT_LINE ('State:     '||zip_rec.state);
      DBMS_OUTPUT.PUT_LINE ('Students: '||
         zip_rec.students);
   END LOOP;
END;
```

In this example, the cursor SELECT statement has been modified so that it returns total number of students for a given city, state, and zipcode. Notice that the

ROWNUM restriction has been removed so that the total number of students is calculated correctly. As a result, the buffer size has been changed from 2000 to 40,000 so that the script does not cause a buffer overflow error.

Consider the partial output retuned by this example:

```
Zip:       07401
City:      Allendale
State:     NJ
Students:  1
Zip:       11373
City:      Amherst
State:     NY
Students:  6
Zip:       48104
City:      Ann Arbor
State:     MI
Students:  1
Zip:       11102
City:      Astoria
State:     NY
Students:  1
Zip:       11105
City:      Astoria
State:     NY
Students:  2
Zip:       11510
City:      Baldwin
State:     NY
Students:  1
Zip:       11360
City:      Bayside
State:     NY
Students:  1
...

PL/SQL procedure successfully completed.
```

Next, assume that just like in the previous version of the script (ch19_1c.sql), you would like to display only four records on the screen. This can be achieved as follows:

```
-- ch19_1e.sql, version 5.0
SET SERVEROUTPUT ON
DECLARE
   CURSOR zip_cur IS
      SELECT city, state, z.zip, COUNT(*) students
        FROM zipcode z, student s
       WHERE z.zip = s.zip
       GROUP BY city, state, z.zip;
```

```
      zip_rec zip_cur%ROWTYPE;
      v_counter INTEGER := 0;
BEGIN
      OPEN zip_cur;
      LOOP
          FETCH zip_cur INTO zip_rec;
          EXIT WHEN zip_cur%NOTFOUND;

          v_counter := v_counter + 1;

          IF v_counter <= 4 THEN
              DBMS_OUTPUT.PUT_LINE ('Zip:       '||
                  zip_rec.zip);
              DBMS_OUTPUT.PUT_LINE ('City:      '||
                  zip_rec.city);
              DBMS_OUTPUT.PUT_LINE ('State:     '||
                  zip_rec.state);
              DBMS_OUTPUT.PUT_LINE ('Students: '||
                  zip_rec.students);
          END IF;
      END LOOP;
END;
```

The SELECT statement defined in the cursor is supported by multiple versions of Oracle. As mentioned previously, Oracle 9i also supports the new ANSI 1999 SQL standard, and the SELECT statement can be modified as follows according to this new standard:

```
SELECT city, state, z.zip, COUNT(*) students
   FROM zipcode z
   JOIN student s
     ON s.zip = z.zip
GROUP BY city, state, z.zip;
```

The preceding SELECT statement uses the ON syntax to specify the join condition between two tables. This type of join becomes especially useful when the columns participating in the join do not have the same name.

You will find detailed explanations and examples of the statements using new ANSI 1999 SQL standard in Appendix E and Oracle help.

19.1.2 ANSWERS

a) Explain the script ch19_2a.sql.

Answer:The declaration portion of the script contains ZIP_CUR cursor, which returns total number of students corresponding to a particular zipcode. Next, it contains the declaration of the user-defined record type, zip_info_type, *which has two fields, and the actual user-defined record,* zip_info_rec.*The executable portion of the script populates the* zip_info_rec *record via the cursor FOR loop.As mentioned earlier, because* zip_info_rec *is a user-defined record, each record field is assigned a value individually.*

b) Modify the script so that zip_info_rec data is displayed on the screen only for the first five records returned by the ZIP_CUR cursor.

Answer:Your script should look similar to the following script. Changes are shown in bold letters.

```
-- ch19_2b.sql, version 2.0
SET SERVEROUTPUT ON
DECLARE
    CURSOR zip_cur IS
        SELECT zip, COUNT(*) students
          FROM student
          GROUP BY zip;

    TYPE zip_info_type IS RECORD
        (zip_code VARCHAR2(5),
         students INTEGER);

    zip_info_rec zip_info_type;
    v_counter INTEGER := 0;
BEGIN
    FOR zip_rec IN zip_cur LOOP
        zip_info_rec.zip_code := zip_rec.zip;
        zip_info_rec.students := zip_rec.students;

        v_counter := v_counter + 1;
        IF v_counter <= 5 THEN
            DBMS_OUTPUT.PUT_LINE ('Zip Code: '||
                zip_info_rec.zip_code);
            DBMS_OUTPUT.PUT_LINE ('Students: '||
                zip_info_rec.students);
            DBMS_OUTPUT.PUT_LINE ('--------------------');
        END IF;
    END LOOP;
END;
```

In order to display information for the first five records returned by the ZIP_CUR cursor, a new variable, `v_counter`, is declared. For each iteration of the loop, the value of this variable is incremented by one. As long as the value of `v_counter` is less than or equal to five, the data of the `zip_info_rec` record is displayed on the screen.

When run, this script produces the following output:

```
Zip Code: 01247
Students: 1
--------------------
Zip Code: 02124
Students: 1
--------------------
Zip Code: 02155
Students: 1
--------------------
Zip Code: 02189
Students: 1
--------------------
Zip Code: 02563
Students: 1
--------------------

PL/SQL procedure successfully completed.
```

c) Modify the script created in the previous exercise (ch19_2b.sql). Change the structure of the `zip_info_rec` record so that it also contains total number of instructors for a given zipcode. Populate this new record and display its data on the screen for the first five records returned by the ZIP_CUR cursor.

Answer: Your script should look similar to the following script. Changes are shown in bold letters.

```
-- ch19_2c.sql, version 3.0
SET SERVEROUTPUT ON
DECLARE
   CURSOR zip_cur IS
      SELECT zip
        FROM zipcode
       WHERE ROWNUM <= 5;

   TYPE zip_info_type IS RECORD
      (zip_code VARCHAR2(5),
       students INTEGER,
       instructors INTEGER);

   zip_info_rec zip_info_type;
BEGIN
```

```
FOR zip_rec IN zip_cur LOOP
   zip_info_rec.zip_code := zip_rec.zip;

   SELECT COUNT(*)
     INTO zip_info_rec.students
     FROM student
    WHERE zip = zip_info_rec.zip_code;

   SELECT COUNT(*)
     INTO zip_info_rec.instructors
     FROM instructor
    WHERE zip = zip_info_rec.zip_code;

   DBMS_OUTPUT.PUT_LINE ('Zip Code:    '||
      zip_info_rec.zip_code);
   DBMS_OUTPUT.PUT_LINE ('Students:    '||
      zip_info_rec.students);
   DBMS_OUTPUT.PUT_LINE ('Instructors: '||
      zip_info_rec.instructors);
   DBMS_OUTPUT.PUT_LINE ('--------------------');
 END LOOP;
END;
```

Consider the changes applied to this version of the script. In the declaration portion of the script, the cursor SELECT statement has changed so that records are retrieved from the ZIPCODE table rather than the STUDENT table. This change allows you to see accurately the total number of students and instructors in a particular zipcode. In addition, because the cursor SELECT statement does not have group function, the ROWNUM restriction is listed in the WHERE clause so that only the first five records are returned. The structure of the user-defined record type, `zip_info_type`, has changed so that total number of instructors for a given zipcode is stored in the `instructors` field.

In the executable portion of the script, there are two SELECT INTO statements that populate `zip_info_rec.students` and `zip_info_rec.instructors` fields, respectively.

When run, this example produces the following output:

```
Zip Code:    00914
Students:    0
Instructors: 0
--------------------
Zip Code:    01247
Students:    1
Instructors: 0
--------------------
Zip Code:    02124
Students:    1
```

```
Instructors: 0
-------------------
Zip Code:    02155
Students:    1
Instructors: 0
-------------------
Zip Code:    02189
Students:    1
Instructors: 0
-------------------
```

PL/SQL procedure successfully completed.

Consider another version of the same script. Here, instead of using two SELECT INTO statements to calculate the total number of students and instructors in a particular zip code, the cursor SELECT statement contains outer joins.

```
-- ch19_2d.sql, version 4.0
SET SERVEROUTPUT ON
DECLARE
   CURSOR zip_cur IS
      SELECT z.zip, COUNT(student_id) students,
             COUNT(instructor_id) instructors
        FROM zipcode z, student s, instructor i
       WHERE z.zip = s.zip (+)
         AND z.zip = i.zip (+)
       GROUP BY z.zip;

   TYPE zip_info_type IS RECORD
      (zip_code VARCHAR2(5),
       students INTEGER,
       instructors INTEGER);

   zip_info_rec zip_info_type;
   v_counter INTEGER := 0;
BEGIN
   FOR zip_rec IN zip_cur LOOP
      zip_info_rec.zip_code := zip_rec.zip;
      zip_info_rec.students := zip_rec.students;
      zip_info_rec.instructors := zip_rec.instructors;

      v_counter := v_counter + 1;
      IF v_counter <= 5 THEN
         DBMS_OUTPUT.PUT_LINE ('Zip Code:    '||
            zip_info_rec.zip_code);
         DBMS_OUTPUT.PUT_LINE ('Students:    '||
            zip_info_rec.students);
         DBMS_OUTPUT.PUT_LINE ('Instructors: '||
            zip_info_rec.instructors);
```

```
                    DBMS_OUTPUT.PUT_LINE ('--------------------');
            END IF;
        END LOOP;
    END;
```

LAB 19.1 SELF-REVIEW QUESTIONS

In order to test your progress, you should be able to answer the following questions.

1) The %ROWTYPE attribute allows you to specify

   a) _____ table-based records only.
   b) _____ cursor-based records only.
   c) _____ table-based and cursor-based records.

2) When creating a user-defined record, you must

   a) _____ initialize all of its fields.
   b) _____ initialize at least one of its fields.
   c) _____ initialize a field only if there is a NOT NULL constraint defined in it.

3) An aggregate assignment statement will cause an error if table-based and cursor-based records have the same structure.

   a) _____ True
   b) _____ False

4) An aggregate assignment statement will cause an error if two user-defined records have the same structure yet different types.

   a) _____ True
   b) _____ False

5) An aggregate assignment statement will cause an error if table-based and user-defined records have the same structure.

   a) _____ True
   b) _____ False

Answers appear in Appendix A, Section 19.1.

L A B   1 9 . 2

NESTED RECORDS

LAB OBJECTIVE

After this Lab, you will be able to:

✔ Use Nested Records

As mentioned in the introduction to this chapter, PL/SQL allows you to define nested records. These are records that contain other records and collections. The record that contains a nested record or collection is called an *enclosing record*.

Consider the following code fragment.

■ FOR EXAMPLE

```
DECLARE
    TYPE name_type IS RECORD
        (first_name VARCHAR2(15),
         last_name VARCHAR2(30));

    TYPE person_type IS
        (name name_type,
         street VARCHAR2(50),
         city VARCHAR2(25),
         state VARCHAR2(2),
         zip VARCHAR2(5));

    person_rec person_type;
```

This code fragment contains two user-defined record types. The second user-defined record type, `person_type`, is a nested record type because its field `name` is a record of the `name_type` type.

Next, consider the complete version of the preceding example.

■ FOR EXAMPLE

```
DECLARE
   TYPE name_type IS RECORD
      (first_name VARCHAR2(15),
       last_name VARCHAR2(30));

   TYPE person_type IS RECORD
      (name name_type,
       street VARCHAR2(50),
       city VARCHAR2(25),
       state VARCHAR2(2),
       zip VARCHAR2(5));

   person_rec person_type;

BEGIN
   SELECT first_name, last_name, street_address, city,
          state, zip
     INTO person_rec.name.first_name,
          person_rec.name.last_name, person_rec.street,
          person_rec.city, person_rec.state, person_rec.zip
     FROM student
     JOIN zipcode USING (zip)
    WHERE rownum < 2;

   DBMS_OUTPUT.PUT_LINE ('Name:    '||
      person_rec.name.first_name||' '||
      person_rec.name.last_name);
   DBMS_OUTPUT.PUT_LINE ('Street: '||
      person_rec.street);
   DBMS_OUTPUT.PUT_LINE ('City:    '||
      person_rec.city);
   DBMS_OUTPUT.PUT_LINE ('State:   '||
      person_rec.state);
   DBMS_OUTPUT.PUT_LINE ('Zip:     '||
      person_rec.zip);
END;
```

In this example, the person_rec record is a user-defined nested record. As a result, in order to reference its field name that is a record with two fields, the following syntax is used:

**enclosing_record.(nested_record or
nested_collection).field_name**

In this case, the person_rec is enclosing record because it contains the name record as one of its fields while the name record is nested in the person_rec record.

This example produces the following output:

```
Name:    James E. Norman
Street:  PO Box 809 Curran Hwy
City:    North Adams
State:   MA
Zip:     01247

PL/SQL procedure successfully completed.
```

LAB 19.2 EXERCISES

19.2.1 USE NESTED RECORDS

In this exercise, you will learn more about nested records.

Create the following PL/SQL script:

```
-- ch19_3a.sql, version 1.0
SET SERVEROUTPUT ON
DECLARE
   TYPE last_name_type IS TABLE OF student.last_name%TYPE
      INDEX BY BINARY_INTEGER;

   TYPE zip_info_type IS RECORD
      (zip VARCHAR2(5),
      last_name_tab last_name_type);

   CURSOR name_cur (p_zip VARCHAR2) IS
      SELECT last_name
        FROM student
       WHERE zip = p_zip;

   zip_info_rec zip_info_type;
   v_zip VARCHAR2(5) := '&sv_zip';
   v_counter INTEGER := 0;
BEGIN
   zip_info_rec.zip := v_zip;

   FOR name_rec IN name_cur (v_zip) LOOP
      v_counter := v_counter + 1;
      zip_info_rec.last_name_tab(v_counter) :=
         name_rec.last_name;
   END LOOP;
END;
```

Answer the following questions:

a) Explain the script ch19_3a.sql.

b) Modify the script so that `zip_info_rec` data is displayed on the screen. Make sure that a value of the zipcode is displayed only once. Provide the value of '11368' when running the script.

c) Modify the script created in the previous exercise (ch19_3b.sql). Instead of providing a value for a zipcode at runtime, populate via the cursor FOR loop. The SELECT statement associated with the new cursor should return zipcodes that have more than one student in them.

LAB 19.2 EXERCISE ANSWERS

This section gives you some suggested answers to the questions in Lab 19.2, with discussion related to how those answers resulted. The most important thing to realize is whether your answer works. You should figure out the implications of the answers here and what the effects are from any different answers you may come up with.

19.2.1 ANSWERS

a) Explain the script ch19_3a.sql.

Answer: The declaration portion of the script contains index-by table type, `last_name_type`, record type, `zip_info_type`, and nested-user-defined record, `zip_info_rec`, declarations. The field, `last_name_tab`, of the `zip_info_rec` is an index-by table that is populated with the help of the cursor, NAME_CUR. In addition, the declaration portion also contains two variables, `v_zip` and `v_counter`. The variable `v_zip` is used to store incoming value of the zipcode provided at runtime. The variable `v_counter` is used to populate the index-by table, `last_name_tab`. The executable portion of the script assigns values to the individual record fields, `zip` and `last_name_tab`. As mentioned previously, the `last_name_tab` is an index-by table, and it is populated via cursor FOR loop.

b) Modify the script so that `zip_info_rec` data is displayed on the screen. Make sure that a value of the zipcode is displayed only once. Provide the value of '11368' when running the script.

Answer: Your script should look similar to the following script. Changes are shown in bold letters.

```
-- ch19_3b.sql, version 2.0
SET SERVEROUTPUT ON
DECLARE
    TYPE last_name_type IS TABLE OF student.last_name%TYPE
        INDEX BY BINARY_INTEGER;

    TYPE zip_info_type IS RECORD
        (zip VARCHAR2(5),
        last_name_tab last_name_type);

    CURSOR name_cur (p_zip VARCHAR2) IS
        SELECT last_name
          FROM student
         WHERE zip = p_zip;

    zip_info_rec zip_info_type;
    v_zip VARCHAR2(5) := '&sv_zip';
    v_counter INTEGER := 0;
BEGIN
    zip_info_rec.zip := v_zip;
    DBMS_OUTPUT.PUT_LINE ('Zip: '||zip_info_rec.zip);

    FOR name_rec IN name_cur (v_zip) LOOP
        v_counter := v_counter + 1;
        zip_info_rec.last_name_tab(v_counter) :=
            name_rec.last_name;

        DBMS_OUTPUT.PUT_LINE ('Names('||v_counter||'): '||
            zip_info_rec.last_name_tab(v_counter));
    END LOOP;
END;
```

In order to display the value of the zipcode only once, the DBMS_OUTPUT.
PUT_LINE statement

```
DBMS_OUTPUT.PUT_LINE ('Zip: '||zip_info_rec.zip);
```

is placed outside the loop.

When run, this script produces the following output:

```
Enter value for sv_zip: 11368
old   15:    v_zip VARCHAR2(5) := '&sv_zip';
new   15:    v_zip VARCHAR2(5) := '11368';
Zip: 11368
Names(1): Lasseter
Names(2): Miller
Names(3): Boyd
Names(4): Griffen
```

```
Names(5): Hutheesing
Names(6): Chatman

PL/SQL procedure successfully completed.
```

c) Modify the script created in the previous exercise (ch19_3b.sql). Instead of providing a value for a zipcode at runtime, populate via cursor FOR loop. The SELECT statement associated with the new cursor should return zipcodes that have more than one student in them.

Answer:Your script should look similar to the following script. Changes are shown in bold letters.

```
-- ch19_3c.sql, version 3.0
SET SERVEROUTPUT ON SIZE 20000
DECLARE
    TYPE last_name_type IS TABLE OF student.last_name%TYPE
        INDEX BY BINARY_INTEGER;

    TYPE zip_info_type IS RECORD
        (zip VARCHAR2(5),
        last_name_tab last_name_type);

    CURSOR zip_cur IS
        SELECT zip, COUNT(*)
          FROM student
        GROUP BY zip
        HAVING COUNT(*) > 1;

    CURSOR name_cur (p_zip VARCHAR2) IS
        SELECT last_name
          FROM student
         WHERE zip = p_zip;

    zip_info_rec zip_info_type;
    v_counter INTEGER;
BEGIN
    FOR zip_rec IN zip_cur LOOP
        zip_info_rec.zip := zip_rec.zip;
        DBMS_OUTPUT.PUT_LINE ('Zip: '||zip_info_rec.zip);

        v_counter := 0;
        FOR name_rec IN name_cur (zip_info_rec.zip) LOOP
            v_counter := v_counter + 1;
            zip_info_rec.last_name_tab(v_counter) :=
                name_rec.last_name;

            DBMS_OUTPUT.PUT_LINE ('Names('||v_counter||'): '||
                zip_info_rec.last_name_tab(v_counter));
```

```
        END LOOP;
        DBMS_OUTPUT.PUT_LINE ('----------');
      END LOOP;
    END;
```

In the preceding script, you declared a new cursor called `zip_cur`. This cursor returns zipcodes that have more than one student in them. Next, in the body of the script, you use nested cursors to populate the `last_name_tab` index-by table for each value of zipcode. First, the outer cursor FOR loop populates the `zip` field of the `zip_info_rec` and displays its value on the screen. Then it passes the `zip` field as a parameter to the inner cursor FOR loop that populates `last_name_tab` table with last names of corresponding students.

Consider the partial output of the preceding example:

```
Zip: 06820
Names(1): Scrittorale
Names(2): Padel
Names(3): Kiraly
--------------------
Zip: 06830
Names(1): Dennis
Names(2): Meshaj
Names(3): Dalvi
--------------------
Zip: 06880
Names(1): Miller
Names(2): Cheevens
--------------------
Zip: 06903
Names(1): Segall
Names(2): Annina
--------------------
Zip: 07003
Names(1): Wicelinski
Names(2): Intal
--------------------
Zip: 07010
Names(1): Lopez
Names(2): Mulroy
Names(3): Velasco
Names(4): Kelly
Names(5): Tucker
Names(6): Mithane
--------------------
...

PL/SQL procedure successfully completed.
```

LAB 19.2 SELF-REVIEW QUESTIONS

In order to test your progress, you should be able to answer the following questions.

1) A record is called a nested record if it contains

a) _____ other records.
b) _____ collections.
c) _____ all of the above
d) _____ none of the above

2) When creating a nested record, you are allowed to nest only a single record or a single collection.

a) _____ True
b) _____ False

3) When creating a nested record, you must initialize

a) _____ all of the fields of the enclosing record.
b) _____ at least one of the fields of the enclosing record.
c) _____ a field of the enclosing record only if there is a NOT NULL constraint defined in it.

4) It is illegal to declare a record field as an index-by table.

a) _____ True
b) _____ False

5) It is illegal to declare a record field as a varray.

a) _____ True
b) _____ False

Answers appear in Appendix A, Section 19.2.

LAB 19.3

COLLECTIONS OF RECORDS

LAB OBJECTIVE
After this Lab, you will be able to:
✔ Use Collections of Records

In the previous lab you have seen an example of the nested record where one of the record fields was defined as an index-by table. PL/SQL also gives you ability to define a collection of records (for example, an index-by table where its element type is a cursor-based record, as shown in the following example).

■ *FOR EXAMPLE*

```
DECLARE
    CURSOR name_cur IS
        SELECT first_name, last_name
          FROM student
         WHERE ROWNUM <= 4;

    TYPE name_type IS TABLE OF name_cur%ROWTYPE
        INDEX BY BINARY_INTEGER;

    name_tab name_type;
    v_counter INTEGER := 0;
BEGIN
    FOR name_rec IN name_cur LOOP
        v_counter := v_counter + 1;

        name_tab(v_counter).first_name := name_rec.first_name;
        name_tab(v_counter).last_name := name_rec.last_name;

        DBMS_OUTPUT.PUT_LINE('First Name('||v_counter||'): '||
            name_tab(v_counter).first_name);
        DBMS_OUTPUT.PUT_LINE('Last Name('||v_counter||'): '||
```

```
                    name_tab(v_counter).last_name);
        END LOOP;
    END;
```

In this declaration portion of the example, you define the `name_cur` cursor, which returns the first and last names of the first four students. Next, you define an index-by table type with its element type based on the cursor defined previously via the %ROWTYPE attribute. Then you define an index-by table variable and the counter that is used later to reference individual rows of the index-by table.

In the executable portion of the example, you populate the index-by table and display its records on the screen. Consider the notation used in the example when referencing individual elements of the index-by table:

name_tab(v_counter).first_name and
name_tab(v_counter).last_name

Notice that to reference each row of the index-by table, you use the counter variable just like in all previous examples. However, because each row of this table is a record, you must also reference individual fields of the underlying record.

This example produces the following output:

```
First Name(1): Fred
Last Name(1): Crocitto
First Name(2): J.
Last Name(2): Landry
First Name(3): Laetia
Last Name(3): Enison
First Name(4): Angel
Last Name(4): Moskowitz

PL/SQL procedure successfully completed.
```

LAB 19.3 EXERCISES

19.3.1 USE COLLECTIONS OF RECORDS

In this exercise, you will learn more about collections of records.

Answer the following questions:

a) Modify the script used earlier in this lab. Instead of using index-by table, use nested table.

b) Modify the script used earlier in this lab. Instead of using index-by table, use a varray.

c) Modify the script used earlier in this lab. Instead of using a cursor-based record, use a user-defined record. The new record should have three fields: `first_name`, `last_name`, `enrollments`. The last field will contain total number of courses in which a student is currently enrolled.

LAB 19.3 EXERCISE ANSWERS

This section gives you some suggested answers to the questions in Lab 19.3, with discussion related to how those answers resulted. The most important thing to realize is whether your answer works. You should figure out the implications of the answers here and what the effects are from any different answers you may come up with.

19.3.1 ANSWERS

a) Modify the script used earlier in this lab. Instead of using index-by table, use nested table.

Answer: Your script should look similar to the following script. Changes are shown in bold letters.

```
-- ch19_4a.sql, version 1.0
SET SERVEROUTPUT ON
DECLARE
   CURSOR name_cur IS
      SELECT first_name, last_name
        FROM student
       WHERE ROWNUM <= 4;

   TYPE name_type IS TABLE OF name_cur%ROWTYPE;

   name_tab name_type := name_type();
   v_counter INTEGER := 0;
BEGIN
   FOR name_rec IN name_cur LOOP
      v_counter := v_counter + 1;
      name_tab.EXTEND;
```

```
        name_tab(v_counter).first_name := name_rec.first_name;
        name_tab(v_counter).last_name := name_rec.last_name;

        DBMS_OUTPUT.PUT_LINE('First Name('||v_counter||'): '||
            name_tab(v_counter).first_name);
        DBMS_OUTPUT.PUT_LINE('Last Name('||v_counter||'): '||
            name_tab(v_counter).last_name);
    END LOOP;
END;
```

In the preceding script, the name_tab is declared as a nested table. As a result, at the time of its declaration it is initialized. In other words, the name_tab is empty but non-null. Furthermore, once the name_tab table is initialized, its size must be increased before it can be populated with the next record.

b) Modify the script used earlier in this lab. Instead of using index-by table, use a varray.

Answer: Your script should look similar to the following script. Changes are shown in bold letters.

```
-- ch19_4b.sql, version 2.0
SET SERVEROUTPUT ON
DECLARE
    CURSOR name_cur IS
        SELECT first_name, last_name
          FROM student
         WHERE ROWNUM <= 4;

    TYPE name_type IS VARRAY(4) OF name_cur%ROWTYPE;

    name_tab name_type := name_type();
    v_counter INTEGER := 0;
BEGIN
    FOR name_rec IN name_cur LOOP
        v_counter := v_counter + 1;
        name_tab.EXTEND;

        name_tab(v_counter).first_name := name_rec.first_name;
        name_tab(v_counter).last_name := name_rec.last_name;

        DBMS_OUTPUT.PUT_LINE('First Name('||v_counter||'): '||
            name_tab(v_counter).first_name);
        DBMS_OUTPUT.PUT_LINE('Last Name('||v_counter||'): '||
            name_tab(v_counter).last_name);
    END LOOP;
END;
```

In this version of the script, the name_tab is declared as a varray with four elements. Just like in the previous version, the collection is initialized and its size is incremented before it is populated with the new record.

Both scripts, ch19_4a.sql and ch19_4b.sql, produce the output identical to the original example:

```
First Name(1): Fred
Last Name(1): Crocitto
First Name(2): J.
Last Name(2): Landry
First Name(3): Laetia
Last Name(3): Enison
First Name(4): Angel
Last Name(4): Moskowitz

PL/SQL procedure successfully completed.
```

c) Modify the script used earlier in this lab. Instead of using a cursor-based record, use a user-defined record. The new record should have three fields: first_name, last_name, enrollments. The last field will contain total number of courses in which a student is currently enrolled.

Answer: Your script should look similar to the following script. Changes are shown in bold letters.

```
-- ch19_4c.sql, version 3.0
SET SERVEROUTPUT ON
DECLARE
    CURSOR name_cur IS
        SELECT first_name, last_name, COUNT(*) total
          FROM student
          JOIN enrollment USING (student_id)
        GROUP BY first_name, last_name;

    TYPE student_rec_type IS RECORD
        (first_name VARCHAR2(15),
         last_name VARCHAR2(30),
         enrollments INTEGER);

    TYPE name_type IS TABLE OF student_rec_type
        INDEX BY BINARY_INTEGER;

    name_tab name_type;
    v_counter INTEGER := 0;
BEGIN
    FOR name_rec IN name_cur LOOP
        v_counter := v_counter + 1;
```

```
        name_tab(v_counter).first_name := name_rec.first_name;
        name_tab(v_counter).last_name := name_rec.last_name;
        name_tab(v_counter).enrollments := name_rec.total;

        IF v_counter <= 4 THEN
           DBMS_OUTPUT.PUT_LINE('First Name('||v_counter||
              '): '||name_tab(v_counter).first_name);
           DBMS_OUTPUT.PUT_LINE('Last Name('||v_counter||
              '): '||name_tab(v_counter).last_name);
           DBMS_OUTPUT.PUT_LINE('Enrollments('||
              v_counter||'): '||name_tab(v_counter).
              enrollments);
           DBMS_OUTPUT.PUT_LINE ('--------------------');
        END IF;
     END LOOP;
  END;
```

In the declaration portion of the script, the cursor SELECT statement has been modified so that for each student it returns total number of enrollments. Next, the user-defined record type, student_rec_type, is declared so that it can be used as the element type for the index-by table type, name_type.

In the executable portion of the script, the index-by table, name_tab, is populated via the cursor FOR loop. Next, the index counter variable, v_counter, is evaluated via the IF-THEN statement so that only first four records of the index-by table are displayed on the screen.

When run, this script produces the following output:

```
First Name(1): A.
Last Name(1): Tucker
Enrollments(1): 1
--------------------
First Name(2): Adele
Last Name(2): Rothstein
Enrollments(2): 1
--------------------
First Name(3): Adrienne
Last Name(3): Lopez
Enrollments(3): 1
--------------------
First Name(4): Al
Last Name(4): Jamerncy
Enrollments(4): 1
--------------------


PL/SQL procedure successfully completed.
```

LAB 19.3 SELF-REVIEW QUESTIONS

In order to test your progress, you should be able to answer the following questions.

1) Collections of records are not supported by Oracle 9i.

   a) _____ True
   b) _____ False

2) A varray of records has an upper bound

   a) _____ that is fixed and cannot be extended to all.
   b) _____ that can be extended to its maximum size.
   c) _____ that can be extended without any limits.

3) There is no need to initialize a nested table of records prior to its use.

   a) _____ True
   b) _____ False

4) There is no need to increase the size of a nested table of records before it is populated with a new record.

   a) _____ True
   b) _____ False

5) It is illegal to use a user-defined record as an element type when creating a collection of records.

   a) _____ True
   b) _____ False

Answers appear in Appendix A, Section 19.3.

**LAB
19.3**

CHAPTER 19

TEST YOUR THINKING

In this chapter, you learned about various types of records, nested records, and collections of records. Here are some projects that will help you test the depth of your understanding.

1) Create the following script. Create an index-by table with the element type of a user-defined record. This record should contain first name, last name, and the total number of courses that a particular instructor teaches. Display the records of the index-by table on the screen.

2) Modify the script created in project (1). Instead of using an index-by table, use a nested table.

3) Modify the script created in project (2). Instead of using a nested table, use a varray.

4) Create the following script. Create a user-defined record with three fields: `course_no`, `description`, `cost`, and `prerequisite_rec`. The last field, `prerequisite_rec`, should be a user-defined record with three fields: `prereq_no`, `prereq_desc`, and `prereq_cost`. For any ten courses that have a prerequisite course, populate the user-defined record with all corresponding data and display its information on the screen.

The projects in this section are meant to have you utilize all of the skills that you have acquired throughout this chapter. The answers to these projects can be found in Appendix D and at the companion Web site to this book, located at http://www.phptr.com/rosezweig2e. Visit the Web site periodically to share and discuss your answers.

APPENDIX A

ANSWERS TO SELF-REVIEW QUESTIONS

CHAPTER 1 PROGRAMMING CONCEPTS

Lab 1.1 ■ Self-Review Answers

Questions	Answers	Comments
1)	A	Machine language is the native language of a particular computer; hence, it is easiest for a computer to understand.
2)	B	Machine language is defined by the hardware of a computer; thus, it is machine-specific.
3)	B	The interpreter translates each statement in the program into machine language and executes it immediately before the next statement is examined.
4)	B	A program must be compiled in order to create an executable that can then run as many times as needed.
5)	A	Because a computer cannot understand statements written in the assembly language, they must be translated into machine language with the help of an assembler.

Lab 1.2 ■ Self-Review Answers

Questions	Answers	Comments
1)	C	
2)	B	Structured programming allows you to organize your program into subroutines so each one focuses on a particular part of the overall problem. The control is then transferred between these subroutines.
3)	B	Linear execution of code assumes that statements are executed in the order they appear.

4)	A	If the test condition does not evaluate to TRUE, the selection statements are not executed.
5)	B	A SELECT statement may be formatted perfectly and still produce incorrect results.

CHAPTER 2 PL/SQL CONCEPTS

Lab 2.1 ■ Self-Review Answers

Questions	Answers	Comments
1)	B	When the SELECT statements are combined into a PL/SQL program, they are sent to the server as a single unit thus reducing network traffic.
2)	B	Executable section is the only mandatory section for a PL/SQL block. As a result,

```
BEGIN
    NULL;   -- null statement
END;
```

is a valid PL/SQL block.

3)	B	When a runtime error occurs in the PL/SQL block, control is passed to the exception-handling section of the block, where the error is evaluated and a specific exception is raised or executed.
4)	A	A PL/SQL compiler is able to detect only syntax errors. It cannot detect any runtime errors because they do not occur prior to the execution of the program.
5)	B	For named PL/SQL blocks, p-code is generated and stored in the database at the time of compilation. When named PL/SQL block is executed, its p-code is retrieved from the database and executed. For anonymous PL/SQL blocks, p-code is not stored in the database and is generated every time the PL/SQL block is executed.

Lab 2.2 ■ Self-Review Answers

Questions	Answers	Comments
1)	B	A semicolon is a terminating symbol of an individual statement in the PL/SQL block.
2)	A	Substitution variables are used for input values only. They cannot be used to output values because no memory is allocated for them.
3)	A	The statement DBMS_OUTPUT.PUT_LINE uses dot notation as follows:

```
package_name.procedure_name
```

where package_name is the name of the package and procedure_name is the name of the procedure defined in the package.

4)	A	When a program completes, the information from the buffer is displayed on the screen.
5)	C	When the SET SERVEROUPUT ON command is used without specifying the size if the buffer, it enables the DBMS_OUTPUT.PUT_LINE statement and the default buffer size is used. The SIZE option changes the default buffer size to the specified size.

CHAPTER 3 GENERAL PROGRAMMING LANGUAGE FUNDAMENTALS

Lab 3.1 ■ Self-Review Answers

Questions	Answers	Comments
1)	A	
2)	B	
3)	A, B, C, E	
4)	D	
5)	A	

CHAPTER 4 SQL IN PL/SQL

Lab 4.1 ■ Self-Review Answers

Questions	Answers	Comments
1)	B, D	
2)	A, D	You cannot create a table or sequence within a PL/SQL block.
3)	C	
4)	A, B, D	A sequence will generate unique numbers, but you cannot count it as a method to generate contiguous number.

Lab 4.2 ■ Self-Review Answers

Questions	Answers	Comments
1)	B	When you issue a ROLLBACK it only applies to the current session of the user you are logged in as. It has no effect on other sessions.
2)	A, C	
3)	D	
4)	B	

CHAPTER 5 CONDITIONAL CONTROL: IF STATEMENTS

Lab 5.1 ■ Self-Review Answers

Questions	Answers	Comments
1)	C	The statements in an IF construct are not executed sequentially. Rather, one group of statements or another will be

selected to execute depending on how a test condition is
evaluated.

2)	A	Only when the condition evaluates to TRUE, the statement of an IF-THEN construct are executed. When the condition evaluates to FALSE or NULL, the control is passed to the first executable statement after the IF-THEN construct. As a result, its statements are not executed at all.
3)	B	When a condition of the IF-THEN-ELSE construct is evaluated to NULL, the statements specified after keyword ELSE will be executed. In other words, the IF-THEN-ELSE construct behaves as if the condition evaluated to FALSE.
4)	B	You can specify only two actions in an IF-THEN-ELSE statement. Furthermore, these actions should be mutually exclusive.
5)	B	The condition of the IF-THEN-ELSE construct can evaluate to TRUE, FALSE, or NULL. When the condition evaluates to TRUE, one group of statements is executed. When the condition evaluates to FALSE or NULL, another group of statement is executed. Hence, the IF-THEN-ELSE construct enables you to specify two and only two mutually exclusive groups of statements.

Lab 5.2 ■ Self-Review Answers

Questions	Answers	Comments
1)	B	An ELSIF construct can have multiple ELSIF clauses, but only one ELSE clause.
2)	B	
3)	C	The ELSE part is executed when none of the conditions evaluate to TRUE.
4)	C	As soon as the first condition evaluates to TRUE, statements associated with it are executed. The rest of the ELSIF statement is ignored.
5)	B	ELSE is an optional part of an ELSIF statement.

Lab 5.3 ■ Self-Review Answers

Questions	Answers	Comments
1)	C	There are no restrictions on how various types of IF statements can be nested one inside another.
2)	C	
3)	B	You can use different logical operators when writing complex conditions. While there are no restrictions on the number of the logical operators present in a condition, you should be aware of precedence rules. For example,

```
x >= 3 OR x <= 5 AND y > 7
```

may produce a result different from

```
(x >= 3 OR x <= 5) AND x > 7
```
for the same values of x and y.

4)	A	There is no need for the conditions of nested IF statements to be mutually exclusive. For example,

```
IF v_num > 0 THEN
    IF v_num < 0 THEN
        ...
    END IF;
END IF;
```

When v_num is greater than 0, the condition of the inner IF statement will evaluate to FALSE. When v_num is less than or equal to 0, the condition of the outer IF statement will evaluate to FALSE. Thus, the inner IF statement will never execute regardless of the value of v_num.

5)	C	The behavior of an IF statement does not change based on its placement in the block. In other words, if a condition of any IF statement (outer or inner) evaluates to FALSE, the control is always passed to the first executable statement after END IF. It is important to remember that this behavior does not apply to IF-THEN-ELSE and ELSIF.

CHAPTER 6 CONDITIONAL CONTROL: CASE STATEMENTS

Lab 6.1 ■ Self-Review Answers

Questions	Answers	Comments
1)	C	The statements in a CASE construct are not executed sequentially. Rather, one group of statements or another will be selected to execute depending on how test conditions are evaluated.
2)	B	
3)	B	The selector is evaluated only once, and the value of each expression is compared to the value of the selector sequentially.
4)	A	The behavior of a searched CASE construct is similar to the behavior of an IF statement. In other words, if all conditions of the CASE construct evaluate to NULL and there is no ELSE clause present, the control will be passed to the first executable statement after END CASE.
5)	A	

Lab 6.2 ■ Self-Review Answers

Questions	Answers	Comments
1)	A	A keyword here is *expression*. You will recall that an expression returns a single value.
2)	C	

3)	B	Similar to CASE statements, there are CASE and searched CASE expressions.
4)	A	The behavior of a CASE expression is similar to the behavior of a CASE statement. In other words, if all conditions of the CASE expression evaluate to NULL and there is no ELSE clause present, the expression returns NULL.
5)	A	As mentioned earlier, the keyword here is *expression*. Because an expression returns a single value, it must return a single datatype.

Lab 6.3 ■ Self-Review Answers

Questions	Answers	Comments
1)	A	
2)	B	The NULLIF function does the opposite of the NVL function. If the first expression is NULL, then NVL returns the second expression. If the first expression is not NULL, then NVL returns the first expression.
3)	B	When the literal NULL is used in the first expression of the NULLIF function, it causes a syntax error.
4)	A	
5)	B	As long as one of the expressions in the COALESCE function does not contain NULL, the COALESCE function executes successfully. For example,

```
COALESCE(NULL, 5)
```

returns the value of 5. On the other hand,

```
COALESCE(NULL, NULL)
```

causes a syntax error.

CHAPTER 7 ERROR HANDLING AND BUILT-IN EXCEPTIONS

Lab 7.1 ■ Self-Review Answers

Questions	Answers	Comments
1)	B	A compiler is able to detect only syntax errors. It cannot detect any runtime errors because they do not occur prior to the execution of the program. Furthermore, a runtime error generally occurs only on some occasions, and not the others.
2)	B	An exception-handling section is an optional section of a PL/SQL block. You will recall that only executable section is a required section of a PL/SQL block.
3)	B	
4)	B	
5)	B, C	Both options are correct. However, you should remember that the value of number 1 is not important. It is number 2

that causes an exception to be raised when its value is equal to zero.

Lab 7.2 ■ Self-Review Answers

Questions	Answers	Comments
1)	A	You will recall that a built-in exception is raised when a program breaks an Oracle rule. In other words, you do not need to specify how to raise a built-in exception, rather, what actions must be taken when a particular built-in exception is raised. A built-in exception will be raised by Oracle implicitly.
2)	B	
3)	B	When a group function is used in the SELECT INTO statement, there is at least one row returned. As a result, exception NO_DATA_FOUND is not raised.
4)	B	Once an exception has been raised in a PL/SQL block, the execution of the block terminates.
5)	B	An exception-handling section may contain multiple exception handlers. For example, NO_DATA_FOUND and OTHERS.

CHAPTER 8 ITERATIVE CONTROL

Lab 8.1 ■ Self-Review Answers

Questions	Answers	Comments
1)	C	If there is no EXIT condition specified, a simple loop becomes an infinite loop. In other words, a sequence of statements will be executed an infinite number of times because there is no statement specifying when the loop must terminate.
2)	B	As soon as the EXIT statement is encountered, the loop is terminated.
3)	A	As long as the EXIT condition does not evaluate to TRUE, the control is never transferred to the EXIT statement. This will prevent a loop from terminating. For example,

```
IF x > 5 THEN
    EXIT;
END IF;
```

In this case, the EXIT condition is a test condition of the IF statement. When the test condition of the IF statement evaluates to FALSE or NULL, the control is passed to the first executable statement after END IF.

Questions	Answers	Comments
4)	C	Once EXIT statement is executed, the control is transferred to the first executable statement after END LOOP.

5)	B	An EXIT condition of a simple loop is located inside the body of the loop. Therefore, the loop will always execute partly before the EXIT condition is evaluated.

Lab 8.2 ■ Self-Review Answers

Questions	Answers	Comments
1)	A	Before a WHILE loop is executed, its test condition is evaluated. If the test condition yields FALSE, the WHILE loop is unable to execute.
2)	C	If a test condition always evaluates to TRUE, the WHILE loop is unable to terminate. As a result, it executes infinite number of times.
3)	B, C	
4)	A	You will recall that a test condition must evaluate to FALSE or NULL for a WHILE loop to terminate. On the other hand, the EXIT condition must evaluate to TRUE. Thus, if the EXIT condition evaluates to TRUE before the test condition evaluates to FALSE, the WHILE loop terminates prematurely.
5)	A	If a test condition of a WHILE loop never evaluates to TRUE, the loop does not execute at all.

Lab 8.3 ■ Self-Review Answers

Questions	Answers	Comments
1)	B	For the first iteration of the loop, the value of the loop counter is equal to the lower limit. For the second iteration of the loop, the value of the loop counter is implicitly incremented by 1. At this point, the value of the loop counter does not satisfy the range specified by the lower limit and the upper limit, so the loop terminates. For example,

```
BEGIN
    FOR i IN 1..1 LOOP
        DBMS_OUTPUT.PUT_LINE ('i = '||i);
    END LOOP;
END;
/
i = 1

PL/SQL procedure successfully completed.
```

Questions	Answers	Comments
2)	A	The loop counter is unable to satisfy the range specified by the lower and upper limits.
3)	C	The loop counter is implicitly defined by the loop construct. As a result, it does not exist anywhere outside the loop.
4)	C	
5)	B	The loop counter is initialized to the upper limit, and it is decremented by 1 for each iteration of the loop.

Lab 8.4 ■ Self-Review Answers

Questions	Answers	Comments
1)	C	
2)	B	Loop labels are optional feature and are used to improve readability.
3)	B	
4)	B	It is considered bad programming practice to use the same name for different variables. When the same name is used for the loop counters, you are unable to reference the outer loop counter in the body of the inner loop. In order to differentiate between two variables having the same name, you must use loop labels when the variables are referenced.
5)	B	You must use loop labels only when outer and inner loop counters have the same name and you want to reference the outer loop counter in the inner loop. In other cases, it is not necessary to use a loop label when referencing the loop counter.

CHAPTER 9 INTRODUCTION TO CURSORS

Lab 9.1 ■ Self-Review Answers

Questions	Answers	Comments
1)	B	
2)	None	Cursor attributes are used for getting information about cursors. They cannot be used to control or close cursors.
3)	1-B Declare, 2-E Open, 3-A Fetch, 4-C Close	
4)	D	Cursor attributes can be use with both implicit and explicit cursors.
5)	D	

Lab 9.2 ■ Self-Review Answers

Questions	Answers	Comments
1)	A	
2)	B	
3)	B	
4)	B	A child cursor in a nested cursor loop will open, loop, and then close for each iteration of the parent loop.
5)	C	

Lab 9.3 ■ Self-Review Answers

Questions	Answers	Comments
1)	A	
2)	A, B, E	
3)	C	
4)	C	
5)	A	A WHERE CURRENT clause in a FOR UPDATE cursor allows you to update a row without having to match the row in the WHERE clause.

CHAPTER 10 EXCEPTIONS

Lab 10.1 ■ Self-Review Answers

Questions	Answers	Comments
1)	C	If an exception is defined in the inner block, it can be raised in the inner block only. The outer block is not included in the scope of such an exception.
2)	B	Once an exception has been raised in the inner block and handled in the outer block, the control is passed to the enclosing environment.
3)	B	Once an exception occurs in the outer block, PL/SQL tries to find its handler in the outer block. PL/SQL will never search the inner block for the exception handler when the exception occurs in the outer block.
4)	B	In order to define an exception inside the body of the loop, you must define the PL/SQL block inside the body of the loop. Therefore, when an exception is raised, it will terminate the block, and the control will be transferred to the first executable statement after END. For example,

```
FOR i IN 1..3 LOOP
    BEGIN
        SELECT first_name
          INTO v_first_name
          FROM student
         WHERE student_id = 123;
    EXCEPTION
        WHEN NO_DATA_FOUND THEN
            DBMS_OUTPUT.PUT_LINE ('Error');
    END;
END LOOP;
```

In this case, if there is no student corresponding to student ID 123, the exception NO_DATA_FOUND is raised. This causes the PL/SQL block to terminate. However, as long as the value of the loop counter ranges between lower and upper limits, the PL/SQL block will be executed repeatedly.

5)	B	When you want to specify the same action for various exceptions, you can combine these exceptions in the single WHEN clause. The exceptions are included in the WHEN clause with the help of the OR operator.

Lab 10.2 ■ Self-Review Answers

Questions	Answers	Comments
1)	B	A user-defined exception is declared and raised. The exception must be declared because it is defined by a programmer and is not provided by the system. The exception must be raised explicitly because it handles violation of application rules, not Oracle rules. For example, a negative value provided by a user for the student ID violates the application rule because an ID cannot be negative, yet it does not violate Oracle rules because a number can be negative.
2)	B	
3)	B	If a user-defined exception has been declared in the inner block, it can be raised in the inner block. However, it ceases to exist once the control is transferred to the outer block, and, as a result, it cannot be raised in the outer block. Any reference to such exception in the outer block will cause a syntax error.
4)	B	A user-defined exception behaves similarly to an Oracle built-in exception.
5)	A	The IF-THEN statement evaluates a condition that causes an application error. Once this condition yields TRUE, the RAISE statement raises a user-defined error associated with the application error. The IF-THEN statement by itself will not raise an exception. On the other hand, the RAISE statement by itself will always raise an exception.

Lab 10.3 ■ Self-Review Answers

Questions	Answers	Comments
1)	B	Once an exception is raised in the declaration section of a block, the control is always transferred to the enclosing environment. In the case of an inner block, the control is transferred to the exception-handling section of the outer block.
2)	B	An exception encountered in the declaration section of any block causes the control to be transferred outside the block. When such a block is not enclosed by another PL/SQL block, the control is transferred to the host environment. This causes a syntax error.
3)	A	

4)	B	Re-raising an exception causes the control to transfer outside the block. In case of an inner block, the control is transferred to the exception-handling section of the outer block.
5)	B	

CHAPTER 11 EXCEPTIONS: ADVANCED CONCEPTS

Lab 11.1 ■ Self-Review Answers

Questions	Answers	Comments
1)	C	RAISE_APPLICATION_ERROR associates an error number with an error text. Therefore, when working with the RAISE_APPLICATION_ERROR there is no need to create an exception name.
2)	C	RAISE_APPLICTION_ERROR has two required parameters, error_number and error_text. The keep_error is an optional parameter that is usually omitted.
3)	A	Generally, Oracle associates negative numbers with run-time errors. For user-defined exceptions, the range of such numbers is from –20,000 to –20,999.
4)	A	When the RAISE_APPLICATION_ERROR procedure is used, control is always passed to the host environment. For example, if an exception is raised in an inner block, it never propagates to the outer block.
5)	C	

Lab 11.2 ■ Self-Review Answers

Questions	Answers	Comments
1)	B	EXCEPTION_INIT pragma is a special instruction to the compiler. It allows handling of unnamed internal exceptions. Such exceptions can also be handled with the help of OTHERS.
2)	B	Because pragma is a special instruction to the compiler, it is processed during compilation time.
3)	C	Some Oracle errors do not have names, and as a result they cannot be referenced in a program. The EXCEPTION_INIT pragma allows you to associate an Oracle error number with a user-defined error.
4)	C	In order to associate an Oracle error with a user-defined exception, the EXCEPTION_INIT pragma requires both error number and name.
5)	C	Error_number is a numeric parameter and should contain any valid Oracle error number; 'ORA' is not a part of an error number.

Lab 11.3 ■ Self-Review Answers

Questions	Answers	Comments
1)	A	
2)	A	
3)	C	
4)	C	
5)	B	When no exception is raised, the SQLCODE function returns 0. When there is a NO_DATA_FOUND exception, SQLCODE function returns 100.

CHAPTER 12 PROCEDURES

Lab 12.2 ■ Self-Review Answers

Questions	Answers	Comments
1)	C	
2)	A, C, D, E	There is no foot section in stored code. The specification can be called the header, but the body is never called footer.
3)	B	An OUT parameter is not a required component of a procedure.
4)	A, B, D	C is a valid definition for the declarative section; all header definitions refer to IN, OUT, or IN/OUT parameters.
5)	B	The USER_SOURCE view shows the text for code in valid and invalid objects.

CHAPTER 13 FUNCTIONS

Lab 13.1 ■ Self-Review Answers

Questions	Answers	Comments
1)	D	
2)	B	A function can have IN, OUT, and IN OUT parameters, but it is considered bad style to have anything but IN parameters in a function.
3)	D	
4)	C	
5)	C, D	

CHAPTER 14 PACKAGES

Lab 14.1 ■ Self-Review Answers

Questions	Answers	Comments
1)	B	When a package is first called, all the procedures and functions in that package are brought into memory and will run quickly when they are used in the same session.

2)	A	
3)	B	Procedures and functions that are not declared in the package specification will be private.
4)	C	
5)	B	A package specification is a database object and must be compiled prior to compiling the package body. This can be done in one or two scripts.

CHAPTER 15 ADVANCED CURSORS

Lab 15.1 ■ Self-Review Answers

Questions	Answers	Comments
1)	True	
2)	A, B, D	%ROWTYPE is only used with declaration of variables.
3)	C	
4)	C	
5)	A	The WHERE CURRENT clause in a FOR UPDATE cursor allows you to update a row without having to match the row in the WHERE clause.

CHAPTER 16 STORED CODE

Lab 16.1 ■ Self-Review Answers

Questions	Answers	Comments
1)	B	The USER_ERRORS view only has details on code that is currently in an invalid state. Once the code becomes valid, it will no longer be present in the USER_ERRORS view.
2)	A	The DESC command can be used on tables and packages. It will give different results for tables and packages.
3)	B	Only functions within packages require pragma restrictions used in SQL statements.
4)	C	
5)	B	

CHAPTER 17 TRIGGERS

Lab 17.1 ■ Self-Review Answers

Questions	Answers	Comments
1)	C	
2)	B	Once a trigger has been defined on a particular table, it fires implicitly when a triggering event occurs. By default, when a trigger is created it is also enabled. Once you disable a trigger, it will not fire when a triggering event occurs.

3)   A   The WHEN condition controls when a trigger should fire. If such a condition does not evaluate to TRUE, the trigger will not fire.

4)   C

5)   D   A trigger fires before or after a triggering event: INSERT, UPDATE, or DELETE. A SELECT operation is not a triggering event. It reads information from a triggering table without modifying it.

Lab 17.2 ■ Self-Review Answers

Questions	Answers	Comments
1)	A	
2)	B	A statement trigger fires once per DML statement issued. In other word, if there is a statement trigger that fires before an UPDATE statement is issued against a triggering table, it will fire once regardless of number of rows affected by the UPDATE statement.
3)	B	
4)	B	It is important to remember that even though an INSTEAD OF trigger is defined on a view, it manipulates underlying database tables.
5)	B	An INSTEAD OF trigger can never be a statement trigger.

Lab 17.3 ■ Self-Review Answers

Questions	Answers	Comments
1)	B	You cannot issue an SQL statement against the triggering table in the body of the trigger.
2)	B	Any SQL statement (INSERT, UPDATE, DELETE, and SELECT) against the triggering table inside the body of the trigger will cause a mutating table error.
3)	B	You are able to issue SQL statements against any table but the triggering table in the body of a trigger. In other words, it there is a trigger defined on the STUDENT table, you can issue a SELECT statement against the ZIPCODE table in the body of the trigger. This will not cause any error. However, if you issue a SELECT statement against the STUDENT table, you will get a mutating table error when the trigger fires. You will recall that a mutating table error is a runtime error and is not be detected by the PL/SQL compiler.
4)	C	
5)	C	You will recall that a constraining table restriction is applicable to Oracle versions prior to 8i.

CHAPTER 18 COLLECTIONS

Lab 18.1 ■ Self-Review Answers

Questions	Answers	Comments
1)	A	
2)	C	You will recall that a following is always used in an index-by table declaration `INDEX BY BINARY_INTEGER;`
3)	A	A nested table is automatically NULL when it is declared. As a result, it must be initialized prior to its use.
4)	C	If a PL/SQL table contains only one element, it is its first and last element. As a result, the FIRST method returns the subscript of the first element, 1, and the LAST method returns the subscript of the last element, 1.
5)	C	It is important to remember that a PL/SQL table in this case is a nested table. You will recall that the DELETE method cannot be used with a nested table.

Lab 18.2 ■ Self-Review Answers

Questions	Answers	Comments
1)	A	You will recall that using a DELETE method on varrays causes a syntax error because varrays are dense.
2)	B	A varray can contain a number of elements, varying from zero (empty array) to its maximum size. In other words, an upper bond of the array can be extended to its maximum size.
3)	A	
4)	C	The COUNT method returns the current number of varray elements, and the LIMIT method returns the maximum number of elements that a varray can contain.
5)	D	Because varrays cannot be sparse, a DELETE method causes a syntax error when it is issued against a varray.

Lab 18.3 ■ Self-Review Answers

Questions	Answers	Comments
1)	A	
2)	B	Regardless of its element type, an upper bound of a varray can be extended to its maximum size.
3)	B	A nested table must be initialized prior to its use regardless its element data type.
4)	C	Consider the statement `varray2(2)(3)` In this statement you are referencing the second element of `varray2` and third element of `varray1`. Each element

of `varray2` is a varray of three integers defined as `varray1`. Recall the following declaration statement:

```
varray2 varray_type2 :=
    varray_type2(varray1, varray_type1
    (4, 5, 6));
```

where `varray_type1(4, 5, 6)` is the second element of the `varray2`. Notice that the third element of `varray1` is 6. As a result, the variable `var1` is assigned a value of 6.

5)   B   You will recall that the PL/SQL block contains the following statements:

```
varray2.EXTEND;
varray2(3) := varray_type1(0);
varray2(3).EXTEND;
```

The first statement increases the size of the `varray2`. In other words, this statement adds the third element to the collection. The second statement initializes the third element of the `varray2` via constructor associated with the varray type `varray_type1`. This is done because each element of the `varray2` is a varray of three integers. This adds one element to the `varray1`. The third statement increases the size of the `varray1` by adding a placeholder for the second element. In other words, it adds the second element to the third element of `varray2`.

CHAPTER 19 RECORDS

Lab 19.1 ■ Self-Review Answers

Questions	Answers	Comments
1)	C	%ROWTYPE means "based on a row." This row may be based on a database table row or on a row returned by a cursor.
2)	C	When a field with a NOT NULL constraint is not initialized, a user-defined record causes an error.
3)	B	You are able to assign a table-based record to a cursor-based record and vice versa. This restriction applies to user-defined records that have the same structure yet different data types.
4)	A	An aggregate assignment statement between two user-defined records causes an error where the records are not based on the same type.
5)	B	A table-based record can be assigned to a user-defined record as long as they have the same structure. This restriction applies to user-defined records that have the same structure yet different data types.

Lab 19.2 ■ Self-Review Answers

Questions	Answers	Comments
1)	C	
2)	B	
3)	C	You must initialize each field that has a NOT NULL constraint specified on it regardless of the record type.
4)	B	A nested record may contain any collection as one of its fields.
5)	B	

Lab 19.3 ■ Self-Review Answers

Questions	Answers	Comments
1)	B	
2)	B	A varray has an upper bound that can be extended to its maximum size. The data type of its individual elements has no effect on how the upper bound is extended.
3)	B	You must always initialize a nested table regardless of its element type.
4)	B	You must always increase the size of a nested table before populating it with a new record regardless of its element type.
5)	B	You can use user-defined, table-based, or cursor-based records when creating a collection of records.

A P P E N D I X   B

PL/SQL FORMATTING GUIDE

PL/SQL CODE NAMING CONVENTIONS AND FORMATTING GUIDELINES

CASE

PL/SQL, like SQL, is case insensitive. The general guidelines here are as follows:

- Use uppercase for keywords (BEGIN, EXCEPTION, END, IF THEN ELSE, LOOP, END LOOP, etc.), datatypes (VARCHAR2, NUMBER), built-in functions (LEAST, SUBSTR, etc.), and user-defined subroutines (procedures, functions, packages).
- Use lowercase for variable names as well as column and table names in SQL.

WHITE SPACE

White space (extra lines and spaces) is as important in PL/SQL as it is in SQL. It is a main factor in providing readability. In other words, you can reveal the logical structure of the program by using indentation in your code. Here are some suggestions:

- Put spaces on both sides of an equality sign or comparison operator.
- Line up structure words on the left (DECLARE, BEGIN, EXCEPTION, and END, IF and END IF, LOOP and END LOOP, etc.). In addition, indent three spaces (use the spacebar, not the tab key) for structures within structures.
- Put blank lines between major sections to separate them from each other.
- Put different logical parts of the same structure on a separate lines even if the structure is short. For example, IF and THEN are placed on one line, while ELSE and END IF are placed on separate lines.

NAMING CONVENTIONS

To ensure against conflicts with keywords and column/table names, it is helpful to use the following prefixes:

- `v_variable_name`
- `con_constant_name`
- `i_in_parameter_name, o_out_parameter_name, io_in_out_parameter_name`
- `c_cursor_name` or `name_cur`
- `rc_reference_cursor_name`
- `r_record_name` or `name_rec`

  `FOR r_stud IN c_stud LOOP...`

  `FOR stud_rec IN stud_cur LOOP`
- `type_name, name_type` (for user-defined types)
- `t_table, name_tab` (for PL/SQL tables)
- `rec_record_name, name_rec` (for record variables)
- `e_exception_name` (for user-defined exceptions)

The name of a package should be the name of the larger context of the actions performed by the procedures and functions contained within the package.

The name of a procedure should be the action description that is performed by the procedure. The name of a function should be the description of the return variable.

■ FOR EXAMPLE

```
PACKAGE student_admin
    -- admin suffix may be used for administration.

    PROCEDURE remove_student
        (i_student_id IN student.studid%TYPE);

    FUNCTION student_enroll_count
        (i_student_id student.studid%TYPE)
    RETURN INTEGER;
```

COMMENTS

Comments in PL/SQL are as important as in SQL. They should explain the main sections of the program and any major nontrivial logic steps.

Use single-line comments "--" instead of the multiline "/*" comments. While PL/SQL treats these comments in the same way, it will be easier for you to debug the code once it is completed because you cannot embed multiline comments within multiline comments. In other words, you are able to comment out portions of code that contain single-line comments, and you are unable to comment out portions of code that contain multiline comments.

OTHER SUGGESTIONS

- For SQL statements embedded in PL/SQL, use the same formatting guidelines to determine how the statements should appear in a block.
- Provide a comment header that explains the intent of the block, lists the creation date and author's name, and have a line for each revision with the author's name, date, and the description of the revision.

■ FOR EXAMPLE

The following example shows the aforementioned suggestions. Notice that it also uses a monospaced font (Courier) that makes the formatting easier. Proportional spaced fonts can hide spaces and make lining up clauses difficult. Most text and programming editors by default use a monospace font.

```
REM ****************************************************************
REM * filename: coursediscount01.sql              version: 1
REM * purpose:  To give discounts to courses that have at
REM *           least one section with an enrollment of more
REM *           than 10 students.
REM * args:     none
REM *
REM * created by:  s.tashi        date: January 1, 2000
REM * modified by: y.sonam        date: February 1, 2000
REM * description: Fixed cursor, added indentation and
REM *              comments.
REM ****************************************************************
DECLARE
   -- C_DISCOUNT_COURSE finds a list of courses that have
   -- at least one section with an enrollment of at least 10
   -- students.
   CURSOR c_discount_course IS
      SELECT DISTINCT course_no
        FROM section sect
       WHERE 10 <= (SELECT COUNT(*)
                      FROM enrollment enr
                     WHERE enr.section_id = sect.section_id
                   );

   -- discount rate for courses that cost more than $2000.00
   con_discount_2000 CONSTANT NUMBER := .90;
```

```
   -- discount rate for courses that cost between $1001.00
   -- and $2000.00
   con_discount_other CONSTANT NUMBER := .95;

   v_current_course_cost course.cost%TYPE;
   v_discount_all NUMBER;
   e_update_is_problematic EXCEPTION;
BEGIN
   -- For courses to be discounted, determine the current
   -- and new cost values
   FOR r_discount_course in c_discount_course LOOP
      SELECT cost
        INTO v_current_course_cost
        FROM course
       WHERE course_no = r_discount_course.course_no;

      IF v_current_course_cost > 2000 THEN
         v_discount_all := con_discount_2000;
      ELSE
         IF v_current_course_cost > 1000 THEN
            v_discount_all :=  con_discount_other;
         ELSE
            v_discount_all := 1;
         END IF;
      END IF;

      BEGIN
         UPDATE course
            SET cost = cost * v_discount_all
          WHERE course_no = r_discount_course.course_no;
      EXCEPTION
         WHEN OTHERS THEN
            RAISE e_update_is_problematic;
      END;    -- end of sub-block to update record
   END LOOP; -- end of main LOOP

   COMMIT;

EXCEPTION
   WHEN e_update_is_problematic THEN
      -- Undo all transactions in this run of the program
      ROLLBACK;
      DBMS_OUTPUT.PUT_LINE
         ('There was a problem updating a course cost.');
   WHEN OTHERS THEN
      NULL;
END;
/
```

A P P E N D I X C

STUDENT DATABASE SCHEMA

TABLE AND COLUMN DESCRIPTIONS

COURSE: Information for a course

Column Name	Null	Type	Comments
COURSE_NO	NOT NULL	NUMBER(8, 0)	The unique course number
DESCRIPTION	NULL	VARCHAR2(50)	The full name for this course
COST	NULL	NUMBER(9,2)	The dollar amount charged for enrollment in this course
PREREQUISITE	NULL	NUMBER(8, 0)	The ID number of the course that must be taken as a prerequisite to this course
CREATED_BY	NOT NULL	VARCHAR2(30)	Audit column—indicates user who inserted data
CREATED_DATE	NOT NULL	DATE	Audit column—indicates date of insert
MODIFIED_BY	NOT NULL	VARCHAR2(30)	Audit column—indicates who made last update
MODIFIED_DATE	NOT NULL	DATE	Audit column—date of last update

SECTION: Information for an individual section (class) of a particular course

Column Name	Null	Type	Comments
SECTION_ID	NOT NULL	NUMBER(8,0)	The unique ID for a section
COURSE_NO	NOT NULL	NUMBER(8,0)	The course number for which this is a section
SECTION_NO	NOT NULL	NUMBER(3)	The individual section number within this course
START_DATE_TIME	NULL	DATE	The date and time on which this section meets
LOCATION	NULL	VARCHAR2(50)	The meeting room for the section
INSTRUCTOR_ID	NOT NULL	NUMBER(8,0)	The ID number of the instructor who teaches this section
CAPACITY	NULL	NUMBER(3,0)	The maximum number of students allowed in this section
CREATED_BY	NOT NULL	VARCHAR2(30)	Audit column—indicates user who inserted data
CREATED_DATE	NOT NULL	DATE	Audit column—indicates date of insert
MODIFIED_BY	NOT NULL	VARCHAR2(30)	Audit column—indicates who made last update
MODIFIED_DATE	NOT NULL	DATE	Audit column—date of last update

STUDENT: Profile information for a student

Column Name	Null	Type	Comments
STUDENT_ID	NOT NULL	NUMBER(8,0)	The unique ID for a student
SALUTATION	NULL	VARCHAR2(5)	This student's title (Ms., Mr., Dr., etc.)
FIRST_NAME	NULL	VARCHAR2(25)	This student's first name
LAST_NAME	NOT NULL	VARCHAR2(25)	This student's last name
STREET_ADDRESS	NULL	VARCHAR2(50)	This student's street address
ZIP	NOT NULL	VARCHAR2(5)	The postal zipcode for this student

PHONE	NULL	VARCHAR2(15)	The phone number for this student, including area code
EMPLOYER	NULL	VARCHAR2(50)	The name of the company where this student is employed
REGISTRATION_DATE	NOT NULL	DATE	The date this student registered in the program
CREATED_BY	NOT NULL	VARCHAR2(30)	Audit column—indicates user who inserted data
CREATED_DATE	NOT NULL	DATE	Audit column—indicates date of insert
MODIFIED_BY	NOT NULL	VARCHAR2(30)	Audit column—indicates who made last update
MODIFIED_DATE	NOT NULL	DATE	Audit column—date of last update

ENROLLMENT: Information for a student registered for a particular section of a particular course (class)

Column Name	Null	Type	Comments
STUDENT_ID	NOT NULL	NUMBER(8,0)	The ID for a student
SECTION_ID	NOT NULL	NUMBER(8,0)	The ID for a section
ENROLL_DATE	NOT NULL	DATE	The date this student registered for this section
FINAL_GRADE	NULL	NUMBER(3,0)	The final grade given to this student for all work in this section (class)
CREATED_BY	NOT NULL	VARCHAR2(30)	Audit column—indicates user who inserted data
CREATED_DATE	NOT NULL	DATE	Audit column—indicates date of insert
MODIFIED_BY	NOT NULL	VARCHAR2(30)	Audit column—indicates who made last update
MODIFIED_DATE	NOT NULL	DATE	Audit column—date of last update

INSTRUCTOR: Profile information for an instructor

Column Name	Null	Type	Comments
INSTRUCTOR_ID	NOT NULL	NUMBER(8)	The unique ID for an instructor
SALUTATION	NULL	VARCHAR2(5)	This instructor's title (Mr., Ms., Dr., Rev., etc.)
FIRST_NAME	NULL	VARCHAR2(25)	This instructor's first name
LAST_NAME	NULL	VARCHAR2(25)	This instructor's last name
STREET_ADDRESS	NULL	VARCHAR2(50)	This instructor's street address
ZIP	NULL	VARCHAR2(5)	The postal zipcode for this instructor
PHONE	NULL	VARCHAR2(15)	The phone number for this instructor, including area code
CREATED_BY	NOT NULL	VARCHAR2(30)	Audit column—indicates user who inserted data
CREATED_DATE	NOT NULL	DATE	Audit column—indicates date of insert
MODIFIED_BY	NOT NULL	VARCHAR2(30)	Audit column—indicates who made last update
MODIFIED_DATE	NOT NULL	DATE	Audit column—date of last update

ZIPCODE: City, state, and zipcode information

Column Name	Null	Type	Comments
ZIP	NOT NULL	VARCHAR2(5)	The zipcode number, unique for a city and state
CITY	NULL	VARCHAR2(25)	The city name for this zipcode
STATE	NULL	VARCHAR2(2)	The postal abbreviation for the U.S. state
CREATED_BY	NOT NULL	VARCHAR2(30)	Audit column—indicates user who inserted data
CREATED_DATE	NOT NULL	DATE	Audit column—indicates date of insert
MODIFIED_BY	NOT NULL	VARCHAR2(30)	Audit column—indicates who made last update
MODIFIED_DATE	NOT NULL	DATE	Audit column—date of last update

GRADE_TYPE: Lookup table of a grade type (code) and its description

Column Name	Null	Type	Comments
GRADE_TYPE_CODE	NOT NULL	CHAR(2)	The unique code that identifies a category of grade (e.g., MT, HW)
DESCRIPTION	NOT NULL	VARCHAR2(50)	The description for this code (e.g., Midterm, Homework)
CREATED_BY	NOT NULL	VARCHAR2(30)	Audit column—indicates user who inserted data
CREATED_DATE	NOT NULL	DATE	Audit column—indicates date of insert
MODIFIED_BY	NOT NULL	VARCHAR2(30)	Audit column—indicates who made last update
MODIFIED_DATE	NOT NULL	DATE	Audit column—date of last update

GRADE_TYPE_WEIGHT: Information on how the final grade for a particular section is computed; for example, the midterm constitutes 50%, the quiz 10%, and the final examination 40% of the final grade

Column Name	Null	Type	Comments
SECTION_ID	NOT NULL	NUMBER(8)	The ID for a section
GRADE_TYPE_CODE	NOT NULL	CHAR(2)	The code which identifies a category of grade
NUMBER_PER_SECTION	NOT NULL	NUMBER(3)	How many of these grade types can be used in this section (i.e., there may be three quizzes)
PERCENT_OF_FINAL_GRADE	NOT NULL	NUMBER(3)	The percentage this category of grade contributes to the final grade
DROP_LOWEST	NOT NULL	CHAR(1)	Is the lowest grade in this type removed when determining the final grade? (Y/N)
CREATED_BY	NOT NULL	VARCHAR2(30)	Audit column—indicates user who inserted data
CREATED_DATE	NOT NULL	DATE	Audit column—indicates date of insert
MODIFIED_BY	NOT NULL	VARCHAR2(30)	Audit column—indicates who made last update
MODIFIED_DATE	NOT NULL	DATE	Audit column—date of last update

GRADE: The individual grades a student received for a particular section (class)

Column Name	Null	Type	Comments
STUDENT_ID	NOT NULL	NUMBER(8)	The ID for a student
SECTION_ID	NOT NULL	NUMBER(8)	The ID for a section
GRADE_TYPE_CODE	NOT NULL	CHAR(2)	The code that identifies a category of grade
GRADE_CODE_ OCCURRENCE	NOT NULL	NUMBER(38)	The sequence number of one grade type for one section. For example, there could be multiple assignments numbered 1, 2, 3, etc.
NUMERIC_GRADE	NOT NULL	NUMBER(3)	Numeric grade value (e.g., 70, 75)
COMMENTS	NULL	VARCHAR2(2000)	Instructor's comments on this grade
CREATED_BY	NOT NULL	VARCHAR2(30)	Audit column—indicates user who inserted data
CREATED_DATE	NOT NULL	DATE	Audit column—indicates date of insert
MODIFIED_BY	NOT NULL	VARCHAR2(30)	Audit column—indicates who made last update
MODIFIED_DATE	NOT NULL	DATE	Audit column—date of last update

GRADE_CONVERSION: Converts a number grade to a letter grade

Column Name	Null	Type	Comments
LETTER_GRADE	NOT NULL	VARCHAR(2)	The unique grade as a letter (A, A–, B, B+, etc.)
GRADE_POINT	NOT NULL	NUMBER(3,2)	The number grade on a scale from 0 (F) to 4 (A)
MAX_GRADE	NOT NULL	NUMBER(3)	The highest grade number that corresponds to this letter grade
MIN_GRADE	NOT NULL	NUMBER(3)	The lowest grade number that corresponds to this letter grade
CREATED_BY	NOT NULL	VARCHAR2(30)	Audit column—indicates user who inserted data
CREATED_DATE	NOT NULL	DATE	Audit column—indicates date of insert
MODIFIED_BY	NOT NULL	VARCHAR2(30)	Audit column—indicates who last made update
MODIFIED_DATE	NOT NULL	DATE	Audit column—date of last update

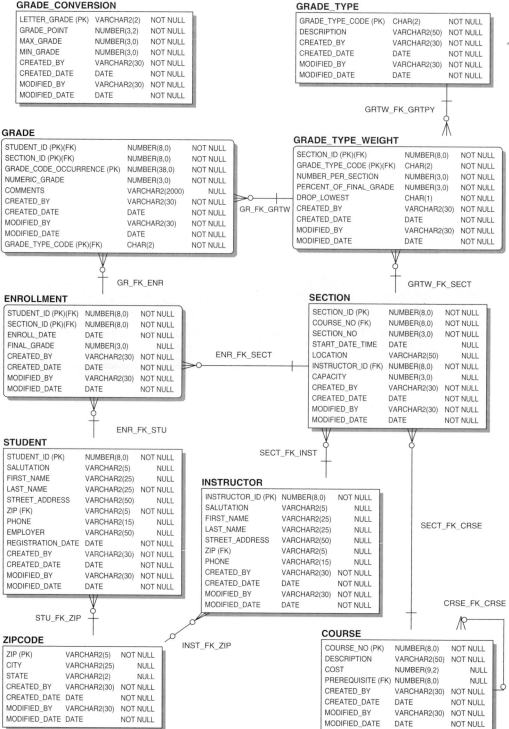

APPENDIX D

ANSWERS TO TEST YOUR THINKING SECTIONS

CHAPTER 1 PROGRAMMING CONCEPTS

1) Create the following structure: Based on the value of a number, determine if it is even or odd. *Hint:* Before you decide how to define even and odd numbers, you should decide what structure must be used to achieve the desired results.

Answer: Your answer should look similar to the following:

```
IF MOD(NUMBER, 2) = 0
    DISPLAY 'THIS NUMBER IS EVEN'
IF MOD(NUMBER, 2) != 0
    DISPLAY 'THIS NUMBER IS ODD'
```

In this example, you are using the selection structure because a decision whether a number is even or odd must be made. This decision can be made with the help of the built-in function MOD. This function returns the remainder of the NUMBER divided by 2. If a number is divisible by 2 (in other words, there is no remainder), then it is an even number. Otherwise, a number is an odd number.

Assume that the number is equal to 16. The value returned by the MOD(16,2) is equal to 0. So the selection structure displays a message 'THIS NUMBER IS EVEN'. Next, assume that the number is equal to 7. The value returned by MOD(7,2) is equal to 1. So the select structure displays a message 'THIS NUMBER IS ODD'.

2) Create the following structure: The structure you created in the previous exercise is designed to work with a single number. Modify it so that it can work with a list of numbers.

Answer: Your answer should look similar to the following:

```
WHILE THERE ARE MORE NUMBERS
   IF MOD(NUMBER, 2) = 0
      DISPLAY 'THIS NUMBER IS EVEN'
   IF MOD(NUMBER, 2) != 0
      DISPLAY 'THIS NUMBER IS ODD'
GO TO THE NEXT NUMBER
```

This structure is a combination of two structures: iteration and selection. The iteration structure repeats its steps for each number in the list. The selection structure makes a decision based on a particular number.

Assume that you have three numbers in your list: 10, 25, and 36. You start with the first number, 10. There are two more numbers left in the list. Next, the control of the flow is passed to the selection structure. Because the current number equals 10, the value returned by the MOD function is equal to 0. As a result, the message 'THIS NUMBER IS EVEN' is displayed. Then the control of the flow passed back to the iteration structure, and you are ready to move to the next number. The next number is equal to 25, and the value retuned by the MOD function is equal to 1. As a result, the message 'THIS NUMBER IS ODD' is displayed. Next, the control of the flow is passed back to the iteration structure to process the last number in the list, 36. This is an even number, so the selection structure displays the message 'THIS NUMBER IS EVEN'.

CHAPTER 2 PL/SQL CONCEPTS

1) In order to calculate the area of a circle, the circle's radius must be squared and then multiplied by π. Write a program that calculates the area of a circle. The value for the radius should by provided with the help of the substitution variable. Use 3.14 for the value of π. Once the area of the circle is calculated, display it on the screen.

Answer: Your answer should look similar to the following:

```
SET SERVEROUTPUT ON
DECLARE
   v_radius NUMBER := &sv_radius;
   v_area NUMBER;
BEGIN
   v_area := POWER(v_radius, 2) * 3.14;
   DBMS_OUTPUT.PUT_LINE
      ('The area of the circle is: '||v_area);
END;
```

In this exercise, you declare two variables, v_radius and v_area, to store the values for the radius of the circle and its area, respectively. Next, you compute the value for the variable v_area with the help of the built-in function POWER and the value of the v_radius. Finally, you display the value of the v_area on the screen.

Assume that number 5 has been entered for the value of the variable v_radius. Then the script produces the following output:

```
Enter value for sv_radius: 5
old   2:    v_radius NUMBER := &sv_radius;
new   2:    v_radius NUMBER := 5;
The area of the circle is: 78.5

PLSQL procedure successfully completed.
```

2) Rewrite the script ch02_2b.sql, version 2.0. In the output produced by the script, extra spaces appear after the day of the week. The new script must remove the extra spaces after the day of the week.

The current output is

```
Today is Friday    , 23:09
```

The new output should have the following format:

```
Today is Friday, 23:09
```

Answer: Your answer should look similar to the following. All changes are shown in bold letters:

```
SET SERVEROUTPUT ON
DECLARE
    v_day VARCHAR2(20);
BEGIN
    v_day := TO_CHAR(SYSDATE, 'fmDay, HH24:MI');
    DBMS_OUTPUT.PUT_LINE ('Today is '|| v_day);
END;
```

In this script, you modify the format in which you would like to display the date. Notice that the word 'Day' is now prefixed by the letters 'fm'. These letters guarantee that extra spaces will be removed from the name of the day. When run, this exercise produces the following output:

```
Today is Tuesday, 18:54

PLSQL procedure successfully completed.
```

CHAPTER 3 GENERAL PROGRAMMING LANGUAGE FUNDAMENTALS

1) Write a PL/SQL block
   a) That includes declarations for the following variables:

   A VARCHAR2 datatype that can contain the string 'Introduction to Oracle PL/SQL'

   A NUMBER that can be assigned 987654.55, but not 987654.567 or 9876543.55

A CONSTANT (you choose the correct datatype) that is auto-initialized to the value '603D'

A BOOLEAN

A DATE datatype auto-initialized to one week from today

b) In the body of the PL/SQL block, put a DBMS_OUTPUT.PUT_LINE message for each of the variables that received an auto initialization value.

c) In a comment at the bottom of the PL/SQL block, state the value of your number datatype.

Answer: Your answer should look similar to the following:

```
SET SERVEROUTPUT ON
DECLARE
    -- A VARCHAR2 datatype that can contain the string
    -- 'Introduction to Oracle PL/SQL'
    v_descript VARCHAR2(35);

    -- A NUMBER that allows for the conditions: can be
    -- assigned 987654.55 but not 987654.567
    -- or 9876543.55
    v_number_test NUMBER(8,2);

    -- [a variable] auto initialized to the value '603D'
    v_location CONSTANT VARCHAR2(4) := '603D';

    -- A BOOLEAN
    v_boolean_test BOOLEAN;

    -- A DATE datatype auto initialized to one week from
    -- today
    v_start_date DATE := TRUNC(SYSDATE) + 7;

BEGIN
    DBMS_OUTPUT.PUT_LINE
        ('The location is: '||v_location||'.');
    DBMS_OUTPUT.PUT_LINE
        ('The starting date is: '||v_start_date||'.');
END;
```

2) Alter the PL/SQL block you just created to conform to the following specs.

a) Remove the DBMS_OUTPUT.PUT_LINE messages.

b) In the body of the PL/SQL block, write a selection test (IF) that does the following (use a nested if statement where appropriate):

i) Check if the VARCHAR2 you created contains the course named 'Introduction to Underwater Basketweaving'.

ii) If it does, then put a DBMS_OUTPUT.PUT_LINE message on the screen that says so.

      iii) If it does not, then test to see if the CONSTANT you created contains
      the room number 603D.

      iv) If it does, then put a DBMS_OUTPUT.PUT_LINE message on the screen
      that states the course name and the room name that you've reached in
      this logic.

      v) If it does not, then put a DBMS_OUTPUT.PUT_LINE message on the
      screen that states that the course and location could not be deter-
      mined.

c) Add a WHEN OTHERS EXCEPTION that puts a DBMS_OUTPUT.PUT_
LINE message on the screen that says that an error occurred.

Answer:Your answer should look similar to the following:

```
SET SERVEROUT ON
DECLARE
    -- A VARCHAR2 datatype that can contain the string
    -- 'Introduction to Oracle PL/SQL'
    v_descript VARCHAR2(35);

    -- A NUMBER that allows for the conditions: can be
    -- assigned  987654.55 but not 987654.567 or
    -- 9876543.55
    v_number_test NUMBER(8,2);

    -- [a variable] auto initialized to the value '603D'
    v_location CONSTANT VARCHAR2(4) := '603D';

    -- A BOOLEAN
    v_boolean_test BOOLEAN;

    -- A DATE datatype auto initialized to one week from today
    v_start_date DATE := TRUNC(SYSDATE) + 7;
BEGIN
    IF v_descript =
       'Introduction to Underwater Basketweaving'
    THEN
        DBMS_OUTPUT.PUT_LINE
           ('This course is '||v_descript||'.');

    ELSIF v_location = '603D' THEN

        -- No value has been assigned to v_descript
        IF v_descript IS NOT NULL THEN
           DBMS_OUTPUT.PUT_LINE ('The course is '||v_descript
                ||'.'||' The location is '||v_location||'.');
        ELSE
```

```
                  DBMS_OUTPUT.PUT_LINE ('The course is unknown.'||
                     ' The location is '||v_location||'.');
           END IF;
        ELSE
           DBMS_OUTPUT.PUT_LINE ('The course and location '||
               'could not be determined.');
        END IF;
     EXCEPTION
        WHEN OTHERS THEN
           DBMS_OUTPUT.PUT_LINE ('An error occurred.');
     END;
```

CHAPTER 4 SQL IN PLSQL

1) Create a table called CHAP4 with two columns; one is ID (a number) and the second is NAME, which is a varchar2(20).

Answer: Your answer should look similar to the following:

```
PROMPT Creating Table 'CHAP4'
  CREATE TABLE chap4
    (id NUMBER,
     name VARCHAR2(20));
```

2) Create a sequence called CHAP4_SEQ that increments by units of 5.

Answer: Your answer should look similar to the following:

```
PROMPT Creating Sequence 'CHAP4_SEQ'
  CREATE SEQUENCE chap4_seq
      NOMAXVALUE
      NOMINVALUE
      NOCYCLE
      NOCACHE;
```

3) Write a PL/SQL block that performs the following in this order:
  a) Declares two variables, one for the v_name and one for v_id. The v_name variable can be used throughout the block for holding the name that will be inserted, realize that the value will change in the course the block.
  b) The block then inserts into the table the name of the student that is enrolled in the most classes and uses a sequence for the ID; afterward there is SAVEPOINT A.
  c) Then the student with the least enrollments is inserted; afterward there is SAVEPOINT B.
  d) Then the instructor who is teaching the maximum number of courses is inserted in the same way. Afterward there is SAVEPOINT C.
  e) Using a SELECT INTO statement, hold the value of the instructor in the variable v_id.

f) Undo the instructor insert by the use of rollback.

g) Insert the instructor teaching the least amount of courses, but do not use the sequence to generate the ID; instead use the value from the first instructor, whom you have since undone.

h) Now insert the instructor teaching the most number of courses and use the sequence to populate his ID.

Add DBMS_OUTPUT throughout the block to display the values of the variables as they change. (This is a good practice for debugging.)

Answer: Your answer should look similar to the following:

```
DECLARE
    v_name  student.last_name%TYPE;
    v_id    student.student_id%TYPE;
BEGIN
   BEGIN
      -- A second block is used to capture the possibility of
      -- multiple students meeting this requirement.
      -- The exception section will handles this situation
      SELECT s.last_name
        INTO v_name
        FROM student s, enrollment e
       WHERE s.student_id = e.student_id
      HAVING COUNT(*) = (SELECT MAX(COUNT(*))
                           FROM student s, enrollment e
                          WHERE s.student_id = e.student_id
                          GROUP BY s.student_id)
      GROUP BY s.last_name;
   EXCEPTION
      WHEN TOO_MANY_ROWS THEN
         v_name := 'Multiple Names';
   END;

   INSERT INTO CHAP4
   VALUES (CHAP4_SEQ.NEXTVAL, v_name);
   SAVEPOINT A;

   BEGIN
      SELECT s.last_name
        INTO v_name
        FROM student s, enrollment e
       WHERE s.student_id = e.student_id
      HAVING COUNT(*) = (SELECT MIN(COUNT(*))
                           FROM student s, enrollment e
                          WHERE s.student_id = e.student_id
                          GROUP BY s.student_id)
      GROUP BY s.last_name;
   EXCEPTION
```

```
    WHEN TOO_MANY_ROWS THEN
        v_name := 'Multiple Names';
END;

INSERT INTO CHAP4
VALUES (CHAP4_SEQ.NEXTVAL, v_name);
SAVEPOINT B;

BEGIN
    SELECT i.last_name
      INTO v_name
      FROM instructor i, section s
     WHERE s.instructor_id = i.instructor_id
    HAVING COUNT(*) = (SELECT MAX(COUNT(*))
                         FROM instructor i, section s
                        WHERE s.instructor_id =
                                i.instructor_id
                        GROUP BY i.instructor_id)
    GROUP BY i.last_name;
EXCEPTION
    WHEN TOO_MANY_ROWS THEN
        v_name := 'Multiple Names';
END;

SAVEPOINT C;

BEGIN
    SELECT instructor_id
      INTO v_id
      FROM instructor
     WHERE last_name = v_name;
EXCEPTION
    WHEN NO_DATA_FOUND THEN
        v_id := 999;
END;

INSERT INTO CHAP4
VALUES (v_id, v_name);
ROLLBACK TO SAVEPOINT B;

BEGIN
    SELECT i.last_name
      INTO v_name
      FROM instructor i, section s
     WHERE s.instructor_id = i.instructor_id
    HAVING COUNT(*) = (SELECT MIN(COUNT(*))
                         FROM instructor i, section s
                        WHERE s.instructor_id =
                                i.instructor_id
```

```
                        GROUP BY i.instructor_id)
     GROUP BY i.last_name;
  EXCEPTION
    WHEN TOO_MANY_ROWS THEN
       v_name := 'Multiple Names';
  END;

  INSERT INTO CHAP4
  VALUES (v_id, v_name);

  BEGIN
     SELECT i.last_name
       INTO v_name
       FROM instructor i, section s
      WHERE s.instructor_id = i.instructor_id
     HAVING COUNT(*) = (SELECT MAX(COUNT(*))
                          FROM instructor i, section s
                         WHERE s.instructor_id =
                                   i.instructor_id
                         GROUP BY i.instructor_id)
     GROUP BY i.last_name;
  EXCEPTION
     WHEN TOO_MANY_ROWS THEN
        v_name := 'Multiple Names';
  END;

  INSERT INTO CHAP4
  VALUES (CHAP4_SEQ.NEXTVAL, v_name);
END;
```

CHAPTER 5 CONDITIONAL CONTROL: IF STATEMENTS

1) Rewrite ch05_1a.sql. Instead of getting information from the user for the variable
v_date, define its value with the help of the function SYSDATE. After it has
been determined that a certain day falls on the weekend, check to see if the time
is before or after noon. Display the time of the day together with the day.

*Answer: Your answer should look similar to the following. All changes are shown in bold
letters.*

```
SET SERVEROUTPUT ON
DECLARE
   v_day VARCHAR2(15);
   v_time VARCHAR(8);
BEGIN
   v_day := TO_CHAR(SYSDATE, 'fmDAY');
   v_time := TO_CHAR(SYSDATE, 'HH24:MI');

   IF v_day IN ('SATURDAY', 'SUNDAY') THEN
```

```
        DBMS_OUTPUT.PUT_LINE (v_day||', '||v_time);
        IF v_time BETWEEN '12:01' AND '24:00' THEN
            DBMS_OUTPUT.PUT_LINE ('It''s afternoon');
        ELSE
            DBMS_OUTPUT.PUT_LINE ('It''s morning');
        END IF;
    END IF;

    -- control resumes here
    DBMS_OUTPUT.PUT_LINE('Done...');
END;
```

In this exercise, you remove variable v_date that was used to store date provided by a user. Instead, you add variable v_time to store the time of the day. You also modify the statement

```
v_day := TO_CHAR(SYSDATE, 'fmDAY');
```

so that 'DAY' is prefixed by letters 'fm'. This guarantees that extra spaces will be removed from the name of the day. Then you add another statement that determines current time of the day and stores it in the variable v_time. Finally, you add an IF-THEN-ELSE statement that checks the time of the day and displays the appropriate message.

Notice that two single quotes are used in the second and third DBMS_OUTPUT. PUT_LINE statements. This allows you to use an apostrophe in your message.

When run, this exercise produces the following output:

```
SUNDAY, 16:19
It's afternoon
Done...

PLSQL procedure successfully completed.
```

2) Create a new script. For a given instructor, determine how many sections he or she is teaching. If the number is greater than or equal to 3, display a message saying that the instructor needs a vacation. Otherwise, display a message saying how many sections this instructor is teaching.

Answer: Your answer should look similar to the following:

```
SET SERVEROUTPUT ON
DECLARE
    v_instructor_id NUMBER := &sv_instructor_id;
    v_total NUMBER;
BEGIN
    SELECT COUNT(*)
```

```
      INTO v_total
      FROM section
     WHERE instructor_id = v_instructor_id;

   -- check if instructor teaches 3 or more sections
   IF v_total >= 3 THEN
      DBMS_OUTPUT.PUT_LINE ('This instructor needs '||
         a vacation');
   ELSE
      DBMS_OUTPUT.PUT_LINE ('This instructor teaches '||
         v_total||' sections');
   END IF;
   -- control resumes here
   DBMS_OUTPUT.PUT_LINE ('Done...');
END;
```

This script accepts a value for instructor's ID from a user. Next, it checks the number of sections taught by given instructor. This is accomplished with the help of the SELECT INTO statement. Next, it determines what message should be displayed on the screen with the help of IF-THEN-ELSE statement. If a particular instructor teaches three or more sections, the condition of the IF-THEN-ELSE statement evaluates to TRUE, and the message 'This instructor needs a vacation' is displayed to the user. In the opposite case, the message stating how many sections instructor is teaching is displayed. Assume that value 101 was provided at the runtime. Then the script produces the following output:

```
Enter value for sv_instructor_id: 101
old    2:    v_instructor_id NUMBER := &sv_instructor_id;
new    2:    v_instructor_id NUMBER := 101;
This instructor needs a vacation

PLSQL procedure successfully completed.
```

3) Execute the following two PL/SQL blocks and explain why they produce different output for the same value of the variable v_num. Remember to issue the SET SERVEROUTPUT ON command before running this script.

```
-- Block 1
DECLARE
   v_num NUMBER := NULL;
BEGIN
   IF v_num > 0 THEN
      DBMS_OUTPUT.PUT_LINE ('v_num is greater than 0');
   ELSE
      DBMS_OUTPUT.PUT_LINE ('v_num is not greater than 0');
   END IF;
END;
```

```
-- Block 2
DECLARE
   v_num NUMBER := NULL;
BEGIN
   IF v_num > 0 THEN
      DBMS_OUTPUT.PUT_LINE ('v_num is greater than 0');
   END IF;
   IF NOT (v_num > 0) THEN
      DBMS_OUTPUT.PUT_LINE ('v_num is not greater than 0');
   END IF;
END;
```

Answer: Consider outputs produced by the preceding scripts:

```
-- Block1
v_num is not greater than 0

PLSQL procedure successfully completed.

-- Block 2
PLSQL procedure successfully completed.
```

The outputs produced by Block 1 and Block 2 are different, even though in both exam-ples variable v_num *has been defined as NULL.*

First, take a closer look at the IF-THEN-ELSE statement used in Block 1:

```
IF v_num > 0 THEN
   DBMS_OUTPUT.PUT_LINE ('v_num is greater than 0');
ELSE
   DBMS_OUTPUT.PUT_LINE ('v_num is not greater than 0');
END IF;
```

The condition v_num > 0 *evaluates to FALSE because NULL has been assigned to the variable* v_num. *As a result, the control is transferred to the ELSE part of the IF-THEN-ELSE statement. So the message 'v_num is not greater than 0' is displayed on the screen.*

Second, take a closer look at the IF-THEN statements used in Block 2:

```
IF v_num > 0 THEN
   DBMS_OUTPUT.PUT_LINE ('v_num is greater than 0');
END IF;
IF NOT (v_num > 0) THEN
   DBMS_OUTPUT.PUT_LINE ('v_num is not greater than 0');
END IF;
```

For both IF-THEN statements their conditions evaluate to FALSE, and as a result none of the messages are displayed on the screen.

CHAPTER 6 CONDITIONAL CONTROL: CASE STATEMENTS

1) Create the following script. Modify the script created in this section in Chapter 5 (Question 1 of the Test Your Thinking section). You can use either the CASE statement or the searched CASE statement. Your output should look similar to the output produced by the example created in Chapter 5.

Answer: Consider the script created in the section in Chapter 5:

```
SET SERVEROUTPUT ON
DECLARE
    v_day VARCHAR2(15);
    v_time VARCHAR(8);
BEGIN
    v_day := TO_CHAR(SYSDATE, 'fmDAY');
    v_time := TO_CHAR(SYSDATE, 'HH24:MI');

    IF v_day IN ('SATURDAY', 'SUNDAY') THEN
        DBMS_OUTPUT.PUT_LINE (v_day||', '||v_time);

        IF v_time BETWEEN '12:01' AND '24:00' THEN
            DBMS_OUTPUT.PUT_LINE ('It''s afternoon');
        ELSE
            DBMS_OUTPUT.PUT_LINE ('It''s morning');
        END IF;

    END IF;

    -- control resumes here
    DBMS_OUTPUT.PUT_LINE ('Done...');
END;
```

Next, consider the modified version of the script with nested CASE statements. For illustrative purposes, this script uses both CASE and searched CASE statements. All changes are shown in bold letters.

```
SET SERVEROUTPUT ON
DECLARE
    v_day VARCHAR2(15);
    v_time VARCHAR(8);
BEGIN
    v_day := TO_CHAR(SYSDATE, 'fmDay');
    v_time := TO_CHAR(SYSDATE, 'HH24:MI');

    -- CASE statement
    CASE SUBSTR(v_day, 1, 1)
        WHEN 'S' THEN
            DBMS_OUTPUT.PUT_LINE (v_day||', '||v_time);
```

```
            -- searched CASE statement
            CASE
               WHEN v_time BETWEEN '12:01' AND '24:00' THEN
                  DBMS_OUTPUT.PUT_LINE ('It''s afternoon');
            ELSE
               DBMS_OUTPUT.PUT_LINE ('It''s morning');
            END CASE;
      END CASE;

      -- control resumes here
      DBMS_OUTPUT.PUT_LINE('Done...');
   END;
```

In this exercise, you substitute nested IF statements with nested CASE statements. Consider the outer CASE statement. It uses a selector expression

```
      SUBSTR(v_day, 1, 1)
```

to check if a current day falls on the weekend. Notice that it derives only the first letter of the day. This is a good solution when using a CASE statement because only Saturday and Sunday start with letter 'S'. Furthermore, without using the SUBSTR function, you would need to use a searched CASE statement. You will recall that the value of the WHEN expression is compared to the value of the selector. As a result, the WHEN expression must return a similar datatype. In this example, the selector the expression returns a string datatype, so the WHEN expression must also return a string datatype.

Next, you use a searched CASE to validate the time of the day. You will recall that, similar to the IF statement, the WHEN conditions of the searched CASE statement yield Boolean values.

When run, this exercise produces the following output:

```
      Saturday, 19:49
      It's afternoon
      Done...

      PLSQL procedure successfully completed.
```

2) Create the following script. Modify the script created in this section in Chapter 5 (Question 2 of the Test Your Thinking section). You can use either the CASE statement or the searched CASE statement. Your output should look similar to the output produced by the example created in Chapter 5.

Answer: Consider the script created in the section in Chapter 5:

```
SET SERVEROUTPUT ON
DECLARE
```

```
   v_instructor_id NUMBER := &sv_instructor_id;
   v_total NUMBER;
BEGIN
   SELECT COUNT(*)
     INTO v_total
     FROM section
    WHERE instructor_id = v_instructor_id;

   -- check if instructor teaches 3 or more sections
   IF v_total >= 3 THEN
      DBMS_OUTPUT.PUT_LINE ('This instructor needs '||
         a vacation');
   ELSE
      DBMS_OUTPUT.PUT_LINE ('This instructor teaches '||
         v_total||' sections');
   END IF;
   -- control resumes here
   DBMS_OUTPUT.PUT_LINE ('Done...');
END;
```

Next, consider modified version of the script with the searched CASE statement instead of the IF-THEN-ELSE statement. All changes are shown in bold letters.

```
SET SERVEROUTPUT ON
DECLARE
   v_instructor_id NUMBER := &sv_instructor_id;
   v_total NUMBER;
BEGIN
   SELECT COUNT(*)
     INTO v_total
     FROM section
    WHERE instructor_id = v_instructor_id;

   -- check if instructor teaches 3 or more sections
   CASE
      WHEN v_total >= 3 THEN
         DBMS_OUTPUT.PUT_LINE ('This instructor needs '||
            a vacation');
      ELSE
         DBMS_OUTPUT.PUT_LINE ('This instructor teaches '||
            v_total||' sections');
   END CASE;
   -- control resumes here
   DBMS_OUTPUT.PUT_LINE ('Done...');
END;
```

Assume that value 109 was provided at runtime. Then the script produces the following output:

```
Enter value for sv_instructor_id: 109
old    2:    v_instructor_id NUMBER := &sv_instructor_id;
new    2:    v_instructor_id NUMBER := 109;
This instructor teaches 1 sections
Done...

PLSQL procedure successfully completed.
```

In order to use the CASE statement, the searched CASE statement could be modified as follows:

```
CASE SIGN(v_total - 3)
    WHEN -1 THEN
        DBMS_OUTPUT.PUT_LINE ('This instructor teaches '||
            v_total||' sections');
    ELSE
        DBMS_OUTPUT.PUT_LINE ('This instructor needs '||
            a vacation');
END CASE;
```

Notice that the SIGN function is used to determine if an instructor teaches three or more sections. You will recall that the SIGN function returns –1 if v_total is less than 3, 0 if v_total equals to 3, and 1 if v_total is greater than 3. In this case, as long as the SIGN function returns –1, the message 'This instructor teaches…' is displayed on the screen. In all other cases, the message 'This instructor needs a vacation' is displayed on the screen.

3) Execute the following two SELECT statements and explain why they produce different output:

```
SELECT e.student_id, e.section_id, e.final_grade,
       g.numeric_grade,
       COALESCE(g.numeric_grade, e.final_grade) grade
  FROM enrollment e, grade g
 WHERE e.student_id = g.student_id
   AND e.section_id = g.section_id
   AND e.student_id = 102
   AND g.grade_type_code = 'FI';

SELECT e.student_id, e.section_id, e.final_grade,
       g.numeric_grade,
       NULLIF(g.numeric_grade, e.final_grade) grade
  FROM enrollment e, grade g
 WHERE e.student_id = g.student_id
```

```
AND e.section_id = g.section_id
AND e.student_id = 102
AND g.grade_type_code = 'FI';
```

Answer: Consider outputs produced by the following SELECT statements:

STUDENT_ID	SECTION_ID	FINAL_GRADE	NUMERIC_GRADE	GRADE
102	86		85	85
102	89	92	92	92

STUDENT_ID	SECTION_ID	FINAL_GRADE	NUMERIC_GRADE	GRADE
102	86		85	85
102	89	92	92	

Consider the output returned by the first SELECT statement. This statement uses the COALESCE function to derive the value of GRADE. It equals the value of the NUMERIC_GRADE in the first row and the value of FINAL_GRADE in the second row.

The COALESCE function compares the value of the FINAL_GRADE to NULL. If it is NULL, then the value of the NUMERIC_GRADE is compared to NULL. Because the value of the NUMERIC_GRADE is not NULL, the COALESCE function returns the value of the NUMERIC_GRADE in the first row. In the second row, the COALESCE function returns the value of FINAL_GRADE because it is not NULL.

Next, consider the output returned by the second SELECT statement. This statement uses the NULLIF function to derive the value of GRADE. It equals the value of the NUMERIC_GRADE in the first row, and it is NULL in the second row.

The NULLIF function compares NUMERIC_GRADE value to the FINAL_GRADE value. If these values are equal, the NULLIF function returns NULL. In the opposite case, it returns the value of the NUMERIC_GRADE.

CHAPTER 7 ERROR HANDLING AND BUILT-IN EXCEPTIONS

1) Create the following script: Check to see whether there is a record in the STUDENT table for a given student ID. If there is no record for the given student ID, insert a record into the STUDENT table for the given student ID.

Answer: Your answer should look similar to the following:

```
SET SERVEROUTPUT ON
DECLARE
    v_student_id NUMBER := &sv_student_id;
    v_first_name VARCHAR2(30) := '&sv_first_name';
    v_last_name VARCHAR2(30) := '&sv_last_name';
    v_zip CHAR(5) := '&sv_zip';
```

```
        v_name VARCHAR2(50);
BEGIN
   SELECT first_name||' '||last_name
     INTO v_name
     FROM student
    WHERE student_id = v_student_id;

   DBMS_OUTPUT.PUT_LINE ('Student '||v_name||
      ' is a valid student');
EXCEPTION
   WHEN NO_DATA_FOUND THEN
      DBMS_OUTPUT.PUT_LINE
         ('This student does not exist, and will be '||
          'added to the STUDENT table');

      INSERT INTO student
         (student_id, first_name, last_name, zip,
          registration_date, created_by, created_date,
          modified_by, modified_date)
      VALUES
         (v_student_id, v_first_name, v_last_name, v_zip,
          SYSDATE, USER, SYSDATE, USER, SYSDATE);
      COMMIT;
END;
```

This script accepts a value for student's ID from a user. For a given student ID, it determines the student's name via the SELECT INTO statement and displays it on the screen. If the value provided by the user is not a valid student ID, the control of execution is passed to the exception-handling section of the block, where the NO_DATA_FOUND exception is raised. As a result, the message 'This student does not exist...' is displayed on the screen, and a new record is inserted in the STUDENT table.

To test this script fully, consider running it for two values of student ID. Only one value should correspond to an existing student ID. It is important to note that a valid zipcode should be provided for both runs. Why do you think this is necessary?

When 319 is provided for the student ID (it is a valid student ID), this exercise produces the following output:

```
Enter value for sv_student_id: 319
old   2:      v_student_id NUMBER := &sv_student_id;
new   2:      v_student_id NUMBER := 319;
Enter value for sv_first_name: John
old   3:      v_first_name VARCHAR2(30) := '&sv_first_name';
new   3:      v_first_name VARCHAR2(30) := 'John';
```

```
Enter value for sv_last_name: Smith
old    4:      v_last_name VARCHAR2(30) := '&sv_last_name';
new    4:      v_last_name VARCHAR2(30) := 'Smith';
Enter value for sv_zip: 07421
old    5:      v_zip CHAR(5) := '&sv_zip';
new    5:      v_zip CHAR(5) := '07421';
Student George Eakheit is a valid student

PLSQL procedure successfully completed.
```

Notice that the name displayed by the script does not correspond to the name entered at runtime. Why do you think this occurs?

When 555 is provided for the student ID (it is not a valid student ID), this exercise produces the following output:

```
Enter value for sv_student_id: 555
old    2:      v_student_id NUMBER := &sv_student_id;
new    2:      v_student_id NUMBER := 555;
Enter value for sv_first_name: John
old    3:      v_first_name VARCHAR2(30) := '&sv_first_name';
new    3:      v_first_name VARCHAR2(30) := 'John';
Enter value for sv_last_name: Smith
old    4:      v_last_name VARCHAR2(30) := '&sv_last_name';
new    4:      v_last_name VARCHAR2(30) := 'Smith';
Enter value for sv_zip: 07421
old    5:      v_zip CHAR(5) := '&sv_zip';
new    5:      v_zip CHAR(5) := '07421';
This student does not exist, and will be added to the
STUDENT table

PLSQL procedure successfully completed.
```

Next, you can select this new record from the STUDENT table as follows:

```
SELECT student_id, first_name, last_name
  FROM student
 WHERE student_id = 555;
```

STUDENT_ID FIRST_NAME	LAST_NAME
---------- -----------------------	-----------------
555 John	Smith

2) Create the following script: For a given instructor ID, check to see whether it is assigned to a valid instructor. Then check the number of sections that are taught by this instructor and display this information on the screen.

Answer: Your answer should look similar to the following:

```
SET SERVEROUTPUT ON
DECLARE
    v_instructor_id NUMBER := &sv_instructor_id;
    v_name VARCHAR2(50);
    v_total NUMBER;
  BEGIN
    SELECT first_name||' '||last_name
      INTO v_name
      FROM instructor
     WHERE instructor_id = v_instructor_id;

    -- check how many sections are taught by this instructor
    SELECT COUNT(*)
      INTO v_total
      FROM section
     WHERE instructor_id = v_instructor_id;

    DBMS_OUTPUT.PUT_LINE ('Instructor, '||v_name||
        ', teaches '||v_total||' section(s)');
  EXCEPTION
    WHEN NO_DATA_FOUND THEN
       DBMS_OUTPUT.PUT_LINE
           ('This is not a valid instructor');
  END;
```

This script accepts a value for instructor's ID from a user. For a given instructor ID, it determines the instructor's name via the SELECT INTO statement. This SELECT INTO statement checks if the ID provided by the user is a valid instructor ID. If this value is not valid, the control of the execution is passed to the exception-handling section of the block, where the NO_DATA_FOUND exception is raised. As a result, the message 'This is not a valid instructor' is displayed on the screen. On the other hand, if the value provided by the user is a valid instructor ID, the second SELECT INTO statement calculates how many sections are taught by this instructor.

To test this script fully, consider running it for two values of instructor ID. When 105 is provided for the instructor ID (it is a valid instructor ID), this exercise produces the following output:

```
Enter value for sv_instructor_id: 105
old   2:    v_instructor_id NUMBER := &sv_instructor_id;
new   2:    v_instructor_id NUMBER := 105;
Instructor, Anita Morris, teaches 10 section(s)

PLSQL procedure successfully completed.
```

When 123 is provided for the instructor ID (it is not a valid student ID), this exercise produces the following output:

```
Enter value for sv_instructor_id: 123
old    2:      v_instructor_id NUMBER := &sv_instructor_id;
new    2:      v_instructor_id NUMBER := 123;
This is not a valid instructor

PLSQL procedure successfully completed.
```

CHAPTER 8 ITERATIVE CONTROL

1) Rewrite script ch08_1a.sql using a WHILE loop instead of a simple loop. Make sure that the output produced by this script does not differ from the output produced by the script ch08_1a.sql.

Answer: Consider the script ch08_1a.sql:

```
SET SERVEROUTPUT ON
DECLARE
   v_counter BINARY_INTEGER := 0;
BEGIN
   LOOP
      -- increment loop counter by one
      v_counter := v_counter + 1;
      DBMS_OUTPUT.PUT_LINE ('v_counter = '||v_counter);

      -- if EXIT condition yields TRUE exit the loop
      IF v_counter = 5 THEN
         EXIT;
      END IF;

   END LOOP;
   -- control resumes here
   DBMS_OUTPUT.PUT_LINE ('Done...');
END;
```

Next, consider a new version of the script that uses a WHILE loop. All changes are shown in bold letters.

```
SET SERVEROUTPUT ON
DECLARE
   v_counter BINARY_INTEGER := 0;
BEGIN
   WHILE v_counter < 5 LOOP
      -- increment loop counter by one
      v_counter := v_counter + 1;
      DBMS_OUTPUT.PUT_LINE ('v_counter = '||v_counter);
   END LOOP;
```

```
   -- control resumes here
   DBMS_OUTPUT.PUT_LINE('Done...');
END;
```

In this version of the script, you replace a simple loop by a WHILE loop. It is important to remember that a simple loop executes at least once because the EXIT condition is placed in the body of the loop. On the other hand, a WHILE loop may not execute at all because a condition is tested outside the body of the loop. So, in order to achieve the same results using the WHILE loop, the EXIT condition

```
v_counter = 5
```

used in the original version is replaced by the test condition

```
v_counter < 5
```

When run, this example produces the following output:

```
v_counter = 1
v_counter = 2
v_counter = 3
v_counter = 4
v_counter = 5
Done...

PL/SQL procedure successfully completed.
```

2) Rewrite script ch08_4a.sql using a simple loop instead of a numeric FOR loop. Make sure that the output produced by this script does not differ from the output produced by the script ch08_4a.sql.

Answer: Recall the script ch08_4a.sql:

```
SET SERVEROUTPUT ON
DECLARE
   v_factorial NUMBER := 1;
BEGIN
   FOR v_counter IN 1..10 LOOP
      v_factorial := v_factorial * v_counter;
   END LOOP;
   -- control resumes here
   DBMS_OUTPUT.PUT_LINE ('Factorial of ten is: '||
      v_factorial);
END;
```

Next, consider a new version of the script that uses a simple loop. All changes are shown in bold letters.

```
SET SERVEROUTPUT ON
DECLARE
    v_counter NUMBER := 1;
    v_factorial NUMBER := 1;
BEGIN
    LOOP
        v_factorial := v_factorial * v_counter;
        v_counter := v_counter + 1;
        EXIT WHEN v_counter = 10;
    END LOOP;
    -- control resumes here
    DBMS_OUTPUT.PUT_LINE ('Factorial of ten is: '||
        v_factorial);
END;
```

In this version of the script, you replace a numeric FOR loop with a simple loop. As a result, there are three important changes that you should make. First, you need to declare and initialize the loop counter, v_counter. This counter is implicitly defined and initialized by the FOR loop. Second, you need to increment the value of the loop counter. This is very important because if you forget to include the statement

```
v_counter := v_counter + 1;
```

in the body of the simple loop, you will end up with an infinite loop. The step is not necessary when using numeric FOR loop because it is done by the loop itself.

Third, you need to specify the EXIT condition for the simple loop. Because you are computing a factorial of 10, the following EXIT condition is specified:

```
EXIT WHEN v_counter = 10;
```

Notice that you could specify this EXIT condition using IF-THEN statement as well:

```
IF v_counter = 10 THEN
    EXIT;
END IF;
```

When run, this example shows the following output:

```
Factorial of ten is: 362880

PL/SQL procedure successfully completed.
```

3) Rewrite the script ch08_6a.sql. A simple loop should be used as the outer loop, and a WHILE loop should be used as the inner loop.

Answer: Consider the script ch08_6a.sql:

```
SET SERVEROUTPUT ON
DECLARE
   v_test NUMBER := 0;
BEGIN
   <<outer_loop>>
   FOR i IN 1..3 LOOP
      DBMS_OUTPUT.PUT_LINE ('Outer Loop');
      DBMS_OUTPUT.PUT_LINE ('i = '||i);
      DBMS_OUTPUT.PUT_LINE ('v_test = '||v_test);
      v_test := v_test + 1;

      <<inner_loop>>
      FOR j IN 1..2 LOOP
         DBMS_OUTPUT.PUT_LINE ('Inner Loop');
         DBMS_OUTPUT.PUT_LINE ('j = '||j);
         DBMS_OUTPUT.PUT_LINE ('i = '||i);
         DBMS_OUTPUT.PUT_LINE ('v_test = '||v_test);
      END LOOP inner_loop;
   END LOOP outer_loop;
END;
```

Next, consider a modified version of the script that uses simple and WHILE loops. All changes are shown in bold letters.

```
SET SERVEROUTPUT ON
DECLARE
   i INTEGER := 1;
   j INTEGER := 1;
   v_test NUMBER := 0;
BEGIN
   <<outer_loop>>
   LOOP
      DBMS_OUTPUT.PUT_LINE ('Outer Loop');
      DBMS_OUTPUT.PUT_LINE ('i = '||i);
      DBMS_OUTPUT.PUT_LINE ('v_test = '||v_test);
      v_test := v_test + 1;
      -- reset inner loop counter
      j := 1;

      <<inner_loop>>
      WHILE j <= 2 LOOP
         DBMS_OUTPUT.PUT_LINE ('Inner Loop');
         DBMS_OUTPUT.PUT_LINE ('j = '||j);
         DBMS_OUTPUT.PUT_LINE ('i = '||i);
         DBMS_OUTPUT.PUT_LINE ('v_test = '||v_test);
         j := j + 1;
      END LOOP inner_loop;

      i := i + 1;
```

```
        -- EXIT condition of the outer loop
        EXIT WHEN i > 3;
     END LOOP outer_loop;
  END;
```

Just like in the previous exercise, there are some changes that are important due to the nature of the loops that are used.

First, both counters, for outer and inner loops, must be declared and initialized. Moreover, the counter for the inner loop must be initialized to 1 prior to the execution of the inner loop, and not in the declaration section of this script. In other words, the inner loop executes three times. *It is important not to confuse the* term execution of the loop *with the term* iteration. *Each execution of the WHILE loop causes the statements inside this loop to iterate twice.* Before each execution, the loop counter j must reset to 1 again. This step is necessary because the WHILE loop does not initialize its counter implicitly like numeric FOR loop. As a result, after the first execution of the WHILE loop is complete, the value of counter j is equal to 3. If this value is not reset to 1 again, the loop will not execute second time.

Second, both loop counters must be incremented. Third, the EXIT condition must be specified for the outer loop, and the test condition must be specified for the inner loop.

When run, the exercise produces the following output:

```
    Outer Loop
    i = 1
    v_test = 0
    Inner Loop
    j = 1
    i = 1
    v_test = 1
    Inner Loop
    j = 2
    i = 1
    v_test = 1
    Outer Loop
    i = 2
    v_test = 1
    Inner Loop
    j = 1
    i = 2
    v_test = 2
    Inner Loop
    j = 2
    i = 2
    v_test = 2
    Outer Loop
    i = 3
```

```
v_test = 2
Inner Loop
j = 1
i = 3
v_test = 3
Inner Loop
j = 2
i = 3
v_test = 3

PL/SQL procedure successfully completed.
```

CHAPTER 9 INTRODUCTION TO CURSORS

1) Write a nested cursor where the parent cursor calls information about each section of a course. The child cursor counts the enrollment. The only output is one line for each course with the course name, section number, and the total enrollment.

Answer: Your answer should look similar to the following:

```
SET SERVEROUTPUT ON
DECLARE
    CURSOR c_course IS
        SELECT course_no, description
          FROM course
         WHERE course_no < 120;

    CURSOR c_enrollment(p_course_no IN
course.course_no%TYPE)
    IS
        SELECT s.section_no section_no, count(*) count
          FROM section s, enrollment e
         WHERE s.course_no = p_course_no
           AND s.section_id = e.section_id
         GROUP BY s.section_no;
BEGIN
    FOR r_course IN c_course LOOP
        DBMS_OUTPUT.PUT_LINE
            (r_course.course_no||' '|| r_course.description);

        FOR r_enroll IN c_enrollment(r_course.course_no) LOOP
            DBMS_OUTPUT.PUT_LINE
                (Chr(9)||'Section:  '||r_enroll.section_no||
                 ' has an enrollment of: '||r_enroll.count);
        END LOOP;
```

```
          END LOOP;
     END;
```

2) Write an anonymous PL/SQL block that finds all the courses that have at least one section that is at its maximum enrollment. If there are no courses that meet that criterion, then pick two courses and create that situation for each.

   a) For each of those courses, add another section. The instructor for the new section should be taken from the existing records in the instruct table. Use the instructor who is signed up to teach the least number of courses. Handle the fact that, during the execution of your program, the instructor teaching the most courses may change.

   b) Use any exception-handling techniques you think are useful to capture error conditions.

   Answer: Your answer should look similar to the following:

```
SET SERVEROUTPUT ON
DECLARE
   v_instid_min instructor.instructor_id%TYPE;
   v_section_id_new section.section_id%TYPE;
   v_snumber_recent section.section_no%TYPE := 0;

   -- This cursor determines the courses that have at least
   -- one section filled to capacity.
   CURSOR c_filled IS
      SELECT DISTINCT s.course_no
        FROM section s
       WHERE s.capacity = (SELECT COUNT(section_id)
                             FROM enrollment e
                            WHERE e.section_id =
                            s.section_id);
BEGIN
   FOR r_filled IN c_filled LOOP
      -- For each course in this list, add another section.
      -- First, determine the instructor who is teaching
      -- the least number of courses. If there are more
      -- than one instructor teaching the same number of
      -- minimum courses (e.g. if there are three
      -- instructors teaching 1 course) use any of those
      -- instructors.
      SELECT instructor_id
        INTO v_instid_min
        FROM instructor
       WHERE EXISTS (SELECT NULL
                       FROM section
                      WHERE section.instructor_id =
                            instructor.instructor_id
```

```
                    GROUP BY instructor_id
                    HAVING COUNT(*) =
                       (SELECT MIN(COUNT(*))
                          FROM section
                        WHERE instructor_id IS NOT NULL
                       GROUP BY instructor_id)
                    )
     AND ROWNUM = 1;

  -- Determine the section_id for the new section
  -- Note that this method would not work in a multi-user
  -- environment. A sequence should be used instead.
  SELECT MAX(section_id) + 1
    INTO v_section_id_new
    FROM section;

  -- Determine the section number for the new section
  -- This only needs to be done in the real world if
  -- thesystem specification calls for a sequence in
  -- a parent. The sequence in parent here refers to
  -- the section_no incrementing within the course_no,
  -- and not the section_no incrementing within
  -- the section_id.
  DECLARE
     CURSOR c_snumber_in_parent IS
        SELECT section_no
        FROM section
       WHERE course_no = r_filled.course_no
     ORDER BY section_no;
  BEGIN
     -- Go from the lowest to the highest section_no
     -- and find any gaps. If there are no gaps make
     -- the new section_no equal to the highest
     -- current section_no + 1.

     FOR r_snumber_in_parent IN c_snumber_in_parent LOOP
       EXIT WHEN r_snumber_in_parent.section_no >
       v_snumber_recent + 1;
       v_snumber_recent := r_snumber_in_parent.
       section_no + 1;
     END LOOP;

     -- At this point, v_snumber_recent will be equal
     -- either to the value preceeding the gap or to
     -- the highest section_no for that course.
  END;
  -- Do the insert.
```

```
        INSERT INTO section
          (section_id, course_no, section_no, instructor_id)
        VALUES
          (v_section_id_new, r_filled.course_no,
           v_snumber_recent, v_instid_min);
        -- COMMIT;
    END LOOP;
  EXCEPTION
    WHEN OTHERS THEN
       DBMS_OUTPUT.PUT_LINE ('An error has occurred');
  END;
```

CHAPTER 10 EXCEPTIONS

1) Create the following script. For each section, determine the number of students registered. If this number is equal to or greater than 15, raise the user-defined exception e_too_many_students and display the error message. Otherwise, display how many students are in a section. Make sure that your program is able to process all sections.

Answer: Your answer should look similar to the following:

```
SET SERVEROUTPUT ON SIZE 5000
DECLARE
   CURSOR section_cur IS
      SELECT section_id
        FROM section;

   v_total NUMBER;
   e_too_many_students EXCEPTION;
BEGIN
   FOR section_rec in section_cur LOOP
      BEGIN
         -- calculate number of students enrolled
         SELECT COUNT(*)
           INTO v_total
           FROM enrollment
          WHERE section_id = section_rec.section_id;

         IF v_total >= 15 THEN
            RAISE e_too_many_students;
         ELSE
            DBMS_OUTPUT.PUT_LINE ('There are '||v_total||
                ' students for section ID '||
               section_rec.section_id);
```

```
            END IF;
        EXCEPTION
            WHEN e_too_many_students THEN
                DBMS_OUTPUT.PUT_LINE ('There are too many '||
                    students for '||section_rec.section_id);
        END;
    END LOOP;
END;
```

In this script, you declare a cursor on the SECTION table. Next, for each section ID returned by the cursor, the number of students enrolled in a given section is computed. If this number equals to or greater than 15, the user-defined exception E_TOO_MANY_STUDENTS is raised. Otherwise, the message specifying how many students are enrolled in a given section is displayed.

When run, this exercise produces the following output (due to the size of the output, only a part of it is shown here):

```
There are 0 students for section ID 79
There are 1 students for section ID 80
There are 3 students for section ID 81
There are 2 students for section ID 82
There are 2 students for section ID 83
There are 2 students for section ID 84
There are 5 students for section ID 85
There are 6 students for section ID 86
There are 7 students for section ID 87
There are 5 students for section ID 88
There are 12 students for section ID 89
...
There are 5 students for section ID 155
There are 8 students for section ID 156

PL/SQL procedure successfully completed.
```

2) Modify the script you created in the previous exercise. Once the exception `e_too_many_students` has been raised in the inner block, re-raise it in the outer block.

Answer: Your answer should look similar to the following. All changes are shown in bold letters.

```
SET SERVEROUTPUT ON SIZE 5000
DECLARE
    CURSOR section_cur IS
        SELECT section_id
            FROM section;
```

```
      v_total NUMBER;
      e_too_many_students EXCEPTION;
   BEGIN
      FOR section_rec in section_cur LOOP
         BEGIN
            -- calculate number of students enrolled
            SELECT COUNT(*)
              INTO v_total
              FROM enrollment
             WHERE section_id = section_rec.section_id;

            IF v_total >= 15 THEN
               RAISE e_too_many_students;
            ELSE
               DBMS_OUTPUT.PUT_LINE ('There are '||v_total||
                  ' students for '||section ID '||
                  section_rec.section_id);
            END IF;
         EXCEPTION
            WHEN e_too_many_students THEN
               RAISE;
         END;
      END LOOP;
   EXCEPTION
      WHEN e_too_many_students THEN
         DBMS_OUTPUT.PUT_LINE ('There are too many students.');
   END;
```

In this exercise, the exception section of the inner has been modified. A DBMS_OUTPUT.PUT_LINE statement has been substituted with the RAISE statement. In addition, an exception section has been added to the outer block. As a result, when an exception is raised in the inner block, it propagates to the outer block, and the cursor loop terminates.

It is important to note that an error message displayed by the DBMS_OUTPUT. PUT_LINE statement must be changed when a E_TOO_MANY_STUDENTS exception is raised in the outer block. In the previous version of this exercise the error message

```
   ('There are too many students for '||section_rec.section_id);
```

was placed inside the body of the cursor FOR loop. If the same error message is placed outside the body of the cursor FOR loop, the following error is generated at runtime:

```
         section_rec.section_id);
         *
ERROR at line 31:
ORA-06550: line 31, column 10:
```

```
PLS-00201: identifier 'SECTION_REC.SECTION_ID' must be
declared
ORA-06550: line 30, column 7:
PL/SQL: Statement ignored
```

Why do you think this error is generated?

CHAPTER 11 EXCEPTIONS: ADVANCED CONCEPTS

1) Create the following script. Modify the script created in this section in Chapter 10 (Question 1 of the Test Your Thinking section). Raise a user-defined exception with the RAISE_APPLICATION_ERROR statement. Otherwise, display how many students there are in a section. Make sure your program is able to process all sections.

Answer: Recall the script created in Chapter 10:

```
SET SERVEROUTPUT ON SIZE 5000
DECLARE
    CURSOR section_cur IS
        SELECT section_id
          FROM section;

    v_total NUMBER;
    e_too_many_students EXCEPTION;
BEGIN
    FOR section_rec in section_cur LOOP
        BEGIN
            -- calculate number of students enrolled
            SELECT COUNT(*)
              INTO v_total
              FROM enrollment
             WHERE section_id = section_rec.section_id;

            IF v_total >= 15 THEN
               RAISE e_too_many_students;
            ELSE
               DBMS_OUTPUT.PUT_LINE ('There are '||v_total||
                  ' students for section ID '||
                  section_rec.section_id);
            END IF;
        EXCEPTION
            WHEN e_too_many_students THEN
                DBMS_OUTPUT.PUT_LINE ('There are too many '||
                   'students for '||section_rec.section_id);
        END;
    END LOOP;
END;
```

Next, consider a modified version of this script. All changes are shown in bold letters:

```
SET SERVEROUTPUT ON SIZE 5000
DECLARE
    CURSOR section_cur IS
        SELECT section_id
          FROM section;

    v_total NUMBER;
BEGIN
    FOR section_rec in section_cur LOOP
        BEGIN
            -- calculate number of students enrolled
            SELECT COUNT(*)
              INTO v_total
              FROM enrollment
             WHERE section_id = section_rec.section_id;

            IF v_total >= 15 THEN
                RAISE_APPLICATION_ERROR (-20000,
                    'A section cannot have 15 '||
                    'or more students enrolled');
            ELSE
                DBMS_OUTPUT.PUT_LINE ('There are '||v_total||
                    ' students for '||section ID '||
                    section_rec.section_id);
            END IF;
        END;
    END LOOP;
END;
```

In this version of the script, you are using the RAISE_APPLICATON_ERROR statement to handle the following error condition: If the number of students enrolled
for a particular section is equal to or greater than 15, the error is raised. It is important to remember that RAISE_APPLICATION_ERROR statement works with
the unnamed user-defined exceptions. Therefore, notice that there is no reference to the exception E_TOO_MANY_STUDENTS anywhere in this script. On the
other hand, an error number has been associated with the error message.

When run, this exercise produces the following output (due to the size of the
output, only a part of it is shown):

```
There are 0 students for section ID 79
There are 1 students for section ID 80
There are 3 students for section ID 81
There are 2 students for section ID 82
There are 2 students for section ID 83
```

```
There are 2 students for section ID 84
There are 5 students for section ID 85
There are 6 students for section ID 86
There are 7 students for section ID 87
There are 5 students for section ID 88
There are 12 students for section ID 89
...
There are 5 students for section ID 155
There are 8 students for section ID 156

PL/SQL procedure successfully completed.
```

2) Create the following script. Try to add a record to the INSTRUCTOR table without providing values for the columns MODIFIED_BY and MODIFIED_DATE. Define an exception and associate it with the Oracle error number so that the error generated by the INSERT statement is handled.

Answer: Consider the following script. Notice that there are no exception handlers in this script:

```
DECLARE
    v_first_name INSTRUCTOR.FIRST_NAME%TYPE :=
        '&sv_first_name';
    v_last_name INSTRUCTOR.LAST_NAME%TYPE := '&sv_last_name';
BEGIN
    INSERT INTO INSTRUCTOR
        (instructor_id, first_name, last_name)
    VALUES (INSTRUCTOR_ID_SEQ.NEXTVAL, v_first_name,
        v_last_name);
    COMMIT;
END;
```

In this version of the script, you are trying to add a new record to the INSTRUCTOR table. The INSERT statement has only three columns: INSTRUCTOR_ID, FIRST_NAME, and LAST_NAME. The value for the column INSTRUCTOR_ID is determined from the sequence INSTRUCTOR_ID_SEQ, and the values for the columns FIRST_NAME and LAST_NAME are provided by the user.

When run, this script produces the following error message:

```
Enter value for sv_first_name: John
old    2:         '&sv_first_name';
new    2:         'John';
Enter value for sv_last_name: Smith
old    3:         '&sv_last_name';
new    3:         'Smith';
DECLARE
```

```
*
ERROR at line 1:
ORA-01400: cannot insert NULL into ("STUDENT".
"INSTRUCTOR"."CREATED_BY")
ORA-06512: at line 5
```

This error message states that a NULL value cannot be inserted in to the column CREATED_BY of the INSTRUCTOR table. Therefore, you need to add an exception handler to the script, as follows. All changes are shown in bold letters:

```
SET SERVEROUTPUT ON
DECLARE
    v_first_name INSTRUCTOR.FIRST_NAME%TYPE :=
        '&sv_first_name';
    v_last_name INSTRUCTOR.LAST_NAME%TYPE := '&sv_last_name';
    e_non_null_value EXCEPTION;
    PRAGMA EXCEPTION_INIT(e_non_null_value, -1400);
BEGIN
    INSERT INTO INSTRUCTOR
        (instructor_id, first_name, last_name)
    VALUES
        (INSTRUCTOR_ID_SEQ.NEXTVAL, v_first_name, v_last_name);
    COMMIT;
EXCEPTION
    WHEN e_non_null_value THEN
        DBMS_OUTPUT.PUT_LINE ('A NULL value cannot be '||
            inserted. Check constraints on the
            INSTRUCTOR table.');
END;
```

In this version of the script, you declare a new exception called E_NON_NULL_ VALUE. Next, you associate an Oracle error number with this exception. As a result, you are able to add an exception-handling section to trap the error generated by Oracle.

When run, the new version produces the following output:

```
Enter value for sv_first_name: John
old    2:          '&sv_first_name';
new    2:          'John';
Enter value for sv_last_name: Smith
old    3:          '&sv_last_name';
new    3:          'Smith';
A NULL value cannot be inserted. Check constraints on the
INSTRUCTOR table.

PL/SQL procedure successfully completed.
```

3) Modify the script created in the previous exercise. Instead of declaring a user-defined exception, add the OTHERS exception handler to the exception-handling section of the block. Then display the error number and the error message on the screen.

Answer: Your script should look similar to the following. All changes are shown in bold letters.

```
SET SERVEROUTPUT ON
DECLARE
    v_first_name INSTRUCTOR.FIRST_NAME%TYPE :=
        '&sv_first_name';
    v_last_name INSTRUCTOR.LAST_NAME%TYPE := '&sv_last_name';
BEGIN
    INSERT INTO INSTRUCTOR
        (instructor_id, first_name, last_name)
    VALUES
        (INSTRUCTOR_ID_SEQ.NEXTVAL, v_first_name, v_last_name);
    COMMIT;
EXCEPTION
    WHEN OTHERS THEN
        DBMS_OUTPUT.PUT_LINE ('Error code: '||SQLCODE);
        DBMS_OUTPUT.PUT_LINE ('Error message: '||
            SUBSTR(SQLERRM, 1, 200));
END;
```

Notice that as long as the OTHERS exception handler is used, there is no need associate an Oracle error number with a user-defined exception. When run, this exercise produces the following output:

```
Enter value for sv_first_name: John
old    2:        '&sv_first_name';
new    2:        'John';
Enter value for sv_last_name: Smith
old    3:        '&sv_last_name';
new    3:        'Smith';
Error code: -1400
Error message: ORA-01400: cannot insert NULL into
("STUDENT"."INSTRUCTOR"."CREATED_BY")

PL/SQL procedure successfully completed.
```

CHAPTER 12 PROCEDURES

1) Write a procedure with no parameters. The procedure will let you know if the current day is a weekend or a weekday. Additionally, it will let you know the user name and current time. It will also let you know how many valid and invalid procedures are in the database.

Answer:Your answer should look similar to the following:

```
CREATE OR REPLACE PROCEDURE current_status
AS
    v_day_type CHAR(1);
    v_user VARCHAR2(30);
    v_valid NUMBER;
    v_invalid NUMBER;
BEGIN
    SELECT SUBSTR(TO_CHAR(sysdate, 'DAY'), 0, 1)
      INTO v_day_type
      FROM dual;
    IF v_day_type = 'S' THEN
        DBMS_OUTPUT.PUT_LINE ('Today is a weekend.');
    ELSE
        DBMS_OUTPUT.PUT_LINE ('Today is a weekday.');
    END IF;
    --
    DBMS_OUTPUT.PUT_LINE('The time is: '||
      TO_CHAR(sysdate, 'HH:MI AM'));
    --
    SELECT user
      INTO v_user
      FROM dual;
    DBMS_OUTPUT.PUT_LINE ('The current user is '||v_user);
    --
    SELECT NVL(COUNT(*), 0)
      INTO v_valid
      FROM user_objects
     WHERE status = 'VALID'
       AND object_type = 'PROCEDURE';
    DBMS_OUTPUT.PUT_LINE
       ('There are '||v_valid||' valid procedures.');
    --
    SELECT NVL(COUNT(*), 0)
      INTO v_invalid
      FROM user_objects
     WHERE status = 'INVALID'
       AND object_type = 'PROCEDURE';
    DBMS_OUTPUT.PUT_LINE
       ('There are '||v_invalid||' invalid procedures.');
END;

SET SERVEROUTPUT ON
EXEC current_status;
```

2) Write a procedure that takes in a zipcode, city, and state and inserts the values
   into the zipcode table. There should be a check to see if the zipcode is already in

the database. If it is, an exception will be raised and an error message will be displayed. Write an anonymous block that uses the procedure and inserts your zipcode.

Answer: Your answer should look similar to the following:

```
CREATE OR REPLACE PROCEDURE insert_zip
   (I_ZIPCODE IN zipcode.zip%TYPE,
    I_CITY    IN zipcode.city%TYPE,
    I_STATE   IN zipcode.state%TYPE)
AS
   v_zipcode zipcode.zip%TYPE;
   v_city zipcode.city%TYPE;
   v_state zipcode.state%TYPE;
   v_dummy zipcode.zip%TYPE;
BEGIN
   v_zipcode := i_zipcode;
   v_city := i_city;
   v_state := i_state;
--
   SELECT zip
     INTO v_dummy
     FROM zipcode
    WHERE zip = v_zipcode;
--
   DBMS_OUTPUT.PUT_LINE('The zipcode '||v_zipcode||
      ' is already in the database and cannot be'||
      ' reinserted.');
--
EXCEPTION
   WHEN NO_DATA_FOUND THEN
      INSERT INTO ZIPCODE
      VALUES (v_zipcode, v_city, v_state, user, sysdate,
              user, sysdate);
   WHEN OTHERS THEN
      DBMS_OUTPUT.PUT_LINE ('There was an unknown error '||
         'in insert_zip.');
END;

SET SERVEROUTPUT ON
BEGIN
   insert_zip (10035, 'No Where', 'ZZ');
END;

BEGIN
   insert_zip (99999, 'No Where', 'ZZ');
END;

ROLLBACK;
```

CHAPTER 13 FUNCTIONS

1) Write a stored function called `new_student_id` that takes in no parameters and returns a `student.student_id%TYPE`. The value returned will be used when inserting a new student into the CTA application. It will be derived by using the formula: `student_id_seq.NEXTVAL`.

Answer: Your answer should look similar to the following:

```
CREATE OR REPLACE FUNCTION new_student_id
   RETURN student.student_id%TYPE
AS
   v_student_id student.student_id%TYPE;
BEGIN
   SELECT student_id_seq.NEXTVAL
     INTO v_student_id
     FROM dual;
   RETURN(v_student_id);
END;
```

2) Write a stored function called `zip_does_not_exist` that takes in a `zipcode.zip%TYPE` and returns a Boolean. The function will return TRUE if the zipcode passed into it does not exist. It will return a FALSE if the zipcode exists. *Hint:* An example of how it might be used is as follows:

```
DECLARE
   cons_zip CONSTANT zipcode.zip%TYPE := '&sv_zipcode';
   e_zipcode_is_not_valid EXCEPTION;
BEGIN
   IF zipcode_does_not_exist(cons_zip) THEN
      RAISE e_zipcode_is_not_valid;
   ELSE
      -- An insert of an instructor's record that
      -- uses of the checked value of zipcode might go here.
      NULL;
   END IF;
EXCEPTION
   WHEN e_zipcode_is_not_valid THEN
      RAISE_APPLICATION_ERROR
         (-20003, 'Could not find zipcode '||
          cons_zip||'.');
END;
```

Answer: Your answer should look similar to the following:

```
CREATE OR REPLACE FUNCTION zipcode_does_not_exist
   (i_zipcode IN zipcode.zip%TYPE)
   RETURN BOOLEAN
AS
```

```
    v_dummy char(1);
BEGIN
    SELECT NULL
      INTO v_dummy
      FROM zipcode
     WHERE zip = i_zipcode;

    -- meaning the zipcode does exits
    RETURN FALSE;
EXCEPTION
    WHEN OTHERS THEN
        -- the select statement above will cause an exception
        -- to be raised if the zipcode is not in the database.
        RETURN TRUE;
END zipcode_does_not_exist;
```

3) Create a new function. For a given instructor, determine how many sections he or she is teaching. If the number is greater than or equal to 3, return a message saying the instructor needs a vacation. Otherwise, return a message saying how many sections this instructor is teaching.

Answer: Your answer should look similar to the following:

```
CREATE OR REPLACE FUNCTION instructor_status
    (i_first_name IN instructor.first_name%TYPE,
     i_last_name IN instructor.last_name%TYPE)
    RETURN VARCHAR2
AS
    v_instructor_id instructor.instructor_id%TYPE;
    v_section_count NUMBER;
    v_status VARCHAR2(100);
BEGIN
    SELECT instructor_id
      INTO v_instructor_id
      FROM instructor
     WHERE first_name = i_first_name
       AND last_name = i_last_name;

    SELECT COUNT(*)
      INTO v_section_count
      FROM section
     WHERE instructor_id = v_instructor_id;

    IF v_section_count >= 3 THEN
        v_status :=
            'The instructor '||i_first_name||' '||
            i_last_name||' is teaching '||v_section_count||
            ' and needs a vaction.';
    ELSE
```

```
            v_status :=
                'The instructor '||i_first_name||'  '||
                i_last_name||' is teaching '||v_section_count||
                ' courses.';
        END IF;
        RETURN v_status;
    EXCEPTION
        WHEN NO_DATA_FOUND THEN
            -- note that either of the SELECT statements can raise
            -- this exception
            v_status :=
                'The instructor '||i_first_name||'  '||
                 i_last_name||' is not shown to be teaching'||
                 ' any courses.';
            RETURN v_status;
        WHEN OTHERS THEN
            v_status :=
                'There has been in an error in the function.';
            RETURN v_status;
    END;
```

Test the function as follows:

```
    SELECT instructor_status(first_name, last_name)
      FROM instructor;
    \
```

CHAPTER 14 PACKAGES

1) Add a procedure to the `student_api` package called `remove_student`. This procedure accepts a `student_id` and returns nothing. Based on the student ID passed in, it removes the student from the database. If the student does not exist or there is a problem removing the student (such as a foreign key constraint violation), then let the calling program handle it.

Answer:

```
    CREATE OR REPLACE PACKAGE student_api AS
        v_current_date DATE;
        PROCEDURE discount;
        FUNCTION new_instructor_id
            RETURN instructor.instructor_id%TYPE;
        FUNCTION total_cost_for_student
            (p_student_id IN student.student_id%TYPE)
            RETURN course.cost%TYPE;
        PRAGMA RESTRICT_REFERENCES
            (total_cost_for_student, WNDS, WNPS, RNPS);
        PROCEDURE get_student_info
```

```
        (p_student_id    IN   student.student_id%TYPE,
         p_last_name     OUT  student.last_name%TYPE,
         p_first_name    OUT  student.first_name%TYPE,
         p_zip           OUT  student.zip%TYPE,
         p_return_code   OUT  NUMBER);
   PROCEDURE get_student_info
        (p_last_name     IN student.last_name%TYPE,
         p_first_name    IN student.first_name%TYPE,
         p_student_id    OUT student.student_id%TYPE,
         p_zip           OUT student.zip%TYPE,
         p_return_code OUT NUMBER);
   PROCEDURE remove_student
        (p_studid IN student.student_id%TYPE);
END student_api;

CREATE OR REPLACE PACKAGE BODY student_api AS
   PROCEDURE discount IS
      CURSOR c_group_discount IS
         SELECT distinct s.course_no, c.description
           FROM section s, enrollment e, course c
          WHERE s.section_id = e.section_id
          GROUP BY s.course_no, c.description,
                   e.section_id, s.section_id
          HAVING COUNT(*) >=8;
   BEGIN
      FOR r_group_discount IN c_group_discount LOOP
         UPDATE course
         SET cost = cost * .95
         WHERE course_no = r_group_discount.course_no;

         DBMS_OUTPUT.PUT_LINE
            ('A 5% discount has been given to'||
             r_group_discount.course_no||' '||
             r_group_discount.description);
      END LOOP;
   END discount;

   FUNCTION new_instructor_id
      RETURN instructor.instructor_id%TYPE
   IS
      v_new_instid instructor.instructor_id%TYPE;
   BEGIN
      SELECT INSTRUCTOR_ID_SEQ.NEXTVAL
        INTO v_new_instid
        FROM dual;
      RETURN v_new_instid;
   EXCEPTION
      WHEN OTHERS THEN
         DECLARE
```

```
         v_sqlerrm VARCHAR2(250) :=
             SUBSTR(SQLERRM,1,250);
      BEGIN
         RAISE_APPLICATION_ERROR
             (-20003, 'Error in instructor_id: '||
                 v_sqlerrm);
      END;
END new_instructor_id;


FUNCTION get_course_descript_private
   (p_course_no   course.course_no%TYPE)
   RETURN course.description%TYPE
IS
   v_course_descript course.description%TYPE;
BEGIN
   SELECT description
     INTO v_course_descript
     FROM course
    WHERE course_no = p_course_no;
   RETURN v_course_descript;
EXCEPTION
   WHEN OTHERS THEN
      RETURN NULL;
END get_course_descript_private;


FUNCTION total_cost_for_student
   (p_student_id IN student.student_id%TYPE)
   RETURN course.cost%TYPE
AS
   v_cost course.cost%TYPE;
BEGIN
   SELECT sum(cost)
     INTO v_cost
     FROM course c, section s, enrollment e
    WHERE c.course_no = c.course_no
      AND e.section_id = s.section_id
      AND e.student_id = p_student_id;
   RETURN v_cost;
EXCEPTION
   WHEN OTHERS THEN
      RETURN NULL;
END total_cost_for_student;


PROCEDURE get_student_info
   (p_student_id    IN   student.student_id%TYPE,
    p_last_name     OUT  student.last_name%TYPE,
    p_first_name    OUT  student.first_name%TYPE,
    p_zip           OUT  student.zip%TYPE,
    p_return_code   OUT  NUMBER)
```

```
IS
BEGIN
   SELECT last_name, first_name, zip
     INTO p_last_name, p_first_name, p_zip
     FROM student
    WHERE student.student_id = p_student_id;
   p_return_code := 0;
EXCEPTION
   WHEN NO_DATA_FOUND THEN
      DBMS_OUTPUT.PUT_LINE
         ('Student ID is not valid.');
      p_return_code := -100;
      p_last_name := NULL;
      p_first_name := NULL;
      p_zip := NULL;
   WHEN OTHERS THEN
      DBMS_OUTPUT.PUT_LINE
         ('Error in procedure get_student_info');
END get_student_info;

PROCEDURE get_student_info
   (p_last_name    IN student.last_name%TYPE,
    p_first_name   IN student.first_name%TYPE,
    p_student_id   OUT student.student_id%TYPE,
    p_zip          OUT student.zip%TYPE,
    p_return_code OUT NUMBER)
IS
BEGIN
   SELECT student_id, zip
     INTO p_student_id, p_zip
     FROM student
    WHERE UPPER(last_name) = UPPER(p_last_name)
      AND UPPER(first_name) = UPPER(p_first_name);
   p_return_code := 0;
EXCEPTION
   WHEN NO_DATA_FOUND THEN
      DBMS_OUTPUT.PUT_LINE
         ('Student name is not valid.');
      p_return_code := -100;
      p_student_id := NULL;
      p_zip := NULL;
   WHEN OTHERS THEN
      DBMS_OUTPUT.PUT_LINE
         ('Error in procedure get_student_info');
END get_student_info;

PROCEDURE remove_student
  (p_studid IN student.student_id%TYPE)
IS
```

```
       BEGIN
          DELETE
            FROM STUDENT
           WHERE student_id = p_studid;
       END;

    BEGIN
       SELECT trunc(sysdate, 'DD')
         INTO v_current_date
         FROM dual;
    END student_api;
```

2) Alter `remove_student` in the `student_api` package body to accept an additional parameter. This new parameter is a VARCHAR2 and is called `p_ri`. Make `p_ri` default to "R." The new parameter may contain a value of "R" or "C." If "R" is received, it represents DELETE RESTRICT and the procedure acts as it does now. If there are enrollments for the student, the delete is disallowed. If a "C" is received, it represents DELETE CASCADE. This functionally means that the `remove_student` procedure locates all records for the student in all of the tables and removes them from the database before attempting to remove the student from the student table. Decide how to handle the situation where the user passes in a code other than "C" or "R."

Answer: Your answer should look similar to the following:

```
CREATE OR REPLACE PACKAGE student_api AS
   v_current_date DATE;
   PROCEDURE discount;
   FUNCTION new_instructor_id
      RETURN instructor.instructor_id%TYPE;
   FUNCTION total_cost_for_student
      (p_student_id IN student.student_id%TYPE)
      RETURN course.cost%TYPE;
   PRAGMA RESTRICT_REFERENCES
      (total_cost_for_student, WNDS, WNPS, RNPS);
   PROCEDURE get_student_info
      (p_student_id   IN  student.student_id%TYPE,
       p_last_name    OUT student.last_name%TYPE,
       p_first_name   OUT student.first_name%TYPE,
       p_zip          OUT student.zip%TYPE,
       p_return_code  OUT NUMBER);
   PROCEDURE get_student_info
      (p_last_name    IN  student.last_name%TYPE,
       p_first_name   IN  student.first_name%TYPE,
       p_student_id   OUT student.student_id%TYPE,
       p_zip          OUT student.zip%TYPE,
       p_return_code  OUT NUMBER);
   PROCEDURE remove_student
```

```
        (p_studid IN student.student_id%TYPE,
         p_ri    IN VARCHAR2 DEFAULT 'R');
END student_api;

CREATE OR REPLACE PACKAGE BODY student_api AS
   PROCEDURE discount IS
      CURSOR c_group_discount IS
         SELECT distinct s.course_no, c.description
           FROM section s, enrollment e, course c
          WHERE s.section_id = e.section_id
          GROUP BY s.course_no, c.description,
                   e.section_id, s.section_id
          HAVING COUNT(*) >=8;
   BEGIN
      FOR r_group_discount IN c_group_discount LOOP
         UPDATE course
         SET cost = cost * .95
         WHERE course_no = r_group_discount.course_no;

         DBMS_OUTPUT.PUT_LINE
            ('A 5% discount has been given to'||
             r_group_discount.course_no||' '||
             r_group_discount.description);
      END LOOP;
   END discount;

   FUNCTION new_instructor_id
      RETURN instructor.instructor_id%TYPE
   IS
      v_new_instid instructor.instructor_id%TYPE;
   BEGIN
      SELECT INSTRUCTOR_ID_SEQ.NEXTVAL
        INTO v_new_instid
        FROM dual;
      RETURN v_new_instid;
   EXCEPTION
      WHEN OTHERS THEN
         DECLARE
            v_sqlerrm VARCHAR2(250) :=
               SUBSTR(SQLERRM,1,250);
         BEGIN
            RAISE_APPLICATION_ERROR
               (-20003, 'Error in instructor_id: '||
                v_sqlerrm);
         END;
   END new_instructor_id;

   FUNCTION get_course_descript_private
      (p_course_no course.course_no%TYPE)
```

```
      RETURN course.description%TYPE
IS
   v_course_descript course.description%TYPE;
BEGIN
   SELECT description
     INTO v_course_descript
     FROM course
    WHERE course_no = p_course_no;
   RETURN v_course_descript;
EXCEPTION
   WHEN OTHERS THEN
      RETURN NULL;
END get_course_descript_private;

FUNCTION total_cost_for_student
   (p_student_id IN student.student_id%TYPE)
   RETURN course.cost%TYPE
IS
   v_cost course.cost%TYPE;
BEGIN
   SELECT sum(cost)
     INTO v_cost
     FROM course c, section s, enrollment e
    WHERE c.course_no = c.course_no
      AND e.section_id = s.section_id
      AND e.student_id = p_student_id;
   RETURN v_cost;
EXCEPTION
   WHEN OTHERS THEN
      RETURN NULL;
END total_cost_for_student;

PROCEDURE get_student_info
   (p_student_id    IN   student.student_id%TYPE,
    p_last_name     OUT  student.last_name%TYPE,
    p_first_name    OUT  student.first_name%TYPE,
    p_zip           OUT  student.zip%TYPE,
    p_return_code   OUT NUMBER)
IS
BEGIN
   SELECT last_name, first_name, zip
     INTO p_last_name, p_first_name, p_zip
     FROM student
    WHERE student.student_id = p_student_id;
   p_return_code := 0;
EXCEPTION
   WHEN NO_DATA_FOUND THEN
      DBMS_OUTPUT.PUT_LINE ('Student ID is not valid.');
```

```
            p_return_code := -100;
            p_last_name := NULL;
            p_first_name := NULL;
            p_zip := NULL;
         WHEN OTHERS THEN
            DBMS_OUTPUT.PUT_LINE
               ('Error in procedure get_student_info');
   END get_student_info;

   PROCEDURE get_student_info
      (p_last_name    IN student.last_name%TYPE,
       p_first_name   IN student.first_name%TYPE,
       p_student_id   OUT student.student_id%TYPE,
       p_zip          OUT student.zip%TYPE,
       p_return_code  OUT NUMBER)
   IS
   BEGIN
      SELECT student_id, zip
        INTO p_student_id, p_zip
        FROM student
       WHERE UPPER(last_name) = UPPER(p_last_name)
         AND UPPER(first_name) = UPPER(p_first_name);
      p_return_code := 0;
   EXCEPTION
      WHEN NO_DATA_FOUND THEN
         DBMS_OUTPUT.PUT_LINE
            ('Student name is not valid.');
         p_return_code := -100;
         p_student_id := NULL;
         p_zip := NULL;
      WHEN OTHERS THEN
         DBMS_OUTPUT.PUT_LINE
            ('Error in procedure get_student_info');
   END get_student_info;

   PROCEDURE remove_student
      -- the parameters student_id and p_ri give user an
      -- option of cascade delete or restrict delete for
      -- the given students records
      (p_studid IN student.student_id%TYPE,
       p_ri     IN VARCHAR2 DEFAULT 'R')
   IS
      -- declare exceptions for use in procedure
      enrollment_present EXCEPTION;
      bad_pri EXCEPTION;
   BEGIN
```

```
-- R value is for restrict delete option
IF p_ri = 'R' THEN
    DECLARE
        -- a variable is needed to test if the student
        -- is in the enrollment table
        v_dummy CHAR(1);
    BEGIN
        -- This is a standard existence check
        -- If v_dummy is assigned a value via the
        -- SELECT INTO, the exception
        -- enrollment_present will be raised
        -- If the v_dummy is not assigned a value, the
        -- exception no_data_found will be raised
        SELECT NULL
          INTO v_dummy
          FROM enrollment e
         WHERE e.student_id = p_studid
           AND ROWNUM = 1;

        -- The rownum set to 1 prevents the SELECT
        -- INTO statement raise to_many_rows
        -- exception
        -- If there is at least one row in enrollment
        -- table with corresponding student_id, the
        -- restrict delete parameter will disallow the
        -- deletion of the student by raising
        -- the enrollment_present exception
        RAISE enrollment_present;
    EXCEPTION
        WHEN NO_DATA_FOUND THEN
            -- The no_data_found exception is raised
            -- when there are no students found in the
            -- enrollment table Since the p_ri indicates
            -- a restrict delete user choice the delete
            -- operation is permitted
            DELETE FROM student
            WHERE student_id = p_studid;
    END;
-- when the user enter "C" for the p_ri
-- he/she indicates a cascade delete choice
ELSIF p_ri = 'C' THEN
    -- delete the student form the enrollment and
    -- grade tables
    DELETE
      FROM enrollment
     WHERE student_id = p_studid;
```

```
                    DELETE
                      FROM grade
                     WHERE student_id = p_studid;

                    -- delete from student table only after
                    corresponding
                    -- records have been removed from the other
                    tables because
                    -- the student table is the parent table
                    DELETE
                      FROM student
                     WHERE student_id = p_studid;
                ELSE
                    RAISE bad_pri;
                END IF;
            EXCEPTION
                WHEN bad_pri THEN
                    RAISE_APPLICATION_ERROR
                        (-20231, 'An incorrect p_ri value was '||
                         'entered. The remove_student procedure can '||
                         'only accept a C or R for the p_ri
                         parameter.');

                WHEN enrollment_present THEN
                    RAISE_APPLICATION_ERROR
                        (-20239, 'The student with ID'||p_studid||
                         ' exists in the enrollment table thus records'||
                         ' will not be removed.');
            END remove_student;

        BEGIN
            SELECT trunc(sysdate, 'DD')
              INTO v_current_date
              FROM dual;
        END student_api;
```

CHAPTER 15 STORED CODE

1) Add a function in `school_api` package specification called `get_course_descript`. The caller takes a `course.cnumber%TYPE` parameter and it returns a `course.description%TYPE`.

Answer: Your answer should look similar to the following:

```
CREATE OR REPLACE PACKAGE student_api AS
    v_current_date DATE;
    PROCEDURE discount;
    FUNCTION new_instructor_id
        RETURN instructor.instructor_id%TYPE;
```

```
FUNCTION total_cost_for_student
    (p_student_id IN student.student_id%TYPE)
    RETURN course.cost%TYPE;
PRAGMA RESTRICT_REFERENCES
    (total_cost_for_student, WNDS, WNPS, RNPS);
PROCEDURE get_student_info
    (p_student_id    IN  student.student_id%TYPE,
     p_last_name     OUT student.last_name%TYPE,
     p_first_name    OUT student.first_name%TYPE,
     p_zip           OUT student.zip%TYPE,
     p_return_code   OUT NUMBER);
PROCEDURE get_student_info
    (p_last_name     IN student.last_name%TYPE,
     p_first_name    IN student.first_name%TYPE,
     p_student_id    OUT student.student_id%TYPE,
     p_zip           OUT student.zip%TYPE,
     p_return_code OUT NUMBER);
PROCEDURE remove_student
    (p_studid IN student.student_id%TYPE,
     p_ri      IN VARCHAR2 DEFAULT 'R');
FUNCTION get_course_descript
    (p_cnumber course.course_no%TYPE)
    RETURN course.description%TYPE;
END student_api;
```

2) Create a function in the `school_api` package body called `get_course_description`. A caller passes in a course number and it returns the course description. Instead of searching for the description itself, it makes a call to `get_course_descript_private`. It passes its course number to `get_course_descript_private`. It passes back to the caller the description it gets back from `get_course_descript_private`.

Answer: Your answer should look similar to the following:

```
CREATE OR REPLACE PACKAGE BODY student_api AS
    PROCEDURE discount IS
        CURSOR c_group_discount IS
            SELECT distinct s.course_no, c.description
              FROM section s, enrollment e, course c
             WHERE s.section_id = e.section_id
             GROUP BY s.course_no, c.description,
                      e.section_id, s.section_id
             HAVING COUNT(*) >=8;
    BEGIN
        FOR r_group_discount IN c_group_discount LOOP
            UPDATE course
            SET cost = cost * .95
            WHERE course_no = r_group_discount.course_no;
```

```
            DBMS_OUTPUT.PUT_LINE
               ('A 5% discount has been given to'||
                 r_group_discount.course_no||' '||
                 r_group_discount.description);
      END LOOP;
   END discount;

   FUNCTION new_instructor_id
      RETURN instructor.instructor_id%TYPE
   IS
      v_new_instid instructor.instructor_id%TYPE;
   BEGIN
      SELECT INSTRUCTOR_ID_SEQ.NEXTVAL
        INTO v_new_instid
        FROM dual;
      RETURN v_new_instid;
   EXCEPTION
      WHEN OTHERS THEN
         DECLARE
            v_sqlerrm VARCHAR2(250) :=
               SUBSTR(SQLERRM,1,250);
         BEGIN
            RAISE_APPLICATION_ERROR
               (-20003, 'Error in instructor_id: '||
                  v_sqlerrm);
         END;
   END new_instructor_id;

   FUNCTION get_course_descript_private
      (p_course_no  course.course_no%TYPE)
      RETURN course.description%TYPE
   IS
      v_course_descript course.description%TYPE;
   BEGIN
      SELECT description
        INTO v_course_descript
        FROM course
       WHERE course_no = p_course_no;
      RETURN v_course_descript;
   EXCEPTION
      WHEN OTHERS THEN
         RETURN NULL;
   END get_course_descript_private;

   FUNCTION total_cost_for_student
      (p_student_id IN student.student_id%TYPE)
      RETURN course.cost%TYPE
   IS
      v_cost course.cost%TYPE;
```

```
BEGIN
   SELECT sum(cost)
     INTO v_cost
     FROM course c, section s, enrollment e
    WHERE c.course_no = c.course_no
      AND e.section_id = s.section_id
      AND e.student_id = p_student_id;
   RETURN v_cost;
EXCEPTION
   WHEN OTHERS THEN
      RETURN NULL;
END total_cost_for_student;

PROCEDURE get_student_info
   (p_student_id    IN  student.student_id%TYPE,
    p_last_name     OUT student.last_name%TYPE,
    p_first_name    OUT student.first_name%TYPE,
    p_zip           OUT student.zip%TYPE,
    p_return_code   OUT NUMBER)
IS
BEGIN
   SELECT last_name, first_name, zip
     INTO p_last_name, p_first_name, p_zip
     FROM student
    WHERE student.student_id = p_student_id;
   p_return_code := 0;
EXCEPTION
   WHEN NO_DATA_FOUND THEN
      DBMS_OUTPUT.PUT_LINE ('Student ID is not valid.');
      p_return_code := -100;
      p_last_name := NULL;
      p_first_name := NULL;
      p_zip := NULL;

   WHEN OTHERS THEN
      DBMS_OUTPUT.PUT_LINE
         ('Error in procedure get_student_info');
END get_student_info;

PROCEDURE get_student_info
   (p_last_name     IN student.last_name%TYPE,
    p_first_name    IN student.first_name%TYPE,
    p_student_id    OUT student.student_id%TYPE,
    p_zip           OUT student.zip%TYPE,
    p_return_code OUT NUMBER)
IS
BEGIN
   SELECT student_id, zip
     INTO p_student_id, p_zip
```

```
           FROM student
         WHERE UPPER(last_name)  = UPPER(p_last_name)
           AND UPPER(first_name) = UPPER(p_first_name);
      p_return_code := 0;
EXCEPTION
   WHEN NO_DATA_FOUND THEN
      DBMS_OUTPUT.PUT_LINE
         ('Student name is not valid.');
      p_return_code := -100;
      p_student_id := NULL;
      p_zip := NULL;

   WHEN OTHERS THEN
      DBMS_OUTPUT.PUT_LINE
         ('Error in procedure get_student_info');
END get_student_info;

PROCEDURE remove_student
   -- the parameters student_id and p_ri give user an
   -- option of cascade delete or restrict delete for
   -- the given students records
   (p_studid IN student.student_id%TYPE,
    p_ri      IN VARCHAR2 DEFAULT 'R')
IS
   -- declare exceptions for use in procedure
   enrollment_present EXCEPTION;
   bad_pri EXCEPTION;
BEGIN
   -- the R value is for restrict delete option
   IF p_ri = 'R' THEN
      DECLARE
         -- a variable is needed to test if the student
         -- is in the enrollment table
         v_dummy CHAR(1);
      BEGIN
         -- This is a standard existence check
         -- If v_dummy is assigned a value via the
         -- SELECT INTO, the exception
         -- enrollment_present will be raised
         -- If the v_dummy is not assigned a value, the
         -- exception no_data_found will be raised

         SELECT NULL
           INTO v_dummy
           FROM enrollment e
          WHERE e.student_id = p_studid
            AND ROWNUM = 1;
```

```
                  -- The rownum set to 1 prevents the SELECT
                  -- INTO statement raise to_many_rows
                  -- exception
                  -- If there is at least one row in enrollment
                  -- table with corresponding student_id, the
                  -- restrict delete parameter will disallow
                  -- the deletion of the student by raising
                  -- the enrollment_present exception
                  RAISE enrollment_present;
            EXCEPTION
                WHEN NO_DATA_FOUND THEN
                      -- The no_data_found exception is raised
                      -- when there are no students found in the
                      -- enrollment table
                      -- Since the p_ri indicates a restrict
                      -- delete user choice the delete operation
                      -- is permitted
                      DELETE FROM student
                        WHERE student_id = p_studid;
            END;
      -- when the user enter "C" for the p_ri
      -- he/she indicates a cascade delete choice
      ELSIF p_ri = 'C' THEN
            -- delete the student from the enrollment and
            -- grade tables
            DELETE FROM enrollment
            WHERE student_id = p_studid;

            DELETE FROM grade
            WHERE student_id = p_studid;

            -- delete from student table only after
            -- corresponding records have been removed from
            -- the other tables because the student table is
            -- the parent table
            DELETE
              FROM student
             WHERE student_id = p_studid;
      ELSE
            RAISE bad_pri;
      END IF;
EXCEPTION
      WHEN bad_pri THEN
            RAISE_APPLICATION_ERROR
                (-20231, 'An incorrect p_ri value was '||
                  'entered. The remove_student procedure can '||
                  'only accept a C or R for the p_ri '
                  'parameter.');
```

```
        WHEN enrollment_present THEN
            RAISE_APPLICATION_ERROR
                (-20239, 'The student with ID'||p_studid||
                ' exists in the enrollment table thus records'||
                ' will not be removed.');
    END remove_student;

    FUNCTION get_course_descript
        (p_cnumber course.course_no%TYPE)
        RETURN course.description%TYPE
    IS
    BEGIN
        RETURN get_course_descript_private(p_cnumber);
    END get_course_descript;

BEGIN
    SELECT trunc(sysdate, 'DD')
        INTO v_current_date
        FROM dual;
END student_api;
```

3) Add a PRAGMA RESTRICT_REFERENCES for `get_course_description` specifying: writes no database state, writes no package state, and reads no package state.

Answer: Your answer should look similar to the following:

```
CREATE OR REPLACE PACKAGE student_api AS
    v_current_date DATE;
    PROCEDURE discount;
    FUNCTION new_instructor_id
        RETURN instructor.instructor_id%TYPE;
    FUNCTION total_cost_for_student
        (p_student_id IN student.student_id%TYPE)
        RETURN course.cost%TYPE;
    PRAGMA RESTRICT_REFERENCES
        (total_cost_for_student, WNDS, WNPS, RNPS);
    PROCEDURE get_student_info
        (p_student_id    IN  student.student_id%TYPE,
         p_last_name     OUT student.last_name%TYPE,
         p_first_name    OUT student.first_name%TYPE,
         p_zip           OUT student.zip%TYPE,
         p_return_code   OUT NUMBER);
    PROCEDURE get_student_info
        (p_last_name     IN student.last_name%TYPE,
         p_first_name    IN student.first_name%TYPE,
         p_student_id    OUT student.student_id%TYPE,
         p_zip           OUT student.zip%TYPE,
```

```
            p_return_code OUT NUMBER);
      PROCEDURE remove_student
         (p_studid IN student.student_id%TYPE,
          p_ri     IN VARCHAR2 DEFAULT 'R');
      FUNCTION get_course_descript
         (p_cnumber course.course_no%TYPE)
         RETURN course.description%TYPE;
      PRAGMA RESTRICT_REFERENCES
         (get_course_descript,WNDS, WNPS, RNPS);
   END student_api;
```

CHAPTER 17 TRIGGERS

I) Create the following trigger. Create or modify a trigger on the ENROLLMENT table that fires before an INSERT statement. Make sure that all columns that have NOT NULL and foreign key constraints defined on them are populated with their proper values.

Answer: Your trigger should look similar to the following:

```
CREATE OR REPLACE TRIGGER enrollment_bi
BEFORE INSERT ON ENROLLMENT
FOR EACH ROW
DECLARE
   v_valid NUMBER := 0;
BEGIN
   SELECT COUNT(*)
     INTO v_valid
     FROM student
    WHERE student_id = :NEW.STUDENT_ID;

   IF v_valid = 0 THEN
      RAISE_APPLICATION_ERROR (-20000, 'This is not a
      valid student');
   END IF;

   SELECT COUNT(*)
     INTO v_valid
     FROM section
    WHERE section_id = :NEW.SECTION_ID;

   IF v_valid = 0 THEN
      RAISE_APPLICATION_ERROR (-20001, 'This is not a
      valid section');
   END IF;

   :NEW.ENROLL_DATE := SYSDATE;
   :NEW.CREATED_BY := USER;
```

```
     :NEW.CREATED_DATE := SYSDATE;
     :NEW.MODIFIED_BY := USER;
     :NEW.MODIFIED_DATE := SYSDATE;
END;
```

Consider this trigger. It fires before the INSERT statement on the ENROLLMENT table. First, you validate new values for student ID and section ID. If one of the IDs is invalid, the exception is raised and the trigger is terminated. As a result, the INSERT statement causes an error. If both student and section IDs are found in the STUDENT and SECTION tables, respectively, the ENROLL_DATE, CREATED_DATE, and MODIFIED_DATE are populated with current date, and columns CREATED_BY and MODIFIED_BY are populated with current user name.

Consider the following INSERT statement:

```
INSERT INTO enrollment (student_id, section_id)
VALUES (777, 123);
```

The value 777, in this INSERT statement does not exist in the STUDENT table and therefore is invalid. As a result, this INSERT statement causes the following error:

```
INSERT INTO enrollment (student_id, section_id)
*
ERROR at line 1:
ORA-20000: This is not a valid student
ORA-06512: at "STUDENT.ENROLLMENT_BI", line 10
ORA-04088: error during execution of trigger
'STUDENT.ENROLLMENT_BI'
```

2) Create the following trigger. Create or modify a trigger on the SECTION table that fires before an UPDATE statement. Make sure that the trigger validates incoming values so that there are no constraint violation errors.

Answer: Your trigger should look similar to the following:

```
CREATE OR REPLACE TRIGGER section_bu
BEFORE UPDATE ON SECTION
FOR EACH ROW
DECLARE
   v_valid NUMBER := 0;
BEGIN
   IF :NEW.INSTRUCTOR_ID IS NOT NULL THEN
      SELECT COUNT(*)
        INTO v_valid
        FROM instructor
       WHERE instructor_id = :NEW.instructor_ID;
```

```
        IF v_valid = 0 THEN
            RAISE_APPLICATION_ERROR (-20000,
                'This is not a valid instructor');
        END IF;
    END IF;

    :NEW.CREATED_BY := USER;
    :NEW.CREATED_DATE := SYSDATE;
    :NEW.MODIFIED_BY := USER;
    :NEW.MODIFIED_DATE := SYSDATE;
END;
```

This trigger fires before the UPDATE statement on the SECTION table. First, you check if there is a new value for an instructor ID with the help of an IF-THEN statement. If the IF-THEN statement evaluates to TRUE, the instructor's ID is checked against the INSTRUCTOR table. If a new instructor ID does not exist in the INSTRUCTOR table, the exception is raised, and the trigger is terminated. Otherwise, all columns with NOT NULL constraints are populated with their re-spected values.

Consider the following UPDATE statement:

```
UPDATE section
   SET instructor_id = 220
 WHERE section_id = 79;
```

The value 220 in this UPDATE statement does not exist in the INSTRUCTOR table and therefore is invalid. As a result, this UPDATE statement when run causes an error:

```
UPDATE section
*
ERROR at line 1:
ORA-20000: This is not a valid instructor
ORA-06512: at "STUDENT.SECTION_BU", line 11
ORA-04088: error during execution of trigger
'STUDENT.SECTION_BU'
```

CHAPTER 18 COLLECTIONS

1) Create the following script. Create an index-by table and populate it with in-structor's full name. In other words, each row of the index-by table should con-tain the first name and last name. Display this information on the screen.

Answer: Your script should look similar to the following:

```
SET SERVEROUTPUT ON
DECLARE
    CURSOR name_cur IS
```

```
        SELECT first_name||' '||last_name name
          FROM instructor;

    TYPE name_type IS TABLE OF VARCHAR2(50)
        INDEX BY BINARY_INTEGER;
    name_tab name_type;

    v_counter INTEGER := 0;
BEGIN
    FOR name_rec IN name_cur LOOP
        v_counter := v_counter + 1;
        name_tab(v_counter) := name_rec.name;

        DBMS_OUTPUT.PUT_LINE ('name('||v_counter||'): '||
            name_tab(v_counter));
    END LOOP;
END;
```

In the preceding example, the index-by table name_tab is populated with instructor full names. Notice that the variable v_counter is used as a subscript to
reference individual table elements. This example produces the following output:

```
name(1): Fernand Hanks
name(2): Tom Wojick
name(3): Nina Schorin
name(4): Gary Pertez
name(5): Anita Morris
name(6): Todd Smythe
name(7): Marilyn Frantzen
name(8): Charles Lowry
name(9): Rick Chow

PL/SQL procedure successfully completed.
```

2) Modify the script created in the preceding exercise. Instead of using an index-by
table, use a varray.

*Answer: Your script should look similar to the following. All changes are highlighted in
bold.*

```
SET SERVEROUTPUT ON
DECLARE
    CURSOR name_cur IS
        SELECT first_name||' '||last_name name
          FROM instructor;

    TYPE name_type IS VARRAY(15) OF VARCHAR2(50);
    name_varray name_type := name_type();
```

```
      v_counter INTEGER := 0;
   BEGIN
      FOR name_rec IN name_cur LOOP
         v_counter := v_counter + 1;
         name_varray.EXTEND;
         name_varray(v_counter) := name_rec.name;

         DBMS_OUTPUT.PUT_LINE ('name('||v_counter||'): '||
            name_varray(v_counter));
      END LOOP;
   END;
```

In this version of the script, you define a varray of 15 elements. It is important to remember to initialize the array before referencing its individual elements. In addition, the array must be extended before new elements are added to it.

3) Modify the script created in the preceding exercise. Create an additional varray and populate it with unique course numbers that each instructor teaches. Display the instructor's name and the list of courses he or she teaches.

Answer: Your script should look similar to the following:

```
SET SERVEROUTPUT ON
DECLARE
   CURSOR instructor_cur IS
      SELECT instructor_id, first_name||' '||last_name name
         FROM instructor;

   CURSOR course_cur (p_instructor_id NUMBER) IS
      SELECT unique course_no course
         FROM section
        WHERE instructor_id = p_instructor_id;

   TYPE name_type IS VARRAY(15) OF VARCHAR2(50);
   name_varray name_type := name_type();

   TYPE course_type IS VARRAY(10) OF NUMBER;
   course_varray course_type;

   v_counter1 INTEGER := 0;
   v_counter2 INTEGER;
BEGIN
   FOR instructor_rec IN instructor_cur LOOP
      v_counter1 := v_counter1 + 1;
      name_varray.EXTEND;
      name_varray(v_counter1) := instructor_rec.name;

      DBMS_OUTPUT.PUT_LINE ('name('||v_counter1||'): '||
         name_varray(v_counter1));
```

```
        -- Initialize and populate course_varray
        v_counter2 := 0;
        course_varray := course_type();
        FOR course_rec in
            course_cur (instructor_rec.instructor_id)
        LOOP
           v_counter2 := v_counter2 + 1;
           course_varray.EXTEND;
           course_varray(v_counter2) := course_rec.course;

           DBMS_OUTPUT.PUT_LINE ('course('||v_counter2||'): '||
              course_varray(v_counter2));
        END LOOP;
        DBMS_OUTPUT.PUT_LINE
           ('============================');
    END LOOP;
END;
```

Consider the script just created. First, you declare two cursors, INSTRUCTOR_CUR and COURSE_CUR. The COURSE_CUR accepts a parameter because it returns a list of course taught by a particular instructor. Notice that the SELECT statement uses function UNIQUE to retrieve distinct course numbers. Second, you declare two varray types and variables, name_varray and course_varray. Notice that you do not initialize the second varray at the time of declaration. Next, you declare two counters and initialize the first counter only.

In the body of the block, you open INSTRUCTOR_CUR and populate name_varray with its first element. Next, you initialize the second counter and course_varray. This step is necessary because you need to repopulate course_varray for the next instructor. Next, you open COURSE_CUR to retrieve corresponding courses and display them on the screen.

When run, the script produces the following output:

```
name(1): Fernand Hanks
course(1): 25
course(2): 120
course(3): 122
course(4): 125
course(5): 134
course(6): 140
course(7): 146
course(8): 240
course(9): 450
============================
name(2): Tom Wojick
course(1): 25
course(2): 100
course(3): 120
```

```
course(4): 124
course(5): 125
course(6): 134
course(7): 140
course(8): 146
course(9): 240
===========================
name(3): Nina Schorin
course(1): 20
course(2): 25
course(3): 100
course(4): 120
course(5): 124
course(6): 130
course(7): 134
course(8): 142
course(9): 147
course(10): 310
===========================
name(4): Gary Pertez
course(1): 20
course(2): 25
course(3): 100
course(4): 120
course(5): 124
course(6): 130
course(7): 135
course(8): 142
course(9): 204
course(10): 330
===========================
name(5): Anita Morris
course(1): 20
course(2): 25
course(3): 100
course(4): 122
course(5): 124
course(6): 130
course(7): 135
course(8): 142
course(9): 210
course(10): 350
===========================
name(6): Todd Smythe
course(1): 20
course(2): 25
course(3): 100
course(4): 122
course(5): 125
```

```
course(6): 130
course(7): 135
course(8): 144
course(9): 220
course(10): 350
===========================
name(7): Marilyn Frantzen
course(1): 25
course(2): 120
course(3): 122
course(4): 125
course(5): 132
course(6): 135
course(7): 145
course(8): 230
course(9): 350
===========================
name(8): Charles Lowry
course(1): 25
course(2): 120
course(3): 122
course(4): 125
course(5): 132
course(6): 140
course(7): 145
course(8): 230
course(9): 420
===========================
name(9): Rick Chow
course(1): 10
===========================

PL/SQL procedure successfully completed.
```

As mentioned earlier, it is important to reinitialize the variable `v_counter2` that is used to reference individual elements of `course_varray`. When this step is omitted and the variable is initialized only once at the time declaration, the script generates the following runtime error:

```
name(1): Fernand Hanks
course(1): 25
course(2): 120
course(3): 122
course(4): 125
course(5): 134
course(6): 140
course(7): 146
course(8): 240
course(9): 450
```

```
name(2): Tom Wojick
DECLARE
*
ERROR at line 1:
ORA-06533: Subscript beyond count
ORA-06512: at line 33
```

Why do you think this error occurs?

4) Find and explain errors in the following script:

```
DECLARE
    TYPE varray_type1 IS VARRAY(7) OF INTEGER;
    TYPE table_type2 IS TABLE OF varray_type1 INDEX BY
    BINARY_INTEGER;

    varray1 varray_type1 := varray_type1(1, 2, 3);
    table2 table_type2 :=
        table_type2(varray1, varray_type1(8, 9, 0));

BEGIN
    DBMS_OUTPUT.PUT_LINE ('table2(1)(2): '||table2(1)(2));

    FOR i IN 1..10 LOOP
        varray1.EXTEND;
        varray1(i) := i;
        DBMS_OUTPUT.PUT_LINE ('varray1('||i||'): '||
            varray1(i));
    END LOOP;
END;
```

Answer: Consider the error generated by the preceding script:

```
    table2 table_type2 := table_type2(varray1,
    varray_type1(8, 9, 0));
                          *
ERROR at line 6:
ORA-06550: line 6, column 26:
PLS-00222: no function with name 'TABLE_TYPE2' exists in
this scope
ORA-06550: line 6, column 11:
PL/SQL: Item ignored
ORA-06550: line 9, column 44:
PLS-00320: the declaration of the type of this expression
is incomplete or
malformed
ORA-06550: line 9, column 4:
PL/SQL: Statement ignored
```

Notice that this error refers to the initialization of `table2`, *which has been declared as an index-by table of varrays. You will recall that index-by tables are not initialized prior to their use. As a result, the declaration of* `table2` *must be modified. Furthermore, additional assignment statement must be added to the executable portion of the block as follows:*

```
DECLARE
    TYPE varray_type1 IS VARRAY(7) OF INTEGER;
    TYPE table_type2 IS TABLE OF varray_type1 INDEX BY
    BINARY_INTEGER;

    varray1 varray_type1 := varray_type1(1, 2, 3);
    table2 table_type2;
BEGIN
    -- These statements populate index-by table
    table2(1) := varray1;
    table2(2) := varray_type1(8, 9, 0);

    DBMS_OUTPUT.PUT_LINE ('table2(1)(2): '||table2(1)(2));

    FOR i IN 1..10 LOOP
        varray1.EXTEND;
        varray1(i) := i;
        DBMS_OUTPUT.PUT_LINE ('varray1('||i||'): '||
            varray1(i));
    END LOOP;
END;
```

When run, this version produces a different error:

```
table2(1)(2): 2
varray1(1): 1
varray1(2): 2
varray1(3): 3
varray1(4): 4
DECLARE
*
ERROR at line 1:
ORA-06532: Subscript outside of limit
ORA-06512: at line 14
```

Notice that this is a runtime error that refers to `varray1`. *This error occurs because you are trying to extend varray beyond its limit. Varray1 can contain up to seven integers. After initialization, the varray contains three integers. As a result, it can be populated with no more than four additional integer numbers. So the fifth iteration of the loop tries to extend the varray to eight elements, which in turn causes a subscript beyond count error.*

It is important to note that there is no correlation between the loop counter and the EXTEND method. Every time the EXTEND method is called, it increases the size of the varray by one element. Since the varray has been initialized to three elements, the EXTEND method adds a fourth element to the array for the first iteration of the loop. At this same time, the first element of the varray is assigned a value of 1 via the loop counter. For the second iteration of the loop, the EXTEND method adds a fifth element to the varray while the second element is assigned a value of 2, and so forth.

Finally, consider the error-free version of the script and its output:

```
DECLARE
    TYPE varray_type1 IS VARRAY(7) OF INTEGER;
    TYPE table_type2 IS TABLE OF varray_type1 INDEX BY
    BINARY_INTEGER;

    varray1 varray_type1 := varray_type1(1, 2, 3);
    table2 table_type2;
BEGIN
    -- These statements populate index-by table
    table2(1) := varray1;
    table2(2) := varray_type1(8, 9, 0);

    DBMS_OUTPUT.PUT_LINE ('table2(1)(2): '||table2(1)(2));

    FOR i IN 4..7 LOOP
        varray1.EXTEND;
        varray1(i) := i;
    END LOOP;

    -- Display elements of the varray
    FOR i IN 1..7 LOOP
        DBMS_OUTPUT.PUT_LINE ('varray1('||i||'): '||
            varray1(i));
    END LOOP;
END;

table2(1)(2): 2
varray1(1): 1
varray1(2): 2
varray1(3): 3
varray1(4): 4
varray1(5): 5
varray1(6): 6
varray1(7): 7

PL/SQL procedure successfully completed.
```

CHAPTER 19 RECORDS

1) Create the following script. Create an index-by table with the element type of a user-defined record. This record should contain the first name, last name, and the total number of courses that a particular instructor teaches. Display the records of the index-by table on the screen.

Answer: Your script should look similar to the following:

```
SET SERVEROUTPUT ON
DECLARE
    CURSOR instructor_cur IS
        SELECT first_name, last_name, COUNT(UNIQUE
        s.course_no) courses
          FROM instructor i
          LEFT OUTER JOIN section s
            ON (s.instructor_id = i.instructor_id)
        GROUP BY first_name, last_name;

    TYPE rec_type IS RECORD
        (first_name INSTRUCTOR.FIRST_NAME%TYPE,
         last_name INSTRUCTOR.LAST_NAME%TYPE,
         courses_taught NUMBER);

    TYPE instructor_type IS TABLE OF REC_TYPE
    INDEX BY BINARY_INTEGER;

    instructor_tab instructor_type;

    v_counter INTEGER := 0;
BEGIN
    FOR instructor_rec IN instructor_cur LOOP
        v_counter := v_counter + 1;

        -- Populate index-by table of records
        instructor_tab(v_counter).first_name :=
            instructor_rec.first_name;
        instructor_tab(v_counter).last_name :=
            instructor_rec.last_name;
        instructor_tab(v_counter).courses_taught :=
            instructor_rec.courses;

        DBMS_OUTPUT.PUT_LINE ('Instructor, '||
            instructor_tab(v_counter).first_name||' '||
            instructor_tab(v_counter).last_name||', teaches '||
            instructor_tab(v_counter).courses_taught||'
            courses.');
    END LOOP;
END;
```

Consider the SELECT statement used in this script. This SELECT statement returns the instructor's name and total number of courses that he or she teaches. The statement is using an outer join so that if a particular instructor is not teaching any courses, he or she will be included in the results of the SELECT statement. Note that the SELECT statement uses ANSI 1999 SQL standard.

You will find detailed explanations and examples of the statements using the new ANSI 1999 SQL standard in Appendix E and in the Oracle help. Throughout this book we try to provide you with examples illustrating both standards; however, our main focus is on PL/SQL features rather than SQL.

In this script, you define a cursor against the INSTRUCTOR and SECTION tables that is used to populate the index-by table of records, `instructor_tab`. Each row of this table is a user-defined record of three elements. You populate the index-by table via the cursor FOR loop. Consider the notation used to reference each record element of the index-by table:

```
instructor_tab(v_counter).first_name
instructor_tab(v_counter).last_name
instructor_tab(v_counter).courses_taught
```

To reference each row of the index-by table, you use the counter variable. However, because each row of this table is a record, you must also reference individual fields of the underlying record. When run, this script produces the following output:

```
Instructor, Anita Morris, teaches 10 courses.
Instructor, Charles Lowry, teaches 9 courses.
Instructor, Fernand Hanks, teaches 9 courses.
Instructor, Gary Pertez, teaches 10 courses.
Instructor, Marilyn Frantzen, teaches 9 courses.
Instructor, Nina Schorin, teaches 10 courses.
Instructor, Rick Chow, teaches 1 courses.
Instructor, Todd Smythe, teaches 10 courses.
Instructor, Tom Wojick, teaches 9 courses.

PL/SQL procedure successfully completed.
```

2) Modify the script created in the preceding exercise. Instead of using an index-by table, use a nested table.

Answer: Your script should look similar to the following. All changes are highlighted in bold.

```
SET SERVEROUTPUT ON
DECLARE
    CURSOR instructor_cur IS
```

```
      SELECT first_name, last_name, COUNT(UNIQUE
   s.course_no) courses
      FROM instructor i
      LEFT OUTER JOIN section s
        ON (s.instructor_id = i.instructor_id)
      GROUP BY first_name, last_name;

   TYPE rec_type IS RECORD
      (first_name INSTRUCTOR.FIRST_NAME%TYPE,
       last_name INSTRUCTOR.LAST_NAME%TYPE,
       courses_taught NUMBER);

   TYPE instructor_type IS TABLE OF REC_TYPE;
   instructor_tab instructor_type := instructor_type();

   v_counter INTEGER := 0;
BEGIN
   FOR instructor_rec IN instructor_cur LOOP
      v_counter := v_counter + 1;
      instructor_tab.EXTEND;

      -- Populate index-by table of records
      instructor_tab(v_counter).first_name :=
         instructor_rec.first_name;
      instructor_tab(v_counter).last_name :=
         instructor_rec.last_name;
      instructor_tab(v_counter).courses_taught :=
         instructor_rec.courses;

      DBMS_OUTPUT.PUT_LINE ('Instructor, '||
         instructor_tab(v_counter).first_name||' '||
         instructor_tab(v_counter).last_name||', teaches '||
         instructor_tab(v_counter).courses_taught||'
         courses.');
   END LOOP;
END;
```

Notice that the `instructor_tab` must be initialized and extended before its individual elements can be referenced.

3) Modify the script created in the preceding exercise. Instead of using a nested table, use a varray.

Answer:Your script should look similar to the following:

```
SET SERVEROUTPUT ON
DECLARE
   CURSOR instructor_cur IS
```

```
SELECT first_name, last_name, COUNT(UNIQUE
s.course_no) courses
  FROM instructor i
  LEFT OUTER JOIN section s
    ON (s.instructor_id = i.instructor_id)
  GROUP BY first_name, last_name;

TYPE rec_type IS RECORD
    (first_name INSTRUCTOR.FIRST_NAME%TYPE,
     last_name INSTRUCTOR.LAST_NAME%TYPE,
     courses_taught NUMBER);

TYPE instructor_type IS VARRAY(10) OF REC_TYPE;
instructor_tab instructor_type := instructor_type();

v_counter INTEGER := 0;
BEGIN
  FOR instructor_rec IN instructor_cur LOOP
    v_counter := v_counter + 1;
    instructor_tab.EXTEND;

    -- Populate index-by table of records
    instructor_tab(v_counter).first_name :=
        instructor_rec.first_name;
    instructor_tab(v_counter).last_name :=
        instructor_rec.last_name;
    instructor_tab(v_counter).courses_taught :=
        instructor_rec.courses;

    DBMS_OUTPUT.PUT_LINE ('Instructor, '||
        instructor_tab(v_counter).first_name||' '||
        instructor_tab(v_counter).last_name||', teaches '||
        instructor_tab(v_counter).courses_taught||'
        courses.');
  END LOOP;
END;
```

This version of the script is almost identical to the previous version. Instead of using a nested table, you are using a varray of 15 elements.

4) Create the following script. Create a user-defined record with three fields: course_no, description, cost, and prerequisite_rec. The last field, prerequisite_rec, should be a user-defined record with three fields: prereq_no, prereq_desc, and prereq_cost. For any ten courses that have a prerequisite course, populate the user-defined record with all corresponding data and display its information on the screen.

Answer: Your script should look similar to the following:

```
SET SERVEROUTPUT ON
DECLARE
    CURSOR c_cur IS
        SELECT course_no, description, cost, prerequisite
          FROM course
         WHERE prerequisite IS NOT NULL
           AND rownum <= 10;

    TYPE prerequisite_type IS RECORD
        (prereq_no NUMBER,
         prereq_desc VARCHAR(50),
         prereq_cost NUMBER);

    TYPE course_type IS RECORD
        (course_no NUMBER,
         description VARCHAR2(50),
         cost NUMBER,
         prerequisite_rec PREREQUISITE_TYPE);

    course_rec COURSE_TYPE;
BEGIN
    FOR c_rec in c_cur LOOP
        course_rec.course_no := c_rec.course_no;
        course_rec.description := c_rec.description;
        course_rec.cost := c_rec.cost;

        SELECT course_no, description, cost
          INTO course_rec.prerequisite_rec.prereq_no,
               course_rec.prerequisite_rec.prereq_desc,
               course_rec.prerequisite_rec.prereq_cost
          FROM course
         WHERE course_no = c_rec.prerequisite;

        DBMS_OUTPUT.PUT_LINE ('Course: '||
            course_rec.course_no||' - '||
            course_rec.description);
        DBMS_OUTPUT.PUT_LINE ('Cost: '|| course_rec.cost);
        DBMS_OUTPUT.PUT_LINE ('Prerequisite: '||
            course_rec.prerequisite_rec. prereq_no||' - '||
            course_rec.prerequisite_rec.prereq_desc);
        DBMS_OUTPUT.PUT_LINE ('Prerequisite Cost: '||
            course_rec.prerequisite_rec.prereq_cost);
        DBMS_OUTPUT.PUT_LINE
            ('=======================================');
    END LOOP;
END;
```

In the declaration portion of the script, you define a cursor against the COURSE table; two user-defined record types, prerequisite_type and course_type;

and user-defined record, `course_rec`. It is important to note the order in which the record types are declared. The `prerequsite_type` must be declared first because one of the `course_type` elements is of the `prerequisite_type`.

In the executable portion of the script, you populate course_rec via the cursor FOR loop. First, you assign values to the course_rec.course_no, course_rec.description, and course_rec.cost. Next, you populate the nested record, prerequsite_rec, via the SELECT INTO statement against the COURSE table. Consider the notation used to reference individual elements of the nested record:

```
course_rec.prerequisite_rec.prereq_no,
course_rec.prerequisite_rec.prereq_desc,
course_rec.prerequisite_rec.prereq_cost
```

You specify the name of the outer record followed by the name of the inner (nested) record followed by the name of the element. Finally, you display record information on the screen.

Note that this script does not contain a NO_DATA_FOUND exception handler even though there is a SELECT INTO statement. Why do you think this is the case?

When run, the script produces the following output:

```
Course: 25 - Intro to Programming
Cost: 1195
Prerequisite: 140 - Structured Analysis
Prerequisite Cost: 1195
========================================
Course: 80 - Structured Programming Techniques
Cost: 1595
Prerequisite: 204 - Intro to SQL
Prerequisite Cost: 1195
========================================
Course: 100 - Hands-On Windows
Cost: 1195
Prerequisite: 20 - Intro to Computers
Prerequisite Cost: 1195
========================================
Course: 120 - Intro to Java Programming
Cost: 1195
Prerequisite: 80 - Structured Programming Techniques
Prerequisite Cost: 1595
========================================
Course: 122 - Intermediate Java Programming
Cost: 1195
Prerequisite: 120 - Intro to Java Programming
Prerequisite Cost: 1195
========================================
```

```
Course: 124 - Advanced Java Programming
Cost: 1195
Prerequisite: 122 - Intermediate Java Programming
Prerequisite Cost: 1195
========================================
Course: 125 - JDeveloper
Cost: 1195
Prerequisite: 122 - Intermediate Java Programming
Prerequisite Cost: 1195
========================================
Course: 130 - Intro to Unix
Cost: 1195
Prerequisite: 310 - Operating Systems
Prerequisite Cost: 1195
========================================
Course: 132 - Basics of Unix Admin
Cost: 1195
Prerequisite: 130 - Intro to Unix
Prerequisite Cost: 1195
========================================
Course: 134 - Advanced Unix Admin
Cost: 1195
Prerequisite: 132 - Basics of Unix Admin
Prerequisite Cost: 1195
========================================

PL/SQL procedure successfully completed.
```

A P P E N D I X E

ORACLE 9i SQL NEW FEATURES

SQL STANDARDS

The American National Standards Institute (http://www.ansi.org) first published a standard SQL specification in 1989. The ANSI SQL standard was later revised in 1992, and this is often referred to as SQL-92 or SQL-2. This was revised again, giving rise to the latest standard, known as SQL-99. Sometimes it is called SQL-3. Database vendors and third-party software companies have had varying levels of conformance to this standard. Most major database vendors support the SQL-92 standard. Generally what you find is that most vendors have their own extensions to the SQL language. Oracle is no exception in this matter. Nonetheless, Oracle has made efforts to maintain the ANSI standard. The reason for this is to provide an easier migration to third-party applications without a need to modify the SQL code. In Oracle 8i and again in Oracle 9i, Oracle has introduced a number of enhancements to conform to the SQL-99 standard. This appendix will review the main enhancements that you will see in this book. Examples will be given. It is important to realize that although many of these features are new to Oracle in version 9i, these constructs have existed in other programming languages. For example, the CASE statement has been a part of MS SQL Server for some time and has been used in Cobol and C since their inception.

JOINS

The 1999 ANSI standard introduced complete JOIN syntax in the FROM clause. The prior method was to list the tables needed in the query in the FROM clause and then to define the joins between these tables in the WHERE clause. However, the conditions of the SQL statement are also listed in the WHERE clause. It was decided to enhance this syntax because listing of the joins and the conditions in the same WHERE clause can be confusing.

The 1999 ANSI join syntax includes cross joins, equijoins, full outer joins, and natural joins.

653

CROSS JOINS

The CROSS JOIN syntax indicates that you are creating a Cartesian product from two tables. The result set of a Cartesian product is usually meaningless, but it can be used to generate a lot of rows if you need to do some testing. The advantage of the new syntax is that it flags a Cartesian product by having the CROSS JOIN in the FROM clause.

■ FOR EXAMPLE

Prior to Oracle 9i, you would create a Cartesian product with the following syntax:

```
SELECT *
  FROM instructor course
```

The new syntax is as follows:

```
SELECT *
  FROM instructor CROSS JOIN
       course
```

The result set from this is 300. This is because the COURSE table has 30 rows and the INSTRUCTOR table has 10 rows. The CROSS JOIN will count all possible combinations resulting in the 300 rows.

EQUI JOINS

The EQUI JOIN syntax indicates the columns that comprise the JOINS between two tables. Prior to Oracle 9i, you would indicate a join condition in the WHERE clause by stating which two columns are part of the foreign key constraint.

■ FOR EXAMPLE

Prior to Oracle 9i, you would join the STUDENT table to the ZIPCODE table as follows:

```
SELECT s.first_name, s.last_name, z.zip, z.city, z.state
  FROM student s, zipcode z
 WHERE s.zip = z.zip
```

The new syntax is as follows:

```
SELECT s.first_name, s.last_name, zip, z.city, z.state
  FROM student s JOIN
       zipcode z USING (zip)
```

The reason for this syntax is that the join condition between the two tables is immediately obvious when looking at the tables listed in the FROM clause. This example is very short, but generally your SQL statements are very long, and it can be time consuming to find the join conditions in the WHERE clause.

Notice that the ZIP column did not have an alias. In the new JOIN syntax, the column that is referenced in the JOIN does not have a qualifier. In the old syntax, if you did not use an alias for column ZIP, as in this example,

```
SELECT s.first_name, s.last_name, zip, z.city, z.state
  FROM student s, zipcode z
 WHERE s.zip = z.zip
```

Oracle would generate the following error:

ORA-00918: column ambiguously defined

In the new JOIN syntax, if you use a qualifier, as in this example,

```
SELECT s.first_name, s.last_name, z.zip, z.city, z.state
  FROM student s JOIN
       zipcode z USING (zip)
```

Oracle generates the following error:

ORA-25154: column part of USING clause cannot have qualifier

The new JOIN syntax also allows you to define the join condition using both sides of the join. This is done with the ON syntax. When using the ON syntax for a JOIN you must use the qualifier. This is also useful when the two sides of the join do not have the same name.

The ON syntax can also be used for three-way joins (or more).

◼ FOR EXAMPLE

```
SELECT s.section_no, c.course_no, c.description,
       i.first_name, i.last_name
  FROM course c
  JOIN section s
    ON (s.course_no = c.course_no)
  JOIN instructor i
    ON (i.instructor_id = s.instructor_id)
```

The syntax for a multiple-table join becomes more complex. Notice that one table is mentioned at a time. The first JOIN lists columns from the first two tables in the ON section. Once the third table has been indicated, the second JOIN lists columns from the second and third tables in the ON clause.

NATURAL JOINS

The NATURAL JOIN is another part of the ANSI 1999 syntax that can be used when joining two tables based on columns that have the same name and datatype. The NATURAL JOIN can only be used when all the columns that have the same name in both tables comprise the join condition between these tables. You cannot use this syntax when the two columns have the same name but a different datatype. Another benefit of this join is that if you use the SELECT * syntax, the columns that appear in both tables will only appear once in the result set.

■ FOR EXAMPLE

```
SELECT *
  FROM instructor NATURAL JOIN zipcode
```

The join that will be used here is not only on the ZIP column of both tables, but the CREATE_BY, CREATED_DATE, MODIFIED_BY, and MODIFIED_DATE columns as well.

The student schema does not support the NATURAL JOIN condition since we have created audit columns that have the same name in each table but are not used in the foreign keys constraints among the tables.

OUTER JOINS

INNER JOIN or EQUI JOIN is the result of joining two tables that contain rows where a match occurred on the join condition. It is possible to lose information through an INNER JOIN because only those rows that match on the join condition will appear in the final result set.

The result set of an OUTER JOIN will contain the same rows as the INNER JOIN plus rows corresponding to the rows from the source tables where there was no match. The OUTER JOIN has been supported by a number of versions of the Oracle SQL language. It had not been a part of the ANSI standard until the 1999 version.

Oracle's OUTER JOIN syntax has consisted of placing a (+) next to the columns of a table where you expect to find values that do not exist in the other table.

■ FOR EXAMPLE

```
SELECT i.first_name, i.last_name, z.state
  FROM instructor i, zipcode z
 WHERE i.zip (+) = z.zip
 GROUP BY i.first_name, i.last_name, z.state
```

In this example, the result set will include all states that are in the ZIPCODE table. If there is no instructor for a state that exists in the ZIPCODE table, the values of FIRST_NAME and LAST_NAME will be blank (NULL). This syntax gets more confusing because it must be maintained if there are more conditions in a WHERE clause. This method can only be used on one side of the outer join at a time.

The new method of OUTER JOINS adopted in Oracle 9i allows the case of an OUTER JOIN on either side or both sides at the same time (for example, if there were some instructors who had zipcodes that were not in the ZIPCODE table, and you wanted to see all the instructors and all the states in both of these tables). This task can be accomplished by using the new OUTER JOIN syntax only. This requires the aforementioned JOIN syntax with addition of new outer join attributes as well. The choice is LEFT/RIGHT/FULL OUTER JOIN. The same OUTER JOIN can now be modified as

```
SELECT i.first_name, z.state
  FROM instructor i RIGHT OUTER JOIN
       zipcode z
    ON i.zip = z.zip
 GROUP BY i.first_name, z.state
```

The RIGHT indicates that the values on the right side of the JOIN may not exist in the table on the LEFT side of the join. This can be replaced by the word FULL if there are some instructors who have zipcodes that are not in the ZIPCODE table.

SCALAR SUBQUERY

A scalar row subquery is a single-row subquery. In other words, it returns a single row. If the scalar subquery returns more than one row, it generates an error. The Oracle 9i version has more support of scalar subqueries than Oracle 8i.

■ FOR EXAMPLE

```
SELECT city, state,
       (SELECT count(*)
          FROM student s
         WHERE s.zip = z.zip) as student_count
  FROM zipcode z
 WHERE state = 'CT'
```

INDEX

inform**IT**

http://www.phptr.com/

Prentice Hall PTR   InformIT   InformIT Online Books   Financial Times Prentice Hall   ft.com   PTG Interactive   Reuters

TOMORROW'S SOLUTIONS FOR TODAY'S PROFESSIONALS

Prentice Hall Professional Technical Reference

| Browse | Book Series | What's New | User Groups | Alliances | Special Sales | Contact Us |

Search | Help | Home

Quick Search

PTR Favorites

Find a Bookstore

Book Series

Special Interests

Newsletters

Press Room

International

Best Sellers

Solutions Beyond the Book

Shopping Bag

Keep Up to Date with

PH PTR Online

We strive to stay on the cutting edge of what's happening in professional computer science and engineering. Here's a bit of what you'll find when you stop by **www.phptr.com**:

! **What's new at PHPTR?** We don't just publish books for the professional community, we're a part of it. Check out our convention schedule, keep up with your favorite authors, and get the latest reviews and press releases on topics of interest to you.

@ **Special interest areas** offering our latest books, book series, features of the month, related links, and other useful information to help you get the job done.

User Groups Prentice Hall Professional Technical Reference's User Group Program helps volunteer, not-for-profit user groups provide their members with training and information about cutting-edge technology.

Companion Websites Our Companion Websites provide valuable solutions beyond the book. Here you can download the source code, get updates and corrections, chat with other users and the author about the book, or discover links to other websites on this topic.

Need to find a bookstore? Chances are, there's a bookseller near you that carries a broad selection of PTR titles. Locate a Magnet bookstore near you at www.phptr.com.

Subscribe today! **Join PHPTR's monthly email newsletter!** Want to be kept up-to-date on your area of interest? Choose a targeted category on our website, and we'll keep you informed of the latest PHPTR products, author events, reviews and conferences in your interest area.

Visit our mailroom to subscribe today! **http://www.phptr.com/mail_lists**